Nineteenth-Century Poetr

MW01257994

This engaging volume provides readers with the essential criticism on nineteenth-century poetry, organised around key areas of debate in the field. The critical texts included in this volume reflect both a traditional and modern emphasis on the study of poetry in the long nineteenth century. These are then tied up by a newly written essay summarising the ideas and encouraging further study and debate.

The book includes:

- Sections on Periodization, 'What is Poetry?', Politics, Prosody, Forms, Emotion, Feeling, Affect, Religion, Sexuality and Science.
- Work by writers such as William Wordsworth, S. T. Coleridge, Percy Bysshe Shelley, Christina Rossetti, Matthew Arnold and Gerard Manley Hopkins.
- Critics and historians including Isobel Armstrong, Richard Cronin, Jason Rudy, Joseph Bristow and Gillian Beer.
- Detailed introductions and critical commentary by Francis O'Gorman, Rosie Miles, Ankhi Mukherjee, Natalie Phillips Hoffman, Martin Dubois, Stefano Evangelista and Gregory Tate.

Providing both the essential criticism along with clear introductions and analysis, this book is the perfect guide to students who wish to engage in the exciting criticism and debates of nineteenth-century poetry.

Jonathan Herapath is an Independent Scholar.

Emma Mason is Professor of English and Comparative Literary Studies at the University of Warwick, UK.

Routledge Criticism and Debates in Literature

The *Routledge Criticism and Debates in Literature* series offers new perspectives on traditional and core subjects from Medieval Literature to Postmodernism. Exploring different approaches and critical directions, essays range from 'classic' and newer criticism to brand new papers. Sections give an essential overview of key topics and inspire lively debate, enhancing subjects through modern takes, angles or arguments against classic debates.

Ideal for students approaching a topic for the first time, the volumes are also useful for those looking for important critical background. Each contains section introductions that usefully situate the topic within wider debates, and glossaries of key terms, people and places. Challenging and provocative, the *Routledge Criticism and Debates in Literature* series shows how subjects and their criticism have travelled into the twenty-first century in an intelligent and accessible way.

Available in this series:

Medieval Literature
Holly Crocker and D. Vance Smith

British Romanticism
Mark Canuel

Victorian Literature
Lee Behlman and Anne Longmuir

Nineteenth-Century Poetry
Jonathan Herapath and Emma Mason

Nineteenth-Century Poetry

Criticism and Debates

Edited by Jonathan Herapath and Emma Mason

Routledge
Taylor & Francis Group

LONDON AND NEW YORK

First published 2016
by Routledge
2 Park Square, Milton Park, Abingdon, Oxon OX14 4RN

and by Routledge
711 Third Avenue, New York, NY 10017

Routledge is an imprint of the Taylor & Francis Group, an informa business

© 2016 Jonathan Herapath and Emma Mason

The right of the editors to be identified as the authors of the editorial
material, and of the authors for their individual chapters, has been asserted
in accordance with sections 77 and 78 of the Copyright, Designs and
Patents Act 1988.

All rights reserved. No part of this book may be reprinted or reproduced or
utilised in any form or by any electronic, mechanical, or other means, now
known or hereafter invented, including photocopying and recording, or in
any information storage or retrieval system, without permission in writing
from the publishers.

Trademark notice: Product or corporate names may be trademarks or
registered trademarks, and are used only for identification and explanation
without intent to infringe.

British Library Cataloguing-in-Publication Data
A catalogue record for this book is available from the British Library

Library of Congress Cataloging-in-Publication Data
Nineteenth century poetry : criticism and debates / edited by Jonathan
Herapath and Emma Mason.
    pages cm. – (The Routledge Criticism and Debates in Literature series)
    Includes bibliographical references and index.
    1. English poetry – 19th century – History and criticism. I. Herapath,
Jonathan, editor. II. Mason, Emma, editor.
    PR583.N55 2015
    821′.809–dc23   2015018927

ISBN: 978-0-415-83129-1 (hbk)
ISBN: 978-0-415-83130-7 (pbk)

Typeset in Times New Roman
by HWA Text and Data Management, London

Printed and bound in the United States of America by
Edwards Brothers Malloy on sustainably sourced paper

Contents

Contributors

Martin Dubois is a Lecturer in Victorian Literature at Newcastle University. He has published articles on a range of Victorian writers, including Hopkins and William Barnes, and is currently completing a monograph on Hopkins and the poetry of religious experience.

Stefano Evangelista is Associate Professor of English at Oxford University and a Fellow of Trinity College, Oxford. His publications include *British Aestheticism and Ancient Greece: Hellenism, Reception, Gods in Exile* (Palgrave, 2009), *The Reception of Oscar Wilde in Europe* (Bloomsbury, 2010) and *A.C. Swinburne: Unofficial Laureate* (Manchester UP, 2013, with Catherine Maxwell). He is currently working on a monograph on literary cosmopolitanism in the 1890s.

Jonathan Herapath is an independent scholar and freelance teacher. He is a contributor to the New Dictionary of National Biography and is the author of 'Lewis' Heritage of Victorian Piety' in Judith E. Tonning and Brenden N. Wolfe, ed., *Lewis and the Church* (T & T Clark, 2011), and 'Henry Francis Lyte', in Jay Parini, ed., *Scribner's British Writers* (Gale, 2013).

Natalie Phillips Hoffmann received her doctorate on nineteenth-century Anglophone poetry and its involvement in shaping global narratives of nationalist identity from the University of Maryland, College Park. Her research interests include Victorian poetry, women's literature, and feminist and postcolonial studies.

Francis O'Gorman is a Professor in the School of English at Leeds. His most recent publications include *Worrying: A Literary and Cultural History* (Bloomsbury, 2015), *The Cambridge Companion to John Ruskin* (Cambridge UP, 2016), and the Oxford Twenty-First Century Authors edition of *Algernon Charles Swinburne* (2016).

Emma Mason is Professor of English and Comparative Literary Studies at the University of Warwick. Publications include *Reading the Abrahamic Faiths: Re-thinking Religion and Literature* (Bloomsbury, 2015); *Elizabeth Jennings: The Collected Poems* (Carcanet, 2012); and *The Cambridge Introduction to Wordsworth* (Cambridge UP, 2010). With Mark Knight, she is general editor of Bloomsbury's monograph series, *New Directions in Religion and Literature*.

Rosie Miles is Reader in English Literature and Pedagogy at the University of Wolverhampton. She is author of *Victorian Poetry in Context* (Bloomsbury, 2013) and co-editor (with Phillippa Bennett) of *William Morris in the Twenty-First Century* (Peter Lang, 2010). She is also a National Teaching Fellow (2011).

Ankhi Mukherjee is Associate Professor of English at Oxford University and a Fellow of Wadham College Oxford. Her publications include *Aesthetic Hysteria: The Great Neurosis in Victorian Melodrama and Contemporary Fiction* (Routledge, 2007) and *What Is a Classic? Postcolonial Rewriting and Invention of the Canon* (Stanford, 2013). She is currently working on an interdisciplinary project that examines the institution of psychoanalysis and its vexed relationship with race and the urban poor.

Gregory Tate is Lecturer in Victorian Literature at the University of St Andrews. He is the author of several publications on literature and science and on nineteenth-century poetry, including *The Poet's Mind: The Psychology of Victorian Poetry* 1830–1870 (Oxford UP, 2012).

Credits

Part I: Periodization

1   Matthew Arnold, Preface to the First Edition of *Poems* (Longman, Brown, Green and Longmans, 1853)
2   Robert Langbaum, 'Romanticism as a Modern Tradition', *The Poetry of Experience: The Dramatic Monologue in Modern Literary Tradition* (W. W. Norton, 1957)
3   Matthew Reynolds, 'Poetry and its Times', *The Realms of Verse 1830–1870: English Poetry in a Time of Nation Building* (Oxford University Press, 2001)
4   Matthew Campbell, 'Introduction: Two Decisions', *Rhythm and Will in Victorian Poetry* (Cambridge University Press, 1999)
5   Michael C. Cohen, 'E. C. Stedman and the Invention of Victorian Poetry', *Victorian Poetry*, 43.2 (2005), 165–188

Part II: 'What is poetry?'

6   P. B. Shelley, *A Defence of Poetry* (1821), Mary Shelley, ed., *Essays, Letters from Abroad, Translations and Fragments, by P. B. Shelley*, 2 vols (Edward Moxon, 1839/40)
7   J. S. Mill, 'What is Poetry?', *Monthly Repository*, 7.73 (January, 1833), 60–70
8   Eric Griffiths, 'The Printed Voice in the Nineteenth Century', *The Printed Voice of Victorian Poetry* (Clarendon Press, 1989)
9   Marion Thain, 'What Kind of a Critical Category is "Women's Poetry"?' *Victorian Poetry*, 41.4 (2003), 575–584
10 Serena Baiesi, 'Female Picturesque and Colonial Settings in the Gift Books', *Letitia Elizabeth Landon and Metrical Romance: The Adventures of a 'Literary Genius'* (Peter Lang, 2010)

Part III: Politics

11 Angela Leighton, 'Elizabeth Barrett Browning', *Victorian Women Poets: Writing Against the Heart* (The University Press of Virginia, 1992)
12 Isobel Armstrong, 'What Kind of Criticism?', *Victorian Poetry: Poetry, Poetics, Politics* (Routledge, 1993)
13 Mike Sanders, 'Introduction', *The Poetry of Chartism: Aesthetics, Politics, History* (Cambridge University Press, 2009)
14 Matthew Bevis, 'Introduction: Literary Persuasions', *The Art of Eloquence: Byron, Dickens, Tennyson, Joyce* (Oxford University Press, 2007)

Part VIII: Sexuality

Part IX: Science

Introduction

Emma Mason

In her essay 'Invective Verse' (1993), the lyric poet Jennifer Moxley urges readers to look past the bind of endlessly 'debating on "where poetry comes from", or what is its "use value"', to instead 'annoy the power mongers by using poetic propaganda to launch a ruthless critique of them and their buddies and to expose the world of contradictions surrounding us'.[1] If, as Moxley writes, poetry 'is the insistence that we partake in the *expression of our lives*', then poets must 'refuse to be insular or troubled', demand free distribution of their work, and abjure narcissism to write 'all freeway signs, tax forms and public awareness leaflets'. Moxley's exit from cul-de-sac questions of poetry's 'value' to argue for its particularity as a form that captures and so confronts the logic of its historical moment is anchored in the nineteenth century. Her emphasis on a poetics that pervades habitual life suggests a continuity between poetry written then and now, answering Arthur Hugh Clough's call for a poetry of 'ordinary feelings, the obvious rather than the rare ... the actual, palpable things with which our every-day life is concerned', and that introduces 'into business and weary task-work a character and a soul of purpose and reality'.[2]

While this soulful purpose might not console or comfort the modern reader, its promise of hope and political optimism connects nineteenth-century poets with their present-day legatees. From the revolutions of 1848 to the Occupy movement, Karl Marx to Thomas Piketty, Christian socialism to liberation theology, political hope shapes the intellectual climate from which nineteenth and twenty-first century poetry emerges. Reading poetry from both periods as a way into the other makes apparent a common poetic thinking that imagines the contents of the world – human and non-human – as points of association and relation. Delimited by the form of the poem, this thinking registers what the poet and Romanticist Peter Larkin calls 'scarcity', a word that appends a shortage of moral, spiritual, ethical and economic assurances in nineteenth-century poetry to warnings about limited resources in twenty-first-century verse.[3] Like Moxley, Larkin reviews 'crises' or scarcities of faith and ontology as moments of insufficiency or lack that poetic form re-inscribes as the call for new ways of imagining and thinking, and that preserves relationships between people and their physical and metaphysical environments. Nineteenth-century poetry makes audible this call for relationship in choral antiphony, the conversation poem, the communal lyric and the dramatic monologue, all forms that articulate urgent questions about gender and race, class and poverty, climate and environment. These are questions that contemporary poetry voices too, but often in relation to its nineteenth-century forebears, both part of an 'aesthetic modernity' in which poetry invades 'unknown territory, exposing itself to the dangers of sudden, shocking encounters, conquering an as yet unoccupied future'.[4] Nineteenth-century poetry is not just 'modern'; it sustains the potential of poetry written now to engender material and affective change.[5]

As a discipline, however, literary criticism divides poetry written since 1780 into chronological 'fields' of study: 'Romantic', 'Victorian' and 'modern' are followed by a wrangle for novelty in the 'New, Newer and Newest Poetries'.[6] The writing and reception of poetry tends not to fall into such neat divisions, as the extracts in the 'Periodization' section disclose. While Harold Bloom's anxiety of influence haunts our understanding of the way one generation of poets responds to another, it is not clear that, for example, Christina Rossetti suffers any anxiety in her poetic responses to William Blake, John Keats, Letitia Landon or Felicia Hemans.[7] Larkin and Moxley's lyrical responses to poetry by Coleridge, Wordsworth and Tennyson also serve to enhance our reading of both, exposing shared dynamics as well as specificity. The specificity of nineteenth-century aesthetic currencies, forms and lexicons are discussed in the 'Forms' and 'Prosody' sections of this book. As suggested in the extracts these sections collect, poetry of this period is characterized by its engagement with the history of poetry and poetics, just as poetry written today looks back to nineteenth-century verse. It follows that poetry from both periods, then, continually tests 'old forms and conventions' to 'see if they are still capable of adding extra volume or direction to a speaker's voice'.[8] As Moxley points out in her reading of *In Memoriam*, Tennyson's elegy makes sense as a collage of 'poetic predecessors' and as an anticipation of *vers libre*, just as her own elegiac poetry looks back to 'Tennyson's sad measure' at the same time as it works within a twenty-first-century reinvention of the lyric.[9]

In introducing this volume of critical excerpts on nineteenth-century poetry through that written in the twenty-first, I make a formal and historical case for reading the two periods in relationship. First, poetry written then and now both discourage interpretation based on paraphrase and narrative, favouring instead a mosaic, layered and synecdochical approach. Second, both are concerned with the study of topics that identify a *longue durée* from the late eighteenth century into our own moment: capitalism, industrialism, technology, ecological devastation, inequality and alienation. As the predominant social form of modernity, poetry registers the structures of feelings and experiences that comprise relationships between people across borders, genders, nations and species, and so advocates a remapping of both our nineteenth-century and twenty-first-century worlds. The nineteenth-century preoccupation with nature, climate, industry and poverty, for example, anticipates our imminent social and environmental collapse in a world where half of the wealth is controlled by only 1 per cent of the population.[10] More than any other genre, poetry is poised to examine this relationship, thinking with the past rather than reinventing it, as subgenres such as Steampunk or Neo-Victorian fiction have done with the novel. As Joshua Clover argues, poetry is ideally placed to 'grasp the current conjuncture' because of its access to the 'essence' of our time: 'increasingly structural, increasingly abstract, increasingly detached from the subjective experience of the individual'.[11] If this 'time' is modernity, poetry's narration of it originates in the late eighteenth and nineteenth centuries, shaped as it is by an analogous anxiety about and resistance to an instrumental world that privileges self-interest and wealth.

My focus on the immediacy of nineteenth-century poetry serves to redress a literary critical history of it that has not always been kind.[12] Denouncements of its outmodedness or triviality especially targeted poets labelled 'Victorian', of which, Arthur Quiller-Couch confessed in his preface to the first *Oxford Book of Victorian Verse*, 'the most of them (I think) will be found on examination to miss being first-rate'.[13] Matthew Arnold even worried that his age was 'not unprofound, not ungrand, not unmoving: but *unpoetical*', an assessment Matthew Bevis links to his sense of the period as one founded on subjects Arnold judged prosaic and mundane: work, money and labour.[14] In a century characterized by the 1851 'Great Exhibition of the Works of Industry in All Nations', poetry held a precarious position in its material culture: poets flourished, but novelists and prose writers dominated the literary market. Philip Davis also notes that nineteenth-century poetry was a form 'in difficulty', fast losing its 'nerve and its place' within a 'new mass industrial and democratic society'.[15] Critics like Oscar Wilde, Aldous Huxley, T. S. Eliot and F. R. Leavis queued up to condemn much of the period's poetic output as sentimental filler: the 'Romantics' were cordoned off from the 'Victorians' as more philosophically serious and reflective ('Though Wordsworth happened to be the first Laureate of Queen Victoria's reign', writes Quiller Couch, 'no one will argue that he belongs to it'[16]); and later nineteenth-century poets struggled to prove their relevance to a newly emergent 'modern poetry'. Self-defined as 'new' and 'anti-lyric', modern poetry reached for an avant-gardism that rejected the previous period's verse as lazily sentimental and indulgently meditative, a critique synonymous with a hostility towards the 'feminine'. Excepting a few canonical 'greats' (Wordsworth, Tennyson, Browning, Rossetti), literary critics suspected that most poetry written before 1900 amounted to frivolous versifying about human 'feelings' and 'beliefs' in a context of esoteric debates over the laws of rhythm and prosody.

The modern construction of nineteenth-century poetry as nostalgic, feminine and sentimental, however, reveals more about a dramatization of literary history in which the novel stars and poetry's nuance is overlooked. Like poetry today, part of the draw of verse written before 1900 was that it was successful with readers even when it made little money. Collections that sold well, such as John Keble's *The Christian Year* (1827), which entered its 122nd edition by 1869, were often not read: even though Keble's book offered solace to many of the period's bereaved, it functioned as much as a ceremonial gift-book than admired volume.[17] Whatever the profit margins, poetry remained central in public discussion about literature and culture, as the extracts in the 'What is poetry?' section convey. Such scrutiny of poetry and poetics was not simply aesthetic, however, and provided the foundation on which it accrued much of its social and political force. Apparent in the extracts comprising the 'Politics' and 'Sexuality' sections is the suggestion that the uneven development of nineteenth-century society gave rise to much of the period's most historically significant poetry: factory poetry, Chartist verse and religious writing. Poets associated with the Oxford Movement, for example, considered pastoral work in poverty-stricken slums bound to their 'literary' faith, its expression in poetry excitedly discussed in the *Tracts for the Times* (1833–41), and also apparent in its influence on poets like Christina Rossetti, Gerard Manley Hopkins and Adelaide Anne Procter. Religion's long association with the rise of capitalism means that religious poetry must consequently have taken capital and the economy as explicit content, a point on which the extracts that comprise the 'Religion' section encourage further thought.[18] The extracts in the 'Science' section too reveal nineteenth-century poetry's implicit critique of a capitalism constituted by ecological regimes as well as its engagement with discourses of nature and technology, and advancements in geology, electricity, optics, physics, biology and energy.

As a mode of critiquing and engaging, exposing and exploring, nineteenth-century poetry is at once transformative and reflective, communal and individual. This aesthetic is directly reworked in twentieth and twenty-first-century poetry. Anne Janowitz, for example, puts the nineteenth-century communitarian lyric into dialogue with W. H. Auden's Anglo-Communist poetry and verse written during the UK miners' strike of 1984–85.[19] David Caplan similarly comments on the popularity of the sonnet with modern gay poets like Adrienne Rich, Marilyn Hacker, Rafael Campo and Henri Cole, all of whom test the elasticity of the form's

Petrarchan past given to them via the nineteenth-century sonnet revival. For poets like Charlotte Smith, Wordsworth and Christina and Dante Gabriel Rossetti, 'sonnettomania' granted them a form through which they could enact and manage emotion, a debate elaborated on in this book's section on 'Emotion, feeling, affect'.[20] Both groups thus petition the sonnet to assert the significance of affective experience through a controlled form that guards its content, whether sexual, religious or political. The dramatic monologue too, reinvented by nineteenth-century women poets like Hemans and Augusta Webster, finds analogy in the power of spoken word and slam poetry in the UK and US, a genre evidently popular with poets who compose from society's margins.[21] As a relational and social form, poetry inscribes historically specific structures of feeling – from protest to affect to identity – that connect the present to the past. Moxley and Wordsworth, for example, both experiment with lyric conventions of expression to articulate the confusion of their kindred moments, both founded on the exploitation of human beings and their environments for the purposes of war and capital. Wordsworth heralded poetry as better suited than other forms to the study of emergent knowledges because it was both familiar to a majority readership (it sounded more like commonplace ecclesiastic, folkloric and political broadsides than the new novel form), while its grammar and rhythms slowed the reading experience to create pauses for questions and reflection.[22] Reflecting on, reciting and memorizing poetry might have served as a mechanism by which readers were instilled with religious, moral and aesthetic norms, but it also served as a firm basis for community and friendship.[23] Samuel Taylor Coleridge, for example, famously recited 'Christabel' (1798) to William and Dorothy Wordsworth, Walter Scott and Henry Crabb Robinson, after which Robinson recited it to Byron, who then read it aloud to Mary Godwin, Percy Bysshe Shelley and John Polidori at the Villa Diodati during their ghost story telling competition in 1816.[24] For Moxley too, poetic form enables connection and intimacy, a 'temporal conduit between the past, present and future. It organizes the senses so that they do not hinder the intellect in its lonely quest toward understanding and, in some cases, unity with something greater than itself'.[25] While this 'greater than itself' is invisible for Moxley, who, intoning Tennyson, claims that her faith is doubt, it nevertheless captures a poetic working with and thinking of the metaphysical and mystical inherited from the poets focused on here.[26]

While this volume introduces readers to a variety of approaches to nineteenth-century poetry, it suggests that readers today require a methodology that allows access to the material and metaphysical. Finding ways to understand and clarify the concrete outcomes of beliefs and convictions that are sacred to some and illusive to others has never been more important for the reading of poetry and the world on which it comments. Certainly the material nature of debates on nineteenth-century poetry have dominated the field since the politicization of literary criticism from the 1960s, focusing as it has on labour and class, gender and sexuality, race and empire, and science and religion. A decade later, new formalism and new historicism reminded readers that questions of aesthetics and form were inseparable from those of history and politics, and that those concerns which preoccupy our lives today – from globalization to the environment – were also urgently examined in the nineteenth century. At a time when the study of poetry threatens to collapse under the banner of creative industries locked within aggressively managed universities, nineteenth-century poetry must be acknowledged not as an antiquated form that requires an imaginative leap into a distant past, but as belonging to a modern world it both fashions and interrogates. For whether a poem enunciates a protest politics or not, its formal nuance and dependence on contemplation and conversation for meaning offers a stay to the impulsive and competitive individualism on which capitalist modernity and neoliberal meritocracy are founded.[27] From Wordsworth's 1802 'Preface' to the *Lyrical Ballads* to Richard Cronin's recent overview of the field in *Reading Victorian Poetry* (2012), the extracts showcased here collectively affirm poetry as experiential and material, extant and historical, and continually in relationship with other forms of writing. Impatient with a linear logic through which current structures of power function, while generative of new ideas by absorbing older ones, nineteenth-century poetry thinks and feels beyond individual freedoms and rights towards an affective and material commons.

Further reading

The volume aims to provide an overview of criticism and debates about nineteenth-century poetry and poetics by including sources from the period alongside modern criticism. As nineteenth-century poetry is arguably the single most important expression of contemporary culture, politics, science, religion and sexuality in the period, articles and essays that touch on its importance are myriad. Below is a chronological list of texts the reader will find helpful in extending her research in poetry and poetics beyond this book, and, for a wider sense of scholarship, the reader is referred to the footnotes of the more recent extracts.

- John Thelwall, *Selections for the Illustration of a Course of Instructions on the Rhythms and Utterance of the English Language* (1812)
- R. B. Roe, *The Principles of Rhythm* (1823)
- W. Crowe, *A Treatise on English Versification* (1827)
- Anna Brownell Jameson, *The Loves of the Poets* (1829)
- W. J. Fox, 'Tennyson's Poems', *Westminster Review* (1831)
- Arthur Hallam, 'On Some Characteristics of Modern Poetry: and on the Lyrical Poems of Alfred Tennyson', *Englishman's Magazine* (1831)
- Letitia Elizabeth Landon, 'On the Character of Mrs Hemans' Writings,' *New Monthly Magazine*, 44 (1835)
- Edwin Guest, *A History of English Rhythms* (1838)
- Thomas Carlyle, 'Hero as Poet', *Heroes and Hero Worship* (1840)
- Margaret Fuller, 'A Dialogue: Poet and Critic', *The Dial* (1841)
- Edgar Allan Poe, 'The Philosophy of Composition', *Graham's Magazine* (1846)
- R. W. Evans, *Treatise on Versification, Ancient and Modern* (1852)
- Arthur Hugh Clough, 'Recent English Poetry', *The North American Review*, 77. 160 (1853)
- Sydney Dobell, 'Lecture on "The Nature of Poetry"' (1857)
- George Marsh, *Lectures on the English Language* (1860)
- Roden Noel, 'On the Use of Metaphor', *Fortnightly Review*, 5. 1 (1866), 670–684
- Alfred Austin, 'The Poetry of the Period: Mr Swinburne', *Temple Bar*, 26 (1869)
- Tom Hood, *The Rules of Rhyme; A Guide to English Versification* (1869)
- Gerard Manley Hopkins, 'Author's Preface on Rhythm', *The Poetical Works* (1870)
- Dora Greenwell, 'An Inquiry: As to how far the spirit of poetry is alien, and how far friendly, to that of Christianity', *Liber Humanitatis: A Series of Essays on Various Aspects of Spiritual and Social Life* (1875)
- E. C. Stedman, *Victorian Poets* (1875–1887)
- Gilbert Conway, *Treatise of Versification* (1878)
- E. Gurney, *The Power of Sound* (1880)
- John Ruskin, *Elements of English Prosody* (1880)
- Friedrich Nietzsche, 'On the Origin of Poetry', in *The Gay Science* (1882)

- J. B. Mayor, *Chapters on English Metre* (1891)
- J. A. Symonds, *Blank Verse* (1895)
- Thomas Stewart Omond, *A Study of Metre* (1903)
- T. E. Hulme, 'Romanticism and Classicism' (1911), in *Speculations: Essays on Humanism and the Philosophy of Art* (1924)
- R. M. Alden, *The Mental Side of Metrical Form* (1914)
- Robert Bridges, *The Necessity of Poetry* (1918)
- G. K. Chesterton, 'The Romance of Rhyme', in *Fancies Versus Fads* (1923)

Notes

1 Jennifer Moxley, 'Invective Verse', *Oblek 12: Writing from the New Coast* (1993); http://www.writing.upenn.edu/~afilreis/88/moxley.html.
2 Arthur Hugh Clough, 'Recent English Poetry', *The North American Review*, 77. 160 (1853), 1–30.
3 See Peter Larkin, *Wordsworth and Coleridge: Promising Losses* (Basingstoke: Palgrave Macmillan, 2012).
4 Jürgen Habermas, 'Modernity – an Unfinished Project', in *The Anti-Aesthetic: Essays on Postmodern Culture*, ed. Hal Foster (Seattle, WA: Bay Press, 1983), p. 3.
5 On the relationship between nineteenth-century poetry and modernity, see, for example: Isobel Armstrong, *Victorian Poetry: Poetry, Poetics and Politics* (London and New York: Routledge, 1993), p. 3; Ivan Kreilkamp, 'Victorian Poetry's Modernity', *Victorian Poetry,* 41.4 (2003), 603–611; Anne Jamison, *Poetics en Passant: Redefining the Relationship between Victorian and Modern Poetry* (New York: Palgrave Macmillan, 2009).
6 Alan Golding, 'New, Newer, and Newest American Poetries', *Chicago Review*, 43.4 (1997), 7–21.
7 Harold Bloom, *The Anxiety of Influence: A Theory of Poetry* (New York: Oxford University Press: 1973).
8 Robert Douglas-Fairhurst, 'Address', in Matthew Bevis, ed., *The Oxford Handbook of Victorian Poetry* (Oxford: Oxford University Press, 2013), pp. 56–73 (p. 65).
9 Jennifer Moxley, 'Too Common! – On Elegy', *LIT* 5, New School University (2001), 74–76; 'On This Side Nothing', in *The Sense Record and Other Poems* (Washington, DC: Edge Books, 2002), pp. 9–10 (p. 10). Many thanks to Jennifer Moxley for granting permission to quote from this poem.
10 Larry Elliott and Ed Pilkington, 'New Oxfam report says half of global wealth held by the 1%', *The Guardian*, 19 January 2015 http://www.theguardian.com/business/2015/jan/19/global-wealth-oxfam-inequality-davos-economic-summit-switzerland.
11 Joshua Clover, '"A Form Adequate to History": Toward a Renewed Marxist Poetics', *Paideuma*, 37.1–2 (2010), 321–348 (324).
12 See Matthew Bevis, 'Introduction: At Work with Victorian Poetry', in Bevis, ed. *Oxford Handbook*, pp. 1–18.
13 Arthur Quiller-Couch, 'Preface', in *The Oxford Book of Victorian Verse* (Oxford: Clarendon Press, 1912), pp. viii–ix.
14 Matthew Arnold, letter to Arthur Hugh Clough, February 1849, quoted in Philip Davis, *The Victorians: The Oxford English Literary History, Volume 8: 1830–1880* (Oxford: Oxford University Press, 2002), p. 456; Bevis, 'Introduction', pp. 3–4.
15 Davis, *The Victorians*, p. 456.
16 Quiller-Couch, *The Oxford Book of Victorian Verse*, p. viii.
17 Susan Matthews, 'Marketplaces', in Bevis, ed., *Oxford Handbook*, pp. 655–672 (p. 664).
18 See R. H. Tawney, *Religion and the Rise of Capitalism* [1926] (London: Verso, 2015); and Philip Goodchild, *Capitalism and Religion: The Price of Piety* (Abingdon: Routledge, 2002).
19 Anne Janowitz, *Lyric and Labour in the Romantic Tradition* (Cambridge: Cambridge University Press, 1998).
20 Anon., 'Sonnettomania,' in the *New Monthly Magazine* (June 1821), 652–6.
21 Armstrong, *Victorian Poetry*, pp. 325–326; Helen Gregory, '(Re)presenting Ourselves: Art, Identity, and Status in U. K. Poetry Slam', *Oral Tradition*, 23.2 (2008), 201–217.

22 Stephen Shapiro, *The Culture and Commerce of the Early American Novel: Reading the Atlantic World-System* (University Park, PA: Pennsylvania State University Press, 2008), p. 3.
23 See Catherine Robson, *Heart Beats: Everyday Life and the Memorized Poem* (Princeton, NJ: Princeton University Press, 2013).
24 See Valerie Purton, *A Coleridge Chronology* (London: Macmillan, 1993).
25 Jennifer Moxley, 'Fragments of a Broken Poetics', *Chicago Review*, 55.2 (2010), 17–27 (18).
26 Jennifer Moxley, interview with Noah Eli Gordon, *Jacket2*, 37 (2009), http://jacketmagazine. com/37/iv-moxley-ivb-gordon.shtml.
27 See David Harvey, *A Brief History of Neoliberalism* (Oxford: Oxford University Press, 2005).

Part I
Periodization

Francis O'Gorman

What would have happened if King William IV had had surviving legitimate children? Or John Keats had not had consumption? Or Percy Bysshe Shelley had not drowned on his way back to Lerici? Such questions—there are plenty of others—remind us of the contingency of categories in literary history. If one of William IV's legitimate heirs had lived, Victoria would not have been Queen. And that heir might not have lived as long as the long-lived Victoria. The 1837–1900 period could have been one with several monarchs, breaking up the convenience of a single reign and forbidding a single title for a rapidly changing but, to us, 'single' era. We do not think of 1937 to 2000 as a unitary period. We do not think of 1901 to 2000 as one either. And it would be useful to apply that same caution when dividing up the nineteenth century. But most literary readers and critics, nevertheless, do not need reminding of the problems of 'periodization', of the taxonomy we mistrust and cannot do without. Literary scholars, like all historians of culture, need parameters and must, rightly, argue about their legitimacy. What more, as Yeats would remark, is there to say?

It is true, all the same, that the 'Victorian' label is peculiarly difficult. This present book concerns 'nineteenth-century poetry'. That may be a neutral label. But it may not be. 'Nineteenth century' may safely avoid the loaded 'Romantic' and 'Victorian' yet still suggest, intentionally or otherwise, an intellectual case, a claim about how literary history should *not* be divided. 'Nineteenth-century poetry' can mean simply 'poetry from the nineteenth century'. Yet it can also mean: 'we are deliberately avoiding the Romantic/Victorian separation because the continuances and development of poetry during this century render them artificial, and what we want to stress is the wholeness of the century not its internal divisions'.

'Victorian' is almost impossible to use neutrally in literary criticism. Despite the best efforts of several generations of scholars, the term remains—even if only at the popular level—freighted with assumptions that leak from the wider culture and, often enough, from modern politics.[1] The 'Romantic' is not that much better—it is hardly assumption-free—but the term does not as frequently serve as a label in contemporary moral or political debate. Both period names, certainly, seem to tell us what, respectively, the poetry of 1780–*c.*1830 and *c.*1830–1900 was like before we read it. And in between those two divisions—the necessary staples of university English literature curricula, publishers' catalogues, commissioning editor's responsibilities, scholarly borderlines—lies the uncertain terrain of the *c.*1830. What happened then? Margaret Oliphant thought it the 'season of lull, of silence and emptiness'.[2] But was it, rather, the supposed 'transition' time *between* the Romantic and the Victorian; or something distinctive, something important in its own right? 'Nineteenth-century poetry' is one of the attempts to keep the 1830s in the academic eye. And concerning transitions, there is an issue at the other end of the century: the 'beginnings' of Modernism. Readers can hardly avoid the argument that a nineteenth-century text 'anticipates' Modernism—Michael Field, Thomas Hardy, James Thomson, Henry James, George Gissing.[3] But we might wonder what this concretely reveals other than that a historical/aesthetic description can be attached to literary writing earlier than is usually thought. The *historical* claim, the exact meaning, of 'pre-figuring' is, to my mind, unclear. What conception or theory of history can tolerate a notion of 'anticipation' in a rigorous analysis of how ideas, practices of writing, and forms of literary representation happen in time? If X occurs in a poem—a poet writes in this way rather than that—nothing precise is gained from arguing that the poem's significance is that it reads more like a text expected from later in time. 'Anticipation' in strictly historical or explanatory terms is a mystificatory word, a description of—seemingly—a piece of historical *prophecy*. And no writer has been able to see into the future.

The placing of a poem in time matters. But the argument about how periods are described is not the same as the broader question of the relationship between poetry and history. Periods, as far as historians really use them, require a thorough and extensive historical argument, a case that between this point in time and that point in time there was enough continuity in significant features of a culture to allow a chronological unit, a 'period' that can be considered as a whole. Recent scholarly arguments among historians have renewed serious debates about the serviceability of 'Victorian' as a historical category of this kind. Does it make sense to see political, social, intellectual, aesthetic, or religious continuities that begin around 1830 and end around 1900? Is this really a historical period? Richard Price thinks not; Martin Hewitt thinks it is.[4] Meanwhile, 'Romantic' hardly features prominently in historiography: it is a category more familiar to literary scholars than historians. The term is also familiar to art historians and musicians—but the nature and duration of the 'Romantic period' for these disciplines is not coincident with the 'Romantic period' of the literary critics. Romantic-period music in Europe, for instance, ended much, much later: Schoenberg's *Verklärte Nacht* was written in 1899; Gustav Mahler died in 1911, Edward Elgar in 1934. In literary studies, one of the difficulties with the 'Romantic' is the way it marks an apparent break with the 'eighteenth century' or is, even now, assumed to signify a reaction *against* the 'eighteenth century'. Wordsworth declared that *Lyrical Ballads* (1798) was sharply new. But modern writing has found it either strongly influenced by earlier poetic practice or even a latecomer to the debates about the scope and language of verse.[5] The assumptions that can be inferred from labels, from claims of new departures and decisive breaks, sometimes take a long time to be challenged.

It is one thing to talk about the historian's view of periods, of whether there is enough cultural continuity to treat a span of time as a serviceable unit in the divisions of national or international histories. But literary critics do not have only this kind of argument in mind when reading historical literature; in fact, they hardly have it in mind at all. Literary periods, as is the case with the 'Victorians', occasionally overlap with a (contested) historical period, but not always. What matters is literary or, here, specifically poetic continuities. What satisfactory, or at least in place-holder terms, define the 'Romantic' in English poetry? Or the 'Victorian'? Or 'the nineteenth century'? There is pedagogic profit in revisiting these topics and not least in the histories of form they matter peculiarly. The Irish Romantic period and the Irish 'Victorian' are not identical with the English, Scottish, or Welsh. The role of myth and ballad, the relationship of poetry and music, of the written with the oral, the identity of radicalism, make that clear. Working-class poetry followed different routes, often enough, from high cultural forms. The working-class poets in England of the early and mid-Victorian period drew largely on neo-Classical models of poetry more than they drew on Romantic and post-Romantic models of verse and conceptions of consciousness. In many cases, sex and gender matter too. Yet, for all that, it is still possible to find value in debating the features—intellectual, aesthetic, formal, together with the patterns of development and change—that help define a literary period even if each has a history and a legacy, and none is merely certain.

Critical questions can usefully be asked about poetic continuities and so can poets' questions, for their apprehension of a literary period in the nineteenth century is worth taking seriously as well. Keats wrote with a version of Spenser in his mind; Shakespeare never left him; Milton was a force to reckon with for Wordsworth and Coleridge.[6] But looking back to the past in this sustaining way is a different thing from thinking that one's poetry is out-of-date, overshadowed by the past. Harold Bloom regards the literary past for poets always as a looming father-figure, threatening the life and independence of the new creative generations.[7] Bloom, in work that remains persuasive, has enumerated imaginative and indeed desperate attempts to resist. But one does not have to accept this theory of the anxiety of influence in all its Freudian complexity to accept that some nineteenth-century poets were distinctively bothered by their date of birth. Tennyson, we know, felt the trouble of the 'Romantics' early in his career and dramatized scenes laden with the heavy sense of being too late—not least in 'The Dying Swan' (1830).[8] There was real difficulty in writing at the end of a generation. Matthew Arnold's verse carried with it the burden of not being 'Romantic' too; the previous generations' confidence in what Arnold called Wordsworth's 'healing power' felt now as inaccessible as miracle-based religions. John Ruskin expected initially to establish himself as a poet: he later remarked that his father had hoped his son would 'write poetry as good as Byron's, only pious'.[10] But Ruskin as a young man found that he had to give poetry up. He could not make a name from it; he had no gift. But there was something greater than personal history, a lack of gift, here too. Ruskin struggled to make an emotional connection between his subject matter and himself. It was a connection he would obtain, luminously, in his later prose. But the problem was not merely Ruskin's. His verse drew on eighteenth-century conventions and on Byron, yet it could not refresh, find a new way of imagining, his immediate poetical forebears. In its affective remoteness, the absence of a secure fusion between subject and object, Ruskin's verse was another indication that the shadow of Wordsworth, Scott, and Byron made life difficult for newcomers.

Romanticism, understood as a set of intellectual and cultural assumptions, was re-interpreted in new terms for the Victorians to satisfy new audiences and new sets of needs and priorities. Ruskin certainly found a way of achieving that repositioning not least through the recognition of what he named—to borrow an early book title—the poetry of architecture. Yet refreshing a legacy is not the same as realising one has not kept up with the times. Periods are useful, if problematic, categories for literary critics and literary historians. But time feels differently for poets themselves. Poets discern they have been left behind as much as they occasionally believe themselves without an audience ready to appreciate their novelty. Hopkins, for one, was not untroubled by his lack of audience even if he did not regard poetry as the central calling of his life. As with historical eras elsewhere, the definitions of 'modern' verse in the nineteenth century shifted so that what was at one point prestigious, fashionable, or marketable ceased to be so. Changes in fashion are not new. Aristotle records in the *Poetics* the shifts in what was most admired in the history of ancient Greek literature: the iambic lampoon, he observes, gave way to comedy and the epic to tragedy as new generations found they were grander forms and, if principally in Athens, *more honoured* (ἔντιμος).[11] Placing oneself as a writer in a literary period can have the awkward consequence of making one seem *passé*. It is as well to reassure oneself that, as a poet, it is not merely for a single period, after all, that one writes.

Algernon Charles Swinburne began in the late 1850s in a Morrisian Pre-Raphaelite mode, and then, quickly, abandoned it. But Swinburne is, more generally, a curious case in relation to the question of keeping pace because he has often been thought a poet whose remarkable early achievements made his *own* future old-fashioned. This problem—assuming for a moment that it is true—has not left Swinburne happily among the critics. John Drinkwater, poet and dramatist, thought Swinburne 'a strange phenomenon in the progress of poetry'[12] because, in fact, there had been no progress. There had only been a remarkable 'fixity in the temper of his language'.[13] Swinburne, regardless of his 'period', had outdated *himself*. More usually writers can seem, in evaluative terms, too much like the period that is past or passing and not enough like the period that is to come. The reputations of poets who live long into a 'new period' are not infrequently uncomfortable. Wordsworth is one example. Walter Savage Landor (1775–1864), 'Barry Cornwall' (1787–1874), and John Clare (1793–1864) in different ways and for different reasons are others, intriguingly 'out of time'. Arthur Symons (1865–1945) is another case. He made his name as a poet of the 1890s but survived, after many of his peers had died young, until the year in which the Second World War concluded. Symons found no easy way of maintaining literary visibility after the years of his greatest fame. W.B. Yeats obtained what Symons did not. But Yeats had had issues of period location early on. His initial poetic writing included Pre-Raphaelite, Tennysonian, and Swinburnian strains. If 'The Falling of the Leaves' had been written by early Swinburne or Tennyson, readers might well have noticed first the deft handling of the music of the line—the echoing of sounds in alliteration and assonance, the distinctive Swinburnean anapaest. Here was sound, even in the opening line, which belonged with the exquisite verbal harmonies for which the Victorian lyric was admired:

> Autumn is over the long leaves that love us,
> And over the mice in the barley sheaves;
> Yellow the leaves of the rowan above us,
> And yellow the wet wild-strawberry leaves.
>
> The hour of the waning of love has beset us,
> And weary and worn are our sad souls now;
> Let us part, ere the season of passion forget us,
> With a kiss and a tear on thy drooping brow.[14]

There was some Rossettian melancholy here too, a Pre-Raphaelite flavour. But the period judgment ('is this poem *of* its period or behind it?') can only result in disappointment. For 'The Falling of the Leaves' was included in Yeats' *Crossways* of 1889, long after Tennysonian melancholy had first been heard, and long after Swinburne had arrived charismatically on the poetic scene. Rossetti had been dead for seven years. Placed in the period when he wrote his early poetry, Yeats seems too much a man of the past and not enough of the new—the coming 'period' of the moderns, of the twentieth century.

Writers, critics, and publishers may worry about freshness and newness more than ordinary readers. Evaluating poetry *against* period can lead to some disabling confusion between the 'new' and the 'good', to evaluation that is based on how far the poetry is and is not of its time rather than, literally, the achievement of the text itself, the words on the page. But there are other productive ways of thinking about poetry and periodization in the nineteenth century that take one not merely into categories but into the experience of reading. The literal business of reading involves, that is, an alternative realisation of time and its passage than that encapsulated by the concept of a historical period. What kinds of pasts and presents can be co-ordinated, made simultaneous in reading poetry is not a question confined to the nineteenth century. But such simultaneity was an absorbing subject in the nineteenth century all the same.[15] Romantics and particularly Victorians searched with ingenuity the matter of how complicated a period can feel from inside a text, of what reading can do to time. Various nineteenth-century poets were, indeed, peculiarly interested in the literary creation of a sense of the simultaneity of historical presents. Reading in this respect provided a nineteenth-century poetry reader with the potential for feeling that the present moment was comprised of the 'now' and belonged to it—yet was also alive with the dead, with the imagined vitality of something apparently gone. The dramatic monologue, an important formal innovation of the 1830s, played vibrantly with the 'living' voice that belonged in the past—Andrea del Sarto, St Simeon Stylites, Ulysses, Pompilia Comparini—yet in the reader's ears those past voices 'speak again'. Writing *The Idylls of the King* (1859–85), Tennyson made the story of Arthur and the Round Table not merely a convenient cover for tackling modern issues of nationhood, the idea of liberalism and government, adultery, or contemporary masculinity, but a way of bringing the contemporary and an imagined ancient British world into a curiously felt simultaneity in the act of reading. *The Idylls* invite their readers to experience historical 'period' in a provocative way because times are interfused imaginatively with each other in a way that is both almost impossible to describe and startlingly real to sense.

Swinburne took such simultaneity further, writing, for instance, two new 'ancient Greek' poetic dramas *Atalanta in Calydon* (1865) and *Erechtheus* (1876). At one level, those pieces (written in English) were of their day: they belong with the classical scholarship that was the common property of the educated Victorian man; they belong in the tormented history of Victorian struggles with Christianity, and the promise of a world shaped by benign intention. Yet *Atalanta in Calydon* and *Erechtheus*, particularly for readers with a grasp of the classical writing on which they drew, also allow a curious, mediated, and disarmingly uncanny experience of two cultures, two histories, two places, read at once and 'lived-in' at once through the reading experience. But sensing the co-ordination of time in reading invites the question of how far creative writers think in terms of their own period in the same way that subsequent critics do. The 'Cockney School' or the 'Lake School' were available terms for poets later generations named 'Romantics'. But belonging to a school or a group is not the same as feeling oneself a signifier or a constituent part of a period. Nevertheless, something important occurs at the end of the nineteenth century when the notion of living in a distinctive period—a Victorian age—emerged visibly into literary critical debate. 'Being Victorian' became, in the end, to be recognized as a lived category of writerly identity. Margaret Oliphant did not question that she was speaking of a period in *The Victorian Age of English Literature* (1892) for it made perfect sense to write about the literature between the accession of the Queen and the end of the nineteenth century just as the great men and women of that age were dying out. The recent death of Tennyson, as Oliphant noted in the 'Preface', 'puts back this record as by the end of the epoch which it treats'.[16] For both *The Victorian Age of English Literature* and the positivist critic and biographer Frederic Harrison, writing in *Studies in Early Victorian Literature* (1895), the important issue was not that 'Victorian literature' had a unity or distinctive intellectual, formal, or aesthetic coherence. 'It is an age', Harrison said, 'peculiarly difficult to label in a phrase'. But for him the 'Victorian' deserved that label simply because the Queen's reign had been distinguished by eminent writers. If the nineteenth century had no Shakespeare, Harrison observed, 'its copious and versatile gifts will make it memorable in the history of modern civilisation'.[17] This sequence of fine writers, a corpus of poets and novelists about whom the whole nation could be proud, signified the existence of a 'period' and that was that. *The Review of Reviews* agreed, adding in March 1894 that the recent death in old age of 'many masters of English prose and verse' was bringing 'to the close [a] great literary epoch'.[18] A literary period was constituted by its practitioners, by its vivid personalities in print: the notion of an 'age' was not an indication of intellectual or aesthetic coherence, of continuities or consistency in politics or principles, but an honorific. The joke in Lytton Strachey's *Eminent Victorians* (1918), then, was that for men of Harrison's temper, the title as far as literature was concerned was tautologous.

As the late Victorian critics defined their own age in literature, so at the end of it, creative writers themselves pondered what was about to leave them. A change of century is an obvious point for self-reflection. But in the history of periodization, the end of the nineteenth century is peculiarly weighted among the poets because it was apprehended as the end of an *age*. Celebrated authors—Alfred Tennyson, Robert Browning, John Ruskin, Matthew Arnold, George Eliot, Anthony Trollope, Oscar Wilde—had died within the last twenty years. Only Swinburne, among the major Victorian poets who had made their name in the middle of the century, continued. It was true that Thomas Hardy, as a poet, had only just begun to publish with *Wessex Poems and Other Verses* (1898), but the air felt heavy with losses and conclusions nevertheless. In 'The Darkling Thrush' ('The Century's End'), Hardy himself was characteristically pensive about what kind of century the faded, etiolated, withered form of the nineteenth could bring to birth. But others echoed the prose critics in thinking not only of the passing of a century but also the ending of an epoch. 'Sound trumpets! sound a peal for the New Year!', wrote Sir Lewis Morris in 'January 1, 1901: An Ode':

> The great New Year which brings another Age;
> The old, the weary Century at last
> Closes its time-worn page;
> Its hopes, its fears, its aspirations dead,
> Deep buried in the irrevocable Past.
> Close, close its eyes, cover its aged head.
> It was an earnest Age; from early youth
> It sought the face of Truth,
> Not as its world-worn sire, it lived and died
> Absorbed in scoffing doubt and scarcely human pride;
> Never it scorned the toiling multitude,
> But loved the general good,
> And dowered the Race with many a gain sublime,
> Grander than any of recorded Time.
> Chant low its dirge awhile! then with loud voice
> Acclaim the coming Sovereign and rejoice!
> Relight hope's waning fires! be of good cheer!
> Put vain regrets aside and chilling fear,
> Sound trumpets! sound a peal for this the great New Year![19]

Morris, born in 1833, would live only to 1907. It was partly his own distinguished, busy life that Morris was remembering on the first day of the new century. He had been a hugely popular poet, one of the most celebrated of the period. But his reputation at the beginning of the new century was already in terminal decline. Yet as the old century closed, there was an unmissable occasion to perceive the past more generally, to frame it, to remember it as something more than seventy individual years but as a whole. Morris—a leading force in the development of the University of Wales—remembered science and politics, an (imperial?) ambition for the 'general good'. And now these values, aspirations, and failings were over. Swinburne, in 'A New Century', gathered into his last volume, *A Channel Passage and Other Poems* (1904), reflected on the passing of what was definitely a period too: 'An age too great for thought of ours to scan', he said, evasively.[20] It was not hard to think of Victoria's long reign as an achievement, a coherence, a narrative, even if, with Swinburne, it was no easy task to describe it. One could speak of 'Victorian literature', though, for a clearer reason because it was a peculiarly writerly time.

Contemporary critics have inherited a label to describe seventy years of the nineteenth century, which, in literary criticism, once had a different, simpler, and evaluative, meaning. In this sense, our usages—sophisticated, contested, liable to ideological misprision, often discarded, often over-run with clichés—are not historical. In literary criticism, we have inherited a Victorian category but in moving it away from its roots we have endeavoured to re-invent it as an argumentative, logically coherent concept that must do more work than it originally did. No wonder we have disagreed with each other.

Notes

1   For some assessment of this, see Gary Day (ed.), *Varieties of Victorianism: The Uses of a Past* (Basingstoke: Macmillan, 1998).
2   Margaret Oliphant, *The Victorian Age of English Literature*, 2 vols (New York: Lovell, Corvell, 1892), I, p. 7.
3   For a recent perspective on this topic in relation to poetry, see Ivan Kreilkamp, 'Victorian Poetry's Modernity', *Victorian Poetry*, 41 (2003), 603–11.
4   See Richard N. Price, *British Society 1680–1880: Dynamism, Containment and Change* (Cambridge: Cambridge University Press, 1999); Martin Hewitt, 'Why the Notion of Victorian Britain Does Make Sense', *Victorian Studies*, 48 (2006), 395–438. Cf. Francis O'Gorman, 'Partly Autonomous? Literary-Historical Reflections on Richard Price, *British Society, 1680–1880*', *Journal of Victorian Culture*, 11.1 (2006), 160–7.
5   Cf. David Fairer, *English Poetry of the Eighteenth Century* (Harlow: Longman, 2003) and *Organising Poetry: The Coleridge Circle, 1790–1798* (Oxford: Oxford University Press, 2009).
6   Cf. Lucy Newlyn, *'Paradise Lost' and the Romantic Reader* (Oxford: Clarendon, 1993).
7   See Harold Bloom, *The Anxiety of Influence: A Theory of Poetry* (New York: Oxford University Press, 1973).
8   On forms of anxiety in this poem, see Catherine Barnes Stevenson 'Tennyson's Dying Swans: Mythology and the Definition of the Poet's Role', *Studies in English Literature, 1500–1900*, 20 (1980), 621–35. See more generally Herbert F. Tucker, *Tennyson and the Doom of Romanticism* (Cambridge, MA: Harvard University Press, 1988).
9   Matthew Arnold, 'Memorial Verses: April, 1850', *The Poems of Matthew Arnold,* ed. Kenneth Allott and Miriam Allott (London: Longman, 1979), p. 242, l. 63. The most recent assessment of Arnold's relationship with the Romantics is Michael O'Neill, '"The Burden of Ourselves": Arnold as a Post-Romantic Poet', *Yearbook of English Studies*, 36 (2006), 109–24.
10 E. T. Cook and Alexander Wedderburn (eds), *The Library Edition of the Works of John Ruskin*, 39 vols (London: Allen, 1903–12), XXXV, p. 185.
11 Aristotle, *Poetics*, 1449, ll., 5–6.
12 John Drinkwater, *Swinburne: An Estimate* (London: Dent, 1913), p. 5.

13 Ibid., p. 9.
14 W.B. Yeats, *The Collected Poems of W.B. Yeats* (London: Macmillan, 1950), p. 16.
15 I am currently writing a sequence of studies of the relationship between time, reading, and forgetting in nineteenth-century literature. See, for instance, Francis O'Gorman, 'Matthew Arnold and Rereading', *The Cambridge Quarterly*, 41 (2012), 245–61.
16 Oliphant, *The Victorian Age,* I, p. vi.
17 Frederic Harrison, *Studies in Early Victorian Literature* (London: Arnold, 1895), p.9. D.F. Hannigan in *The Westminster Review* took exception to this assertion about Shakespeare, noting: 'but we have a Browning—and who shall say that he is not a supremely great poet?' 'The Victorian Age of Literature and Its Critics', *The Westminster Review,* 145 (January 1896), 519–25.
18 'The Victorian Age in Literature', *The Review of Reviews* (March 1894), p. 256.
19 *The Works of Sir Lewis Morris* (London: Kegan Paul, Trench, Trübner, 1904), p. 760.
20 Algernon Charles Swinburne, *A Channel Passage and Other Poems* (London: Chatto & Windus, 1904), p. 142, l.1. The poem was originally printed in *The Saturday Review*, 5 January 1901, p. 1.

1   Preface to the First Edition of *Poems* (1853)

Matthew Arnold

'The poet,' it is said,[1] and by an intelligent critic, 'the poet who would really fix the public attention must leave the exhausted past, and draw his subjects from matters of present import, and *therefore* both of interest and novelty.'

Now this view I believe to be completely false. It is worth examining, inasmuch as it is a fair sample of a class of critical dicta everywhere current at the present day, having a philosophical form and air, but no real basis in fact; and which are calculated to vitiate the judgment of readers of poetry, while they exert, so far as they are adopted, a misleading influence on the practice of those who make it.

What are the eternal objects of poetry, among all nations, and at all times? They are actions; human actions; possessing an inherent interest in themselves, and which are to be communicated in an interesting manner by the art of the poet. Vainly will the latter imagine that he has everything in his own power; that he can make an intrinsically inferior action equally delightful with a more excellent one by his treatment of it. He may indeed compel us to admire his skill, but his work will possess, within itself, an incurable defect.

The poet, then, has in the first place to select an excellent action; and what actions are the most excellent? Those, certainly, which most powerfully appeal to the great primary human affections: to those elementary feelings which subsist permanently in the race, and which are independent of time. These feelings are permanent and the same; that which interests them is permanent and the same also. The modernness or antiquity of an action, therefore, has nothing to do with its fitness for poetical representation; this depends upon its inherent qualities. To the elementary part of our nature, to our passions, that which is great and passionate is eternally interesting; and interesting solely in proportion to its greatness and to its passion. A great human action of a thousand years ago is more interesting to it than a smaller human action of to-day, even though upon the representation of this last the most consummate skill may have been expended, and though it has the advantage of appealing by its modern language, familiar manners, and contemporary allusions, to all our transient feelings and interests. These, however, have no right to demand of a poetical work that it shall satisfy them; their claims are to be directed elsewhere. Poetical works belong to the domain of our permanent passions; let them interest these, and the voice of all subordinate claims upon them is at once silenced.

Achilles, Prometheus, Clytemnestra, Dido, – what modern poem presents personages as interesting, even to us moderns, as these personages of an 'exhausted past?' ... It may be urged, however, that past actions may be interesting in themselves, but that they are not to be adopted by the modern poet, because it is impossible for him to have them clearly present to his own mind, and he cannot therefore feel them deeply, nor represent them forcibly. But this is not *necessarily* the case. The externals of a past action, indeed, he cannot know with the precision of a contemporary; but his business is with its essentials. The outward man of Œdipus or of Macbeth, the houses in which they lived, the ceremonies of their courts, he cannot accurately figure to himself; but neither do they essentially concern him. His business is with their inward man; with their feelings and behaviour in certain tragic situations, which engage their passions as men; these have in them nothing local and casual; they are as accessible to the modern poet as to a contemporary.

The date of an action, then, signifies nothing; the action itself, its selection and construction, this is what is all-important. This the Greeks understood far more clearly than we do. The radical difference between their poetical theory and ours consists, as it appears to me, in this: that, with them, the poetical character of the action in itself, and the conduct of it, was the first consideration; with us, attention is fixed mainly on the value of the separate thoughts and images which occur in the treatment of an action. They regarded the whole; we regard the parts. With them, the action predominated over the expression of it; with us, the expression predominates over the action. Not that they failed in expression, or were inattentive to it; on the contrary, they are the highest models of expression, the unapproached masters of the *grand style.* But their expression is so excellent because it is so admirably kept in its right degree of prominence; because it is so simple and so well subordinated; because it draws its force directly from the pregnancy of the matter which it conveys. For what reason was the Greek tragic poet confined to so limited a range of subjects? Because there are so few actions which unite in themselves, in the highest degree, the conditions of excellence: and it was not thought that on any but an excellent subject could an excellent poem be constructed. A few actions, therefore, eminently adapted for tragedy, maintained almost exclusive possession of the Greek tragic stage. Their significance appeared inexhaustible; they were as permanent problems, perpetually offered to the genius of every fresh poet. This too is the reason of what appears to us moderns a certain baldness of expression in Greek tragedy; of the triviality with which we often reproach the remarks of the chorus, where it takes part in the dialogue: that the action itself, the situation of Orestes, or Merope, or Alcmæon, was to stand the central point of interest, unforgotten, absorbing, principal; that no accessories were for a moment to distract the spectator's attention from this; that the tone of the parts was to be perpetually kept down, in order not to impair the grandiose effect of the whole. The terrible old mythic story on which the drama was founded stood, before he entered the theatre, traced in its bare outlines upon the spectator's mind; it stood in his memory, as a group of statuary, faintly seen, at the end of a long and dark vista: then came the poet, embodying outlines, developing situations, not a word wasted, not a sentiment capriciously thrown in: stroke upon stroke, the drama proceeded: the light deepened upon the group; more and more it revealed itself to the riveted gaze of the spectator: until at last, when the final words were spoken, it stood before him in broad sunlight, a model of immortal beauty.

[...]

How different a way of thinking from this is ours! We can hardly at the present day understand what Menander meant, when he told a man who enquired as to the progress of his comedy that he had finished it, not having yet written a single line, because he had constructed the action of it in his mind. A modern critic would have assured him that the merit of his piece depended on the brilliant things which arose under his pen as he went along. We have poems which seem to exist merely for the sake of single lines and passages; not for the sake of producing any total impression. We have critics who seem to direct their attention merely to detached expressions, to the language about the action, not to the action itself. I verily think that the majority of them do not in their hearts believe that there is such a thing as a total impression to be derived from a poem at all, or to be demanded from a poet; they think the term a common-place of metaphysical criticism. They will permit the poet to select any action he pleases, and to suffer that action to go as it will, provided he gratifies them with occasional bursts of fine writing, and with a shower of isolated thoughts and images. That is, they permit him to leave their poetical sense ungratified, provided that he gratifies their rhetorical sense and their curiosity.

[…]

The confusion of the present times is great, the multitude of voices counselling different things bewildering, the number of existing works capable of attracting a young writer's attention and of becoming his models, immense. What he wants is a hand to guide him through the confusion, a voice to prescribe to him the aim which he should keep in view, and to explain to him that the value of the literary works which offer themselves to his attention is relative to their power of helping him forward on his road towards this aim. Such a guide the English writer at the present day will nowhere find. Failing this, all that can be looked for, all indeed that can be desired, is, that his attention should be fixed on excellent models; that he may reproduce, at any rate, something of their excellence, by penetrating himself with their works and by catching their spirit, if he cannot be taught to produce what is excellent independently.

Foremost among these models for the English writer stands Shakespeare: a name the greatest perhaps of all poetical names; a name never to be mentioned without reverence. I will venture, however, to express a doubt, whether the influence of his works, excellent and fruitful for the readers of poetry, for the great majority, has been of unmixed advantage to the writers of it. Shakespeare indeed chose excellent subjects; the world could afford no better than Macbeth, or Romeo and Juliet, or Othello; he had no theory respecting the necessity of choosing subjects of present import, or the paramount interest attaching to allegories of the state of one's own mind; like all great poets, he knew well what constituted a poetical action; like them, wherever he found such an action, he took it; like them, too, he found his best in past times. But to these general characteristics of all great poets he added a special one of his own; a gift, namely, of happy, abundant, and ingenious expression, eminent and unrivalled: so eminent as irresistibly to strike the attention first in him, and even to throw into comparative shade his other excellences as a poet. Here has been the mischief. These other excellences were his fundamental excellences *as a poet;* what distinguishes the artist from the mere amateur, says Goethe, is *Architectonicè* in the highest sense; that power of execution, which creates, forms, and constitutes: not the profoundness of single thoughts, not the richness of imagery, not the abundance of illustration. But these attractive accessories of a poetical work being more easily seized than the spirit of the whole, and these accessories being possessed by Shakespeare in an unequalled degree, a young writer having recourse to Shakespeare as his model runs great risk of being vanquished and absorbed by them, and, in consequence, of reproducing, according to the measure of his power, these, and these alone. Of this preponderating quality of Shakespeare's genius, accordingly, almost the whole of modern English poetry has, it appears to me, felt the influence. To the exclusive attention on the part of his imitators to this it is in a great degree owing, that of the majority of modern poetical works the details alone are valuable, the composition worthless… .

Let me give an instance of what I mean. I will take it from the works of the very chief among those who seem to have been formed in the school of Shakespeare: of one whose exquisite genius and pathetic death render him for ever interesting. I will take the poem of Isabella, or the Pot of Basil, by Keats. I choose this rather than the Endymion, because the latter work, (which a modern critic has classed with the Fairy Queen!) although undoubtedly there blows through it the breath of genius, is yet as a whole so utterly incoherent, as not strictly to merit the name of a poem at all. The poem of Isabella, then, is a perfect treasure-house of graceful and felicitious words and images: almost in every stanza there occurs one of those vivid and picturesque turns of expression, by which the object is made to flash upon the eye of the mind, and which thrill the reader with a sudden delight. This one short poem contains, perhaps, a greater number of happy single expressions which one could quote than all the extant tragedies of Sophocles. But the action, the story? The action in itself is an excellent one; but so feebly is it conceived by the poet, so loosely constructed, that the effect produced by it, in and for itself, is absolutely null. Let the reader, after he has finished the poem of Keats, turn to the same story in the Decameron: he will then feel how pregnant and interesting the same action has become in the hands of a great artist, who above all things delineates his object; who subordinates expression to that which it is designed to express.

[…]

The present age makes great claims upon us; we owe it service, it will not be satisfied without our admiration. I know not how it is, but their commerce with the ancients appears to me to produce, in those who constantly practise it, a steadying and composing effect upon their judgment, not of literary works only, but of men and events in general. They are like persons who have had a very weighty and impressive experience; they are more truly than others under the empire of facts, and more independent of the language current among those with whom they live. They wish neither to applaud nor to revile their age; they wish to know what it is, what it can give them, and whether this is what they want. What they want, they know very well; they want to educe and cultivate what is best and noblest in themselves; they know, too, that this is no easy task … and they ask themselves sincerely whether their age and its literature can assist them in the attempt. If they are endeavouring to practise any art, they remember the plain and simple proceedings of the old artists, who attained their grand results by penetrating themselves with some noble and significant action, not by inflating themselves with a belief in the preeminent importance and greatness of their own times. They do not talk of their mission, nor of interpreting their age, nor of the coming poet; all this, they know, is the mere delirium of vanity; their business is not to praise their age, but to afford to the men who live in it the highest pleasure which they are capable of feeling. If asked to afford this by means of subjects drawn from the age itself, they ask what special fitness the present age has for supplying them. They are told that it is an era of progress, an age commissioned to carry out the great ideas of industrial development and social amelioration. They reply that with all this they can do nothing; that the elements they need for the exercise of their art are great actions, calculated powerfully and delightfully to affect what is permanent in the human soul; that so far as the present age can supply such– actions, they will gladly make use of them; but that an age wanting in moral grandeur can with difficulty supply such, and an age of spiritual discomfort with difficulty be powerfully and delightfully affected by them.

A host of voices will indignantly rejoin that the present age is inferior to the past neither in moral grandeur nor in spiritual health. He who possesses the discipline I speak of will content himself with remembering the judgments passed upon the present age, in this respect, by the men of strongest head and widest culture whom it has produced; by Goethe and by Niebuhr. It will be sufficient for him that he knows the opinions held by these two great men respecting the present age and its literature; and that he feels assured in his own mind that their aims and demands upon life were such as he would wish, at any rate, his own to be; and their judgment as to what is impeding and disabling such as he may safely follow. He will not, however, maintain a hostile attitude towards the false pretensions of his age; he will content himself with not being overwhelmed by them. He will esteem himself fortunate if he can succeed in banishing from his mind all feelings of contradiction, and irritation, and impatience; in order to delight himself with the contemplation of some noble action of a heroic time, and to enable others, through his representation of it, to delight in it also.

I am far indeed from making any claim, for myself, that I possess this discipline; or for the following poems, that they breathe its spirit. But I say, that in the sincere endeavour to learn and practise, amid the bewildering confusion of our times, what is sound and true in poetical art, I seemed to myself to find the only sure guidance, the only solid footing, among the ancients. They, at any rate, knew what they wanted in art, and we do not... .

Two kinds of *dilettanti,* says Goethe, there are in poetry: he who neglects the indispensable mechanical part, and thinks he has done enough if he shows spirituality and feeling; and he who seeks to arrive at poetry merely by mechanism, in which he can acquire an artisan's readiness, and is without soul and matter. And he adds, that the first does most harm to art, and the last to himself. If we must be *dilettanti:* if it is impossible for us, under the circumstances amidst which we live, to think clearly, to feel nobly, and to delineate firmly: if we cannot attain to the mastery of the great artists; – let us, at least, have so much respect for our art as to prefer it to ourselves. Let us not bewilder our successors; let us transmit to them the practice of poetry, with its boundaries and wholesome regulative laws, under which excellent works may again, perhaps, at some future time, be produced, not yet fallen into oblivion through our neglect, not yet condemned and cancelled by the influence of their eternal enemy, caprice.

Note

1 In the *Spectator* of April 2, 1853. The words quoted were not used with reference to poems of mine.

2 Romanticism as a Modern Tradition (1957)

Robert Langbaum

"In English writing we seldom speak of tradition," T. S. Eliot complained back in 1917.[1] Nowadays, thanks largely to Mr Eliot's influence, an opponent of his might complain, we seldom speak of anything else. But we do not have to be opponents of Eliot to recognize that the volume of talk about tradition has increased considerably since World War I, that the word which, as Eliot tells us, seldom appeared "except in a phrase of censure" now appears almost always in phrases of approval, phrases which mark the approver of tradition as a man of advanced ideas.

Why, we may well ask, should a word which used to carry associations of stale orthodoxy carry for us the shine of novelty? Because the word has been used, more frequently and emphatically than before 1917, to remind us that tradition is the thing we have not got, to remind us of our separation from the past, our modernity. The word helps construct for us that image of ourselves which constitutes the modern pathos, the image of ourselves as emancipated to the point of forlornness, to the point where each is free to learn for himself that life is meaningless without tradition.

> I can connect
> Nothing with nothing

says Eliot's modern equivalent for Ophelia, after she has been seduced. Ophelia is pathetic because her inability to make connections is a sign of madness. But the inability of Eliot's ruined lady to make connections is a sign of the times. It expresses perfectly the meaning of *The Waste Land,* as of all those poems and novels which ring most poignantly of the new age. For we have used the contrast with tradition to define not only our separateness from the whole heritage of the West but to define also our separation from the immediate past, to define the special character of the twentieth century as an age distinct from the nineteenth. The curious thing about the twentieth century's reaction against the nineteenth is that we have levelled against the nineteenth century two apparently opposite charges. On the one hand, we have accused the nineteenth century of not being untraditional enough, of trying to compromise with the past, to cling through a false sentimentality to values in which it no longer really believed. On the other hand, we have accused the nineteenth century of breaking with the past, of rejecting *the* tradition, the "main current," to use Eliot's phrase, of Christian and humanist culture.

The apparent contradiction can be reconciled, however, once we realize the special nature of modern traditionalism, that it is built upon an original rejection of the past which leads to an attempt to reconstruct in the ensuing wilderness a new principle of order. If the nineteenth century ought to have swept away the sentimentally sustained debris of the past, it was because the debris hindered the work of discerning the really enduring patterns of human existence. Thus, Eliot's *Waste Land* and Joyce's *Ulysses* are at once more nihilistic and more deliberately traditional than any nineteenth-century works. In their accounts of the present, Eliot and Joyce show with uncompromising completeness that the past of official tradition is dead, and in this sense they carry nineteenth-century naturalism to its logical conclusion. But they also dig below the ruins of official tradition to uncover in myth an underground tradition, an inescapable because inherently psychological pattern into which to fit the chaotic present.

Eliot, in reviewing *Ulysses* for *The Dial* of November 1923, showed how modern anti-traditionalism clears the ground for modern traditionalism. Taking issue with Richard Aldington's condemnation of Joyce as a "prophet of chaos," Eliot calls *Ulysses* "the most important expression which the present age has found" precisely because Joyce has shown us how to be "classical" under modern conditions. He has given us the materials of modern disorder and shown us how to impose order upon them.

In using the myth, in manipulating a continuous parallel between contemporaneity and antiquity, Mr Joyce is pursuing a method which others must pursue after him…. It is simply a way of controlling, of ordering, of giving a shape and a significance to the immense panorama of futility and anarchy which is contemporary history. It is a method already adumbrated by Mr Yeats, and of the need for which I believe Mr Yeats to have been the first contemporary to be conscious. It is a method for which the horoscope is auspicious. Psychology (such as it is, and whether our reaction to it be comic or serious), ethnology, and *The Golden Bough* have concurred to make possible what was impossible even a few years ago. Instead of narrative method, we may now use the mythical method. It is, I seriously believe, a step toward making the modern world possible for art, toward that order and form which Mr Aldington so earnestly desires. And only those who have won their own discipline in secret and without aid, in a world which offers very little assistance to that end, can be of any use in furthering this advance.

The passage indicates the special nature of modern traditionalism in that Eliot does not talk about adherence to a publicly acknowledged tradition. He talks about a tradition which the past would not have recognized, a tradition tailored for a modern purpose by modern minds. And he talks, in the final sentence, of a sense of order won as a personal achievement in the face of external chaos.

The interesting thing is that both ideas, the idea of the past and of the superior individual as giving meaning to an otherwise meaningless world, derive from that same nineteenth-century romanticism against which Eliot is in reaction. Whatever the difference between the literary movements of the nineteenth and twentieth centuries, they are connected by their view of the world as meaningless, by their response to the same wilderness. That wilderness is the legacy of the Enlightenment, of the scientific and critical effort of the Enlightenment which, in its desire to separate fact from the values of a crumbling tradition, separated fact from all values—bequeathing a world in which fact is measurable quantity while value is man-made and illusory. Such a world offers no objective verification for just the perceptions by which men live, perceptions of beauty, goodness and spirit. It was as literature began in the latter eighteenth century to realize the dangerous implications of the scientific world-view, that romanticism was born. It was born anew in at least three generations thereafter as men of genius arrived intellectually at the dead-end of the eighteenth century and then, often through a total crisis of personality, broke intellectually into the nineteenth. As literature's reaction to the eighteenth century's scientific world-view, romanticism connects the literary movements of the nineteenth and twentieth centuries.

[…]

Although one dreads reopening at this late date the quarrel over the definition of romanticism, it nevertheless remains impossible to talk long about modern literature without employing, whether explicitly or implicitly, some working definition of the term. Such a working definition can, I think, be achieved at the lowest common denominator of agreement, once we distinguish between romanticism as a permanently recurring characteristic of personalities and artistic periods, and romanticism as that unprecedented shift of mind and sensibility which began in the latter eighteenth century. In the first sense, romanticism is one pole of the eternal alternation between emotion and intellect, freedom and discipline. In the second, it is the attempt of modern man to reintegrate fact and value after having himself rejected, in the experience of the Enlightenment, the old values. Post-Enlightenment romanticism does, to be sure, make use of emotion and freedom, but only as means incidental to the main and, as far as one can make out, historically unique purpose of the movement, which is not in the end to reject intellect and discipline but to renew them by empirical means.

Post-Enlightenment romanticism is historically unique just to the extent that it uses for its reconstructive purpose the same scientific or empirical method which is itself unique to the modern world. Like the scientist's hypothesis, the romanticist's formulation is evolved out of experience and is continually tested against experience. The difference is that the scientist's experiment is a selected and analysed experience, whereas experience for the romanticist is even more empiric because less rationalized. It is what happens before selection and analysis take place. Romanticism is in this sense not so much a reaction against eighteenth-century empiricism as a reaction within it, a corrected empiricism. It is, as Mill suggested, the necessary corrective for the skeptical analytic intellect.

Thus the empiricist Locke, spelling out the philosophical implications of Newton's physics, says that the world of our ordinary perception is largely illusory, that the only objective reality consists of particles of matter moving in space. He gives us a world without aesthetic, moral or spiritual significance. Against such a world-view, the romanticist protests by appealing not to tradition but to his own concrete experience of nature, his own insight into "the life of things." It is *matter* which is the abstraction, the mere theoretical concept derived from an analysis of experience; whereas "the life of things" is what we perceive at the moment when experience is immediate and unanalysed.

"An atom," says Blake, is "a thing which does not exist."[2] For Blake, the "form" or "image," the object not in itself but as perceived, is the concrete fact. The object in itself is an abstraction, a rationalization after the fact, what Blake calls the "memory of an image," which is less certain than the "perception of an image." Wordsworth makes the same point in *The Tables Turned.* "We murder to dissect," he complains, meaning that nature is a living organism and you lose its truth, which is its life, once you analyse it. Goethe makes the same complaint in *Faust:*

> The man who wants to know
> organic truth and describe it well
> seeks first to drive the living spirit out;
> he's got the parts in hand there,
> it's merely the breath of life that's lacking.[3]

The romanticist is not against science. He is merely trying to limit the applicability of its findings. He is objecting to what Whitehead, in *Science and the Modern World,* calls the Fallacy of Misplaced Concreteness—the fallacy by which the eighteenth century mistook an analysis of reality, made because the intellect is too weak to comprehend it as a whole, with the concrete totality by which we must live. "To thee," says Wordsworth to Coleridge in *The Prelude:*

> Science appears but what in truth she is,
> Not as our glory and our absolute boast,
> But as a succedaneum and a prop
> To our infirmity. No officious slave
> Art thou of that false secondary power
> By which we multiply distinctions, then
> Deem that our puny boundaries are things
> That we perceive, and not that we have made.

(II, 211–19)

"A man, born and bred in the so-called exact sciences," says Goethe, "will, on the height of his analytical reason, not easily comprehend that there is also something like an exact concrete imagination."[4] This "exact concrete imagination" Goethe employed not only for his poetry but for his scientific investigations as well.

[...]

It would hardly be necessary to insist on this line of continuity with the nineteenth century, were it not that the rejection of romanticism has been the issue with which the twentieth-century literary movement, especially in poetry, has declared its independence of its nineteenth-century predecessor. The main charges against romantic poetry have been that it is subjective, that it is sentimental, that its diction is inflated, and that it lacks form. In regard to the first charge I have, I believe, already said enough to indicate that it is an historical mistake to accuse the romanticists of subjectivism. It is to misunderstand the *direction* of romantic thought. For subjectivity was not the program but the inescapable condition of romanticism. No sooner had the eighteenth century left the individual isolated within himself—without an objective counterpart for the values he sensed in his own will and feelings—than romanticism began as a movement toward objectivity, toward a new principle of connection with society and nature through the imposition of values on the external world. Wordsworth wrote *The Prelude,* the model in English of the subjective or autobiographical poem, not because he believed in autobiographical poetry but in order to prepare himself for a long philosophical poem treating of the "mind of man." He wrote it because he felt as yet inadequate to the objective undertaking, out of "real humility": "Here, at least, I hoped that to a certain degree I should be sure of succeeding, as I had nothing to do but describe what I had felt and thought."[5]

The whole conscious concern with objectivity as a *problem,* as something to be achieved, is in fact specifically romantic. Objectivity presented no problem to an age of faith like the Middle Ages, which considered the object and its value as equally *given.* Nor did it present a problem to a critical and rationalist age like the Enlightenment, the whole point of which was to undermine the established order of values by driving a wedge between the object and its value. It was the romanticists with their new reconstructive purpose who, starting with an inherited split between object and value and wanting to heal the breach, saw objectivity as desirable and as difficult to achieve. When subjectivity came to be called a disease (*la maladie du siècle*), the Romantic period had begun. "Look you, the end of this disease is death!" said Goethe,[6] who as early as 1774 sought to deliver himself from the disease by writing *Werther.* The complaint continued throughout the next century into our own. Goethe had his Faust pass through the *sickness* (subjectivity) of Part I in order to achieve the *health* (objectivity) of Part II. Coleridge suffered from subjectivity:

> Such punishments, I said, were due
> To natures deepliest stained with sin,—
> For aye entempesting anew
> The unfathomable hell within.[7]

Byron, "the wandering outlaw of his own dark mind," tried to exorcise the devil of subjectivity with the laughter of *Don Juan.* Carlyle preached Work as an escape from subjectivity. Arnold found in his own *Empedocles* the example of what was wrong with modern poetry—that it deals with situations

> in which the suffering finds no vent in action; in which a continuous state of mental distress is prolonged, unrelieved by incident, hope, or resistance; in which there is everything to be endured, nothing to be done.[8]

And in our own time a militant insistence upon objectivity characterizes the leading critical doctrines: Yeats' *mask*, that the poet must not write about himself but about the antithesis of himself; Eliot's *catalyst,* that the poet acts like a catalyst to bring the poetic elements into combination but remains himself outside the poem; and Eliot's *objective correlative,* that emotion cannot be stated as a description of subjectivity but must be presented through

> a set of objects, a situation, a chain of events which shall be the formula of that *particular* emotion; such that when the external facts, which must terminate in sensory experience, are given, the emotion is immediately evoked … this is precisely what is deficient in *Hamlet.* Hamlet (the man) is dominated by an emotion which is inexpressible, because it is in *excess* of the facts as they appear.[9]

One is reminded here of Arnold's strictures on *Empedocles.*

It should be clear, then, that the desire to overcome subjectivity and achieve objectivity is by no means peculiar to the twentieth century, but has determined the direction of poetic development since the end of the Enlightenment. Certain twentieth-century poets have, it is true, tried to escape the post-Enlightenment condition by attaching their poetry to dogmas. Yeats with his cosmology of cones and gyres, Eliot with his Anglo-Catholicism, the Auden circle of the 'thirties with their Marxism, all sought to create for their poetry the external condition enjoyed by the Middle Ages and the Renaissance. By positing an objective order of values, they sought to make their poetry not so much an externalization of their own minds as an imitation of an external system of ideas.

Yeats, for example, once he had established his cosmology, was not in his own view making metaphors but, like Dante, describing objectivity. Yet Yeats can hardly be said to have succeeded in his aim, since his cosmology remained after all a private one; while the Auden circle, in renouncing Marxism, have admitted the failure of their aim. Eliot apparently rests secure on the rock of Christian dogma, but his success is no less characteristic of the romantic movement than the failure of the others. For if the others failed because of the romantic condition, he has apparently succeeded in accordance with the romantic prescription—in having intellectually worked his way back from the Enlightenment, in having achieved the goal of the romantic quest for commitment. His poetry is romantic in that it gives a history of that quest and is more consistent in its autobiographical development than any poetry in English since Wordsworth's.

Once we grant that the return to objectivity is a purpose distinctive of the literature since the Enlightenment, then the poetry of the last one hundred and seventy-five years or so can be understood as belonging to a single developing tradition in which the romantic idea, far from having been rejected, is being perpetually realized through isolation from incidental accretions—from eighteenth-century accretions in the nineteenth century, and from nineteenth-century accretions in the twentieth. It is, for example, as eighteenth-century accretions that we can explain the sentimentalism and inflated diction of which romantic poetry has been accused.

Sentimentalism is an eighteenth-century phenomenon in that it belongs to Locke's world where the push and pull of atoms was considered the only reality. In such a world the individual fell back upon the feelings, but with the fundamental acknowledgment that they did not reflect reality. Even today sentimentalism flourishes among the so-called Philistines—in just those circles, that is, where the Lockian world-view persists, where respect for beauty is at its lowest and the *real* is equated with the ugly and mechanistic, with whatever is antithetical to human wishes. But the romanticists were prepared precisely to take up the issue that the sentimentalists were content to let lie. They were out to transform reality, to show that it had no existence apart from the emotional apprehension of it. It is where the romantic transformation does not come off, where emotion remains opposed to an object that will not yield it back, that a poem falls into sentimentalism or bathos. But the point is that sentimentalism is the failure of romantic poetry, not its characteristic. The sentimental poem has not achieved the romantic fusion, it has been unable to win out over the eighteenth century.

In the same way, there is nothing new or distinctively nineteenth-century in the inflated diction of which there was certainly plenty. To the extent that there were innovations in diction, they were in the direction of plainness and colloquialism, as in Wordsworth, Browning and Hopkins. The nineteenth-century poets who were not innovators of diction simply continued with the cluster of Spenser, Milton and the neo-classicists which had constituted the norm of mid-eighteenth-century style. It is that mid-eighteenth-century style which is most often meant when "romantic" diction is criticized. But to the extent that poets take over a conventional style, they are not being romantic at all but quite traditional.

It may be argued that the romanticists were responsible for the revival of archaic diction. But insofar as this was a revival of what had become extinct, as distinguished from a continuation of what was becoming stale, the archaic revival was surely as beneficial for refreshing the language and enlarging its resources as, say, the introduction of scientific words by twentieth-century poets. The use of archaic diction is sufficiently justified by *The Ancient Mariner*; while Eliot himself has shown how effective it can be, in *East Coker:* "In daunsinge, signifying matrimonie," and in that bewitching quotation in *Little Gidding:* "Sin is Behovely."

There remains still the charge of formlessness which has been levelled against romantic poetry. If, however, we consider form as existing not only around the edges of a poem but in the relation of all its parts, it is hardly possible for a poem which has meaning to be formless, to have no discernible relation between its parts.[10] It is possible for a poem not to adhere to established forms, or to have no relation (though this is unlikely) to the forms of other poems. It is also possible for a poet not to be aware of the relation between one poem of his and another, or between his poetry and that of his contemporaries. It is possible for poets and critics not yet to have generalized the rationale of a new kind of poetry.

This is, I think, the case with the romantic poets and their critics. In making their new kind of poetry, many romanticists announced that they were sacrificing form in the interest of *sincerity.* They announced an ideal of artlessness—Coleridge finding the perfect poet in the Eolian harp which being played on by the wind makes music without intervention of art, Shelley finding him in the skylark which pours out its

> full heart
> In profuse strains of unpremeditated art,

Faust teaching the pedantic classicist, Wagner, that sincerity is the only effective rhetoric:

> but you'll never move others, heart to heart,
> unless your speech comes from your own heart.[11]

Yet the anti-rhetorical style is itself a rhetoric. For there remains, between the sincere feeling in the heart and the effect of sincerity on the page, the art of communication. Literary scholarship has by now discounted the popular illusion that the best romantic poetry sprang full-blown from the poet's heart, unrevised and unlaboured (that the illusion existed is a sign of the success of the romantic rhetoric). The point therefore in understanding the form of romantic poetry is to understand how the sincere, unpremeditated effect is achieved—the history of romanticism being largely the history of the attempt of poets and critics to arrive at that understanding. The fact that the so-called reactions against romanticism, from the Victorian reaction to the reaction of our own time, have all called for more objectivity and more form is a sign that they have been attempts to articulate a form potential in romantic poetry from the start.

For it is with form as with objectivity; at the same time that the romanticists broke away from both, they were also preoccupied to a degree unknown before with working back to both. Goethe was for most of his career a professed classicist, who sought to emulate in his poetry the abstraction and pure formalism of Greek sculpture; and we owe to German romanticism generally the unprecedented glorification of Greece in modern times. It is too often forgotten that romanticism was as much responsible for a Greek as for a medieval revival, the former having had as a matter of fact the more widespread and enduring effect. It should also be remembered that the Greek interest of most nineteenth-century literary men was in the formal aspects of Greek aesthetics, as distinguished from the Renaissance interest in the Greek ethos. For the Renaissance, Greece offered an alternative way of life to Christian culture (Shelley's Greek interest was in this respect Renaissance); but for the nineteenth century, Greece came to represent objectivity and form as opposed to modern subjectivity and naturalism. Toward the end of the century, the aesthetic capital shifted for some people from Greece to Byzantium or Japan, because they found as they moved eastward a more extreme stylization.

Yeats' *Sailing to Byzantium* is less a reaction against Keats' *Ode on a Grecian Urn* than it is a more extreme articulation of Keats' essential idea. Where Keats sees in the formal perfection of Greek plastic art an idealization of nature, Yeats sees in the two-dimensional golden abstractness of the Byzantine mosaics a rejection of nature. The difference is of degree not kind. Both poets recognize the Lockian split between the real and the ideal, and both see that the artist must transform the real into the ideal. The difference is in the amount of transformation which each considered necessary. Yeats required a more radical transformation because he saw the split as wider. The fact that Yeats had to turn Keats' recognition of the split between art and nature into a belligerently anti-naturalistic position is a sign that his is, if anything, the more extreme romanticism, the more radical solution of the more radical problem.

For if romanticism gave rise to the poetry of artlessness, spontaneity, and sincerity, to the "spasmodic" poets, Whitman and free verse; it also gave rise, and this has been its more enduring contribution, to Keats, the pre-Raphaelites, and the aesthetic and symbolist movements, to the poetry of art, even of artifice and insincerity. The doctrine of insincerity that characterized the aesthetic movement is a sign of the connection of that movement with romanticism and the doctrine of sincerity. Neither would have been conceivable as classical doctrine. The classical poet could afford to distinguish between the subjectivity of his lyric poetry and the objectivity of his narrative and dramatic poetry, because he had no trouble being objective when he wanted to be. It is only when meaning is in the epistemological sense a personal creation that the distinction between the subjective and objective statement breaks down and the poet feels it necessary to mask the subjective origin of his idea, to expend art to objectify it. *Insincerity* together with its offshoot Yeats' *mask,* in fact the whole literary attempt since the late nineteenth century to escape from personality, have created a literature in which sincerity and autobiography are encoded, written backwards.[12]

We would therefore require, to talk intelligently about the form of romantic poetry, a theory which could account for both the artlessness and the artifice, the sincerity and the insincerity, the subjectivity and the objectivity, of poetry since the Enlightenment. We would require, in other words, a theory to connect the poetry of the nineteenth and twentieth centuries, to connect romanticism with the so-called reactions against it. We are now in a position to advance such a theory. For having seen the poetry which set out to be different from romantic poetry, we can find in the core that remains unchanged the essential idea of romanticism. That essential idea is, I would suggest, the doctrine of experience—the doctrine that the imaginative apprehension gained through immediate experience is primary and certain, whereas the analytic reflection that follows is secondary and problematical. The poetry of the nineteenth and twentieth centuries can thus be seen in connection as a poetry of experience—a poetry constructed upon the deliberate disequilibrium between experience and idea, a poetry which makes its statement not as an idea but as an experience from which one or more ideas can be abstracted as problematical rationalizations.

Much could be learned from the isolation of a poetry of experience. It would reveal for the first time, in addition to the distinctively romantic sensibility and subject matter which we already know, a distinctively romantic form in poetry—a form of which the potentials are realized in the so-called reactions against romantic poetry, in the dramatic monologues of the Victorians and the symbolist poems of the moderns. Such a form, furthermore, if it were treated as a way of meaning, a way of establishing the validity of a poetic statement, would become the best index of a distinctively modern tradition. What better sign can there be, after all, of a culture's real belief than the principle by which it establishes the validity of its statements of value? And what better sign can there be of its coherence than the fact that it can make such statements, statements combining its unspoken convictions on the nature of truth, goodness and beauty? Form is a better index of a tradition than subject matter in that subject matter is often controversial; it is often an index of what people think they believe, whereas form is an index of what is believed too implicitly to be discussed.

Since a new culture, like a new art, looks disorderly until we discover its principle of order, and since the principle which gives order to a culture is intimately related to the principle which gives order to its art, the critic who finds the latter principle is by implication at least helping to find the former. If in addition to isolating the poetry of experience as a form, as a way of establishing in an anti-dogmatic and empiricist age a truth based on the disequilibrium between experience and idea, he could show that there emerges from this deliberate disequilibrium a correspondingly new moral and aesthetic symmetry—he would have suggested at least one line of coherence by which to discern in the bewildering heterogeneity of modern culture a distinctively modern tradition. Such a tradition would present a curious paradox in that it would have been created out of the rejection of tradition and the preoccupation with its loss. We would find that the artists and thinkers of the last one hundred and seventy-five years or so have, in proclaiming the freedom of modern life, actually laid down new rules for it, that they have, in proclaiming its meaninglessness and disunity, formulated for it a new meaning and a new unity.[13]

Notes

1   "Tradition and the Individual Talent," *Selected Essays 1917–1932* (London: Faber and Faber, 1932), p. 13; (New York: Harcourt, Brace, 1938), p. 3.

2   To George Cumberland, 12 April 1827, *Poetry and Prose,* ed. Geoffrey Keynes (London: Nonesuch Press, 1939), p. 927. See also Northrop Frye, *Fearful Symmetry: A Study of William Blake* (Princeton: Princeton University Press, 1947), Chap. I, "The Case Against Locke."

3   Part I, "Faust's Study," trans. C. F. MacIntyre (Norfolk, Conn.: New Directions, 1949), p. 60.

4   Quoted in Erich Heller, *The Disinherited Mind* (Cambridge: Bowes and Bowes, 1952), p. 26.

5   To Sir George Beaumont, 1 May 1805, *The Early Letters of William and Dorothy Wordsworth (1787–1805)*, ed. Ernest deSelincourt (Oxford: Clarendon Press, 1935), p. 489.

6   Quoted in Karl Viëtor, *Goethe the Poet* (Cambridge, Mass: Harvard University Press, 1949), p. 28.

7   *The Pains of Sleep.*

8   Preface to the 1853 edition of his *Poems* (London: Oxford University Press, 1945), pp. 2–3.

9   "Hamlet," *Selected Essays* (London: Faber and Faber), p. 145; (New York: Harcourt, Brace), pp. 124–25. For the *catalyst,* see "Tradition and the Individual Talent" in the same volume. For Yeats' doctrine of the *mask,* see T. R. Henn, *The Lonely Tower* (London: Methuen, 1950), and Richard Ellman, *Yeats: The Man and The Masks* (New York: Macmillan, 1948).

10 For a discussion of this idea, see Jacques Barzun, "The Fetish of Form: An Example from Music," *Kenyon Review,* Winter 1950.

11 Part I, "Night," p. 13. See Coleridge's *The Eolian Harp* and Shelley's *To a Skylark.*

12 For a discussion of the aesthetic movement's doctrine of insincerity in connection with Yeats' doctrine of the mask, see Ellman, *Yeats: The Man and the Masks,* Chap. VI.

13 The work of counting up the cultural treasure of the nineteenth and twentieth centuries and formulating from it a modern tradition may well fall upon the now emerging literary generation—a generation already recognizable as more critical than creative just because we of that generation have, I think, been rendered silent by our reverence for the immediate past, by our sense of having inherited a modern tradition, of having to master an impressive canon of modern "classics" before we can speak out in our own right.

3   Poetry and its Times (2001)

Matthew Reynolds

When Garibaldi visited Britain in 1864, he found time to call on the Poet Laureate. For Tennyson's son Hallam, then 11 years old, this was 'the great event of the year'; the poet himself was still proud of the occasion two decades later, mentioning, in some verses about his garden, the 'waving pine' planted by 'the warrior of Caprera'.[1] In their admiration for their visitor, the Tennysons were not alone. Garibaldi had become famous throughout Europe as the commander of two key enterprises in the Italian Risorgimento: the defence of republican Rome in 1849 and, in 1860, the extraordinary conquest of Sicily and southern Italy by 'the Thousand'.[2] As the Illustrated London News observed, these exploits had provoked remarkable enthusiasm in British hearts: 'the name of Garibaldi exerts a talismanic influence of unprecedented potency over all classes of society, and inspires a common sentiment of affectionate, we may even say passionate, admiration into the bosoms of the nobility, the middle classes, and the toiling millions.'[3] Lurking beneath such unanimous acclaim was some disagreement as to quite what Garibaldi was being applauded for. Whigs and Tories emphasized his loyalty to the King of Piedmont—and later of Italy—Vittorio Emmanuele II, and interpreted Italian unification as an assertion of British-style constitutional monarchy. Radicals, on the other hand, took comfort from his humble background and his association with the republican revolutionary Mazzini: for them, Italian unification was at once an instance and a symbol of the shift of European (including British) politics towards self-determination and democracy. These conflicting views came face to face in 1864 when Garibaldi's presence in Britain caused such popular agitation that he was encouraged by powerful friends to curtail his trip.[4] Not, however, before he had met the Tennysons. [...]

The encounter of Tennyson and Garibaldi on the Isle of Wight suggests two factors that a historically sensitive approach to the Idylls, and to other mid-nineteenth-century English poems, should keep in view. First, their interest in and relevance to the politics and literature of the continent. Secondly, that there was greater continuity between poetry and high politics than there is today, and that people active in the two kinds of endeavour treated each other with more respect. It was not only that poets thought of themselves as being politically engaged: their claims to be, in some more or less figurative way, legislators, were taken seriously by those men (they were of course all men) who were involved in the day-to-day business of actual legislation. As Gladstone observed, recalling 'Love thou thy land' and its companion poems at the beginning of his review of the 1859 Idylls: 'never has political philosophy been wedded to the poetic form more happily than in the three short pieces on England and her institutions, unhappily without title, and only to be cited, like writs of law and papal bulls, by their first words.'[5] The *Illustrated London News* recalled the same group of poems when it remarked:

> If we know Tennyson and Garibaldi, they could not long confer together without speculating on the prospects of a successful assertion of the liberty of nations ... No other English poet has so thoroughly comprehended the public spirit of this country; in none is the love of freedom more richly tempered with a loyal respect for the ancient laws, customs, and institutions of old England, and her venerable traditions of 'the storied past';

> Where freedom broadens slowly down
> From precedent to precedent.[6]

The choice of quotation suggests just how much Tennyson's and Garibaldi's thoughts on the liberty of nations are likely to have differed, for the phrasing 'from precedent to precedent' contrives to envisage the progress of freedom as a return into the past, and the generally calmative rhetoric ('broadens slowly down') now seems almost comical in its determination to shut out any hint of the kind of revolution (a quick rising from below) in which Garibaldi was a specialist.

As even a brief look at the readings which Tennyson and Garibaldi exchanged in shared appreciation and guarded disagreement makes clear, nineteenth-century poetry was, in its political bearings, often considerably more subtle and enquiring than the skillfully versified opinions of 'Love thou thy land'. Idylls of the King is typical of the poems which are the focus of this book in that it both requires and resists insertion into contemporary debates. The Round Table clearly has some connection with Prince Albert and also some doubtless more tenuous link to Garibaldi. But to suggest that the work was simply about these contemporary figures would be to make it a travesty, as Swinburne well knew when he proposed the alternative title Idylls of the Prince Consort.[7] The ambivalent imaginative and conceptual location of much Victorian poetry has been well described by Isobel Armstrong: 'Art occupied its own area, a self-sufficing aesthetic realm over and against practical experience ... And yet it was at once apart and central, for it had a mediating function, representing and interpreting life.'[8] Idylls of the King, like many mid-nineteenth-century poems, was designed both to speak to the practical concerns of its times, and to hold itself apart from them so as to make itself available to more wide-ranging and multivalent interpretations.

The title of Professor Armstrong's own wide-ranging volume, *Victorian Poetry: Poetry, Poetics and Politics*, appears to herald a consideration of the overlaps between Tennyson's realms of activity and those of Gladstone or Garibaldi. In fact, the word 'politics', as it appears in the book, takes on a partial and specialized definition: 'the task of a history of Victorian poetry is to restore the questions of politics, not least sexual politics, and the epistemology and language which belong to it.'[9] In practice, 'not least' often hardens into 'that is to say'. The virtue of this approach is that it allows even the most apparently uncommitted of works to be placed in relation to political issues. Of Tennyson's 'The Kraken', Armstrong remarks— having adduced a variety of contexts—that 'according to which of the myths are activated, utopian or conservative, the Kraken is the principle of transformation, of mindless destruction, or evil, or the helpless victim of external forces', and suggests that this multifariousness is the sign of 'a peculiarly radical conservatism, which dreads change and sees its necessity, even the necessity of violence'. Such observations support her claim that 'one of the subliminal themes' of Tennyson's 1830 *Poems, Chiefly Lyrical* is 'what revolutionary change is, how it comes about and what its consequences are'.[10] The shortcoming of this line of argument, however, is that it tends to reduce, even annihilate the distance between imaginative changes registered in the seclusion of the page and the developments that were debated in the public space of Parliament, or that were demonstrated for and fought over in the even more public streets of London, Dublin, Paris, Milan, and elsewhere. To emphasize that sexual relations, epistemology, and language are—as we now think—themselves intrinsically 'political' is to play down the question of how they connect with what people in the nineteenth century generally meant by politics: 'the science and art of government ... Political affairs or business ... The political principles, convictions, opinions, or sympathies of a person or party' (OED). Indeed, such an emphasis makes it possible to write a book about poetry and 'politics' without taking parliamentary debates and such like into consideration at all. Armstrong has little to say about politicians—she mentions neither Gladstone nor Garibaldi—and barely comments on the works in which Victorian poets most obviously confronted politics in the public sense, and which will, for that reason, be at the heart of this volume: *Aurora Leigh, Amours de Voyage, The Ring and the Book, The Princess*, and *Idylls of the King*. Her book virtually concurs with the old view that the Victorian poetry which matters is confined to the personal life; with this difference, that the personal is now understood to be political.

If private life is already shot through with political implications, the possibility of conflict between a realm thought of as 'private', and a 'public' realm which is the location of politics, will disappear; with the result that everything will be seen to have a political aspect. The very mysteriousness of 'The Kraken', the difficulty of associating it with any political attitude, itself makes the poem the embodiment of a political position. However, it has long been recognized that in the mid-nineteenth century the disjunction between 'private' and 'public', although neither fixed nor unbridgeable, was strongly maintained, and was fundamental to people's experience of their lives.[11] The contrast was felt with particular acuity by poets, for poetry, though not simply 'private' discourse, was not straightforwardly 'public' either. Sometimes coinciding, and sometimes contrasting with the paradox 'at once apart and central', was another paradox: at once private and public. Awareness of this double status appears throughout Tennyson's 1830 volume, and registers most creatively in the poems' allusions to the transfer out of the private realm which they themselves undergo upon publication. Tennyson's unease about what the public will make of his work brings him, in 'The Poet's Mind', to the point of insulting them:

> Vex not thou the poet's mind
>   With thy shallow wit:
> Vex not thou the poet's mind;
>   For thou canst not fathom it.

It is only at the beginning of the second stanza that we are offered the possibility of deflecting this tirade onto a 'dark-browed sophist' who threatens to invade and blight a flourishing garden of the mind, hedged (aptly enough) with 'laurel-shrubs', where a 'merry bird chants' and a 'fountain ... springs', 'drawn | From the brain of the purple mountain' which, in turn, 'draws it from Heaven above'. This endearing ecology of the imagination prompts us to configure the sophist, in whose 'eye there is death', and 'frost' in his 'breath', as a rationalistic psychologist, someone like James Mill, whose *Analysis of the Phenomena of the Human Mind* appeared in 1829.[12] However, we cannot escape so easily, for to advance such an interpretation is itself to claim to have fathomed the work, and so to make us again vulnerable to the abuse launched in the opening four lines. Even so slight a creation as 'The Poet's Mind', a poem which appears to tell you its interpretation in its title, turns out not only to resist understanding but to make a demonstration of resistance. It is in the paradoxical situation of having been published but wanting not to be understood, perhaps not even to be read.

The unease about exposure which is dramatized in 'The Poet's Mind' continues to be manifest throughout Tennyson's career. Forty years later he was to complain about interpreters of Idylls of the King, 'I hate to be tied down to say, *"This means that,"* because the thought within the image is much more than any one interpretation'.[13] His remark suggests how the familiar story of the conflict between the two Tennysons, aesthete and prophet, gives rise, at the level of text, to a question about the multivalence or otherwise of his writing. If, as he insisted, 'poetry is like shot-silk with many glancing colours', it cannot straightforwardly have a public voice, for it is not, in the usual sense of the phrase, saying something.[14] On the other hand, as 'The Palace of Art' and the many laureate poems make clear, Tennyson was determined that his verse should assume a civic role. As we will see, works such as The Princess and Idylls of the King operate a tug of war between these two imperatives, so as to be 'political poems' with the full weight of both those words. This duality, and the internal conflict which it engenders, is shadowed forth in the poem which anticipates so much of the later narrative writing: 'The Lady of Shalott'.

When Lancelot irrupts into the Lady's consciousness she is liberated and energized: such at least is the implication of the sudden burst of movement, and profusion of active verbs: 'She left the web, she left the loom, | She made three paces through the room', and so on.[15] As Tennyson remarked, 'the new-born love for something, for some one in the wide world from which she has been so long secluded, takes her out of the region of shadows into that of realities'.[16] However, this vigorous adoption of a subject position is also a 'curse', and results in the attenuation and eventual loss of her existence.[17] If, as readers have generally agreed, the lonely weaving in the first, predominantly lyric half of the poem has as its main implication the self-sufficing activity of the artistic imagination, the second, narrative half in which the Lady floats along the river to the town of Camelot, dying on the way, suggests the process by which poetic imaginings are written down and made available to the public. 'Singing in her song she died', whereupon she becomes no longer the origin of a melody that was heard occasionally echoing in the distance, but an object to be observed with the eye, and whose name is written and can be read: *The Lady of Shalott'*. Lancelot's judgement at Camelot that she has 'a lovely face', and the action of the crowd, who cross themselves 'for fear', are not presented with so unequivocally negative a spin as the endeavours of the sophist in 'The Poet's Mind'.[18] Nonetheless, as acts of interpretation they seem unsatisfactory, and hint to us that we should make our readings different from them by travelling, as it were, back up the river and entrancing ourselves in the poem's weave. This, the geography of the work implies, is a matter of momentarily leaving behind our social roles with all their commitments and opinions. The poem relies on the fact that its readers, when they are reading, will generally be alone, silent, imaginatively alert and comparatively abstracted from their usual duties. It asks them, therefore, to identify more with the Lady than with Lancelot. On the other hand, it also recognizes that it is destined to have its spell broken by being summed up and thought 'lovely' or otherwise as it becomes a counter in the intellectual and commercial exchanges of society at large.

As a poem, 'The Lady of Shalott' moves between the two extremes represented by Shalott and Camelot. It is not so much 'at once apart and central' as a journey from one position to the other and then perhaps back again. Its two locations are not unlike the two places which figure prominently in Garibaldi's descent on Farringford: the isolated study, where the latter-day Lancelot retired with the poet to indulge in shared aesthetic delight and private conversation, and the crowded garden where they adopted their civic roles and conducted a public ceremony. Like the visit, the poem helps us to understand the kind of relationship which much of Tennyson's writing—and indeed that of his contemporaries—has with its social and political contexts. *The Princess* and *Idylls of the King* are located away from their times in a mythical elsewhere. To read anything is, in some degree, to abstract one's attention from one's immediate surroundings; but what is special about these poems is the extent to which they make readers aware that what we are doing in reading is departing from the real and inhabiting a place of the imagination. When Leavis wrote that 'nineteenth-century poetry ... was characteristically preoccupied with the creation of a dream-world' he was right; but only in part.[19] What Tennyson's contemporaries found in that other place continually threw light back on the circumstances they were encouraged to think they had left behind them. This does not happen in any systematic way: it would be wrong to think of the works as being allegorical. One might rather say, as Tennyson did of the *Idylls*, that they have a 'parabolic drift', meaning that they are in the nature of a parable, and also that they have a tangential relation to the present, like a parabola.[20] The parabolic mode allowed him, and with variations some of his contemporaries, to produce writing that was politically relevant and yet avoided the simplicities and stridencies of direct address. In order to understand this kind of poetry, we must give full weight to both aspects of the dilemma that Tennyson felt himself to be in: he had to speak to his contemporaries, so as to be politically relevant; and he had to hold himself apart from them, so as to be a poet.

If, in Isobel Armstrong's argument, Victorian verse is all Shalott, with the proviso that Shalott is inherently political (the Lady's predicament, she suggests, is like that of workers in the recently mechanized weaving industry),[21] the other dominant understanding of the relationship between poetry and politics in the nineteenth century sees nothing but Camelot. For the critics of this school, 'every poem is a social event', which 'organizes communication oriented toward reciprocal action, and itself reacts'. The significance of a poem's 'communication' can be deduced by attention to the context of its 'point of origin'— which is sometimes the moment of composition (if that can be identified) and sometimes the date of first publication. Thus, in Jerome McGann's opinion, Keats's 'To Autumn', is a direct reaction to Peterloo: 'the poem's autumn is an historically specified fiction dialectically called into being by John Keats as an active response to, and alteration of, the events which marked the late summer and early fall of a particular year in a particular place.' Being an 'active response' it has a clear polemical significance: 'its message is that the fine arts, and by extension imagination generally, are more humanly productive than any of the other more practical sciences of the artificial.' Critics who adopt this point of view have little track with the multiplicities of meaning which are so subtly drawn out in Professor Armstrong's book. As Tom Paulin remarks, approvingly: 'this makes the poem look less like an urn in a national museum and more like a pamphlet or a piece of journalism.'[22]

What we might call the poetry-as-journalism approach adopts for literature the practice of historical contextualization pioneered by Quentin Skinner for the history of political thought. Skinner's methodology considers works of political theory to be analogous to speech acts, whose meaning can be gauged only in relation to a detailed reconstruction of the context for which they are taken to have been produced: 'any statement ... is inescapably the embodiment of a particular intention, on a particular occasion, addressed to the solution of a particular problem, and thus specific to its situation in a way that it can only be naïve to try to transcend.' Works of political theory lend themselves to this kind of analysis because they generally respond to contemporary political problems and engage in a debate whose terms have been laid down by their predecessors. But works of literature are not to the same degree bound in to a definable context, as Professor Skinner recognizes when he observes that 'any example of the application of this rule to a work of literature is liable either to look very crude or to be very complicated'.[23] In the first place, the kind of intention which poets can be thought to embody in their writing is usually different from that which may be extrapolated from a work of political thought. We find it quite reasonable that a poet should declare 'I hate to be tied down to say, "This means that"'; such an admission would, however, be fatal to a political theorist. Correspondingly, poems do not on on the whole address themselves to 'the solution of a particular problem'. The stimuli to which they are responses and the questions upon which they bear are usually various and not easily definable. What are the issues confronted by 'The Lady of Shalott', or for that matter 'My Last Duchess'? Certainly they are more wide-ranging than those tackled by, say, Hobbes in his chapter 'Of the Rights of Soveraignes by Institution'.[24]

Admittedly, some pieces of writing which we are accustomed to call 'poems' do not differ very greatly from journalism. Tennyson's lines entitled 'The Third of February, 1852'— published four days later in the Examiner—are a versified argument against a House of Lords' decision rejecting a Bill for the organization of a militia to defend Britain against a supposed threat from France:

> We love not this French God, the child of hell,
>   Wild War, who breaks the converse of the wise;[25]

—it proclaims. This work does have a particular intention which is specific to its occasion. For that very reason, it announces itself as possessing a particular generic character as just one of the many distinguishable kinds of writing covered by the word 'poetry': it is an 'occasional poem', or a 'polemical poem'. When we recognise a text's genre we determine how it should be taken: as comedy or journalism or a piece of abstract logical reasoning or a lyric; in determining how it should be taken, we make a judgement about how it relates to its context and what that context is. 'The Lady of Shalott' sends out different generic signals from 'The Third of February, 1852', and asks to be read according to other expectations: its symbolic mode and its rhetorical distance from the immediate circumstances of its composition let readers know that it is not likely to be making a direct response to contemporary political developments; rather, it has to do with longer-running questions about subjectivity, gender, interpretation, and so on, as its extensive critical history makes clear.[26] The poetry-as-journalism approach assumes that, whatever a poem's genre, its defining context is always provided by its immediate historical surroundings. On this view, if only you look closely enough, all poems are like 'The Third of February, 1852'.

Certainly there may be illumination to be gained from reconstructing the historical circumstances of any piece of writing, perhaps even (very occasionally) a mathematical equation. However, the degree of illumination will vary according to the contextual requirements of the work's genre. 'The Lady of Shalott' was written at a time of rural agitation: in consequence, its peaceful vision of 'reapers, reaping early | In among the bearded barley' may well have given Tennyson a specially calmative pleasure of the sort Keats is supposed to have found in composing 'To Autumn' soon after Peterloo.[27] The poem cannot therefore satisfactorily be described as an 'active response' to this circumstance with a 'message' to deliver. The rural connection is one element in the work's multifarious and uncertain range of concern.

The poems which I will be discussing characteristically maintain a generic distance from their immediate historical surroundings. Yet they did not thereby turn their back on politics, for by abstracting themselves from the present, so as to open up a longer timescale for the imagination, they brought themselves into proximity with perhaps the most momentous political concept in the nineteenth century: 'nation'. As Edmund Burke had explained: 'a nation is not an idea only of local extent, and individual momentary aggregation; but it is an idea of continuity, which extends in time as well as in numbers and in space'.[28] In the mid-nineteenth century, 'poetry', like 'nation', was strongly felt to be an 'idea of continuity'.

Benedict Anderson has written perceptively of the importance of language in creating a sense of national community subsisting through time:

> No one can give a date for the birth of any language. Each looms up imperceptibly out of a horizonless past … If English-speakers hear the words 'Earth to Earth, ashes to ashes, dust to dust'—created almost four-and-a-half centuries ago—they get a ghostly intimation of simultaneity across homogeneous, empty time. The weight of the words derives only in part from their solemn meaning; it comes also from an as-it-were ancestral 'Englishness'.[29]

As Anderson's choice of quotation implies, nationhood is fostered, not only by continuity of language, but by the persistence in a culture of particular usages of that language. An extract from a sixteenth-century broadside pamphlet would not carry quite the same weight as those very familiar words from the Book of Common Prayer.

The lifetime of canonical poetry in Western culture is not dissimilar to that of liturgy. In consequence, when, in the late eighteenth and early nineteenth centuries, the idea of nationhood began to command the thoughts of intellectuals and the hopes of revolutionaries, poets were ascribed a central role. In his very influential lectures On Heroes and Hero-Worship (1840), Carlyle declared: 'poor Italy lies dismembered, scattered asunder, not appearing in any protocol or treaty as a unity at all; yet the noble Italy is actually one: Italy produced its Dante; Italy can speak!'[30] A fantastical claim, one might think. However, more recent theorists have attributed to creative writers a no less significant part in the construction of nationhood—although they have generally eschewed the idealist terminology adopted by Carlyle. 'Who, more than poets, musicians, painters and sculptors, could bring the national ideal to life and disseminate it among the people?'—asks Anthony D. Smith:[31] not only living poets, he might have added, but dead ones also, and perhaps more effectively. Generations of Italian schoolchildren who have been under the happy obligation of reading through the Divine Comedy one canto per week at school would testify to the persistence of such ideas in contemporary practice.

Mid-nineteenth-century English poets were excited by the new conception of poetry's nation-building power. If the realms of verse were also the dwelling-places of a national spirit, the commitment to generic abstraction and the desire for political influence might be reconciled. In order to understand what poets made of this possibility, we must precisely not limit ourselves to asking how their work may have reacted to and altered 'the events which marked … a particular year in a particular place'. Poets were attracted by the thought of creating comparatively general and enduring myths or archetypal narratives which, while having relevance to contemporary affairs, might also throw light on many other, past and future events—in the way that, to give a small example, Tennyson found the 1859 Idylls to be apposite to Garibaldi in 1864. It is not so much that the book would have taken on a different implication in that particular context, as that the book is offered as being itself a context, in relation to which Garibaldi and many other people can be understood and judged: the Idylls present themselves as occupying 'homogeneous, empty time', the time of 'Englishness'. Equally, however, poets were—to differing degrees—suspicious of the potential for coercion in such writing, and uncertain about the large claims for national unity made by propagandists such as Mazzini. Browning gained critical purchase on the ideas of 'as-it-were ancestral' nationhood and of poetry's role in its evocation, by setting his verse in a different elsewhere: Italy. Even Tennyson was creatively aware of the large element of make-believe in the myths which he nonetheless continued to produce. The challenge for a historically sensitive criticism is to trace the filaments by which these works are linked to contemporary political matters, while not flattening their enquiring and expansive textures into the blankness of a 'message.'

Notes

1   Hallam, Lord Tennyson, *Alfred Lord Tennyson: A Memoir: By his Son*, 2 vols. (Macmillan, 1897: cited as Memoir hereafter), ii. 2; Alfred Tennyson, 'To Ulysses', 25–6. Tennyson's poems are quoted from *The Poems of Tennyson*, 2nd edn., ed. Christopher Ricks, 3 vols. (Longman, 1987).

2   See Giorgio Candeloro, *Storia dell'Italia Moderna*, 2nd edn., 11 vols. (Milan: Feltrinelli, 1988–91), iii. 425–53; iv. 427–526; G. M: Trevelyan, *Garibaldi's Defence of the Roman Republic* (Longmans, Green and Co., 1907) and *Garibaldi and the Thousand* (Longmans, Green and Co., 1909).

3   *Illustrated London News*, 44/1256 (23 Apr. 1864), 382.

4   Derek Beales, 'Garibaldi in England: The Politics of Italian Enthusiasm', in John A. Davis and Paul Ginsborg (eds.), *Society and Politics in the Age of the Risorgimento* (Cambridge: Cambridge University Press, 1991), 199–208. On divergent understandings of the Risorgimento.

5   W. E. Gladstone, *Gleanings of Past Years, 1843–78* (John Murray, 1879), ii, 133.

6   *Illustrated London News*, 44/1256 (23 Apr. 1864), 398. 'The storied past' is from 'Love thou thy land, with love far-brought', 2; the succeeding two lines are 'You ask me, why, thought ill at ease', 11–12, with altered indentation: Tennyson wrote 'Past' and 'Freedom' with initial capitals.

7   John D. Jump (ed.), *Tennyson: The Critical Heritage* (Routledge and Kegan Paul, 1967), 339.

8   Isobel Armstrong, *Victorian Poetry: Poetry, Poetics, and Politics* (Routledge, 1993), 4.

9   Ibid. 7.

10 Ibid. 56, 51.

11 Karl Marx, *Critique of Hegel's Philosophy of Right*, ed. Joseph J. O'Malley (Cambridge: Cambridge University Press, 1970), 32; John Tosh, *A Man's Place: Masculinity and the Middle-Class Home in Victorian England* (New Haven: Yale University Press, 1999), 27–31.

12 'The Poet's Mind', 1–4, 8, 14, 22, 24, 31, 28–9, 32, 17–18.

13 *Memoir*, ii. 127.

14 Ibid.

15 'The Lady of Shalott', 109–10.

16 *Memoir*, i. 117.

17 'The Lady of Shalott', 116.

18 'The Lady of Shalott', 152, 162, 169, 166.

19 F. R. Leavis, *New Bearings in English Poetry: A Study of the Contemporary Situation* (1932; Harmondsworth: Penguin, 1972), 14.

20 *Memoir*, ii. 127.

21 Armstrong, *Victorian Poetry*, 84–5.

22 Jerome J. McGann, *The Beauty of Infections: Literary Investigations in Historical Method and Theory* (Oxford: Clarendon Press, 1985), 24, 19, 59, 61, 60; Tom Paulin, *Minotaur: Poetry and the Nation-State* (Faber and Faber, 1992), 137.

23 James Tully (ed.), *Meaning and Context: Quentin Skinner and his Critics* (Cambridge: Polity Press, 1988), 65, 77.

24 Thomas Hobbes, *Leviathan* (1651), ed. Richard Tuck (Cambridge: Cambridge University Press, 1991), 121.

25 'The Third of February, 1852', 7–8.

26 See Edgar F. Shannon, 'Poetry as Vision: Sight and Insight in "The Lady of Shalott"', *Victorian Poetry*, 19 (1981), 207–8; Kirk H. Beetz, Tennyson: A Bibliography, 1827–1852 (Scarecrow, 1984).

27 Robert Bernard Martin, *Tennyson: The Unquiet Heart* (Oxford: Clarendon Press, 1983), 125; 'The Lady of Shalott', 28–9.

28 Quoted in Raymond Williams, *Culture and Society: Coleridge to Orwell* (1958; Hogarth Press, 1993), 11.

29 Benedict Anderson, *Imagined Communities: Reflections on the Origin and Spread of Nationalism*, 2nd edn. (Verso, 1991), 144–5.

30 Thomas Carlyle, *On Heroes, Hero-Worship and the Heroic in History* (1840; Chapman and Hall, 1897), 114.

31 Anthony D. Smith, *National Identity* (Harmondsworth: Penguin, 1991), 92.

4   'Two Decisions', Introduction to *Rhythm and Will in Victorian Poetry* (1999)

Matthew Campbell

With characteristic humility, Hallam Tennyson omits to name himself as the recipient of this advice from his father:

> I cannot refrain from setting down his talk to a young man who was going to the University. – 'If a man is merely to be a bundle of sensations, he had better not exist at all. He should embark on his career in the spirit of selfless and adventurous heroism; should develop his true self by not shirking responsibility, by casting aside all maudlin and introspective morbidities, and by using his powers cheerfully in accordance with the obvious dictates of his moral consciousness, and so, as far as possible, in harmony with what he feels to be the Absolute Right.'[1]

This advice is familiar in the Victorian public school fiction which promotes a 'muscular Christianity'. Heroism is selfless before it is adventurous; responsibility exists in facing the morbid, and bowing to the moral necessity of 'the Absolute Right'. This is an example of something that John R. Reed might describe as moving from the Romantic to the Victorian, from 'aggressive heroism, or what might be called the imperial will, to controlled heroism, or the reflective will'.[2] Napoleon and Wellington are replaced by the model citizens of Samuel Smiles' *Self Help*.

In the midst of such counsel from his father, Hallam includes these lines from 'Oenone':

> Self-reverence, self-knowledge, self-control,
> These three alone lead life to sovereign power.
> Yet not for power (power of herself
> Would come uncalled for) but to live by *law*,
> *Acting* the law we live by without fear;
> And, because right is right, to follow right
> Were wisdom in the scorn of consequence.
>
> (142–8)

(The text here is Hallam's *Memoir* of his father; the italics are Hallam's.) This is a key passage for Tennyson, and also for his family. Yet the very status of these lines, as moral instruction, impairs the quality of the verse. The yoking of the self into reverence, knowledge and control to achieve 'sovereign power' is easily said, but harder done. Even the ease which is supposedly a characteristic of Tennyson's verse has difficulty with this. There is a straining after self-evident truth, almost to tautology: 'because right is right, to follow right /

Were wisdom …' Hallam's emphases, on 'law' and 'Acting', bringing together as they do necessity and freedom, or the freedom to act in acknowledgement of necessity, overstress the already strenuous at the very point at which the calm of conviction should hold.

In 'Oenone', these lines are related by the outcast and powerless heroine who speaks in the main body of what is a partially realised dramatic monologue. They come from the speech of Pallas Athene, describing the benefits which will follow if Oenone's lover Paris decides to opt for the way of will. The speech continues in the poem (not quoted by Hallam) a few lines after this, describing just what the bodily experience of this will might be:

> '… rest thee sure
> That I shall love thee well and cleave to thee,
> So that my vigour, wedded to thy blood,
> Shall strike within thy pulses, like a God's,
> To push thee forward through a life of shocks,
> Dangers, and deeds, until endurance grow
> Sinewed with action, and the full-grown will,
> Circled through all experience, pure law,
> Commeasure perfect freedom.'
>
> (156–64)

The quality of these lines is their very strenuousness, an imitation of the difficulty of the task proposed. The blank verse courts rhyme as the line ending 'like a God's' is picked up with a close sonic echo in 'life of shocks'. The verse itself admits its subject matter as one of great struggle: 'cleave … vigour … blood … strike … pulses … push … shocks … Sinewed'. The experience of will in the masculine body is experienced in the sonic body of the verse as it strikes off these vital signs of power. Yet this is a hard task, and pictures a life of great strain. 'Power of herself', gendered in this poem, will be given by the goddess to this man, as she says to Paris that she will 'push thee forward'. Her way is towards law, wisdom and power through a strengthening of habits of will.

Oenone, passive narrator of the poem, cries out that Paris, her former lover, should give the golden apple to Pallas, and we can hear the older Tennyson and his son concurring at this point, along probably with the majority of their Victorian readership. Choices to be made, or moments of will like this one, have both the watching speaker Oenone, as well as an imaginary audience, urging them on. These are particularly Victorian moments, and they can be caricatured in the terms of Kipling's exhortation to the future officer class in 'If' ('And so hold on when there is nothing in you / Except the Will which says to them: "Hold on!"'[3]) or in the handbook for self-improving capitalism which is *Self Help:*

> there is no power of law that can make the idle man industrious, the thriftless provident, or the drunken sober; though every individual can be each and all of these if he will, by the exercise of his own powers of action and self-denial. Indeed all experience serves to prove that the worth and strength of a State depend far less upon the form of its institutions than upon the character of its men.[4]

For Kipling and Smiles, as well as for Tennyson and Browning, the first mover behind such an ideology of resilience and activity is Thomas Carlyle, who posits a conception of heroism revealing itself to the hero-worshipper, thus acting as a powerful example to all. In his lecture, 'The Hero as King', Carlyle works no less than the meaning of life, for all of his audience, around the importance of vital and active willing:

> And yet, I say, there is an irrepressible tendency in every man to develop himself according to the magnitude which Nature has made of him; to speak out, to act out, what Nature has laid in him. This is proper, fit, inevitable; nay, it is a duty, and even the summary of duties for a man. The meaning of life here on earth might be defined as consisting in this: to unfold your *self,* to work what thing you have the faculty for. It is a necessity for the human being, the first law of our existence.[5]

Duty and necessity both go out to meet volition and individualism. We can actively control our destiny, but only insofar as that destiny reveals itself to us. We are not prompted to act by will, as a first cause, but by what, as Carlyle's rhyming prose stresses it, 'Nature has made' of us, what 'Nature has laid' in us.

Yet such exhortations are as much the source of an anxious sense of powerlessness in the writing of the nineteenth century, and the centrality of individual agency in the unfolding of the self is often inspected to reveal a hollowness, a sense of being without just such a centre. For every official exhortation of Tennyson, Carlyle, Kipling or Smiles, there is a voice, like Arthur Hugh Clough's, which might ask that the struggle nought availeth, or as his speaker confronts the issue in *Sa Majesté Très Chrétienne,*

> Alas, and is it true
> Ought I can purpose, say, or will, or do,
> My fancy choose, my changeful silly heart
> Resolve, my puny hand enact,
> To that great glory can in ought conduce
> Which from the old eternities is Thine?
> Ah never, no!
>
> (52–8)[6]

This drama of weakness before the imperatives of action, and the sense of failure in purpose, speech, will, action, choice, resolve is trapped here where 'can' meets 'ought', and issues only in passive denial. With duty laid before him, Clough's speaker can only turn to an intuited sense of a contained subjectivity which may never have to engage in a world in which it may fail: 'Somehow I think my heart within is pure' (122).

Decisions such as face Paris in Tennyson's 'Oenone' are founded in a testing of the will, a version of self which is held up in a dramatic verse which allows itself to work as mimic, counterpoint, enemy or ally, of the efforts of poet or speaker to work their way into a position of informed choice carried through with a strong will. These moments are marked in the poems discussed in this book by their rhythms in the way that a speech such as Pallas Athene's is conveyed in a poetry which seeks for a rhythm of will. The dilemma which is presented to Paris captures not only a Carlylean account of history as the individual responding to crisis, but it captures the way in which the poetry that wished to work within such moments sought to find form, here narrative as well as prosodic, for insight into processes of mind which were dependent not only upon thought and feeling, but also on will. Tennyson is not alone in such a seeking, and as John R. Reed and Isobel Armstrong, to name but two, have recently told us, the will is a central and often unquestioned part of Victorian accounts of self and mind. The implicit logical shift in equating volitional power with moral strength in

Tennyson's advice to his son, and the related terms of Pallas' offer show this: the ethical, the psychological and the means of describing action as experience and necessity meet in a strenuously argued medium.[7] That medium is a Victorian poetry, which, as Dennis Taylor and Eric Griffiths have also stated, is one which has been concerned with moving towards the rhythmic representation of the human voice.[8] Add to this the moral and psychological preoccupations of a poetry which explores character in dramatic monologue and loss in elegy, and we have a concern with sounding a sense of self or character through the experience of that character's volitional abilities or failings.

This book presents readings of a number of poems in order to discuss varying Victorian accounts of agency through comparable accounts of voiced rhythm. Bringing these concerns together, it describes the workings of human will through poetic effect both in the narrative and lyrical forms which move towards dramatic monologue and in Victorian versions of elegy. The means of sounding the many voices which the poetry of Tennyson, Browning, Hopkins and Hardy presents us, is through an ear for prosodic innovations. These innovations are concerned with laying the line of a lyric or dramatic consciousness within the line of poetry, working one with or against the other, within or outside metrical norms or inventions. An attention to prosodic practice in Victorian poetry is no mere technical matter. Rather, it enables us to listen for the rhythms of will which emerge from the representation of experiences of self through the bodily experience of a poetry which is conscious of itself as voiced sound.

The dramatic and elegiac poetry of the nineteenth century investigates agency through speech, a sense of agency which is posited as central to the identity of the self. The self, in turn, strives to make its presence felt in the speech which is recreated in Victorian verse. This happens both in the individual decision and in the greater sense of the marking of these decisions in history. What is sounded along the line of poetry aspires to be either the sound of the self facing the moment of decision or a life spent avoiding such decisions. Before poet and speaker the options for change are always open. The possibilities of new life for the subject in the poem, or new form available to the subject who is the artist, tug this poetry into the challenge of something that we might call modernity, but the Victorians would call the future. Passionate about the past as they were, the attitude to the will as the faculty which places the agency of the individual in a position to determine the future, to effect change, to bring into form the new, is represented with the ambivalence shown in many poems discussed in this book. The poems do find rhythms for representing agency in crisis, but they might just as easily sound the inertia attendant upon a conception of the agent existing only in a scene of aftermath.

Robert Browning's *Sordello,* a poem so innovative it is still nearly unreadable, sees action, event and character often circling around themselves with varying degrees of crisis, inertia and obscurity. Book V attempts to move the poem away from the enervation which threatens its poet-hero, and out to its story of a European civilisation emerging from the Dark Ages. Speaking directly to his hero 'in modern speech', the 'low voice' of Browning's narrator counsels the despondent Sordello to take a part in the history of man. He advances a theory of history which will exemplify how 'collective man / Outstrips the individual' (103–4) and points to 'The Multitude to be materialized' (124–5). History is 'loose eternal unrest' (126) and while it needs individuals to bring it to form, those individuals are destined to be subsumed both by the materialized multitude for which they work and a human progress which will in its turn need other individuals to advance it. So the narrator, steeling himself to make his point clearly for once ('Speak plainer!'), shows Sordello how from one specific of policy, a single Pope's decision to take the responsibility for ecclesiastical appointments, the position of Roman power in history has been secured:

'Speak plainer! Is't so sure
God's church lives by a King's investiture?
Look to last step! A staggering – a shock –
What's mere sand is demolished, while the rock
Endures: a column of black fiery dust
Blots heaven – that help was prematurely thrust
Aside, perchance! – but air clears, naught's erased
Of the true outline. Thus much being firm based,
The other was a scaffold'

(v, 153–61)

The cataclysmic blotting of heaven here is due to the process of the realignment of social organisations into their true forms. A critical moment of upheaval clears to show, in a conflation of two passages from St Matthew, the destruction of the house made of sand (vii, 24–7) and the surviving outline of the rock of Peter's Church (xvi, 18). The scaffold of a temporal organisation makes way for the true outline of eternal forms, in this case Rome.

This reorganisation contributes to an emergence of what is prophesied in scripture from what is temporary. The expedient of the scaffold is no longer needed, and history progresses, further revealing the eternal, an achievement in time which reveals the timeless. Yet that achievement, the revelation of the outline of truth from the clearing air, is one which has to be realised by an individual, even though that individual is obeying what history will reveal to be necessity. The individual reveals this truth from the processes of his own body. The passage continues:

'See him stand
Buttressed upon his mattock, Hildebrand
Of the huge brain-mask welded ply o'er ply
As in a forge; it buries either eye
White and extinct, that stupid brow; teeth clenched,
The neck tight-corded, too, the chin deep-trenched,
As if a cloud enveloped him while fought
Under its shade, grim prizers, thought with thought
At dead-lock, agonizing he, until
The victor thought leap radiant up, and Will,
The slave with folded arms and drooping lids
They fought for, lean forth flame-like as it bids.
Call him no flower – a mandrake of the earth,
Thwarted and dwarfed and blasted in its birth,
Rather, – a fruit of suffering's excess,
Thence feeling, therefore stronger: still by stress
Of Strength, work Knowledge!'

(v, 161 77)

Writing from the nineteenth century, Browning pictures key moments which assist him in his version of history as eternal progress. To do this he pictures not only the government of the 'Multitude' but also of the self, and the critical moment of history is placed in the eleventh century body of the 'suffering', 'feeling' Pope Gregory VII. That body has come dramatically to the decisions which here burst into the present tense at 'thought leap radiant up', and show a contorting rhythmic portrait of the mechanisms of will.

Browning portrays an intellectual strife within the self. Processes of mind are shown allying power with will: at one point decision-making is compared to a prize fight. The body of the Pope is locked into its processes of thought, vigorously disputing with itself and showing the fierceness of that dispute in brain, eye, brow, teeth, neck and chin. The rhyming verse chafes with the strain: 'ply/eye', 'clenched'/'trenched', 'fought'/'thought'. These rhymes hold the couplets into the deliberating body that the rhythms of the passage scan. Those rhythms are chopped up into seemingly random caesura, sudden substitutions and enjambments which, due to the semantic emphasis of the couplets, never really allow the verse to throw off its constraint. They work with the mind which is stressing its body so. 'Teeth clenched / The neck tight-corded, too, the chin deep-trenched': the lines pack their metrical stresses around the moments of physical stress shown in the hyphenated tension of the tightened neck and impacted chin. They must relax, and do. 'At dead-lock, agonizing he, until / The victor thought leap radiant up, and Will': the strain is released gradually into that isolated iamb, and the 'until/Will' rhyme works us out of the impasse of thought, through decision, and into action. This action results from the capitalised 'Will', a faculty which, the decision taken, 'bids' with the sudden destructiveness of a flame. This faculty is in the service of one who knows an excess of suffering, of one who feels. It only increases his strength to work Knowledge.

This is exactly what Pallas Athene promises Paris in 'Oenone', the abilities of a 'full-grown will', and the corresponding civic and political virtues which will involve hard decisions, but decisions that Paris can make. As I have said, these would be the virtues that an official version of a strong will would hold up before a society keen to materialise a multitude of autonomous individuals. Such choice is a necessary fiction of the newly liberal society which was then in its infancy in Victoria's Britain. Yet choice may be compromised by other factors. Oenone has told us of the 'clear and bared limbs' of Pallas, a candid nudity which is, we suspect, mediated by what is undoubtedly the sort of advice you give to young men going to the university. The way of will is open, but other factors can influence the way in which we make decisions.

The allure of overpowering sexuality may be one of them. Thus Paris is faced with the half-naked, half-shadowed body of Aphrodite, slowly drawing back her hair in a tempting display of erotic dissemblance. She,

> 'With rosy slender fingers backward drew
> From her warm brows and bosom her deep hair
> Ambrosial, golden round her lucid throat
> And shoulder: from the violets her light foot
> Shone rosy-white, and o'er her rounded form
> Between the shadows of the vine-bunches
> Floated the glowing sunlights, as she moved.'

(172–8)

It takes four enjambed lines of rolling blank verse, so different in rhythmic style from Pallas' speech, to effect this revelation. Even Aphrodite's foot is 'light', the pun stressing the growing brightness that this goddess' nudity brings to the scene. She offers a single sentence as her speech to Paris, 'The fairest and most loving wife in Greece', and this and the above erotic picture (narrated to us by a woman) make up his mind. He chooses to reject the faculty which will make more and better choices part of his personality. The option of power is given up in favour of the option to continue as a 'bundle of sensations'.

Unlike Hildebrand's effort, which rights the course of the history of Western Europe, this is an instance of incontinence, the choice of a course of action taken against the agent's better judgement. Paris surrenders to sexual attraction, giving up the opportunity of divine assistance towards absolute moral control. Pallas Athene had offered an intermingling of godly power with the human body: her vigour and his blood are shown in the internalised image of a perpetual adrenalin rush of power which will 'strike within thy pulses', and then give Paris the moral muscularity of one who is 'Sinewed with action'. However, the method which Pallas uses to tell Paris how he can have a full grown will is one which does not sweeten the facts of a life spent struggling towards it. The 'shocks, / Dangers, and deeds' are hardly attractive, and the strenuous rhythms and straining syntax of that speech too perfectly mimic the harshness of what she is outlining. Neither the myth nor Tennyson can allow us to see what might happen if Paris were to take up Pallas' offer. The cataclysmic effects of his choice are elsewhere well documented, ready to meet with the consequences of another action, and, as Yeats says, 'The broken wall, the burning roof and tower / And Agamemnon dead'.[9] Rhythmically acknowledged human shortcomings cannot allow Paris to grasp fully the idea, or even the physicality, of the metaphors used to express Pallas' offer and the consequences in history of his decision.

It takes only a split-second shutting of Oenone's 'sight for fear' (184) for Paris to give the apple to Aphrodite, and for her narrative to come to a close. This is a decision which goes desperately wrong for the poem's heroine, who has had no part in the drama enacted in front of her. A passive spectator to a process of choosing, her complaint is the complaint of the powerless, one who has had no opportunity to choose, no option of will. Alluding to the last line of 'Ulysses', Gerhard Joseph summarises a tradition of criticism of 'Oenone' and Tennyson's early poetry, in terms which are applicable to the marginalised yet titular heroine: she is in 'that hovering state between the fatality of suffering victim and the striving, seeking, unyielding hero'.[10] Her grieving situation is the result of the denial of Pallas' offer. Another's choice leaves her alone, and her predicament is one where another's actions have irrevocably affected her circumstances.

Oenone cannot know what Tennyson called 'The happiness resulting from power well exercised'. This phrase appears in the fragment of a letter that he sent to his fiancée Emily Selwood in 1839, one of the few remaining pieces of evidence we have of a relationship which nearly foundered on circumstance. The letter works from power on earth to silence in eventual knowledge:

> The happiness resulting from power well exercised must in the end far exceed the mere physical happiness of breathing, eating and sleeping like an ox. Can we say that God prefers higher happiness in some to a lower happiness in all? It is a hard thing that if I sin and fail I should be sacrificed to the bliss of the saints. Yet what reasonable creature, if he could have been asked beforehand would not have said 'Give me the metaphysical power, let me be the lord of my decisions: leave physical quietude and dull pleasure to lesser lives'? All souls methinks would have answered thus and so had men suffered by their own choice, as now by necessity of being born what they are, but there is no answer to the question except in a great hope of universal good ... Let us be silent for we know nothing of these things and we trust there is one who knows all.[11]

Writing within a particularly difficult moment in his relationship, Tennyson asks to be lord of its decisions. He moves at first towards the orthodox Christianity of the recipient of the letter, but then veers away in claims of ignorance, and the assertion only of 'trust'. The 'reasonable creature' asks for power and will, yet questioningly. The sacrifice of the self in failure is the 'hard thing' of responsibility, but 'all souls methinks' would want it. Suffering and necessity do condition such freedoms, and they exist only as the 'great hope of universal good'. Paris repudiates just such an opportunity, and Oenone is shown to possess very little in the way of 'the metaphysical power'.

Power, decision and choice are all placed before characters such as these in Victorian poetry; often they remain ungraspable, held there either only by a 'trust' in 'one who knows all', or in the merely intuited sense of a need to pursue a progress barely to be felt in the hero's own lifetime. The 'low voice' of Browning's narrator wonders whether Sordello himself might effect the move to the final stage of human progress:

> 'Knowledge by stress of merely Knowledge? No –
> E'en were Sordello ready to forego
> His life for this, 'twere overleaping work
> Some one has first to do, howe'er it irk,
> Nor stray a foot's breadth from the beaten road.'
>
> (v, 211–15)

The theme is that Rome wasn't built in a day, but it is also one which allows the self to play a crucial part in its construction. That part may be neither an easy nor an attractive option. For the first time in Book V, Browning rhymes 'work' with 'irk' (he does it again at lines 305–6), and suggests the labour that is required to achieve a task, and the necessity of keeping to its already beaten road. Such achievement may not be possible, and much that follows in this book may be a record of failure. But the option of foregoing a life for such tasks was always before the Victorians, and their poetry tries to sound the experience of its strenuous difficulty.

Notes

1 Hallam Tennyson, *Alfred Lord Tennyson, A Memoir By His Son,* 2 vols. (London: Macmillan, 1897), vol. 1, p. 317.
2 John R. Reed, *Victorian Will* (Athens: Ohio University Press, 1989), p. 9. On muscular Christianity, see Norman Vance, *Sinews of the Spirit: The Ideal of Christian Manliness in Victorian Literature and Religious Thought* (Cambridge: Cambridge University Press, 1985).
3 Quoted from *Selected Poems of Rudyard Kipling,* ed. T. S. Eliot (London: Faber, 1942).
4 Samuel Smiles, *Self Help* (London: John Murray, 1859), p.2.
5 Thomas Carlyle, *Heroes and Hero-Worship* (London: Chapman and Hall, 1898), p.225.
6 Quoted from *The Poems of Arthur Hugh Clough,* ed. A. L. P. Norrington (Oxford: Oxford University Press, 1968).
7 Isobel Armstrong, *Victorian Poetry: Poetry, Poetics and Politics* (London: Longman, 1993), the early chapters of which are concerned with establishing 'the critical necessity of will'.
8 Dennis Taylor, *Hardy's Metres and Victorian Prosody* (Oxford: Oxford University Press, 1988), and Eric Griffiths, *The Printed Voice of Victorian Poetry* (Oxford: Oxford University Press, 1989).
9 'Leda and the Swan', from *The Collected Poems of W. B. Yeats,* 2nd edn (London: Macmillan, 1950).
10 Gerhard Joseph, *The Weaver's Shuttle: Tennyson and the Text* (Cambridge: Cambridge University Press, 1992), p. 172.
11 *The Letters of Alfred Lord Tennyson,* ed. Cecil Y. Lang and Edgar F. Shannon, 3 vols. (Oxford: Oxford University Press, 1982–90), vol. 1, pp. 175–6. The letter is dated 24 October 1839.

5 E. C. Stedman and the Invention of Victorian Poetry (2005)

Michael C. Cohen

Critics have long despised "the genteel tradition" of the American nineteenth century. According to the vast majority of American literary histories written since 1915 (when Van Wyck Brooks published his polemic *America's Coming of Age*), the genteel tradition (and nineteenth-century America more generally) derived its poetic norms and ideals from the forms, imagery, and language of foreign sources, and it expressed a sentimental, bourgeois ideology at odds with the subversive work of truly great American writers. Only after the liberating Modernist revolution of the early twentieth century would America have its own poetic tradition. As Andrew DuBois and Frank Lentricchia tell the story, "to many appreciative American readers at the end of the nineteenth century," the genteel writers

> were synonymous with poetry. Other readers—Eliot, Frost, and especially Pound among them—saw things differently, saw these displaced late Victorians, this genteel cabal, filling the day's major magazines of culture, saw these fat old hens styling themselves as wise old owls ... saw these men squatting out the inadequate eggs of the day, their boring poems. Against this intolerable situation, the modernists made their attack. When the feathers finally settled, a handful of expatriates and the scattered nativist and homebody had already proved that the young century might be an American century, for poetry at least.... . The day was won by this historical movement, this *modernism*.[1]

The Modernists, then, resented not only the "boring poems" of the genteel writers but more significantly the cultural control they exercised, and by breaking the power of this "cabal," Modernism effected much more than a revolution in taste. In other words, the key target of Modernist rage was not genteel poems but genteel poetics, a system of "values," which DuBois and Lentricchia indict without really specifying. But the phrase "displaced late Victorians" is telling: not only do the genteel poets hold on to a set of values hopelessly out of date (hence "late"), they also mistakenly endorse a tradition that is not even theirs (hence they are "displaced Victorians"). Looking to Britain, the Victorian American "cabal" endorsed a sense of American poetry that only (and weakly) met the terms of a foreign poetics, and in so doing they missed the vital work being created at home, so that only in the twentieth century would the real American literature (*Walden, Moby Dick, Leaves of Grass*) be recognized. Besides being generally incorrect', this thesis fails to acknowledge an important implication of its terms, namely that "looking eastward" from America might be creative and productive as well as derivative. Americans did not look eastward to an autonomous or pre-existent field or discourse of Victorian poetry; rather, their looking eastward called that field into being. In other words, Americans did look to Britain during the Victorian era, but these Americans did not imitate, they created Victorian poetry. Rather than merely adopting pre-existing British poetic models as paradigms for American poetry, American writers helped to create those models by theorizing and defining Victorian poetry.[2]

The first modern critical work on the field—the first work to treat nineteenth-century British poetry as a field, separate and separable from the poetry of earlier times and places— was Edmund Clarence Stedman's 1875 *Victorian Poets,* Shortly after its publication, Stedman wrote to Moncure Conway that "it is the first attempt thus far to survey the whole course of recent British poetry, from the *rise* of Tennyson, down to the latest aspirants, upon a consistent method—with analysis of the period, etc., etc., including careful study into both the works and the lives of the leading poets."[3] Not only was it the first professional book on the subject, prior to it "the *prefix 'Victorian' had not previously become familiar"* (*LL*, p. 1; emphasis in the text). And while Victoria would reign nearly thirty more years, Stedman emphasized that he had been led "to complete the present work" because "I saw that what I term the Victorian period is nearly at an end, and that no consecutive and synthetic examination of its schools and leaders had yet been made."[4] The striking fact of an American inventing Victorian poetry is not accidental: Stedman's treatise followed a logic of periodization that went beyond the convenient fact of Victoria's reign, while the transatlanticism embedded in the origins of Victorian poetry played a causal role in the origins of *Victorian Poets*. His critical work had begun with an effort to review "the course of American poetry, since it may be said to have had a pathway of its own" (*VPoets*, p. xvi), but he quickly found that "with regard to the causes of the success and failure of our own poets … some of the most important were not special, but general: belonging to the period, and equally affecting the verse of the motherland. This led me to make a study of a few British poets.… . In order to formulate my own ideas of poetry and criticism, it seemed to me that I could more freely and graciously begin by choosing a foreign paradigm than by entering upon the home-field" (*VPoets*, p. xvii).

The transatlantic interdependence of nineteenth-century poetry became the ground on which to articulate the various national poetic fields. Not only were *Victorian Poets* and *Poets of America* (1885) the first major synthetic treatments of Victorian poetry, they also helped to mark the emergence of literary criticism as a profession. In his letter to Conway, Stedman claimed that while his treatment of nineteenth-century British poetry may not have been absolutely original, it did mark the origin of a new type of writing on the subject: "English books on the subject have chiefly been compiled by barristers, college-professors, and other *laymen…* . [*Victorian Poets*] is in a certain sense, professional—not amateur— criticism" (*LL*, p. 3; emphasis in text). Stedman understood his work to be professional not because he himself made a living writing criticism (he was in fact a broker on the New York Stock Exchange) but because his critical writing followed fully theorized principles: "The *real purpose* of both the 'Victorian Poets' and 'Poets of America' has been to give the author's *views* and *canons of poetry* and the *poetic art*, and to study a *poetic era,* and *poetic temperaments"* (*LL*, p. 54; emphasis in text).

Victorian Poets and *Poets of America* thus serve as foundational works not only for their respective poetic fields of study, but for the modern practice of literary criticism itself—a practice characterized by, among many other things, a reliance on periodization, national fields, and literary theories. Yet if Stedman mapped out terrain for the modern professionalized study of poetry, he was not therefore a proponent of what came to be important features of modern literary-critical discourse. For instance, Stedman never taught at a university. [...] Even if he did not teach at a university, he did (enthusiastically) participate in the emerging academic discourse of literary criticism—most notably by delivering the inaugural Turnbull lectures on poetry at the Johns Hopkins University in 1891.

[…]

In the introduction to *The Nature and Elements of Poetry,* the published edition of his Turnbull lectures at Johns Hopkins, Stedman defined poetry as "a specific manifestation of that all-pervading force, of which each one possesses a share at his control, and which communicates the feeling and thought of the human soul to its fellows." If this assertion seems like pale genteel effusing, Stedman intended, in fact, to cut through this sort of language by way of an "applied criticism" that would demand "the sincere and even ascetic mood that wishes no illusions and demands a working basis." Such sincerity and asceticism demand that the critic understand poetic form as an extension of the material history surrounding it; rather than imagining form as existing outside of time (or in opposition to it), the critic must read form as the highest index of time and history:

> *Expression* is the avowed function of all the arts, their excuse for being; out of the need for it, art in the rude and primitive forms has ever sprung… . At the same time, the [poet] cannot invent forms and methods and symbols out of keeping with what we term the nature of things; such inventions, if possible, would be monstrous, baleful, not to be endured.
>
> (*NEP*, pp. 44–45)

Genre and history are linked in this formulation, and the dialectical progression of one coincides with the dialectical progression of the other in standard Hegelian fashion—"objective" forms like epics and ballads give way to "subjective" forms like lyrics and dramas as a race becomes more self-conscious and as a nation achieves full internal coherence. The "objective masterpieces … are so naturally inwrought with history and popular traits that they seem growths rather than works of art" (*NEP*, p. 78). Such masterpieces ("the Indian epics, the Northern sagas, the early ballads of all nations, and of course the Homeric poems of Greece") embody a people because they come into existence prior to history, before that people understand themselves as a people. When the dialectical progression has advanced the people into a nation with an historical self-consciousness, these early objective works function as the indices that maintain the distinctive identity of the people who constitute the nation. The early literary tradition thus enables a people to remain a people and allows a nation to continue as a nation. The subjective poetry of later periods must work to continue the identity embodied in the early literature. These later works will need to contend with the historical and material forces of their own time, but they will only have lasting value if they maintain the prehistorical identity of the nation embodied in the early literature. "It seems, then, I say, the lot of each nation, as if an individual, and of each period, as if a modish season, to discover the beauty conformed both to the general laws and to specific needs and impulse; to create, moreover, its proper forms in every art, thus making new contributions to the world's thesaurus of poetry and design" (*NEP*, p. 164). And because material circumstances, such as national institutions like democracy, affect poetic production, the value of institutions will be determined by the poetry with which they coincide:

> In the Old World [poetic production] has been accomplished through the instrumentality of central governments. In a democracy the individual imagination has the liberty, the duty, of free play and achievement. Therefore, we say that in this matter our republicanism is on trial; that, with a forecast more exultant, as it is with respect to our

own future, than that of any people on earth, our theory is wrong unless through private impulse American foundations in art, learning, humanity, are not even more continuous and munificent than those resulting in other countries from governmental promotion.

(*NEP*, p. 229)

Far from seeing democracy or liberty as the ground of American identity that great American literature must express in order to be great American literature (as F. O. Matthiessen might argue), Stedman makes such institutions subsequent to an America grounded in literary genres (most prominently the ballad) that exist apart from historical manifestations like democratic government. And not only do such historical manifestations not embody America, Stedman implies that they should be discarded if they cannot soon produce a poetry able to continue American identity. Of course, the constitution of American identity has been a fraught subject throughout Stedman's work—first it is a continuation of an Anglo-Saxon identity that begins in England (in *Victorian Poets*); later it is based on the Yankee folk, distinct from English ancestry yet only in the process of unifying the many regional sub-types found in America; later still Stedman models the American identity on the Scottish example, but since America must first discover national melodies like those that embody and enable Scottish identity, Stedman finally locates American identity—or more specifically, America—in literary genres. The Hegelian historicism of *The Nature and Elements of Poetry* thus allows Stedman to produce both an American identity and an American literature in one critical treatise, and it also explains the urgency with which he argues for a new, vital poetic spirit in America, since without a new era of vital national poetry, America itself becomes a tentative phenomenon.

Critics of the genteel tradition are therefore wrong to see late-nineteenth-century poetics as solely a defense of bourgeois domestic mores. While it is true that Stedman disliked the dirty parts of *Leaves of Grass* and encouraged Whitman to publish an expurgated edition (which Whitman did),[5] his critical work was not concerned with defending the values of genteel decency. The values Stedman advocated were "imagination" and "expression," and, as I have argued, he asserted these values in the service of a nationalistic literary tradition that saw America and American poetry as the same. This program was not defensive in the sense that it did not urge normative literary values for the sake of shoring up normative cultural values. Rather, it was productive in the sense that it urged the creation of American poetry according to a paradigm that emphasized genres like the ballad. According to the theoretical program underwriting Stedman's paradigm, the focus on key poetic genres would call into being both an American people and an American nation.

In this light, Stedman seems to have pre-empted the principle thesis of anti-genteel criticism. The major focus of such criticism is not genteel culture's sentimentalism or consumerism, but the schizophrenic split between American ideals (literary, religious, etc.) and the reality of everyday life in America (economic competition, political corruption, etc.) that begins during the Victorian era. Critiques grounded in an analysis of this bifurcation of culture into genteel ideals and pragmatic reality run through twentieth-century polemics against the nineteenth century, beginning with George Santayana, and including Van Wyck Brooks, V. L. Parrington, Perry Miller, Ann Douglas, T. J. Jackson Lears, and the contributors to the latest *Cambridge History of American Literature*. This critical tradition (which can of course be modified to include, for instance, critiques of the evasion of race in American literary history like those by Toni Morrison or Eric Sundquist) forms one major strand of twentieth-century Americanist criticism.[6] The striking point is not that these polemical accounts of Victorian American culture are wrong, but that they replicate Stedman's own major anxieties. One of Stedman's major desires in his critical work was to keep poetry as a driving force in American culture. In the face of a mounting consumerism—which he sometimes calls "science" and sometimes "material progress"—and an American public that seemed to him increasingly uninterested in poetry, Stedman searches for a "usable past" (in Brooks's words) that will vitalize an American literary tradition and prevent the splits within culture that later critics deplore.

We can see how Stedman anticipates later anti-Victorian criticism if we compare his argument with Ann Douglas' account, which is particularly interesting since it replicates so many of Stedman's concerns. According to Douglas, American culture was based on the "self-evasion of a society both committed to laissez-faire industrial expansion and disturbed by its consequences," and, because it was "younger and less formed than that of any European country," Victorian American culture "had not yet developed sufficiently rich and diversified secular traditions to serve as carriers for its ongoing intellectual life."[7] Douglas attacks nineteenth-century culture for its failure to come to terms with the Puritan theological heritage of seventeenth-and eighteenth-century New England, a failure that, among other things, disabled "the transfer of energy formerly assigned to theological tasks into the service of history" (*F*, p, 175) begun by antebellum historians like Jared Sparks and George Bancroft. Such historicism "constituted an undisputedly serious effort toward American self-realization" at a time when "rapid and apparently promising intellectual, economic, and social development necessitated the at least partial adoption of historicism" (*F*, p. 180). But the self-evasion of Victorian America blocked this historicist self-realization and produced in its stead a genre of "clerical-feminine biography" that replaced the "grand view of Hegelian intellectual history" with a "psychological topography of [the] era" (*F*, p. 189). The result was that "as a genre ... the clerical-feminine biographies ... [used] the biographical form as [a] calculatedly therapeutic indulgence in the experience of ordinary human personality" (*F*, pp. 189–190). In the culture of Victorian America, the articulation of a national self-consciousness, heralded in the Hegelian historicism of the antebellum historians, lost out to the palliative comforts of the sentimental ideology endorsed in the clerical-feminine biographies. The defeat happens on the level of genre: the serious genre—history—loses to the non-serious or popular genre. Structurally Douglas' critique repeats Stedman's, since he also deplored the replacement of good, national poetic genres with bad, artificial ones. For both Douglas and Stedman, this sort of generic defeat made American culture a tenuous proposition.

The structural similarity also highlights the specific differences in the generic struggle that Douglas and Stedman focus on. In *The Feminization of American Culture*, the debate is entirely between prose genres. By replacing theology and history with the sentimental novel and the clerical-feminine biography, America loses its political and historical consciousness and becomes little more than bourgeois marketing enterprise; Victorian American culture is "a tragic dead-end" (*F*, p. 253), and only those (prose) writers (Melville, Fuller) who "rebel" against middle-class culture are of value today. The benefit of pairing Douglas' version with Stedman's is not only to show that Victorian America did make a "serious effort toward American self-realization," but also to show how in the nineteenth century such an effort came through the production of an American literary tradition based on poetic genres, while in the twentieth century the same effort (to produce a usable American past) must, almost by definition, be dominated by prose genres. "By definition," since "poetic genre" conjures up notions of formal conventionalism that are, in their most benign twentieth-century iterations, imagined as non-American and thoroughly domesticated; "almost" since, of course, there are at least two notable exceptions to the prose domination of the

American canon. But the canonicity of these poets has also long depended, at least within the anti-genteel tradition, on their rebelliousness against popular culture and poetic form. This rebelliousness accommodates these poets to the twentieth-century norms that mark an author's status as canonically American: Whitman's break with form in the chants and catalogues of the 1855 *Leaves of Grass* makes him the democratic leveler; Dickinson, in the increasingly lyricized or unedited manifestations that have marked the twentieth-century history of her poems, becomes one of the great antinomians. For the anti-genteel critics, poetic individualism equals a hostility to genre. Great American poetry must therefore be "novelistic" in Bakhtin's sense of "three-dimensionality" and formal "openendedness."[8] But this resistance to genre is not in any sense an escape from genre: Whitman and Dickinson must be read a certain way—that is, read according to a certain set of norms—to highlight the distinctively American features of their poems. The normative intent of anti-genteel writers still conflates Americanness and genre, only "genre" in the anti-genteel critique has largely lost any specific content and often means nothing more than high or serious literature (as opposed to popular or sentimental literature) or even simply "literature" as such.[9] The anti-genteel tradition thus replicates the genteel tradition's association of genre with national identity even as it assumes itself to be repudiating the genteel.

While a return to Stedman's criticism makes clear the connection between genteel and anti-genteel discourse, this does not mean that the genteel tradition simply authorizes the terms of its later repudiation. The two traditions are not, after all, the same, and one important difference is that genteel writing grounded its claims about literature and national literary traditions in an historical theorization of poetic genres, while the anti-genteel tradition, by and large, has emphasized either prose genres or novelistic poetics. Stedman's work defined literary criticism as a distinct domain of study by taking poems as objects of great cultural power. This power was the ability to bring races and nations into being by providing them with a shared expressive consciousness, and it resided in exemplary poetic genres like the ballad. Stedman's poetics thus offers a counterstatement to contemporary critical unease about poetry and poetic genres. This unease has received its most rigorous articulation in Paul de Man's poetics, with its premise that "generic terms … as well as pseudo-historical period terms … are always terms of resistance and nostalgia, at the furthest remove from the materiality of actual history."[10] In "Anthropomorphism and Trope in the Lyric," de Man's profound skepticism about critical discourse emerges out of a project that takes aim at the "uncertain status of the lyric as a term for poetic discourse in general" by interrogating "the structure of the tropes on which the claim to lyricism depends" (*RR*, p. 254), namely the anthropomorphic attribution of voice as subject. This tropological act must be the opening move in any further claim to knowledge: "the union of aesthetic with epistemological properties," de Man argues, "is carried out by the mediation of the metaphor of the self as consciousness of itself" (*RR*, p. 256). Revealing this false naturalisation leads to the conclusion that "the lyric is not a genre, but one name among several to designate the defensive motion of understanding" (*RR*, p. 261). The problem, which provides the impetus for de Man's hermeneutics, is that claims for poetic language—and, following the example of Nietzsche, truth and knowledge more generally—have come to rely un-self-consciously on a naturalized sense of the lyric subject. This mistake allows "the aesthetic ideologization of linguistic structures" to act as though it were "an empirical historical event" (*RR*, p. 253), an illustration of the proposition that "tropes are the producers of ideologies that are no longer true" (*RR*, p. 242). The asceticism of de Man's poetics demands some alternative to the false referentiality or ideology (the "fallacious lyrical reading of the unintelligible") that constitutes poetic language, an alternative de Man characterizes as "*historical* modes of language power" (*RR*, p. 262).

Stedman provides an alternative to de Man's poetics by providing a non-lyrical reading practice for poetry, one based on a notion of historically forceful poetic genres that are something more than theoretical (or false) constructs. This non-lyrical reading practice makes poems and poetic traditions dialectical entities, never totally immanent to their context and yet not transcendent of it either. As such, it gives genre a potent relation to human life. This understanding of poetic genres as functional, historical agents may prove to be the most shocking characteristic of genteel literary criticism, far more so than any perceived sense of its sentimentalism or conventionality. To Stedman, the purpose of literary criticism was to provide a system of analysis that could describe the historical products of this generic power, and also prescribe its uses for the future—a normative, which is to say a nationalistic or even nativistic intent, one far different from that most often aligned with the genteel tradition. Stedman's ambivalence about the discourse he helped create came from the fear that literary criticism would be deprived of this normative purpose, and given over simply to debates among pedants. By giving literary criticism both a purpose and an analytical approach, Stedman enabled twentieth-century Americanist critics to dismantle the nineteenth century in a search for a more usable past. Much has been obscured in this search: the genteel origins of modern literary study; the transatlantic relationship that formed the national fields of Victorian British and American poetry; and most importantly the multiform cultural role of poetic genres in the creation of national, racial, historical, and literary traditions. This obscuration, which can also be known as the lyricization of genre, could help to explain the malaise so often associated with the discursive (if not pedantic, but most certainly normative) debates of modern literary study, a malaise that has much to do with literary study's imagined sense of its own history as a discourse. Re-examining the origins of literary study, national literary traditions, and poetic discourse may not provide answers to contemporary critical problems—whither Victorian poetry? does literature matter? is theory dead?—but it will reveal that such problems were built into the very history of literary criticism as a discipline. In consequence, the genteel tradition may come to herald the future of American literary criticism, and Stedman to seem like the newest Americanist critic.

Notes

My thanks to Viriginia Jackson and Mary Poovey for their help with this essay.

1 Andrew DuBois and Frank Lentricchia, "Modernist Lyric in the Culture of Capital." *The Cambridge History of American Literature,* gen. ed. Sacvan Bercovitch, vol. 5 (Cambridge: Cambridge Univ. Press, 2003), p. 174.

2 In this emphasis on dialectical transatlanticism, this essay will differ from Joseph Bristow's very interesting recent essay on the development of the adjective "Victorian" as a period-marker. Though he links the development of the term with late-nineteenth-century theories about post-1842 British poetry and though he gives attention to Stedman's *Victorian Poets* as the first major treatise to use the term, Bristow does not examine the transatlantic implications of this innovation. See Joseph Bristow, "Whether 'Victorian' Poetry: A Genre and Its Period," *Victorian Poetry* 42, no. 1 (2004): 81–109.

3 Laura Stedman and George M. Gould, eds., *Life and* Letters *of Edmund Clarence Stedman* (New York; Moffat, Yard and Company, 1910), 2:3. Hereafter abbreviated *LL* and cited in the text.

4 E. C. Stedman, *Victorian Poets* (Boston: Houghton Mifflin, 1903). p. xviii. Hereafter abbreviated *VPoets* and cited in the text.

5 See Ed Folsom, "Leaves of Grass Junior: Whitman's Compromise with Discriminating Taste," *American Literature* 63, no. 4 (December 1991): 641–663. The editor of the expurgated *Leaves of Grass* was Stedman's son Arthur.

6 There are, of course, other ways of talking about nineteenth-century culture; see, for instances Jane Tompkins, *Sensational Designs* (Durham: Duke Univ. Press, 1984), and Walter Benn Michaels, *The Gold Standard and the Logic of Naturalism* (Berkeley: Univ. of California Press, 1987). The interesting point for my purpose is that counter-arguments for the nineteenth century are grounded in prose fiction and ignore poetry, which belies the historical centrality of poetic genres in the formation of American literature and American literary culture. Paula Bennett's *Poets in the Public Sphere* (Princeton: Princeton Univ. Press, 2003) provides one recent exception to this tendency.

7 Ann Douglas, *The Feminization of American Culture* (New York: Farrar, Strauss and Giroux, 1998), p. 12. Hereafter abbreviated *F* and cited in the text.

8 M.M. Bakhtin, *The Dialogic Imagination: Four Essays, trans.* Caryl Emerson and Michael Holquist (Austin: Univ. of Texas Press, 1981), p. 11.

9 I am in agreement with Harrington's assessment that contemporary Americanist literary histories, despite their efforts to be "new," repeat the old Americanist literary histories they had ostensibly outmoded, and thus function as "literary histories of American literary history." Donald Pease would probably be unhappy to learn that Stedman early on refers to his own critical project as "the New Americanism" (*PA*, p. 10) because it works toward a more expansive and less localized idea of American literature. So long as revisionary interventions into the Americanist canon continue to exclude poetic genres, they will not be new—they will not even be genteel.

10 Paul de Man, *The Rhetoric of Romanticism* (New York: Columbia Univ. Press, 1984), p. 262. Hereafter abbreviated *RR* and cited in the text.

Part II
What is Poetry?

Rosie Miles

> Poetry needs no Preface: if it do not speak for itself, no comment can render it explicit.
> – L.E.L. (Letitia Landon)[1]

Romanticism is in itself a Victorian term coined to describe the sensibilities of art (and particularly) poetry from the 1790s–1820s. The Romantic poets reacted against the epigrammatic 'finish' of neo-classicism (exemplified by Pope and Dryden), to the coming of the industrial revolution, and became an integral part of the Romantic assertion of a self which turns to nature – its power and simplicity – as a rebellion against the mechanisation of the human spirit.

J. R. Watson writes of the 'extraordinary sense of life and energy, of freshness and excitement' as the Romantic poets grapple with questions of the self and/in the world.[2] William Wordsworth and Samuel Taylor Coleridge were aware they were doing something new with *Lyrical Ballads* in 1798, and the 1800 edition carried the famous Preface (revised and expanded 1802) which is, in effect, *the* poetic manifesto to which all other nineteenth-century accounts of poetry are explicitly or implicitly responding. The Preface states that *Lyrical Ballads* aimed to use 'a selection of language really used by men' and there is a concern to bring the speaking voice into poetry, as there will be in the blank verse of Wordsworth's autobiographical work *The Prelude* (published posthumously in 1850; mostly written 1804–6). Most famously, in terms of still-quoted poetry soundbites, the Preface speaks of poetry as 'the spontaneous overflow of powerful feelings', making the link between poetry and emotion definitive. If this appears to justify any blurting out onto the page as poetry, it is important to remember that the Preface repeats this phrase, but the second time allies it to an equally well-known line that appears to contradict it: 'I have said that poetry is the spontaneous overflow of powerful feelings; it takes its origin from emotion recollected in tranquillity'.[3] This latter phrase is embodied in such an iconic poem as Wordsworth's poem about daffodils but also gestures towards the thought necessary to turn such unstoppable affect into a poem. The poem's utterance must be crafted and shaped and the Preface affirms the *pleasure* inherent in 'the music of harmonious metrical language'.

The Romantic poet does not just reflect the world, but transforms and acts upon that which is perceived through the creative (and thus God-like) power of the imagination. In M. H. Abrams' terms, the central metaphor is of poetry (and thus art) not as a mirror but a lamp. This he derives from Hazlitt:

> The light of poetry is not only a direct but also a reflected light, that while it shews us the object, throws a sparkling radiance on all around it: the flame of the passions,

communicated to the imagination, reveals to us, as with a flash of lightning, the inmost recesses of thought, and penetrates our whole being.[4]

The eternal optimism of the imagination, its never-ending capacity for revelation, is captured in Wordsworth's eulogy to 'Imagination!' ('a shout of recognition, or wonder') in Book VI of *The Prelude*:

> With hope it is, hope that can never die,
> Effort, and expectation, and desire,
> And something evermore about to be.
>
> (ll.540–2)

If the Preface to *Lyrical Ballads* is Wordsworth's poetic manifesto, then Coleridge's consideration of the same is mapped out in his *Biographia Literaria* (1817). As he succinctly notes, to ask 'What is poetry? is so nearly the same question with, what is a poet? that the answer to the one is involved in the solution of the other'. He also suggests that 'A poem is that species of composition, which is opposed to works of science, by proposing for its *immediate* object pleasure, not truth'.[5]

Shelley's 'A Defence of Poetry' concludes a triumvirate of key Romantic manifestos, but it is important to remember that despite its strong assertions of faith in the power of poetry – it has been described as 'for many … the most exalted celebration of poetry ever written'[6] – the 'Defence' is a reaction to an attack on poetry's continuing value, and thus it is already marked with what will soon more explicitly emerge: a sense of having to champion poetry's cause. It is a rebuttal of Thomas Love Peacock's 'The Four Ages of Poetry' appeared in the first (and only) number of *Ollier's Literary Miscellany* in 1820. Peacock's essay suggests that the current is an age of brass, as opposed to former epochs of iron, gold and silver. He traces poetry's emergence from the primitive to its pinnacle and then decline through both the classical and modern eras. There are frequent recourses in nineteenth-century accounts of poetry and poets to lists of ever-declining greatness, starting with Homer and progressing through Virgil, Dante, Shakespeare and Milton. While Peacock is mocking of 'that egregious confraternity of rhymesters, known by the name of the Lake Poets', his real concern is that the appropriate readership for poetry is diminishing. The finest minds are interested in 'useful art and science, and … moral and political knowledge', but not poetry.[7]

This, in essence, is the challenge facing all who respond to the question 'what is poetry?' in the first half of the nineteenth century. Romanticism makes high claims for the centrality of poetry and the poet as the one who can apprehend and communicate the finest truths through it. On this side of the divide we find imagination, fancy, creativity, the divine, feeling, truth, nature, song and transcendence. But as the juggernaut of Victorian progress rolls into view, a whole other world order appears antithetically opposed, epistemologically committed to empiricism, utilitarianism, science, fact, truth, reason and materialism. At stake are also two very different conceptions of truth and how truth is arrived at and, as Alba Warren notes, there is still a desire in the early Victorian period 'to conceive of poetry as an effective social and moral force'.[8] For Shelley, poetry is behind all, a fundament of primitive civilisation: 'In the infancy of society every author is necessarily a poet because language itself is poetry'.[9] The poet is thus elevated to a transcendent position of power and influence: 'Poets … were called, in the earlier epochs of the world, legislators or prophets', and the poet 'participates in the eternal, the infinite, the one'.[10] The 'Defence' also addresses the question of utility. In one sense it is not the poet's concern to ask what use-value or impact poetry has: 'a poet is a nightingale, who sits in darkness and sings to cheer its own solitude with sweet sounds'.[11] At the same, time poetry is also part of what morally and essentially improves the world. While philosophy and science may do some good, realms of knowledge-making which neglect the poetic faculty in favour of 'the accumulation of facts and calculating processes' ultimately enslave the 'internal world' of humanity.[12]

Angela Leighton notes how Shelley's view of poetry in the 'Defence' 'raises it above the particular work and presents it instead as the original energy of creativity ... poetry itself is the very spirit of change and progress'.[13] As such, and despite Shelley's atheism, poetry 'is indeed something divine'.[14] All systems of thought – including science – are rooted in it. Thus poetry is not somehow set against science, or the material, or empiricism, but subsumes and transcends them all. The illuminating lamp for Shelley is not just the imagination but beauty: 'poetry is a mirror which makes beautiful that which is distorted';[15] it 'turns all things to loveliness'.[16] Perhaps the most famous section of the 'Defence' is its rousing conclusion. In contrast to Peacock's suggestion that the present represents a degraded modern era of poetry, Shelley sees 'an energetic development' in the literature of his time.[17] He affirms that poetry is forever on the side of social, moral (and implicitly political) good: it is 'the most unfailing herald, companion, and follower of the awakening of a great people to work a beneficial change in opinion or institution'. Poetry is inherently radical, and what poetry and poets were in the past, they are still now. Shelley asserts the eternal, unchanging greatness of poetry. If once poets were the law-makers, they actually still are (even if some now don't recognise this): 'Poets are the unacknowledged legislators of the world'.[18]

Richard Cronin writes that:

> Shelley focussed so many key Victorian concerns; on the relationship between the poet and his works, on whether the artist should address the many or the few, on whether art was an affair of the body or the spirit, on whether poems should be valued for the justice or the intensity of the sentiments they express.[19]

His influence on the youthful Robert Browning is seen in the latter's admiring 'An Essay on Percy Bysshe Shelley' (1852), which introduced a selection of Shelley's letters. The letters turned out to be forgeries, but the essay afforded Browning the opportunity to formulate a distinction between the objective and subjective poet: the objective focusses upon 'the doings of men' while the subjective poet's 'study has been himself'.[20] This is significant in Browning's subsequent contribution to the development of the dramatic monologue. His early poem 'Pauline' (1833) also specifically addresses Shelley in tribute. While Carlyle appeared to be dismissive of Shelley, his conception of 'The Hero as Poet' is very close to that of Shelley.[21] The Poet (capital P) is one of the leaders the changing age needs.

The belatedness of Victorian poetry is often noted.[22] Sandwiched between two literary eras that appear to define their difference from what preceded them more clearly, Victorian poetry and poetic theory is post-Romantic (certainly from the 1830s–50s). This volume puts paid to any notion that Victorian poets, commentators and critics had nothing of any interest to say about poetry. Treatises abound.[23] Isobel Armstrong notes that the proliferation of periodicals as the nineteenth century progresses affords opportunities for a new kind of criticism (by way of reviews) which is often 'closer to cultural pressures than the abstract treatises'.[24] These critics also 'were confronted with a social ... environment which seemed to be peculiarly hostile to the writing of poetry'.[25] Jeremy Bentham's utilitarianism (associated with the greatest good of the greatest number), 'represents a culmination of a tendency of the new philosophy in England, empirical in pretension and practical in orientation, to derogate poetry in comparison with science'.[26] Bentham concedes that poetry does have a use in that it can give pleasure, but as fewer people enjoy poetry (apparently) than the child's game of push-pin, then its value is limited: everybody can play at push-pin; poetry and music are relished only by a few. [27] A utilitarian perspective is also highly suspicious of the Romantic notion of poetry's excitation of the imagination and fancy, and the valorising of emotion over reason. These are incitements to falsehood, not empiricist, verifiable truth. So pervasive is this view that until the 1860s Victorian poetics are put on the defensive, attempting to defend poetry on the very terms that utilitarian thinking has laid down. E. S. Dallas' *Poetics* (1852), for example, opens by saying that its aim is to 'plac[e] … criticism upon something like a scientific footing; in brief, towards a science of poetry and of poetic expression, I desire to contribute a mite'.[28]

John Stuart Mill's *Autobiography* (1873) provides helpful context for understanding the two essays he wrote on poetry for the *Monthly Repository* in 1833. Mill's father, James, was a Benthamite disciple, and 'professed the greatest contempt' for 'passionate emotions of all sorts'.[29] As a young man, Mill was also a card-carrying Benthamite, but aged twenty-five he experienced what we would now refer to as a form of psychological breakdown. Mill describes his loss of purpose and meaning as a direct result of an education and upbringing entirely devoid of the recognition of feeling. In an oedipal overthrowing of his father's principles of which Freud would have been proud, Mill reorients his own sense of self such that 'the cultivation of the feelings became one of the cardinal points in my ethical and philosophical creed'. Crucial to this is a new-found sense of 'the importance of poetry and art as instruments of human culture'.[30] Specifically it is through the poetry of Wordsworth that he literally finds healing: 'What made Wordsworth's poems a medicine for my state of mind, was that they expressed, not merely outward beauty, but states of feeling, and of thought coloured by feeling, under the excitement of beauty'.[31] Mill's indebtedness to the *Lyrical Ballads* 'Preface' here is also evident in 'What is Poetry?' Following Wordsworth, Mill pits the realm of science against that of poetry, and affirms poetry as on the side of feeling and ultimate truth. Most famously, Mill distinguishes between eloquence and poetry, and suggests that 'eloquence is *heard*, poetry is *over*heard. Eloquence supposes an audience; the peculiarity of poetry appears to us to lie in the poet's utter unconsciousness of a listener'.[32] This appears to be an argument on the side of the poet's separation from the world: if the poet happens to be overheard, all to the good, but this is not a prerequisite of creation (see again Shelley's 1820 'To a Skylark'). In a similarly Wordsworthian formulation, Mill suggests that 'poetry … is the natural fruit of solitude and meditation'.[33] Mill's second essay, 'The Two Kinds of Poetry', distinguishes between Wordsworth and Shelley. Where Wordsworth is more measured, Shelley is 'the most striking example ever known of the poetic temperament', who turns his sensations into an exuberant, inexhaustible imagery.[34] In saying that 'the susceptibility of [Shelley's] nervous system … made his emotions intense',[35] however, Mill gestures towards one of the Victorian period's other problems with poets: the poet's mind. Mill's definitions in 'What is Poetry?' also point to poetry as connected to the hidden and interior self (see also Matthew Arnold's 'The Buried Life'), and the Victorians find this association of poetry with the mind and interiority troubling. Either morbid or diseased, the poet's mind is suspect as the scientific study of the mind emerges in psychiatry and psychology.[36] As Gregory Tate notes, it is not until the 1850s–60s that commentators start to applaud the use of poetry as a vehicle for introspection, and indeed indeterminacy, for example in responses to Arthur Hugh Clough's poetry.[37] But the (in)famously negative 'dialogue of the mind with itself' bemoaned by Arnold in his 1853 'Preface' is by then well underway.[38]

Eric Griffiths encapsulates this well when he highlights the Victorian period's 'contradictory attitudes to poetry – [as both] prophecy and disease'.[39] His work on the printed voice gestures towards close readings (of Tennyson, Robert Browning, Elizabeth Barrett Browning, Hardy and Hopkins) that are interested in 'the movement between speech and print'.[40] Written poetry, marked with metre and stress, holds within itself the signs of its spoken origins, which are forever lost. Excepting a shaky wax cylinder recording of Tennyson reading 'The Charge of the Light Brigade' available online,[41] we have no way of knowing how the Victorians voiced their poems, thus the printed voice is always already 'an archived pattern on the page, salvaged from an evanescence of the voice in the ear'.[42] As a critical approach to Victorian poetry, this embodies its own sense of loss just as Victorian poets themselves – most of all Arnold – felt deeply their own sense of no longer being able to inhabit the same certainties as the Romantics before them. Matthew Bevis cites Arnold's coinage of his own term to describe the 'unpoetrylessness' of the age.[43]

Griffiths also reads that most characteristic of Victorian poetic forms, the inherently doubled dramatic monologue, as 'hing[ing] on a difference between the sorts of weight we can rightly give to something spoken and the same words when written down. Writing down what has been said constitutes a judgement of speech ... In writing, speech is brought to book.[44] *The Printed Voice* is slightly in advance of a criticism focussed on the material textuality of literary works (Romantic scholar Jerome McGann's *The Textual Condition* was published in 1991), but implicitly looks towards this. Victorian poetry is central to subsequent understandings of word and image working together, particularly in the work of poets such as Dante Gabriel Rossetti, Christina Rossetti and William Morris. [45]

Hovering over all of this, however, is the crucial issue of gender in relation to nineteenth-century poetry. From the late 1980s onwards, critics have questioned the construction of Romanticism as solely based on the poetry and poetics of the 'big six': Wordsworth, Coleridge, Blake, Byron, Shelley, Keats. The feminist critique of Romanticism has at least two key strands: one is the analysis of how gender functions within 'masculine Romanticism', and how male poets appropriate and subsume the traditionally female realm of affect (for example) into their own version of the Hero-as-Poet/Prophet. As Anne Mellor says, 'After these canonised Romantic poets had stolen their emotions, their intuition, their capacity for imagination and fancy, their romances, and their affinity with nature, what did women have left?'.[46] The second strand, paralleling the rediscovery of dozens of forgotten Victorian women poets, is the re-evaluation of many Romantic women poets, including Anna Barbauld, Charlotte Smith, Phillis Wheatley, Mary Robinson, Felicia Hemans and Letitia Landon.[47] The breaking open of the canons of Romantic and Victorian poets enables new questions to be asked. For example, traditionally the dramatic monologue has been regarded as originating in the 1830s via Robert Browning and Tennyson. A broader perspective might well see the monologue as emergent in the work of Felicia Hemans and Letitia Landon.[48] Indeed, the question 'what is poetry?' must be answered differently once women's poetry is recognised as part of the mix. However, as this current volume demonstrates, the most well-known and long-lasting prose statements on poetry in the period are made almost exclusively by men. Women's voices appear pretty much absent from the construction of a Romantic or Victorian poetics. As the Romantic poet with his (sic) 'sword[s] of lightning'[49] is by definition male, and women are mostly excluded from the educational trajectories that would enable them to write 'high' forms of poetry or reviews for the periodicals, women poets had to find other outlets for publication.

Mellor has argued that 'We need to learn ... how to read these alternative poetic genres in a way that acknowledges ... their creation of a *popular* culture that perhaps more than any other literary productions defined Romanticism to itself.[50] In particular annuals and gift books (*The Keepsake*, *Forget-Me-Not*, the *Literary Souvenir* and others) flourished in the 1830s and:

> In professional and financial terms [they] were of immense significance in the lives of Hemans and L.E.L. and many other women writers because they provided, for the first time for women, a reliable source of income, a practical working world, a professional status, and a framework of supportive literary friendships.[51]

As poetry by women contributed to their success, the annuals gave women poets access to networks and publication opportunities which the masculine literary establishment denied them. Letitia Landon (L.E.L.) has been regarded as 'one of the most fully developed examples of the popular Victorian poetess', who defines what the term comes to mean to an entire generation.[52] More recently she has been seen as 'play[ing] the role of a poetess' self-consciously, in that the poetess 'label' does not have to be interpreted as limiting feminine expression but it can also delineate a more political self-fashioning.[53]

Glennis Byron rightly says that 'gender articulated the whole field of early Victorian poetry'.[54] Hence critical discussions of poetry are almost always implicitly (if not explicitly) also engaged with matters of gender. As I have suggested elsewhere, 'calls for a renewed, revitalised poetry in the period are often a rallying cry for the "manly"' poet to rise up (sic) and write the masculine epic (as opposed to lyric) poetry that the nation needs'.[55] The challenge for the female poet is the taking on of the male mantle of 'Poet', or the negotiating of the poetess tradition; the problem for the male poet is the association with a language of emotion, interiority and sensuous beauty which tips into a dangerous effeminacy. Both are legacies of Romanticism.

A poetics which will delineate the later nineteenth century starts to emerge in the 1860s.[56] As Marion Thain notes, by the end of the nineteenth century the poetic landscape is diverse enough that both male *and* female poets are more able to inhabit this terrain together, without the need to separate out male and female traditions.[57] In her essay on 'Women's Poetry' as a critical category, Thain aims to go beyond 'the unity implied by the term "women's poetry"'[58] to show how women poets of the *fin de siècle* are writing in multiple ways, and how anthologies of the period such as Elizabeth Sharp's *Women Poets of the Victorian Era* (1890) are also articulating a new poetics that recognises more complexity for women poets than solely their relationship to the earlier poetess tradition. Developing Isobel Armstrong's notion of the Victorian poem as inherently double and sceptical,[59] Thain uses a lyric by May Kendall to exemplify her notion of a triple poem, which highlights 'the dilemma of the *fin-de-siècle* woman poet who writes self-consciously … within a New Woman poetic, but who still has to negotiate the dominant poetess tradition from which she distances herself'.[60] If poetry started out at the beginning of the nineteenth century as being about mountain heights and daffodils, by the end of the century it is articulating gaslights, omnibuses and hothouse orchids. Women poets are writing modernity every bit as much as men.

Despite this essay's attempts in prose to explore some of what poetry and the poet meant in the nineteenth century, I still largely endorse L.E.L.'s epigraph quote which says poetry always best speaks its own poetics. While numerous nineteenth-century poems do this, none better takes on Romantic male traditions and transforms them in the name of gender than Barrett Browning's *Aurora Leigh* (1856). In the central fifth book, Aurora offers her own poetic philosophy, and asserts poetry's absolute concern with the present in a powerfully feminised language:

Their [the poets'] sole work is to represent the age,
Their age, not Chalemagne's, -- this live, throbbing age,
That brawls, cheats, maddens, calculates, aspires,
[…]
Never flinch,
But still, unscrupulously epic, catch
Upon the burning lava of a song
The full-veined, heaving, double-breasted Age …

(ll.202–4, 213–16)

Many of the concerns which Romantic poetry sets down and which the Victorians then pick up and modify are still with us. Can poetry still heal our unquiet minds, as it did for Wordsworth? Anthologies such as Bloodaxe's *The Poetry Cure* (2005) and Rachel Kelly's memoir *Black Rainbow: How Words Healed Me* (2014) suggest this is popularly so. In David Constantine's *Poetry* (2013), written as part of a series on 'The Literary Agenda' in the face of governmental retrenchment and withdrawal of funding to university humanities courses in the UK, he writes of poetry's continued resistance to the market and instrumentalism: 'Poetry cannot be had'.[61] And the question of whether poetry is on the wane seems to be a perennial sport. It is likely one that the nineteenth century invented. As Simon Armitage says, 'the demise of poetry remains poetry's favourite subject. Like someone in a state of manic hypochondria, it continues to search for signs of its own ill-health'.[62]

Notes

1 L.E.L., Advertisement at the front of *The Improvisatrice and Other Poems* (London: Hurst, Robinson & Co., 1825), n.p.
2 J. R. Watson, *English Poetry of the Romantic Period 1789–1830* (Harlow: Longman, 1985), p. 2.
3 William Wordsworth, 'Preface' to *Lyrical Ballads, with Pastoral and Other Poems* (1802), in Stephen Gill, *William Wordsworth: The Major Works* (Oxford: Oxford World Classics, 2008), p. 611.
4 M. H. Abrams, *The Mirror and the Lamp: Romantic Theory and the Critical Tradition* (Oxford: Oxford University Press, 1953), p. 53.
5 S. T. Coleridge, *Biographia Literaria* 2 vols. (Oxford: Clarendon Press, 1907), pp. 12 & 10.
6 Stuart Curran, 'Romantic Poetry: Why and Wherefore?' in Stuart Curran ed., *The Cambridge Companion to British Romanticism* 2nd ed. (Cambridge: Cambridge University Press, 2010), pp. 209–28.
7 H. F. B. Brett-Smith (ed.), *Peacock's 'Four Ages of Poetry'; Shelley's 'Defence of Poetry'; Browning's 'Essay on Shelley'* (Oxford: Basil Blackwell, 1947), pp. 14 & 19.
8 Alba H. Warren, *English Poetic Theory 1825–1865* (Princeton, NJ: Princeton University Press), p. 20.
9 Brett-Smith, *Peacock's*, p. 26.
10 Ibid., p. 27.
11 Ibid., 31. This sentiment is echoed in Shelley's 'To a Skylark', which was composed shortly after the 'Defence' in 1820. A Shelleyan poetics in itself, the skylark is compared, *inter alia*, to being:

Like a poet hidden
In the line of thought,
Singing hymns unbidden,
Till the world is wrought
To sympathy with hopes and fears it heeded not;

(ll.36–40)

This early affirmation of what the later nineteenth century will term aestheticism – arts for art's sake – can be traced through Arthur Hallam's significant review of Tennyson's *Poems, Chiefly Lyrical* (1830), which allies Tennyson with Keats and Shelley as 'Poets of Sensation'. See Arthur Henry Hallam, unsigned review, *Englishman's Magazine* 1 (August 1831), pp.616–28. Reprinted in John D. Jump (ed.), *Tennyson: The Critical Heritage* (London: Routledge, Kegan & Paul, 1969), pp. 34–49.

12 Ibid., p. 52.
13 Angela Leighton, *Shelley and the Sublime* (Cambridge: Cambridge University Press, 1984), pp. 40–1.
14 Brett-Smith, *Peacock's*, p. 53.
15 Ibid., p. 31.
16 Ibid., p. 55.
17 Ibid., p. 51.
18 Ibid., p. 59.
19 Richard Cronin, 'Shelley and the Nineteenth Century' in Michael O'Neill and Anthony Howe (eds), *The Oxford Handbook of Percy Bysshe Shelley* (Oxford: Oxford University Press, 2012), p. 618.
20 Brett-Smith, *Peacock's*, p. 66.
21 See Ronald A. Duerksen, *Shelleyan Ideas in Victorian Literature* (London: Mouton & Co, 1966).
22 Isobel Armstrong, *Victorian Poetry: Poetry, Poetics and Politics* (London: Routledge, 1993), p. 3.
23 See Joseph Bristow (ed.), *The Victorian Poet: Poetics and Persona* (London: Croom Helm, 1987).
24 The interested reader is strongly encouraged to pursue periodical reviews of Victorian poetic texts as an expansion of their understanding of Victorian poetic theories. Isobel Armstrong *Victorian Scrutinies* (London: Athlone Press, 1972) and Donald Thomas (ed.), *The Post-Romantics* (London: Routledge, 1990) contain key reviews of canonical male poets (Tennyson, Browning, Arnold, Clough, Swinburne). The Critical Heritage series (mostly published in the 1960s and 1970s) also provides contemporary reviews of major Victorian poets.
25 Isobel Armstrong, *Victorian Scrutinies: Reviews of Poetry 1830–1870* (London: Athlone Press, 1972), p. 3–4.
26 Abrams, *The Mirror and the Lamp*, p. 390.
27 'The Rationale of Reward', 1825; cited in Abrams, *The Mirror and the Lamp* p. 391.
28 E. H. Dallas, *Poetics* (London: Smith, Elder & Co., 1852), p. 3.
29 John Stuart Mill, *Autobiography* (London: Penguin, 1989), p. 56.
30 Ibid., p. 26.
31 Ibid., p. 121.
32 John Stuart Mill ('Antiquus'), 'What is Poetry?' *Monthly Repository,* 7.73 (1833), p. 64.
33 Ibid., p. 65.
34 John Stuart Mill, 'The Two Kinds of Poetry', *Monthly Repository*, 7.80 (1833) p. 717.
35 Ibid., p. 720.
36 See Ekbert Faas, *Retreat into the Mind:Victorian Poetry and the Rise of Psychiatry* (Princeton, NJ: Princeton University Press, 1988).
37 Gregory Tate, *The Poet's Mind: The Psychology of Victorian Poetry 1830–1870* (Oxford: Oxford University Press, 2012), p. 17.
38 Matthew Arnold, *Selected Prose* (London: Penguin, 1987), p. 41.
39 Eric Griffiths, *The Printed Voice of Victorian Poetry* (Oxford: Clarendon Press, 1989), p. 154.
40 Ibid., p. 194.
41 See http://www.poetryarchive.org/poem/charge-light-brigade.
42 Griffiths, *Printed Voice*, p. 61.
43 Matthew Bevis, 'At Work with Victorian Poetry' in Matthew Bevis (ed.), *The Oxford Handbook of Victorian Poetry*, (Oxford: Oxford University Press, 2013), p. 3.
44 Griffiths, *Printed Voice*, p. 201.
45 See Elizabeth Helsinger, *Poetry and the Pre-Raphaelite Arts: Dante Gabriel Rossetti and William Morris* (London: Yale University Press, 2008); Lorraine Janzen Kooistra, *Christina Rossetti and Illustration: A Publishing History* (Athens, OH: Ohio University Press, 2002) and Jerome McGann, *Black Riders: The Visible Language of Modernism* (Princeton, NJ: Princeton University Press, 1993).

46 Anne K. Mellor, *Romanticism and Gender*, London: Routledge, 1993), p. 29. See also: Anne K. Mellor, *Romanticism and Feminism* (Bloomington, IN: Indiana University Press, 1998) and Marlon B. Ross, *The Contours of Masculine Desire: Romanticism and the Rose of Women's Poetry* (Oxford: Oxford University Press, 1993).
47 See Duncan Wu (ed.), *Romantic Women Poets: An Anthology* (Oxford; Blackwell, 1997).
48 See Armstrong, *Victorian Poetry*; and Glennis Byron, *Dramatic Monologue* (London: Routledge, 2003).
49 Brett-Smith, *Peacock's*, p. 38.
50 Mellor, *Romanticism and Gender*, p. 11.
51 Margaret Reynolds, 'Introduction I', in Angela Leighton and Margaret Reynolds (eds), *Victorian Women Poets: An Anthology* (Oxford: Blackwell, 1995), p. xxxiv.
52 Glennis Stephenson, *Letitia Landon: The Woman Behind L.E.L* (Manchester: Manchester University Press, 1995), p. 2.
53 Serena Baiesi, *Letitia Elizabeth Landon and Metrical Romance* (Bern: Peter Lang, 2009), p. 39.
54 Byron, *Dramatic Monologue*, p. 56.
55 Rosie Miles, *Victorian Poetry in Context* (London: Bloomsbury, 2013), p. 10.
56 See Carol Christ, 'Introduction: Victorian Poetics', in Richard Cronin, Alison Chapman and Anthony H. Harrison (eds), *A Companion to Victorian Poetry*, (Oxford: Blackwell, 2002).
57 See Marion Thain, 'Poetry' in Gail Marshall (ed), *The Cambridge Companion to the Fin de Siècle* (Cambridge: Cambridge University Press, 2007).
58 Thain, p. 577.
59 Armstrong, 1993, p. 13.
60 Thain, 'Poetry', p. 582.
61 David Constantine, *Poetry* (Oxford: Oxford University Press, 2013), p. 70.
62 Dennis O'Driscoll (ed.), *The Bloodaxe Book of Poetry Quotations* (Newcastle: Bloodaxe Books), p. 236.

6   A Defence of Poetry (1821)

Percy Bysshe Shelley

According to one mode of regarding those two classes of mental action, which are called reason and imagination, the former may be considered as mind contemplating the relations borne by one thought to another, however produced, and the latter, as mind acting upon those thoughts so as to colour them with its own light, and composing from them, as from elements, other thoughts, each containing within itself the principle of its own integrity. The one is the το ποιειν, or the principle of synthesis, and has for its objects those forms which are common to universal nature and existence itself; the other is the το λογιςειν, or principle of analysis, and its action regards the relations of things simply as relations; considering thoughts, not in their integral unity, but as the algebraical representations which conduct to certain general results. Reason is the enumeration of qualities already known; imagination is the perception of the value of those qualities, both separately and as a whole. Reason respects the differences, and imagination the similitudes of things. Reason is to imagination as the instrument to the agent, as the body to the spirit, as the shadow to the substance.

Poetry, in a general sense, may be defined to be "the expression of the imagination": and poetry is connate with the origin of man. Man is an instrument over which a series of external and internal impressions are driven, like the alternations of an ever-changing wind over an Æolian lyre, which move it by their motion to ever-changing melody. But there is a principle within the human being, and perhaps within all sentient beings, which acts otherwise than in the lyre, and produces not melody alone, but harmony, by an internal adjustment of the sounds or motions thus excited to the impressions which excite them. It is as if the lyre could accommodate its chords to the motions of that which strikes them, in a determined proportion of sound; even as the musician can accommodate his voice to the sound of the lyre. A child at play by itself will express its delight by its voice and motions; and every inflexion of tone and every gesture will bear exact relation to a corresponding antitype in the pleasurable impressions which awakened it; it will be the reflected image of that impression; and as the lyre trembles and sounds after the wind has died away; so the child seeks, by prolonging in its voice and motions the duration of the effect, to prolong also a consciousness of the cause. In relation to the objects which delight a child these expressions are what poetry is to higher objects. The savage (for the savage is to ages what the child is to years) expresses the emotions produced in him by surrounding objects in a similar manner; and language and gesture, together with plastic or pictorial imitation, become the image of the combined effect of those objects, and of his apprehension of them. Man in society, with all his passions and his pleasures, next becomes the object of the passions and pleasures of man; an additional class of emotions produces an augmented treasure of expressions; and language, gesture, and the imitative arts, become at once the representation and the medium, the pencil and the picture, the chisel and the statute, the chord and the harmony. The social sympathies, or those laws from which, as from its elements, society results, begin to develop themselves from the moment that two human beings coexist; the future is contained within the present, as the plant within the seed; and equality, diversity, unity, contrast, mutual dependence, become the principles alone capable of affording the motives according to which the will of a social being is determined to action, inasmuch as he is social; and constitute pleasure in sensation, virtue in sentiment, beauty in art, truth in reasoning, and love in the intercourse of kind. Hence men, even in the infancy of society, observe a certain order in their words and actions, distinct from that of the objects and the impressions represented by them, all expression being subject to the laws of that from which it proceeds. But let us dismiss those more general considerations which might involve an inquiry into the principles of society itself, and restrict our view to the manner in which the imagination is expressed upon its forms.

In the youth of the world, men dance and sing and imitate natural objects observing in these actions, as in all others, a certain rhythm or order. And, although all men observe a similar, they observe not the same order, in the motions of the dance, in the melody of the song, in the combinations of language, in the series of their imitations of natural objects. For there is a certain order or rhythm belonging to each of these classes of mimetic representation, from which the hearer and the spectator receive an intenser and purer pleasure than from any other: the sense of an approximation to this order has been called taste by modern writers. Every man in the infancy of art observes an order which approximates more or less closely to that from which this highest delight results: but the diversity is not sufficiently marked, as that its gradations should be sensible, except in those instances where the predominance of this faculty of approximation to the beautiful (for so we may be permitted to name the relation between this highest pleasure and its cause) is very great. Those in whom it exists in excess are poets, in the most universal sense of the word; and the pleasure resulting from the manner in which they express the influence of society or nature upon their own minds, communicates itself to others, and gathers a sort of reduplication from that community. Their language is vitally metaphorical; that is, it marks the before unapprehended relations of things and perpetuates their apprehension, until the words which represent them, become, through time, signs for portions or classes of thoughts instead of pictures of integral thoughts; and then if no new poets should arise to create afresh the associations which have been thus disorganized, language will be dead to all the nobler purposes of human intercourse. These similitudes or relations are finely said by Lord Bacon to be "the same footsteps of nature impressed upon the various subjects of the world" ["De Augment. Scient.," cap. i, lib. iii—Shelley]—and he considers the faculty which perceives them as the store-house of axioms common to all knowledge. In the infancy of society every author is necessarily a poet, because language itself is poetry; and to be a poet is to apprehend the true and the beautiful, in a word, the good which exists in the relation, subsisting, first between existence and perception, and secondly between perception and expression. Every original language near to its source is in itself the chaos of a cyclic poem: the copiousness of lexicography and the distinctions of grammar are the works of a later age, and are merely the catalogue and the form of the creations of poetry.

But poets, or those who imagine and express this indestructible order, are not only the authors of language and of music, of the dance, and architecture, and statuary, and painting: they are the institutors of laws, and the founders of civil society, and the inventors of the arts of life, and the teachers, who draw into a certain propinquity with the beautiful and the true that partial apprehension of the agencies of the invisible world which is called religion. Hence all original religions are allegorical, or susceptible of allegory, and, like Janus, have a double face of false and true. Poets, according to the circumstances of the age and nation in which they appeared, were called, in the earlier epochs of the world, legislators, or prophets: a poet essentially comprises and unites both these characters. For he not only beholds intensely the present as it is, and discovers those laws according to which present things ought to be ordered, but he beholds the future in the present, and his thoughts are the germs of the flower and the fruit of latest time. Not that I assert poets to be prophets in the gross sense of the word, or that they can foretell the form as surely as they foreknow the spirit of events: such is the pretence of superstition, which would make poetry an attribute of prophecy, rather than prophecy an attribute of poetry. A poet participates in the eternal, the infinite, and the one; as far as relates to his conceptions, time and place and number are not. The grammatical forms which express the moods of time, and the difference of persons, and the distinction of place, are convertible with respect to the highest poetry without injuring it as poetry; and the choruses of Aeschylus, and the book of Job, and Dante's "Paradise" would afford, more than any other writings, examples of this fact, if the limits of this essay did not forbid citation. The creations of sculpture, painting, and music are illustrations still more decisive.

Language, colour, form, and religious and civil habits of action, are all the instruments and materials of poetry; they may be called poetry by that figure of speech which considers the effect as a synonym of the cause. But poetry in a more restricted sense expresses those arrangements of language, and especially metrical language, which are created by that imperial faculty, whose throne is curtained within the invisible nature of man. And this springs from the nature itself of language, which is a more direct representation of the actions and passions of our internal being, and is susceptible of more various and delicate combinations, than colour, form, or motion, and is more plastic and obedient to the control of that faculty of which it is the creation. For language is arbitrarily produced by the imagination, and has relation to thoughts alone; but all other materials, instruments, and conditions of art have relations among each other, which limit and interpose between conception and expression. The former is as a mirror which reflects, the latter as a cloud which enfeebles, the light of which both are mediums of communication. Hence the fame of sculptors, painters, and musicians, although the intrinsic powers of the great masters of these arts may yield in no degree to that of those who have employed language as the hieroglyphic of their thoughts, has never equalled that of poets in the restricted sense of the term; as two performers of equal skill will produce unequal effects from a guitar and a harp. The fame of legislators and founders of religions, so long as their institutions last, alone seems to exceed that of poets in the restricted sense; but it can scarcely be a question, whether, if we deduct the celebrity which their flattery of the gross opinions of the vulgar usually conciliates, together with that which belonged to them in their higher character of poets, any excess will remain.

We have thus circumscribed the word poetry within the limits of that art which is the most familiar and the most perfect expression of the faculty itself. It is necessary, however, to make the circle still narrower, and to determine the distinction between measured and unmeasured language; for the popular division into prose and verse is inadmissible in accurate philosophy.

Sounds as well as thoughts have relation both between each other and towards that which they represent, and a perception of the order of those relations has always been found connected with a perception of the order of the relations of thoughts. Hence the language of poets has ever affected a certain uniform and harmonious recurrence of sound, without which it were not poetry, and which is scarcely less indispensable to the communication of its influence, than the words themselves, without reference to that peculiar order. Hence the vanity of translation; it were as wise to cast a violet into a crucible that you might discover the formal principle of its colour and odor, as seek to transfuse from one language into another the creations of a poet. The plant must spring again from its seed, or it will bear no flower—and this is the burden of the curse of Babel.

An observation of the regular mode of the recurrence of harmony in the language of poetical minds, together with its relation to music, produced metre, or a certain system of traditional forms of harmony and language. Yet it is by no means essential that a poet should accommodate his language to this traditional form, so that the harmony, which is its spirit, be observed. The practice is indeed convenient and popular, and to be preferred, especially in such composition as includes much action: but every great poet must inevitably innovate upon the example of his predecessors in the exact structure of his peculiar versification. The distinction between poets and prose writers is a vulgar error. The distinction between philosophers and poets has been anticipated. Plato was essentially a poet—the truth and splendor of his imagery, and the melody of his language, are the most intense that it is possible to conceive. He rejected the measure of the epic, dramatic, and lyrical forms, because he sought to kindle a harmony in thoughts divested of shape and action, and he forebore to invent any regular plan of rhythm which would include, under determinate forms, the varied pauses of his style. Cicero sought to imitate the cadence of his periods, but with little success. Lord Bacon was a poet. [See the "Filum Labyrinthi," and the "Essay on Death" particularly—Shelley] His language has a sweet and majestic rhythm, which satisfies the sense, no less than the almost superhuman wisdom of his philosophy satisfies the intellect; it is a strain which distends, and then bursts the circumference of the reader's mind, and pours itself forth together with it into the universal element with which it has perpetual sympathy. All the authors of revolutions in opinion are not only necessarily poets as they are inventors, nor even as their words unveil the permanent analogy of things by images which participate in the life of truth; but as their periods are harmonious and rhythmical, and contain in themselves the elements of verse; being the echo of the eternal music. Nor are those supreme poets, who have employed traditional forms of rhythm on account of the form and action of their subjects, less capable of perceiving and teaching the truth of things, than those who have omitted that form. Shakespeare, Dante, and Milton (to confine ourselves to modern writers) are philosophers of the very loftiest power.

A poem is the very image of life expressed in its eternal truth. There is this difference between a story and a poem, that a story is a catalogue of detached facts, which have no other connection than time, place, circumstance, cause and effect; the other is the creation of actions according to the unchangeable forms of human nature, as existing in the mind of the Creator, which is itself the image of all other minds. The one is partial, and applies only to a definite period of time, and a certain combination of events which can never again recur; the other is universal, and contains within itself the germ of a relation to whatever motives or actions have place in the possible varieties of human nature. Time, which destroys the beauty and the use of the story of particular facts, stripped of the poetry which should invest them, augments that of poetry, and forever develops new and wonderful applications of the eternal truth which it contains. Hence epitomes have been called the moths of just history; they eat out the poetry of it. A story of particular facts is as a mirror which obscures and distorts that which should be beautiful; poetry is a mirror which makes beautiful that which is distorted.

[…]

The production and assurance of pleasure in this highest sense is true utility. Those who produce and preserve this pleasure are poets or poetical philosophers.

The exertions of Locke, Hume, Gibbon, Voltaire, Rousseau [although Rousseau has been thus classed, he was essentially a poet. The others, even Voltaire, were mere reasoners.—

Shelley's note], and their disciples, in favor of oppressed and deluded humanity, are entitled to the gratitude of mankind. Yet it is easy to calculate the degree of moral and intellectual improvement which the world would have exhibited, had they never lived. A little more nonsense would have been talked for a century or two; and perhaps a few more men, women, and children burnt as heretics. We might not at this moment have been congratulating each other on the abolition of the Inquisition in Spain. But it exceeds all imagination to conceive what would have been the moral condition of the world if neither Dante, Petrarch, Boccaccio, Chaucer, Shakespeare, Calderon, Lord Bacon, nor Milton, had ever existed; if Raphael and Michael Angelo had never been born; if the Hebrew poetry had never been translated; if a revival of the study of Greek literature had never taken place; if no monuments of ancient sculpture had been handed down to us; and if the poetry of the religion of the ancient world had been extinguished together with its belief. The human mind could never, except by the intervention of these excitements, have been awakened to the invention of the grosser sciences, and that application of analytical reasoning to the aberrations of society, which it is now attempted to exalt over the direct expression of the inventive and creative faculty itself.

We have more moral, political, and historical wisdom than we know how to reduce into practice; we have more scientific and economical knowledge than can be accommodated to the just distribution of the produce which it multiplies. The poetry in these systems of thought is concealed by the accumulation of facts and calculating processes. There is no want of knowledge respecting what is wisest and best in morals, government, and political economy, or at least, what is wiser and better than what men now practise and endure. But we let *I dare not* wait upon *I would,* like the poor cat in the adage. We want the creative faculty to imagine that which we know; we want the generous impulse to act that which we imagine; we want the poetry of life; our calculations have outrun conception; we have eaten more than we can digest. The cultivation of those sciences which have enlarged the limits of the empire of man over the external world, has, for want of the poetical faculty, proportionally circumscribed those of the internal world; and man, having enslaved the elements, remains himself a slave. To what but a cultivation of the mechanical arts in a degree disproportioned to the presence of the creative faculty, which is the basis of all knowledge, is to be attributed the abuse of all invention for abridging and combining labor, to the exasperation of the inequality of mankind? From what other cause has it arisen that the discoveries which should have lightened, have added a weight to the curse imposed on Adam? Poetry, and the principle of Self, of which money is the visible incarnation, are the God and Mammon of the world.

The functions of the poetical faculty are twofold: by one it creates new materials of knowledge, and power, and pleasure; by the other it engenders in the mind a desire to reproduce and arrange them according to a certain rhythm and order which may be called the beautiful and the good. The cultivation of poetry is never more to be desired than at periods when, from an excess of the selfish and calculating principle, the accumulation of the materials of external life exceed the quantity of the power of assimilating them to the internal laws of human nature. The body has then become too unwidely for that which animates it.

Poetry is indeed something divine. It is at once the centre and circumference of knowledge; it is that which comprehends all science, and that to which all science must be referred. It is at the same time the root and blossom of all other systems of thought; it is that from which all spring, and that which adorns all; and that which, if blighted, denies the fruit and the seed, and witholds from the barren world the nourishment and the succession of the scions of the tree of life. It is the perfect and consummate surface and bloom of all things; it is as the odor and the colour of the rose to the texture of the elements which compose it, as the form and splendor of unfaded beauty to the secrets of anatomy and corruption. What were virtue, love, patriotism, friendship—what were the scenery of this beautiful universe which we inhabit; what were our consolations on this side of the grave—and what were our aspirations beyond it, if poetry did not ascend to bring light and fire from those eternal regions where the owl-winged faculty of calculation dare not ever soar? Poetry is not like reasoning, a power to be exerted according to the determination of the will. A man cannot say, "I will compose poetry." The greatest poet even cannot say it; for the mind in creation is as a fading coal, which some invisible influence, like an inconstant wind, awakens to transitory brightness; this power arises from within, like the colour of a flower which fades and changes as it is developed, and the conscious portions of our natures are unprophetic either of its approach or its departure. Could this influence be durable in its original purity and force, it is impossible to predict the greatness of the results; but when composition begins, inspiration is already on the decline, and the most glorious poetry that has ever been communicated to the world is probably a feeble shadow of the original conceptions of the poet. I appeal to the greatest poets of the present day, whether it is not an error to assert that the finest passages of poetry are produced by labor and study. The toil and the delay recommended by critics can be justly interpreted to mean no more than a careful observation of the inspired moments, and an artificial connection of the spaces between their suggestions by the intertexture of conventional expressions; a necessity only imposed by the limitedness of the poetical faculty itself; for Milton conceived the "Paradise Lost" as a whole before he executed it in portions. We have his own authority also for the Muse having "dictated" to him the "unpremeditated song." And let this be an answer to those who would allege the fifty-six various readings of the first line of the "Orlando Furioso." Compositions so produced are to poetry what mosaic is to painting. This instinct and intuition of the poetical faculty are still more observable in the plastic and pictorial arts; a great statue or picture grows under the power of the artist as a child in a mother's womb; and the very mind which directs the hands in formation is incapable of accounting to itself for the origin, the gradations, or the media of the process.

Poetry is the record of the best and happiest moments of the happiest and best minds. We are aware of evanescent visitations of thought and feeling sometimes associated with place or person, sometimes regarding our own mind alone, and always arising unforeseen and departing unbidden, but elevating and delightful beyond all expression: so that even in the desire and the regret they leave, there cannot but be pleasure, participating as it does in the nature of its object. It is as it were the interpretation of a diviner nature through our own; but its footsteps are like those of a wind over the sea, which the coming calm erases, and whose traces remain only as on the wrinkled sand which paves it. These and corresponding conditions of being are experienced principally by those of the most delicate sensibility and the most enlarged imagination; and the state of mind produced by them is at war with every base desire. The enthusiasm of virtue, love, patriotism, and friendship is essentially linked with such emotions; and whilst they last, self appears as what it is, an atom to a universe. Poets are not only subject to these experiences as spirits of the most refined organization, but they can colour all that they combine with the evanescent hues of this ethereal world; a word, a trait in the representation of a scene or a passion will touch the enchanted chord, and reanimate, in those who have ever experienced these emotions, the sleeping, the cold, the buried image of the past. Poetry thus makes immortal all that is best and most beautiful in the world; it arrests the vanishing apparitions which haunt the interlunations of life, and veiling them, or in language or in form, sends them forth among mankind, bearing sweet news of kindred joy to those with whom their sisters abide—abide, because there is no portal of expression from the caverns of the spirit which they inhabit into the universe of things. Poetry redeems from decay the visitations of the divinity in man.

Poetry turns all things to loveliness; it exalts the beauty of that which is most beautiful, and it adds beauty to that which is most deformed; it marries exultation and horror, grief and pleasure, eternity and change; it subdues to union under its light yoke all irreconcilable things. It transmutes all that it touches, and every form moving within the radiance of its presence is changed by wondrous sympathy to an incarnation of the spirit which it breathes: its secret alchemy turns to potable gold the poisonous waters which flow from death through life; it strips the veil of familiarity from the world, and lays bare the naked and sleeping beauty, which is the spirit of its forms.

All things exist as they are perceived: at least in relation to the percipient. "The mind is its own place, and of itself can make a heaven of hell, a hell of heaven." But poetry defeats the curse which binds us to be subjected to the accident of surrounding impressions. And whether it spreads its own figured curtain, or withdraws life's dark veil from before the scene of things, it equally creates for us a being within our being. It makes us the inhabitants of a world to which the familiar world is a chaos. It reproduces the common universe of which we are portions and percipients, and it purges from our inward sight the film of familiarity which obscures from us the wonder of our being. It compels us to feel that which we perceive, and to imagine that which we know. It creates anew the universe, after it has been annihilated in our minds by the recurrence of impressions blunted by reiteration. It justifies the bold and true words of Tasso—"Non merita nome di creatore, se non Iddio ed il Poeta" [none but God and the poet deserve the name of Creator—ed.].

A poet, as he is the author to others of the highest wisdom, pleasure, virtue, and glory, so he ought personally to be the happiest, the best, the wisest, and the most illustrious of men. As to his glory, let time be challenged to declare whether the fame of any other institutor of human life be comparable to that of a poet. That he is the wisest, the happiest, and the best, inasmuch as he is a poet, is equally incontrovertible: the greatest poets have been men of the most spotless virtue, of the most consummate prudence, and, if we would look into the interior of their lives, the most fortunate of men: and the exceptions, as they regard those who possessed the poetic faculty in a high yet inferior degree, will be found on consideration to confine rather than destroy the rule. Let us for a moment stoop to the arbitration of popular breath, and usurping and uniting in our own persons the incompatible characters of accuser, witness, judge, and executioner, let us decide without trial, testimony, or form, that certain motives of those who are "there sitting where we dare not soar," are reprehensible. Let us assume that Homer was a drunkard, that Vergil was a flatterer, that Horace was a coward, that Tasso was a madman, that Lord Bacon was a peculator, that Raphael was a libertine, that Spenser was a poet laureate. It is inconsistent with this division of our subject to cite living poets, but posterity has done ample justice to the great names now referred to. Their errors have been weighed and found to have been dust in the balance; if their sins "were as scarlet, they are now white as snow"; they have been washed in the blood of the mediator and redeemer, Time. Observe in what a ludicrous chaos the imputations of real or fictitious crime have been confused in the contemporary calumnies against poetry and poets; consider how little is as it appears—or appears as it is; look to your own motives, and judge not, lest ye be judged.

Poetry, as has been said, differs in this respect from logic, that it is not subject to the control of the active powers of the mind, and that its birth and recurrence have no necessary connection with the consciousness or will. It is presumptuous to determine that these are the necessary conditions of all mental causation, when mental effects are experienced unsusceptible of being referred to them. The frequent recurrence of the poetical power, it is obvious to suppose, may produce in the mind a habit of order and harmony correlative with its own nature and with its effects upon other minds. But in the intervals of inspiration, and they may be frequent without being durable, a poet becomes a man, and is abandoned to the sudden reflux of the influences under which others habitually live. But as he is more delicately organized than other men, and sensible to pain and pleasure, both his own and that of others, in a degree unknown to them, he will avoid the one and pursue the other with an ardor proportioned to this difference. And he renders himself obnoxious to calumny, when he neglects to observe the circumstances under which these objects of universal pursuit and flight have disguised themselves in one another's garments.

But there is nothing necessarily evil in this error, and thus cruelty, envy, revenge, avarice, and the passions purely evil have never formed any portion of the popular imputations on the lives of poets.

I have thought it most favorable to the cause of truth to set down these remarks according to the order in which they were suggested to my mind, by a consideration of the subject itself, instead of observing the formality of a polemical reply; but if the view which they contain be just, they will be found to involve a refutation of the arguers against poetry, so far at least as regards the first division of the subject. I can readily conjecture what should have moved the gall of some learned and intelligent writers who quarrel with certain versifiers; I confess myself, like them, unwilling to be stunned by the Theseids of the hoarse Codri of the day. Bavius and Mævius undoubtedly are, as they ever were, insufferable persons. But it belongs to a philosophical critic to distinguish rather than confound.

The first part of these remarks has related to poetry in its elements and principles; and it has been shown, as well as the narrow limits assigned them would permit, that what is called poetry, in a restricted sense, has a common source with all other forms of order and of beauty, according to which the materials of human life are susceptible of being arranged, and which is poetry in an universal sense.

The second part will have for its object an application of these principles to the present state of the cultivation of poetry, and a defence of the attempt to idealize the modern forms of manners and opinions, and compel them into a subordination to the imaginative and creative faculty. For the literature of England, an energetic development of which has ever preceded or accompanied a great and free development of the national will, has arisen as it were from a new birth. In spite of the low-thoughted envy which would undervalue contemporary merit, our own will be a memorable age in intellectual achievements, and we live among such philosophers and poets as surpass beyond comparison any who have appeared since the last national struggle for civil and religious liberty. The most unfailing herald, companion, and follower of the awakening of a great people to work a beneficial change in opinion or institution, is poetry. At such periods there is an accumulation of the power of communicating and receiving intense and impassioned conceptions respecting man and nature. The person in whom this power resides, may often, as far as regards many portions of their nature, have little apparent correspondence with that spirit of good of which they are the ministers. But even whilst they deny and abjure, they are yet compelled to serve, that power which is seated on the throne of their own soul. It is impossible to read the compositions of the most celebrated writers of the present day without being startled with the electric life which burns within their words. They measure the circumference and sound the depths of human nature with a comprehensive and all-penetrating spirit, and they are themselves perhaps the most sincerely astonished at its manifestations; for it is less their spirit than the spirit of the age. Poets are the hierophants of an unapprehended inspiration; the mirrors of the gigantic shadows which futurity casts upon the present; the words which express what they understand not; the trumpets which sing to battle, and feel not what they inspire; the influence which is moved not, but moves. Poets are the unacknowledged legislators of the world.

7   What is Poetry? (1833)

John Stuart Mill

It has often been asked, What is Poetry? And many and various are the answers which have been returned. The vulgarest of all—one with which no person possessed of the faculties to which Poetry addresses itself can ever have been satisfied—is that which confounds poetry with metrical composition: yet to this wretched mockery of a definition, many have been led back, by the failure of all their attempts to find any other that would distinguish what they have been accustomed to call poetry, from much which they have known only under other names.

That, however, the word 'poetry' *does* import something quite peculiar in its nature, something which may exist in what is called prose as well as in verse, something which does not even require the instrument of words, but can speak through those other audible symbols called musical sounds, and even through the visible ones, which are the language of sculpture, painting, and architecture; all this, as we believe, is and must be felt, though perhaps indistinctly, by all upon whom poetry in any of its shapes produces any impression beyond that of tickling the ear. To the mind, poetry is either nothing, or it is the better part of all art whatever, and of real life too; and the distinction between poetry and what is not poetry, whether explained or not, is felt to be fundamental.

Where every one feels a difference, a difference there must be. All other appearances may be fallacious, but the appearance of a difference is itself a real difference. Appearances too, like other things, must have a cause, and that which can *cause* anything, even an illusion, must be a reality. And hence, while a half-philosophy disdains the classifications and distinctions indicated by popular language, philosophy carried to its highest point may frame new ones, but never sets aside the old, content with correcting and regularizing them. It cuts fresh channels for thought, but it does not fill up such as it finds ready made, but traces, on the contrary, more deeply, broadly, and distinctly, those into which the current has spontaneously flowed.

Let us then attempt, in the way of modest inquiry, not to coerce and confine nature within the bounds of an arbitrary definition, but rather to find the boundaries which she herself has set, and erect a barrier round them; not calling mankind to account for having misapplied the word 'poetry,' but attempting to clear up to them the conception which they already attach to it, and to bring before their minds as a distinct *principle* that which, as a vague *feeling*, has really guided them in their actual employment of the term.

The object of poetry is confessedly to act upon the emotions; and therein is poetry sufficiently distinguished from what Wordsworth affirms to be its logical opposite, namely, not prose, but matter of fact or science. The one addresses itself to the belief, the other to the feelings. The one does its work by convincing or persuading, the other by moving. The one acts by presenting a proposition to the understanding, the other by offering interesting objects of contemplation to the sensibilities.

This, however, leaves us very far from a definition of poetry. We have distinguished it from one thing, but we are bound to distinguish it from everything. To present thoughts or images to the mind for the purpose of acting upon the emotions, does not belong to poetry alone. It is equally the province (for example) of the novelist: and yet the faculty of the poet and the faculty of the novelist are as distinct as any other two faculties; as the faculty of the novelist and of the orator, or of the poet and the metaphysician. The two characters may be united, as characters the most disparate may; but they have no natural connexion.

Many of the finest poems are in the form of novels, and in almost all good novels there is true poetry. But there is a radical distinction between the interest felt in a novel as such, and the interest excited by poetry; for the one is derived from *incident,* the other from the representation of *feeling.* In one, the source of the emotion excited is the exhibition of a state or states of human sensibility; in the other, of a series of states of mere outward circumstances. Now, all minds are capable of being affected more or less by representations of the latter kind, and all, or almost all, by those of the former; yet the two sources of interest correspond to two distinct and (as respects their greatest development) mutually exclusive characters of mind. So much is the nature of poetry dissimilar to the nature of fictitious narrative, that to have a really strong passion for either of the two, seems to presuppose or to superinduce a comparative indifference to the other.

At what age is the passion for a story, for almost any kind of story, merely as a story, the most intense?—in childhood. But that also is the age at which poetry, even of the simplest description, is least relished and least understood; because the feelings with which it is especially conversant are yet undeveloped, and not having been even in the slightest degree experienced, cannot be sympathised with. In what stage of the progress of society, again, is story-telling most valued, and the story-teller in greatest request and honour?—in a rude state; like that of the Tartars and Arabs at this day, and of almost all nations in the earliest ages. But in this state of society there is little poetry except ballads, which are mostly narratives that is, essentially *stories,* and derive their principal interest from the *incidents.* Considered as poetry, they are of the lowest and most elementary kind: the feelings depicted, or rather indicated, are the simplest our nature has; such joys and griefs as the immediate pressure of some outward event excites in rude minds, which live wholly immersed in outward things, and have never, either from choice or a force they could not resist, turned themselves to the contemplation of the world within. Passing now from childhood, and from the childhood of society, to the grown-up men and women of this most grown-up and unchildlike age—the minds and hearts of greatest depth and elevation are commonly those which take greatest delight in poetry; the shallowest and emptiest, on the contrary, are, by universal remark, the most addicted to novel-reading. This accords, too, with all analogous experience of human nature. The sort of persons whom not merely in books but in their lives, we find perpetually engaged in hunting for excitement from without, are invariably those who do not possess, either in the vigour of their intellectual powers or in the depth of their sensibilities, that which would enable them to find ample excitement nearer at home. The same persons whose time is divided between sightseeing, gossip, and fashionable dissipation, take a natural delight in fictitious narrative; the excitement it affords is of the kind which comes from without. Such persons are rarely lovers of poetry, though they may fancy themselves so, because they relish novels in verse. But poetry, which is the delineation of the deeper and more secret workings of the human heart, is interesting only to those to whom it recalls what they have felt, or whose imagination it stirs up to conceive what they could feel, or what they might have been able to feel, had their outward circumstances been different.

Poetry, when it is really such, is truth; and fiction also, if it is good for anything, is truth: but they are different truths. The truth of poetry is to paint the human soul truly: the truth of fiction is to give a true picture of *life*. The two kinds of knowledge are different, and come by different ways, come mostly to different persons. Great poets are often proverbially ignorant of life. What they know has come by observation of themselves; they have found *there* one highly delicate, and sensitive, and refined specimen of human nature, on which the laws of human emotion are written in large characters, such as can be read off without much study: and other knowledge of mankind, such as comes to men of the world by outward experience, is not indispensable to them as poets: but to the novelist such knowledge is all in all; he has to describe outward things, not the inward man; actions and events, not feelings; and it will not do for him to be numbered among those who, as Madame Roland said of Brissot, know man but not *men*.

All this is no bar to the possibility of combining both elements, poetry and narrative or incident, in the same work, and calling it either a novel or a poem; but so may red and white combine on the same human features, or on the same canvass; and so may oil and vinegar, though opposite natures, blend together in the same composite taste. There is one order of composition which requires the union of poetry and incident, each in its highest kind—the dramatic. Even there the two elements are perfectly distinguishable, and may exist of unequal quality, and in the most various proportion. The incidents of a dramatic poem may be scanty and ineffective, though the delineation of passion and character may be of the highest order; as in Goethe's glorious 'Torquato Tasso;' or again, the story as a mere story may be well got up for effect, as is the case with some of the most trashy productions of the Minerva press: it may even be, what those are not, a coherent and probable series of events, though there be scarcely a feeling exhibited which is not exhibited falsely, or in a manner absolutely common-place. The combination of the two excellencies is what renders Shakespeare so generally acceptable, each sort of readers finding in him what is suitable to their faculties. To the many he is great as a story-teller, to the few as a poet.

In limiting poetry to the delineation of states of feeling, and denying the name where nothing is delineated but outward objects, we may be thought to have done what we promised to avoid—to have not *found*, but *made* a definition, in opposition to the usage of the English language, since it is established by common consent that there is a poetry called *descriptive*. We deny the charge. Description is not poetry because there is descriptive poetry, no more than science is poetry because there is such a thing as a didactic poem; no more, we might almost say, than Greek or Latin is poetry because there are Greek and Latin poems. But an object which admits of being described, or a truth which may fill a place in a scientific treatise, may *also* furnish an occasion for the generation of poetry, which we thereupon choose to call descriptive or didactic. The poetry is not in the object itself, nor in the scientific truth itself, but in the state of mind in which the one and the other may be contemplated. The mere delineation of the dimensions and colours of external objects is not poetry, no more than a geometrical ground-plan of St. Peter's or Westminster Abbey is painting. Descriptive poetry consists, no doubt, in description, but in description of things as they appear, not as they *are;* and it paints them not in their bare and natural lineaments, but arranged in the colours and seen through the medium of the imagination set in action by the feelings. If a poet is to describe a lion, he will not set about describing him as a naturalist would, nor even as a traveller would, who was intent upon stating the truth, the whole truth, and nothing but the truth. He will describe him by *imagery,* that is, by suggesting the most striking likenesses and contrasts which might occur to a mind contemplating the lion, in the state of awe, wonder, or terror, which the spectacle naturally excites, or is, on the occasion, supposed to excite. Now this is describing the lion professedly, but the state of excitement of the spectator really. The lion may be described falsely or in exaggerated colours, and the poetry be all the better; but if the human emotion be not painted with the most scrupulous truth, the poetry is bad poetry, i.e. is not poetry at all, but a failure.

Thus far our progress towards a clear view of the essentials of poetry has brought us very close to the last two attempts at a definition of poetry which we happen to have seen in print, both of them by poets and men of genius. The one is by Ebenezer Elliott, the author of 'Corn-Law Rhymes,' and other poems of still greater merit. 'Poetry,' says he, 'is impassioned truth.' The other is by a writer in *Blackwood's Magazine*, and comes, we think, still nearer the mark. We forget his exact words, but in substance he defined poetry 'man's thoughts tinged by his feelings.' There is in either definition a near approximation to what we are in search of. Every truth which man can announce, every thought, even every outward impression, which can enter into his consciousness, may become poetry when shewn through any impassioned medium, when invested with the colouring of joy, or grief, or pity, or affection, or admiration, or reverence, or awe, or even hatred or terror: and, unless so coloured, nothing, be it as interesting as it may, is poetry. But both these definitions fail to discriminate between poetry and eloquence. Eloquence, as well as poetry, is impassioned truth; eloquence, as well as poetry, is thoughts coloured by the feelings. Yet common apprehension and philosophic criticism alike recognize a distinction between the two: there is much that every one would call eloquence, which no one would think of classing as poetry. A question will sometimes arise, whether some particular author is a poet; and those who maintain the negative commonly allow, that though not a poet, he is a highly *eloquent* writer.

The distinction between poetry and eloquence appears to us to be equally fundamental with the distinction between poetry and narrative, or between poetry and description. It is still farther from having been satisfactorily cleared up than either of the others, unless, which is highly probable, the German artists and critics have thrown some light upon it which has not yet reached us. Without a perfect knowledge of what they have written, it is something like presumption to write upon such subjects at all, and we shall be the Foremost to urge that, whatever we may be about to submit, may be received, subject to correction from *them*.

Poetry and eloquence are both alike the expression or uttering forth of feeling. But if we may be excused the seeming affectation of the antithesis, we should say that eloquence is *heard*, poetry is *over*heard. Eloquence supposes an audience; the peculiarity of poetry appears to us to lie in the poet's utter unconsciousness of a listener. Poetry is feeling confessing itself to itself, in moments of solitude, and bodying itself forth in symbols which are the nearest possible representations of the feeling in the exact shape in which it exists in the poet's mind. Eloquence is feeling pouring itself forth to other minds, courting their sympathy, or endeavouring to influence their belief, or move them to passion or to action.

All poetry is of the nature of soliloquy. It may be said that poetry, which is printed on hot-pressed paper, and sold at a book-seller's shop, is a soliloquy in full dress, and upon the stage. But there is nothing absurd in the idea of such a mode of soliloquizing. What we have said to ourselves, we may tell to others afterwards; what we have said or done in solitude, we may voluntarily reproduce when we know that other eyes are upon us. But no trace of consciousness that any eyes are upon us must be visible in the work itself. The actor knows that there is an audience present; but if he act as though he knew it, he acts ill. A poet may write poetry with the intention of publishing it; he may write it even for the express purpose of being paid for it; that it should *be* poetry, being written under any such influences, is far less probable; not, however, impossible; but no otherwise possible than if he can succeed in excluding from his work every vestige of such lookings-forth into the outward and every-day world, and can express his feelings exactly as he has felt them in solitude, or as he feels that he should feel them, though they were to remain for ever unuttered. But when he turns round and addresses himself to another person; when the act of utterance is not itself the end, but a means to an end,—viz., by the feelings he himself expresses to work upon the feelings, or upon the belief, or the will of another,—when the expression of his emotions, or of his thoughts, tinged by his emotions, is tinged also by that purpose, by that desire of making an impression upon another mind, then it ceases to be poetry, and becomes eloquence.

Poetry, accordingly, is the natural fruit of solitude and meditation; eloquence, of intercourse with the world. The persons who have most feeling of their own, if intellectual culture have given them a language in which to express it, have the highest faculty of poetry; those who best understand the feelings of others, are the most eloquent. The persons, and the nations, who commonly excel in poetry, are those whose character and tastes render them least dependent for their happiness upon the applause, or sympathy, or concurrence of the world in general. Those to whom that applause, that sympathy, that concurrence are most necessary, generally excel most in eloquence. And hence, perhaps, the French, who are the *least* poetical of all great and refined nations, are among the *most* eloquent: the French, also, being the most sociable, the vainest, and the least self-dependent.

If the above be, as we believe, the true theory of the distinction commonly admitted between eloquence and poetry; or though it be not *that,* yet if, as we cannot doubt, the distinction above stated be a real *bona fide* distinction, it will be found to hold, not merely in the language of words, but in all other language, and to intersect the whole domain of art.

Take, for example, music: we shall find in that art, so peculiarly the expression of passion, two perfectly distinct styles; one of which may be called the poetry, the other the oratory of music. This difference being seized would put an end to much musical sectarianism. There has been much contention whether the character of Rossini's music—the music, we mean, which is characteristic of that composer—is compatible with the expression of passion. Without doubt, the passion it expresses is not the musing, meditative tenderness, or at pathos, or grief of Mozart, the great poet of his art. Yet it is passion, but *garrulous* passion—the passion which pours itself into other ears; and therein the better calculated for *dramatic* effect, having a natural adaptation for dialogue. Mozart also is great in musical oratory; but his most touching compositions are in the opposite style—that of soliloquy. Who can imagine 'Dove sono' *heard?* We imagine it *over*-heard. The same is the case with many of the finest national airs. Who can hear those words, which speak so touchingly the sorrows of a mountaineer in exile:—

'My heart's in the Highlands—my heart is not here;
My heart's in the Highlands, a-chasing the deer,
A chasing the wild-deer, and following the roe—
My heart's in the Highlands, wherever I go.'

Who can hear those affecting words, married to as affecting an air, and fancy that he *sees* the singer? That song has always seemed to us like the lament of a prisoner in a solitary cell, ourselves listening, unseen, in the next. As the direct opposite of this, take 'Scots wha hae wi' Wallace bled,' where the music is as oratorical as the poetry.

Purely pathetic music commonly partakes of soliloquy. The soul is absorbed in its distress, and though there may be bystanders it is not thinking of them. When the mind is looking within, and not without, its state does not often or rapidly vary; and hence the even, uninterrupted flow, approaching almost to monotony, which a good reader, or a good singer, will give to words or music of a pensive or melancholy cast. But grief, taking the form of a prayer, or of a complaint, becomes oratorical; no longer low, and even, and subdued, it assumes a more emphatic rhythm, a more rapidly returning accent; instead of a few slow, equal notes, following one after another at regular intervals, it crowds note upon note, and often assumes a hurry and bustle like joy. Those who are familiar with some of the best of Rossini's serious compositions, such as the air 'Tu che i miseri conforti,' in the opera of 'Tancredi,' or the duet 'Ebben pen mia memoria,' in 'La Gazza Ladra,' will at once understand and feel our meaning. Both are highly tragic and passionate; the passion of both is that of oratory, not poetry. The like may be said of that most moving prayer in Beethoven's 'Fidelio'—

> 'Komm, Hoffnung, lass das letzte Stern
> Der Müde nicht erbleichen;

in which Madame Devrient, last summer, exhibited such consummate powers of pathetic expression. How different from Winter's beautiful 'Paga pii,' the very soul of melancholy exhaling itself in solitude; fuller of meaning, and, therefore, more profoundly poetical than the words for which it was composed—for it seems to express not simple melancholy, but the melancholy of remorse.

If, from vocal music, we now pass to instrumental, we may have a specimen of musical oratory in any line military symphony or march: while the poetry of music seems to have attained its consummation in Beethoven's Overture to Egmont. We question whether so deep an expression of mixed grandeur and melancholy was ever in any other instance produced by mere sounds.

In the arts which speak to the eye, the same distinctions will be found to hold, not only between poetry and oratory, but between poetry, oratory, narrative, and simple imitation or description.

Pure *description* is exemplified in a *mere* portrait or a *mere* landscape—productions of art, it is true, but of the mechanical rather than of the fine arts, being works of simple imitation, not *creation*. We say, a *mere* portrait, or a *mere* landscape, because it is possible for a portrait or a landscape, without ceasing to be such, to be also a *picture*. A portrait by Lawrence, or one of Turner's views, is not a mere copy from nature: the one combines with the given features that particular expression (among all good and pleasing ones) which those features are most capable of wearing, and which, therefore, in combination with them, is capable of producing the greatest positive beauty. Turner, again, unites the objects of the given landscape with whatever sky, and whatever light and shade, enable those particular objects to impress the imagination most strongly. In both, there is *creative* art—not working after an actual model, but realizing an idea.

Whatever in painting or sculpture expresses human feeling, or *character*, which is only a certain state of feeling grown habitual, may be called, according to circumstances, the poetry or the eloquence of the painter's or the sculptor's art; the poetry, if the feeling declares itself by such signs as escape from us when we are unconscious of being seen; the oratory, if the signs are those we use for the purpose of voluntary communication.

The poetry of painting seems to be carried to its highest perfection in the Peasant Girl of Rembrandt, or in any Madonna or Magdalen of Guido; that of sculpture, in almost any of the Greek statues of the gods; not considering these in respect to the mere physical beauty, of which they are such perfect models, nor undertaking either to vindicate or to contest the opinion of philosophers, that even physical beauty is ultimately resolvable into expression; we may safely affirm, that in no other of man's works did so much of soul ever shine through mere inanimate matter.

The narrative style answers to what is called historical painting, which it is the fashion among connoisseurs to treat as the climax of the pictorial art. That it is the most difficult branch of the art, we do not doubt, because, in its perfection, it includes, in a manner, the perfection of all the other branches. As an epic poem, though, in so far as it is epic (i.e. narrative), it is not poetry at all, is yet esteemed the greatest effort of poetic genius, because there is no kind whatever of poetry which may not appropriately find a place in it. But an historical picture, as such, that is, as the representation of an incident, must necessarily, as it seems to us, be poor and ineffective. The narrative powers of painting are extremely limited. Scarcely any picture, scarcely any series even of pictures, which we know of, tells its own story without the aid of an interpreter; you must know the story beforehand; *then,* indeed, you may see great beauty and appropriateness in the painting. But it is the single figures which, to us, are the great charm even of a historical picture. It is in these that the power of the art is really seen: in the attempt to *narrate,* visible and permanent signs are far behind the fugitive audible ones which follow so fast one after another, while the faces and figures in a narrative picture, even though they be Titian's, stand still. Who would not prefer one Virgin and Child of Raphael, to all the pictures which Rubens, with his fat, frouzy Dutch Venuses, ever painted? Though Rubens, besides excelling almost every one in his mastery over all the mechanical parts of his art, often shows real genius in *grouping* his figures, the peculiar problem of historical painting. But, then, who, except a mere student of drawing and colouring, ever cared to look twice at any of the figures themselves? The power of painting lies in poetry, of which Rubens had not the slightest tincture—not in narrative, where he might have excelled.

The single figures, however, in an historical picture, are rather the *eloquence* of painting than the poetry: they mostly (unless they are quite out of place in the picture) express the feelings of one person as modified by the presence of others. Accordingly the minds whose bent leads them rather to eloquence than to poetry, rush to historical painting. The French painters, for instance, seldom attempt, because they could make nothing of, single heads, like those glorious ones of the Italian masters, with which they might glut themselves day after day in their own Louvre. They must all be *historical*; and they are, almost to a man, attitudinizers. If we wished to give to any young artist the most impressive warning our imaginations could devise, against that kind of vice in the pictorial, which corresponds to rant in the histrionic art, we would advise him to walk once up and once down the gallery of the Luxembourg; even now when David, the great corrupter of taste, has been translated from this world to the next, and from the Luxembourg, consequently, into the more elevated sphere of the Louvre. Every figure in French painting or statuary seems to be showing itself off before spectators: they are in the worst style of corrupted eloquence, but in no style of poetry at all. The best are stiff and unnatural; the worst resemble figures of cataleptic patients. The French artists fancy themselves imitators of the classics, yet they seem to have no understanding and no feeling of that *repose* which was the peculiar and pervading character of Grecian art, until it began to decline: a repose tenfold more indicative of strength than all their stretching and straining; for strength, as Thomas Carlyle says, does not manifest itself in spasms.

There are some productions of art which it seems at first difficult to arrange in any of the classes above illustrated. The direct aim of art as such, is the production of the *beautiful;* and as there are other things beautiful besides states of mind, there is much of art which may seem to have nothing to do with either poetry or eloquence as we have defined them. Take for instance a composition of Claude, or Salvator Rosa. There is here *creation* of new beauty: by the grouping of natural scenery, conformably indeed to the laws of outward nature, but not after any actual model; the result being a beauty more perfect and faultless than is perhaps to be found in any actual landscape. Yet there is a character of poetry even in these, without which they could not be so beautiful. The unity, and wholeness, and aesthetic congruity of the picture still lies in singleness of expression; but it is expression in a different sense from that in which we have hitherto employed the term. The objects in an imaginary landscape cannot he said, like the words of a poem or the notes of a melody, be the actual utterance of a feeling; but there must be some feeling with which they harmonize, and which they have a tendency to raise up in the spectator's mind. They must inspire a feeling of grandeur, a loveliness, a cheerfulness, a wildness, a melancholy, a terror. The painter must surround his principal objects with such imagery as would spontaneously arise in a highly imaginative mind, when contemplating those objects under the impression of the feelings which they are intended to inspire. This, if it be not poetry, is so nearly allied to it, as scarcely to require being distinguished.

In this sense we may speak of the poetry of architecture. All architecture, to be impressive, must be the expression or symbol of some interesting idea; some thought, which has power over the emotions. The reason why modern architecture is so paltry, is simply that it is not the expression of any idea; it is a mere parroting of the architectural tongue of the Greeks, or of our Teutonic ancestors, without any conception of a meaning.

To confine ourselves, for the present, to religious edifices: these partake of poetry, in proportion as they express, or harmonize with, the feelings of devotion. But those feelings are different according to the conception entertained of the beings, by whose supposed nature they are called forth. To the Greek, these beings were incarnations of the greatest conceivable physical beauty, combined with supernatural power: and the Greek temples express this, their predominant character being graceful strength; in other words, solidity, which is power, and lightness which is also power, accomplishing with small means what seemed to require great; to combine all in one word, *majesty*. To the Catholic, again, the Deity was something far less clear and definite; a being of still more resistless power than the heathen divinities; greatly to be loved; still more greatly to be feared; and wrapped up in vagueness, mystery, and incomprehensibility. A certain solemnity, a feeling of doubting and trembling hope, like that of one lost in a boundless forest who thinks he knows his way but is not sure, mixes itself in all the genuine expressions of Catholic devotion. This is eminently the expression of the pure Gothic cathedral; conspicuous equally in the mingled majesty and gloom of its vaulted roofs and stately aisles, and in the 'dim religious light' which steals through its painted windows.

There is no generic distinction between the imagery which is the *expression* of feeling and the imagery which is felt to *harmonize* with feeling. They are identical. The imagery in which feeling utters itself forth from within, is also that in which it delights when presented to it from without. All art, therefore, in proportion as it produces its effects by an appeal to the emotions partakes of poetry, unless it partakes of oratory, or of narrative. And the distinction which these three words indicate, runs through the whole field of the fine arts.

The above hints have no pretension to the character of a theory. They are merely thrown out for the consideration of thinkers, in the hope that if they do not contain the truth, they may do somewhat to suggest it. Nor would they, crude as they are, have been deemed worthy of publication, in any country but one in which the philosophy of art is so completely neglected, that whatever may serve to put any inquiring mind upon this kind of investigation, cannot well, however imperfect in itself, fail altogether to be of use.

8   The Printed Voice in the Nineteenth Century (1989)

Eric Griffiths

John Hollander marks the critical importance of illocutionary re-description when he writes that 'speaking and writing are both language … it is the region between them which poetry inhabits'.[1] He is thinking of poetry which is not purely oral, the poetry which Yeats believed to be distinctively English: '… English literature, alone of great literatures, because the newest of them all, has all but completely shaped itself in the printing-press'.[2] Yeats's testimony about the history of literatures is not entirely reliable, and his 'all but completely' (which manages to make a reservation sound like a redoubled assertion) conceals several major questions. English literature does not stand alone in having shaped itself in the printing-press. Despite its exaggerations, Yeats's insight remains considerable, and considering it, even in application only to poetry, involves a great deal.

The spoken voice, more richly than writing, conveys, in emphasis and intonation, by stress and juncture, and so on, much of the illocutionary force of any utterance. Not that the wealth of such features in vocal utterance is always only an advantage; creative opportunities may also arise from the comparative absence of vocal quality in print. The semantic role of prosodic features, as I have argued so far, renders them integral to the study, whether linguistic or philosophical, of utterances. For literary critics, I shall now argue, acknowledgement of the printed character of the poetic voice in most texts involves a recognition of the very conditions of poetic meaning. The reader must inform writing with a sense of the writer it calls up—an ideal body, a plausible voice. How this is done repays study, as Leavis thought it might when he reviewed Eliot's recording of *Four Quartets*: 'These records should call attention to the problem of reading *Four Quartets* out. The problem deserves a great deal of attention, and to tackle it would be very educational'.[3] Whatever else poetry may be, it is certainly a use of language that works with the sounds of words, and so the absence of clearly indicated sound from the silence of the written word creates a double nature in printed poetry, making it both itself and something other—a text of hints at voicing, whose centre in utterance lies outside itself, and also an achieved pattern on the page, salvaged from the evanescence of the voice in air. Browning names this double nature in a phrase from *The Ring and the Book*—'the printed voice'.

He describes the odd system of trial which his poem records, a trial in which written depositions were made to the judges but

> … there properly was no judgment-bar,
> No bringing of accuser and accused,
> And whoso judged both parties, face to face
> Before some court, as we conceive of courts.[4]

In literature shaped by the printing-press, writer and reader do not 'properly' face each other. But this sense of a lost community, felt as a form of death by some writers when their voice fails to be manifest in print, is the germ of a further community and a new life; it prompts the reader to interpret and resuscitate. Browning notes that the absence of voices from the trial he reports allows 'the trial Itself, to all intents,' to be 'then as now Here in the book and nowise out of it'; his poem truly perpetuates in its own phantasmal character the meaning of what then went on:

> 'T was the so-styled Fisc began.
> Pleaded (and since he only spoke in print
> The printed voice of him lives now as then)[5]

We may come to find the same thing true of the voices of poets.

They were often baffled themselves. Yeats wrote, remembering early days: 'I spoke them [the lines of Yeats's poems] slowly as I wrote and only discovered when I read them to somebody else that there was no common music, no prosody.'[6] Though Browning had confidence that the voice of the Fisc spoke in his lines, G. H. Lewes felt that Browning's own voice failed to ring in the poems: 'And respecting his versification, it appears as if he consulted his own ease more than the reader's; and if by any arbitrary distribution of accents he could make the verse satisfy his own ear, it must necessarily satisfy the ear of another.'[7] Poets were not always good at hearing each other. Coleridge thought the young Tennyson had no metrical sense: 'The misfortune is, that he has begun to write verses without very well understanding what metre is ... I can scarcely scan some of his verses'[8] (this after Tennyson had published the book of poems which contains such masterpieces of versification as 'The Lady of Shalott' and 'To J. S.').

Problems of translating the intended music of a voice into the scant notation of the written word posed themselves even in such rudiments of writing as the punctuation of a text. Masters of the language felt at times like schoolboys. Yeats wrote to Bridges:

> I chiefly remember you asked me about my stops and commas. Do what you will. I do not understand stops. I write my work so completely for the ear that I feel helpless when I have to measure pauses by stops and commas.[9]

Perhaps the 'Do what you will' sounds more lordly than helpless, but the problem remains, though attitudes to it may vary. Wordsworth's letter to Humphry Davy on the same subject strikes a different note:

> You would greatly oblige me by looking over the enclosed poems and correcting any thing you find amiss in the punctuation, a business at which I am ashamed to say I am no adept.[10]

The different characters of the two poets show in their distinct approaches to the task of getting your point across by getting your pointings right: Yeats faces the academically correct: Bridges, feels conscious of his lack of an education in the punctilio of written language (he had not been to university) and yet makes that lack a blazon of what he wishes to consider the direct and rooted nature of his own poetry, direct in its address to the ear, rooted in the community of his imagined Irish speech;[11] Wordsworth is humbly formal, exasperated, no doubt, by the mechanics of committing his voice to print—a tinge of that exasperation in the phrase 'a business' and in the slightly flowery 'adept' with its mild intimation of sarcasm about such expertise, but submitting none the less to correction. It is not surprising that much should hinge, for poets, and so for readers of poetry on these minutiae; they compose the fibre of communication.

Francis Berry in his pioneering book, *Poetry and the Physical Voice,* insists: 'Most, poetry is vocal sound ... and not the signs *for* vocal sound printed on a page...'.[12] Whatever most poetry is, most poems are in fact 'signs *for* vocal sound printed on a page'. Berry recognizes the intonational ambiguity of many written lines but thinks such uncertainty of voice only a hurdle and never a resource: 'Normally, the qualities of a voice, which are resistant to mensuration and notation, should declare themselves in a valid poem without attempting the inadequate aid of marks usually employed in the scoring of music, the whole context determining those qualities.'[13] Wordsworth's 'She dwelt ...', for example, does not work 'normally', but only in the sense that it is an unusually good poem. Berry expects the 'whole context' to compel vocal quality to appear and he fails to allow that sometimes contexts are not so readily to hand or mouth—because they are in doubt (the writer's and/or the reader's doubt). 'She dwelt ...' creates a sense of 'not being sure what to say', a reflective absence of an instantly declared tone. It may be, roughly speaking, that 'through the totality of the printed signs on the page the poet conveys his voice',[14] but he may also convey the absence of his voice which it can be quite as important for us to hear as that individual physical timbre which Berry celebrates.

His argument gets into a tangle. At times, it seems that he wants the reader to try to hear 'the actual physical voice of the poet',[15] at others, the poet's voice matters not 'as it actually was, as it actually sounded to others, that is, but as the poet himself heard it, or experienced it, or ... as he supposed it to sound to others when he was employing it to good effect'.[16] The many coils of Berry's qualifications show how hard it is to hear a voice, whether your own or someone else's, and that it is not only notation which makes it hard but also a web of hopes and fears between the self and others. We will never hear another's voice as it sounded to him if only because we cannot hear from inside the acoustic of another's body, but then the voice too intimately sounds of me self for us to be certain that we hear it always 'as it actually was' and me speaker always only as it sounds to him. Uncertainties of voice are amongst the excursions of the self, and a voice, poetic and otherwise, can no more be strictly identified with me physical voice than a person with his body. Berry's thesis comes adrift on two connected snags: his underestimate of the inherent problems of vocal transcription, and his failure to recognize these problems as problems of individuality and the voice's role as a sign of that individuality, the linguistic impress of an agent.

[...]

Wordsworth is the great discoverer in English lyric poetry of these conditions of 'human nature'. He could no more do without the term than earlier writers, but he felt the shock it got, and he contributed to giving it that shock. He wrote to John Wilson, after Wilson had complained of 'The Idiot Boy' that its story was 'almost unnatural' because 'We are unable to enter into [Betty Foy's] feelings; we cannot conceive ourselves actuated by the same feelings ...':

> People in our rank of life are perpetually falling into one sad mistake, namely, that of supposing that human nature and the persons they associate with are one and the same thing. Whom do we generally associate with? Gentlemen, persons of fortune, professional men, ladies, persons who can afford to buy or can easily procure, books of half a guinea price, hot-pressed, and printed upon superfine paper. These persons are, it is true, a part of human nature, but we err lamentably if we suppose them to be fair representatives of the vast mass of human existence.[17]

The prose shivers with an indignation it can hardly contain or render plain. Consider the shade of distinction between 'People in our rank of life' and 'the persons they associate with', 'persons of fortune', 'persons who can afford', and 'These persons'. What is the difference between people and persons? None, it seems, except the degree of kindliness Wordsworth can muster in contemplating them. The sentence beginning 'Gentlemen' gathers annoyance as it goes along, huffing and puffing rather ('half ... price', 'hot-pressed') as Wordsworth thinks of the complicity between social arrogance and the institution of literature. This kind of reader, it seems, filches literature from Wordsworth, degrading it from its task of reflective apprehension to the level of a luxurious commodity ('superfine paper') with a novelty value ('hot-pressed') and a use as a symbol of status ('can afford to buy') in a well-oiled machine of supply and demand ('easily procure'). He checks the momentum of his vexation—'These persons are, it is true, a part of human nature'—because it will not do to discard the polite world as not truly human. He was, after all, a gentleman himself and not the writer to forsake his own past, the culture in which his personality had grown. Indeed, when Wordsworth in this letter turns from the irritatingly familiar 'persons' whose manners he knows so well that he can insinuate them into his own prose with great economy and dexterity of language, he faces something quite blank—'the vast mass of human existence'. The difficulty of much of his prose writing, and especially the Prefaces to *Lyrical Ballads*, faces the task of a precarious adjustment between 'human nature' and 'the vast mass of human existence', as he takes the strain put on the concept of human nature by the recognition of the diversities of this incalculable 'vast mass'. Particularly, that strain sets him the question of how poets might be 'fair representatives' of the 'vast mass'.

William Empson succinctly imagined what happens to a writer when he tries to write as a mediator between distinct, and sometimes mutually uncomprehending, groups within a society:

> Large societies need to include a variety of groups with different moral codes or scales of value, and it is part of the business of a writer to act as a go-between; so their differences are liable to become a conflict within himself.[18]

He also brilliantly suggests that these distinctions, introjected into the practical consciousness of the poet, may produce a condition of 'Neurotic Guilt'; 'The Rime of the Ancient Mariner' is, Empson claims, 'the first major study of that condition, recognized as such'.[19] Such introjection sets in high relief the separation between the actual voice of the person who is a poet and the poetic voice in the sense I have previously outlined. For our voices greatly bear the marks of social particularity—gender, regional and class origin, diversities of cult, degree of education, and so forth. A go-between who speaks too completely in the accents of one group may thereby move less well between groups. Trying to speak, if only briefly, in the accents of neither party, the poet develops a style which relies on the reticences of the written word to postpone the identification of his own socially fractional position and give time (a breathing space on the page) for ampler sympathies to be felt.

Coleridge dramatizes the predicament of poetic mediation, the practical task of speaking for other people in their variety, of being, as a poet, a 'fair representative', at that moment in his poem when the Mariner shies from utterance:

> And I quak'd to think my own voice
> How frightful it would be!'[20]

This draws on lines from Cowper's poem about the eloquence of castaways, the 'Verses, supposed to be written by Alexander Selkirk, during his solitary abode in the Island of Juan Fernandez':

> I am out of humanity's reach,
> I must finish my journey alone,
> Never hear the sweet music of speech,
> I start at the sound of my own.[21]

Here too, the loss of a hold on humanity troubles the person's relation to his own voice. The printed page which retains the poetic voice ('retains' in the double sense of 'keeps back' and 'preserves') becomes the dramatic scene of this searched and searching utterance; we can, as it were, see the blank space around Selkirk's self-startled words. Cowper's poem was praised by Wordsworth: '... the Reader has an exquisite pleasure in seeing such natural language so naturally connected with metre.'[22] It may be just casualness that made Wordsworth write 'seeing' rather than 'hearing' at this point, but the word is felicitous, for the ear might be less gratified by a recitation of the piece, its slightly bland mellifluousness consorts uneasily with the subject of isolation from speech. The poem's tune seems more sociable than its tenor, whereas on the page the merely potential tune has a redolence of longing about it which beautifully imagines how Selkirk might like to speak, were there anyone to hear.

I'm not suggesting that Cowper's poem should be seen and not heard; it 'asks' to be read aloud. The nature of that request, though, plays a small, imaginative drama about speaking, a drama on the page and for the voice elicited from the page. Perhaps because poets like calling their works 'songs', critics tend to write as if the only important sound-quality of poems is that they should be 'grateful' to the voice, as we say that Mozart's lines are 'grateful' to a singer or 'lie' well on the voice. Coleridge was inclined to that view when he complained about some of Wordsworth's verse:

> Among the possible effects of practical adherence to a theory that aims to *identify* the style of prose and verse ... we might anticipate the following as not the least likely to occur. It will happen ... that the metre itself, the sole acknowledged difference, will occasionally become metre to the eye only. The existence of *prosaisms*, and that they detract from the merits of a poem, *must* at length be conceded, when a number of successive lines can be rendered, even to the most delicate ear, unrecognizable as verse, or as having even been intended for verse, by simply transcribing them as prose ...'[23]

Coleridge stands in distinguished company when he makes this complaint, echoing Dr Johnson's sentiments:

> The variety of pauses, so much boasted by the lovers of blank verse, changes the measures of an English poet to the periods of a declaimer; and there are only a few skilful and happy readers of Milton, who enable their audience to perceive where the lines end or begin. *Blank verse,* said an ingenious critick, *seems to be verse only to the eye.*[24]

It could fairly be asked whether Johnson and Coleridge are not right to think that metre must be audible, and that metre to the eye only must be factitiously added to words which are not really poetry at all. Well, Johnson thought Milton's verse was verse only to the eye but had the sense to admit, 'I cannot prevail on myself to wish that Milton had been a rhymer;

for I cannot wish his work to be other than it is'.[25] If Milton falls victim to the argument that metre must be audible, then the argument rather than Milton may be at fault. Its fault lies in the implicit conviction it contains that unless metre is guiding vocalization it can be doing nothing creatively genuine in a poem. To check this conviction, we should refer to Wordsworth's account of the work of metre in his 1802 Preface to *Lyrical Ballads*:

> The end of Poetry is to produce excitement in coexistence with an overbalance of pleasure. Now, by the supposition, excitement is an unusual and irregular state of the mind; ideas and feelings do not in that state succeed each other in accustomed order. But, if the words by which this excitement is produced are in themselves powerful, or the images and feelings have an undue proportion of pain connected with them, there is some danger that the excitement may be carried beyond its proper bounds. Now the co-presence of something regular, something to which the mind has been accustomed in various moods and in a less excited state, cannot but have great efficacy in tempering and restraining: the passion by an intertexture of ordinary feeling, and of feeling not strictly and necessarily connected with the passion. This is unquestionably true, and hence, though the opinion will at first appear paradoxical, from the tendency of metre to divest language in a certain degree of its reality, and thus to throw a sort of half consciousness of unsubstantial existence over the whole composition, there can be little doubt but that, more pathetic situations and sentiments, that is those which have a greater proportion of pain connected with them, may be endured in metrical composition, especially in rhyme, than in prose.[26]

Metre tends to 'divest language in a certain degree of its reality' because it provides, as it were, an alibi for the words in a poem—they are there both as their expressive and significant selves, but also elsewhere, half-absent, tokens of rhythmical units. The metrical form of a poem records the poet's compositional activity which may or may not entirely square with the drift of what is said, or the state of mind implicit in that drift. (Wordsworth neglected to observe that much the same can be said of the Augustan diction he so disliked.) An awareness of compositional activity enables us to distinguish, say, cries of pain from poetic lamentation, and thus makes 'pathetic situations and sentiments' more tolerable. This is, as Wordsworth claimed, 'unquestionably true', but the truth has often been not even questioned but simply ignored, because it runs counter to an emphasis, derived from Coleridge, on the organic unity of poems and the unity of consciousness in the poet which the wholeness of his works is called to witness: 'The poet, described in *ideal* perfection, brings the whole soul of man into activity ...'.[27]

When Wordsworth admits into the poem 'an intertexture ... of feeling not strictly connected with the passion', he puts in doubt the Coleridgean unity both of his work and of his self at work. The 'intertexture of feeling' will be the metrical record of composition, the 'passion', the expressive tenor of the poem. Wordsworth, then, envisages the possibility of a created double consciousness within the poem, and that doubleness may respond to divisions in the poet himself or to divisions between the poet and the imagined subject of his poem, or to both. There are at least two reasons why Wordsworth may have been moved to this. In the first place, the social diversities of his time, turned into conflicts within his self, as Empson describes the process, result in a need for poetic forms which speak to the divided soul of man. Since many people, then and now, have divided souls, it seems a respectable thing for a poet to call them into activity. Secondly, the particular form of such calling into activity required Wordsworth to dramatize poetical composition itself, and this is, in part, effected by a doubled consciousness of metrical language itself, the divesting of 'reality' from, the poetic voice which cannot remain singly the voice of 'quelque homme qui parle'. And Wordsworth stands in distinguished company too—Hamlet:

> Speake the Speech I pray you, as I pronounc'd it to you trippingly on the Tongue: But if you mouth it, as many of your Players do, I had as live the Town-Cryer had spoke my Lines. Nor do not saw the Ayre too much your hand thus, but use all gently; for in the verie Torrent, Tempest, and (as I may say) the Whirle-winde of Passion, you must acquire and beget a Temperance that may give it Smoothnesse.[28]

Wordsworth essentially attempted, by the metrical intertexture of feeling not strictly connected with the passion, to give to the lyric a dramatic self-consciousness of its own voice such as Hamlet recommends to the players. For example, though he defended 'The Idiot Boy' with grave moral splendour—'... I have indeed often looked upon the conduct of fathers and mothers of the lower classes of society towards Idiots as the great triumph of the human heart. It is there that we see the strength, disinterestedness, and grandeur of love, nor have I ever been able to contemplate an object that calls out so many excellent and virtuous sentiments without finding it hallowed thereby and having something in me which bears down before it, like a deluge, every feeble sensation of disgust and aversion'— he also said of it simply, 'in truth, I Never wrote anything with so much glee'.[29] The conjunction of 'strength, disinterestedness and grandeur' with 'glee' provides one instance of the compositional drama which can be played between 'passion' and 'smoothness' by virtue of a break with organic functions of metre, by virtue of rendering the passage from visible to audible rhythmic patterns less secure than Johnson and Coleridge recommended.

There was great prescience in Coleridge's regret that Wordsworth showed an 'undue predilection for the *dramatic* form'.[30] He was thinking particularly of the personative works such as 'The Thorn', but much of Wordsworth's early writing is dramatic in the deeper and more elusive sense that it makes even the most lyrical utterance, utterance that might be thought to spring from the fullness of an 'I', dramatically self-conscious, watched, by a 'he'. Coleridge's prescience lies in so exactly anticipating the direction Wordsworth's influence would take—it led to the discovery of the most characteristic and fertile of nineteenth-century poetic forms: the dramatic monologue.

The tendency Wordsworth noted metre had 'to divest language in a certain degree of its reality, and thus to throw a sort of half consciousness of unsubstantial existence over the whole composition' explains in part the particular subtlety of the double nature of the printed voice in poetry. For the 'half consciousness of unsubstantial existence' imparted by metre joins with the retention of voice by the page to enable the poet to fashion, and not merely to suffer from, bafflements of voice, lacks and flusterings in speech, the burdens of address. Poetry in the line of Wordsworth takes shape from, and makes shapes of, what Harry in *The Family Reunion* suffers from as a sheer predicament:

> To be living on several planes at once
> Though one cannot speak with several voices at once.[31]

The sounds of one person's actual voice must happen one after another (I contrast 'actual voice' with a recorded voice and what is now possible by way of dubbing and multi-track superimposition). This makes it difficult to achieve in fact a simultaneity of different voices to meet the simultaneity of different demands on your voice. But the 'unsubstantial existence' of poetic voice in print creates the chance of a polyphony, the chance for a divided soul to speak with something better than a forked tongue.

Notes

1 John Hollander, *Vision and Resonance: Two Senses of Poetic Form* (New York: Oxford University Press 1975), p. x.
2 W. B. Yeats, 'Literature and the Living Voice' (1906), repr. in *Explorations* (London: Macmillan, 1962), p. 206.
3 F. R. Leavis, 'Poet as Executant', *Scrutiny,* 15/1 (1947), 80.
4 Robert Browning, *The Ring and the Book,* 1. 167 and 1. 155–8. I quote from the edition of R. D. Altick (Harmoodsworth, 1971), hereafter referred to as Altick.
5 Ibid. 1. 165–7.
6 W. B. Yeats, *Reveries over Childhood and Youth* (1915), repr. in *Autobiographies* (London: Macmillan, 1955), p. 67.
7 G. H. Lewes, unsigned review, *British Quarterly Review* (1847), repr. in Boyd Litzinger and Donald Smalley, ed., *Browning: The Critical Heritage* (London: Routledge and Kegan Paul, 1970), p. 122.
8 S. T. Coleridge, entry for 24 Apr. 1833 in *Specimens of the Table Talk of Samuel Taylor Coleridge,* ed. H. N. Coleridge (1837, 3rd eds. 1851), 236–7.
9 W. B. Yeats, letter to Robert Bridges, July 1915, in *The Letters of W. B. Yeats,* ed. A. Wade (New York: Macmillan, 1954), p. 598.
10 William Wordsworth, letter to Humphry Davy, 29 Sept. 1800, in *The Letters of William and Dorothy Wordsworth: The Early Years 1787–1805,* ed. E. de Selincourt (Oxford: Oxford University Press, 1935), 2nd edn., rev. C. L. Shaver, 2 vols. (Oxford: Oxford University Press, 1967), i. 289; the poems were 'Hart-Leap Well', 'There was a Boy', 'Ellen Irwin', and part of 'The Brothers'.
11 See, for example, Yeats's comments in 'A Literary Causerie' (1893), repr. in *W. B. Yeats: Uncollected Prose* ed. J. P. Frayne, 2 vols (London: Macmillan, 1970), I, p. 288 and in *Explorations,* p. 206; also the conversation recorded (not without malice) in G. Moore's *Ave* (1911), ch. 1.
12 Francis Berry, *Poetry and the Physical Voice* (New York: Oxford University Press, 1962), p. 34.
13 Ibid. p. 178.
14 Ibid. p. 193.
15 Ibid. p. 3.
16 Ibid. p. 189.
17 William Wordsworth, letter to John Wilson, 7 June 1802, in *The Letters of William and Dorothy Wordsworth: The Early Years 1787–1805* (Oxford: Clarendon Press, 1967), p. 355.
18 William Empson, Introduction to *Coleridge's Verse: A Selection,* ed. W. Empson and D. Pirie (London: Faber and Faber, 1972). p. 39.
19 Ibid.
20 'The Rime of the Ancyent Marinere', 1798 text, ll. 337–8; I quote from *Wordsworth and Coleridge: Lyrical Ballads,* ed. R. L. Brett and A. R. Jones (London: Methuen, 1963), 23.
21 (1782). I quote from *The Poems of William Cowper,* ed. John D. Baird and Charles Ryskamp, 3 vols. (Oxford: Clarendon Press, 1980–95), i. p. 403.
22 'Appendix' to *Lyrical Ballads* (1802), in Brett and Jones op. cit. p. 318.
23 Samuel Taylor Coleridge, *Biographia Literaria* (1817). I quote from the edition of J. Engell and W. J. Bate, 2 vols. (New Jersey: Princeton University Press, 1983), ii. p. 79.
24 'Life of Milton', in *Lives of the English Poets* (1779–81, repr. in 2 vols., 1906), i. p. 133.
25 Ibid.
26 Brett and Jones, *Lyrical Ballads,* op. cit. p. 264.
27 *Biographia Literaria,* ii. p. 16.
28 iii. ii. 1 ff.; Folio, ll. 1849–56.
29 *The Letters of William and Dorothy Wordsworth: The Early Years,* i. 357; note dictated to Isabella Fenwick, 1843, in Brett and Jones, op. cit. p. 292.
30 *Biographia Literaria,* ii. p. 135.
31 (1939). I quote from T. S. Eliot, *The Complete Poems and Plays* (London: Faber and Faber, 1969), p. 324.

9 What Kind of a Critical Category is 'Women's Poetry'? (2003)

Marion Thain

When Ana Parejo Vadillo and I decided to organize the 2002 conference "Women's Poetry and the Fin-de-siècle," several of my colleagues asked whether this focus on women's writing was not rather old-fashioned now. For many in Britain "women's writing" is seen to signify purely a feminist political stance in which one argues for the value of women's writing against an assumption that it is forgotten or undervalued. Yet this is not just a category created for a late-twentieth-century political gesture, which can therefore be discarded when that act of recuperation is deemed to be over: it is, as we shall see with particular reference to the work of May Kendall, a category which existed to shape poetic identity and a framework for reading in the later nineteenth century. It is the shifting critical currency of the term "women's poetry," within the field of late-Victorian studies, that I want to explore here.

The differences between the conception of "women's poetry" represented at Isobel Armstrong, Virginia Blain, and Laurel Brake's 1995 "Rethinking Women's Poetry: 1730–1930" conference and that apparent at the 2002 "Women's Poetry and the Fin-de-siècle" conference might be a useful starting point. Certainly in 1995 the sense in which "women's poetry" was a recuperative term was still in the air.[1] In contrast, the discourse of the forgotten was hardly in evidence by the 2002 conference. But if the 1995 conference was an important marker of that initial moment of rediscovery, it was also to act as a catalyst for the critical trajectory which we followed thereafter. Armstrong and Blain's book is subtitled *Gender and Genre, 1830–1900*; the emphasis of the volume is on "the poetic investigation of gender and its interplay with genre" (Preface, p. xiv). Charting the involvement of women's poetry in a wide range of discourses and debates has occupied us since.

If there was a change apparent in the 2002 conference from the agenda aired in 1995, it might be the subtle twist of the focus from "Gender and Genre" to, more specifically, "Gender *as* Genre." The debate about the genre of gender was, of course, already apparent in the 1995 conference in the concern of several speakers with the historical role played by the category "women's poetry" and the necessity, to current critical thinking, of understanding the generic qualities of this label. Yopie Prins' published paper from this conference begins by stating the need to "theorize and historicize a category that we assume to be self-evident: namely, the woman poet."[2] Anne Mellor, writing about Romantic literature, adds to this discussion of the woman poet as a generic category by arguing for the need to distinguish between the tradition of the poetess and "female-authored poetry which does not conform to this poetic practice": the tradition of the "female poet."[3] It is this attempt to interrogate the deceptively unified term "women's poetry" which interests me here. The questions raised in these papers have become more and more insistent in our thinking about "women's poetry" as we have moved farther away from the importance of the term as a recuperative one. Susan

Brown, in her extremely useful chapter on "The Victorian Poetess" (2000), does much to provide an overview of the recent growth in the number of personas recognized as possible positions for the Victorian woman poet. For Brown, even the one category of the "poetess" contains many possible personas.[4] She goes on to make the chronological claim that "from the 1870s onward, the explicit invocation of the poetess is more critical than poetic" (p. 196). She cites Elizabeth Sharp's 1890 *Women Poets of the Victorian Era* as an accurate reflection of the "mood of the previous two decades." What we have here, writes Brown, is a "new poetess," "rather like her fictional counterpart the New Woman" (p. 197).[5]

This sense of "women's poetry" referring to a multiplicity of established poetic personas became one of the recurring themes of the 2002 conference on fin-de-siècle women's poetry. Brown's "new poetess" has not caught on as a label, but the "New Woman poet" figure she recognized with this term appeared in eight papers delivered at the conference under that name (this persona was put firmly on the map of women's poetry with the publication, in 2001, of Linda Hughes's *New Woman Poets: An Anthology*).[6] Another possibility for the Victorian woman poet which has emerged fully after 1995—and was cited in several papers at the 2002 conference— is, of course, the female aesthete (thanks to excellent work by Talia Schaffer, Kathy Psomiades, and others). Aestheticism poses an intriguing challenge to the "poetess" by consciously declaring an interest in artifice, intense experience, beauty, and the desire to experience life itself as art, and so being in danger of parodying what Brown describes as the "commodified aestheticism that frequently conflates the woman poet's body with her literary corpus" (p. 181).[7]

Whether or not we want to see the New Woman poet and the "female aesthete," like the "poetess," as fully-fledged gender-based literary genres by the end of the century, I want to raise the possibility that, given more study, these poetic personas might entail distinctive literary conventions (of form and style as well as content) which distinguish them from purely social types and which might enable us to identify through them distinctive poetic alternatives to the poetess tradition. This challenge to the unity implied by the term "women's poetry" is an important part of appreciating the diversity of opportunity available for the woman writer at the end of the century, and a way of peopling the literary critical scene with a number of personas which mark a broader sense of the importance of "women's poetry."

Furthermore, by examining late-nineteenth-century anthologies, I will suggest that this discernment of "women's poetry" as containing more than one type of female poetics was one which underlay principles of engagement with poetry at its time of composition. Alfred Miles's ten volumes of nineteenth-century poetry, published between 1891 and 1897 under the title *The Poets and The Poetry of the Century*, give us the opportunity to see a late-nineteenth-century editor making choices about gender and genre on a large scale.[8] Volumes one to six contain a chronological anthology of the poetry of the century, or rather of the poetry by men written in the century. The final four volumes are devoted to types of poetry which are seen as marginal: humorous verse, sacred verse, the verse of Robert Bridges and his contemporaries, and women's poetry. The Robert Bridges volume was one of the last to be published and contained contemporary poetry, by men and women, which could not have been assimilated into the earlier volumes. In the later 1905–7 edition of the work Miles did away with this mixed volume, devoting volumes 1 to 7 to male poets, 8 to 9 to female poets, and 10 to 12 to humorous and sacred verse, thus showing that this mixed volume of contemporary poets had been motivated by the pragmatics of multi-volume publishing over a long period of time rather than a sense that fin-de-siècle women's poetry could be mixed with that of men in a way not possible with earlier Victorian poetry.[9]

Why did Miles feel it necessary to separate women's poetry from that of men? What did this category "women's poetry" mean for Miles? It is immediately apparent that the term is not simply one which refers to poetry written by women, as some women poets are occasionally placed in other volumes of the anthology, not in the core volumes 1–6, granted, but certainly in the other volumes of marginal genres. "Sacred, Moral, and Religious verse" is, perhaps unsurprisingly, also well populated with women poets, and, more interestingly, "Humour, Society, Parody and Occasional Verse" contains work by just one woman: May Kendall. Miles himself wrote the introduction to the selection of Kendall's poems and explains that

> a deeper note is touched in some of the psychological poems, the writer dealing with serious issues without becoming morbid, and treating all her subjects without losing the dominating influence of a robust common sense. It is this faculty, associated with a true sense of humour, which not only projects itself into her writings, but which prevents her from taking herself too seriously, and qualifies her for the office of self-criticism that distinguishes her from the sentimental school of the women poets of the past.
>
> (pp. 613–614).

It seems that Miles's explanation, in the preface to the series, of the segregated women's poetry volume—that "the poetess [was] a development of the period" (p. iv)—really does in some sense show a recognition of a certain kind of poetic genre (as do the other volumes outside the core chronology). Indeed, in the introduction to the volume of women poets itself—"Joanna Baillie to Mathilde Blind" —he goes on to express his concern to show the "progress and development" of a "characteristic feature" of the century's literature within this volume (p. iii). His overall vision seems to be one as much concerned with genre as with gender, and the astonishing introduction to May Kendall makes this particularly clear as he distinguishes her "from the sentimental school of the woman poet of the past" which he maps in the "poetess" volume. What we see in his volume of "women poets" is not simply the female sex being sidelined, but a genre being recognized, categorized.

But what about Susan Brown's claim that from the 1870s onward, the poetess became a less important category, and Elizabeth Sharp's new anthology was more in keeping with the mood of the age? Did the poetess give way to new configurations of the "woman poet" toward the end of the nineteenth century? It certainly does seem that Sharp is recognizing quite a different genre of women's poetry in her anthology to that which constitutes "women's poetry" in the above example. She sees the "poetess" as existing in the past, a product of the "general mild sentiment then in vogue." What she represents is "modern women-poets," whose work needs no apology. May Kendall is included within her version of the woman poet, because here the late-nineteenth-century "woman poet" is very much a New Woman type (and quite different to Miles's woman poet), with Kendall's "Woman's Future" proudly on display under the explanation: "From the standpoint of 'Woman's Rights.'" That Kendall's poem is emblematic for this volume can be seen in the way Sharp seems to echo Kendall's poem in the language of her introduction:

> But who shall predict what woman will do in the future? Daily, yearly, prejudices are being broken down, fetters are falling off; women are ushered into knowledge and to experiences of life through wider doors; legitimate freedom is now partly theirs, and before long it will be theirs as wholly as it belongs to men. Who, therefore, can predict exactly what will be or will not be the outcome of these growing possibilities?[10]

A comparison with Eric S. Robertson's contemporaneous anthology, *English Poetesses* (1883), is striking. Even if one knew nothing about the content of the poems listed on the two contents pages, the titles alone seem to suggest that the two anthologers have a different agenda. The complete lack of poems by fin-de-siècle women poets about science in Robertson's anthology can instantly be seen to contrast with a number of poems dealing with evolution in Sharp's collection: Emily Pfeiffer's "Evolution," Constance Naden's "The Pantheist's Song of Immortality," A. Mary F. Robinson's "Darwinism." Often the same poets are represented by Robertson, but by different poems. His selection of Robinson includes "Maiden Love" and "Love's epiphany" rather than "Darwinism" and "The Idea." Similarly, Robertson's picture of Jean Ingelow contains poems such as "Wedlock," while Sharp's contains one called "Work." Just as Kendall's "Woman's Future" and "Education's Martyr" could not have found a place within Robertson's collection, neither could Meynell's "The Modern Poet." Robertson's biographical focus, with added poems, can similarly be contrasted with Sharp's discrete separation of life and work, with short biographies given only in the back of the book.

Yet, throughout the later nineteenth century this type of New Woman poetry—recognized and categorized by Sharp—seems to coexist with the "poetess." Robertson's anthology may confess itself to be peddling a "very old-fashioned doctrine," in its conviction that "children are the best poems Providence meant women to produce,"[11] but such assertions were still being made, very publicly, in 1902 when Hannah Lynch wrote her long and similarly conservative review of A. Mary F. Robinson.[12] Gladstone, in 1890, was also writing about contemporaneous "poetesses" making remarkable additions "to the train of Sappho";[13] and Oscar Wilde was also declaiming about the Poetess in 1888, when he too traced the Sapphic persona.[14] Women poets at the end of the century could write poems from a number of generic positions and often played with more than one of them.

If the poetess continues to be an important idea, poetically and critically, through to the end of the century, then this is not to say that she continued to play the same role in women's poetry. In arguing for the demise of the poetess, Brown writes that toward the end of the century, "women no longer need define themselves against the figure of the poetess" (p. 198). Yet, I think women poets, even New Women poets, do continue to engage with the role of the poetess, and measure themselves against it (even if only to mark their distance from it) through to the end of the century. The development of the poetess genre toward the end of the century needs to be as much a part of the critical exploration of this area as is the recognition of other, alternative, personas available to women poets at this time. I will briefly discuss one short poem which may be used to raise some questions along these lines.

"In The Drawing Room"[15] is by May Kendall—the poet whose name has appeared so important in marking the boundaries between types: so conspicuously placed outside Miles's category of "women's poetry," while so emblematic of Sharp's New Woman category, and so significantly absent from Robertson's work.[16] The poem is a very evocative picture of the absence of a woman in a room. One can almost still hear the dust settling from her departure:

> Furniture with the languid mien,
> On which life seems to pall—
> With your insipid grey and green
> And drab, your cheerless wall—
> To think that she has really been
> An hour among you all.

Focussing on how dull the room is in her absence is a very effective, indirect, method of implying her liveliness and vibrancy. While she is never described, we get a very strong impression of her presence from this room still warm from her occupation. In a nice touch at the end the narrator sees echoes of the life she used to bring to the room:

> I see the dingy curtains stir
> With a faint memory,
> The grand piano dreams of her
> In a drowsy minor key.

But who is this absent woman and what is the point of the poem?

In her essay "The Damsel, the Knight, and the Victorian Woman Poet," Dorothy Mermin presents the dilemma of the Victorian woman poet as having to be "two things at once, or in two places, whenever she tries to locate herself within the poetic world."[17] She has to play two opposing roles at one time: "both knight and damsel, both subject and object" (p. 65). This is the dilemma well known from more recent discussions of the "poetess": that if woman is the object, the muse, of a poem, to become its author and subject is to take on an extra role, not an alternative one. As Brown comments, "Poetry is for women a mode, not an occupation": "For women writers, the major problem in this formulation is that women *are* poetry" (p. 181). Mermin argues that the quest to become the active subject cannot work while the poetess is still the poem's object: she must relinquish the role of the object of poetry. The importance of Kendall's poems is, I think, that she does precisely refuse to perform from within the poem in the conventional way. The careful, almost loving, evocation of the space around the missing object is, I suggest, a celebration of Kendall's own absence from the role of poetess and an inscription of her position as the subject or author of the poem: poem has become poet. "In The Drawing Room" ends on a triumphant note: having suggested that the woman may be back in the room some day, she declares that "To-night it may not be!" Perhaps this poem should be seen as working against poems such as those by Letitia Landon which depict women in pictures; "freezing women in a static but intense moment.... They become objects whose life is in suspension," comments Isobel Armstrong.[18] Kendall, by contrast, animates this woman and allows her to resume her life, leaving only a sense of her recent departure in the frame.

It is important to note in this poem that the absence is entirely without explanation. This lack of specificity, the generic sense of loss, is important to my reading of the poem. We are alerted to the possibilities of such ambiguity by Isobel Armstrong's writing on the "double poem," and it is just such a dialogue "of the poem with itself" that I am tracing here (*Victorian Poetry*, p. 14). While the poetess was trapped within the realm of the object, the depicted (the "room" of the "drawing"), the author of this poem has found her own theoretical space in which she can depict ("room" for "drawing"). Facile word play aside, we should remember that the drawing room was originally the "withdrawing" room; a private space into which to withdraw from the public sphere. That the woman of this poem has deserted that place of reticence implies a move into a space where she can find her voice (remember Michael Field's plea to avoid being "stifled in drawing-room conventionalities").[19] The woman's relocation from object to subject is inscribed at many levels within the poem. The joke in this poem is very much on the reader. If we see only an absence in the heart of these poems, then we are missing the point, which is the inscription of the presence of the woman poet outside the poem.

Or is it? Absence—or the abandoned Sapphic woman—has become recognized as a crucial part of a poetess poetics. Lawrence Lipking in *Abandoned Women and Poetic Tradition* suggests the abandoned woman offers a challenge to traditional poetics by being outside it. Poetry needs abandoned women to remind us of what is left out, what is absent or missing: "typically poems of abandoned women tend to embody the emptiness within them."[20] "Women poets" he says, "create from a sense of loss; the myth, not of hope pursued, but of hope abandoned" (p. 180). So, are we to read Kendall's poem as a woman abandoning her prescribed role, or a woman drawing attention to the fact that her role is to be abandoned? More recently, Virginia Jackson and Yopie Prins in their fascinating essay "Lyrical Studies" have continued this exploration of the emptiness of the "poetess" category in the nineteenth century: the poetess "is not the content of her own generic representation: not a speaker, not an 'I,' not a consciousness, not a subjectivity, not a voice, not a persona, not a self."[21] Far from negotiating the problem of being endlessly and explicitly on display as the contents of the poem, the poetess, argue Jackson and Prins, has to contend with being displaced by the genre she uses. "Victorian British and American poetesses (the very figures accused of being most personal and subjective, and thus most historically obscure)" are simply evaded through the act of composition: "the presentation [within poetry] of those subjects as already gone reveals their ideal emptiness as well as the lyric's historical function as vehicle for transporting, and potentially displacing, representative identities" (p. 529). If the woman poet is erased through her performance of the poetess genre, then is the absent woman in Kendall's poem a parody of the poetess's own displacement by lyric conventions?

What we have here is a "triple poem": a poem which is at the most literal level a light verse describing a drawing room; and at a more self-reflexive level is about the celebratory loss of the New Woman who refuses to be objectified in her own poem; while also at some level invoking ideas about the ironic displacement of the woman who cannot be present through the conventions of the poetess. This poem seems to me to capture particularly concisely the dilemma of the fin-de-siècle woman poet who writes self-consciously (and sometimes parodically) within a New Woman poetic, but who still has to negotiate the dominant poetess tradition from which she distances herself. It is perhaps no coincidence that in my exploration of late Victorian anthologies it was Kendall's work, particularly, which marked the boundaries between the different types of "woman poet" recognized by the Victorian mind. However, Kendall's poem is, of course, part of a larger group of poems by late Victorian women writers which suggests a knowing manipulation of multiple female poetic personas. In short, what I want to suggest is a translation—at least a mental one—of the term "women's poetry," whenever we hear it, into "women's poetries," which explicitly acknowledges the multiple, gendered positions which women poets could assume towards the end of the century.[22] Where critical texts offer one chapter on "women's poetry," we get a false sense of female unity pitched against male poetic diversity. Further exploration of women poets' sense of the multiple positions available to them, and the conventions established around those positions would, I suggest, enrich and expand discussions of "women's poetry" in the period.

Notes

1 Indeed, the final section of Armstrong and Blain's book of papers from the conference *Women's Poetry, Late Romantic to Late Victorian* is titled "Re-reading Forgotten Poets" (New York: St. Martin's Press, 1999).

2 Yopie Prins, "Personifying the Poetess: Caroline Norton, 'The Picture of Sappho,'" *Women's Poetry, Late Romantic to Late Victorian*, p. 50.

3 Anne Mellor, "The Female Poet and the Poetess: Two Traditions of British Women's Poetry, 1780–1830," *Women's Poetry in the Enlightenment: The Making of a Canon, 1730–1820*, ed. Isobel Armstrong and Virginia Blain (New York: St. Martin's Press, 1999), p. 82.

4   Susan Brown, "The Victorian Poetess," in *The Cambridge Companion to Victorian Poetry*, ed. Joseph Bristow (Cambridge: Cambridge Univ. Press, 2000), p. 184, 186.

5   Brown also acknowledges Eric S. Robertson's *English Poetesses* (1883), with its radically different "poetess"' gender politics, yet she argues that although Robertson was influential for some critics, "his polemic seems outmoded" (p. 197).

6   Linda Hughes, ed., *New Woman Poets: An Anthology* (London: The Eighteen Nineties Society, 2001). In *Poetry of the 1890s* (London: Penguin, 1997), R.K.R. Thornton and I also included a short section on the poetic New Woman which begins to map the territory so much more comprehensively handled by Hughes. Of course, including the New Woman on our list of suggested topics on the call for papers might be considered to have engineered this situation, but that list of topics was formed from a sense of areas that had recently been gaining critical interest.

7   Talia Schaffer suggests that the position of the female aesthete could achieve a fine balance between demands of poetess femininity and New Woman politics: "To turn-of-the-century observers, Meynell was the living proof of the female aesthetes' theory that New Womanism and traditional femininity could merge seamlessly" (*The Forgotten Female Aesthetes* [Charlottesville: Univ. Press of Virginia, 2000], pp. 160–1).

8   *The Poets and The Poetry of the Century*, ed. Alfred H. Miles, 10 vols. (London, 1891–7).

9   This gives a very straight-forward answer to M. Lynda Ely's recent question as to why A. Mary F. Robinson's poetry was "inexplicably" "tucked away in volume eight" of Miles' anthology (the volume of Robert Bridges and his contemporaries), instead of appearing in volume seven, the volume of women's poetry of the period ("'Not a Song to Sell': Re-Presenting A. Mary F. Robinson," *VP* 38 [2000]: 98).

10 *Women Poets of the Victorian Era*, ed. Mrs. William Sharp (London: Walter Scott, ?1890), pp. xxxii-xxxiii.

11 Eric S. Robertson, *English Poetesses: A Series of Critical Biographies, with Illustrative Extracts* (London, 1883), p. xiii.

12 Hannah Lynch, "A. Mary F. Robinson," *The Fortnightly Review* 71, New Series (February 1902): 260–76.

13 W. E. Gladstone, "British Poetry of the Nineteenth Century," *The Speaker* 1 (1890): 34–5.

14 Oscar Wilde, "English Poetesses," in *The Artist as Critic: Critical Writings of Oscar Wilde*, ed. Richard Ellmann (New York: Random House, 1969), p. 102; originally in *Queen*, December 8, 1888.

15 May Kendall, *Songs From Dreamland* (London, 1894) pp. 6–7.

16 For a brief biography see my entry on Kendall in *Late Nineteenth- and Early Twentieth-Century British Women Poets*, ed. William B. Thesing, vol. 240 of the *Dictionary of Literary Biography* (Detroit: Gale, 2001), pp. 118–23.

17 Dorothy Mermin, "The Damsel, the Knight, and the Victorian Woman Poet," *CritI* 31 (1986): 67.

18 Isobel Armstrong, *Victorian Poetry: Poetry, Poetics and Politics* (New York: Routledge, 1993), pp. 327–8.

19 *Works and Days: From the Journal of Michael Field*, ed. T. and D. C. Sturge Moore (with an introduction by Sir William Rothenstein) (London: John Murray, 1933), p. 6.

20 Lawrence Lipking, *Abandoned Women and Poetic Tradition* (Chicago: Univ. of Chicago Press, 1988), p. 26.

21 Virginia Jackson and Yopie Prins, "Lyrical Studies," in *The Cambridge Companion to Victorian Poetry*, ed. Joseph Bristow (Cambridge: Cambridge Univ. Press, 2000), p. 523.

22 Or at least, perhaps, an explicit acknowledgement of when we are using the term "women's poetry," as Alfred Miles used it, to denote a particular poetess tradition, rather than an inclusive gender category.

10 Female Picturesque and Colonial Settings in the Gift Books (2010)

Serena Baiesi

Female aesthetics of the picturesque in the representation of colonial space

Oriental tales set in India were widespread in England during the second phase of British colonial expansion. This was after 1815 – following the Hastings impeachment of 1795 – when English settlement in the subcontinent was politically stable and flourishing economically. To the English, India was, in geographical terms, only a distant reality; but despite the remote location, the Eastern colony had a strong influence upon the English imaginary, reflected in social and literary tastes. Both those who had travelled to or settled in India and those who had never been there found themselves attracted by, and curious about, everything that was Indian. As Nigel Leask discusses in his study on *Curiosity and the Aesthetics of Travel Writing,* this 'curiosity' incorporated two distinct senses as it was employed in eighteenth-and nineteenth-century discourses of travel:

> The first bound to a negative account of the wonder aroused by distant lands, associated with a socially exclusive desire to posses the 'singular' object or else […] a vulgar, popular interest in exotic objects for commercial profit. The second – employed more positively – denotes an inclination to knowledge of foreign singularities.[41]

The colonial fascination translated into exotic attraction was manifested in several social files, including literature. However, the romantic enthusiasm for India was focused more on an idealized and imaginary colonial space than on a real existing country with its own traditions, culture, religion and civilization. Colonial narratives during the eighteenth and nineteenth centuries integrated literary and scientific discourses, even though the subjectivity of the writer frequently clouded a more objective and scientific approach to the cultural encounter. A fictionalized colonial world was reproduced in literature and visual art through romantic aesthetics, employing the dynamics of the sublime or, more specifically, the picturesque.

Revd William Gilpin, together with Sir Uvedale Price, and Richard Payne Knight were the major theorists of this aesthetic category, which influenced nineteenth century British visual arts and literature. In their painting, Richard Wilson and Gainsborough applied the picturesque aesthetic combining Italian landscapes – taking as models Claude Loraine's and Salvator Rosa's paintings – with the Dutch style. In literature, Ann Radcliffe – who admired Gilpin – was one of the chief followers of the picturesque dictates, which she effectively applied to landscape descriptions in her gothic romances. The notion of the observer having multiple perspectives, together with the principle of movement and the interplay of light and shade were new aesthetic perspectives the painter had to associate with any kind of scenery, from English landscapes to colonial.

Applied to the colonial context, the picturesque was translated into the observation and mimicking of exterior reality through the imperial gaze. This aesthetic, which started in relation to visual arts and then spread out into literary descriptions, had a profound influence on Indian travel writing in the romantic period and thereafter. It was Richard Knight who, in his *Analytical Inquiry* (1805), compared the visual effect to the sensorial experience produced by colonial depictions. Limiting the colonial encounter to an external appreciation, the eye of the English observer had the possibility of separating the pleasing optical impressions derived from the picturesque object from the negative physical perceptions related to that very reality.[42] As a consequence, the spectator activated the so-called 'screening effect' to colonial representations, perceiving the territory without the dangers, horrors and discomforts to be found in the real India of the time.[43] From the British imperialistic point of view, the picturesque becomes, as Sara Suleri has discussed in *The Rhetoric of English India:*

> Synonymous with a desire to transfix a dynamic cultural confrontation into a still life, converting the pictorial imperative into a gesture of self-protection that allows the colonial gaze a license to convert his ability not to see into studiously visual representations.[44]

The aesthetic curiosity exemplified by the visual picturesque was readily provided by a number of narrations, written or illustrated, which described visions, sounds, and colours linked to the Indian colony and which were made available for mass consumption in the imperial motherland.[45]

Imaginary travel in India became possible for a large audience, especially with the publication of tales, poems and illustrations in widespread editions. At the time, travel writing was developing into a literary genre, second only to novels and romances in popularity. It mingled literary and scientific discourses, without omitting a moralistic purpose; but it also aimed to entertain and instruct by means of appealing to the imagination and to sentiment. Travel accounts and travelogues were published in literary journals and periodicals and enjoyed great success amongst a wide audience from all levels of society and literary culture. Circulating libraries also helped in the transmission of colonial literature, and they created a popular taste for the genre, especially among those who could not afford the price of an illustrated catalogue.

Travel literature was supposed to recreate and relocate colonial settings – objects, people, animals and plants – back home, transforming the different, distant, unknown, wild, and faithless into something familiar, ordered and converted. However, even if curiosity about the colonial and the exotic compelled the artist to encounter and reproduce the otherness, there was a certain distance he or she would keep, as part of the spatial dynamic of travel writing. Temporalization was one of the literary devices employed by writers to maintain a 'safe distance' from the disturbing colonial reality: the picturesque was represented as the past landscape manifesting the ruinous agency of time. Colonial ruins were depicted in terms of their former splendour, which the picturesque stillness had immobilized, in order to arrest the turmoil of history and to contemplate its passing in the spirit of nostalgic detachment.[46]

The melancholic contemplation of collapsed Hindoo temples and graveyards was one of the most recurrent motifs of Indian landscape description. Displays of ruins linked to former empires demonstrated the triumph of British liberty over oriental despotism, and gave the assurance of colonial conquest from past to present times: 'Indian ruins figured the historical triumph of liberty over tyranny, rather than the guilt of colonial dispossession'.[47] The picturesque 'commodified' the Indian landscape for sentimental consumption in England, through its associative power over distance, screening out the history of violent conquest and usurpation from colonial picturesque, and communicating with the imperial viewer through sites of domesticity, sentimentality and nostalgia.

Women writers of the romantic period were particularly skilled in colonial representations, and Letitia Landon was one of them. Even though imperial space was traditionally conceived as male, women played an important role in building up the British empire, with their physical presence – living and working in the colonies – and in creating an imaginary and aesthetic background – publishing literary accounts concerned with colonial subjects. In their writing, women unveiled a different reality from that usually described by men, who were mostly concerned with public life; instead, women interpreted their colonial experiences by relating them to their gender and social status. As a consequence, they developed specific aesthetic practices in order to define, understand and relate to readers an idea of Empire that was significantly different from the one maintained by their male counterparts. Women were zealous observers of the private sphere, female spaces, and their own role in society. When discussing Anglo-Indian women writers, Suleri argues that they employed the devices of the 'orientalist picturesque' with the aim of 'aestheticizing rather than analyzing' colonial reality:

> To produce both visual and verbal representations of India that could alleviate the more shattering aspects of its difference, romanticizing its difficulties into the greater tolerability of mystery, and further regarding Indian cultures and communities with a keen eye for the picturesque.[48]

Women felt explicitly attracted by colonial alterity — although they feared it at the same time — and often dedicated themselves to writing on various colonial subjects, either because they were travellers or simply because they were avid readers of travel literature. They seem to have avoided straightforward political and economic analysis; however, they used discourse strategies focusing on the domestic sphere to discuss public matters.

Moreover, women exploited colonial alterity in order to discuss their own condition as women and as inferior social beings in British society. The feminine picturesque developed a dual discourse: on one level, it showed obedience to the imperialistic ideology by following the structures of sentimentality and accepting its own minority status. What was depicted in oriental tales was a pattern of allegories of empire, a sort of 'domesticated' reality, studded with racist and imperialist attitudes: the worst of Indian threats were temporally suspended in colonial tales, and portrayed as if in watercolours, so that they were domesticated, and fitted into a less disturbing system of belonging.[49] However, on a more subversive level, female writers manipulated the terminology of the picturesque to lend a new violence to fragility, implicitly questioning the symbolic relevance of women to a colonial discourse.[50]

Representations of Indian women in Letitia Landon's poems

Letitia Landon's oriental poems fit the aesthetic category of the colonial picturesque, but they also negotiate with official imperial and paternalistic aesthetic discourses, so that her resistance to the latter is figured through a variety of Indian female characters. In her Indian representations, the poet relocates alterity so that it has a domestic identity, and she employs discursive devices, such as sentimentality and nostalgia linked to temporalization of objects and landscape, as a means of dialogue and confrontation with empire.

Poems referring to Indian scenery and culture were published in a very specific editorial tradition, which much influenced and directed Landon's own poetical inspiration and purposes. In fact, the majority of her oriental poems were written for Fisher's illustrated annual *Drawing Room Scrap-Book*, which Landon edited from 1832 to 1838. As we have already remarked, gift-books were a fashionable phenomenon from the 1820s to the 1840s, and Indian themes drew a lot of attention in these illustrated publications. A large number of engravings were dedicated to Indian landscapes, especially in Fisher's annual, who gave the poet the literary commission for each of them. Sometimes Landon demanded the assistance of a friend, Crofton Croker – a writer of Irish legends – to find the right link between the illustrations she received from the publisher, and the subjects she had to choose for the complementary poem. Croker explains his support in these terms:

> The favour alluded to in the annexed note was an offer which I made to Miss Landon to assist her by writing some verses, or notes, or otherwise attempting a literary illustration of any of the plates sent to her by Messrs Fisher & Co for the Drawing Room Scrap Book, which she might feel a difficulty about, what is called 'writing up to'. – Altho' the imagination of Miss Landon, when once kindled shed a poetical light upon every thing it touched, I think she was rather slow in seeing at the first glance all the capabilities of a subject. It was not until she had dwelt upon a subject, or it had been placed before her in a poetical aspect, that she felt even a hope of being able to treat it successfully. But a subject – I may say any subject, having once taken hold of her mind, a thousand unseen beauties unfolded themselves before her, and crowded upon her extraordinary fertility.[51]

Letitia Landon might have struggled to accomplish all her literary commitments, not only because she could have a lack of literary imagination, but also due to the amount of writing she was busy publishing. In a letter dated 1831 she writes:

> I am in the agonies of my last volume, unable to sleep for thinking of my preface, and unable to eat for mediating my dedication; also, I know not which way to turn for a motto. Moreover, this is my very busiest time, writing for the annuals. [...] I am fairly fagged out of my life.[52]

The volume Landon was working on was her novel *Romance and Reality,* published in November 1831, but during that summer she was also hectically arranging the editorship for the *Drawing Room Scrap-Book.* Its publication was scheduled before December, to allow readers to buy it as a Christmas gift.

Landon remarked on the difficulty of her literary task in the Preface to the *Drawing Room Scrap-Book* published in 1832. In this issue the poet received a large number of oriental drawings, so she had to extend her poetical imagination to match all the exotic illustrations:

> It is not an easy thing to write illustrations to prints, selected rather for their pictorial excellence than their poetic capabilities; and mere description is certainly not the most popular species of composition. I have endeavoured to give as much variety as possible, by the adoption of any legend, train of reflection, which the subject could possibly suggest.[53]

The following year, the poet had to deal with another *Scrap-Book* edition full of different geographical scenery from all over the world. If England and Europe were well known places to describe, China, on the contrary, was too distant from her cultural and literary imagination. Commenting on an illustration of the city of Macao, Letitia Landon began her poem with some ironic lines, which reveal her dejection dealing with such a subject:

> Good Heaven! whatever shall I do?
> I must write something for my readers;
> What has become of my ideas?
> Now, out upon them for seceders!
> Of all the places in the world,
> To fix upon a port in China;
>
> Celestial empire, how I wish
> I had been christened Celestina![54]

Later she found another Chinese illustration for the same issue, which she accompanied by a poem entitled 'The Chinese Pagoda'. Again, Landon finds it an effort to create an original composition, and she makes a joke about the conflict between the poet, who is struggling to find suitable verses to accompany the engravings, and the publisher, who cannot afford to replace a costly illustration for the sake of the poet's inspiration:

> Now, I who thought the first [Macao] vexatious,
> Despaired, and knew not what to do,
> Abused the stars, called fate ungracious –
> Here is a second Chinese view!
>
> I sent to Messr. Fisher, saying
> The simple fact – I could not write;
> What was the use of my inveighing? –
> Back came the fatal scroll that night.
>
> 'But, Madam, such a fine engraving,
> The country, too, so little known!'
> One's publisher there is no braving -
> The plate was work'd, 'the dye was thrown'.[55]

Landon closes the poem with a resigned tone knowing that the will of a poet is unheard when business is concerned: 'If in this world there is an object, / For pity which may stand alone, / It is a poet with no subject, / Or with a picture worse than none'.[56]

In the *Scrap-Book's* 1834 edition, Landon decided to alter the editorial rule of the annual. Instead of inventing single poems for each engraving, she composed one single narrative tale, which matched all the illustrations. She justifies her editorial choice in the Preface:

The present volume is so different from its predecessors, that I shall venture, in a few words, to explain my motive for such alteration. Of all soils, a literary one is the soonest exhausted, and a change of subjects is as much needed as a change of crops. The magnificent ruins in the Indian Views suggested at first so much of melancholy reflection on the instability of human glories, that the poems which sought to illustrate 'the fallen temple of the lonely tomb', naturally took a sad and thoughtful cast. But as my knowledge of Oriental history increased, I found it full of rich material for narrative; abounding with incidents of interest and of wild adventure. I am therefore determined on accompanying the Plates of Eastern Scenery this year with a connected tale. Hope, love, and sorrow for the staple of the poet's song; and though I have adhered as accurately as possible to character, costume, and scenery, it is on the expression of universal feelings that I place reliance, in any attempt of mine to win the sympathy of my readers. I trust the attempt will be its own apology.[57]

Landon is referring to the tale entitled *The Zenana,* a long poem based on Indian locations and Indian female characters. The decision to insert women protagonists who were not physically portrayed in the illustrations was necessary in order to create a romance. Moreover the poet deliberately chose Indian women in very specific living conditions: the domestic sphere of the zenana. This was the traditional Indian system of female confinement, where women lived isolated from the rest of society. Landon chose this subject matter because it allowed her to employ her favourite literary genre – the metrical romance – together with female characters as the main protagonists, and exotic locations outside English social and cultural boundaries.

In a letter dated 1833, and addressed to her friend Anna Maria Hall, Letitia Landon commented on her work for this very issue of the *Drawing Room Scrap-Book* praising her skilfulness in having found a successful editorial strategy:

> I have been just hurried out of my life with getting my 'Drawing-room Scrap-book' finished. [...] The volume just completed contains one long poem founded in Indian history; a connected story called the 'Zenana'. [...] How my ingenuity has been taxed to introduce the different places! And, pray, forgive this little tender effusion of vanity, I do pique myself on contriving to get from Dowlutabad to Shusher, and Penawa, and the Triad Figure in the Caves of Elephante, and from thence to Ibrahim Padshah's tomb, etc. etc. But I am too sick of all these hard names to inflict any more upon you. It is four years since I have written a long poem. I cannot describe to you the enjoyment of going back to 'my first-love and my last'. I can only say that writing poetry is like writing one's native language, and writing prose, writing in a strange tongue.[58]

This extract shows how Landon was devoted to her work for the annuals and had to negotiate her way between financial and artistic interests: firstly she had to care about her business relationship with her publisher – on whom she depended economically – and secondly she had to relate her own poetical taste and inspiration to the visual images of the gift-book. However, in this edition she managed to express the full potentiality of her writing, employing her most favourite poetical genre.

Although the illustrations of the 1834 issue of the *Scrap-Book* were mostly of Indian scenery, especially ruins and temples, Landon composed a metrical romance solely about women, which she set in the enclosed world of an Indian zenana. In order to justify her digression from the general rules of an annual's composition – one illustration followed by a poem or a tale – Landon links the main story of women's lives to the engravings of Indian settings through the use of footnotes. She applies to her narration the principle that 'distant places, events, and objects must be rendered mobile, so that they can be moved back and forth without decay or distortion resulting from decontextualization'.[59] Through her narration Landon relocates Indian plants, ruins, caves and temples from their original context (the illustration) into a dynamic context (the poem) combining their meaning with her own imagination. Landon skilfully employs the literary device of including Indian objects and locations into the poem, managing to manipulate the temporalization of external scenes belonging to the traditional oriental picturesque, and dislocating the objects into fictional commodities. Thereby she reveals and reduces colonial distance by using Indian scenery mingled with invented Indian female characters.

The metrical tale *The Zenana* portrays the life of Indian women in an isolated and secret place, which is self-contained, self-governing and completely autonomous from the rest of the world:

> What is there that the world hath not
> Gather'd yon enchanted spot?
> Where, pale, and with languid eye,
> The fair Sultana listlessly
> Leans on her silken couch, and dreams
> Of mountain, airs, and mountain streams.[60]

Among the women, there are two main protagonists whose stones lead the central narration. However, the poem is intermingled with a series of other narratives, so it becomes difficult to trace a single plot.

The first protagonist is a young bride, Nadira, the sultana, who, comforted by her companions, is awaiting the return of her husband, who is dangerously engaged in the battlefield. His death or his survival will affect Nadira's own life. In fact, following the Hindoo tradition, a wife will live or die depending on her husband's destiny. The customary immolation of the Indian widow on the funeral pyre of the deceased husband is not a new topic in Landon's poetry, in fact it was staged in several other compositions before *The Zenana*.[61] Letitia Landon exploited the reference to this cruel religious practice that required the sacrifice of the wife's life to denounce indirectly the subordinate condition of women in patriarchal societies more in general.

Landon does not involve herself in a moral or religious dispute concerning this practice; on the contrary, she reverses the subordination of the woman seen as an innocent victim of society, giving to this brutal practice, which otherwise would simply compel her to surrender to a masochistic and patriarchal custom, a new unexpected interpretation. Surprisingly the heroine asserts her right to die: her death becomes a voluntary sacrifice of her life following not a primitive and sad tradition, but acting according to her own free will. Therefore Indian widows become symbols of revolutionary liberty, being driven by love and faithfulness. As a consequence, Landon's Indian female characters only appear to be passive women, instead they behave as brave protagonists, who resolve to sacrifice themselves to fulfil their own destiny, and enjoy love in the afterlife.

The second main protagonist of the story is a woman artist, Zilara, who entertains the sultana and the other girls with music, songs and traditiotnal Indian tales. Her duty is that of alleviating the sultana's distress as she waits for the return of her beloved husband, so she recites several stories of female experiences of submission, despondency, dejection but also self-fulfilment. Zilara refers to women alternatively as slaves, and devoted lovers, but also as resolute and brave wives, who even if not engaged in warfare, fight their own battle. Their struggles are linked to the domestic sphere, specifically the zenana in this case: the idea is that even if a woman is isolated, she must deal with an external world, dominated by violence and misery.

As a female performer Zilara recalls another character of Landon's: the protagonist of the *The Improvisatrice,* a long poem the author published in 1824. The woman of the zenana is a singer and actress, and she wears the clothes of other female characters each time she improvises a story for her audience. Again, it is interesting to note that Landon already described Indian settings and Hindoo women before the publication of *The Zenana.* In the narrative poem published in 1824 the protagonist, the Improvisatrice, happens to go to a masked ball dressed-up as a Hindoo girl, where she sings the song 'The Hindoo Girl's Song' for the guests, and recites a tale entitled The Indian Bride'.

Within Landon's *Zenana* Hindoo women are allowed to express their feelings, manifest their artistic talents, and confess their intimate desires. Even though the zenana is described as a luxurious prison, Landon transforms it into a private place where women can freely articulate their power. Here Indian women play an active role, they are assertive discursive subjects, while men become 'objects' and topics of discussions and prayers. Life seems suspended: stillness, boredom and often mourning are the key elements of Landon's zenana, where Indian rituals like that of the floating boats on the river Ganges are perpetuated. This was a superstitious ceremony, which attracted the attention of several English women writers, since it was narrated in many poems by different authors.

Letitia Landon refers to this custom in at least two different compositions, among the several she wrote for the annuals on Hindoo practices: in *The Zenana,* and in 'The Hindoo Girl Song'. In this last poem she introduces the rite as 'a well-known superstition among the young Hindoo girls':

They make a little boat out of a coconut shell, place a small lamp and flower within this tiny ark of the heart, and launch it upon the Ganges. If it floats out of sight with the lamp still burning, the omen is prosperous: if it sinks, the love of which it questions, is ill-fated.[62]

Elizabeth Barrett Browning also depicted this ceremony in a poem entitled 'India. A Romance of the Ganges', published in 1837. Browning's poem was composed for the annual *Findens' Tableaux* at the request of Mary Russell Mitford, who was the editor of that issue. In turn, Mitford too dealt with oriental scenes and Indian culture in Findens' annual, which she edited and contributed to. However, all these exotic representations were second-hand versions of colonial reality, because none of these poets had ever been to India. Instead, Emma Roberts – Landon's close friend and a poet herself – was one of the few writers who really had the chance to witness what she described in her oriental poems, since she lived in Calcutta from 1828 to 1832. Roberts was a contributor to the annuals – *Forget-Me-Not, Friendship's Offering, The Amulet* and *Literary Souvenir* – but she also wrote her own collection of *Oriental Scenes* (1830) dedicated to L.E.L. In 1839 she edited a posthumous publication of Landon's poems entitled *The Zenana and Minor Poems,* collecting all major colonial poems written by Landon during her lifetime. Additionally, Roberts introduced this edition with a long preface on L.E.L.'s life, personality and literary accomplishments.

Landon describes the feminine world of colonial India by applying the devices of the oriental picturesque. However, she also tries to domesticate the colonial reality to get a closer look at it, rather than keeping it at a safe distance. She skilfully includes comments on the colonial system in her works, referring, for example, to the damsels of the zenana as slaves, denouncing traditions that keep women – English women included – in subordinate positions. Furthermore describing the bravery of men in battle, she refers to colonial war as cruel and as inhuman. In this way, Landon crosses the limits of the detached picturesque of colonial literature and challenges male imperialistic ideology by employing a colonial background in order to display female sympathy for alterity. Ironically the poet concludes her romance not with the death of the waiting wife, the sultana, who happily reconciles with her beloved husband on his return from the war, but with that of the woman artist, Zilara, who dies of a broken heart from a betrayed love. In this way Landon re-stages the enduring conflict between fame and happiness for a woman artist.

In a poem published in the introduction to the 1835 *Scrap-Book* edition, Landon seems to summarize her position on colonial discourse, supporting universality and human sympathy instead of division and separation:

> For now I find in foreign scenes
> What foreign scenes can be,
> And truth with fancy intervenes,
> To bring them home to me.
> A few short miles, a few salt waves,
> How strange a change there came –
> Our lives as separate as our grave;
> Is then our kind the same?
>
> Ah, yes; a thousand sympathies
> Their general birth-place find,
> And nature has a thousand links
> To beautify and bind.
> I deeply felt that song should make
> One universal link,
> Uniting, for each other's sake,
> All those who feel and think.[63]

Landon's approach to colonial discourse can be interpreted from two perspectives: if on the one hand she deals with stereotypes and second-hand information about Indian culture and society; on the other hand, she uses exotic locations and foreign habits in order to discuss with metaphors and symbols the broader condition women suffered in her society. Landon best articulated gendered issues using the genre she mastered the most, the metrical romance. By displacing her characters outside English society – as she did in her preceding romances – she is able to expand her argument on women and their role inside and outside the domestic sphere.

However, in the publications dated in the 1830s we can detect a further development of the genre. As we have already remarked the genre of metrical romance is transformed into a dramatic monologue for single poems in the annuals, and also for *The Zenana*. The main protagonist – who recites a story – is more focused on the attention of the audience/listener than on her own voice. The interplay between the characters carried out in these poems is more concise in terms of length and dramatization, exactly because of the kind of publication in which they were meant to appear. Letitia Landon's poetical aesthetic was very much influenced by marketing strategies and audience requests, and was thus transformed in terms of form and language. During the 1820s the poet was experimenting with the genre of the metrical romance following Scott's and Byron's examples, and orienting the content of her story towards gender and social issues. In the metrical romances and short poems composed for annuals during the 1830s, she adapts the literary strategies of the Romantic period to those of the newest fashion – the gift-book – which was to become emblematic of the Victorian era.

Notes

41 Nigel Leask, *Curiosity and the Aesthetics of Travel Writing, 1770–1840,* Oxford: Oxford University Press, 2002, p. 4.
42 See Richard Payne Knight, *An Analytical Inquiry into the Principies of Taste,* 4th ed., London, 1808.
43 Leask, *Curiosity and the Aesthetics of Travel Writing,* p. 169.
44 Sara Suleri, *The Rhetoric of English India* (Chicago: Chicago University Press, 1992), p. 76.
45 Leask, *Curiosity and the Aesthetics of Travel Writing,* p. 169.
46 Ibid., p. 174.
47 Ibid.
48 Suleri, *The Rhetoric of English India,* p. 75.
49 Ibid., p. 76.
50 Ibid., p. 78.
51 Letitia Elizabeth Landon, *Letters,* ed. F. J. Sypher (Ann Arbor : Scholars' Facsimiles & Reprints, 2001), p. 67.
52 *Ibid.,* pp. 65–6.
53 *Fisher's Drawing Room Scrap-Book, with Poetical Illustrations by L.E.L.* (London: Fisher, Son, and Jackson, Newgate Street, 1832); Landon edited *Fisher's Drawing Room Scrap-Book* from 1832–1838.
54 Ibid., p. 42.
55 Ibid., p. 49.
56 Ibid., pp. 49–50.
57 *Drawing Room Scrap-Book,* 1834.
58 Landon, *Letters,* p. 91.
59 Leask, *Curiosity and the Aesthetics of Travel Writing,* p. 21.
60 Letitia Elizabeth Landon, *The Poetical Works of Miss Landon* (Philadelphia: E. L. Carey and A. Hatt, 1838), p. 261.
61 See 'Immolation of a Hindoo Widow', 'The Bayadere', and 'The Indian Bride'.
62 *Drawing Room Scrap-Book,* 1836, p. 16.
63 *Fisher's Drawing Room Scrap-Book,* 1835.

Part III
Politics

Ankhi Mukherjee

The politics of Victorian poetry is perhaps not dissociable from the politics of reading Victorian poetry. As Isobel Armstrong points out, 'the most arresting discussions of Victorian poetry recently have come from Marxists, feminists, and deconstruction'.[1] Armstrong cautions against the instrumentalities of motivated criticism in the same breath, on the grounds that attempts to pin a poet to his or her ideology nullifies the conscious and unconscious ambiguities of poetic language, and valorises a very narrow form of intentionality. The arbitrariness of the interpretive process which determines a poem's politics is demonstrated by the manifest differences in a Marxist and, say, a queer theoretical reading of a piece, revealing the different selection criteria and priorities in play. Armstrong points out the self-defeating nature of critical practices that simplify a text's projects in order to invoke the complexities of the work: 'A text is not quite like a patient in analysis and actually anticipates these strategies of deconstruction by enabling them to take place'.[2] A more fruitful approach would be to treat the poem 'as struggle', Armstrong suggests, between the text's multiple viewpoints, clashing imperatives and ideologies, and the inherent contradictions of language. Armstrong's way of reading Victorian poetry follows the deconstructive logic of the 'double poem', whose two readings unseat fixed categories of thought and language. It is 'an expressive model and an epistemological model simultaneously': hermeneutic questions structure it while its lyric expressivity destabilises any structure with anxieties, ambiguities, and the 'confounding complexities of language'.[3] The double form is one which splits in enunciation, making utterance both a subject and an object: the Victorian dramatic poem, Armstrong asserts, 'is not the dialogue of the mind with itself so much as the dialogue of the poem with itself'.[4] The double poem is post-teleological in the way it flouts the *telos* of transcendent signifiers and meta-narratives. It is post-revolutionary and post-industrial in its commitment to democratic forms of power and its epistemological unease with subject-object relations. Finally, Armstrong argues, the double poem is post-Kantian in its disdain of instrumental energies. It is art for art's sake, innocent of practical experience.

Armstrong draws attention also to the dynamism of language in Victorian poetry, crucial to the genesis of the double form: 'to read a Victorian poem is to be made acutely aware of the fact that it is made of language'.[5] Though the unstinted textuality of the poem can sometimes seem to subsume the poet, Armstrong argues that the linguistic excess of Victorian poetry is not to be read as anarchy and flux but as systematic and self-reflexive: 'It is not the disorganised expression of subjectivity but a way of exploring and interrogating the grounds of its representation'.[6]

Victorian criticism did not view the poem as a hermetic identity on which its moral and social formations did not impinge. John Sterling famously began a discussion of Tennyson's

1842 volume in the *Quarterly Review* with a survey of his society: 'The time, among us at least, is an essentially unpoetic one – one which, whatever may be the worth of its feelings, finds no utterance for them in melodious words'.[7] Poetry, in the best critical discussions, was inseparable from its cultural referents and this confusion between art and life, which, according to Isobel Armstrong, is 'also what gives the best criticism a rich amplitude and seriousness, a largeness of concern'.[8] Matthew Arnold's Preface to the first edition of *Poems* (1853), very much concerned with questions of poetry and the age, argues that the main aim of poetry is to give pleasure by the representation of an action that appeals to the affections of the reader. Such an action can be taken from any age in human history, and Arnold objects strongly to the view that only the nineteenth-century modern could furnish the materials of poetry. Reacting adversely to a review of Edwin Arnold's poems by R. S. Rintoul in the *Spectator*, which urges the poet to 'leave the exhausted past' and draw on 'matters of present import',[9] Arnold claims that the past is inexhaustible, especially those cultural resources 'which appeal to the great primary human affections: to those elementary feelings which subsist permanently in the human race'. Arnold's 1853 Preface is unique in the way it urges political engagement and action through a return to the past. Writing of those who engage in active cultural traffic with the ancients, Arnold states:

> They are told that it is an era of progress, an age commissioned to carry out the great ideas of industrial development and social amelioration. They reply that with all this they can do nothing; that the elements they need for the exercise of their art are great actions, calculated powerfully and delightfully to affect what is permanent in the human soul; that so far as the present age can supply such actions, they will gladly make use of them; but that an age wanting in moral grandeur can with difficulty supply such, and an age of spiritual discomfort with difficulty be powerfully and delightfully be affected by them.[10]

Arnold's emphasis on action offers a corrective to that element of contemporary poetry that he condemned, the subjective poetry that revolved around 'the dialogue of the mind with itself'.[11] Such a dialogue is morbid and lowering, Arnold argues, and proceeds to urge an 'architectonicé', a severity of form and chastity of style, which would pre-empt 'self-complacent reverie' and create enduring art.[12]

The Arnold of the 1853 Preface is not entirely certain as to what will 'bear directly upon the cravings and ideas of the age ... and transform it into melody', as Charles Kingsley put it in an unsigned review in the May 1849 issue of *Fraser's Magazine*.[13] What sort of poetry does the age need? Philip Davis sees the relationship of the Victorian poet to the world outside as marked by opposing tendencies: the desire to establish the autonomy and singularity of literature and a counter-tendency 'which internally recommitted art – in its content, in its urgency – to the service of the world outside'.[14] In *The Art of Eloquence*, Matthew Bevis examines how writers sought to reconcile these opposing tendencies and how they cultivated the critical distance that would allow them to engage with political arguments without being ideologically compromised by them. Bevis claims that Arnold's presence at many of the 1866–7 reform debates in the Parliament inspired him to write the essays that would make up *Culture and Anarchy* (1869), a book that objected vehemently 'to the uncultured polemics of contemporary political argument'.[15] In direct contradistinction to the vicissitudes of parliamentary debate, Arnold proposes the power of disinterested play of consciousness. He urges the believer in culture to 'get the present believers in action, and lovers of political talking and doing, to make a return on their own minds'.[16] This return to the self seems at first to be at odds with the 'dialogue of the mind with itself' that Arnold had condemned in the 1853 Preface, and in which 'disinterested objectivity' is dissipated, not intensified, by a situation that evokes passive endurance. For Arnold, Bevis argues, 'literature must lend its peculiar eloquence to "the opposite side of the question", but this eloquence must not tend toward a reflexivity that turns political amplitude into a passive or unprincipled loss of bearings'.[17] Arnold's 'Empedocles on Etna' is the model of the overstrained, morbid thinker who fails to be an inadequate interpreter of his age. His mental distress, unrelieved by 'incident, hope, or resistance', to cite Arnold's words from the 1853 Preface, fails to transform the painful into the tragic, and his perpetual (private and political) *agon* into poetry.

In his 1853 Preface, Arnold condemned critics 'who seem to direct their attention merely to detached expressions, to the language about the action, not to the action itself':

> They will permit the Poet to select any action he pleases, and to suffer that action to go as it will provided he gratifies them with occasional bursts of fine writing, and with a shower of isolated thoughts and images. That is, they permit him to leave their poetical sense ungratified, provided that he gratifies their rhetorical sense and their curiosity.[18]

In his insistence that poets narrate an action, rather than indulge in 'occasional bursts of fine writing', and in his commitment to an engaged poetical sense, mistaken often for the flourishes of 'rhetorical sense', Arnold seems aligned with the worker-poets of the Chartist movement. This is not to say that Arnold subscribed to the ideology of the Chartists. As Peter Scheckner points out, 'during the height of the Chartist militancy, Arnold became the private secretary to Lord Landsdowne, the president of the council in the ministry of the Chartists' most notable enemy – Lord John Russell'.[19] However, he would unequivocally agree with the Chartists that poetry should never 'become the allegory of the state of one's own mind'.[20] According to Scheckner, 'Arnold moved with such determination toward an objective view of the world that eventually he gave up writing poetry entirely, and instead concentrated on prose and the essay format'.[21] For the Chartist poets – workers and agitators in England, Scotland, and Wales – the themes of poetry could not be dissociated from social struggles and structured political resistance. During the late 1830s and 1840s, writers, publicists, politicians, as well as unknown workers published thousands of essays and poems. The most famous and widely read of these were William James Linton, Ernest Jones, Ebenezer Elliott, Gerald T. Massey, and Thomas Cooper. Influenced by communal music and Christian hymnology, the politically committed and iconoclastic poetry of Milton, Marvell, Pope, Burns, Shelley, Byron, and Scott, among others, political theory, philosophy, and increasingly democratic principles and structures of education, the Chartists 'were using poetry – their own and their predecessors' – to continue the political struggle between themselves and the ruling classes'.[22] The August 1, 1840 issue of *The Chartist Circular*, which ran a regular column titled 'The Politics of Poets,' lauded the 'deeply, essentially, entirely Radical poetry' of Wordsworth, who, like the Chartist poets, had extrapolated his poetic materials 'from the lowest and simplest walks of life', and whose heroes were 'waggoners, strollers, pedlars, beggars, hedgers and ditchers, and shepherds'.[23]

Chartist verse, penned by self-educated industrial and artisan workers and disseminated in Chartist journals, magazines, and newspapers, was public poetry that sought primarily to uphold the rights of the people amongst democratic nations. As the editors, Fergus O'Connor and Ernest Jones, of an 1847 issue of *The Labourer: A Monthly Magazine of Politics, Literature, and Poetry*, put it: 'What is Robert Browning doing? … has he nothing to say for popular rights? Let him eschew his kings and queens – let him quit the pageantry of courts – and *ascend* into the cottage of the poor'.[24] As this shows, the Chartist response was to contemporary class struggles as well as to the middle-class response to and mediation of the same. For the Chartist poets, thought and feeling in poetry were necessarily soldered to political activism, which is not to say that the poetry strained always to be a trigger for political action. In fact, the predominant themes of the poetry of Chartism were freedom, social equality, and an equitable society, and international cooperation and fraternity. It was animated by a millennial confidence in the humane working conditions that would reverse the oppression and alienation of industrial labour. Brian Maidment sees this 'post-revolutionary consciousness' of Chartist poetry manifesting itself in a subversion of lyric assumptions by playing them against 'quite complex *symbolic* modes of writing'.[25] He describes the formal features of Chartist poetry as:

> a strong sense of orality [and] of communal occasion and the appropriate rhetoric, or a willingness to align the devices of popular literature – pathos, melodrama, refrains, and catchphrases – with quite sophisticated literary skills in order to convey ideas or abstractions by emotional as well as intellectual means.[26]

The politics of Chartist poetry was not merely presentist: the vision of 'group identity and political solidarity', it sought to forge was inseparable from its belief in self-causing and self-sustaining people's power and its idealism for a better social order to come, a future state.[27] Writing on Gerald Massey, a poet whose works capture the intense euphoria and despair associated with the Chartist experience from 1848 to 1852, Mike Sanders relates his conception of revolution to Walter Benjamin's reflections on messianism in 'Theses on the Philosophy of History' (1940). Benjamin's messianism involves a reordering of temporality, whereby what he terms the 'homogeneous empty time' of capitalist modernity, and which produces a futurity that is a repetition of the same rather than a harbinger of the new, is corrected through the redemption of a real historical past. In a poem like Massey's 'The Three Voices', Sanders aptly identifies a messianic drive to supplant the 'empty time' of the present with a more meaningful realignment of the past and future. The poem, which enjoins 'Yoke-fellows' to, in turn, 'Weep', 'Work', and 'Hope', sees history as both inexorable and reversible through human agency. By presenting the time-states of the past, the present, and the future as 'a sequence of discrete yet continuous stages', Gerald Massey's poetry envisions the present 'in dualistic terms as both a site of oppression and domination and as a site of resistance and change'.[28] In the Introduction to his *The Poetry of Chartism*, included in this collection, Sanders claims that 'Chartist poetry constitutes both a distinctive form of agency and a unique form of knowledge'.[29]

'The heroine, instead of waiting at home for her husband to return from the Crusades, disguises herself as a boy and goes to fight at his side.' This is Angela Leighton describing Elizabeth Barrett Browning's 'The Romaunt of the Page', whose emancipatory politics is viewed transversally through domestic, patriarchal structures, and not in their absence. Barrett Browning did write poetry on political subjects, but this ballad demonstrates how she would deploy dominant discourses to 'generate innovative ideological effects through their subtextual operations'.[30] 'Romaunt' reverses the marriage plot-driven structure of the traditional ballad: in fact, the female protagonist's ordeals start with her nuptials, conducted with undue haste, after which she decides to follow her husband to the Crusades dressed as his page. When the husband hears that the page's 'sister' had disguised herself as a boy to fight by her husband's side, he calls such a wife 'Unwomaned' and adds that forgive her though he might, he would only love her as a 'servitor', 'but little as my wife'. Saracens approach, and the gallant page tells her master to ride on, saving the small-minded husband by dying in his place. The poem seems to reinforce conventional values, but only for the obtuse reader who has missed the bitter indictment of a romance tradition whose libidinal investment in epigrams and imaginary women, 'So high, so pure, and so apart', does grievous wrong to the needs of real women. The virgin-wife's sacrifice could just as easily be interpreted as an act of liberating herself from the domestic carceral in an androgynous flight into chivalric death. Leighton reads 'The Romaunt of the Page' as the 'Victorian woman's version of the story of [Byron's] *Lara*, the forgotten story – "tale untold" – of a loyal female page accompanying her master into battle'; 'not aloof superiority but disappointing conventionality is the reaction in men which blocks women's ambition' in Browning's retelling.[31]

If her eminent contemporaries, L.E.L and Felicia Hemans, write of the vicissitudes of love, Browning offers a more cynical, worldly, and witty take on the disillusionments and disenchantment besetting the relation between the sexes. Barrett Browning said of Hemans that, despite her redoubtable powers, there is 'a sense of sameness which goes with the excellence ... a feeling [that] "this writer has written her best", – or "It is very well – but it can never be better"'.[32] Her pastoral elegy for Hemans, written in a reactive mode to Miss Landon's 'Stanzas on the Death of Mrs Hemans', offers a correction to her predecessors' diffuse sentimentality and tired amatory discourse in its self-conscious and self-reflexive assessment of the place of women's poetry in the hypertrophic literary tradition (of Milton's *Lycidas* and Shelley's *Adonais*, in particular) and the contemporary world. As Harrison notes, Barrett parodies Landon by appropriating her stanzaic form, making 'stately four-line stanzas out of the more diffuse eight-line stanzas used by Landon'.[33] The revisionary elegy stands out for its frankness and candour. To Landon's injunction to bring flowers 'to greet the bride' of Christ, Barrett archly retorts: 'Lay only dust's stern verity upon the dust undreaming'. Pouring withering scorn at Landon's excessive grief, she advises her peer to 'be happy, crowned and living one!' The last line of the poem, where she wishes that Landon will emulate from Hemans a softer, less brazen style, thereby earning England's praise that the 'foot-fall of her parting soul is softer than her/singing', is nothing short of 'killing off her remaining rival by prematurely inscribing her epigraph'.[34]

'The Romaunt of the Page' similarly rejects 'stultified poses', Leighton argues, in this case pertaining to the 'waiting game of woman's love'.[35] Again, in *Aurora Leigh*, the eponymous heroine comes of age through her radical refusal of the discursive constructions – the clasping 'green wreath' of leaves, the infantilising and trivialising 'clean white morning dresses' (II. 93, 96) – that keep her in her gendered place in the marital home as well as the Palace of Art. Barrett Browning's poetry is political not necessarily by virtue of its subject matter or even its rhetoric but in the agonistic struggle between 'desire and fact, between the individual and the system' it gives form to.[36] Leighton traces the influence of George Sand in Barrett Browning's break from the self-centred sensibility of the de Staël romance tradition toward a new boldness of imagination and articulation. *Aurora Leigh* celebrates the 'triumph of the poet', whose utterance 'burns you through / With special revelation', and 'shakes the heart / Of all the men and women in the world' (I: 902–7). Aurora's cousin Romney, the personification of the abstract reason and Christian socialism she so hates, is blinded by a fire. Unlike Jane Eyre, Aurora Leigh does not become the nurse of her blinded companion but this sensory deprivation leads to his transformation by Aurora's imaginative social vision. *Aurora Leigh* seems to sanction both 'the affective, and the aggressive',[37] the poem's valorisation of an expressive, imaginative passion co-existing with its forceful disavowal of the degeneration of the emotive life into self-abnegating femininity. Barrett

Browning's politics are best encapsulated in the double poem, wherein contrarieties can abound and radicalisms juxtapose with affective insight. 'Perhaps because women in the nineteenth century were confronted with contradictory experience they use the double poem persistently', Armstrong concludes.[38]

'[A] single shelf of a good European library was worth the whole native literature of India and Arabia', said Thomas Macaulay in his infamous Education Minute of 2 February 1835.[39] Macaulay, well-versed in the Western classics but utterly ignorant of Sanskrit and Arabic literature, foreshadows the perils of Orientalist scholarship that Edward Said delineates in *Orientalism*, whereby comparative evaluations would be unfairly weighted in favour of one culture and not the other, which in turn would justify and perpetuate the asymmetrical power structures of native governance. English language poetry written in India exhibits the inevitable anxieties associated with its unwanted and belated arrival and the hauntology of Macaulay's mimic men, a class of interpreters Indian in blood but English in taste. English was the metropolitan language in India, 'the chief cultural and communicational instrument for the centralization of the bourgeois state',[40] and English poetry, a crucial component of the educational curriculum in colonial India, was implicated in the ideology of empire in a way that the novel, circulating outside the immediate sphere of the colonial state apparatus, was not.

English poetry in India in the colonial era occupied a heteroglot space, the poets drawing on both classical languages (Persian, Arabic, Sanskrit, Greek, and Latin) and Indian vernaculars. It was further differentiated by markers of social class, gender, birth, and education. Both rooted to the spot and curiously out-of-place, poetry in English in India exhibited heterogeneous influences and what Patrick Williams calls 'simultaneous uncontemporaneities'.[41] Devoid of the constellations of literary movements, regional groups, or schools, the history of Indian poetry in English in the long nineteenth century is 'scattered, discontinuous, and transnational', as Arvind Mehrotra puts it. In the introduction to her *Indian Angles: English Verse in Colonial India from Jones to Tagore*, Mary Ellis Gibson looks at the webs of 'affiliation and rupture'[42] – identifications and misidentifications with the Western canon – structuring English language poetry written outside Great Britain. Correcting the historical tendency to include poems written by poets born in India of Indian parents, Gibson includes both 'Indian' and 'British' poets in her study, the scare quotes drawing attention to the proleptic and changeable nature of avowed national identifications. Gibson argues that scholars of Indian English such as Eunice de Souza and Sisir Kumar Das, seduced by linguistic parochialism and a recursive nationalist ideology, have paid little attention 'to the mutually constitutive history of British and Indian poets working on the subcontinent in the nineteenth century'.[43] While an understanding of the various reckonings of linguistic and cultural nationalism is indispensable when it comes to interpreting and contextualising Indian writing in English, Gibson argues that twentieth-century postcolonial nationalism makes some poets and poems visible while rendering others obscure. Alongside usual suspects like H. L. V. Derozio, Toru Dutt, and Rabindranath Tagore, Gibson argues it is time to include the Orientalist Sir William Jones, the second-generation Irish poet Mary Seyers Carshore, and Sir John Horsford, who left his Oxford fellowship to enlist in the Indian army, in the imagined unity that is English language poetry.

Poetry, which Gibson describes as 'a kind of pressure cooker for historical and ideological contradictions',[44] seems especially suitable for studying the ambivalences, rifts and fissures of colonial writing. Borrowing Tracy Davis's formulation on 'repertoire', Gibson sees English language poetry in India as signifying accretions of practice and what Davis identifies as the 'multiple, circulating recombinative discourses of intelligibility'.[45]

This manifests itself in the traces of a wide variety of Western and non-Western languages, classical and vernacular, and in the proliferation of paratexts – 'footnotes, endnotes, glosses, prefaces, and dedications'[46] – through which Indian poets sought to make their palimpsestic versifying practices legible to a local and global audience. 'Repertoire' also refers to affective communities, largely overlooked in critical appraisals of English language poetics, wherein the rich continuities or marked discontinuities between poets who shared a cultural space are further explored. Indian poetry in English of the nineteenth century, whether penned by Indian natives or British colonials (and the changing terminology to demarcate this genre, as seen in the varying fortunes of 'Anglo-Indian', 'Indo-Anglian', and 'Indo-English' alongside the more recent 'Indian-English' and 'Anglophone' would testify to this anxiety of origin) is invaluable for studying the politics of Victorian writing in the empire. It provides complex evidence as to how, to quote Leela Gandhi, 'the substance of imperial self-articulation was in fact furnished by the materials of non-Western difference'.[47] Testifying to the cross-cultural exchanges between, say, the Indian poet Sarojini Naidu and the Decadent Arthur Symons, it captures a genuine cosmopolitan space between Victorian poetry of two nationalist derivations.

'Before beginning this study, I regarded Chartist proclamations of the importance of poetry with a large measure of scepticism', Sanders writes in his introduction.[48] The assumption fell away in the course of Sanders's sustained engagement with the Chartist press, convincing him that poetry played a primary role in galvanizing the movement. The politics of Victorian poetry, or the poetics of Victorian politics, seems to urge two questions in the same breath: 'why poetry?' and 'why politics?' While the essays collected here do not provide straightforward answers to this, a productive and constitutive dilemma of poetic endeavour down the ages, they engage with various manifestations of the imbrications of the aesthetic and the political in Victorian poetry. They provide valuable insights into the dominant ideological forms that went into the making of the Victorian modern, and the ways in which works of art supplanted the same with emergent values and structures of feelings from marginalized ideological positions. The coming together of poetic ambition with political proclivities was, of course, not always conscious or avowed. Elizabeth Barrett Browning concludes a letter of 1837, bristling with controversial political insights, thus: 'I would rather … write of any other subject than politics – altho' you may not think so, after all this!'[49]

Notes

1 Isobel Armstrong, *Victorian Poetry: Poetry, Poetics and Politics* (London: Routledge, 1993), p. 9.
2 Ibid., p. 10.
3 Ibid., pp. 13, 16.
4 Ibid., p. 14.
5 Ibid., p. 11.
6 Ibid., p. 12.
7 Isobel Armstrong, ed., *Victorian Scrutinies: Reviews of Poetry 1830–1870* (London: Athlone Press, 1972), pp. 125–6.
8 Ibid., p. 5.
9 Ibid., p. 32.
10 Matthew Arnold, 'Preface to the First Edition of Poems 1853' in R.H. Super (ed.), *Matthew Arnold: The Classical Tradition* (Ann Arbor, MI: University of Michigan, 1960), p. 13.
11 Ibid., p. 2.
12 Ibid., p. 9.
13 Armstrong, *Scrutinies*, p. 36.

14 Matthew Bevis, *The Art of Eloquence* (Oxford: Oxford University Press, 2007), p. 5.
15 Ibid., p. 6.
16 Ibid., p. 6.
17 Ibid., p. 7.
18 Arnold, 'Preface', pp. 7–8.
19 Peter Scheckner, ed., *An Anthology of Chartist Poetry: Poetry of the Working Class 1830s–1850s* (Madison, NJ: Fairleigh Dickinson University Press, 1989), p. 33.
20 Arnold, 'Preface', p. 8.
21 Scheckner, *Anthology* p. 33.
22 Ibid., p. 30.
23 Ibid., p. 31.
24 Ibid., p. 17.
25 Brian Maidment (ed.), *The Poor House Fugitives* (Manchester: Carcanet, 1992), p. 38.
26 Ibid., p. 24.
27 Ibid., p. 37.
28 Mike Sanders, *The Poetry of Chartism* (Cambridge: Cambridge University Press, 2009), pp. 212–213.
29 Ibid., p. 3.
30 Anthony H. Harrison, *Victorian Poets and the Politics of Culture: Discourse and Ideology* (Charlottesville, VA: University of Virginia Press,1998), p. 85.
31 Angela Leighton, *Victorian Women Poets: Writing Against the Heart* (Charlottesville, VA: University of Virginia Press, 1992), p. 84.
32 Philip Kelley and Ronald Hudson (eds), *The Brownings' Correspondence*, 14 vols (Winfield, KS: Wedgestone Press, 1983–1997), I, p. 235.
33 Harrison, *Victorian Poets*, p. 97.
34 Ibid., p. 98.
35 Leighton, *Victorian Women Poets*, p. 83.
36 Ibid., p. 87.
37 Armstrong, *Victorian Poetry*, p. 370.
38 Ibid., p. 368.
39 G. M. Young (ed.), *Macauley: Prose and Poetry* (Cambridge, MA: Harvard University Press, 1967), p. 722.
40 Aijaz Ahmed, *In Theory: Classes, Nations, Literatures* (New York: Verso, 1992), p. 74.
41 Mary Ellis Gibson, *Indian Angles: English Verse in Colonial India from Jones to Tagore* (Athens, OH: Ohio University Press, 2011), p. 7.
42 Ibid., p. 2.
43 Ibid., p. 3.
44 Ibid., p. 8.
45 Ibid., p. 8.
46 Ibid., p. 9.
47 Ibid., p. 4.
48 Sanders, *Poetry of Chartism,* p. 3.
49 Kelley and Hudson, *Browning's Correspondence,* III, p. 217.

11 Elizabeth Barrett Browning (1992)

Angela Leighton

Towards the end of her life, Barrett Browning wrote a ballad which 'shows how far she had travelled from the archaisms of sensibility the sexual politics of the contemporary world. In 1861, 'Lord Walter's Wife' was rejected by Thackeray as unsuitable for family reading in the *Cornhill Magazine*. 'Thackeray has turned me out of the "Cornhill" for indecency' (*Letters:* II, 443), Elizabeth triumphantly reported. Clearly the 'indecency' of 'Lord Walter's Wife', in which nothing indecent ever occurs, stems from the extra-marital situation it insinuates. The poem, as the very title suggests, is about the emotional property values of marriage. Lord Walter is absent throughout, though he 'owns' both title and wife. The woman who speaks and the friend she addresses are both nameless, known only in their relation to the absent lord. The poem is interesting because, while it sets up the opportunity for an adulterous affair between wife and friend, its purpose is ultimately neither to condemn adultery nor to reaffirm the sanctity of marriage. It is, rather, to expose the double standards of men. 'Why are women to be blamed if they act as if they had to do with swindlers?' (*RB:* I, 341) Elizabeth once demanded of Robert. Lord Walter's friend proves to be not so much a seducer as a swindler. He is corrupt precisely because he does *not* feel the adulterous passion he disingenuously proposes.

The poem opens with the lady asking why her friend must go so soon. She receives, for answer, a series of reasons in which sexual gallantry barely disguises accusation:

'Because I fear you,' he answered; – 'because you are far too fair,
And able to strangle my soul in a mesh of your gold-coloured hair.'

(*CM:* VI, 9–14, ll. 3–4)

He thus plunges the conversation into sexual meanings at the first opportunity. However, instead of receiving the coy protestation of innocence which he expects, and which would have ensured a safe passage for his one-sided game of seduction, the lady answers him with apparently reciprocal interest: '"Oh, that," she said, "is no reason! Such knots are quickly undone"' (5). Both her hair and her marriage, she suggests, are easily unknotted. When the friend starts to protest, '"I value your husband, Lord Walter"' (8), the laws of property making themselves heard in that loaded verb, she precipitates his insinuations into a real possibility of unfaithfulness:

'Oh, that,' she said, 'is no reason. You smell a rose through a fence:
If two should smell it, what matter? who grumbles, and where's the pretence?'

(9–10)

As she crudely literalises each of the hints he has dropped, meeting his proposals more than halfway, the friend suddenly turns on her as the guilty party in a fantasy he had thought entirely his own:

> At which he rose up in his anger, – 'Why, now, you no longer are fair!
> Why, now, you no longer are fatal, but ugly and hateful, I swear.'

(19–20)

The reasoning is exquisite. The contemporary slang of 'fatal' to mean only sexually alluring and not 'fatal' at all when it comes to it, shows up the selfish level of his thinking. The woman is only beautiful and fatal for as long as she remains innocent and inaccessible. He is another Mr Hunter who 'talks epigrams' of sexual gallantry in the safety of his assumptions that women are not sexual beings in any way, but angels in the clouds or faithful wives in the kitchen.

The contradiction between the man's rhetoric and his feelings is then exposed, word for word, by the lady herself:

> 'If a man finds a woman too fair, he means simply adapted too much
> To use unlawful and fatal. The praise! – shall I thank you for such?
>
> 'Too fair? – not unless you misuse us! and surely if, once in a while,
> You attain to it, straightway you call us no longer too fair, but too vile.'

(29–32)

Though no more than a verbal encounter in a garden, the episode is rich in the other meaning of real sexual use and abuse. It is the woman who brings into the open ground of straight speaking the double standard which is the very condition of the man's desire. He desires her only as a modest wife and adoring mother, yet at the same time the drift of his speeches is that she might be willing to be something else. '"You take us for harlots, I tell you, and not for the women we are"' (50), she accuses. The whole event of seduction emerges as a complacent and self-regarding fantasy of male power (as it does in Doris Lessing's short story, 'One Off the Short List' (1965: 7–33) which it curiously foreshadows). As in 'The Romaunt of the Page', the language of the heart proves wholly mediated by other, socio-political structures of desire.

Thackeray, perhaps, was right in detecting in the poem a subject not fit for family reading. For it is as much a critique of marriage as of adultery, of ownership as of unfaithfulness. As Mary Poovey puts it: 'Modesty announces purity in a virgin, promises fidelity in a wife, and thus will continue to be a reflection of her husband's power (1984: 22). In this poem, the man's game of seduction relies on the whole structure of marriage, motherhood, title, purity, property and, of course, male friendship, remaining intact. '"I value your husband ..."' is the crucial admission. The object of the friend's attentions is precisely 'Lord Walter's *Wife*'. Adultery, Barrett Browning might almost be hinting, is not so much the threatening opposite of marriage, as its hidden reaffirmation.

As a poet, she learned early to distrust the iconic postures of romance in favour of a socialised and contextualised account of desire. She perceives love, not as a conclusive emotional absolute, but as a mixture of lust, ambition, rhetoric, fear and, above all, conventionality. Hers is thus an essentially politicised poetry, not because politics is its dominant subject matter and not because she shows herself in any sense a political radical (as some critics have complained[1]), but because the tensions between desire and fact, between the individual and the system, can be felt in it. Those tensions were missing in the work of de Stael, Hemans and L.E.L., whose sense of morality was identical with the claims of the heart, but Barrett Browning found them in the novelist who, in a sense, provided her with a much needed counterbalance: George Sand.

Elizabeth lighted on 'the new French literature' (*MRM:* II, 85) comparatively late, in 1842, but thereafter was a confirmed devotee, who tried to convert both Miss Mitford and Robert Browning, though she kept her French enthusiasms secret from her increasingly puritanical father. In particular it seems to have been, as Patricia Thomson points out, not so much the Corinne-like *Consuelo* which drew her admiration, but Sand's novels about class and politics (1977: 57). 'Such a colossal nature in every way – ', she exclaimed to Robert, 'with all that breadth & scope of faculty which women want – magnanimous, & loving the truth & loving the people' (*RB:* I, 114). When she visited Sand in Paris in 1852 she was struck, above all, by the novelist's indifference to appearances: 'A scorn of pleasing she evidently had; there never could have been a colour of coquetry in that woman. Her very freedom from affectation and consciousness had a touch of disdain. But I liked her' (*Letters*: II 56–7). After the narcissistic monumentalism of *Corinne,* the sheer emotional and political variety of Sand's writing must have seemed like an opening into that 'experience of life & man' (*RB:* I, 41) which Elizabeth herself so much craved. The story of *Aurora Leigh,* her long epic poem about the development of the woman poet, contains, among other things, the drama of Barrett Browning's own imaginative emancipation from the self-centred sensibility of de Staël's romance into the 'breadth & scope' of vision she envied in George Sand. Such an emancipation is achieved through sceptically reproducing many of the old figures of female sensibility: the myth of Italy, the figurative anatomisation of the woman's body, the interlocking of the narratives of love and fame, but such devices are now put in the context of a diminishing and sometimes discrediting reality.

As Ellen Moers has shown, the crowning scene in the garden of Book II is a prolonged, literary in-joke about the Corinne myth (1978: 182). Aurora, on her twentieth birthday, persuades herself of her poetic vocation by playing the part of Corinne at the Capitol, and crowning herself poet in her aunt's garden. She is then caught in the classic pose of a statue by the unexpected audience of her sceptical and disdainful cousin, Romney:

> I stood there fixed, –
> My arms up, like the caryatid, sole
> Of some abolished temple, helplessly
> Persistent in a gesture which derides
> A former purpose. Yet my blush was flame,
> As if from flax, not stone.

> (II, 60–5)

In this moment of triumph turned silly, Barrett Browning seems to be enjoying a joke against all the Corinnes whose art consisted of standing in attitudes. 'Her arms were transcendently beautiful; her figure tall' (1836: 20), de Staël wrote. At the end of 'A History of the Lyre', L.E.L. reproduced the same posture:

> There was a sculptured form; the feet were placed
> Upon a finely-carved rose wreath; the arms
> Were raised to Heaven, as if to clasp the stars ...

> (*PW:* 231)

But instead of a tragic funerary monument, Aurora looks like a useless 'caryatid', whose hands are empty and whose arms carry nothing. Purposeless and pretentious, her moment of triumph has the opposite effect to Corinne's, for Romney is not impressed. The temple of the old poetic goddesses has been 'abolished', and the 'former purpose' of uplifted arms, if there ever was one, has somehow been forgotten. Barrett Browning takes the classical imagery of the myth and turns it into an imagery of purely archaeological interest (see Cooper, 1988: 157–8). Aurora's vocation is to be a poet, not a statue.

Yet it is interesting that, in the argument which follows, Romney tries to recuperate the myth for his own domestic purposes. He tells Aurora:

> 'Keep to the green wreath,
> Since even dreaming of the stone and bronze
> Brings headaches, pretty cousin, and defiles
> The clean white morning dresses.'
>
>   (II, 93–6)

The '"green wreath"' of leaves represents, for Romney, an Aurora who will stay '"pretty"' and '"clean"' in her '"white morning dresses"', and thus be a more picturesque and pleasing wife. Like Gilfillan, who praised Hemans for saving him from 'the ludicrous image of a double-dyed Blue … sweating at some stupendous treatise' (*Tait's*, 14 (1847), 361), Romney treacherously advises Aurora to avoid the '"headaches"' and dirty dresses of real work, and to keep to the pose of creativity which shows her person off to more advantage. To stand still in a wreath is thus turned back into the attitude, not of solitary poetic triumph as Aurora had fantasised, but of sexual and domestic appeal. It is as if Barrett Browning has found out the ideology behind her old favourite novel. By putting a man in the scene, she entirely changes its meaning. It is Romney's eye which both devalues Aurora's pose and then cunningly re-evaluates it in terms of its domestic propriety. The old double purpose of sensibility is thus exposed as Barrett Browning hints that, in the long run, it is Romney, not Aurora, who desires to play at statues. It is he who justifies, but only in his own terms, this standing about in a 'white' dress. Through such a deft reversal, which comments on the whole critical reception of women's poetry, she points out that, in fact, Romney's appreciation is worse than his scorn, for it traps the aspiring poet in the same formulas of romance as her predecessor, who sang to implore 'the protection of a friend' (de Staël, 1833: 21).

However, it is at this point that Aurora makes her break with the whole debilitating collusion of work and love which *Corinne* had encouraged. She tells Romney that she would rather be dead,

> 'than keep quiet here
> And gather up my feet from even a step
> For fear to soil my gown in so much dust.
> I choose to walk at all risks.'
>
>   (II, 103–6)

To rise and walk is a gesture full of defiance, not only of all the self-conscious statuary of the myth, but also of all the men in Elizabeth's own life: her father, brothers and Mr Hunter, who had a vested interest in her not 'daring to tread in the dust' (*MRM:* III, 81). Aurora, instead of being rejected, herself rejects the cousin who offers her a wreath as a plaything or an ornament, and goes in search of the real one with all its 'headaches'. *Aurora Leigh* is

Barrett Browning's poem of escape, both from the marital home and the Palace of Art (the two often subtly confused by critics) where, as a woman, she risks becoming a permanent fixture, whether angel or art work. In order not to be a Galatea but a Pygmalion, she must '"walk at all risks"'. Her declared aesthetic aim of rejecting 'togas and the picturesque' (V, 209) in order to capture her own 'live, throbbing age' (203) is connected with this rejection of an iconic poetic identity which ultimately only justifies the condescensions of male praise.

The scene of reunion between Aurora and Romney in Book VIII intriguingly parallels this first garden scene. But although it is June again, the place is Italy, Aurora has achieved fame in her writing and Romney is blind. This change is driven home in an image which crucially reverses the old roles:

> he, the man, appeared
> So pale and patient, like the marble man
> A sculptor puts his personal sadness in ...
>
> (VIII, 1099–101)

Now it is Romney who is the art object, the statue, and Aurora who walks free. Her reward at the end is not a triumphal crowning in public, but, almost its opposite: an invisibility which the darkness of the garden and the blindness of the man both emphasise. 'He had to be blinded, observe, to be made to see' (*Letters:* II, 242), Barrett Browning explained. Romney, who voices many of the prejudices and epigrams of the men Elizabeth knew and of the reviewers she had read, is deprived of the sense which lies behind the whole aesthetic of sensibility: the sense of sight. The eye of Phaon, for whom Sappho supposedly killed herself, the eye of Oswald, for whom Corinne paraded her art round Italy, the eye of Lockhart, which dissolved in tears at the frontispieces of women's poems, the eye of Mr Hunter, dogmatically fixed on women as clouds, and the eye of Romney himself, who once preferred Aurora to stand prettily in a garden rather than labour in the dust of the real world, are all forms of a controlling, external viewpoint, which turns women's art into a sight for men. Where Hemans and L.E.L. had played to a double audience, encoding a message to other women through their ritual appeals for one man's love, Barrett Browning, characteristically, exposes the contradiction. By blinding Romney, she attacks the whole sexually appreciating voyeurism of the literature she inherits.

To read this episode as part of a developing aesthetics rather than as a crude revenge of the plot is to avoid the embarrassment, either of Aurora seeming to be thus proved 'right' (Tompkins, 1961–2: 19) or of her seeming to be thus turned into another of Milton's daughters (Gilbert and Gubar, 1979: 578). Her triumphant invisibility at the end is, instead, a sign that she has freed herself from the applause of the Capitol. She has learned to write of something other than herself, and Romney's praise, which was once only praise of her looks, is now honest praise of her work. '"But, in this last book, / You showed me something separate from yourself"' (VIII, 606), he tells her. To gaze 'on Self apart' (1989: 187), as George Eliot puts it in 'Erinna', is to have achieved the artist's necessary breadth and scope of feeling. Romney's blindness is Aurora's sight, in a symbolic disequilibrium which runs through Victorian women's writing. Aurora has learned to see precisely because she has learned the insignificance of being seen; she has learned to write because she has learned the insignificance of being loved. She gets both love and fame in the end, but only because she has found them to be separate and different, each with their own requirements and their own rewards. Furthermore, she has learned the 'hard & cold thing', that love may be only an elaborate convention of feeling or a flattering fantasy of power. *Aurora Leigh* thus continues the work of the ballads in rescuing the woman from the thrall of being seen, or rather not seen, for all the angels, clouds and statues of men's eyes. It offers a drastic revision of the terms of romance, even if it is a revision for which Romney pays a high and somewhat obvious price.

It is this sceptical awareness of the sexual politics of sensibility which marks out Barrett Browning's poetry from that of her predecessors. Love, in her work, is not a sacred ideal, removed from the contingencies of the world, but is dragged in the dust of that reality which was itself so hard-won an experience and a theme for her.

Notes

1   In particular, Cora Kaplan, in her Introduction to *Aurora Leigh* (London: The Women's Press, 1978), takes Barrett Browning to task for her 'reactionary' rejection of Romney's socialism and for her middle-class lack of sympathy for the poor in the church scene (32). Deirdre David, in *Intellectual Women and Victorian Patriarchy* (London: Macmillan, 1987), is even more politically inquisitional, though her terms are somewhat baffling. She writes that 'As a political conservative favouring the values of the landowning classes in England, as a conservative poet lamenting the "defilement" of a once heroic culture, Barrett Browning speaks as a Gramscian traditional intellectual and abhors the liberalism and mercantilism of the swelling middle classes' (136). The problem with such anachronistic judgments is that they ignore the political realities and terminologies of Barrett Browning's own times.

Abbreviations

(Primary works are given in parenthesis in the text)

Elizabeth Barrett Browning:

- *Letters: The Letters of Elizabeth Barrett Browning,* 2 vols., ed. Frederic G. Kenyon, London, 1897.
- *CW: The Complete Works of Elizabeth Barrett Browning,* 6 vols., ed. Charlotte Porter and Helen A. Clarke, New York: Crowell, 1900.
- *RB: The Letters of Robert Browning and Elizabeth Barrett Browning 1845–1846,* 2 vols., ed. Elvan Kintner, Cambridge, Mass.: Harvard University Press, 1969.
- *AL: Aurora Leigh and Other Poems,* intro. Cora Kaplan, London: The Women's Press, 1978.
- *MRM: The Letters of Elizabeth Barrett Browning to Mary Russell Mitford: 1836–1854,* 3 vols., ed. Meredith B. Raymond and Mary Rose Sullivan, Winfield, Kans.: Wedgestone Press, 1983.

Works Cited

Cooper, Helen, *Elizabeth Barrett Browning, Woman & Artist* (Chapel Hill and London: The University of North Carolina Press, 1988)

de Staël, Mme., *Corinne: or Italy,* trans. Isabel Hill, with metrical versions of the odes by L. E. Landon (London 1836)

Eliot, George, *George Eliot: Collected Poems,* ed. Lucien Jenkins (London: Skoob Books, 1989)

Gilbert, Sandra M. and Susan Guber, *The Madwoman in the Attic: The Woman Writer and the Nineteenth-Century Literary Imagination* (New Haven and London: Yale University Press, 1979)

Gilfillan, George, 'Female Authors – Mrs. Hemans', *Tait's Edinburgh Magazine* 14 (June 1847), 359–63

Lessing, Doris, *A Man and Two Women* (St Albans: Panther, 1965)

Moers, Ellen, *Literary Women* (London: Women's Press, 1978)

Poovey, Mary, *The Proper lady and Woman Writer: Ideology as Style in the Works of Mary Wollstonecraft, Mary Shelley and Jane Austen* (Chicago and London: The University of Chicago Press, 1984)

Thomson, Patricia, *George Sand and the Victorians: Her Influence and Reputation in Nineteenth Century England* (London: Macmillan, 1977)

Tomkins, J. M. S., *Aurora Leigh, The Fawcett Lecture* (London, 1961–1962)

12 What Kind of Criticism? (1993)

Isobel Armstrong

What kind of criticism?

The most arresting discussions of Victorian poetry recently have come from Marxists, feminists and deconstruction. A critical history cannot be written from outside these debates with a false neutrality, for these are the contexts in which readers will read new discussions and the poets themselves.

Alan Sinfield's *Alfred Tennyson* is an impressive Marxist intervention which has quite properly shaken up accounts of Victorian poetry.[1] He reads Tennyson as a cultural materialist and inevitably sees him, as he was, as a conservative poet. Sinfield's hindsight enables him to argue that Tennyson's aesthetic solutions to political problems were either timid or straightforwardly reactionary. The poet's evasiveness leads to a perpetual emptying out of signification in which language resorts to a fetishistic preoccupation with its own surfaces rather than being deployed in the service of exploring meaning. Two difficulties emerge in the necessity to establish an unequivocally reactionary Tennyson. First, in order to pin Tennyson to political and religious positions, Sinfield has to eliminate the possibility of ambiguity in poetic language. Or when confronted with two contending meanings he has to opt for one as being 'really' the intended meaning. Similarly, in order to argue Tennyson's political bad faith he has to argue that Tennyson's 'real' interests as a sympathiser with the landed gentry and as a supporter of nationalism and imperialistic interests must give a poem a particular historical meaning even when it appears to be struggling against it. Thus he virtually makes Tennyson personally responsible for the colonialist ravaging of Tahiti as a result of 'The Lotos-Eaters'. He excludes the element of struggle with the element of ambiguity. Eve Sedgwick's brilliant feminist reading of *The Princess* in *Between Men* adopts rather the same strategy.[2] She argues that far from being a para-feminist poem, as the stated project of *The Princess* insists, Tennyson's poem actually or 'really' deals with the patriarchal homosocial bonding which makes women an object of exchange between men. She makes an impressive analysis of the structure of the poem in order to demonstrate the case. However, rather like Sinfield, she makes her argument stick by first excluding ambiguity, or staying with those elements of ambiguity which corroborate the case. Secondly, the deconstruction of the poem has to take place by the introduction of a very narrow form of intentionality. Tennyson 'meant' to write a poem in celebration of women but the manifest intention of the text is subverted by its latent homosocial desires. This distinction between what is meant and what happens assumes that the text has a manifest and a latent content, a conscious and unconscious desire. The difficulty about this is that everything that is observed is all there in the text anyway, and it is a strangely arbitrary decision which makes some elements of the text manifest and some latent, some conscious and some unconscious, since all elements of the text are actually manifest. A process of selection has gone on, in which the critic has decided to select an intentional and an unintentional project. To simplify a text's projects and then to invoke the complexities of the text itself to undermine the simple project is an odd procedure. A text is not quite like a patient in analysis and actually anticipates these strategies of deconstruction by enabling them to take place.

The problem of deciding what is 'really' a poet's interests politically or what is 'really' intentional as against unconscious can be circumvented by a more generous understanding of the text as struggle. A text is endless struggle and contention, struggle with a changing project, struggle with the play of ambiguity and contradiction. This is a way of reading which gives equal weight to a text's stated project and the polysemic and possibly wayward meanings it generates. 'The Lotos-Eaters', for instance, can be read as a struggle with an impossible ideology of consciousness, labour and consumption which lays bare the poverty of accounts of social relationships underlying these conceptions in a language which libidinously orchestrates the deranged perceptions and desires of the subject, who is either consumed by work or destroyed by cessation from it. Rather than longing for retreat, the poem struggles with what constitutes the self as divided between labour and the cessation of labour. Its exploration is nearer to Marx's understanding of the estranged labour which converts all energy expended outside work into subhuman or animal experience than to an account of the text as a simple desire for escape and exploitation of resources. The desire for escape is involved, of course, in the struggle with the nature of work. But it is not the primary 'intentional' project of the poem.

To see the text as a complex entity defining and participating in an area of struggle and contention is to make intentionality a much wider and more complex affair and to include the contradictions and uncontrolled nature of language within the text's project. For the escape of language from univocal order becomes one of the text's areas of contention and not part of its latent unconscious. (And, as I have suggested in my discussion of Carlyle, the advantage of this strategy is that the Victorians themselves were aware of the 'escape' of language from control.) Perhaps this encounters the danger of accepting complexity to the extent that we can map deconstructive processes on to the text, and, as it were, leave the text alone with its intricacies and to its ludic activities. To do this, however, would be to attribute to the text a composure with its difficulties which few texts have. It would be precisely not to engage in that understanding of the unsettled nature of the text which deconstruction has elicited. And it ignores the ideological struggles of the text. Post-Derridean criticism, however, tends to ignore the aspect of active struggle in a text. Volosinov, taking up a different form of the Hegelian tradition than the one from which deconstruction stems, puts the struggle with language at the centre of a text, and such a concentration on language should help in the rereading of Victorian poetry.[3]

A clever critic of Browning, Herbert Tucker, has noticed the linguistic intricacy of Victorian poetry and used the strategies of deconstruction in *Browning's Beginnings* to elicit Browning's complexities, but he tends to stay with them rather than to probe what is problematical and conflicting.[4] To concentrate on the ludic energies of language rather than its conflicts is to miss the underlying element of struggle in poetry of this period, its engagement with a content, its political awareness. What is linguistically and formally complex in Victorian poetry seems to me to arise from stress. To understand what is stressful, and why, it is important to link linguistic and formal contradictions to the substantive issues at stake in the poems – issues of politics, gender and epistemology, the problem of relationship and the continual attempts to reinvest the content of self and other. An earlier generation of writers attempted to understand the form of Victorian poetry as the function of a complex of social and psychosocial problems.

E. D. H. Johnson, in *The Alien Vision of Victorian Poetry,* explored the terms of Victorian poetry in relation to an increasingly severe lesion between the poet and society.[5] Robert Langbaum in *The Poetry of Experience* studied the dramatic monologue as an attempted solution to a cultural crisis in which the conceptualisation of the self and its relations acknowledged a split between insight and judgement, empathy and detachment.[6] Though Johnson tends to remain too narrowly with existential subjectivity and Langbaum's readings return a trifle rapidly to the ethical, these books are important in their attempts to read Victorian poetry in a sophisticated way in terms of a cultural analysis, attempts which, along with Morse Peckham's readings of Victorian poetry, seem to have terminated the valuable project they began.[7]

Perhaps what was lacking in these studies (and which may account for the subsequent lack of creative followers) was an account of the language of Victorian poetry in relation to both formal and cultural problems, an attempt to see these things as inseparable from one another. The link between cultural complexities and the complexities of language is indirect but can be perceived. We might start with the nature of language in Victorian poetry. For to read a Victorian poem is to be made acutely aware of the fact that it is made of language. Whether it is the strange, arcane artifice of Tennyson's early poems or the splutter of speech in Browning, the limpid economy of Christina Rossetti, Swinburne's swamping rhythms, Hopkins's muscle-bound syntax, the sheer verbalness of poetry is foregrounded. It is as if the poet's secondariness takes a stand on the self-conscious assertion of the unique discourse of poetry. This is connected with the overdetermination of ambiguity. The open nerve of exposed feeling in Tennyson is registered in a language fraught with ambiguity. Christina Rossetti's distilled exactitude analyses into an equally precise ambiguity. Signification in Browning shifts and lurches almost vertiginously. The structural ambiguities of Romantic syntax have intensified to an extent that coalescing syntax and semantic openness is the norm. In an age of 'movable type' and mechanical reproduction in which signification moves beyond the immediate control of the writer it is as if the writer can only resort to an openness in advance of the reader, testing out the possibilities of systematic misprision. Such language draws attention to the nature of words as a medium of representation. In the same way poets resort to songs and speech, as if to foreground the act of reading a secondary text, for the song is not sung but read, and the speech is not spoken but written.

Hopkins saw the openness of his contemporaries as anarchy and flux and desperately tried to arrest it, reintroducing an agonised, sundered language of ambiguity in spite of himself.[8] Arnold saw it as the product of disorganised subjectivity, and in a brilliant phrase, summed up nineteenth-century poetry as 'the dialogue of the mind with itself', and attempted to freeze poetry back into classical form.[9] Neither, however, saw that this was a systematic and organised ambiguity. The doubleness of language is not local but structural. It must be read closely, not loosely. It is not the disorganised expression of subjectivity but a way of exploring and interrogating the grounds of its representation. What the Victorian poet achieved was often quite literally two concurrent poems in the same words.

Schopenhauer wrote of the lyric poet as uttering between two poles of feeling, between the pure undivided condition of unified selfhood and the needy, fracturing self-awareness of the interrogating consciousness.[10] The Victorian poet does not swing between these two forms of utterance but dramatises and objectifies their simultaneous existence. There is a kind of duplicity involved here, for the poet often invites the simple reading by presenting a poem as lyric expression as the perceiving subject speaks. Mariana's lament or Fra Lippo Lippi's apologetics are expressions, indeed, composed in an expressive form. But in a feat of recomposition and externalisation the poem turns its expressive utterance around so that it becomes the opposite of itself, not only the *subject's* utterance but the *object* of analysis and critique. It is, as it were, reclassified as drama in the act of being literal lyric expression. To re-order lyric expression as drama is to give it a new content and to introduce the possibility of interrogation and critique. Mariana's torture in isolation, for instance, is the utterance of a subjective psychological condition, but that psychological expression is reversed into being the object of analysis and restructured as a symptomatic form by the act of narration, which draws attention to the reiterated refrain of the poem as Mariana's speech, speech which attempts to arrest temporality while time moves on in the narrator's commentary. The poignant expression of exclusion to which Mariana's state gives rise, and which is reiterated in the marking of barriers – the moat itself, the gate with clinking latch, the curtained casement, the hinged doors – is simultaneously an analysis of the hypersensitive hysteria induced by the coercion of sexual taboo. These are hymenal taboos, which Mariana is induced, by a cultural consensus which is hidden from her, to experience as her own condition. Hidden from her, but not from the poem, the barriers are man-made, cunningly constructed through the material fabric of the house she inhabits, the enclosed spaces in which she is confined. It is the narrative voice which describes these spaces, not Mariana as speaker.

The dramatic nature of Victorian poetry was understood by its earliest critics, by W. J. Fox and Arthur Hallam in particular, but seems to have been lost to later readers.[11] Twentieth-century readers have been right to see the dramatic monologue as the primary Victorian genre, even though they have too often codified it in terms of technical features. Other devices, such as the framed narrative or the dream, dialogue or parody, are related to it. All enable double forms to emerge. Rather than to elicit its technical features, it is preferable to see what this dramatic form enabled the poet to explore. By seeing utterance both as subject and as object, it was possible for the poet to explore expressive psychological forms simultaneously as psychological conditions *and* as constructs, the phenomenology of a culture, projections which indicate the structure of relationships. I have called this objectification of consciousness a phenomenological form because phenomenology seeks to describe and analyse the manifestations of consciousness rather than its internal condition. Thus such a reading relates consciousness to the external forms of the culture in which it exists. The gap between subjective and objective readings often initiates a debate between a subject-centred or expressive and a phenomenological or analytical reading, but above all it draws attention to the act of representation, the act of relationship and the mediations of language, different in a psychological and in a phenomenological world.

The struggle between two kinds of reading is highly complex. It is not a question of a simple dialogue or dialectic form in which the opposition between two terms is fixed and settled. Such an opposition too often is what the dialogic has come to mean. But we have only to look at 'Mariana' to see that the cultural or phenomenological reading which changes the status of Mariana's utterance as lyric expression is subject to unsettling pressures in its turn. In the phenomenological reading, Mariana's anguish becomes no longer something for which she is psychologically responsible. When under the scrutiny of phenomenological critique the terrible privacy of her obsessional condition, her inability to gaze on the external world except at night, becomes the function of a death wish to which she has been induced without fully realising that she has been driven to it. On the other hand, this suicidal condition asks questions of the cultural reading. Is not the phenomenological reading too ready to concede that this is a situation 'without hope of change', too ready to metaphorise Mariana's emotions in terms of projection onto the external world ('blackest moss', 'blacken'd water'), which becomes an extension of her condition even though the landscape operates quite independently of her? The external world becomes both her psychic environment and an existence from which she is irretrievably estranged. The phenomenological reading seems uncertain of these relations. Is it not too ready to narrow the grounds of feminine sexuality as the passive object of experience (notice the 'wooing wind')? Thus it arrives at a self-fulfilling reading of estrangement in which Mariana *must* be alienated. And so the status of the phenomenological reading is changed. It cannot be metacommentary with clean hands entirely in charge of the grounds of debate. And this reflects back onto Mariana as subject. Her loathing of the day and the derangement of her perception is a rebellious act in this context, and questions have to be asked about her autonomy and the extent of her passivity. It might well be that the fragmented self she becomes is both cause and effect of a particular way of conceiving of feminine subjectivity. And it is difficult to say whether Mariana's condition is a violent protest or a passive response to such conceptions of the feminine. What is here is nothing so straightforward as a simple opposition but a dynamic text in which lyric description and analysis are repeatedly redefining the terms of a question and contending for its ground. To probe the status of one form of utterance is to call forth an analysis of the status of *that* interpretation, and so on. If this is a dialogue or a dialectical form it is so in all the antagonistic complexity of the Hegelian master-slave dialectic in which the mediations between different positions are so rapid and subtle, so continually changing places in the relationship of authority, that the play of difference can hardly be resolved.

To see the text as struggle continually investing terms with a new content is to see it as a responsive rather than as a symptomatic discourse. Both the Marxist and feminist readings to which I have referred consider the Victorian poem in different ways as a symptom of the political unconscious and thus irrevocably blind to its own meaning. No text can account for the way it is read in future cultures but it can establish the grounds of the struggle for meaning. There is a difference between what is blindfold and what is unpredictable. What I would call a new Hegelian reading avoids symptomatic interpretations, just as it avoids the endless ludic contradictions which sometimes emerge from deconstruction. A text which struggles with the logic of its own contradictions is in any case arguably nearer, though not identical with, Derridean principles, in which a text is threatened by collapse from internal oppositions, than to the systematic incoherence which deconstruction sometimes elicits.

True to its status as a transitional form Victorian poetry has either been used to confirm a general critical theory, as in the readings of Bloom, or been seen simply as an instance of a particular historical case, for which a particular critical reading is necessary, as in the readings of Johnson or Langbaum. What I have done is to develop the political implications of Johnson's work and the epistemological implications of Langbaum. Langbaum is also concerned with the double reading, though his way of seeing the judgemental reading as a *control* on the empathetic reading seems to me to state the problem too rigidly in moral rather than analytical terms. It is without that sense of a new content which evolves when the subjective reading reverses into critique and so back and forth between critique and expressive form. 'Mariana' is an exemplary case of this process.

When the full importance of Victorian poetry is recognised, however, it becomes apparent that it need not be discussed either as illustrative material for theory or as a particular case. It surely marks an extraordinarily self-conscious moment of awareness in history. A poetic form and a language were evolved which not only make possible a sophisticated exploration of new categories of knowledge in modern culture but also the philosophical criticism adequate to it. The sense of secondariness with which Victorian poetry comes into being produces the double poem, two poems in one. The double poem, with its systematically ambiguous language, out of which expressive and phenomenological readings emerge, is a structure commensurate with the 'movable type' which Carlyle saw as both the repercussion and the cause of shifts in nineteenth-century culture. The double poem belongs to a post-teleological, post-revolutionary, post-industrial and post-Kantian world and its interrelated manifestations. The double poem signifies a godless, non-teleological world because as soon as two readings become possible and necessary, the permanent and universal categories of the 'type' dissolve. For the 'type' is of course an ancient theological word, meaning those fixed categories of thought and language ordained by God which governed relationships, well before it becomes associated with print. The double reading inevitably dissolves such fixity, just as it means a shift from ontology to epistemology, a shift from investigating the grounds of being to a sceptical interrogation of the grounds of knowledge, which becomes phenomenology, not belief. In a post-revolutionary world in which power is supposedly vested in many rather than a privileged class, the double poem dramatises relationships of power. In the twofold reading, struggle is structurally necessary and becomes the organising principle, as critique successively challenges and redefines critique. Movable type, where technology mobilises the logos, makes the process of signification a political matter as it opens up a struggle for the meaning of words which is part of the relations of power explored through the structures of the poem. Hence the poet's systematic exploration of ambiguity. This reveals not only the confounding complexities of language and the anxieties this generates but boldly establishes that play of possibility in which meaning can be decided. It draws attention to the fact that meaning *is* decided by cultural consensus even while its ambiguity offers the possibility of challenging that consensus through the double reading. The poem of the post-industrial world recognises the displacement of relationships in its structure as well as in its language. The formal ploy in which the uttering subject becomes object and the poem reverses relationships not once but many times indicates that epistemological uneasiness in which subject and object, self and world, are no longer in lucid relation with one another but have to be perpetually redefined. The structure of the double poem emerges from the condition in which self-creation in the world is no longer straightforward but indirect and problematical and in which, as Carlyle said, 'nothing is done directly'. Finally, the double structure inevitably draws attention to the act of interpretation, since one reading encounters another and moves to a new content in the process. Hermeneutic self-consciousness leads in its turn to concentration on the nature of representation, for if interpretation is in question as a construct, so also are the categories of thought it deals with. In a post-Kantian world the double poem becomes a representation of representation, not only secondary historically but a second-order activity in itself. Mariana's poignant utterance is framed as the solipsistic constructions of her world and this reflects back on the complexity of the framing process which presents that self-enclosed utterance. It too cannot be exempted from the second-order status. If one utterance is a representation, so is the other. Both are ideological and both confront one another.

It would not be too much to claim that the genesis of modern form and its *problems* arise in the double poem, just as the possibilities for a criticism which interrogates the nature of the speaking subject and deconstructs the contradictory assumptions of the text are generated out of the double reading. The philosophical premises for a criticism commensurate with this complexity arise in the twentieth century and not in the nineteenth century but they follow from nineteenth-century poetic experiment which, I suggest, is bolder and more self-conscious than most poetry subsequent to it. This is not to argue neatly that Victorian poetry should be studied because it 'produces' and confirms the deconstructive moment and that here we have the 'original' deconstructive form. Rather it should be recognised that the deconstructive moment *is* a historical moment, and that Victorian poetry anticipates its strategies and moves beyond it. For, committed to going through the process of 'movable type', the double poem confronts the scepticism of the deconstructive moment and challenges it. Victorian poems are sceptical and affirmative simultaneously for they compel a strenuous reading and assume an active reader who will participate in the struggle of the lyric voice, a reader with choices to make, choices which are created by the terms of the poem itself. The active reader is compelled to be internal to the poem's contradictions and recomposes the poem's processes in the act of comprehending them as ideological struggle. There is no end to struggle because there is no end to the creative constructs and the renewal of content which its energy brings forth.

Rereading Victorian poetry, then, involves a reconsideration of the way we conceptualise history and culture, and the way we see the politics of poetry. It also involves rethinking some of the major criticism of this century, Marxist and feminist criticism and deconstruction, and considering how the language and form of Victorian poetry question the theories they have developed.

Notes

1 Alan Sinfield, *Alfred Tennyson,* Rereading Literature Series, Oxford, 1986.
2 Eve Kosofsky Sedgwick, *Between Men: English Literature and Male Homosocial Desire,* New York, 1985.
3 V. N. Volosinov, *Marxism and the Philosophy of Language,* trans. L. Matejka, I. R. Titanik, Cambridge, Mass., 1986. Volosinov's contention that both written and spoken language participates in a struggle for the sign long precedes, of course, the work of deconstruction, but the possibilities of his work, even though he excluded poetry from the activity of struggle, are only comparatively recently being discovered. In saying that both Volosinov's work and that of Derrida stem from Hegel I am oversimplifying both. Volosinov is a Marxist in contention with linguistics, but his concept of struggle goes back to Hegel's master-slave dialectic. Derrida develops and transforms the premises of Sausserean linguistics, as Volosinov does not, and he dissents from the master-slave dialectic and develops the alternative concept of *différance.* Arguably, however, *différance* as the constant repositioning of relationship arrests a stage of Hegelian thought. The strength of Volosinov is that he finds a way of conceptualising linguistic struggle.
4 Herbert S. Tucker Jnr, *Browning's Beginnings: The Art of Disclosure,* Minnesota, 1980.
5 E. D. H. Johnson, *The Alien Vision of Victorian Poetry; Sources of the Poetic Imagination in Tennyson, Browning and Arnold,* Princeton, N.J., 1952.
6 Robert Langbaum, *The Poetry of Experience: The Dramatic Monologue in Modern Literary Tradition,* London, 1957.
7 There is much valuable uncollected work by Morse Peckham, for example, his centenary essay on Browning's *The Ring and The Book,* 'Historiography and *The Ring and The Book',* Victorian Poetry 6 (1968), 243–57.
8 G. M. Hopkins believed that the looseness of the language of nineteenth-century poetry reflected the lax relativism of the age, which he describes in some of his earliest writings. 'The probable future of metaphysics', *The Journals and Papers of Gerard Manley Hopkins,* Humphrey House, Graham Strong, eds, London, 1959, 118–21.
9 Arnold's brilliant but limited diagnosis of modernity and its problems appears in the Preface to his *Poems* of 1853, in which he explained his reasons for withdrawing that modern poem, *Empedocles on Etna* (1852), from his volume: 'the dialogue of the mind with itself has commenced; modern problems have presented themselves'. *The Poems of Matthew Arnold* (Longman Annotated English Poets), Kenneth Allott, ed., London, 1965, 591.
10 Nietzsche quotes Schopenhauer's account of lyric critically in *The Birth of Tragedy:* 'It is the subject of the will, i.e. his own volition, which fills the consciousness of the singer, often as a released and satisfied desire (joy), but still oftener as an inhibited desire (grief), always as an affect, a passion, a moved state of mind ... the stress of desire, which is always restricted and always needy'. *The Birth of Tragedy* (1872), trans. Walter Kaufmann, New York, 1967, 51.
11 Both W. J. Fox and A. H. Hallam conducted sophisticated analyses of Tennyson's early poems in terms of drama. See *Victorian Scrutinies: Reviews of Poetry 1830–70,* Isobel Armstrong, ed., London, 1972, 75–9, 99–101.

13 Introduction to *The Poetry of Chartism: Aesthetics, Politics, History* (2009)

Mike Sanders

Introduction

The *Northern Star's* poetry column for 18 May 1839, carries a factory reform poem written by a woman known to history only as E. H., 'a Factory Girl of Stalybridge'. In this poem entitled, 'On Joseph Rayner Stephens', E. H. compares her position with that of the millowners' children and wives. The contrast she draws between their advantages purchased, she believes, at the cost of her own class's impoverishment is a common rhetorical device in early Victorian social discourse. Less familiar, perhaps, is the content of this trope, for E. H. protests her cultural deprivation as bitterly as any material deprivation:

> Their children, too, to school must be sent,
> Till all kinds of learning and music have learnt;
> Their wives must have veils, silks dresses, and cloaks,
> And some who support them can't get linsey coats.

Two stanzas later E. H. returns to the question of cultural entitlement – 'If they had sent us to school, better rhyme we could make, / And I think it is time we had some of their cake'. In this simple rhyming couplet E. H. attests to poetry's importance in the working-class movement. Here poetry is figured as a luxury rather than a fundamental necessity – cake rather than bread – but nonetheless it is something to which E. H. believes she is entitled. In her imagination, poetry equates with plenty; it signifies the desire for 'something more', the 'something better' which impelled Chartism.

Precisely because the history of all hitherto existing society is the history of scarcity, we have grown accustomed to hearing the cries for bread. In comparison the call for cake sounds anomalous. The inability to appreciate the difference between the two has entered popular consciousness as one of the causes of the French Revolution. If the call for cake seems outlandish as a popular demand, then the call for poetry seems equally improbable. To imagine a nineteenth-century workers' movement demanding the right to versify alongside the demand for the vote and better working and living conditions seems incredible. Yet for E. H. these demands were inseparable, and she ends her poem by returning to the subject:

> We factory lasses have but little time,
> So I hope you will pardon my bad written rhyme.
> God bless him for striving to get us our rights,
> And I wish the world over were true Stephenites.

A Stephenite I am from the ground of my heart,
And I hope from the same I shall never depart.
May God spare your life till the tyrants are ended,
So I bid you good bye, till my verses I've mended.

E. H. knows she is writing 'bad' poetry and wants to write better verse; aesthetic standards mattered to her as they did to the rest of the Chartist movement. A dozen years later, at the end of the period covered by this study, a similar note is struck by the better-known Chartist poet, Gerald Massey. Addressing a poetic comrade in the preface to his first collection of Chartist verse, *Voices of Freedom and Lyrics of Love* (1851), Massey simultaneously acknowledges and excuses his poetic shortcomings. He identifies a lack of education and limited exposure to poetry's 'great masters' as the causes of the intellectual and aesthetic weakness of his poetry which, he asserts, is nonetheless justified by its truthfulness and sincerity:

> No one knows better than myself how unworthy [these poems] are of our common cause; no one knows so well as myself how far I have fallen short of what I had thought to perform; but the builder can only erect his edifice according to his material, and I have not much book lore ... until of late, I have been quite shut out from the great masters of the lyre, and the mighty in the realms of thought. In my 'Voices of Freedom' I have endeavoured to utter what is stirring in poor men's hearts. The thoughts may be unripe, and the utterance crude, but what is written, is written in my own life's-blood; and you, at least, will not despise my earnest sincerity.[1]

E. H. and Massey assume that the political struggle to which they were committed, required not just poetry – but the best poetry. This study originates in a desire to understand the terms of this conjunction of aesthetics and politics effected by the Chartist movement. In addition, it seeks to abandon the defensive formulations of E. H. and Massey by celebrating the aesthetic and political achievements of Chartist poetry – to join with *The Chartist Circular* in denying 'that the union of poetry with politics is always hurtful to the politics, and fatal to the poetry', and with *The Friend of the People* in affirming the value of those 'eloquent outpourings of the complaints of the people, passionate appeals for justice, [and] lofty dreamings of the great future, when SLAVERY and MISERY shall be no more'.[2]

Before beginning this study, I regarded Chartist proclamations of the importance of poetry with a large measure of scepticism and privileged the political over the aesthetic as the site of significant Chartist activity. This assumption fell away in the face of a prolonged encounter with the Chartist press in general, and its leading newspaper the *Northern Star* (NS) in particular, which convinced me that poetry played an active, primary role within the movement. Chapter 1, The Chartist imaginary: 'talking by turns of politics and poetry', is the result of the realisation that for the Chartist movement, the political and the aesthetic are not just closely related concepts but are thoroughly imbricated practices. The chapter provides the theoretical underpinning for this study's claim that Chartist poetry constitutes both a distinctive form of agency and a unique form of historical knowledge. The unity of these twin facets of Chartist poetry constitutes the realm of the Chartist imaginary.

Chapter 2 examines the reception and critical history of Chartist poetry over the past century and a half. It charts the fluctuating visibility of Chartist poetry over this period and discusses the work of the most significant critics working in this field. It notes that the existing critical tradition has tended to concentrate on the work of a handful of 'labour laureates' (most notably Ernest Jones, Thomas Cooper, Gerald Massey and W. J. Linton) who are atypical

Chartist poets insofar as the overwhelming majority of Chartist poets enjoyed at best a limited, local rather than national reputation, and published their work in the periodical press rather than in single volumes. Therefore, this study takes the poetry column of a given journal rather than the individual poet as its object of analysis. Chapter 3 represents the methodological outgrowth of this argument. It provides an empirical analysis of the poetry column of the leading Chartist newspaper, the *Northern Star,* quantifying the number of poems and poets published on an annual basis as well as the ratio of Chartist to non-Chartist poetry in its columns. In addition, Chapter 3 seeks to reconstruct the poetry column's editorial policy, paying particular attention to its attempts to raise the quality of Chartist poetic production from 1844 onwards.

Chapters 4, 5 and 6 examine the *Northern Star's* poetry column during the periods of political crisis which accompanied the presentation of each of the three national petitions in 1839, 1842 and 1848. Chapter 4 deals with the aftermath of the 'Newport uprising' in November 1839 and focuses in particular on the insurrection's ideological afterlife in the *Northern Star.* It examines the role of the poetry column in explaining and interpreting Newport and its treatment of the themes of exile and return following the transportation of the uprising's leader, John Frost. Chapter 5 deals with Chartism's resurgence in 1842 when a massive strike-wave in the aftermath of the rejection of the second petition constituted one of the most serious challenges to the British state in the entire nineteenth century. It demonstrates the crucial role played by the *Northern Star's* poetry column both in the reconstruction of Chartist identity in the post-Newport period, and in the emergence of a more sophisticated economic and political critique. It examines the reworking of established Chartist poetic tropes in relation to the unresolved contradictions in Chartist strategy, before ending with an analysis of the role of 'nostalgia' in the Chartist imaginary in 1842. Chapter 6 examines the poetry column during the year of European revolutions, 1848. It traces Chartism's response to the revolutionary nationalism which swept both Ireland and continental Europe, and to the defeat of those same forces in the latter half of that turbulent year. It examines the consolidation of a new structure of feeling – 'red republicanism' – and analyses its accompanying new poetic, which consolidates the emergent political and economic critique identified in the previous chapter.

Chapter 7 differs from the preceding three chapters by concentrating on the work of an individual Chartist poet, Gerald Massey, rather than the *Northern Star's* poetry column. It does so in order to capture the idiosyncratic qualities of late (post-1848) Chartist poetry, with its distinctive figuring of the relationship between forms of temporal understanding and political activity. In particular, this chapter seeks to differentiate between the 'messianic' (used in its Benjaminian sense) and the 'millenarian' in Massey's poetry, as exemplifying the ideological trajectory of the wider Chartist movement in this period. Massey's attempt to preserve hope at a moment of profound historical defeat provides a fitting coda for the Chartist imaginary:

> 'All's well!' saith the sentry on tyranny's tower,
> 'Even Hope by their watch-fire is grey and tear-blind.'
> Aye, all's well! Freedom's altar burns hour by hour –
> Live brands for the fire-damps with which ye are mined.[3]

Notes

1 Gerald Massey, *Voices of Freedom and Lyrics of Love* (J. Watson, 1851), i.
2 *The Chartist Circular*, 11 July 1840, 170. *The Friend of the People,* 3 May 1851, 187.
3 Gerald Massey, 'Our Symbol', *Voices of Freedom*, 10. This poem also appeared in the first number of *The Red Republican* under the title 'The Red Banner'.

14 'Literary Persuasions', Introduction to *The Art of Eloquence: Byron, Dickens, Tennyson, Joyce* (2007)

Matthew Bevis

Disinterested parties

In *Great Expectations* (1860–1), Pip and Herbert watch Mr Wopsle perform the lead role in *Hamlet.* Nearly everything that could go wrong does go wrong, and soon even the Prince of Denmark himself is the subject of the audience's laughter:

> Upon my unfortunate townsman all these incidents accumulated with playful effect. Whenever that undecided Prince had to ask a question or state a doubt, the public helped him out with it. As for example; on the question whether 'twas nobler in the mind to suffer, some roared yes, and some no, and some inclining to both opinions said 'toss up for it;' and quite a Debating Society arose. When he asked what should such fellows as he do crawling between earth and heaven, he was encouraged with loud cries of 'Hear, hear!'[1]

The drama begins to resemble a scene from the floor of the House of Commons, with some members chiming in 'Hear, hear', others murmuring their disapproval from the back benches. Wopsle is translated from player to orator, and Pip finds himself 'feeling keenly for him, but laughing, nevertheless, from ear to ear' (p. 255); even Pip's recollection is inflected with the audience's cries, for 'ear to ear' echoes 'Hear, hear'. After the farcical performance, Herbert and Pip dine with Wopsle, sitting up with him until two in the morning to indulge him in his pipe dreams for 'reviving the Drama'. When Pip retires to bed, mulling over his chances with Estella, we begin to sense one reason why he felt so keenly for the actor. The chapter ends as he falls asleep: '[I] miserably dreamed that my expectations were all cancelled, and that I had to give my hand in marriage to Herbert's Clara, or to play Hamlet to Miss Havisham's Ghost, before twenty thousand people, without knowing twenty words of it' (p. 258). It's as though Pip sees his own predicament in Wopsle's—full of great expectations, haunted as well as taunted by voices off-stage, a public figure faced by the nightmare of a demanding audience.

This scene, like many others in *Great Expectations,* is itself haunted by a book that appeared a year before it began its serial run: Samuel Smile's *Self-Help* (the phrase 'great expectations' is employed by an orator in the first chapter of Smiles's book).[2] *Self-Help* (1859) tells of another who was trying to make his way in the world, Benjamin Disraeli:

> As an orator too, his first appearance in the House of Commons was a failure. It was spoken of as 'more screaming than an Adelphi farce'. Though composed in a grand

and ambitious strain, every sentence was hailed with 'loud laughter'. 'Hamlet' played as a comedy were nothing to it. But he concluded with a sentence which embodied a prophecy. Writhing under the laughter with which his studied eloquence had been received, he exclaimed, 'I have begun several things many times, and have succeeded in them at last. I shall sit down now, but the time will come when you will hear me.'[3]

The Times report of the speech makes for entertaining reading—'"Nothing was so easy as to laugh" (Increased laughter)'[4]—and when Disraeli finishes up with the prophecy 'you will hear me', his audience eagerly chimes in: 'Hear, hear.'[5] Like Wopsle's, Disraeli's 'grand and ambitious strain' is the occasion for 'playful effects', something akin to *Hamlet* performed as a comedy of errors. But Disraeli was proved right (this is why Smiles is telling the story), rising to the top of the greasy pole of politics despite his inauspicious start. Significantly, when we come across Wopsle again later in Dickens's novel, we find that he is no longer playing the Prince who loiters at the edge of court, but 'a plenipotentiary of great power' who has 'a gracious dignity' and is addressed as 'Your Honour' (pp. 383–4).

Much of Dickens's fiction—and much other nineteenth-century writing—is shadowed in this way by oratorical trials and tribulations. When Wopsle finds his soliloquies reshaped into dialogues by a 'Debating Society', his predicament is a miniature version of a larger development that sees literary rumination involved in scenes of debate and persuasion. On the jubilee of the Oxford Union in 1873, a reporter for *The Times* enthused:

> In the course of these fifty years we have become a nation of public speakers. Everyone speaks now ... Eloquence is but a facility, or instrument, or weapon, or accomplishment, or, in academic terms, an art ... We are now more than ever a debating, that is, a Parliamentary people.[6]

These multiple definitions of 'eloquence' invite a question. If eloquence might be an art in a nation of public speakers, then what could art become? During the nineteenth century, a commitment to literary eloquence involved consideration of how far it might, or should, be both a 'weapon' and an 'art'. This book explores how four writers responded to a debating, parliamentary people, and examines the ways in which they and their publics conceived the relations between political speech and literary endeavour. It envisages literary 'persuasion' not just as an attempt to get someone to adopt a position (although it is sometimes that), but also as a certain kind of disposition—one drawn to the study of conflicting allegiances and principles. Such a persuasion—asking questions, stating doubts—partakes of the nature of 'that undecided Prince' that Wopsle was playing, and it echoes throughout the period.

[...]

In a speech on 'Politics and Literature', William Gladstone hinted at these seemingly opposed trends. The politician hoped that

> the *absolute integrity of mental labour and enquiry* might never be compromised in whole or in part by the seductions of immediate popular applause. (Hear, Hear). With this reservation he rejoiced that men like Sir Walter Scott, Charles Dickens and Alfred Tennyson had received from the public such an acknowledgement of their works as was a substantial evidence of gratitude, if not an adequate reward, and in the nature of an *absolute guarantee of the freedom and independence* of the modern literary work. (Cheers).[7]

The studied sentences and polished periods have their charm, but 'Hear, Hear' follows so quickly on the heels of Gladstone's worries about 'applause' that we are perhaps inclined to smile rather than to cheer. Having more time than the audience, a reader can note that the orator's 'absolute's point to a mixed state of affairs: the first suggests that literature's relations with the 'immediate' are to be avoided; the second asserts that, for these writers, the contemporary public has been the guarantee of 'freedom'.

The writers who appear in the following chapters would not have been entirely at ease with Gladstone's eulogy. Their negotiations with an increasingly political public show that the integrity of 'the modern literary work' often involved a mediation between the 'immediate' and the 'independent'. The politician may vaunt the 'freedom' of literature from immediate public debate, but the cost of such freedom might entail a view of literary achievement that precludes formative socio-political influence. Even as they felt the need for a form of eloquence in which immediate commitment could be tempered by other considerations, Byron, Dickens, Tennyson, and Joyce were aware that a disinterested independence might shade into an irresponsible indifference. One reason for focusing on these writers is that their struggles are representative of a dilemma faced by others in the period. As Philip Davis has observed:

> Two opposite but mutually linked tendencies were going on at the same time, as though struggling to belong together: on the one hand, the establishment of literature as a distinct and defended area, also a separate profession and even an industry; on the other, within those forms, a counter-tendency which internally recommitted art—in its content, in its urgency—to the service of the world outside.[8]

My interest lies in how writers sought to bring these opposing tendencies into fruitful dialogue, and in how they aimed to cultivate a 'literary' detachment that could gain critical purchase on political arguments without being conceived as a culpable isolation from them. Such a study needs to reflect on the kinds of responsibility that writers have when they seek to address political issues in their work, and to examine the ways in which a style of writing might act as a spur to, or disclaimer of, political sympathies.

Matthew Arnold's deliberations over the value of 'Culture' and 'disinterestedness' bring these questions into sharper focus. Arnold's presence at many of the 1866–7 reform debates in Parliament prompted him to write those articles that would make up *Culture and Anarchy* (1869), a book that continually objected to the uncultured polemics of contemporary political argument. 'Culture is of like spirit with poetry,' he claimed, and this spirit was being neglected by the party spirit at Westminster. Arnold's book takes its bearings from the speech it hears, opening with the words 'In one of his speeches a short time ago ...', going on to criticize those orators who were for and those who were against reform, and dreaming at its close of an eloquence that would contain a 'power of disinterested play of consciousness' to answer 'any House of Commons' orator, or practical operator in politics'.[9] This emphasis on the 'power' of disinterestedness and the alignment of 'culture' with 'poetry' suggest that the aesthetic realm might help to address and redress political problems.

This suggestion is full of promise and fraught with danger. Arnold asserts that the disinterested business of the believer in culture is 'to get the present believers in action, and lovers of political talking and doing, to make a return on their own minds'.[10] This mention of 'a return' is a return to a passage in Arnold's earlier lecture 'The Function of Criticism at the Present Time' (1864). There he asked writers to cultivate an impulse that pulls against the polemical. His gloss on Burke's ending to *Thoughts on French Affairs* (1791) explains the quality of this impulse:

> That return of Burke upon himself has always seemed to me one of the finest things in English literature, or indeed in any literature. That is what I call living by ideas: when one side of the question has long had your earnest support, when all your feelings are engaged, when you hear all round you no language but one, when your party talks this language like a steam-engine and can imagine no other,—still to be able to think, still to be irresistibly carried, if so it be, by the current of thought to the opposite side of the question.[11]

Just as Kant felt that rhetoric could 'move people, like machines', so Arnold fears the growth of party political language that can encourage you to talk like 'a steam-engine'. This 'return upon' the self is praised as a model of *'disinterestedness'*,[12] but admirers of such a return should also note its proximity to what Arnold in his 'Preface to *Poems*' (1853) denounces as 'the dialogue of the mind *with* itself, a dialogue in which 'disinterested objectivity' is not intensified but dissipated by a situation where 'there is everything to be endured, nothing to be done'.[13] For Arnold, literature must lend its peculiar eloquence to 'the opposite side of the question', but this eloquence must not tend towards a reflexivity that turns political amplitude into a passive or unprincipled loss of bearings. In the passage above, Arnold's own oscillation between active and passive voices ('still to be able to think, still to be irresistibly carried') gives distilled expression to this dilemma.

Arnold's enquiries into the varying implications of disinterestedness point to how difficult it is to achieve—and to define—a balance between affirmation and concession that is at once politically responsive and responsible. As Henry Sidgwick astutely observed in a review of Arnold's work: 'All this criticism of action is very valuable; but it is usually given in excess, just because, I think, culture is a little sore in conscience, is uncomfortably eager to excuse its own evident incapacity for action.'[14] Such excuses can also lead to claptrap, as George Eliot (an admirer of Arnold and of disinterestedness) suggests when her narrator swoops on Mr Brooke in *Middlemarch* (1871–2):

> And here I must vindicate a claim to philosophical reflectiveness, by remarking that Mr Brooke on this occasion little thought of the Radical speech which, at a later period, he was led to make on the incomes of the bishops … if he had foreknown this speech, it might not have made any great difference. To think with pleasure of his niece's husband having a large ecclesiastical income was one thing—to make a Liberal speech was another thing; and it is a narrow mind which cannot look at a subject from various points of view.[15]

From this angle, a return upon the self that goes beyond the language of 'your party' is a disingenuous rhetorical manœuvre: self-interest masquerades as large-mindedness. Still, Eliot's wry take on Brooke's pale imitation of disinterestedness is itself disinterested, for the free indirect style through which we learn that 'it is a narrow mind which cannot look at a subject from various points of view' is a model of what it describes. The compound narrative voice belongs to the author and to Mr Brooke, acknowledging the value of Arnold's ideal even as it draws attention to how it might be misused.

The ideal has fared less well since Sidgwick and Eliot offered their even-handed contributions to the debate. A hundred years later, Paul Goodman conceded that 'Some of us … have been fighting a losing fight to save "disinterested"', before stressing that the term should not be seen as a synonym for either 'uninterested' or 'impartial', but might be better defined as a 'non-attached attitude'.[16] William Empson also spotted a sea-change when reviewing Raymond Williams's *Keywords* (1976) a few years later. Williams had expressed consternation that 'Disinterested is still used, with what are intended to be positive implications' by 'those' who wish to associate the word with '"undogmatic" concern'. Empson intimates that '"Those" are the bosses … deceiving the workers with their tainted words', and he is bracingly direct about the tainted aspect of Williams's own words: 'why *still,* and where does *dogma* come from? Surely, at any date, in a football match, you want a ref who hasn't been nobbled by either side? … I grant that the ref should not be too bored to pay attention, but an appearance of decent coolness is expected of him.'[17]

Empson's metaphor usefully conceives disinterestedness as a form of engaged yet fair-minded arbitration, but subsequent contributions to the debate by both deconstructive and Marxist critics tend towards suspicion. Jacques Derrida sees those who appeal to the concept as making a disingenuous claim to 'interestlessness', while Pierre Bourdieu claims that the term 'really' means 'indifference … the refusal to invest oneself and take things seriously'.[18] The term is, I think, redeemable, and it can be made to allow for a more capacious sense of how literary writers conduct their political investigations. But it needs to be considered less as a specific ideology or as a set of prescriptions, more as a method—a *form* of enquiry, rather than a repository for a settled political *content.* Hazlitt, for example, would have baulked at some aspects of Arnold's politics, but his passionate defence of disinterestedness as a fulcrum, not a terminus, is based on his faculty, as David Bromwich puts it, 'of holding two opposed ideas in his mind at the same time': 'he believed "disinterestedness" meant not excluding all interests but being open to an unpredictable plurality of them … if [the action] is responsive to many interests, and settled in its service to none, we are making sense when we praise it as disinterested.'[19]

Instead of approaching or reproaching literary texts primarily for their political commitments, we might focus on how writers negotiate contending political demands in and through their work, and on how the literary arena can be considered one in which political questions are raised, entertained, and tested—not only decided or 'settled'. The conflicts and divided loyalties embodied in this arena need not be construed as a merely impracticable or disingenuous hedging of bets. They might also be seen as models of responsible political conduct, for their willingness to engage with multiple and sometimes contradictory value can prepare the ground for a richer political response in future.

[…]

This book is primarily concerned to chart how writers envisaged their work in relation to contemporary political voices, but it also considers how modern debates about relations between poetics and rhetoric are inflected by classical forbears. Three of the four authors studied were classically trained, and Dickens's early years as a parliamentary reporter involved prolonged exposure to the voices of those who were educated in the same tradition. This tradition acknowledged that poetics could inform and enrich political debate—Aristotle, Cicero, and Quintilian all recommended the study of poetry as part of a sound rhetorical training and quoted poets as examples of procedure to be emulated. As Jeffrey Walker has recently shown, even as distinctions were made between poetics and rhetoric, epideictic 'literaturized' forms of rhetoric (concerned with the 'forming' of opinions) were also seen as the foundation of pragmatic modes of persuasion in parliaments or courts (concerned with making decisions). That is, civic eloquence was descended from poetic discourse—epideictic modes were formative influences rather than ornamental afterthoughts.[20] The emergence of the categories of the 'literary' and the 'aesthetic' in the nineteenth century is informed by this heritage. Post-Romantic discussions are full of oppositions—as Walker puts it, '"Rhetoric" and "poetry" align with the practical and the aesthetic, the mundane and the ineffable, manipulation and truth, constraint and freedom, and so forth.'[21] However, these oppositions are constantly being tested by writers who sense the value of forms of literary eloquence that may seek to shape opinion by offering something more than the clear statement of an opinion.

When Aristotle defended the central ideal of classical rhetoric, he observed: 'One should be able to argue persuasively on either side of a question … in order that it may not escape our notice what the real state of the case is.'[22] Like Arnold and his contemporaries, Aristotle had concerns about the ethical and socio-political dangers of such reflexive and reflective powers, but considered that—if rhetoric was to be an 'art'—it would need to face these dangers rather than to avoid them by abandoning the ideal. A commitment to arguing on both sides is an acknowledgement of the inescapability of conflicting attachments and callings: rhetoric 'is concerned with the sort of things we debate … And we debate about things that seem to be capable of admitting two possibilities.'[23]

The art of modern literary eloquence shares this perspective, and is founded on an appreciation of literary style as a form of conduct as well as a mode of persuasion. Eugene Garver writes:

> An art of rhetoric never stops being a capacity for arguing both sides of a question … despite this ethically troubling status, rhetorical activity … is itself valuable, even if not all its products are valuable … An art which proves opposites creates mistrust. Today we don't need to be reminded of this mistrust. But we do need to know about its nobility.[24]

Literary eloquence can embody this nobility, for it offers us a form of expression that stands by what it says in two senses: we 'stand by' our utterances when we commit ourselves to them; but we also 'stand by' such utterances when we reconsider them, stand back to survey them from a more disinterested perspective, acknowledging and incorporating counter-claims. As Empson once wrote, such an imagining 'combines breadth of sympathy with energy of judgment; it can keep its balance among all the materials for judging'.[25] This is the poised conviction that a literary persuasion may carry.

Notes

1 Charles Dickens, *Great Expectations,* ed. Charlotte Mitchell (London: Penguin, 1996), 254. Subsequent page references are given parenthetically in the text.
2 Samuel Smiles, *Self-Help: With Illustrations of Character, Conduct, and Perseverance,* ed. Peter W. Sinnema (Oxford: Oxford World's Classics, 2002), 19.
3 Ibid. 34.
4 *The Times*, 8 Dec. 1837, 3e–f.
5 Ibid. 3f.
6 *The Times,* 23 Oct. 1873, 7b.
7 *The Times,* 16 June 1879, 6a; my emphasis.
8 Philip Davis, *The Victorians* (Oxford; Oxford University Press, 2002), 238.
9 Matthew Arnold, *Culture and Anarchy and Other Writings,* ed. Stefan Collini (Cambridge: Cambridge University Press, 1993), 67, 55, 186.
10 See Paul Guyer, *Kant and the Experience of Freedom: Essays on Aesthetics and Morality* (Cambridge: Cambridge University Press, 1993).
11 Ibid. 35.

12 Ibid. 37; Arnold's emphasis. This quality is again conceived by Arnold as 'keeping aloof from what is called "the practical view of things" … leav[ing] alone all questions of practical consequences and application'.

13 Matthew Arnold, 'Preface to *Poems*', in *The Poems of Matthew Arnold,* ed. Miriam Allott, 2nd edn. (London: Longman, 1979), 656; my emphasis.

14 Henry Sidgwick, 'The Prophet of Culture', *MacMillan's Magazine*, 16 (Aug. 1867), 271–80, pp. 279–80.

15 George Eliot, *Middlemarch*, ed. David Carroll (Oxford: Oxford World's Classics, 1998), 61.

16 Paul Goodman, *Speaking and Language: Defence of Poetry* (New York: Random House, 1971), 132–3.

17 William Empson, 'Compacted Doctrines' (1977), in *Argufying: Essays on Literature and Culture,* ed. John Haffenden (Londen: Chatto & Windus, 1987), 185–6.

18 Jacques Derrida, 'Economimesis', *Diacritics,* 11 (June 1981), 3–25, p. 15; Pierre Bourdieu, *Distinction: A Social Critique of the Judgement of Taste,* trans. Richard Nice (London; Routledge & Kegan Paul, 1984), 34.

19 David Bromwich, *Hazlitt: The Mind of a Critic,* 2nd edn. (New Haven and London: Yale University Press, 1999), 22, 80, 86.

20 Jeffrey Walker, *Rhetoric and Poetics in Antiquity* (Oxford: Oxford University Press, 2000).

21 Ibid. 329.

22 Aristotle, *On Rhetoric*, 1, i. 12.

23 Ibid.

24 Eugene Garver, *Aristotle's Rhetoric: An Art of Character* (Chicago: University of Chicago Press, 1994), 180, 212, 248.

25 William Empson, *Some Versions of Pastoral* (1935; repr. New York: New Directions, 1974), 64.

15 Introduction to *Indian Angles: English Verse in Colonial India from Jones to Tagore* (2011)

Mary Ellis Gibson

Introduction

In the years since Indian independence, scholars have collected and anthologized poems by important nineteenth-century poets writing English language verse in India. But this scholarship includes, with one exception, only those poems written by poets born in India of Indian parents. The exception, Henry Louis Vivian Derozio, is claimed as the "father" of Indian English poetry—as the first Indian poet to write in English—despite the fact that his mother was born in Hampshire and his father's parents were of Portuguese and Indian extraction. Derozio called himself an "East Indian," and those who admired him called him, after his early death, "the Indian Keats." It is ironic—but absolutely right—that a poet of complex political views and of complex ethnic, religious, and familial identifications should be thought of as the paterfamilias of Indian English poetry.

I argue here that all poets writing in English in India worked necessarily in a web of affiliation and rupture, identifications and disidentifications. They inhabited polyglot locations. They defined themselves within, against, and across canonical understandings that included much of the British poetic canon, classical European and modern European poetry, and classical and contemporary poetry in the languages of the subcontinent. Writing English language poetry in India is, at best, an uneasy undertaking—and was so from its beginning, both for poets we understand now as "Indian" and for those totally forgotten poets we might now understand as "British." I use scare quotes here to emphasize that the meanings of nation are always in the making. For the writers I discuss here, whether they were born in India of Irish Catholic parents (Mary Carshore) or schooled in England from the age of ten (Manmohan Ghose), what it meant to be Indian or British or something else was always at issue, never a given. I want to hold in abeyance for the moment—insofar as possible—the taken-for-granted categories of nationalism to look afresh, often for the first time in decades, at poets who made English verse in colonial India. If we were to look only at the current canon of "Indian English poets," who are, in any case, scarcely known to North American readers, we would be missing at least half the conversation that shaped their practices. Conversely, if we were to follow the lead of an old anthology, *Poets of John Company,* in focusing only on poets associated with the East India Company, we would ignore both Indian poets and the considerable number of British women who wrote poetry on the subcontinent in the long nineteenth century. My aim here is to bring back into conversation all those who were, in fact, parties to literary exchanges in this period.

Scholars of Indian English have shaped the canon of English language verse to the contours of nationalism. Constructing a canon in this way, however, renders *invisible* poets who are not claimed as Indian. It renders *illegible* many nuances of poetic form and influence shaping the texts of those poets who are claimed as Indian. Scholars in India and very recently in the United States and in Britain are beginning to rethink these canonical boundaries and the nationalist discourses that necessarily shaped earlier critical writing. In particular, Rosinka Chaudhuri and the scholars whose work is represented in Arvind Mehrotra's *Illustrated History of Indian Literature in English* have begun to critique the nationalist and linguistic assumptions that shaped and at the same time delegitimated English language poetry written in India. Building on their work, I double the scope of English language poetry in India to re-create the mutually constitutive history of British and Indian poets working on the subcontinent in the nineteenth century.

The very awkwardness of the phrase "English language poetry" points to significant historical and critical issues, and I retain it here to clarify and to navigate the vexed territory marked by such phrases as "Indian English poetry" and "Indo-Anglian" and "Anglo-Indian poetry." The first two phrases conventionally designate poets that include H. L.V. Derozio, Toru Dutt, and Rabindranath Tagore and exclude Sir William Jones and Rudyard Kipling. The third has an ambivalent history. "Anglo-Indian poetry" could be understood in two contradictory ways. Before independence, it would have designated poems written by British people in India; postindependence, it typically indicates poetry in English either by Indian writers or by those who in some circumstances were called "Eurasians." As a result of this confusion, the category "Indo-Anglian" was sometimes—and awkwardly—used as a marker for English language poetry written in India, excluding poetry written by the British. I want to talk here about poetry written in the English language in India, hence I use the seemingly redundant phrase "English language poetry."

Describing the family backgrounds of the poets themselves is equally awkward. Some of the poets I discuss here, beginning with Derozio, would once have been described as "Eurasian." I prefer here to use either the name current among the community in 1820s Calcutta, "East Indian," or simply—if wordily—to refer to persons of mixed ethnicity. No category is ever innocent of its past or free of the ideology of its own construction. My ostensibly neutral "English language poetry" entails its own polemic, its own claims and disclaimers. Through its very pleonasm, I want to drive a wedge between the nationalist claims of "English" and its denotative linguistic claim, between adjective and noun. I hope in this way to make possible a new understanding of the canon, and here, too, I refer to the notion of canon in its most capacious sense—as poems known and discussed, whatever judgments might further be made about their political efficacy or aesthetic value.

I claim that poetry written in colonial situations can tell us as much as or even more than novels can about figuration, multilingual literacies, and histories of nation and nationalism. In making this claim, I seek to redress what I believe has been a disproportionate emphasis on fiction in the study of colonial, postcolonial, and transnational literatures. From the beginning, poetry was the most important belletristic English form in India. Writing English language poetry, being educated in British poetic tradition, and translating poetry from various Asian and European languages into English were central to the development of Indian English.Taking fiction as the primary form of both colonial and postcolonial Indian English writing obscures the contours of the literary canon as it was experienced by writers in the nineteenth century and as it is often still experienced by Indian poets and novelists. This study (and the anthology that accompanies it—*Anglophone Retry in Colonial India, 1780–1913*) recovers and makes available carefully edited texts; it provides a new historical approach to understanding poems written in English in nineteenth-century India; and it argues for an understanding of a canon that takes nationalism as a subject of inquiry rather than a criterion for selection.

The canon of English language poetry in India was in the twentieth century constructed almost entirely on nationalist lines. Poems written by persons identified as "Indian" were read in the context of each other but only incidentally in relationship to poems written by persons identified as "British." This practice was both useful and problematic. It led to such anthologies as Eunice de Souza's recent *Early Indian Poetry in English* and to Sisir Kumar Das's magisterial history of Indian English literature, published by the Sahitya Akademi. Under the categories of "Indian English," Anglo-Indian, or Indo-Anglian poetry, many poets have been discovered, discussed, and defended from the wider charge—a common feature of linguistic nationalism in India—that no good poetry can be written in English on the subcontinent. Yet despite the critique of linguistic nationalism that is implicit in any defense of poets such as Derozio and Toru Dutt, this poetic canon was itself built on a nationalist foundation. The result is a curious dehistoricization effacing the contestation and conversation that in fact created English language literary culture in India.

Like the scholars I implicitly critique, I too argue for the importance of nationalisms in reading any number of poems, but with the caveat that twentieth-century post-colonial nationalism makes some poets and some poems legible while rendering others mute, uninteresting, or obscure. Attaining an Archimedean point from which to leverage nationalist presuppositions would be impossible: my intention here is to survey the complexities of their construction and to render visible a wide swath of English language poetry, its literary and linguistic contexts, its formal claims, its place in the social formation. Even the idea of "English language" in the phrase "English language poetry in India" contains more ambiguity than at first meets the eye, for there was a reasonably significant infusion of Scots poetry and, to a lesser extent, of Irish sentiment into the construction of Indian English. I share the premise of Elleke Boehmer and Katie Trumpeter that globalization must be understood not only as a late twentieth-century development but also as a phenomenon of the late eighteenth and early nineteenth centuries, a time when metropolis and colonial peripheries were constituted also by transperipheral relationships—among, for example, London, Calcutta, the American colonies, Edinburgh, and Dublin. Trumpener is primarily concerned with bardic nationalism as it played out in Scotland and Ireland and to some extent in North America; building on her work, I show how the tropes of bardic nationalism, integral to linguistic and cultural identities marked as Scottish and Irish and recuperated in a depoliticized way by the English, were reprised in nineteenth-century India. The distinctions between the peripheries of internal colonialism and the metropole were important to writers of English language poetry in colonial India. That one might identify with Scots bards or, later, with Irish nationalists meant that British domination had internal fissures and that British, Indian, and East Indian writers responded to these differences.

It is true that when military action was at issue in India, the common identity of "Britishness" overcame the ideological divisions of English internal colonialism; but in political appointments, in what we might call cultural activity, and sometimes in political activity, such differences mattered. Take, for example, John Leyden, who came to India to make his fortune when he found that a career in the Scottish church was impossible. Born a "peasant," as one of his biographers puts it, he was (like his contemporary Thomas Carlyle) a product of Scots education and his own intellectual ambition.[1] Leyden aspired to rival the great linguist Sir William Jones in classical and oriental learning and might have done so had he not died in 1811, at age thirty-six. Just before he boarded the *Hugh Inglis* bound for Madras, Leyden published his long poem, *Scenes of Infancy, Descriptive of Teviotdale*. The last section of this poem places Leyden's emigration in a context of enclosures and enforced peasant displacement; the poet identifies with the Scots of his generation who have left their homes, whether to farm in North America or to fight in the Scottish regiments. He identifies too with the "sons of Erin" in the wake of the Act of Union (1801), which followed the bloody rebellion of 1798, and he makes common cause with the Cherokees of North America, who have been turned out of their land in the process of enclosure by some of these same Scots and Irish settlers:

> Long may the Creek, the Cherokee, retain
> The desert woodlands of his old domain,
> Ere Teviot's sons, far from their homes beguiled
> Expel their wattled wigwams from the wild!
> For ah! not yet the social virtues fly,
> That wont to blossom in our northern sky,
> And, in the peasant's free-born soul, produce,
> The patriot glow of Wallace and of Bruce;
> Not yet our swains, their former virtues lost,
> In dismal exile roam from coast to coast;
> But soon, too soon, if lordly wealth prevail,
> The healthy cottage shall desert the dale,
> The active peasants trust their hardy prime
> To other skies, and seek a kinder clime.
>
> (*Poems,* 200–201)

Leyden's *Scenes of Infancy,* written in English rather than in Scots, followed his work assisting Walter Scott collect materials for the *Minstrelsy of the Scottish Border. Scenes of Infancy* at once captured and resisted the long-term economic and cultural consequences of the Scottish Act of Union (1707). And it drew the lines connecting the Scots diaspora with the fate of those inhabiting the reaches of empire.

Leyden found that it was a long road from a cottage in the Borders even to the drawing rooms of Edinburgh, much less to the shores of India. When he was promoted from his post in Madras to a better one in Calcutta, Leyden experienced yet another sort of displacement. Upon arriving in Calcutta in 1805, he was given friendly advice by his fellow Scot, General Sir John Malcolm, who later recounted this exchange: "I was most solicitous regarding his reception in the society of the Indian capital. 'I entreat you, my dear friend; I said to him the day he landed, 'to be careful of the impression you make on entering this community; for God's sake, learn a little English, and be silent upon literary subjects except among literary men.' 'Learn English!' he exclaimed—'no, never; it was trying to learn that language that spoilt my Scotch.'"[2] Though Leyden learned to write "proper" English (he, unlike Burns, was persuaded that his best poetry was written in English rather than Scots), he considered his *speech* too precious to lose. Leyden's stubborn insistence on his "Scotch" makes clear that even the "English language" in the Indian context comprised competing dialects and identifications, from Teviotdale to Calcutta, from Edinburgh to Madras, from Cherokee lands to the Scottish Borders, highlands, and islands, the transperipheral was as important as the metropole/colony exchange in making the cultural space of English poetry.

As is obvious in Leyden's experience, the English language in India consisted of multiple regional and class dialects, and these dialects were in turn situated in a thoroughly multilingual space. Though few people on the subcontinent were even literate, those who wrote English language poetry operated among multiple classical languages (Persian, Arabic, Greek, Latin, and sometimes Sanskrit) and vernaculars (Hindustani and Bangla principally, though also in South Indian languages). In entering this multilingual space, poets choosing to write in English had widely different access to language depending on their place of birth, education, religion, gender, and social class or caste. Religion, class, and gender were crucial markers of access to literacy, to belletristic writing, and to participation in constructions of nation and nationalism. In the chapters that follow, I attend to these differences as I delineate the material and social contours that shaped the scene of writing.

Moving among the multiple vernaculars, not to mention classical languages, at play on the subcontinent and moving within and outside of discourses of nation, poets were sometimes tempted to claim a kind of valorizing indigeneity for a particular vernacular or dialect—whether that vernacular be identified, for example, as Scottish or as Bengali. And yet, as Sheldon Pollock has argued, recourse to ideas of the indigenous (for example, to the "mother tongue") functions as a powerful illusion: "No form of culture can therefore ever be 'indigenous'; that term, it bears repeating, is only the name we give to what exhausts our capacity for historicization. When taken as anything more than this, the idea inhibits our perceiving that all cultures participate in what are ultimately global networks of begging, borrowing, and stealing, imitating and emulating—all the while constructing themselves precisely by sublating this history and affirming a specious autogenesis... From this processual perspective culture becomes ... a freeze frame in a film taken for the whole story" (*Language,* 539). Pollock defines cultures as sites for "reprocessing cultural goods that are always already someone else's" (539). A processual perspective, moreover, suggests a corrective to a singular reliance on spatial metaphors in the historiography of empire.

It is tempting, as I have done above, to think of the multilingual dimensions of empire in spatial metaphors—in terms of center/periphery and transperipheral spaces—but another crucial way of thinking these differential connections is temporal. Patrick Williams argues, following Elleke Boehmer and Ernst Bloch, that global interconnections were also marked by "simultaneous uncontemporaneities" (31). This notion of fissures within what we take to be contemporaneous phenomena allows us to think of the empire as a heterogeneous space—heterogeneous as to technologies of publishing and distribution, as to reception and reading practices, as to language itself.

To capture both temporal and spatial heterogeneity, I move among three registers here: the material histories of uneven development; the geocultural history of the transperipheral; and the psychic history of what Homi Bhabha calls "unhomeliness" (*Location,* 13). These theoretical strands are drawn through each chapter, though with differing emphases. With respect to the histories of uneven development, I am particularly interested in the technologies of publishing and distribution and the development of cultural institutions, including English medium schools and libraries. A focus on the geocultural histories of imperial space brings into view institutions of literary sociality, including the differential reception of English language poetry in Indian and metropolitan periodicals. Finally, a focus on the psychic history of "unhomeliness" allows me to trace the differentials suggested in experiences of displacement, marginalization, and migration and in gendered access to culture. In all these registers, I attend to the consequences for literary conventions, tropes, and formal choices. I ask, for example, what conventions were available to poets writing in India, what forms or tropes were dominant, what other languages or dialects could be evoked through the medium of English language verse, and whether or how these elements of English poetics shifted over time and in their "simultaneous uncontemporaneity" from one social location to another.

Fundamental to this argument is the assumption that poetry is crucial to an understanding of the development of English language culture in India. In colonial India at least through about 1860, poetry was the most important form of English language belletristic writing. As I show in more detail in subsequent chapters, from the eighteenth century onward, English language newspapers printed much more poetry than fiction, and printers in the presidencies—Madras, Bombay, and especially Calcutta—brought out various volumes of verse. The publishing of English language verse began in Calcutta, though authors were also eager to print collections in Britain that were then imported to India. Graham Shaw shows that practical items and government regulations, not surprisingly, formed the preponderance of books printed in Calcutta before 1800, but he notes that the majority of belletristic volumes were "collections of very mediocre poetry" or plays (*Printing,* 19). Such titles as *The Oriental Masonic Muse* (1791), *The Oriental Asylum for Fugitive Pieces* (1788). *The Oriental Miscellany* (collecting "airs of Hindoostan"), and Sir William Jones's translation of *Śakuntalā* indicate the variety of this early publishing.[3] Fiction was often imported but seldom locally produced, at least before the 1860s.

More important for my purposes than its relatively strong place in the world of colonial publishing is the nature of poetry itself. Although all literary forms—novel, story, novella, verse—exist only through convention, formal verse makes still greater claims than fiction on an understanding of convention, operating through meter and rhyme even at the level of lexical choice and syntax. And of course verse genres (epic, elegy, and ballad) and verse forms (ballad stanza, Spenserian stanza, sonnet, and blank verse) have particular histories through which these conventions and poetic practices are transmitted. The result, I believe, is that poetry can be thought of as a kind of pressure cooker for historical and ideological contradictions. I claim here not only that poetry has been understudied and largely untheorized in colonial and postcolonial scholarship but that poetry provides an important site for investigating the cultural contradictions of empire. The pressure of poetic convention makes especially evident the rifts and fissures within the colonial scene of writing. Finally, I argue, poetry is crucial to our understanding of the colonial scene precisely because it is, of all genres, the one most fully understood through writers' and readers' repertoires.

Here I borrow Tracy Davis's extremely useful definition of repertoire, which she has developed to account for the ways an audience finds innovation or invention intelligible. Davis argues that repertoire can be thought of as mutual knowledge and accretions of practice through which, in her case, theatrical performances are made legible. In a recent lecture, she defined repertoire as the "multiple, circulating recombinative discourses of intelligibility that habituate audiences to understand performative tropes, recognizing and incorporating the unfamiliar."[4] Repertoire, then, is not simply the accumulation of texts (songs, roles, and so forth) to which a performer has access; rather, it can be understood as an accretion of possibilities made through reiteration, revision, and citation.

In the chapters that follow, a central concern is precisely this process of reiteration, revision, and citation. Indeed, I argue that reiteration entails revision. For example, when the trope of exile, much favored by early nineteenth-century British poets writing in India, is repeated by Michael Madhusudan Dutt at midcentury, it is radically revised, almost reversed. The teenaged poet living in Calcutta who sighed "for Albion's distant shore" did not long for a family he had lost. Rather, he manufactured a family he was loath to leave. A more subtle kind of reiteration and revision is evident in Kasiprasad Ghosh's metrical experiments, which turn such forms as Spenserian stanza to his own purposes. And a complex web of citations in their most literal sense is constructed in hundreds of orientalist footnotes attached to hundreds of poems during this period.

The processes of repetition, citation, and revision are key to the development of English language poetry in India, but the divisions within the colonial scene of writing and the divisions between the colony and the metropole often rendered poems illegible or differently legible to audiences in India and in Britain. The repertoire of colonial English language poetics was built from the intersection of British, classical and vernacular European, and classical and vernacular Indian canons. In this heteroglot and often ambilingual scene of writing, legibility was a moving target. As a result, poets in India surrounded their verse with an extraordinary number of paratexts: footnotes, endnotes, glosses, prefaces, and dedications. This can be understood generally as the poets' attempts to establish the forms of knowledge from which repertoire is built. These paratexts both deflect and invite criticism, both justify the poetic undertaking and excuse its failings. Paratexts are put to a variety of uses in these poems; they create ironies, they apologize, they rhetorically situate poets and readers. But often they also point to poets' insecurities about the very audience that the notion of shared repertoire necessarily takes for granted. Who exactly was the audience for this verse? Where was the audience located? Would the poet be judged by virtue of his attempt to write English poetry in the first place? Would she be judged by her distance from the metropole?

Notes

1 See W. W. Tulloch, 'Biographical Sketch of the Author,' in John Leyden, *Scenes of Infancy, Descriptive of Teviotdale* (Edinburgh: J. Ballantyne for T. N. Longman and O. Rees, 1803).
2 John Malcolm, 'To the Editor of the Bombay Courier,' quoted in Walter Scott, 'Supplementary Memoir,' which introduces John Leyden, *Poems and Ballads* (Kelso, Scotland: J. and J. H. Rutherfurd, 1858), xli.
3 Graham W. Shaw's *Printing in Calcutta* is an invaluable resource from which we can extrapolate the importance of institutions of literary sociality, including, for example, the Masons and the Highland Society, whose Rules and membership list were published in 1788 in not one, but two editions; see *Printing in Calcutta to 1800: A Description and Checklist of Printing in Late 18th-Century Calcutta* (London: Bibliographical Society, 1976), p. 120.
4 Tracy Davis, 'Sonic Repertoire', Conference Paper. North American Victorian Studies Association, Yale University, November 2008.

Part IV
Prosody

Natalie Phillips Hoffmann

Broadly defined as the rhythms and sound patterns of poetry, prosody has long both captivated and exasperated literary scholars. Almost all people—even very young children—can hear, feel, and replicate rhythmic sound patterns. Yet, prosody has historically been, and some would argue remains, more difficult to interpret than nearly any other aspect of poetry studies. In the nineteenth and early twentieth centuries, treatises on prosody were plentiful, with such tomes often running to a thousand pages and published in multiple editions. George Saintsbury's *A History of English Prosody from the Twelfth Century to the Present* (1906) looms large in both size and influence, but his work joined a critical field so crowded that titles were often recycled with only the slightest modifications.[1] The staggering number of pages devoted to prosodic study, however, seemed to complicate rather than clarify how nineteenth-century critics understood the features of poetry that, for most of them, distinguished it from all other kinds of writing. Crucial prosodic terms remained deeply contested and technical debates, particularly surrounding whether meter should be measured by syllabic accent or quantity, outlived the century. Yet, despite all the tumult, poetry held fast to its special place in English national and imperial life as the definitive measure of English identity and cultural accomplishment.[2]

Looking back, we now see reflected in the instability of nineteenth-century prosodic discourse the most central social, cultural, and political preoccupations of the period: shifts in national and imperial identity, tensions between religious traditions and scientific discovery, strains in class relations, and anxieties about change generally that intensified as the end of the century drew nearer. In fact, the nineteenth-century examinations of prosody that follow—cloaked as they are in esoteric and ever-shifting terms—reveal the heart of English national and cultural life. For this reason, much is at stake for today's poetry scholars in making sense of nineteenth-century prosodic discourse. The contemporary pieces included here, by Meredith Martin and Adela Pinch, illustrate the two dominant critical modes between which today's scholars of poetry and prosody mediate. Indeed, this collection's juxtaposition of nineteenth-century and contemporary critical work on prosody reveals an important continuity: the extent to which prosody remains a lively site for the contestation of ideas about poetry and, more broadly, about history, politics and identity.[3] My introduction here offers a brief discussion of these nineteenth-century texts and their tensions, interactions, and consequences.

As their presence in this collection must suggest, Samuel Taylor Coleridge, Coventry Patmore, and Sidney Lanier are part of the same ongoing debate about English prosody; however, they write from very different places within a dynamic, even volatile, century. Written in the opening decades of the century, Coleridge's *Biographia Literaria* (1817) predates the political, scientific, religious, and social upheavals of the mid- to late-nineteenth century. Coleridge's time was one of relative geopolitical confidence for Britain. At home, the Second Treaty of Paris (November 20, 1815) officially ended the Napoleonic Wars (1803–1815), bringing an end to the financial drain and emotional grind of more than a decade of war, and significantly bolstering British national and military pride. Further afield in the colonies, the British could still imagine themselves as benevolent, welcome bringers of civilization to eager subjects. By mid- to late- century, when Patmore and Lanier published the bulk of their works, the Indian Mutiny (1857) had badly shaken British imperial and martial confidence. By the turn of the century, which neither Patmore nor Lanier lived to see, the Second Boer War (1899–1902) made Britain's geopolitical situation seem even grimmer. In terms of science and religion, Coleridge wrote at a time when the two fields were not yet experienced as antagonistic in the literary or popular imaginary. Postulating the theory of a watchmaker god whose designs were evident in the operations of natural law, William Paley's *Natural Theology* (1802) was the most widely circulated treatise on the implications of scientific discovery on faith. At the century's end—after the dinosaur discoveries of the 1820s and 1830s, Darwin's *On the Origin of Species* (1859), and scores of groundbreaking discoveries in the fields of disease identification and treatment— the spirit of the age was better captured in the title of Andrew White's 1896 *A History of the Warfare of Science with Theology in Christendom*: that is one of intense and enduring conflict between science and religion. Coleridge's work is also separated from Patmore and Lanier by the landmark Reform Act of 1832, which expanded suffrage and awakened political activism amongst the English middle classes, and the Chartist Movement (1838– 1848), which revealed the danger of continued political and economic repression of the lower classes. The years following Coleridge's major publications witnessed the emergence of a powerful national movement for women's suffrage; a movement, it should be noted, that took pleasure in deriding Patmore's most (in)famous poem, *The Angel in the House* (1854). In short, many of the foundational truths that structured English national and cultural life when Coleridge published *Biographia Literaria* underwent profound alterations by the time Patmore and Lanier wrote their own reflections on prosody. Nevertheless, Coleridge's work is foundational for nineteenth-century engagements with prosody, and most critics in the field (including Patmore and Lanier) engaged directly with his ideas.

Set out in the eighteenth chapter of *Biographia Literaria*, entitled 'Language of Metrical Composition', Coleridge's theory of prosody invests most heavily in reasserting and explaining the difference between poetry and prose. The long-accepted distinction had recently been blurred by none other than Coleridge's closest friend and poetic collaborator, William Wordsworth (1770–1850). Their collaboration, *Lyrical Ballads* (1798), marks the beginning of the poetic ascendency of English Romanticism; its poems react against the classicism of Enlightenment poetry, and turn toward simpler poetic forms and personal expression. In 1800, Wordsworth brought out a second edition that included a new 'Preface', an extended discussion of Romantic poetic philosophy that seemed to advocate the use of broadly accessible poetic language and verse structures. Of prosody, he claimed 'there neither is nor can be any essential difference between the language of prose and metrical composition'. Of Coleridge, Wordsworth writes, 'our opinions on the subject of poetry do almost entirely coincide'.[4] For Coleridge, however, Wordsworth's move to downplay the difference between poetry and prose could scarcely be further off the mark. 'Language of Metrical Composition' is Coleridge's counter to his friend.

Adopting Wordsworth's own language, Coleridge contends 'the language of poetry … is *essentially* different from that of prose'.[5] In fact, poetry only arises from the intellectual exercise of expressing the high, intense emotions that are proper to poetry through the rigorous structures of metered verse. In Coleridge's words, poetry's particular challenge and gift is 'the interpenetration of passion and of will, of *spontaneous* impulse and of *voluntary* purpose'; the 'blending of *delight* with emotion, so the traces of present *volition* remain', 'discernable'. Coleridge imagines poetic genre conventions as a '*compact* between poet and reader', whereby readers are 'entitled to expect' and poets are 'bound to supply' poetry in its 'proper', metered form.[6] For Coleridge, metered language signals to readers that what follows is, indeed, poetry; poetry because it excites through a juxtaposition of elevated emotions and intellectual rigor impossible to replicate in any other genre. In the opening decades of the century, Coleridge defends prosody as necessary to poetry and claims for poetry particular expressive possibilities unavailable to prose.

As the century wore on, most scholars held fast to the notion that meter was essential to poetic expression; however, their expectations of what poetry needed to express and to what ends changed. For Coleridge, poetry was particularly suited to expressing intense emotional states, and at mid-century, some of the most intense emotions in England were patriotism and, along with it, imperial zeal.[7] As the work of poet-critic Coventry Patmore shows, metrical theories became increasingly bound up with national and, by extension, imperial identity. In his reverence for meter, Patmore's debt to Coleridge is clear. In fact, he frames what has become the most oft-cited claim from his most famous essay, *English Metrical Law* (1857)—'the language should always seem to *feel*, though not to *suffer from* the bonds of verse'—as a 'neglected corollary' of Coleridge.[8] The best poets, according to Patmore, should not only write in meter; they should write in meter that is simultaneously understated and obvious. Yet, in an important shift away from Coleridge, Patmore's main work in his essay concerns not how one might write such meters but how one might properly read, hear, feel, or experience such meters. To properly hear or attend to meter is, for Patmore, no esoteric or particularly poetic task: it is necessary for basic communication. Meter is 'natural to [all] spoken language', and, while there are many ways of reading a sentence, there is only one way that rightly attends to the 'meter and melody of prose' in its 'common and intelligible delivery'.[9] Indeed, Patmore's illustrative question—'shall you walk out to-day?'—warrants the time it takes to test for oneself his contention that even in prose the subtlest of changes in accent result in significant changes in meaning.[10]

Turning from prose to poetry, Patmore argues that poetry's emotional intensity makes its meters even more 'conspicuous', demanding from its readers not only a command of 'common and intelligible delivery', but an inherent ability to sense the proper beats of a metered line. For Patmore, meter arises from the 'marking, *by whatever means*, certain isochronous intervals' within poetic lines. Isochrony, the rhythmic division of 'vocal utterance…into equal or proportionate spaces', was not a new idea; however, Patmore's contention that such division was 'made manifest by an ictus or beat…actual or mental' was paradigm-shifting. Herein is Patmore's most influential contribution to nineteenth-century prosody studies: he argues that while poetry may be heard through the ear, meter exists most perfectly in the mind—and not just any mind. For Patmore, the ictus (the 'time-beater' that makes verse verse) resides within the properly trained English mind which 'craves measure in everything'.[11] The English mind's notion of meter is so powerful that Patmore claims most English readers prefer not to hear poetry read aloud because its music is more perfect in their minds than in even the best oral recitation.

Patmore's *English Metrical Law* was a foundational text for what came to be called the 'New Prosody', the critical mode that dominated British prosodic thinking in the mid- to late- nineteenth century. New Prosodists, maintaining Coleridge's notion of poetry's necessary emotiveness, believed that metrical patterns (and, especially, variations in those patterns) directly transmitted affect from poet to reader. However, the New Prosodists also argued that to achieve its intended affects and effects, poetry required, in instances of public performance, a proper reading and, in all instances, a properly trained reader.[12] The transformation of meter from rhythms that are heard to abstract patterns that are known to the English mind, of course, had important nationalist and class overtones. Most innocuously, Patmore and other critics invested in the New Prosody aimed to elevate English prosody by marking its distinctiveness from classical prosody and by codifying its special properties into law. For them, there was something particularly English and, thus, particularly appealing about a theory of prosody that understood meter in isochronic terms. However, the New Prosody's insistence on flawless elocution and its metaphysical theory of meter also seemed to turn English poetry into a kind of insider's club, available in its most perfect iterations only to English elites whose mouths could read lines with accentual exactitude and whose minds came 'inherently' to feel its meters after years of rigorous training in exclusive public schools. The exclusionary implications of New Prosody's poetics were vexing to many critics, especially non-English ones, and fueled turns to science—and, by extension, the physical body—as a new, more democratic means of dissecting, studying, and understanding poetry's rhythms of sound and silence.[13]

American poet, musician, and academic Sidney Lanier (1842–1881) offers one of the most comprehensive and eloquent responses to New Prosody poetics, moving away from the more abstract theories of Coleridge and Patmore and attempting instead to formulate 'a science of verse'. In the opening chapter of *The Science of English Verse* (1880), Lanier argues that poetry need not be concerned with elevated or impassioned emotion or even with conveying ideas. Lanier claims that the words of a poem may be substituted for any other set of words with identical sound patterns without altering the poem at all. For him, poetry, like music, is solely a function of sound. Lanier reacts against notions, like Patmore's, of a prosody that exists in the mind apart from the material reality of sound and hearing. In his own words, verse is 'a set of specially related sounds' that 'impresses itself upon the ear as verse...purely as sounds, without reference to...associated ideas'.[14] In an essay permeated with scientific language and structured much like a lab report, Lanier relies on physical science and anatomy to explain how ears distinguish different kinds of sounds and, thus, experience music and meter. Yet, for Lanier, subjecting poetry to the rigors of scientific study does not, as many including Patmore had claimed, blunt prosody's mysterious beauty. Instead, in his stirring chapter 'Of rhythm throughout all those motions which we call nature', Lanier connects the rhythms of poetic lines to the governing rhythms of the natural world and, most interestingly, of man's moral universe.[15] In Lanier's hands, scientific study works to bind together poetry and, by extension, the ears and bodies of its readers with everything from the minute and observable movements of cells to the cosmic and remote movements of planets and solar systems. By rejecting the centrality of Coleridge's impassioned, elevated emotions and Patmore's meter of the mind, Lanier's *fin-de-siècle* essay concerns itself with 'the ear of average persons' and imagines the metered pleasures of poetry as arising, at least in part, from the connections it forges among readers and between readers and their world.[16]

As I hope my discussions of Coleridge, Patmore, and Lanier suggest, the intricate connections between nineteenth-century poetry and a host of structuring narratives hold out the promise of rich critical rewards for scholars across a number of subject areas. The two critical pieces included here, Meredith Martin's 'Prosody Wars' (2011) and Adela Pinch's 'Rhyme's End' (2011), model the breadth of that range. They also model the distinct critical approaches—broadly described as New Historicism and New Criticism—that most powerfully shape our approaches to making contemporary meaning from nineteenth-century prosody. Martin's 'Prosody Wars' shows how texts about prosody—particularly Saintsbury's *History of English Prosody from the Twelfth Century to the Present Day*—were constitutive with questions of English national identity and of English educational and class politics. Martin is interested, primarily, in how nineteenth-century poetry and prosody operate in broad socio-political and historical contexts. Her essay is, of course, about prosody, but it does not contain a single poetic line. In contrast, in 'Rhyme's End', Pinch builds her prosodic and philosophic arguments upon close readings of poems. Pinch is invested in poetry's and prosody's participation in overarching philosophic questions about time and selfhood, but her starting point is not at the level of discourse but at the level of the line. While Martin and Pinch model distinct schools of critical thought, their work—and in fact the work of most contemporary scholars—mediates between New Historicist and New Critical reading practices. Elsewhere, Martin practices methodologies more closely aligned with the New Criticism, just as Pinch positions her close readings and philosophic engagements within broader cultural and historical frameworks.[17] My intention here is to depict their negotiation of scholarly approaches not in zero-sum terms but as questions of strategic emphasis. By framing Martin's and Pinch's work in terms of their engagements with particular critical methodologies, I hope to make entry into prosodic criticism—steeped as it is in voluminous and technical vocabulary and vexed as it is by enduring questions about how to read meter— at least somewhat less daunting to the newcomer.

In keeping with New Historicist practices, Martin's 'Prosody Wars' situates nineteenth-century poetry and discussions about prosody at the nexus of larger debates about English education and, by extension, English national identity. Nineteenth-century social reforms brought about unprecedented expansion in educational availability and, with it, the opening of pedagogical debates about the appropriateness of public-school-style classical education for the English masses. As Martin shows, this movement of education from the elite fringes to the mainstream had especially pronounced impacts on poetry instruction. Long seen by pedagogical theorists, including Matthew Arnold, as formative of moral character, poetry became in the new educational environment a primary means of developing national character. Yet, as Martin illustrates, poetry scholars' disagreements about basic terminology, about how English meters evolved (in relationship to Anglo-Saxon and classical meters), and about how English lines should be scanned (accent, quantity, or a combination approach) made them seem ill-equipped for the serious job of inculcating national character. Consequently, Martin argues, men like Patmore, Lindley Murray, Edwin Guest and Saintsbury felt compelled to put an end to the destabilizing debates that had come to surround prosody.[18] Martin provides a clear, succinct summary of the intricacies of the 'prosody wars'; however, what interests her most are the forces that fueled both the contentiousness of prosodic debates and the fervent desire to have done with them, as expressed through attempts, like Saintsbury's, at exhaustiveness.

Depicting Saintsbury as a savvy prosodic politician, Martin shows how he navigates between competing metrical traditions and, more importantly, between competing theories of metrical pedagogy in order to position English poetry as both a reflection of and a tool for teaching English national character. To settle the dogged questions of the origins of the English foot and how best to scan it, Saintsbury forwards the notion of 'blended originality', becoming in Martin's words 'the representative for standard English meter based on a subtle blending of classical (foreign, quantitative) and Anglo-Saxon (native, accentual) meters'.[19] Yet, Martin notes that Saintsbury's insistence on retaining the connection between English meter and classical verse raises a stubborn problem for him: how can English poetry, with its classical indebtedness, instill national character in English school children unfamiliar with Greek or Latin verse? Saintsbury's solution, in a rare agreement with Patmore, was the idea of the 'English ear'. Martin reads Saintsbury's reliance on the innate ability of the English ear to hear English meters as a revealing dodge of actual engagement with questions of prosody—a dodge that exposes the extent to which Saintsbury longs to use his ethos as an eminent scholar of prosody to close down prosodic debates and, thereby, to reassert poetry's fitness to be at the forefront of English character education. In Martin's words, Saintsbury's chief aim is not to make arguments about prosody (though he does that too), but instead to lend 'stabilization for the healthy, collective, patriotic view of English meter and, by extension, English poetry's role as a stabilizing, patriotic force in national culture'.[20] Ultimately, Saintsbury's work and the prosody wars more generally are most important for what they tell us about why and how ever-fluctuating concepts—like meter or national identity—are so frequently and laboriously constructed as innate or natural.

Pinch's 'Rhyme's End' is, as she explicitly notes, a response to recent increases of interest in nineteenth-century prosody, especially among scholars (like Martin) eager to approach prosody through its relationship to broader social or political trends. Pinch frames her work as an initial step towards elevating a more concrete feature of the poetic line—specifically, end-rhyme—to the same level of critical consideration now accorded to meter. Pinch invests in individual lines, showing through the closest of readings how rhyme—more specifically, short, rhymed lines—can manipulate (create, lengthen, or shorten) time. Through readings of Mary Elizabeth Coleridge's (1861–1907) short poems, Pinch argues that rhyme has the power to literally 'open up or compress time' by either 'leaving a long interval between sound A and sound A, or by having sound A return quickly'. Rather than a 'metrical pattern' of any kind, Pinch argues that rhyme determines the length of Coleridge's lines, which demand from the reader as much time as 'it takes the line to get around to the final end-rhyme'.[21] Pinch's primary poetic work in 'Rhyme's End' illustrates how rhyming strategies enable lines of poetry to intervene in the world by altering a reader's sense of time's progression.

For Pinch, Coleridge's use of end-rhyme both reflects nineteenth-century experimentations with non-linear understandings of time, and challenges twenty-first century narratives of time's ceaseless advance. Pinch resists creating an elaborate context for her theorization of rhyme, trusting in only the sparsest of historical detail to suggest that poets and readers at the *fin de siècle* would be particularly interested in time and in poems intended to 'heighten our subjective experience of duration, and its existential pangs'.[22] Similarly, while Pinch acknowledges nineteenth-century debates about rhyming strategies, she is less interested in providing an overview or exploration of such debates than in citing the views of certain participants (Saintsbury chief among them) as supporting evidence for her own interest in the association between rhyme and ending. For Pinch, the most relevant contexts for her engagement with end-rhyme are nineteenth-century and contemporary philosophies of time and self. The poems of anxious Victorians facing the end of their century, according to Pinch, reflect a fascination and fear about ending—ultimately about dissolution and death—that is as real and present for us now as it was for them. Drawing on the theories of Giorgio Amgaben, Pinch reads the poem as constantly under threat: threat of dissolving into prose, of losing its identity as a poem at its conclusion, and of being engulfed by the vast nothingness of white margins. Located, of course, at the end of the line, end-rhyme occupies the frontlines of poetry's existential struggle with its margins and, ultimately, with its own ending. And, as Pinch shows, end-rhyme can—as in Coleridge's poems, which she describes as 'little time machines'—prevail in forestalling the march of time by making lines seem to 'slow down' or 'unfurl extra time'.[23] For Pinch, then, prosody is important because it empowers the poet—if only momentarily—to stave off a host of inevitable endings and, thereby, to challenge the ubiquitous narrative of time's uninterruptable progression.

Martin's and Pinch's work point to the dynamism—of the different critical directions and reading practices at work—in nineteenth-century prosody studies. Following the Victorians, today's scholars understand prosody studies as much more than contests over accent versus quantity, Anglo-Saxon versus classical origins, or simpler versus more complex poetic forms. Following nineteenth-century prosodists and poets, contemporary critics recognize prosody as deeply imbricated with political, social, and philosophic discourses. There are, in fact, a number of important continuities extending from Coleridge, Patmore, and Lanier through to Martin and Pinch. Pinch—like Patmore and Lanier before her—enters the debate over how line length should be determined, suggesting that contests over scansion (while not the whole of the debate) are as lively and unresolved as ever. Both Coleridge and Pinch invest in poetry's distinctiveness from prose, each claiming that the antagonistic forces at work in poetic lines enable a kind of emotional expressiveness or engagement with time (respectively) that is particular to poetry. Both Martin and her subject, Saintsbury, intervene politically in prosodic discourse, reframing how we understand poetry's relationship to and role in national identity formation. In the excerpts from Martin and Coleridge presented here, the question of what poetry expresses dwarfs the more technical questions in which Patmore, Lanier, and Pinch are interested. Indeed, as this collection's juxtaposition of nineteenth-century and contemporary texts intends to show, the contentions that animate today's prosodic debates are extensions of the concerns that so vexed nineteenth-century critics. The 'Prosody Wars', it seems, continue in new variations. They remain vibrant because today's critics share with their nineteenth-century predecessors the conviction that prosody 'by whatever means' (to borrow from Patmore) forges human connections and shapes identity, conditioning our understanding of the world and our relationship to it.

Notes

1 Consider, as just three examples, William Crowe's *A Treatise on English Versification* (1827), Robert Wilson Evans's *Treatise on Versification, Ancient and Modern* (1852), and Gilbert Conway's *Treatise of Versification* (1878).

2 For only two (of hundreds of potential) examples of how nineteenth-century critics discussed and contested poetry's crucial role in English national and political consciousness, see 'Poetry as a Motive Force in National Life', *Saturday Review of Politics, Literature, Science and Art*, 61.1585 (1886), 364–5; and John William Courthope, 'Poetry and Politics: Form and Subject', *The National Review*, 6.35 (1886), 640–65.

3 For readers interested in a book-length treatment of prosody's critical importance both then and now, Jason David Hall's *Meter Matters: Verse Cultures of the Long Nineteenth Century* (Athens, OH: Ohio University Press, 2011) offers a recent and wide-ranging collection of essays from many of the prominent voices in the field of nineteenth-century studies.

4 William Wordsworth, 'Preface to *Lyrical Ballads, with Pastoral and Other Poems* (1802)', in Stephen Gill, *William Wordsworth: The Major Works* (Oxford: Oxford World Classics, 2008), pp. 595, 602.

5 Samuel Taylor Coleridge, *Biographia Literaria, or Biographical Sketches of my Literary Life and Opinions* [1817] (New York: Leavitt, 1834), p. 210.

6 Coleridge, *Biographia Literaria*, p. 212.

7 The Indian Mutiny, which occurred three months before Patmore's publication of *English Metrical Law*, destabilized British imperial narratives and shook the nation's confidence. An almost frenzied need to reassert British national and imperial identity followed, leading (in no small part) to the turn to poetry as a necessary reinforcement of English identity. For a broad discussion of the impact of the Munity on English popular, political, and fictional narratives of national identity,

see Gautam Chakravarty, *The Indian Mutiny and the British Imagination* (Cambridge: Cambridge University Press, 2005).

8   Coventry Patmore, *Essay on English Metrical Law* [1857] (Washington, DC: The Catholic University of America Press, 1961), p. 8.

9   Patmore, *Metrical Law*, p. 11.

10   Patmore, *Metrical Law*, p. 11.

11   Patmore, *Metrical Law*, p. 15.

12   For a more in-depth discussion of Patmore and his relationship to the New Prosody, see Joshua King, 'Patmore, Hopkins, and the Problem of the *English Metrical Law*', *Victorian Poetry*, 49.2 (2011), 31–49.

13   The 'Science' section of this volume offers an extended exploration of the relationship between poetry, prosody, and nineteenth-century scientific discourse. For a book-length examination of the connections between meter and the body, see Kirstie Blair, *Victorian Poetry and the Culture of the Heart* (Oxford: Oxford University Press, 2006).

14   Sidney Lanier, *The Science of English Verse* (New York: Charles Scribner's, 1880), pp. 21, 22.

15   Lanier, *English Verse*, pp. 246ff.

16   Lanier, *English Verse*, p. 36; on Lanier's theorization of prosody's ability to forge collective identity, see Yopie Prins, 'Historical Poetics, Dysprosody, and "The Science of English Verse"', *PMLA* 123.1 (2008), 229–34; and Jason Rudy, 'Manifest Prosody', *Victorian Poetry*, 49 (2011), 253–66.

17   For an example of Martin's scholarship in which close reading features prominently, see 'Gerard Manley Hopkins and the Stigma of Meter', *Victorian Studies*, 50.2 (2008), 243–53. For an example of Pinch's scholarship that positions her close readings in a detailed context of nineteenth-century socio-political discourse, see 'Love Thinking', *Victorian Studies*, 50.3 (2008), 379–97.

18   Here, Martin focuses on the nationalist politics that shape prosodic discourse. For a theorization of how the nationalist or imperialist politics of specific nineteenth-century poets—including Barrett Browning, Browning, Tennyson, and Clough—impacted their metrical styles, see Matthew Reynolds, *The Realms of Verse, 1830–1870: English Poetry in a Time of Nation-Building* (Oxford: Oxford University Press, 2001): his chapter, 'Poetry and its Times', appears in Part I of this volume.

19   Meredith Martin, 'Prosody Wars', in Hall, *Meter Matters*, pp. 237–62 (p. 248).

20   Martin, 'Prosody Wars', p. 257. Bringing the prosody debates under control and, thereby, making clear the connection between English poetry and English national identity was a matter of both domestic and international importance. Several recent contributions to nineteenth-century prosody studies have examined the ways in which poets writing in colonial (or formerly colonial) spaces sought to understand their own relationship with English national identity by engaging with English metrical forms. See especially Meredith McGill, *The Traffic in Poems: Nineteenth-century Poetry and Transatlantic Exchange* (New Brunswick, NJ: Rutgers University Press, 2008); and Mary Ellis Gibson, *Indian Angles: English Verse in Colonial India from Jones to Tagore* (Athens, OH: Ohio University Press, 2011). The *Indian Angles* is available in Part III of this volume.

21   Adela Pinch, 'Rhyme's End', *Victorian Studies*, 53.3 (2011), 485–94 (p. 488).

22   Pinch, 'Rhyme's End', p. 486.

23   Pinch, 'Rhyme's End', p. 493.

16 Language of Metrical Composition (1817)

Samuel Taylor Coleridge

Essence, in its primary signification, means the principle of individuation, the inmost principle of the possibility of any thing, as that particular thing. It is equivalent to the idea of a thing, whenever we use the word *idea*, with philosophic precision. Existence, on the other hand, is distinguished from essence, by the superinduction of reality. Thus we speak of the essence, and essential properties of a circle; but we do not therefore assert, that any thing, which really exists, is mathematically circular. Thus too, without any tautology we contend for the existence of the Supreme Being; that is, for a reality correspondent to the idea. There is, next, a secondary use of the word essence, in which it signifies the point or ground of contra-distinction between two modifications of the same substance or subject. Thus we should be allowed to say, that the style of architecture of Westminster Abbey is essentially different from that of St. Paul, even though both had been built with blocks cut into the same form, and from the same quarry. Only in this latter sense of the term must it have been denied by Mr. Wordsworth (for in this sense alone is it affirmed by the general opinion) that the language of poetry (that is the formal construction, or architecture, of the words and phrases) is essentially different from that of prose. Now the burden of the proof lies with the oppugner, not with the supporters of the common belief. Mr. Wordsworth, in consequence, assigns as the proof of his position, "that not only the language of a large portion of every good poem, even of the most elevated character, must necessarily, except with reference to the metre, in no respect differ from that of good prose, but likewise that some of the most interesting parts of the best poems will be found to be strictly the language of prose, when prose is well written. The truth of this assertion might be demonstrated by innumerable passages from almost all the poetical writings, even of Milton himself." He then quotes Gray's sonnet—

> "In vain to me the smiling mornings shine,
> And reddening Phœbus lifts his golden fire;
> The birds in vain their amorous descant join,
> Or cheerful fields resume their green attire.
> These ears, alas! for other notes repine;
> *A different object do these eyes require;*
> *My lonely anguish melts no heart but mine;*
> *And in my breast the imperfect joys expire.*
> Yet morning smiles the busy race to cheer,
> And new-born pleasure brings to happier men;
> The fields to all their wonted tribute bear;

> To warm their little loves the birds complain:
> *I fruitless mourn to him that cannot hear,*
> *And weep the more, because I weep in vain;"*

and adds the following remark:—"It will easily be perceived, that the only part of this Sonnet which is of any value, is the lines printed in italics; it is equally obvious, that, except in the rhyme, and in the use of the single word 'fruitless' for fruitlessly, which is so far a defect, the language of these lines does in no respect differ from that of prose."

An idealist defending his system by the fact, that when asleep we often believe ourselves awake, was well answered by his plain neighbour, "Ah, but when awake do we ever believe ourselves asleep?" Things identical must be convertible. The preceding passage seems to rest on a similar sophism. For the question is not, whether there may not occur in prose an order of words, which would be equally proper in a poem; nor whether there are not beautiful lines and sentences of frequent occurrence in good poems, which would be equally becoming as well as beautiful in good prose; for neither the one nor the other has ever been either denied or doubted by any one. The true question must be, whether there are not modes of expression, a construction, and an order of sentences, which are in their fit and natural place in a serious prose composition, but would be disproportionate and heterogeneous in metrical poetry; and, *vice versa,* whether in the language of a serious poem there may not be an arrangement both of words and sentences, and a use and selection of (what are called) figures of speech, both as to their kind, their frequency, and their occasions, which on a subject of equal weight would be vicious and alien in correct and manly prose. I contend, that in both cases this unfitness of each for the place of the other frequently will and ought to exist.

And first from the origin of metre. This I would trace to the balance in the mind effected by that spontaneous effort which strives to hold in check the workings of passion. It might be easily explained likewise in what manner this salutary antagonism is assisted by the very state, which it counteracts; and how this balance of antagonists became organized into metre (in the usual acceptation of that term), by a supervening act of the will and judgment, consciously and for the foreseen purpose of pleasure. Assuming these principles, as the data of our argument, we deduce from them two legitimate conditions, which the critic is entitled to expect in every metrical work. First, that, as the elements of metre owe their existence to a state of increased excitement, so the metre itself should be accompanied by the natural language of excitement. Secondly, that as these elements are formed into metre artificially, by a voluntary act, with the design and for the purpose of blending delight with emotion, so the traces of present volition should throughout the metrical language be proportionately discernible. Now these two conditions must be reconciled and co-present. There must be not only a partnership, but a union; an interpenetration of passion and of will, of spontaneous impulse and of voluntary purpose. Again, this union can be manifested only in a frequency of forms and figures of speech, (originally the offspring of passion, but now the adopted children of power), greater than would be desired or endured, where the emotion is not voluntarily encouraged and kept up for the sake of that pleasure, which such emotion, so tempered and mastered by the will, is found capable of communicating. It not only dictates, but of itself tends to produce a more frequent employment of picturesque and vivifying language, than would be natural in any other case, in which there did not exist, as there does in the present, a previous and well understood, though tacit, compact between the poet and his reader, that the latter is entitled to expect, and the former bound to supply this species and degree of pleasurable excitement. We may in some measure apply to this union the answer of Polixenes, in the Winter's Tale, to Perdita's neglect of the streaked gilliflowers, because she had heard it said,

"There is an art, which, in their piedness, shares
With great creating nature.

Pol   Say there be;
Yet nature is made better by no mean,
But nature makes that mean; so, o'er that art,
Which, you say, adds to nature, is an art,
That nature makes. You see, sweet maid, we marry
A gentler scion to the wildest stock;
And make conceive a bark of baser kind
By bud of nobler race. This is an art,
Which does mend nature,—change it rather; but
The art itself is nature."

Secondly, I argue from the effects of metre. As far as metre acts in and for itself, it tends to increase the vivacity and susceptibility both of the general feelings and of the attention. This effect it produces by the continued excitement of surprise, and by the quick reciprocations of curiosity still gratified and still re-excited, which are too slight indeed to be at any one moment objects of distinct consciousness, yet become considerable in their aggregate influence. As a medicated atmosphere, or as wine during animated conversation, they act powerfully, though themselves unnoticed. Where, therefore, correspondent food and appropriate matter are not provided for the attention and feelings thus roused there must needs be a disappointment felt; like that of leaping in the dark from the last step of a staircase, when we had prepared our muscles for a leap of three or four.

The discussion on the powers of metre in the preface is highly ingenious and touches at all points on truth. But I cannot find any statement of its powers considered abstractly and separately. On the contrary Mr. Wordsworth seems always to estimate metre by the powers, which it exerts during, (and, as I think, in consequence of), its combination with other elements of poetry. Thus the previous difficulty is left unanswered, what the elements are, with which it must be combined, in order to produce its own effects to any pleasurable purpose. Double and tri-syllable rhymes, indeed, form a lower species of wit, and, attended to exclusively for their own sake, may become a source of momentary amusement; as in poor Smart's distich to the Welsh Squire who had promised him a hare:

"Tell me, thou son of great Cadwallader!
Hast sent the hare? or hast thou swallow'd her?"

But for any poetic purposes, metre resembles, (if the aptness of the simile may excuse its meanness), yeast, worthless or disagreeable by itself, but giving vivacity and spirit to the liquor with which it is proportionally combined.

The reference to THE CHILDREN IN THE WOOD by no means satisfies my judgment. We all willingly throw ourselves back for awhile into the feelings of our childhood. This ballad, therefore, we read under such recollections of our own childish feelings, as would equally endear to us poems, which Mr. Wordsworth himself would regard as faulty in the opposite extreme of gaudy and technical ornament. Before the invention of printing, and in a still greater degree, before the introduction of writing, metre, especially alliterative metre, (whether alliterative at the beginning of the words, as in PIERCE PLOUMAN, or at the end, as in rhymes,) possessed an independent value as assisting the recollection, and consequently the preservation, of any series of truths or incidents. But I am not convinced by the collation of facts, that THE CHILDREN IN THE WOOD owes either its preservation, or its popularity, to its metrical form. Mr. Marshal's repository affords a number of tales in prose inferior in pathos and general merit, some of as old a date, and many as widely popular. TOM HICKATHRIFT, JACK THE GIANT-KILLER, GOODY TWO-SHOES, and LITTLE RED RIDING-HOOD are formidable rivals. And that they have continued in prose, cannot be fairly explained by the assumption, that the comparative meanness of their thoughts and images precluded even the humblest forms of metre. The scene of GOODY TWO-SHOES in the church is perfectly susceptible of metrical narration; and, among the θαυματα θαυμαστότατα even of the present age, I do not recollect a more astonishing image than that of the "whole rookery, that flew out of the giant's beard," scared by the tremendous voice, with which this monster answered the challenge of the heroic TOM HICKATHRIFT!

If from these we turn to compositions universally, and independently of all early associations, beloved and admired; would the MARIA, THE MONK, or THE POOR MAN'S ASS of Sterne, be read with more delight, or have a better chance of immortality, had they without any change in the diction been composed in rhyme, than in their present state? If I am not grossly mistaken, the general reply would be in the negative. Nay, I will confess, that, in Mr. Wordsworth's own volumes, the ANECDOTE FOR FATHERS, SIMON LEE, ALICE FELL, BEGGARS, and THE SAILOR'S MOTHER, notwithstanding the beauties which are to be found in each of them where the poet interposes the music of his own thoughts, would have been more delightful to me in prose, told and managed, as by Mr. Wordsworth they would have been, in a moral essay or pedestrian tour.

Metre in itself is simply a stimulant of the attention, and therefore excites the question: Why is the attention to be thus stimulated? Now the question cannot be answered by the pleasure of the metre itself: for this we have shown to be conditional, and dependent on the appropriateness of the thoughts and expressions, to which the metrical form is superadded. Neither can I conceive any other answer that can be rationally given, short of this: I write in metre, because I am about to use a language different from that of prose. Besides, where the language is not such, how interesting soever the reflections are, that are capable of being drawn by a philosophic mind from the thoughts or incidents of the poem, the metre itself must often become feeble. Take the last three stanzas of THE SAILOR'S MOTHER, for instance. If I could for a moment abstract from the effect produced on the author's feelings, as a man, by the incident at the time of its real occurrence, I would dare appeal to his own judgment, whether in the metre itself he found a sufficient reason for their being written metrically?

And, thus continuing, she said,
"I had a Son, who many a day
Sailed on the seas; but he is dead;
In Denmark he was cast away;
And I have travelled far as Hull to see
What clothes he might have left, or other property.

The Bird and Cage they both were his:
'Twas my Son's Bird; and neat and trim
He kept it: many voyages
This Singing-bird hath gone with him;
When last he sailed he left the Bird behind;
As it might be, perhaps, from bodings of his mind.

He to a Fellow-lodger's care
Had left it, to be watched and fed,
Till he came back again; and there
I found it when my Son was dead;
And now, God help me for my little wit!
I trail it with me, Sir! he took so much delight in it."

If disproportioning the emphasis we read these stanzas so as to make the rhymes perceptible, even tri-syllable rhymes could scarcely produce an equal sense of oddity and strangeness, as we feel here in finding *rhymes at all* in sentences so exclusively colloquial. I would further ask whether, but for that visionary state, into which the figure of the woman and the susceptibility of his own genius had placed the poet's imagination,—(a state, which spreads its influence and colouring over all, that co-exists with the exciting cause, and in which

"The simplest, and the most familiar things
Gain a strange power of spreading awe around them,")[1]

I would ask the poet whether he would not have felt an abrupt downfall in these verses from the preceding stanza?

"The ancient spirit is not dead;
Old times, thought I, are breathing there;
Proud was I that my country bred
Such strength, a dignity so fair:
She begged an alms, like one in poor estate;
I looked at her again, nor did my pride abate."

It must not be omitted, and is besides worthy of notice, that those stanzas furnish the only fair instance that I have been able to discover in all Mr. Wordsworth's writings, of an actual adoption, or true imitation, of *the real and very language of low and rustic life,* freed from provincialisms.

Thirdly, I deduce the position from all the causes elsewhere assigned, which render metre the proper form of poetry, and poetry imperfect and defective without metre. Metre, therefore, having been connected with poetry most often and by a peculiar fitness, whatever else is combined with metre must, though it be not itself essentially poetic, have nevertheless some property in common with poetry, as in *intermedium* of affinity, a sort, (if I may dare borrow a well-known phrase from technical chemistry), of *mordant* between it and the super-added metre. Now poetry, Mr. Wordsworth truly affirms, does always imply passion: which word must be here understood in its most general sense, as an excited state of the feelings and faculties. And as every passion has its proper pulse, so will it likewise have its characteristic modes of expression. But where there exists that degree of genius and talent which entitles a writer to aim at the honours of a poet, the very act of poetic composition itself is, and is allowed to imply and to produce, an unusual state of excitement, which of course justifies and demands a correspondent difference of language, as truly, though not perhaps in as marked a degree, as the excitement of love, fear, rage, or jealousy. The vividness of the descriptions or declamations in Donne or Dryden, is as much and as often derived from the force and fervour of the describer, as from the reflections, forms or incidents, which constitute their subject and materials. The wheels take fire from the mere rapidity of their motion. To what extent, and under what modifications, this may be admitted to act, I shall attempt to define in an after remark on Mr. Wordsworth's reply to this objection, or rather on his objection to this reply, as already anticipated in his preface.

Fourthly, and as intimately connected with this, if not the same argument in a more general form, I adduce the high spiritual instinct of the human being impelling us to seek unity by harmonious adjustment, and thus establishing the principle that *all* the parts of an organized whole must be assimilated to the more *important* and *essential* parts. This and the preceding arguments may be strengthened by the reflection, that the composition of a poem is among the imitative arts; and that imitation, as opposed to copying, consists either in the interfusion of the same throughout the radically different, or of the different throughout a base radically the same.

Lastly, I appeal to the practice of the best poets, of all countries and in all ages, as authorizing the opinion, (deduced from all the foregoing,) that in every import of the word essential, which would not here involve a mere truism, there may be, is, and ought to be an *essential* difference between the language of prose and of metrical composition.

In Mr. Wordsworth's criticism of Gray's Sonnet, the reader's sympathy with his praise or blame of the different parts is taken for granted rather perhaps too easily. He has not, at least, attempted to win or compel it by argumentative analysis. In my conception at least, the lines rejected as of no value do, with the exception of the two first, differ as much and as little from the language of common life, as those which he has printed in italics as possessing genuine excellence. Of the five lines thus honourably distinguished, two of them differ from prose even more widely, than the lines which either precede or follow, in the position of the words.

> *"A different object do these eyes require;*
> My lonely anguish melts no heart but mine;
> *And in my breast the imperfect joys expire."*

But were it otherwise, what would this prove, but a truth, of which no man ever doubted?— *Videlicet,* that there are sentences, which would be equally in their place both in verse and prose. Assuredly it does not prove the point, which alone requires proof; namely, that there are not passages, which would suit the one and not suit the other. The first line of this sonnet is distinguished from the ordinary language of men by the epithet to morning. For we will set aside, at present, the consideration, that the particular word "smiling" is hackneyed, and, as it involves a sort of personification, not quite congruous with the common and material attribute of *shining.* And, doubtless, this adjunction of epithets for the purpose of additional description, where no particular attention is demanded for the quality of the thing, would be noticed as giving a poetic cast to a man's conversation. Should the sportsman exclaim, "Come boys! the rosy morning calls you up:"—he will be supposed to have some song in his head. But no one suspects this, when he says, "A wet morning shall not confine us to our beds." This then is either a defect in poetry, or it is not. Whoever should decide in the affirmative, I would request him to re-peruse any one poem, of any confessedly great poet from Homer to Milton, or from Æschylus to Shakespeare; and to strike out, (in thought I mean), every instance of this kind. If the number of these fancied erasures did not startle him; or if he continued to deem the work improved by their total omission; he must advance reasons of no ordinary strength and evidence, reasons grounded in the essence of human nature. Otherwise, I should not hesitate to consider him as a man not so much proof against all authority, as dead to it.

The second line,

> "And reddening Phœbus lifts his golden fire;—"

has indeed almost as many faults as words. But then it is a bad line, not because the language is distinct from that of prose; but because it conveys incongruous images; because it confounds the cause and the effect, the real thing with the personified representative of the thing; in short, because it differs from the language of good sense! That the "Phœbus" is hackneyed, and a school-boy image, is an accidental fault, dependent on the age in which the author wrote, and not deduced from the nature of the thing. That it is part of an exploded mythology, is an objection more deeply grounded. Yet when the torch of ancient learning was re-kindled, so cheering were its beams, that our eldest poets, cut off by Christianity from all accredited machinery, and deprived of all acknowledged guardians and symbols of the great objects of nature, were naturally induced to adopt, as a poetic language, those fabulous personages, those forms of the[2] supernatural in nature, which had given them such dear delight in the poems of their great masters. Nay, even at this day what scholar of genial taste will not so far sympathize with them, as to read with pleasure in Petrarch, Chaucer, or Spenser, what he would perhaps condemn as puerile in a modern poet?

I remember no poet, whose writings would safelier stand the test of Mr. Wordsworth's theory, than Spenser. Yet will Mr. Wordsworth say, that the style of the following stanza is either undistinguished from prose, and the language of ordinary life? Or that it is vicious, and that the stanzas are *blots* in THE FAERY QUEEN?

> "By this the northern wagoner had set
> His sevenfold teme behind the stedfast starre,
> That was in ocean waves yet never wet,
> But firme is fixt and sendeth light from farre
> To all that in the wild deep wandering arre:
> And chearfull chaunticlere with his note shrill
> Had warned once that Phœbus' fiery carre
> In hast was climbing up the easterne hill,
> Full envious that night so long his roome did fill."
>
> *Book I. Can. 2. St. 2*

> "At last the golden orientall gate
> Of greatest heaven gan to open fayre,
> And Phœbus fresh, as brydegrome to his mate,
> Came dauncing forth, shaking his deawie hayre,
> And hurl'd his glist'ring beams through gloomy ayre;
> Which when the wakeful elfe perceived, straightway
> He started up, and did him selfe prepayre
> In sun-bright armes and battailous array;
> For with that pagan proud he combat will that day."
>
> *Book I. Can. 5. St. 2*

On the contrary to how many passages, both in hymn books and in blank verse poems, could I, (were it no invidious), direct the reader's attention, the style of which is most unpoetic, because, and only because, it is the style of prose? He will not suppose me capable of having in my mind such verses, as

> "I put my hat upon my head
> And walk'd into the Strand;

And there I met another man,
Whose hat was in his hand."

    To such specimens it would indeed be a fair and full reply, that these lines are not bad, because they are unpoetic; but because they are empty of all sense and feeling and that it were an idle attempt to prove that "an ape is not a Newton, when it is self-evident that he is not a man." But the sense shall be good and weighty, the language correct and dignified, the subject interesting and treated with feeling; and yet the style shall, notwithstanding all these merits, be justly blamable as prosaic, and solely because the words and the order of the words would find their appropriate place in prose, but are not suitable to metrical composition.

Notes

1 "Altered from the description of Night-Mair in the REMORSE.
"Oh Heaven! 'twas frightful! Now ran down and stared at
By hideous shapes that cannot be remembered;
Now seeing nothing and imagining nothing;
But only being afraid—stifled with fear!
While every goodly or familiar form
Had a strange power of spreading terror round me!"

N.B.—Though Shakespeare has, for his own *all-justifying* purposes, introduced the Night-*Mars* with her own foals, yet Mair means a Sister, or perhaps a Hag.

2 But still more by the mechanical system of philosophy which has needlessly infected our theological opinions, and teaching us to consider the world in its relation to God, as of a building to its mason, leaves the idea of omnipresence a mere abstracts notion in the state-room of our reason.

17 Essay on English Metrical Law (1857)

Coventry Patmore

The adoption, by Surrey and his immediate successors, of certain foreign metres[1] into our poetry, and the unprecedented attempt of that accomplished writer to establish 'blank verse' as a narrative vehicle, first aroused conscious and scientific interest in the subject of the mechanism of English verse. From that time to this, the nature of modern verse has been a favourite problem of enthusiasts who love to dive in deep waters for diving's sake. A vast mass of nondescript matter has been brought up from the recesses visited, but no one has succeeded in rendering any sufficient account of this secret of the intellectual deep. I have made it my business to ascertain whether any of the musical grammarians,[2] whose science is, in great part, a mere abstraction of the laws of metre, have supplied the deficiencies of the prosodians. The sum total of my inquiries in both fields of criticism, musical and poetical, amounts to this, that upon few other subjects has so much been written with so little tangible result. Without for a moment questioning the value of certain portions of the writings of Puttenham, Gascoigne, Campion, Webbe, Daniel, Crowe, Foster, Mitford, Guest,[3] and others, it must be confessed that no one of these writers renders anything like a full and philosophical account of the subject; and that, with the exception of Daniel, the admirable author of the 'Civil Wars,' and Mitford, none has treated the question, even on the superficial ground in most cases assumed, with the combined ability and competence of information from which alone any important fruit can be looked for in such investigations. George Puttenham's 'Art of English Poesy' is by very much the most bulky and laborious of the early metrical essays; but at least nine-tenths of this book consist of as unprofitable writing as ever spoilt paper. His chapter on the arrangement of rhymes to form staves[4] is worthy of the poetical student's attention; and there is in the outset of his work an explicit acknowledgment[5] of the fact, so often lost sight of by his successors, that English verse is not properly measurable by the rules of Latin and Greek verse.[6] Indeed, the early poetical critics commonly manifest a much clearer discernment of the main importance of rhyme[7] and accentual stress, in English verse, than is to be found among later writers. Their views are, for the most part, far from being expressed with that positiveness and appearance of system characterising the school of critics[8] which received its data from Pope and his compeers; but they are, upon the whole, considerably more in accordance with the true spirit[9] of English verse, as it appears in its highest excellence in the writings of the poets of Elizabeth and James. The dissertations of the second class of critics, of whom Foster was the best example, are rendered comparatively useless by the adoption of false or confused opinions as the groundwork of their theories; such, for instance, as Foster's assumption that the time of syllables in English[10] keeps the proportion usually attributed to long and short quantities in Greek and Latin, and that the metrical ictus or stress in English is identical with elevation of tone;[11]—mistakes which seem also to have been made by Dr. Johnson in the prosody prefixed to his Dictionary,[12] and by various other writers of his time. Joshua Steele[13] has the praise of having propounded more fully than had hitherto been done, the true view of metre, as being primarily based upon isochronous division by ictuses or accents;[14] and he, for the first time, clearly declared the necessity of measuring pauses[15] in minutely scanning English verse. He remarked the strong pause[16] which is required for the proper delivery of adjacent accented syllables, and without which the most beautiful verses must often be read into harsh prose. But the just and important views of this writer were mingled with so much that was erroneous and impracticable, that they made little or no general impression. Mitford's careful work on the Harmony of Language is perhaps the most significant book which has appeared upon the subject. This work, though far from containing the whole, or the unmixed truth, has not yet been superseded by any of the several elaborate essays on the same theme which have since appeared. Mr. Guest's work on English Rhythms is a laborious and, in some respects, valuable performance; but many of his observations indicate an ear defective to a degree which seriously impairs their value, when they concern the more subtle kinds of metrical effect. The value of his work is further diminished by a singular unskilfulness in the mode of arranging his materials, and communicating his views. He has fallen into the great error of endeavouring to simplify and abbreviate his statements by adopting, for the indication of different species of verse, a notation[17] which few persons can fairly be called upon to take the pains to comprehend and follow.

The radical faults of nearly all the writers I have mentioned, and of those who have followed in their steps, are, first, the mistake of working in ignorance of the truth declared by Quintilian, 'that mere literature, without a knowledge of sounds, will not enable a man to treat properly of metre and rhythm;'[18] and, secondly, that of having formed too light an estimate of their subject, whereby they have been prevented from sounding deep enough for the discovery of the philosophical grounds and primary laws of metrical expression. No one, with any just sense of the exalted but unobtrusive functions of art,[19] will expect to derive much artistic instruction from the writings of men who set about their work, perhaps their life's work, with such sentiments as Dr. Burney was not ashamed to avow at the commencement of that laborious treatise which is still deservedly a text-book of musical history: 'I would rather be pronounced trivial than tiresome; for music being, at best, but an amusement, its history merits not, in reading, the labour of intense application.'[20] And again: 'What is music? An innocent luxury, unnecessary indeed to existence, but a great improvement and gratification to our sense of hearing.'[21]

The nature of the relation between the poet's peculiar mode of expression and the matter expressed[22] has engaged the curiosity of many philosophic minds. Hegel,[23] whose chapters on music and metre contain by far the most satisfactory piece of writing I know of on the subject, admirably observes, that versification affords a necessary counterpoise[24] to the great spiritualisation of language in poetry. 'It is false,' he adds, 'that versification offers any obstacle to the free outpouring of poetic thought. True genius disposes with ease of sensible materials, and moves therein as in a native element, which, instead of depressing or hindering, exalts and supports its flight.'[25] Art, indeed, must have a body as well as a soul;[26] and the higher and purer the spiritual, the more powerful and unmistakable should be the corporeal element;—in other words, the more vigorous and various the life, the more stringent and elaborate must be the law[27] by obedience to which life expresses itself.

The co-ordination of life and law, in the matter and form of poetry, determines the different degrees and kinds[28] of metre, from the half-prosaic dramatic verse to the extremest elaboration of high lyric metres. The quality of all emotion which is not ignoble is to boast of its allegiance to law. The limits and decencies of ordinary speech will by no means declare high and strong feelings with efficiency. These must have free use of all sorts of figures and latitudes of speech; such latitudes as would at once be perceived by a delicately constituted mind to be lax and vicious, without the shackles of artistic form.[29] What in prose would be shrieks and vulgar hyperbole, is transmuted by metre into graceful and impressive song. This effect of metre has often been alluded to, with more or less exactness of thought and expression. 'Bacon,' says Mr. Dallas, 'regards metre as a curb or shackle, where everything else is riot and lawless revelling; Wordsworth regards it as a mark of order, and so an assurance of reality needed in such an unusual state of mind as he takes poetry to be; and Coleridge would trace it to the balance struck between our passions and spontaneous efforts to hold them in check.'[30] From the truth which is implied alike in these several propositions, an important and neglected corollary follows: metre ought not only to exist as the becoming garment[31] of poetic passion, but, furthermore, it should continually make its existence recognized. Some writers, by a peculiar facility of language, have attained to write perfect metre with almost as little metrical effect[32] as if it were prose. Now this is no merit, but very much the reverse. The language should always seem to *feel,* though not to *suffer from* the bonds of verse. The very deformities produced, really or apparently, in the phraseology of a great poet, by the confinement of metre, are beautiful, exactly for the same reasons that in architecture justify the bossy Gothic foliage,[33] so unlike Nature, and yet, indeed, in its place and purpose as art, so much more beautiful than Nature.[34] Metre never attains its noblest effects when it is altogether unproductive of those beautiful exorbitancies on the side of law. Milton and Shakspeare are full of them; and we may declare the excellence of these effects without danger to the poorer proprieties of the lower walks of art, since no small poet can originate them, or even copy them, without making himself absurd. Wordsworth's erroneous critical views[35] of the necessity of approximating the language of poetry, as much as possible, to that of prose, especially by the avoidance of grammatical inversions, arose from his having overlooked the necessity of manifesting, as well as moving in, the bonds of verse. In the finest specimens of versification, there seems to be a perpetual conflict[36] between the law of the verse and the freedom of the language, and each is incessantly, though insignificantly, violated for the purpose of giving effect to the other. The best poet is not he whose verses are the most easily scanned, and whose phraseology is the commonest in its materials, and the most direct in its arrangement; but rather he whose language combines the greatest imaginative accuracy[37] with the most elaborate and sensible[38] metrical organization, and who, in his verse, preserves everywhere the living sense of metre, not so much by unvarying obedience to, as by innumerable small departures from, its *modulus.*[39] The over-smooth[40] and 'accurate' metre of much of the eighteenth century poetry, to an ear able to appreciate the music of Milton and the best parts of Coleridge, is almost as great a defect as the entire dissolution of metre[41] displayed by some of the writers of our own century.

The reader will already have discovered that I am writing under a conviction that the musical and metrical[42] expression of emotion is an instinct, and not an artifice. Were the vulgar[43] and infantine delight in rhythm insufficient to justify that conviction, history itself would prove it. The earliest writings of all nations possessing regularly constituted languages have been rhythmical in that high degree which takes the form of verse.[44] 'Verse,' as Ellis well observes, 'is anterior to prose, because our passions are anterior to reason and judgment; because vocal sounds are the natural expression of emotion, not of reflection.'[45] On examination, however, it will be found that the most ordinary speaking involves the musical and metrical element[46] in an easily appreciable degree, and as an integral part of language, and that this element commonly assumes conspicuousness and importance in proportion to the amount of emotion intended to be expressed. Metre, in the primary[47] degree of a simple series of isochronous intervals,[48] marked by accents, is as natural to spoken language as an even pace is natural to walking. Prose delivery, without this amount of metre, is like a drunkard's walk, the irregularity of which is so far from being natural to a person in his senses, that it is not even to be imitated without effort. Now, as dancing is no more than an increase of the element of measure which already exists in walking,[49] so verse is but an additional degree of that metre[50] which is inherent in prose speaking. Again, as there is this difference between prose and verse generically, so the same difference gives rise to specific kinds of prose and of verse; and the prose of a common law report differs from that of an impassioned piece of oratory, just in the same way that semi-prosaic dramatic verse differs from on elaborate lyric.

[…]

Let me now ask, What do we mean by 'accent,' as the word is commonly used in speaking of its function in English verse?—for I may dismiss the Greek meaning as being well defined in its independence of ours, which, whatever it is, is certainly not *pure tone*. Some writers have identified our metrical accent with long quantity;[51] others have placed it in relative loudness: others have fancied it to consist, like the Greek, in pure tone; others have regarded it as a compound of loudness and elevation of tone; and others, as a compound of height and duration of tone; others, again, have regarded it as the general prominence acquired by one syllable over another, by any or all of these elements in combination. Now, it seems to me that the only tenable view of that accent upon which it is allowed, with more or less distinctness, by all, that English metre depends, in contradistinction to the syllabic[52] metre of the ancients, is the view which attributes to it the function of marking, *by whatever means*, certain isochronous intervals. Metre implies something measured; an assertion which sounds like a truism; but to a person much read in our metrical critics, it will probably seem a startling novelty. It is one, however, which can afford to stand without any further recommendation than its obvious merits, for the present. The thing measured is the time occupied in the delivery of a series of words. But time measured implies something that measures, *and is therefore itself unmeasured*;[53] an argument before which those who hold that English accent and long quantity are identical[54] must bow. These are two indispensable conditions of metre,—first, that the sequence of vocal utterance, represented by written verse, shall be divided into equal or proportionate spaces;[55] secondly, *that the fact of that division shall be made manifest* by an 'ictus' or 'beat,'[56] actual or mental, which, like a post in a chain railing, shall mark the end of one space, and the commencement of another. This 'ictus' is an acknowledged condition of all possible metre;[57] and its function is, of course, much more conspicuous in languages so chaotic in their syllabic quantities as to render it the *only* source of metre. Yet, all-important as this time-beater is, I think it demonstrable that, for the most part, *it has no material and external existence*[58] *at all*, but has its place in the mind, which craves measure in everything, and, wherever the idea of measure is uncontradicted, delights in marking it with an imaginary 'beat.' The Greeks, it appears, could tolerate, and even delight, in that which, to our ear, would confuse and contradict measure. Our habits require that everything which gives preponderance to a syllable shall, as a rule, be concentrated upon one, in order to render it duly capable of the mental 'ictus.' Those qualities which, singly, or in various combination, have hitherto been declared to *be* accent, are indeed only the *conditions of accent;* a view which derives an invincible amount of corroboration from its answering exactly to the character and conditions of accent in vocal and instrumental music, of which the laws cannot be too strictly attended to, if we would arrive at really satisfactory conclusions concerning modern European metre. People are too apt to fancy they are employing a figure of speech when they talk of the music of poetry. The word 'music' is in reality a much more accurate expression for that which delights us in good verse, apart from the meaning, than the word 'rhythm,' which is commonly employed by those who think to express themselves with greater propriety. Rhythm, when the term is not meant to be synonymous with a combination of varied tone and measured time, must signify an abstraction of the merely metrical character extremely difficult to realise, on account of the curious, though little noticed, tendency of the mind to connect the idea of tone with that of time or measure. There is no charm in the rhythm of monotones, unless the notion of monotone can be overcome; and, when that is the case, it is not rhythm, but rhythmical melody, whereby we are pleased. If Grétry, when a child, danced to the pulsations of a waterfall,[59] it was because his fancy abolished their monotony. The ticking of a clock[60] is truly monotonous; but when we listen to it, we hear, or rather seem to hear, two, or even four, distinct tones, upon the imaginary distinction of which, and the equally imaginary emphasis of one or two, depends what we call its rhythm. In the case of the beat of a drum, this ideal apprehension of tone is still more remarkable: in imitating its tattoo, the voice expresses what the mind imagines, and, in doing so, employs several varieties of tone. In all such cases, however, the original sounds, though monotonous, are far from being pure monotones; they are metrical recurrences of the same *noise*, rather than the same tone;[61] and it is very interesting to observe, that we cannot evoke what we thus erroneously term 'rhythm' from the measured repetition of a perfectly pure tone. The tattoo of a knuckle upon the table will lose most, if not all, of its rhythm, if transferred to a bell. The drum gives 'rhythm;' but the clear note of the 'triangle' is nothing without another instrument, *because it does not admit of an imagined variation.*

The relation of music to language[62] ought to be recognised as something more than that of similarity, if we would rightly appreciate either. 'The musical art,' says G. Weber, 'consists in the expression of feelings by means of tones.'[63] Now, all feelings have relation to thought or facts which may be stated, or at least suggested, in words; and the union of descriptive words with an expressive variation and measurement of tones, constitutes, according to the amount and kind of feeling, and the truth[64] of its vocal expression, song, poetry,[65] and even the most ordinary spoken language. *Perfect poetry and song are, in fact, nothing more than perfect speech[66] upon high and moving subjects*; a truth upon which Grétry, one of the soundest, as well as by very much the most amusing of modern musical critics, inferentially insists, when he says, 'Il est une musique qui ayant pour base la declamation des paroles, est vraie comme les passions,'[67] which is as much as to say, that there is no right melody which is not so founded. And again, 'La parole est un bruit ou le chant est renfermé;'[68] a statement which is the converse of the other, and amounts to a charge of imperfection against our ordinary modes of speaking, in so far as, when concerned with the expression of the feelings, they do not amount to pure song. Who has not heard entire sentences, and even series of sentences, so spoken by women, who are usually incomparably better speakers[69] than men, as to constitute a strain of melody which might at once be written down in notes,[70] and played, but with no increase of musical effect, on the piano? Where was the 'bruit' in Rachel's delivery[71] of an impassioned passage of Racine? Her rendering of such passages was not commonly recognised as pure song because, in modern times (it was not so with the Greeks), song, by having been long regarded as an 'artificial' mode of expression, has fallen into extravagance and falsehood, and is now very rarely 'vrai comme les passions.' Modern singing and modern declamation, as a rule, are equally far removed from that just[72] medium at which they coalesce and become one. In song, we have gradually fallen into the adoption of an extent of scale, and a diversity of time, which is simply *nonsensical*;[73]

for such variations of tone and time correspond to no depths or transitions of feeling of which the human breast is cognisant. The *permanent* popular instinct, which is ever the best test of truth in art, recognises the falsehood of these extremes; and Grétry well asks, 'N'avons nous pas remarqué que les airs les plus connus sont ceux qui embrassent le moins d'espace, le moins de notes, le plus court diapason? Voyez, presque tous les airs que le temps a respectés, il sont dans ce cas.'[74] The musical shortcomings of ordinary recitation are not nearly so inexcusable as the extravagancies of most modern song. *Perfect* readers of high poetry are as rare as fine singers and good composers,[75] for the sufficient reason, that they *are* fine singers and good composers, though they may not suspect it in an age of unnatural divorce of sound and sense. What is commonly accounted good reading—what indeed is such when compared with the inanimate style of most readers—falls immeasurably short of the musical sense of really fine verse. The interval between the veriest mouther and an ordinarily accomplished elocutionist,[76] is scarcely greater than that which separates the latter from the *ideal* actor, who should be able to effect for the poetry of Shakspeare what Rachel did for, here and there, a line of Racine. Hence, few lovers of good poetry care to hear it read or acted; for, although themselves, in all likelihood, quite unable to give such poetry a true and full vocal interpretation, their unexpressed imagination of its music is much higher than their own or any ordinary reading of it would be. Poets themselves have sometimes been very bad readers[77] of their own verses; and it seems not unlikely that their acute sense of what such reading ought to be, discomposes and discourages them when they attempt to give their musical idea a material realisation. In this matter of the relationship of music and poetry, the voice of theory is corroborated by that of history. 'These two arts,' writes Dr. Burney, 'were at first so intimately connected, and so dependent on each other, that rules for poetry were in general rules for music; and the properties and effects of both were so much confounded together that it is extremely difficult to disentangle them.'[78]

Notes

Title ESSAY ON ENGLISH METRICAL LAW. *English Metrical Critics NBR;* PREFATORY STUDY ON ENGLISH METRICAL LAW. (*with footnote:*) This Essay appeared, almost as it now stands, in vol. xxvii. of the *North British Review. Am;* PREFATORY STUDY ON ENGLISH METRICAL LAW. *Pi*

NBR has heading and introductory paragraph: ART. VI—1. The Art of Elocution. By GEORGE VANDENHOFF. London: 1S55. 8vo.

2. *A History of English Rhythms.* By E. GUEST. London: 1838. 8vo.

3. *The Ancient Rhythmical Art Recovered.* By WILLIAM O'BRIEN. Dublin: 1843. 8vo.

Verses, good or bad, at one time or another have exercised the power of delighting and impressing all persons. It seems, therefore, somewhat singular that all theories and criticisms of the nature of verse, and canons for its composition, should hitherto have been found the most dreary of reading: prosaic *par excellence,* "prosody," in short—a word scarcely proper to be spoken within hearing of the ladies, a necessary evil of academic days, a subject which pedantry itself seldom dreams of obtruding upon ears polite. The reason seems to be, that in this department of learning investigators have failed to reach, often even to seek, those fundamental truths, which, if discovered, must confer connection and unity, and consequently intellectual interest, on all the less general facts.

1 THE] The *indented, NBR*
2 a favourite] the pet *NBR*
3 of enthusiasts] of a large part of that peculiar class of enthusiasts *NBR*
4 A vast] An infinite *NBR*
5 no one has succeeded in] none of the divers has succeeded, to the complete satisfaction of any but himself, in *NBR*

6 any sufficient account] an account *NBR*
7 I] we *NBR*
8 my] our *NBR*
9 supplied the deficiencies] sounded the depths *NBR*
10 the prosodians.] this department of their art. *NBR*
11 my] our *NBR*
12 few other subjects] no other subject with which we are acquainted *NBR*
13 Daniel, Crowe,] Daniel Crowe, *Am*
14 there is] we find *NBR*
15 characterising] characterizing *NBR*
16 best] most notable *NBR*
17 English] English, *NBR, Am, P1*
18 Dr.] Dr *NBR*
19 his] that *NBR*
20 Mr.] Mr *NBR*
21 great] grave *NBR*
22 follow.] *NBR continues paragraph:* He throws, however, much new and interesting light upon the history of versification, and no student of the subject will omit to give his volumes a respectful reading. Mr Dallas brings metrical criticism up to the present day. His "Poetics" is a clever and amusing volume, made up of much fun, much metaphysics, and a good many observations to the purpose. Indeed the balance between the metaphysics and the fun is hard to strike. When we feel ourselves disposed to object to the style of such criticisms as "the centrifugal force wherewith the mind rushes forth into the objective, acting on the centripetal force of self-consciousness, generates the circling numbers of the revolving harmonies of poesy—in one word, a roundelay,"— we ought, perhaps, to satisfy ourselves as Charles Lamb, in a stutter, is said to have consoled a free-thinking friend who had just been irritated by one of Coleridge's "properer-for-a-sermon" philosophical monologues, and to conclude that all such criticisms are only Mr Dallas's ph-ph-ph-*fun!*
23 I] we *NBR*
24 and, secondly,] secondly, *NBR*
25 exalted] ex *at line end,* alted *on next line, om hyphen, NBR*
26 Dr.] Dr *NBR*
27 metre contain] metre, in the third volume of his Æsthetics, contain *NBR*
28 I] we *NBR*
29 outpouring] out-pouring *NBR*
30 unmistakable] unmistakeable *NBR*
31 law] law, *NBR*
32 itself.] *NBR continues paragraph:* The defective balance of these powers, the failure being on the material side, produces the effect of license in Shelley, and slovenliness in Wordsworth, and of much waste of the great spiritual powers of both; the opposite kind of failure, namely, the preponderance of form, has few examples among the writings of first-class English poets, but very many among those of Germany, whose prevailing error is that of causing form to weigh down and conceal, instead of expressing and supporting spirit. In this we do not allude only to metre, which is often over-elaborated by the best German poets, but to that which may be justly regarded as the continuation and development of the metrical element, namely, a highly and obviously artificial arrangement and unfolding of the subject.
33 half-prosaic] half prosaic *NBR*
34 ignoble] ignoble, *NBR*
35 delicately] finely *NBR*
36 vulgar] vular *NBR*
37 graceful and impressive song.] graceful song. *NBR*
38 Mr.] Mr *NBR*
39 propositions, an] propositions, it seems to us that an *NBR*
40 beautiful,] beautiful and noble, *NBR*
41 same reasons] same artistic reasons *NBR*
42 Gothic] gothic *NBR*
43 Nature] nature *NBR*
44 Nature.] nature herself. *NBR*

45 Shakspeare] Shakespeare *NBR*
46 himself absurd.] himself obviously absurd. *NBR*
47 scanned,] scannible, *NBR*
48 organisation,] organization, *NBR*
49 some of the writers] most of the versifiers *NBR*
50 century.] time. *NBR*
51 I am] we are *NBR*
52 found that] found out that *NBR*
53 And,] And *NBR*
54 my] our *NBR*
55 speaking] talking *NBR*
56 *Gentilhomme*] gentilhomme *NBR*
57 quantity:] quantity; *NBR, Am, P1*
58 me] us *NBR*
59 case] case, *NBR*
60 in English, generally indicative] in English generally, indicative *NBR*
61 me] us *NBR*
62 verse?—] verse? *NBR*
63 I] we *NBR*
64 me] us *NBR*
65 distinctness,] distinctness *NBR*
66 I] we *NBR*
67 habits require] grosser sense requires *NBR*
68 corroboration] corroboration, *NBR*
69 to,] to *NBR*
70 realise,] realize, *NBR*
71 two, or even four, distinct] two distinct *NBR*
72 one or two, depends] one, depends *NBR*
73 all,] all *NBR*
74 either.] either, *Am, P1*
75 *Perfect poetry and song are,*] *Perfect song is, NBR*
76 inferentially] emphatically *NBR*
77 ou] [*sic*]
78 women, who are usually incomparably better speakers than men,] women (who are incomparably better speakers than men), *NBR*

18 Investigation of Sound as Artistic Material (1880)

Sidney Lanier

It will now be useful to combine the two last propositions in a statement made from a different point of view. *A formal poem is always composed of such sounds and silences*[1] *(or of the signs, or of the conceptions, of such sounds and silences) as can be co-ordinated by the ear.*

By "sounds which can be co-ordinated by the ear" are meant sounds which the ear can perceive with such clearness that it is able to compare them with reference to some one or more particulars. For example, if, in strolling, we hear first the quick chirp of a sparrow and then the slow shrilling of the field-cricket in the grass, our ear can compare the two sounds as to *time,* and can decide that the latter is longer than the former: that is to say, the ear can co-ordinate these two sounds with reference to the particular of their *duration.*

Again: if, immediately afterwards, we hear the cry of a jay, our ear can compare it with the previous sounds as to the point of *loudness,* and can decide that the jay's sound is louder than the other two: that is to say, the ear can co-ordinate these three sounds with reference to the particular of their *intensity.*

Again: if we now hear in succession the grave coo of a dove and the keen piping of a field-lark, our ear can compare them as to the point of their relative *shrillness* or trebleness, and can decide that the latter is the shriller, or more treble, of the two: that is to say, the ear can co-ordinate these two sounds with reference to the particular of their *pitch.*

Again: if we now hear in succession the whirr of the grasshopper poised above the grass and the whistle of the partridge down the field, our ear can compare the two sounds as to the point of *tone-color,* and can decide that the grasshopper's note is somewhat like the low tones of the clarinet (having a certain fluttering quality characteristic of the reed-instruments), while the partridge's note has more likeness to the smoother flute: that is to say, the ear can co-ordinate these two tones with reference to the particular of their tone-color.

The foregoing are examples of the general co-ordination, or indefinite comparison, of sounds. But the reader is now asked to observe that in none of the instances given could the ear make any *exact co-ordination,* or definite measurement, of the sounds compared. To recur to the first example: while the ear could recognize that the song of the cricket was in a general way longer than that of the sparrow, it was unable to pronounce exactly how many times as long. So, in the second example, though we could say immediately that the jay's cry was more intense — that is, louder— than the sparrow's, we could not say how much more intense. In the third example, while we could pronounce the field-lark's note certainly higher in pitch than the dove's, we have no scale of degrees, like the musical scale, to which we could refer these two tones and ascertain their precise distance from each other, or musical "interval." And finally, in the fourth example, while the tone-color of the grasshopper's whirr is sufficiently distinct from that of the partridge's whistle, it is not so distinct as to admit of more than a general classification as reedy.

But the art of tone, which includes the art of music and the art of verse, depends upon exact co-ordinations by the ear. It is therefore necessary for us to advance beyond the consideration of such sounds as are capable merely of general co-ordination, or indefinite comparison, by the ear, to the consideration of such sounds as are further capable of exact co-ordination, or definite measurement, by the ear.

[…]

Stating the same purpose in different terms: since the four particulars mentioned (duration, intensity, pitch, and tone-color) comprise all the possible variations of sound and of silence, let us now inquire as to which of these particulars, if any, the ear of average persons has the power of *exactly co-ordinating* sounds. By the power of exact co-ordination is meant the power of conceiving the relations of sounds in terms of number, or in terms of degree. Thus if, of two sounds occupying different lengths of time, the ear is able to perceive that one was exactly twice as long as the other, it may be said that the ear has exactly co-ordinated, or definitely measured, those two sounds as to their duration, and has conceived the result in terms of number. If, again, any key of a piano be struck, and then another, and the ear recognizes the latter tone as lying at exactly six degrees (according to the musical scale of degrees) above the former, it may be said that the ear has exactly co-ordinated, or definitely measured, these two sounds with reference to their pitch, and has arrived at a conception of such co-ordination in terms of a precise scale of degrees. These illustrations will be carried farther in the next proposition.

Actual observation reveals that there are three particulars, and only three, as to which the ear has the power of exactly coordinating sounds. These three are duration, pitch, and tone-color.

Example of exact co-ordination with reference to the particular of duration. If a musician be asked to strike any key of a piano so that two of its sounds will exactly fill the time of one second, as marked off by a clock ticking seconds, he is able to do so without trouble: if, between any two ticks of the clock, he should hold the key down longer than its legitimate time of half a second, the deviation from the proper time is immediately observed: if he be told to make four sounds to the second, instead of two, he distributes them thus with ease: indeed, these are the simplest forms of example, and the musician can interpose between each tick of the clock, with unerring precision, sounds bearing to each other much more complex relations of duration. It is obvious that his power to do so, as well as the power to recognize *when* he does so, depends upon the remarkable capacity of the ear (affirmed in the first clause of this proposition) to co-ordinate sounds exactly with reference to their duration.

Example of exact co-ordination with reference to the particular of pitch. If any two keys of a piano be struck in succession, the musician will immediately name the relation of the latter to the former in terms of the musical scale, by his ear alone. Thus if the first key struck be the middle C, and the next be the second white key to the right of it, he will announce the second as a major third above the first, or E: if the second key struck be the seventh white key to the right, he will announce it as the octave of the first; and so on. In other words, the human ear has the power of exactly co-ordinating sounds with reference to the particular of pitch, and of forming precise conceptions thereof which can be accurately expressed in degrees of the musical scale.

Example of exact co-ordination with reference to the particular of tone-color. If a given tone, say the middle C, be sounded on the piano, and the same tone — that is to say, a tone of the same duration (or length), of the same intensity (or loudness), and of the same pitch — be sounded on the violin, the ear instantly recognizes a difference; if the same tone be then sounded on the flute, the ear recognizes a difference from both the others; if it be further sounded on the clarinet, the ear recognizes a difference from all the preceding. This difference, being by the supposition neither a difference of duration nor of intensity nor of pitch, must belong to the only other class of differences of which sounds are capable, namely, the class known as tone-color. We have already found that the difference between one vowel-sound and another in speech — the difference between *a,* for instance, and *o,* or that between *i* and *e* — belongs to this class of sound relations. The ability of the ear to discriminate the most delicate shades of difference in this particular constitutes one of the most remarkable of our faculties, and leads to some very interesting fields of thought. All the phenomena of rhyme and of alliteration, and several allied verse-effects which will be found herein treated for the first time, are due to this capacity of the ear for exactly co-ordinating sounds with reference to their tone-color.

While, as noted in the last proposition, the ear is capable of exactly co-ordinating sounds with reference to their duration, their pitch, and their tone-color, it is not capable of exactly co-ordinating them with reference to the other particular mentioned — intensity. We have already seen that a general or inexact co-ordination in respect of intensity was possible: indeed, it is not a matter requiring further illustration, that of two given sounds every ear can in a general way pronounce one to be louder or softer than the other. But *how much* louder or softer; whether twice as loud, or three times as soft; whether louder or softer according to the degrees of any given scale or standard of measurement: for such exact co-ordinations of intensity in sounds the ear has no means. There is here possible neither an appeal to terms of number, as when, in the case of duration, we can say that two sounds occupying a given time are followed by two sounds occupying exactly the same time, and so on; nor an appeal to a given scale of degrees, as when, in the case of pitch, the musician's ear pronounces definitely the relation of one tone to another by referring them to the fixed degrees of the musical scale (which is really a kind of primordial tune, always carried in the memory of the ear, and always available as a sort of graduated auditory yardstick for measurement); nor, finally, an appeal to those easily-preserved and fixed conceptions of tone-color which the ear retains, and by which it compares a given tone with recollected tones so as instantly to recognize them as flute-tones, as piano-tones, as violin-tones, and so on. We have no standard within the mind for the precise measurement of intensity in sound; that is, the ear is not capable of exactly co-ordinating sounds with reference to the particular of intensity.

Since an art of sound must depend primarily upon exact co-ordinations by the ear, and since these exact co-ordinations are, as just shown, possible only in respect of duration, pitch, and tone-color, it is evident that these three sound-relations constitute three distinct principles to one or the other of which all the primary phenomena of this art must be referred. They thus afford us three fundamental principles of classification for the effects of sound in art. The effects ordinarily known as "rhythm" depend primarily upon duration;[2] those known as "tune" depend upon pitch; those known as "colors" in music, and as "rhymes" and "alliterations" in verse, — besides many allied effects of verse which have never been named, — depend upon tone-color. Stated in other terms: —

I.

When the ear exactly co-ordinates a series of sounds and silences with primary reference to their duration, the result is a conception of ... RHYTHM.

II.

When the ear exactly co-ordinates a series of sounds with primary reference to their pitch, the result is a conception of ... ... TUNE.

III.

When the ear exactly co-ordinates a series of sounds with primary reference to their tone-color, the result is a conception of (in music, flute-tone as distinct from violin-tone, and the like; in verse, rhyme as opposed to rhyme, vowel varied with vowel, phonetic syzygy, and the like), in general ... TONE-COLOR.

[...]

Rhythm not only thus appears as perhaps the widest artistic instinct in man: it would seem to be a universal principle throughout nature. Perhaps every one, in these days, is more or less familiar with the complete way in which modern physical science has reduced all that enormous and complex mass of phenomena which we call physical nature to a series of motions. Older conceptions of substance as opposed to form have resolved themselves into the general conception of force producing motion in certain modes.

It would seem that the general primordial mode of all these motions which we assemble under the general term "nature" is rhythm. The essential principle of rhythm — the student must have observed — is recurrence at an interval of time which furnishes a unit of measure by which all the times marked-off by the recurrences may be co-ordinated. Mr. Herbert Spencer claims to have observed such a prevalence of this rhythmic periodicity throughout nature as to convince him that it is universal and states that this belief is shared by Mr. Tyndall. It would indeed seem that every thing moves to measure (ὀνθμὸς). The spiral distribution of the remote nebulæ hints at rhythmic motion: the variable stars brighten and pale at rhythmic intervals; planet, satellite, comet, revolve and return in proportionate periods; the seasons, the magnetic variations, the sun-spots, come and go, orderly; the great tides in the sea, the great trade-winds in the air, flow by rhythmic rule; the terrible sawyer in the Mississippi marks a vertical rhythmus, the sweet long grasses in running brooks a horizontal one; the lungs of the man, the heart of the beast, the cilia of the animalcule, play to and fro with rhythmic systole and diastole.

And even those forms of motion which seem at first view most lawless appear to range themselves under this orderly principle at last. Storms, earthquakes, upheavals of continents, recessions of waters, would seem to show some traces of recurrence at ordered intervals. Even disease,— as I am informed by observant physicians, — the more it is studied, appears to show the tendency to take on this yoke, from the well-marked periodicities of the ague to the vaguer and more baffling exacerbations and remissions of obscure fevers and ills. And so from the prodigious recurrences of the great worlds in space which are measured by ages, to the inconceivably rapid recurrences of the vibrating string or air-column in the production of sound which are measured by thousandths of a second, or those of the ether in the production of light which are measured by hundredths-of-thousandths of a second, everywhere we find rhythm.

One of the most striking similes in all literature involves this rhythmic idea. Edgar Poe, in his fantastic *Eureka,* after having detailed the process of the primal diffusion of matter in space, the aggregation of atoms into worlds, the revolution of these worlds for a time, their necessary return after that time into the central sun, and the then necessary re-diffusion of the atoms into space, again to aggregate into worlds, to fall into the central sun, and to be again re-diffused — ever contracting, ever expanding — closes his raptus of thought with declaring that this prodigious process is nothing more than the rhythmic beating of the heart of God.

It is curious, indeed, to find another assertion in this connection, almost as vague as Poe's dream, meeting confirmation in the exacter views of modern science. Puttenham, in beginning his chapter "Of Proportion Poeticall" says: "It is said by such as profess the Mathematicall sciences, that all things stand by proportion, and that without it nothing could stand to be good or beautiful. The Doctors of our Theologie to the same effect, but in other termes, say: that God made the world by number, measure and weight: some for weight say tune, and peradventure better."

And there is yet a more general view of the rhythmic principle which hints that this proportion in which the worlds move and by which "things stand to be good or beautiful" is due to antagonism, Mr. Herbert. Spencer has formulated the proposition that where opposing forces act, rhythm appears, and has traced the rhythmic motions of nature to the antagonistic forces there found, such as the two motions which carry the earth towards, and away from, the sun and so result in the periodicity of the earth's progress, and others.

Perhaps this view may be made, without strain, to bind together even facts so remote from each other as the physical and the moral. When we compare what one may call the literal rhythm which rules throughout physical nature with that metaphorical rhythm or proportion which governs good behavior as well as good art; when we find that opposition in the physical world results in rhythm, and that so opposition in the moral world — the fret, the sting, the thwart, the irreconcilable me as against all other me's, the awful struggle for existence, the desperate friction of individualities, the no of death to all requests — may also result in rhythm; when we perceive that through all those immeasurable agitations which constitute both moral and physical nature this beautiful and orderly principle of rhythm thus swings to and fro like the shuttle of a loom and weaves a definite and comprehensible pattern into the otherwise chaotic fabric of things: we may be able to see dimly into that old Orphic saying of the seer, "The father of metre is rhythm, and the father of rhythm is God."

Notes

1 These "silences" are included in Proposition I, under the term "specially related sounds." For example, if a couplet of sounds be separated by a silence of one minute in duration, while another couplet is separated by a silence of two minutes in duration, these differing silences constitute an independent means of comparison between the two couplets; and, as such, the measured silence or rest may be considered one species of relations between sounds with sufficient accuracy for a proposition in which the most general terms are desirable.

2 For detailed proof of which see the special discussion of rhythm in Part I. following.

19 Prosody Wars (2011)

Meredith Martin

[…]

The problem of fixing the terms for poetic form was an issue to which George Saintsbury devoted an enormous amount of energy, not only because he felt strongly that the history of English poetry would clearly prove his opinions about English prosody but also because he was invested in a reading practice that he took for granted as shared. Taught Greek and Latin and even Hebrew at a young age, George Saintsbury, like most other young men of his generation, learned, in just three or four years of school, "the first three books of the *Aeneid,* the Odes of Horace, some Homer, and most of the iambic part, with some of the choruses, of two or three Greek plays," which he described as "large patterns and examples of the most perfect literary form that the world has produced."[1] This is a typical assessment from a student educated at King's College School, London, and Merton College Oxford, where there was not yet regular instruction in English literature when Saintsbury finished his studies in 1868. Saintsbury asserted that he had formed his ideas about English prosody solely by reading English poetry.[2] And as this proclaimed prosodic autodidact's 1878 review of Coventry Patmore's *Essay on English Metrical Law* reveals, even at the young age of thirty-three, not only was Saintsbury (like Patmore, Robert Bridges, and Gerard Manley Hopkins) fully aware of the complicated nineteenth-century prosodic debates; he had already formed strong opinions about them. He also displayed what would become his characteristic style of dismissing prosodic systems that did not satisfy his nascent ideas of what an English foot should be and do:

> Mr. Patmore does not seem to have made quite as valuable a contribution to the literature of the subject as he might have made; the fatal old quarrel between accent and quantity has drawn him to take part in it with the usual result. The truth seems to be that English verse is to be scanned both by quantity and accent, and that no verse is really good which does not answer to this double test. Those who rely only upon accent give us slipshod doggerel; those who rely only upon quantity give us variations on the original "Tityus happily thou," and so on.[3]

Though he gave no further information to back up his claim that the "truth seems to be" that English meter is scanned by both accent and quantity, less than ten years later, in his *History of Elizabethan Literature* (1887), he asserted his belief in an English foot measurable by both accent and quantity and based explicitly on classical meters: "I must entirely differ with those persons who have sought to create an independent prosody for English verse under the head of 'beats' or 'accents' or something of that sort."[4] For Saintsbury, English verse must not rely solely on accent or else it loses its link to the classical languages. But why would this assertion be important in a book about Elizabethan literature? A mere five years earlier, one of Saintsbury's main interlocutors in the prosody wars, Walter Skeat, had reissued Edwin Guest's imposing and "epoch-making" *A History of English Rhythms* (1882). Old English rhythms were generating considerable interest among German scholars; there was even some speculation as to whether Skeat edited the second edition of Guest's book to show that English scholars could analyze English rhythms with more authority than Germans.[5] Guest believed accent to be "the *sole* principle"[6] that regulates English rhythm and that English has no metrical quantity.[7] The competing histories of English prosody in the late nineteenth century were also competing histories of English literature and Englishness: were our literary and national origins in the great Shakespeare and Milton or in the Anglo-Saxon, Old English tradition? Both literary narratives were attempting to create a canon, an origin for the study of English literature and culture: the continuous line of poetic thought between Shakespeare and Swinburne and the narrative of the steady beating Anglo-Saxon rhythms that should be preserved against the foreignness of classical verse forms. One critic wondered if Guest's theories would be given the credit they deserved due to the new edition: "It remains to be seen whether, now that the interest in the formal study of English versification is more widely diffused, this remarkable achievement of erudition and speculative force will meet with a worthier reception."[8] Saintsbury's mission was to guarantee that it would not, not only by undermining Guest's *History* and arguing vehemently against the accentual system but also by replacing Guest's looming two-volume project with three volumes of his own.

In prosodic manuals, size does matter. In Saintsbury's next step in foot domination, he published *A Short History of English Literature* (1898). Guest's *History* was 738 pages; Saintsbury's "short" history vas 818 pages (the later, three-volume *History of English Prosody* runs to a staggering 1,577 pages). In the *Short History,* Saintsbury makes clear his view that, in English prosody's history, just as in the history of the English language and people, there was a distinct break with Anglo-Saxon; therefore, there was also a break with Guest's solely accentual basis for English meter. In his introductory section "The Making of English Literature," Saintsbury claims that "the true and universal prosody of English instead of the cramped and parochial rhythm of Anglo-Saxon"[9] came about from the influence of Latin. This section, referred to as "the transition" (39), is in many ways a blueprint for the section titled "The Mothers" in the larger *History of English Prosody.* (The *Short History* was in its eighth edition by 1913.) Between 1898 and 1905, when his next explicit statement about English feet appeared, Saintsbury published *A History of Nineteenth-Century Literature* (1900) and *A History of English Criticism* (1901). Both were reprinted several times. The latter is a direct engagement with Guest and other critics, laying both the groundwork and the justification for his forthcoming *History of English Prosody.* The former shows Saintsbury trying to balance the accessibility (and thus ensure the posterity) of his version of foot prosody, while at the same time subtly trying to distinguish between the kinds of meters that are detectable by a "good English ear" versus a "general ear" or, even worse, "no ear" at all. Macaulay's verses, for example, appeal to the "general ear": "They are *popular;* they hit exactly that scheme of poetry which the general ear can appreciate and the general brain understand."[10] But how could Saintsbury disseminate his faith in the English foot to the "general brain"?

Saintsbury's remarks, titled simply "English Versification," are quite possibly the most succinct summary of his views on the matter. Yet they were not published as part of his three-volume *History,* nor did they appear as an English Association Pamphlet. Rather, this essay serves as the introduction to a handbook for poets by Andrew Loring titled *The Rhymer's*

Lexicon (1905). "English Versification" was at once an advertisement for Saintsbury's forthcoming three volumes as well as a clear distillation of them. Saintsbury here defines the history of English versification not as "a struggle between native and foreign rhythm, but of the native material of language adapting itself to the pressure of the foreign moulds, and modifying those moulds themselves by the spring and 'thrust' of its natural qualities."[11] The result, he writes, "is one of the most interesting things in literature... . By looking both ways—from earliest to latest and from latest to earliest—we can distinguish a new form of verse, characteristically English in its blended originality, which takes the general rhythmical form of Low Latin and French, but which adapts them to, or adapts to them, the primaeval English tendency to syllabic equivalence" (viii). The "blended originality" of English verse form is a point of pride in his longer *History;* by 1905, Saintsbury was becoming the representative for standard English meter based on a subtle blending of classical (foreign, quantitative) and Anglo-Saxon (native, accentual) meters. As a founding member of the English Association and a professor at the University of Edinburgh, Saintsbury was balancing more than just Anglo-Saxon accents and classical quantities; he was blending a characteristic Englishness that could value the classical languages as a necessary part of English literature at a time when they were under siege; there had been a loud and angry reaction against the reinstatement of compulsory Latin after the 1902 Education Act,[12] and Saintsbury was performing the role of the English literary historian while at the same time trying to preserve the connection between English literature and its competing pasts.

Increasingly, the foreign names for classical feet were called into question and students were taught to feel English poetry according to its "natural" accents (traced to an Anglo-Saxon past), divorced from the valueless and hegemonic classical system. What American prosodist C. E. Andrews in 1918 called "prosodic wars"[13] enlisted, in one battle, those committed to moving the concept of English meter away from its classical origins, and even away from the popular concept of feet, into a more capacious metrical system, sometimes syllabic, sometimes accentual, that could reflect varieties of dialects and even welcome other languages. These hopes for English meter were not altogether new, but they certainly took on a more nationalistic and a more defensive stance in the Edwardian era. The quick rise of English education—and the uncertainty, after the failures of the Boer War, that the education system was not doing its proper job to create a strong, competitive, and patriotic class of potential soldiers[14]—accelerated the pace and passion of prosodic debate outside the classroom and increased the circulation of and demand for texts that would teach English poetry and English meter along purely national lines. Pamphlets and tracts from the English Association, established in part by Henry Newbolt in 1906, and the Society for Pure English, established in part by Robert Bridges in 1913, worried over the fate of English pronunciation, English spelling, and English reading practices—issues that they believed might help to solve the prolific and zealous debates over defining English meter. Educators and poets alike had high expectations that Saintsbury's three-volume *History of English Prosody from the Twelfth Century to the Present Day* (1906–10), in which the issue, for Saintsbury, was no longer explicitly the contest between Anglo-Saxon or classical measures but rather how the blend of these two metrical heritages could constitute a characteristic English meter and, more important, could most accurately measure the ideal English character.

The English Ear

Saintsbury wanted to have it both ways. He wanted to popularize the foot-based system as natural for those with an English ear, and he wanted all Englishmen to possess an ear like his, despite his bitter awareness that they did not. In his introduction to Loring's 1905 *The Rhymer's Lexicon,* Saintsbury lays out his metrical principles clearly:

> "Lines" … possess a definite rhythm based on what is called double and triple time; that these integers (the lines) are made up of corresponding or proportionate fractions to which it has been usual to give the name of "feet," though some object; that they are as a rule tipped with rhyme, whether in simple sequences or pairs or in more complicated sets called stanzas. It is upon the nature and constitution of these fractions that the hottest and most irreconcilable difference prevails among prosodists. Some prefer to regard them merely from the point of view of the accented syllables which they contain, while others consider them as made up of "long" and "short" syllables precisely as classical feet are, though not combined on quite the same systems; and yet others hold different views. (x)

Five pages later, he returns to the battlefield in stating, "The central knot, the *crux,* the battle-field, the bone of contention—a hundred other phrases may be applied to it—is the principle on which these aggregations of words or syllables are differentiated from prose—made to become 'lines' in themselves, and to be fit material for the construction in couplets and stanzas" (xv). The "central knot," therefore, is the question of how poetry is distinct from prose. Whereas meter is summoned by Saintsbury and others to act as the simple mediator in the particular battle between verse and prose, or as its boundary or border. English meter is also the subject of its own internal battles between various national pasts or educational backgrounds that, as we have seen, Saintsbury attempts to mediate through his insistence on the portability of the "foot" across time. Yet for those readers without a classical education, these feet may still seem foreign. Promoting a kind of national metrical intuition over formal training, Saintsbury finds a way around this dilemma: the English ear. He writes that "the ear recognizes for itself, or is made to recognize by the sleight-of-hand of the poet, one broad distinction of value between syllables—the distinction which is denoted, in classical prosody, by the terms 'long' and 'short'" (xvi). But here Saintsbury makes his plea: whether the distinction has to do with time in utterance, a sharper or graver tone, a lighter or heavier weight, a louder or softer sound, or a thinner and denser substance does not matter, for "everybody (if he would only admit it) recognizes the fact of the broad difference" (xvi). We hear them, he says, but we might not admit that we do. These divisions, or "sub-integers," are generally called by the "inoffensive" word *feet,* which he describes as "an obvious and innocent metaphor—they being what the line (verse) *runs* upon" (xvi). This metaphor should be obvious and familiar because it is the same metaphor used by both Sheridan and Murray, and it is not necessarily innocent. The idea of rise voice, via an artificial—indeed a prosthetic "foot"—running naturally across a line is here transformed into a line of verse overlaid on the already existing skeleton, the historical expectation and backbone of the metrical foot. But despite the metaphors to stepping stones, fence posts, and walking to which that word *foot* lends itself, Saintsbury throws up his hands and distracts attention from his obvious and innocent move: "Call them feet, spaces, isochronous intervals, or abracadabras, every English verse can be divided up … into so many groups of 'long' and 'short' syllables which have metrical correspondence with each other in the line and in other lines … . Call the name iamb or abracadabra, trochee or tomfool, the *thing* is there from the *Brut* to the *Barrack-Room Ballads"* (xix). From the earliest rhymed history of England to patriotic tales of soldiers, Saintsbury asserts that the history of English meter and of England is unified, indivisibly, by these groups of syllables that preexist and predate even our ability to name them—name them whatever you like, but Saintsbury likes to call them *feet.* The English ear, as he construes it, is particularly adapted to detect and judge them.

But what are these feet? When, in 1905, Saintsbury announced that he would write *A History of English Prosody from the Twelfth Century to the Present Day,* the news was reported on both sides of the Atlantic. Perhaps, with his extensive project, Saintsbury would put to rest many of the underlying problems in the study of English prosody. Reviewers noted that prosodists and amateur readers alike anticipated that Saintsbury's book would not only settle the question of English meter once and for all but also provide a model that would be clear, understandable, and free of the pitfalls of the overly technical discourse produced by the prosody wars. The central idea that Saintsbury stated in 1906 was that "English accent is a *cause* of quantity, but not the only cause, and not a stable one" and that "by calling these sound-values 'long' and 'short' [he did] not intend to beg the question as to their origin and differentia," nor in using the term *feet* did he wish to cause offense.[15] But his prose is defensive, and his "tribunal" turns out to be, once again, "that of the fairly sensitive and well-trained ear. How would such an ear 'scan' (again, no malice in the word) each line? And when such an ear has pronounced, what most rational rationale presents itself as a formula to express the scansion? Of these answers to these questions, and the working-out necessary to get those answers, I hope to make the stuff and substance of this book" (1:10). Addressing the "accent-men" directly, he writes that "something had survived from the old versicular prosody which the national ear, modified as it had been, was not prepared to abandon" (1:77).

Saintsbury, then, clearly states his claim that meter is the measure of the English nation: "It seems to me, on the evidence of the facts only and wholly, that just as Saxon and Norman and Celtic constituents, with political and ecclesiastical influence from Rome, were blending and coalescing to form the English nation, so corresponding influences (though in each case the Celtic might not make much show) were blending and coalescing to make English language in the first place, and English prosody in the next" (1:78). The story of English prosody is the story of the English nation. To use any system other than the system Saintsbury espouses would be to apply something truly artificial and foreign to the native tongue; indeed, English ears and English feet are what England is all about.

But even if Saintsbury gives plenty of examples of the best poetry in English with his descriptions and praise, the book itself cannot provide the "ear training" of the native English man who is, though Saintsbury does not say this directly, classically trained. That is, implicit everywhere in the three volumes is the fact that the classical methods through which Saintsbury was trained prepared him for what he then translates into an innate sense of rhythmic sound that haunted his thinking about rhythm and meter. This "innate sense" also played extremely well into the way that the national education system was teaching English poetry. For Saintsbury, an "English ear" that could naturally hear metrical feet based loosely on a classical measure of scansion was the true English ear—the true, classically trained, public-school-educated, elite English ear. History, as far as metrical training is concerned, is transformed into nature, but only if you have had access to a classical education. As Saintsbury makes a case for the appreciation of Langland, the writer of *Piers Plowman,* he cannot help but insert that foot-arrangement makes a difference "as any one whose eye and ear are well enough fitted naturally, and well enough trained artificially, will soon discover," which is a direct intervention and attack on Guest and his editor (who also famously edited Langland), Walter Skeat.[16] Here Saintsbury argues that though there is a natural English ability to both see and hear the beauty of English verses, some artificial training is beneficial. Buried in a note to *A History of English Prosody* is this admission: "I hope it is not impertinent or pedantic once more to recommend strongly this joint eye-and-ear reading. It does not at all interfere with the understanding of the sense or enjoyment of the poetry, and it puts the mind in a condition to understand the virtue and the meaning of the prosody as nothing else can. One of the innumerable privileges of those who have received the older classical education is that they have been taught (in at least some cases) to read scanningly" (1:182). The eye and an ear are a "combined instrument" that when "properly tuned" will reveal English meter to be "a real and living rhythmical organism" (1:184). But if the choice is between a theory of scansion, which is intended for the eye, and a theory of pronunciation, intended for the ear, the remaining two volumes lean toward the ear. The eye, directed by signs that may be visible to all and therefore would be less interpretive, less dependent on an elite education, might be frighteningly democratic.

Saintsbury did not invent the concept of an "English ear" (it was already evident in school books and elocution manuals). Nor did this concept resemble the "natural" pronunciation that Murray may have intended in his *Grammars;* for Saintsbury, the "English ear" meant a certain kind of pronunciation coupled with a certain kind of hearing, quite refined. As Yopie Prins has noticed, Saintsbury's discussion of Tennyson's "Hollyhock song" in volume 3 of his *History of English Prosody* is especially striking for the way it emphasizes a particularly English reader: "One reads it, wondering how any human ear could be 'tortured' by it, but wondering still more how any *English* ear could be in the least puzzled by its metre"[17]— above mere human understanding, the English ear is undeniably privileged. In this statement, Saintsbury claims that the true "English ear" is able to detect true English meter. He exclaims, "Our business is with English; and I repeat that, *in English,* there are practically no metrical fictions, and that metre follows, though it may sometimes slightly force, pronunciation" (3:188). Though at times he focuses on the regular combination and alternation of metrical feet in various forms, the book also makes a case for iambic meter and, particularly, for ballad meter, as particularly English. The ballad meter is "very much ours" and "the ballad quatrain, or common measure … [is] perhaps the most definitely English—blood and bone, flesh and marrow—of all English metres. It comes the most naturally of all to an English tongue and an English ear" (3:247). Joining the forms of English verse to the forms of English bodies, Saintsbury emphasizes the instinct, the internal feeling that English speakers and hearers should have for prosodic forms. These forms do not merely prove that you are an Englishman; they bind you to other Englishmen, with whom you also share "blood," "bone," "flesh," "marrow," "tongue," and "ear."

Not only must your ear be tuned, like Saintsbury's, to hear, for example, blended classical feet in English verse, but also you must understand and absorb the character that these blended, natural feet create. Saintsbury's narrative of the evolution of English feet is imbued with the same militaristic swagger as the patriotic poems that were being taught in state-funded schools: English feet evolved into their "orderly and soldierly fashion" over time, grouped into syllables and then into lines like so many regiments. Indeed, English metrical feet form "vast armies" that English citizens, future armies, are conditioned to hear "naturally." It is a matter of national pride that English readers should, can, and do cultivate their faculties to correctly appreciate poetry Saintsbury's three volumes echo the movements in the Victorian and Edwardian classrooms by giving a patriotic historical context to the glories of England's poetry without going into too much detail about the application of an overarching prosodic theory; if a student is blessed with an English ear, then he has access to the glories of English meter.

But if Saintsbury's idealized and "natural" English ear is, in fact, a classically trained organ, how does he promote the English foot-soldier among the general reading public, the majority of whom did not have access to (much less sustained training in) classical languages and literatures? The answer is simple: he *believes* in it, and you should as well. His position, though it seems conciliatory in the first two volumes (in a nod to Patmore, he even consented to call a foot an "isochronous interval" in volume 2)[18] becomes staunch and uncompromising by the third volume and thereafter. Rather than define explicitly what he means by "feet," Saintsbury again and again insists on an innate sense of rhythm—what Saintsbury would have learned in the Latin classroom and, perhaps, what English schoolchildren were learning through patriotic songs, recitation, and drills. In the main text, Saintsbury refers to feet as both "breath-units" and "time-units" that exist in a common English imaginary, the only ruling characteristic being that they are, at heart, part of an alternating pattern of stressed and unstressed syllables. These combinations of syllables make up feet, but how these feet are employed or scanned is, again, only considered in an appendix—"Is the base-foot of English iamb or trochee?" Despite high hopes, one reviewer admits, after the publication of the first volume,[19] "We are a little disappointed. We expected more—we expected that in it, something at least should be done toward the settlement of metrical theory; that some at least of those questions which have puzzled all who have ever attempted the subject should be dealt with, if they could not be solved. Of this there is nothing."[20] Another reviewer laments. "That the work will bring peace in the 'fair field full of fighting folk' whereon modern scholars of Prosody 'clang battleaxe and clash brand' is not to be hoped; rather it will bring a sword, for the central idea of the book runs counter to many widely-received and much debated theories."[21]

What Saintsbury does give us, in 1906, is a justification, along militaristic lines, of the ascendancy of his favorite metrical foot, the iamb: "To get the vast armies, the innumerable multitudes of [iambic verse] that exist in English, into trochaic form, or in most cases even into a suggestion of trochaic rhythm, you have to play the most gratuitous, unliterary, and unnatural tricks upon them, and you often produce positively ludicrous or nauseous results" (1:529). Saintsbury, as one might expect, prefers iambic to trochaic rhythm, but he values the trochee highly as the necessary variant for the iamb. However, his ability to diagnose English verse as iambic rather than trochaic is dependent only on his ability to hear meter; he states simply and vexingly "my ear informs me" (530). In this early appendix to the first volume, he also makes his first declaration of the self-evident truths of English feet. The iamb is the "ruling constituent," the anapest "omnipresent." Of the dactyl he has "no doubt ... at all," despite its tendency to "tip up" into an anapest; why does it do this? He writes, "I do not know why; and though it would not cost me five minutes to turn the statement of the fact into a jargonish explanation thereof on principles very popular to-day, I decline to do anything of the kind. The English language is made so and I accept the fact," and thus he insists that we accept the fact as well (1:402–3). Saintsbury does not merely dispense with the prosody wars tout court—the burgeoning science of English verse reduced to a passing fad—he explicitly, deliberately, commingles what he sees as historical metrical fact with something akin to a declaration of prosodic faith. In an extraordinary statement (that nevertheless belies his constant shuttling between classical and "English" scansion), Saintsbury proclaims that "the amphibrach is a clever foot, but I do not (in English) believe in the amphibrach" (403). Though part of Saintsbury's inherent charm is his confidence that we will take his word for it, his lack of technical guidance leaves us with the one thing he has been convincing us we have—our ear. Our understanding of English prosody is at once intensely individual, therefore, but also, because of our race, necessarily collective. Rather than being taught, as a student in a classical classroom would have been, what the iamb *is* (or was) and how to mark it and memorize it, Saintsbury infuses his concept of English meter with an Edwardian article of faith in the steadfast and sturdy nature of English, of an England in which the iamb is and has always been the ruling constituent. Just like the narratives of military glory through which schoolchildren learned about English poetry, like the countless histories of England that justified and extolled imperial expansion, Saintsbury's English meter spoke to and fostered what he imagined was a specifically English national character.

Notes

1 George Saintsbury, *Last Vintage* (London; Methuen. 1950), 116; and Saintsbury, *Last Scrap Book* (London: Macmillan, 1924), 88–91 (both quoted in Dorothy Richardson Jones, *King of Critics: George Saintsbury, 1845–1933* [Ann Arbor: University of Michigan Press, 1992], 8).
2 Saintsbury, *History of English Prosody,* 3:575.
3 Saintsbury, review of *Essay on English Metrical Law,* by Coventry Patmore, *Athenaeum* 2642 (June 1878): 757. The last line refers to translating Horace's Odes into English.
4 George Saintsbury, *A History of Elizabethan Literature,* 2nd ed. (New York: Macmillan, 1912), 14. He continued, emphatically, "Every English metre since Chaucer at least can be scanned, within the proper limits, according to the strictest rules of classical prosody: and while all good English metre comes out scatheless from the application of those rules nothing exhibits the badness of bad English metre so well as that application" (14). Saintsbury's *History of Elizabethan Literature* was part of a four-part series that proved to be extremely popular in the 1890s, with reprints appearing nearly every year until the late 1920s (twenty-two reprints in all and two editions).
5 Jakob Schipper's *Englische Metrik; Altenglische Metrik,* vol. 1, appeared in 1881 and was reprinted in 1888.
6 Edwin Guest, *A History of English Rhythms,* 2nd ed., ed. Walter Skeat (London: George Bell, 1882), 108.
7 An archaeologist and philologist, Guest established the Philological Society in 1842 that eventually began working on the *New English Dictionary.* A reviewer noted that "compilers of histories of English language and literature have quarried in Dr. Guest and appropriated his results" and that Guest refused to reprint the edition in his lifetime. William Minto, review of *A History of English Rhythms,* by Edwin Guest, *Academy* 22, no. 548 (4 November 1882): 323.
8 Ibid.
9 George Saintsbury, *A Short History of English Literature* (London: Macmillan, 1898), 39–47; the quotation is from 44.
10 George Saintsbury, *A History of Nineteenth-Century Literature* (London: Macmillan, 1900), 227.
11 George Saintsbury, introduction to Andrew Loring, *The Rhymer's Lexicon* (London: Routledge and Sons, 1905), iv.
12 Eric Eaglesham writes that the authors of the act—Robert Laurie Morant, James Wycliffe Headlam, and John William Mackail (classicists all)—believed that true mental discipline could be learned only through mastery of Latin grammar; English education had grown too quickly and without standards, and after the failures of the Boer War, Latin might get the country back on track. Eaglesham, "Implementing the Education Act of 1902," *British Journal of Education Studies* 10, no. 2 (1962): 153–75. Christopher Stray makes a similar assertion: "Underlying the attachment to Latin grammar was a powerful emotional conviction that it was the exemplar of 'real' knowledge—discipline as opposed to furniture, forming the mind rather than filling it with facts. And in the Edwardian period, the defense and reassertion of the disciplinary position belonged to a politics of culture in which pressures for change and for social incorporation generated reactive ideological constructions. The stress on the power of discipline needs to be seen in this context, as a reassertion of permanence and stability." Stray, *Classics Transformed,* 258.
13 C. E. Andrews, *The Reading and Writing of Verse* (New York: D. Appleton and Company, 1918), ix.
14 See especially Matthew Hendley, "'Help Us to Secure a Strong, Healthy, Prosperous and Peaceful Britain': The Social Arguments of the Campaign of Compulsory Military Service in Britain, 1899–1914," *Canadian Journal of History* 30, no. 2 (1995): 261–88. See also J. O. Springhall, "Lord Meath, Youth, and Empire," *Journal of Contemporary History* 5, no. 4 (1970): 97–111; and R. J. Q. Adams, "The National Service League and Mandatory Service in Edwardian Britain," *Armed Forces and Society* 12, no. 1 (1985): 53–74.

15 George Saintsbury, *A History of English Prosody from the Twelfth Century to the Present Day*, vol. 1 (London: Macmillan, 1906), 4.
16 Saintsbury, *History of English Prosody*, 1:182.
17 Saintsbury, *History of English Prosody*, 3:188. See also Yopie Prins, "Victorian Meters", in *Cambridge Companion to Victorian Poetry*, ed. Joseph Bristow (Cambridge: Cambridge University Press, 2000), 89–113 (89–106).
18 George Saintsbury, *A History of English Prosody from the Twelfth Century to the Present Day*, vol. 2 (London: Macmillan, 1908), 550–51.
19 In order, the three volumes are titled *From the Origins to Spenser, From Shakespeare to Crabbe*, and *From Blake to Mr. Swinburne*.
20 R. B. McKerrow, "Review: A History of English Prosody," *Modern Language Review* 2, no. 1 (1907): 65.
21 G. C. Macaulay, "English Prosody," *Academy* 70 (2 June 1906): 523.

20 Rhyme's End (2011)

Adela Pinch

Fin-de-siècle poets were experts at measuring short lines against long. They did so in order to meditate on scale, on perspective, and above all, as the end of the century seemed to loom both near and far, they used the interplay of short and long to meditate on perspectives on time. In these opening lines from Margaret Veley's "A Japanese Fan" (1888), the odd interplay of octosyllabic and trisyllabic lines lends its uneven rhythm to the speaker's startled consciousness of time passing simultaneously quickly and slowly:

> How time flies! Have we been talking
> For an hour?
> Have we been so long imprisoned
> By the shower
> In this old oak-panelled parlour?
> Is it noon?
> Don't you think the rain is over
> Rather soon? (1–8)

The shorter rhymed lines—is it noon? Rather soon?—do the work of this passage by both bringing us up short, and, in their chiming resonance, extending the duration at least of sound. In these lines and elsewhere, the fin-de-siècle poem's short poetic line impresses itself upon us, upon our ears as much as our eyes, making conspicuous the effects of rhyme. These are lines that milk the conjunction of metrical brevity with reverberating sound to heighten our subjective experience of duration, and its existential pangs.

Thanks to a renewal of interest in Victorian meters we have learned how deeply Victorian metrical theory and practice were allied with major intellectual trends: trends toward quantification, abstraction, and enumeration that spanned discourses and disciplines from economics to music to philosophy, particularly toward the century's end.[1] But if late-Victorian meters processed thinking about time at the century's end, so, I hope to show here, did late-Victorian practices of rhyme. It is not really possible, of course, to separate effects of rhyme from effects of line-length governed by meter (as the passage from Veley's "Japanese Fan," above, attests). But theorizing rhyme has often seemed a less sophisticated field than theorizing meter, and I hope, by isolating rhyme as a topic, to challenge this, and to suggest the richness of fin-de-siècle verse and culture in this regard.

Fin-de-siècle theorizing of rhyme took place in a number of arenas, and, to cite just one, we might consider the incredible clustering of collections and treatises about nursery rhymes in the last decade of the century and the first decade of the new one. Men of letters such as Andrew Lang theorized the rhymes of nursery rhymes as ways of counting people and counting time, of passing time and making time; they were survivals of past time in the present, their sounds produced by the passage of time. "Thus," wrote Lang, "our old nursery rhymes are smooth stones from the brook of time, worn round by constant friction of tongues long silent" (*The Nursery Rhyme Book* 278).

In the remainder of this paper I invite you to think through with me some of the ways in which poetic practices of rhyming at the fin-de-siècle might also be seen not as made by time or as survivals of past time but as ways of making, extending time at the century's end. While the work of any number of poets writing at the fin-de-siècle—Thomas Hardy, Arthur Symons, Alice Meynell, Michael Field—might serve as illustrations, I focus here on the spare, late poetry of Mary Elizabeth Coleridge. Coleridge used rhyme in remarkable ways to tell the story of ends and of resistances to ends. She seems to have viewed her often irregularly metered but interestingly rhymed stanzas as "happy hours" in which, in the words of one of her late poems, "I shall have gathered all the world can give / Unending Time and Space!" ("Chillingham, III," *Collected Poems* 247).

Coleridge was highly attuned, in both poetry and life, to the philosophical relation of sound to self. In an essay "On Noises" (1886) she wrote of the necessity of seeing a continuum (rather than an opposition) between what she called "all of those different noises, little and great, which make the chorus of life" such as "the squeak of a slate pencil, a pig, a violin in the hands of a young gentleman of tender age," on one end, and poetry and music on the other, thus refusing to distinguish between noxious "noise" and musical "sound" (*Gathered Leaves* 169). "Outside our own selves, there is nothing so pleasant, so genial, so friendly, as a noise," she wrote; "the sounds, even more than the sights we are accustomed to … pass into our very being, and become one with us" (170–71). Noises and sounds, in this view, cling to us like a kind of second skin. Coleridge begins to theorize rhyme in her remarks about repetition of sounds. "And then," she says, "there is the romantic side of noise. Echo will lend it the curious charm that reflection lends to an ordinary object" (171). Coleridge used the curious charm of echoing sounds in her economical poems to make time, to make up for lost time, and to make time yet to be gained: for her, the end of rhyme is the making of endings.

The articulation of rhyme and time in her poems from the turn of the century took a number of forms. It is most programmatic in this somewhat awkward, little allegorical poem, "Sounds" (1906), in which sound is explicitly coordinated with modes of experiencing time:

> The clock!
> A crowing cock!
> And under these
> The murmur of the wind among the trees,
> The hum of bees.
>
> The clock is busy Man with Time at strife,
> Wasting brief hours to measure out his life!
> The cock vainglorious Man chanting his praise
> Forgetful of the time—how short the days!
>
> The wind is Man, dreaming and dreaming still,
> Silence with music evermore to fill.
> The bee is Man that neither hastes nor shirks,
> Not happy and unhappy as he works. (1–13)

It goes without saying that this poem called "Sounds" is a sound- and specifically rhyme-driven poem. The layering of sounds—clock/cock/ wind/bees—unfolds in the first, irregular stanza, as "clock" produces "cock," and as the these/trees/bees rhyme generates the lines the sounds anchor. As is often the case in Coleridge's irregular stanzas, line length is determined not by a metrical pattern, but by end rhyme. The line is determined, that is, by how long it takes the line to get around to the final end-rhyme. As in the *bouts-rimés*—the Victorian parlor game popular with, among others, the Rossetti family circle, in which players are challenged to make a poem out of a given set of rhymes—Coleridge's poems often seem to start with the end rhyme and then move leftward across the page, rather than the reverse. End rhymes are truly the ends of the poem, the rest of the lines merely the means to those ends.

Why do the particular sounds of "Sounds"—the clock, the cock, the wind, the bees—represent these different relations to time: obsessing about time, and thus wasting it; heedless of time, and hence also wasting it; filling up time; and lastly, finding some kind of just-right, unconscious, in-between, adequate relation to time? There is indeed something forced and awkward about Coleridge's little allegory, unless we stop to think about the ways in which the sounds of the sounds in the poem "Sounds" do their own dance with time. One way to think about rhyme is to notice the ways in which it seems to open up or to compress time by either creating a long interval between sound A and sound A, or by having sound A return quickly. The story of "Sounds" goes from rhymes that return hastily ("The Clock! A crowing cock!") to the somehow laggardly gap between "these" and "trees," and "bees," to the neither hasting nor shirking, metrically regulated return of the couplets of the second and third stanzas. In one turn-of-the-century verse manual and rhyming dictionary, *Orthometry* by R. F. Brewer (1893), the key to rhyming rightly is all about the timing: avoiding too "quick a return of the same sound," which though pleasing "is inconsistent with the gravity and sublimity that characterize the higher forms of poetic expression," while avoiding too long an interval (173). "No definite rules bearing upon the subject" can be deduced, and "little more can be said with certainty," he continues (173), but we can see in Coleridge's "Sounds" exactly this kind of consideration of rhyming and timing.

A poem of 1900, "No Newspapers," also demonstrates Coleridge's use of rhyme to shrink and expand the poetic line, sound, and time:

> Where, to me, is the loss
> Of the scenes they saw—of the sounds they heard;
> A butterfly flits across,
> Or a bird;
> The moss is growing on the wall,
> I heard the leaf of the poppy fall. (1–6)

Where, indeed, is the loss, in this poem about being newspaper-deprived, which hangs the word "loss" daringly at the end of the first enjambed line? The suspension of that enjambment, and the unbalanced length of line 2 it causes, in turn magnifies the imbalance between line 2, and its rhyme-pair, line 4. We are asked to experience the difference between newspaper-time, presumably both daily and event-focused, and the very slow (moss is growing) or very fast (bird flits) time of the poet. This is poetry time, rhyme time.

The final couplet of "No Newspapers" is striking for the conjunction between the improbable auditory claim of the last line (she heard the leaf of the poppy fall?), and the extraordinary self-assurance and authority of the declaration. We exit the poem, it seems to me, fully convinced that a life with "no newspapers"—even in the game-changing year of 1900—is no loss at all. This speaker, unlike Dorothy in *The Wizard of Oz*, who falls to the powers of the field of poppies, is still standing at the end, awake to hear the leaf of the poppy fall. The self-assurance of this turn-of-the-century poem brings to mind a comment from Elaine Scarry's beautiful essay on the urgency of numbers and time in the poetry of various fins-de-siècle, "Counting at Dusk": "The end of the century … far from contracting one's belief in one's own agency, seems instead to prompt the desire to reconstitute the world linguistically" (10). In "No Newspapers," this self-assurance about remaking the world— and specifically the experience of time—linguistically makes itself felt through rhyme: not only the striking internal rhyme by which the "moss" replaces the "loss" of the first stanza, but also Coleridge's repurposing of the wall/fall rhyme. Normally an apocalyptic pairing—in which either it is the walls themselves falling, or, as in Humpty-Dumpty, someone falling *off* the wall—Coleridge's wall/fall is emphatically anti-apocalyptic. And this, I would emphasize, is another lesson about how we should read Coleridge's use of rhyme: she understood how rhyme can make a kind of argument, not only through its temporal spacing (as in "Sounds"), but also through manipulating our awareness of rhyme's conventions and the semantic contents that have been built up through usage. The speaker of "No Newspapers" ends by hearing the leaf of the poppy fall; we end with hearing a rhyme effect whose semantic significance is palpable but subliminal. As Simon Jarvis puts it: "Melodics is the way verse thinks at the limit of explicability" ("Melodics" 619; see also Jarvis, "Why Rhyme Pleases").

At the same time, however, some of the apocalyptic, inevitable, ends-oriented feel of the wall/fall rhyme clings to the end of "No Newspapers." For both late-Victorian, and late-twentieth-century commentators on rhyme, there is a strong connection between rhyming and ending. The Victorian prosodist George Saintsbury had a strong aversion to internal rhyme, rhyme, that is, involving words not at the end of the line. (He would have objected to Coleridge's "moss" in "No Newspapers, which rhymes internally with the end rhymes "loss" and "cross.") Saintsbury ends his massive treatise's appendix on rhyme by stipulating that "on the whole, rhyme should come at the end of something" (*A History of English Prosody* 3: 539), and elsewhere refers to internal rhyme as "treacherous," and as "a most disintegrating and revolutionary thing" (Introduction xxi). The idea that rhyming is about ending is central to Giorgio Agamben's essay, "The End of the Poem." For Agamben, rhymes not only take place at the ends of poetic lines but are central both to the ends of poetry—in the sense of its goals—and to the crisis that implicitly occurs in each poem as it comes to its own ending: that moment when it is about to lose its identity as a poem. In his view rhyme is "a disjunction between a semiotic event (the repetition of sound) and a semantic event (words which ought to have no connection of meaning)," which is, for Agamben, along with enjambment, the essence of poetry (110). At the ends of poems, there is no enjambment; poems threaten to lose their identity and become prose; final rhymes often—as is the case with Coleridge's wall/fall pair—threaten to become freighted with semantic content, incorporating "the element of sound into the very lap of sense," collapsing the disjunction of sound and sense that is poetry's life support (112). At this moment, in this "event" that is "the end of the poem," there is an apocalypse indeed: in Agamben's words it is a "catastrophe and loss of identity" (112). After the "fall" at the end of "No Newspapers," for example, we are left to face a free-fall into a place where there is not only no newspaper but also no poetry: nothing but the eternity of the white blank page that dwarfs Coleridge's tiny poem.

Coleridge wrote a number of poems that exploit the apocalyptic end-game of end rhyme to figure the ending not only of the poem but of existence. In "One Day in Every Year" (1894), for example, the skinny lines, the chiming, simple rhymes figure the hearing of the approach of one's own death—something that is, once again, both near and far:

> One day in every year
> A hope that is a fear
> Comes very near.
>
> Once, every year, I say,
> "Less long now the delay
> Shorter the way."
>
> Whether for joy or woe
> I say that this is so
> I do not know.
>
> Only one thing is clear:
> A hope that is a fear
> Comes near. (1–12)

Not unlike contemporary American poet W. S. Merwin's "For the Anniversary of My Death" (1967), Coleridge's poem acknowledges the strangeness of looking forward to the unknown moment of one's own death. The identity of the constricted, repeated rhyme sounds comes to figure the indifference as to whether that moment will come soon, or not soon enough, is to be hoped or feared. By the end of the poem, the indeterminacy of deixis clings to the final "near"—we have no idea exactly how soon "near" might be, but it rings in our ears. In Coleridge's spare, precise poems, rhyme fills up the border between the end of the poet's consciously abbreviated line and a blank space that is often figured as death.

The last poem I will look at, "From My Window," may be seen as a kind of companion poem to "One Day Every Year." In this poem from 1907—the year Coleridge died suddenly of appendicitis at the age of forty-five—the question of how to manage the unknown amount of time left before one's death is displaced onto another person. It is an old man, who must be viewed as a close kinsman of the one whom Wordsworth contemplated in "Old Man Travelling" (1798). Here is Coleridge's old man:

> An old man leaning on a gate
> Over a London mews—to contemplate—
> Is it the sky above—the stones below?
> Is it remembrance of the years gone by,
> Or thinking forward to futurity
> That holds him so?
> Day after day he stands,
> Quietly folded are the quiet hands,
> Rarely he speaks.
> Hath he so near the hour when Time shall end,
> So much to spend?
> What is it he seeks?

> Whate'er he be,
> He is become to me
> A form of rest.
> I think his heart is tranquil, from it springs
> A dreamy watchfulness of tranquil things,
> And not unblest. (1–18)

The comparison to "Old Man Travelling" is instructive: where Wordsworth captured his old man's combination of glacial slowness, passivity, and edge-of-existence precariousness through skillful manipulation of blank verse—particularly via enjambed line endings—Mary Elizabeth Coleridge conveys hers through jagged line endings, rhyme, and the play of short and long. Rhyme sounds—either between metrically matched lines (as in for example the third and last lines of the last stanza, or the two penultimate lines of the last stanza), or unmatched lines (as in "Hath he so near the hour when Time shall end / So much to spend?")—make time close in on this man. The sense of a narrowing down, counting down, or closing in is assisted as well by the use of rhyme's alien double: repeated words ("day after day," "quietly folded are the quiet hands," the use of "tranquil" twice in the penultimate lines)—these repetitions I call rhyme's alien double because they so curiously don't seem to "rhyme," though of course they sound the same. The sense of closing in is assisted as well by the shape of the stanzas on the page in which the longer lines are framed or clasped by shorter ones, as in a vise.

However, the uneven, rhyme-driven form of the lines of "From My Window" also pushes back against the hastening of the end. One of the effects of an uneven pair is that the short second line, paradoxically, seems to slow down, as we unwittingly let it fill a time frame equivalent to the longer line. This effect creates, to use the phrase Coleridge uses to describe the man himself in line 15, "a form of rest." Whether or not the old man has "time to spend" depends on the ways in which Coleridge "makes time" for him, not only through the act of witnessing and observing him, but through her rhyme's time-effects. The creation of extension and duration through rhyme takes place also through Coleridge's prominent use of what one theorist of rhyme has called "promotion": rhyme pairs that match—often imperfectly—monosyllabic words with multi-syllabic ones such as gate/contemplate, by/futurity, below/so, and finally rest/unblest (Harmon, "Rhyme in English Verse" 389–90). Such rhymes—particularly in their most common form, in which the monosyllable comes before the multisyllable—seem to unfurl extra time, an ending beyond the end. Saintsbury referred to rhyme as "a very-influential *time-beater*," challenging our assumption that it is meter, not rhyme, through which verse beats out time (Introduction xxii, emphasis original). But some of Mary Elizabeth Coleridge's poems, including the ones I've touched on today, suggest that the end of rhyme is the beating, the vanquishing of time.

Fin-de-siècle poets, writing in the few years at the end of the century "so near the hour when Time [or at least the century] shall end," pushed back against the hastening of the days, hours, and minutes by devising forms that slowed time, and expanded the experience of duration. Their spare, gem-like poems are little time machines. In their will to make time, their work bears comparison to that of another great fin-de-siècle writer, the British idealist philosopher, John McTaggart Ellis McTaggart. During the same period—the 1890s and first years of the twentieth century—that Coleridge was writing her late poems, McTaggart was laboring away on his famous essay on "The Unreality of Time" (1908), which, in a curious use of my own time, I listened to on my iPod while writing this paper. Reading—or, rather, listening—to this essay in the context of writing this paper affirmed that McTaggart's rejection of the reality of time—the rejection of what he called "the A series" (past, present, and future) and "the B series" (earlier and later)—in favor of what he called "the C series" (abstract, non-temporal seriality)—must really be seen as a phenomenon of fin-de-siècle thinking with provocative implications for how we might theorize rhyme, rather than as a crazy philosophical exercise. To listen to it expanding in my ears, while watching the little timeline on my iPod counting down the minutes, transfixed me with the always curious differences between the time of writing and the time of sound, which is the province of poetry.

Notes

1 See especially recent critical work by Blair; Harrington; Prins; and Rudy.

Works cited

Agamben, Giorgio. "The End of the Poem." *The End of the Poem*. Trans. Daniel Heller-Roazen. Stanford: Stanford UP, 1999. 109–15.

Blair, Kirstie. *Victorian Poetry and the Culture of the Heart*. Oxford: Oxford UP, 2006.

Brewer, R. F. *Orthometry: A Treatise on the Art of Versification*. London: C. W. Deacon, 1893.

Coleridge, Mary Elizabeth. *Gathered Leaves from the Prose of Mary E. Coleridge*. London: Constable, 1910.

Coleridge, Mary Elizabeth. *The Collected Poems of Mary Coleridge*. Ed. Theresa Whistler. London: Rupert Hart-Davis, 1954.

Harmon, William. "Rhyme in English Verse: History, Structures, Functions." *Studies in Philology* 84 (1987): 365–93.

Harrington, Emily. "The Measure of Time: Rising and Falling in Victorian Meters." *Literature Compass* 4.1 (Jan. 2007): 336–54.

Jarvis, Simon. "The Melodics of Long Poems." *Textual Practice* 24 (2010): 607–21.

Jarvis, Simon. "Why Rhyme Pleases." *Thinking Verse* 1 (2010). 18 Oct. 2010. <http://www.thinkingverse.com>.

Lang, Andrew, ed. *The Nursery Rhyme Book*. London: Frederick Warne, 1897.

McTaggart, John McTaggart Ellis. "The Unreality of Time." *Mind: A Quarterly Review of Psychology and Philosophy* 17 (1908): 456–73.

Prins, Yopie. "Victorian Meters." *The Cambridge Companion to Victorian Poetry*. Ed. Joseph Bristow. Cambridge UP, 1999. 89–113.

Rudy, Jason. *Electric Meters: Victorian Physiological Poetics*. Athens: Ohio UP, 2009.

Saintsbury, George. *A History of English Prosody*. Vol. III. London: Macmillan, 1910.

Saintsbury, George. "Introduction." *The Rhymer's Lexicon*. Comp. and ed. Andrew Loring. London: Routledge, 1904. v–xxvi.

Scarry, Elaine. "Counting at Dusk (Why Poetry Matters When the Century Ends)." *Fins de Siecle: English Poetry in 1590, 1690, 1790, 1890, 1990*. Baltimore: Johns Hopkins UP, 1995. 1–36.

Veley, Margaret. *A Marriage of Shadows and Other Poems*. London: Smith, 1888.

Part V
Forms

Martin Dubois

> What form is best for poems? Let me think
> Of forms less, and the external. Trust the spirit,
> As sovran nature does, to make the form;
> For otherwise we only imprison spirit,
> And not embody.[1]

Thinking of form, the eponymous protagonist of Elizabeth Barrett Browning's epic poem *Aurora Leigh* (1856) offers what is a familiar argument in nineteenth-century poetics: that form should not be a mechanical imposition, but instead derived from an internal law or logic, something integral to the poem and self-evolved from it. The critical essays gathered in this section are concerned with form in terms of genres or modes of poetry, as opposed to what is partly at issue for Aurora Leigh: form as the close structure of individual poems, in aspects such as metre and rhythm. Yet these senses of form are evidently allied, and—as the essays included below show in their discussion of the hymn, the epic, the sonnet, and the dramatic monologue—the notion that poets should 'Trust the spirit ... to make the form' vitally shapes and inspires nineteenth-century poetic modes and genres, even (and perhaps especially) when it is being undermined or resisted.

What lies behind this notion is the aspiration that the writing of poetry should be as far as possible a natural act. E. S. Dallas thinks in a similar vein in his book *Poetics* (1852) when he comments that 'since the imagination is a copy of sense, its forms must be those of its pattern'.[2] Part of Dallas's importance as a literary theorist is to have attempted to marry the Romantic concept of organic form with emerging mid-Victorian ideas about consciousness. Dallas associates creativity with unconsciousness, describing 'unconsciousness as the last and highest law of poetry'—an argument further developed by his later, equally remarkable and eccentric study, *The Gay Science* (1866).[3] Not all were enamoured by this turn to psychology. *Poetics* sparked a famous controversy with David Masson's claim (made in a review of Dallas's book, along with the poems of Alexander Smith) that 'a true allegory of the state of one's own mind in a representative history is perhaps the highest thing that one can achieve in the way of poetry'.[4] Such praise for introspection drew the ire of Matthew Arnold, who retorted that 'no great poetical work has ever been produced with such an aim', and proposed action, not mind, as the proper sphere of poetry.[5] As many of the extracts included in this volume show, the debate over the merits of subjectivity is among the most abiding of nineteenth-century poetics. That *Poetics* can also be understood within these terms indicates that Dallas's unconventionality does not make him a marginal figure.

Like Nietzsche's *The Gay Science*, the ambition of *Poetics* is classificatory and taxonomic, seeking in this case to distinguish laws of imagination, harmony, activity, unconsciousness, as well as genres and modes of poetry. Its significance in relation to the subject of this chapter resides in the distinction Dallas attempts between what he identifies as the three kinds of poetry: the drama, the epic, and the lyric. They appear in *Poetics* in a kind of ascending order, given that the lyrical is allied for Dallas with the unconscious, whereas the dramatic is tied to imagination, and the epic to harmony. Each is further shown to be associated with particular periods of literature, and said to look in a different direction temporally: the epic to the past, the dramatic to the present, and the lyric to the future. The discussion of this ranges freely and eclectically, taking in aspects of hermit life and the nature of personal pronouns before fixing the three kinds of poetry into metaphysical categories (the beautiful, the true, the good).[6] Finding that its creative ambition is only imitative in nature, Dallas assigns the dramatic the lowest place among the three. The epic is found to have greater significance, because it attends to the causes that lie behind what it represents, but it still falls some way short of the lyric, which is absorbed with 'the inward life alone'.[7] English poetry is less essentially lyrical than Scottish poetry, Dallas surprisingly argues, for it is often tainted by a dramatic strain which means that its poets tend to run shy of speaking in their own characters. That this is regrettable is shown by the contrast it presents with sacred songs and hymns. According to Dallas, these constitute pure lyric—a fact which leads him on, finally, to the assertion that 'the lyric sees in God the ultimate end of all things'.[8] It is a claim with which many writers of hymns in the period would surely have agreed.

Hymn

Her sense of identity disturbed by the topsy-turvy world she encounters, Alice in Lewis Carroll's *Alice's Adventures in Wonderland* (1865) attempts to find reassurance in what she knows by heart: multiplication tables, the names of European capital cities, and children's hymns. She begins to recite a familiar example of the latter—the verse beginning '*How doth the little*'—only to find that 'her voice sounded hoarse and strange, and the words did not come as they used to do':

> *How doth the little crocodile*
> *Improving his shining tail,*
> *And pour the waters of the Nile*
> *On every golden scale!*
>
> *How cheerfully he seems to grin,*
> *How neatly he spreads his claws,*
> *And welcomes little fishes in,*
> *With gently smiling jaws!*[9]

This is a bad mangling of the original, Isaac Watts's 'Against Idleness and Mischief' (1715), beginning 'How doth the little busy Bee / Improve each shining Hour'. The bee is a model of industry to which, in Watts's original, children everywhere should aspire: 'For Satan finds some mischief still / For idle hands to do.' Such moralizing provided Carroll with an easy target, but that he should think it worth parodying indicates something of the prevalence and importance of hymns in nineteenth-century religious and literary culture. As J. R. Watson explains in his 2005 article 'Ancient or Modern, Ancient and Modern:

The Victorian Hymn and the Nineteenth Century', hymns became an increasingly constant presence in everyday life, as matter to be read, learned, recited, and sung, in individual as well as collective acts of worship. This was in many ways Watts's legacy, for, along with Charles and John Wesley, he stands at the head of the tradition of English hymn-writing that originated in eighteenth-century religious revival. In Watts's own day, hymnody was largely the preserve of evangelicalism, a state of affairs that continued into the early decades of the nineteenth century. Fervent hymn-singing was an identifying mark of this religion of the heart.[10] Metrical psalmody otherwise held sway in the Church of England, led (especially in rural areas) by gallery bands and choirs, often of less than certain musical talent. Frustration with the inadequacies of psalmody provided the opening for the hymn's general use in church as well as chapel. Gradually it assumed a position of dominance across a range of denominations that it still maintains to this day.

Hymns crossed confessional lines in the nineteenth century, but, as Watson makes clear, they were also a means of staking out differences between and within the major Christian traditions, both Protestant and Roman Catholic. Hymns were only considered appropriate to Church of England worship once removed from their evangelical context. The new interest in Latin hymnody drew its energy from the Oxford Movement, and formed part of the effort to revive Catholic principles in the Church of England: in this context, Watson observes, Latin hymns were found to be 'capable of bringing into the nineteenth century the riches of the early Church, which was regarded as purer than its confused and divided contemporary counterpart'.[11]

The nineteenth-century hymn has received very little attention in literary studies. One possible cause of its neglect is the sheer quantity of hymns and hymn books the period produced: it is hard to know where to begin. Watson chooses to focus on *Hymns Ancient and Modern* (1861), a best-selling hymn book, and also (as he explains) one that sought by its breadth to appeal to different factions within the established church. The importance of studying Victorian hymnody is here suggested to be principally historical (the essay opens with a plea to 'the historian who would consider the impact of literature on the culture of the Victorian period').[12] Elsewhere Watson has entered a different claim about the hymn, distinguishing between its historical interest and its literary quality, and opposing the idea 'that the hymn is a poor relation of poetry, a limited and circumscribed art'.[13] The claim is made in the context of an old debate—Watson would say a tired debate—about what another major critic of the hymn, Donald Davie, writing in 1978, terms the 'intrinsic virtues' of hymns, a category he sets apart from 'their historical significance'.[14] Talk of 'intrinsic virtues' is nowadays relatively rare in literary-critical discussion, and is at risk of appearing out-dated. That Watson's book *The English Hymn* is almost never found outside the religion section of libraries who own it, however, does suggest that the battle to have hymns considered as literary artefacts is not yet won. In many ways the hymn faces the same difficulty as devotional verse, running up against an essentially post-Romantic resistance to the idea that poetry can serve as a conduit for the public and collective as well as the private and individual. For hymns to receive their literary due requires that complexity and variety not be the sole measures of interest and value. For while, as Watson shows, many nineteenth-century hymns share these attributes, others do not, being closer to the 'plain style' Davie praises in his tough-minded introduction to *The New Oxford Book of Christian Verse* (1981), a style that is said to engage 'the most direct and unswerving English'.[15]

There is the added complication, as there is not with devotional verse, that the significance of hymns can only ever be partially registered by scholarship that seeks to understand them only as text, without reference to music. Watson's article does not attempt to discuss the latter, perhaps for the same reason declared in *The English Hymn*: that much scholarship has been undertaken in this area already. This is undoubtedly the case, but it is possible that an increasing trend towards interdisciplinarity in nineteenth-century studies has now created an opportunity for words and music, text and tune, to be seen as mutually dependent and reciprocal in creating a hymn's meaning.

Epic

Epic was for a long time supposed to have died with Milton, only to be reborn in the twentieth century with the advent of literary modernism in T. S. Eliot's *The Waste Land* (1922) and Ezra Pound's *The Cantos* (1925–1969). That, in Hegel's influential theorization, epic is a 'primitive' form, the expression of a nation's collective life and shared values,[16] means it appears ill-suited to the conditions of modernity. Where epic survives into the nineteenth century, it survives (so the argument runs) as an exception—Wordsworth's *The Prelude* (1805, published 1850) is most often mentioned here—and an exception turned more towards individual experience than to commonality and wholeness, the traditional preserves of classical epic, even as Wordsworth sustains the long convention of using the form to reflect upon the nature of poetic vocation. Another cause of epic's long displacement, according to customary interpretation, is the emergence of the novel, a genre that Georg Lukács in his *Theory of the Novel* (1916) sees as signalling the loss of integrity upon which classical epic depends: 'The novel is the epic of an age in which the extensive totality of life is no longer directly given, yet which still thinks in terms of totality.'[17]

Herbert F. Tucker tells a very different story in *Epic: Britain's Heroic Muse 1790–1910* (2008), lamenting 'the categorical erasure of the epic genre from our working picture of the nineteenth century', and contending that the transformation of classical epic in modern poetry can only be understood with reference to the radical shifts and changes seen in its rich continued life in the preceding period.[18] His determinedly revisionist book continues the work of recovery begun by Simon Dentith's study of epic primitivism, *Epic and Empire in Nineteenth-Century Britain* (2008). For Dentith, the bardic recitation of a heroic past connotes its difference from the present: 'epic becomes the foremost evidence of the historical alterity of the barbaric world; by the same token, it becomes a principal indicator of our own modernity'.[19] Tucker's much bigger book (it is 737 pages long) conducts the argument on a larger scale, asserting that epic's facility for consensus and fusion meant that it was the 'nineteenth century's preferred form of organizing whatever it knew'.[20] In a similar vein to Dentith, Tucker suggests that epic's 'associations with the old and with the primitive helped nineteenth-century lays do the essential work of rendering perceptible … the complex wholeness of the materials they handled'.[21] The introduction to his study, excerpted here, is mostly concerned with tricky matters of definition, finally resting the book's selection of material on length and scope; but it also gives a thumbnail sketch of the altering nature and status of epic in the period, from the 'newly experimental frame of mind' seen in the aftermath of the French Revolution all the way to epic's 'Edwardian efflorescence'.[22] There are also hints of the astonishing range of Tucker's reading, which involves him delving deep into previously unexplored recesses of nineteenth-century epic to bring to light the extent and variety with which the genre was deployed in the period.

Not the less remarkable is Tucker's facility in moving between close poetic details and large cultural contexts. His example has been crucial to proponents of so-called critical 'new formalism', who argue that 'close reading of the very best sort takes literary form as a subtle and often neglected vehicle for broader cultural forces'.[23] Epic might provide a test case of what this method of interpretation makes possible—and of what it needs to keep in mind. The editors of a special issue on epic in the *Journal of Victorian Culture* in 2009 propose that the way epic itself changed and altered in the nineteenth century, moving beyond its traditional confines in order to survive the challenge presented by new forms of knowledge, proves instructive for literary studies in the twenty-first century: 'Going outside itself, the study of literary form might survive best by continuing to learn much from the historical disciplines, even as the historical disciplines can learn much from formalist lines of enquiry.'[24] That absolute even-handedness is in practice very hard to achieve is shown by the fact that the editors go on to acknowledge that their issue 'places form at the centre of historical ways of thinking' rather than making 'the aesthetic dimensions of the text the main subject of investigation'.[25] The argument about where the emphasis should lie in the study of epic will not be easily resolved.

Sonnet

The sonnet, as Joseph Phelan observes early in his study of the form in the nineteenth century, occupies an ambiguous position in the poetics of the period: 'It is both spontaneous and rule-governed, both personal and conventional. It is a throwaway form of little intrinsic value, written to fill up a spare page, and at the same time the most intrinsically valuable of poetic utterances.'[26] The Romantic emphasis on sincere and authentic self-expression in poetry made the conventionality and artificiality of the form appear the more suspect. It is all the more remarkable, then, that the nineteenth century is rich in sonnets, and in theories of sonnet writing. Having earlier fallen into disuse, the slow revival of the form begun in the eighteenth century (led in particular by Thomas Gray and Thomas Warton) and gathered pace towards the turn of the century, most notably in the work of female poets such as Anna Seward, Charlotte Smith, Helen Maria Williams, and Mary Robinson. For a long time, their contribution to the nineteenth-century sonnet revival was overshadowed by that of male Romantic poets, especially Wordsworth, who wrote more than 500 sonnets, and whose sonnets upon the sonnet (such as 'Scorn Not the Sonnet' of 1827) provide famed defences of the form. A major development in recent criticism has been the recognition of how far the recovery in status of the sonnet in this period was bound up with the efforts of women writers to secure their position in a literary world in which they themselves were gradually becoming more prominent.[27] A fierce preference for the Petrarchan over the Shakespearean sonnet was more than narrowly technical: adopting a purist's stance towards what counted as a 'legitimate sonnet' (Mary Robinson's term in her preface to the 1796 sonnet sequence *Sappho and Phaon*) was a means for Seward, Smith, and others to legitimize themselves as poets.[28] The feminization of the sonnet during the late eighteenth century and the way in which its later development relates to gender continues to be a key concern of scholars.[29]

Debates about the nature of the sonnet feature heavily in the critical writing of the period. A letter written by Gerard Manley Hopkins in 1881 gives as 'the equation of the best sonnet' as '(4+4) + (3+3) = 2.4 + 2.3 = 2 (4+3) = 2.7 = 14'.[30] The idea of the sonnet this connotes is highly unusual in a century in which vigorous efforts were being made to prove its organicism. Most writers on the sonnet sought to establish what Wordsworth in a letter of 1833 beautifully describes as the 'intense Unity' of the form: the sonnet as 'the image of an orbicular body,—a sphere—or a dew drop'.[31] What might at first glance appear mechanical—a fixed form, requiring adherence to certain set rules, regardless of subject—according to this view actually provides a natural pattern for expression. Victorian theorisations of the sonnet likewise suggested that its coherence should be unforced, with 'every part ... but a member of a vital organism', in which the *volta*, if observed, should at most be 'a turning-point at which the subject is to be gently transferred to a further stage, as in walking we progress in shifting the centre of gravity from one side to the other'.[32] This emphasis aligns with the increasing tendency to see the sonnet as a universal lyric rather than as tied to specific historic circumstances, as manifested, for instance, in the decline in biographical readings of Shakespeare's sonnets occurring across the period.[33]

Phelan places both Wordsworth and Hopkins as inheritors of Milton's view of the sonnet as balancing the need for creative freedom with formal discipline. By contrast, he proposes that the revival of the sonnet sequence also occurring during this period (it was enlisted by poets such as Elizabeth Barrett Browning, George Meredith, Christina Rossetti, and Dante Gabriel Rossetti) involved a return to medieval and Renaissance practice 'for instruction in and sanction for dissenting attitudes and beliefs.'[34] As with lyric sequences such as Tennyson's *In Memoriam* (1850), the sonnet sequence requires that individual poems not be seen in isolation, yet it also often leaves the nature of the larger unity they comprise uncertain, meaning that the tension between the individual and the whole is often left unresolved. In that sense it can often be an ideal vehicle of doubt and ambiguity—as John Holmes has shown to be the case in Dante Gabriel Rossetti's *House of Life* (1881).[35]

Overall, Phelan's book reveals how the development of the sonnet across the nineteenth century cuts across the traditional Romantic/Victorian divide—something which is also true of the other major study of the form in the nineteenth century, Jennifer Wagner's jargon-heavy 1996 study *A Moment's Monument: Revisionary Poetics and the Nineteenth-Century English Sonnet*, which posits a shift 'from a compensatory to a revelatory function for the sonnet':

> its occasion not an expression of loss, necessarily, but a moment of heightened consciousness; the emergence of figures of space, light, and instrumentality that self-reflexively describe the form and its new mode; and the emphasis, through these figures, not so much on the brevity and constraint of the form as on its potential for expansiveness.[36]

Dramatic monologue

There is wide agreement that the dramatic monologue is the most significant Victorian innovation in poetry, but that its defining characteristics are difficult to identify exactly. Efforts at categorising the form sometimes appear too broad to be meaningful (e.g., 'a poem in the first person spoken by ... someone who is indicated not to be the poet'); they can just easily arrive at a narrow taxonomy that excludes all but a few monologues by Tennyson and Robert Browning.[37] Robert Langbaum's classic treatment in his 1957 book *The Poetry of Experience* proposes that we can know the form by its effects, in the tension between sympathy and judgment such poems elicit from their readers. According to Langbaum, we first enter into the speaker's subjectivity, but before long find ourselves passing judgment on it: a rift emerges between how the speaker intends their words and how we as readers comprehend them.[38] In that sense, the dramatic monologue is an instance of what Isobel Armstrong has influentially called the Victorian 'double poem', a mode of writing at once expressive and epistemological. It both extends and undermines the Romantic lyric of experience. Dramatic monologues are double poems in that they provide an encounter with an individual self and at the same time force us to reflect on how that self comes to be made. Indeed, in this way, speakers of dramatic monologues can be seen not only to give themselves away, but, as Herbert F. Tucker has observed, 'also [to] give the self away': 'The business of articulation, of putting oneself into words, compromises the self it would justify; it disintegrates the implicit claim of self-presence in the lyric into a rhetorical fabric of self-presentation'.[39]

This last remark refers to Robert Browning, the poet with whom efforts to classify and categorise the dramatic monologue have tended above all to be concerned. His achievement in the form is unparalleled, but by no means all Victorian poets followed in the manner of his example—a fact which older accounts of the dramatic monologue, such as Langbaum's, have sometimes neglected. The wealth of examples discussed by Richard Cronin in his chapter on the dramatic monologue in *Reading Victorian Poetry* (2012) highlights the variety in Victorian experimentation with the dramatic monologue. At its most fundamental, Cronin sees the form as a means to exploring self-division, and as the most prominent instance of an increasingly vexed relationship between poets and their speakers evident in this period more widely. What applies in the case of poems about poets—Cronin discusses the 'teasing relationship between Elizabeth Barrett's poem and Aurora's poem' in Elizabeth Barrett Browning's epic *Aurora Leigh* (1856)—also holds true of the dramatic monologue generally: in each case it becomes impossible wholly to identify poet with speaker, but also equally problematic to distance them entirely.[40] This uncertainty is especially apparent in the form of such poems (Cronin discusses how in Robert Browning 'rhyme and metre serve formally to secure the difference between the poet and the speaker, but they do not build between the two a fence high enough to keep them quite apart'; he makes a similar point in respect of Dante Gabriel Rossetti's 'Jenny' [1870]).[41]

As is common in interpretations of the dramatic monologue, Cronin sees that the form places a high responsibility upon the reader in weighing the words of the speaker they encounter. (As is also true of Langbaum's account, a fairly universal reader is assumed, perhaps problematically.) This responsibility, he suggests, can be felt especially keenly in the case of Elizabeth Barrett Browning's anti-slavery poem 'The Runaway Slave at Pilgrim's Point' (1850). As is clear from Cronin's discussion, Barrett Browning's poem does not follow in the pattern described by Langbaum; rather, it is one of a number of dramatic monologues by women poets which, as Linda K. Hughes observes, 'explore unusual psychological states and social, theological, or philosophical problems with a crucial difference: it is not women who are perverse but the society that limits their choices and brands them as tainted goods if they resist.'[42] The way nineteenth-century women poets adopt and adapt the dramatic monologue has been one recent area of major critical interest; another has been the effort to understand how the speech acts of dramatic monologues might be performative—intended to achieve certain goals, or a means of enacting relationships of power.[43] As this suggests, we have come a long way from assuming (as some early critics of the form did) that what speakers reveal of themselves in dramatic monologues is both unconscious and unwitting. What constitutes a dramatic monologue appears less certain than ever, a fact that ensures interpretative approaches to the form continue to multiply.

Notes

1 Elizabeth Barrett Browning, *Aurora Leigh* in John Robert Glorney Bolton and Julia Bolton Holloway (eds), *Aurora Leigh and Other Poems* (London: Penguin, 1995), 5: l. 223.
2 E.S. Dallas, *Poetics, An Essay on Poetry* (London: Smith, Elder & Co., 1852), p. 157.
3 Dallas, *Poetics*, p. 61.
4 David Masson, Review of E.S. Dallas, *Poetics*, and Smith, *Poems*, *North British Review*, 20 (1852), 297–344 (p. 338).

5   Matthew Arnold, Preface to *Poems*, in R.H. Super (ed.), *Complete Prose Works*, 11 vols. (Ann Arbor. MI: University of Michigan Press, 1960–1977), I (1960), p. 8. On Arnold's response to Masson, see Gregory Tate, *The Poet's Mind: The Psychology of Victorian Poetry 1830–1870* (Oxford: Oxford University Press, 2012), pp. 84–89.

6   Dallas's insights into the changing use of pronouns from classical epic onwards are 'surprisingly innovative', according to W. David Shaw: see Shaw's discussion of this in *The Lucid Veil: Poetic Truth in the Victorian Age* (London: Athlone Press, 1987), pp. 252–256.

7   Dallas, *Poetics*, p. 146.

8   Dallas, *Poetics*, p. 150. The religious strain to *Poetics* allows Dallas to be accommodated within what Cynthia Scheinberg calls 'Victorian theological poetic theory': see her *Women's Poetry and Religion in Victorian England: Jewish Identity and Christian Culture* (Cambridge: Cambridge University Press, 2002), pp. 53–54.

9   Lewis Carroll, *Alice's Adventures in Wonderland and Through the Looking-Glass*, Hugh Haughton (ed.) (London: Penguin, 1998), p. 19.

10 See Elisabeth Jay, *The Religion of the Heart: Anglican Evangelicalism and the Nineteenth-Century Novel* (Oxford: Clarendon Press, 1979), p. 124.

11 J.R. Watson, '"Ancient or Modern": The Victorian Hymn and the Nineteenth Century', *The Yearbook of English Studies*. 36 (2006), 1–16 (p. 8).

12 Watson, '"Ancient or Modern"', p. 1.

13 J.R. Watson, *The English Hymn: A Critical and Historical Study* (Oxford: Clarendon Press, 1997), p. 4.

14 Donald Davie, *A Gathered Church: The Literature of the English Dissenting Interest, 1700–1930* (London: Routledge, 1978), p. 47.

15 Donald Davie, 'Introduction' to *The New Oxford Book of Christian Verse* (1981; repr. Oxford: Oxford University Press, 1988), p. xxix.

16 See G.W.F. Hegel, *Aesthetics: Lectures on Fine Art*, trans. T.M. Knox, 2 vols. (Oxford: Clarendon Press, 1975), II, pp. 1040–1110.

17 Georg Lukács, *The Theory of the Novel*, trans. Anna Bostock (Cambridge, MA: MIT Press, 1977), p. 56.

18 Herbert F. Tucker, *Epic: Britain's Heroic Muse 1790–1910* (Oxford: Oxford University Press, 2008), p. 10.

19 Simon Dentith, *Epic and Empire in Nineteenth-Century Britain* (Cambridge: Cambridge University Press, 2006), p. 1.

20 Tucker, *Epic*, p. 310.

21 Tucker, *Epic*, p. 21.

22 Tucker, *Epic*, pp. 11–12.

23 Jason R. Rudy, 'On Cultural Neoformalism, Spasmodic Poetry, and the Victorian Ballad', *Victorian Poetry*, 41 (2003), 590–596 (p. 590).

24 Adelene Buckland and Anna Vaninskaya, 'Introduction: Epic's Historic Form', *Journal of Victorian Culture*, 14 (2009), 163–172 (p. 170).

25 Ibid., p. 170.

26 Joseph Phelan, *The Nineteenth-Century Sonnet* (Basingstoke: Palgrave Macmillan, 2005), p. 2.

27 See on this Daniel Robinson, 'Reviving the Sonnet: Women Romantic Poets and the Sonnet Claim', *European Romantic Review*, 6:1 (1995), 98–127.

28 Mary Robinson, *Selected Poems*, Judith Pascoe (ed.) (Ontario: Broadview, 2000), p. 144.

29 See especially Marianne Van Remoortel, *Lives of the Sonnet, 1787–1895: Genre, Gender and Criticism* (Farnham: Ashgate, 2011).

30 Lesley Higgins and Michael F. Suarez, S.J. *et al.* (eds), *The Collected Works of Gerard Manley Hopkins* 8 vols, (Oxford: Oxford University Press, 2006–), I (2013), p. 476.

31 William Wordsworth, letter to Alexander Dyce of 22 April 1833, in Ernest de Selincourt (ed.), Alan G. Hill, Chester L. Shaver, Mary Moorman *et al.* (rev. eds), *The Letters of Dorothy and William Wordsworth*, 8 vols (Oxford: Clarendon Press, 1967–1993), V (1979), pp. 604–605.

32 James Ashcroft Noble, 'The Sonnet in England', *Contemporary Review*, 38 (September 1880), 446–71 (p. 450); Mark Pattison, editorial introduction to *The Sonnets of John Milton* (London: Kegan Paul, 1883), pp. 30–31.

33 See on this Rhian Williams, '"Pyramids of Egypt": Shakespeare's *Sonnets* and a Victorian Turn to Obscurity', *Victorian Poetry*, 48 (2010), pp. 509–521.

34 Phelan, *Nineteenth-Century Sonnet*, p. 4.
35 John Holmes, *Dante Gabriel Rossetti and the Late Victorian Sonnet Sequence: Sexuality, Belief and the Self* (Aldershot: Ashgate, 2005).
36 Jennifer Ann Wagner, *A Moment's Monument: Revisionary Poetics and the Nineteenth-Century English Sonnet* (Madison, NJ: Fairleigh Dickinson University Press, 1996), p. 14.
37 Alan Sinfield, *Dramatic Monologue* (London: Methuen, 1977), p. 9.
38 See his *The Poetry of Experience: The Dramatic Monologue in Modern Literary Tradition* (London: Chatto and Windus, 1957).
39 Herbert F. Tucker, 'From Monomania to Monologue: "St. Simeon Stylites" and the Rise of the Victorian Dramatic Monologue', *Victorian Poetry*, 22 (1984), 121–137 (p. 125).
40 Richard Cronin, *Reading Victorian Poetry* (Chichester: Wiley-Blackwell, 2012), p. 42.
41 Cronin, *Reading Victorian Poetry*, p. 47.
42 Linda K. Hughes, *The Cambridge Introduction to Victorian Poetry* (Cambridge: Cambridge University Press, 2010), p. 19.
43 See E. Warwick Slinn, *Victorian Poetry as Cultural Critique: The Politics of Performative Language* (Charlottesville, VA: University of Virginia Press, 2002); and Cornelia D.J. Pearsall, 'The Dramatic Monologue', in Joseph Bristow (ed.), *The Cambridge Companion to Victorian Poetry*, (Cambridge: Cambridge University Press, 2000), pp. 67–88.

21 Poetics, An Essay on Poetry (1852)

E. S. Dallas

On the defence of poesy

The defence of poesy has already more than once been written; and with more than usual power by a Sidney and a Shelley. Without any slight to these able works, it may, however, be said, that they can have little weight with those who push poetry to defend its own. They are mostly written from the whereabouts of the poet; and the weapon employed is the unsearchable logic of poesy—a logic most true, but too brief for common purposes, a logic swift and untraceable as electricity, flying straight from point to point, unmindful of the turns, the stoppages, and the stages, the ifs, buts, and therefore, of ordinary argument. Such reasoning will seldom hit those who drive poets to the defensive. The poet is thus pressed by two very different personages; by the philosopher, and by one who stands between philosopher and poet, of neither gender, the proser. The proser has been dipt in some unknown Styx that has case-hardened him against almost every weapon—all but the heel; and there is no way of dealing with him but by putting motion into those heels, I mean, by arousing his activities; and then he will turn, according to his degree, either a poet or a philosopher. If he takes the part of the poet, good and well, nothing more has to be said. If he becomes a philosopher, and still decries the poet, he must be met on the side of his arithmetical understanding with common logic and the rule of three.

In the foregoing pages, it is hoped that somewhat has been advanced, which, in this regard, may be of service; since if anything need and be worthy of defence, the best that can be given is to make known its real nature, and show its true colours. Having already at some length (in Books Third and Fourth) put forward doctrines that illustrate the *positive* worth of poesy, it will here be sufficient to stand wholly on the defensive. Not that in every case, and from every mind, it will be possible to remove objections; but at least they may be silenced. We may spike the guns which we cannot take away.

There is no denying that, however much poesy may be ill-spoken of by some, it has always been well received by the wide world; more heartily welcomed than aught else the work of man; more lastingly kept, and never willingly forgotten. This is not (although it might be) brought forward as a plea in favour of poetry, lest any one should think that plea in danger of Bacon's remark, that man has in him more of the fool than of the wise, and is more strongly influenced by his foolish than by his reasonable powers; but simply to show, that on the whole poets have no ground for quarrelling with their treatment and their lot on this earth. Pindar, for his poesy, is said to have been loved of Pan, and even to have heard one of his own odes chanted by the god: there is a truth in the story.

Any direct and formal charge is seldom brought against poetry: it is generally assailed by means of clever backstrokes and passing lounges. Oftenest of all, however, with inarticulate sneers. And these attacks come not merely from such as Sir Edward Coke, who, in the exercise of his judicial functions, foredoomed to everlasting pain five classes of men, namely, Chemists, Monopolists, Concealers, Promoters, and Rhyming Poets; but even from such writers as Bacon. The latter have keenly felt the power of poetry, but have been unwilling to own because unable satisfactorily to account for that power, and have fretted and chafed under the yoke. They have often been gifted with no small share of the poetic faculty, and in anticipation of Hahnemann have sought by a small dose of poetic language to cure the poetry of their fellows. Like the monkeys, that, to keep the sailors from landing on their island, pelted them with cocoa-nuts, the very and only thing which was wanted, Bacon pelted the poet with flowers, and tried to stop his mouth with pleasant words: while others, beside, in rich and glowing language, seek to overwhelm the imagination and its works. They are bent on the same error as the wise men of Gotham, who set about the drowning of an eel. Upon all such, the scorners of poesy, Sir Philip Sidney, in closing the treatise above mentioned, has pronounced a curse which would certainly be very frightful if it would only take effect: "Thus much curse I must lend you in the behalf of all poets, that while you live you live in love, and never get favour for lacking skill of a sonnet; and when you die, your memory die from the earth for want of an epitaph."

Whenever these assailants come to close quarters, and give us a clue to their meaning, it will be found that their objections naturally range themselves under three heads. They say that poesy is not Beautiful, or not True, or not Good. An attempt has already been made in these pages to show that it is all three. It is now behoveful to show the insufficiency of those grounds upon which the doctrine is denied.

Beauty of poesy

It is objected that Poesy is not beautiful. The objection, indeed, is never stated thus plainly, but rather implied, and implied in such a way, that it might almost be regarded as impugning either the truth or the good of poesy even more than its beauty. Thus parasitically entwined with other and bolder objections, it is not possible to grapple with it singly; and we must therefore consider it as entangled, in the first place with a question of Truth, in the second place with a question of Good.

Of the many forms which objections of the former class may take, the Puritanic seems not yet to have spent itself. "The imaginations of men's hearts are only evil continually," it is said; and therefore from the delights of the imagination we are to call a solemn, a perpetual fast. Such a fast is simply impossible; at best it can only be a Ramazan, which forbids food during the day, but allows it after sunset, since, if dreams may be banished in our waking hours, they will yet return in the night. Here, the objector, desirous of wielding the lash of William Prynne, or the cudgel of Jeremy Collier, will perhaps point significantly to the license of certain poems, or certain plays, and ask if, with such before his eyes, any right-minded man can allow himself to indulge in the reading of poesy. The foulness of many a poem and many a play is undeniable. Great part of the famous Alexandrian library, which was turned into fuel for the public baths, was unworthy even thus remotely of being applied to a cleanly purpose; and if a Jew had bathed in waters thus warmed, he might with reason have deemed himself unclean as a leper for the remainder of his days. But the fact of certain poems and certain plays being bad, is no more an argument against poesy, than it is an argument against the produce of the hive to say that the bees of Trebisonde feed on poisonous flowers and brew poisonous honey.

It will then be said that at least the imagination is a very unhealthy faculty, and that we ought by all means to keep it down. Even poets have said as much. Shenstone is a delightful companion to all who can relish the manliness, the freedom, the unaffected ease of a hearty, well-witted, and tasteful country gentleman. He deserves to be better known than he is, and not every one will resist the following pleasant invitation, here given as in a manner showing that, when he chose, he could regard poetry in the light of a healthy and familiar feeling.

"You who can frame a tuneful song,
And hum it as you ride along;
And, trotting on the king's highway,
Snatch from the hedge a sprig of bay;
Accept this verse, howe'er it flows,
From one that is your friend in prose."

Yet the man who could so write, could at another time bring himself to speak of poetry, if not in his very heart to regard it, as a mere sickly hankering. "Poetry and Consumption," he says, "are the most flattering of diseases." Therefore, let poetry yield to philosophy; let the imagination give place to the understanding. It is quite true, that in some minds poetry may become a disease; but so also in other minds may philosophy. And there cannot well be a greater mistake than to oppose Judgment to Imagination, or to consider them, as often they are considered, in the light of a madman and his keeper. It would not be a greater to place knowledge, which is so clear of eye, in opposition to love, which we have been taught to regard as blind; and it is the very same mistake which sets up reason against faith, and makes ignorance the mother of devotion, enlightenment its enemy. Is there, then, it may be asked, no such thing as a wild imagination? In unhealthy minds there is, but nowhere else. If it be answered, that this unhealthiness of mind, and consequent wildness of fancy, is owing to a lack of judgment, an appeal to facts will show that it is not; for then would the mind of the unjudging boy be very-sickly, and his imagination crazed; whereas, even when his imagination is most daring, it is sounder than that of the most thoughtful man. In truth, the imagination has very seldom to be curbed; it is continually needing the spur. Very often, from the mere feebleness of this faculty, Dugald Stewart has well said, and not from any coldheartedness, arises that want of feeling with or for others, which is but too frequently charged against our fellow-men; they do not, they cannot, imagine the situation of other people. The idea, indeed, that a poetic imagination is something very weakly, very sickly, will be found to rest upon some vitiated taste, some mistaken view of the nature of poesy. After all that Wordsworth has said, after all that he and others have done, it is too much the fashion to regard poetry as something very unreal, skyhigh, and out of the way; an opinion greatly strengthened, if not chiefly caused, by the habit of looking into a poem, above everything, for the made-pleasure derived from happy and abundant images. Abundant images no more make a poem than any number of swallows make a summer. Doubtless, in its own place, the pleasure of tracing resemblances may be natural enough; it has delighted every one to think the passing cloud a weasel, backed as a camel, or very like a whale. But artificial and absurd most decidedly it is when desired for its own sake, and regarded, as children regard the sweetmeats at a feast, best and chief. True poetry is as real, as needful, and naturally as common to every man as the blood of his heart and the breath of his nostrils. If poetry were not part and parcel of our being, poesy would not be so widely felt and admired; and it is always but short-lived when, as with Donne and Cowley, it is addressed not to feelings universal and irrepressible, but to the passing taste of a little circle. Of all such poesy, of all poesy whatsoever, we may say that it will "fit audience find, though few;" but this in a sense the very opposite of that which Milton intended; in the sense in which we might also say that it will fit welcome find, though small.

As thus far considered, the objection, by casting a slur upon the *origin* of poetic pleasure, is connected with a question of truth. It comes to this: Poesy may be very beautiful, but it is the offspring of disease. The fact for which we contend is here admitted in words, denied in reality; since that which others may regard as beautiful can awaken no admiration, but rather contempt, in the mind of one who associates it with a corrupt source.

Unable to hold this, the objector falls back upon the other ground above mentioned. Harping no longer upon the evil cause, he now begins to harp upon the worthless effect. Thus, instead of connecting his denial of the beauty with a denial of the truth of poesy, he now connects it with a denial of the good: Poesy may be very fine, very beautiful; but where is the use of it? Here again, the point at issue is in so many words admitted, in reality is denied; since what to another may be beautiful is not so to the man who can see in it no use whatsoever.

The utilitarian is not the only, nor is it the highest test of beauty; but rightly understood and applied, it is trustworthy, and it is a test by which the lovers of poesy would be willing to abide. They do not complain of the test, but of its wrong application. They complain that poesy is measured by utilities of the very lowest order. It is often valued at nothing, because its effect is not bodily before our eyes. Bartholin declared that ailments, chiefly the falling sickness, were curable by rhymes; Dr Serenus Sammonicus offered to cure a quartan ague by laying the fourth book of Homer's Iliad under the head of the patient; and Virgil was once believed to be an excellent fortune-teller. But since poesy can do no such marvels, it is regarded as a mere game of words, a solemn trifling, wilder far than the wildest and most foolish extravagances on which the old scholastic philosophers wasted their time and blunted their wits. Of persons who so think it is enough to say that they utterly mistake the calling, the aim, and the work of the poet. The Troubadour gave to his calling the name of El Gai Saber, the gay science: to suppose however that gravity of purpose may not exist under this gayety of mien is to imitate the poor satyr who was so greatly puzzled to understand how a man could blow hot and cold with one and the same mouth. The avowed object of the poet is pleasure; but he has laid in ambush other ends as mighty and as earnest as any that rule mankind. If he seems to have his eye set upon the world, it is only as a rower who is pulling further and further away. The readers of the Tatler were in an early number informed that when any part of that paper appeared dull they were to believe that the dullness had a design. It was not a bad joke; but will it not be far more credible, as it is most true, that the poet under the air of frolic has more or less consciously a serious purpose? Shenstone truthfully paints the village schoolmistress as sitting disguised in looks profound: on the contrary, the greatest of all teachers comes masked in smiles, a winebibber, half drunken with joy. Therefore he is unknown. Therefore, also, his work is constantly misjudged; deemed most useless when haply it is most useful; and deemed shallowest where perhaps it is deepest. A very weighty thought, if it have ornament sufficient, may rise like a balloon till it go out of sight and none but sharp eyes can see it. By itself it is heavy as ballast; when joined to the volatile gas it seems to be lighter than air.

22 Ancient or Modern, Ancient and Modern: The Victorian Hymn and the Nineteenth Century (2006)

J. R. Watson

Religion in Victorian times was political. Every gesture, every assumption, every allegiance to a belief, was accompanied by a set of assumptions about society, often unspoken but always present, in ideas about wealth and power, in attitudes to the Empire and its peoples, in pressure for reform, in attitudes to education, in temperance movements, or just in the desire to be left alone (as Sir William Heathcote and Keble, despotic squire and conservative parson, evidently wished at Hursley). It was into this confused and fevered world that *A&M* was born. It contained 273 hymns, arranged as follows: a preliminary section: Morning and Evening, Sundays (5 hymns) and the days of the week (1 each); then the church year, from Advent to Trinity Sunday, followed by hymns labelled 'General Use'; then hymns on the Sacraments and Special Occasions (Harvest, Dedication of a Church, for example); and finally, hymns for Saints' Days, and for Apostles, Evangelists, and Martyrs. It was clearly a book for the Church, but—in such a politico-religious age—what kind of church? We may start by considering the 'Ancient' of the title, which meant principally Latin.

Latin hymns had been lost to the Church since the Reformation. There had been a few isolated examples of translation, such as John Cosin's 'Come, Holy Ghost, our souls inspire' and Dryden's 'Creator Spirit, by whose aid', both translations of 'Veni, creator spiritus'. But the real revival of Latin hymnody began in the nineteenth century. It was a statement of the value of tradition: it was as much a part of the nineteenth-century fascination with the past as was the interest in the Middle Ages. The difference was that whereas the Middle Ages were valued as a time of prosperity and community life, as well as being picturesque, the Latin past was a time of Roman virtue and imperial achievement, followed by centuries of monasticism and scholarship.

Latin was the tongue of saints and scholars. It was also the language of Roman Catholicism, and therefore suspect in the eyes of Protestant England. For example, some verses of 'Adeste, fideles, laeti triumphantes', including the first, come from an eighteenth-century collection called 'The Jacobite Manuscript', probably originating in Douai and entitled 'A Prayer for James', referring to James III, the Old Pretender. The tune was often played in the chapel of the Portuguese Embassy in London, and became so associated with a foreign embassy of a Roman Catholic country that it was called 'Portuguese'. During the French Revolution, French Roman Catholics took refuge in England: one of them, Abbé Etienne Jean François, Monsignor de Borderies, added another verse to the Latin text. It was a splendid hymn for Christmas, but its origins were suspect.

But if Latin brought with it a suggestion of Papist infiltration, it also had the distinction of being the language of an educated person. It was the language of the Universities of Oxford and Cambridge. Newman published a collection of Latin hymns from the Roman and Paris

Breviaries, *Hymni Ecclesiae,* in 1838. Keble's lectures as Professor of Poetry at Oxford from 1832 to 1841 were given in Latin, and not translated into English until 1912. Isaac Williams, another of the major figures in the Oxford Movement and author of 'Be thou my guardian and my guide', said that during his schooldays at Harrow he 'received no religious instruction of any kind', but that his preference for Latin was so great that when he had to write an English exercise he had to think it out, or write it out, in Latin, and then translate it into English.

In 1829 Williams began translating hymns from the Paris Breviary of 1736. He noted that at the time 'there prevailed a general horror among Church people of unauthorized hymns being sung in church, and I remember I put them often into unrhythmical harsh metres to prevent this'.[1] He published some of his translations in a religious periodical, the *British Magazine,* where they attracted the attention of John Chandler, Fellow of Corpus Christi College, Oxford. Chandler acquired a copy of the Paris Breviary for himself, and began translating from it, publishing *The Hymns of the Primitive Church* in 1837, with an enlarged edition in 1841. It contained hymns such as 'On Jordan's bank the Baptist's cry' and 'The heavenly child in stature grows'. In the same year as Chandler's first edition, Richard Mant, then Bishop of Down and Connor, published *Ancient Hymns from the Roman Breviary, for Domestick Use.*

Williams, Chandler, and Mant were Latin scholars, Oxford men. They were willing to accept the disapproval of the evangelicals and Nonconformists for the sake of the material which they had unearthed. They were pioneers in a venture to bring to the Church of England hymns of a different kind from those then in use, primarily among evangelical churches where they had been introduced unofficially into services. Suspicion of this practice was considerable among the senior clergy: when Reginald Heber, then a Shropshire vicar, asked permission in 1820 to compile a collection of hymns for the Church's year, he was refused. Meanwhile evangelical churches used unofficial books, often compiled by local clergy, or written by them: the best-known example was by a Sheffield incumbent, Thomas Cotterill, whose *Selection of Psalms and Hymns* was published in 1810, with many successive printings and enlargements. A classic hymn book of this kind was *Olney Hymns,* written by Newton and Cowper and published in 1779, which was one of the books which furnished material for these selections.

Williams and Chandler were entering this field in different ways. Williams by stealth, printing translations that no one could sing; Chandler more boldly. In his orotund preface to *Hymns of the Primitive Church* he addressed himself to the Church of England with a kind of heavy playfulness:

> It will not, I trust, be unpleasing or unedifying to her members to see a Morning Hymn by a Bishop of Milan of the fourth century [Ambrose] joined to one on the same subject by a Bishop of Salisbury of the seventeenth [probably Chandler meant Ken here, though Ken was Bishop of Bath and Wells]. Perhaps, if the authorities of our Church carry on the design, we may see next to them a hymn by a Bishop of Calcutta of the nineteenth [Heber], (p. x).

The reference to Heber points to his *Hymns Written and Adapted to the Weekly Church Service of the Year,* published in 1827. Heber, after some hesitation, had accepted appointment as Bishop of Calcutta in 1823, dying suddenly in India in 1826. His unexpected death, caused by overwork (more immediately by plunging into a cold swimming pool on a hot day), shocked the country, and his widow, Amelia, took advantage of his position as a heroic martyr of the mission field to override episcopal objections and bring out his hymn book. It contained hymns such as 'Brightest and best of the sons of the morning', 'Holy, holy, holy! Lord God Almighty', both of which are still sung, and the missionary hymn 'From Greenland's icy mountains' which is not, although it was once a compulsory hymn for every mainstream hymn book. Its second verse, in particular, was so well known that it was parodied by Kipling ('The 'eathen in 'is blindness bows down to wood an' stone; 'E don't obey no orders unless they is 'is own'):

> What though the spicy breezes
>   Blow soft through Ceylon's isle:
> Though every prospect pleases,
>   And only man is vile;
>   In vain with lavish kindness
> The gifts of God are strewn;
>   The heathen in his blindness
> Bows down to wood and stone!

Missionary work was one way of distracting attention from the anxieties at home, as Dickens's Mrs Jellyby in *Bleak House* comically demonstrates; and its Christian expansionism is often unattractive, although the heroism of nineteenth-century missionaries, going out to countries where they had a life expectancy of a few years or even a few months, is often forgotten.

Chandler's reference to Heber is significant, indicating a readiness to see contemporary hymnody as part of a tradition stretching back to St Ambrose. It is evidence of a slow discovery that hymns were not necessarily the preserve of evangelicals, dissenters, or Methodists, but capable of bringing into the nineteenth century the riches of the early Church, which was regarded as purer than its confused and divided contemporary counterpart:

> Christ's Church was holiest in her youthful days
>   Ere the world on her smiled.

That poem was no. 131 in *Lyra Apostolica,* the volume published in 1836 by Newman in conjunction with like-minded religious associates—Hurrell Froude, Keble, Isaac Williams, and others. It was part of the growing interest in the poetry of religion that accompanied the Tractarian movement. The interest had begun almost ten years before, with *The Christian Year* of 1827, the same year as Heber's *Hymns.* Although Keble appeared in it, *Lyra Apostolica* was markedly different from *The Christian Year.* As G. B. Tennyson has pointed out, it was more aggressive and polemical. The title, as he says, 'calls to mind a common Romantic image, the poet as inspired singer':

> Theirs is an *apostolic* lyre, one in harmony with the stirrings of the Apostolic Church, which is both Newman's Church of the Fathers and the Church that secured its perpetuity even to the present through the apostolic succession, a principle of enormous importance to the Tractarians and the source for their arguments on behalf of the authority of the visible Church and the validity of the Church of England as part of the Church Catholic.[2]

The gathering cloud of Tractarian disquiet with the state of the English Church burst with Newman's conversion of 1845, after which all became clearer. Newman himself tried to entice Keble to follow him, in a clever and seductive review of Keble's *Lyra Innocentium* of 1846, arguing that the Roman Catholic Church was the most 'poetical' of all churches and that Keble, who had done so much to bring poetry to the Church of England, would find his true place in Rome.[3] At this point hymns and poems were becoming weapons in the battle for the hearts and minds of British Christians. One convert, F. W. Faber, who published *Jesus and Mary; or, Catholic Hymns for Singing and Reading* in 1849, and a collected edition of his hymns in 1862, wanted his hymns to do for Roman Catholics what *Olney Hymns* had done for evangelical Protestants. The 1849 preface acknowledged the power of hymns over them, while completely failing to understand the glories of Wesley or the subtlety of Cowper:

> There is scarcely anything which takes so strong a hold upon people as religion in metre, hymns or poems on doctrinal subjects. Every one, who has had experience among the English poor, knows the influence of Wesley's hymns and the Olney collection. Less than moderate literary excellence, a very tame versification, indeed often the simple recurrence of a rhyme is sufficient: the spell seems to lie in that.[4]

Another convert, Edward Caswall, published *Lyra Catholica* in 1849, the title proclaiming his new allegiance. It contained hymns such as 'Bethlehem! of noblest cities', translated from the Latin of Prudentius, 'O sola magnarum urbium', and 'Hark! an awful voice is sounding', a translation of 'Vox clara ecce intonat'. In the first flush of his new allegiance, Caswall was investigating the possibilities of ancient hymnody, and in translating them he was not only making them available to the British Christian community but also promulgating the idea of the continuity of the Church.

The greatest of these translators was John Mason Neale (1818–66). At Cambridge he was one of the founders of the Cambridge Camden Society (later the Cambridge Ecclesiological Society), with aims that were not dissimilar to those of Newman and his associates at Oxford. Prevented through ill health from taking up the living of Crawley in Sussex, he became Warden of Sackville College, a small sisterhood at East Grinstead, where his High Church practices aroused the wrath of the Bishop of Chichester, who denounced his furnishing of the chapel as 'spiritual haberdashery'. But because the chapel and sisterhood were part of a private foundation, the bishop had no jurisdiction over it, and Neale lived a quietly productive life, writing the history of the Eastern Church and a novel, *Theodora Phranza*, and publishing *Mediaeval Hymns and Sequences* in 1851 and *Hymns, Chiefly Mediaeval, on the Joys and Glories of Paradise* in 1865. He was also considerably involved in a production of the Cambridge Ecclesiological Society, *the Hymnal Noted*, which appeared in two parts (1852, 1854). His enthusiasms may be seen from the preface to the first of these, which introduced Sequences to the British Church:

> It is a magnificent thing to pass along the far-stretching vista of hymns, from the sublime self-containedness of S. Ambrose to the more fervid inspiration of S. Gregory, the exquisite typology of Venantius Fortunatus, the lovely painting of S. Peter Damiani, the crystal-like simplicity of S. Notker, the scriptural calm of Godelascus, the subjective loveliness of S. Bernard, till all culminate in the full blaze of glory which surrounds Adam of S. Victor, the greatest of them all.[5]

Neale translated hymns that became universally known and loved, such as 'Jerusalem the golden', 'Of the Father's love begotten', 'O come, O come, Emmanuel', and 'The royal banners forward go'. In the first edition of *A&M* he was the most represented author. Like Faber he was commendably interested in 'the poor', and wrote *A Short Commentary on the Hymnal Noted, from Ancient Sources, Intended Chiefly for the Use of the Poor* in 1852. It explained the aims of the *Hymnal Noted,* and condemned the metrical psalms created by the Reformers, who 'put the psalms into verse, and sang them by way of hymns'. This led to the neglect of 'the old hymns of the Church of England' (those written before the Reformation), 'and so a great number of "collections", that have no authority, came into the Church'.[6] The 'no authority' phrase referred to the many unofficial collections made by clergy for their individual churches: it was this proliferation of hymn books that the publication of *A&M* was intended to stop.

Latin was a resource for these hymn writers that emphasized their shared status as educated men. One book, *Clavis Dominica* (1884), contained translations of some hymns from *A&M* into Latin, including two by the Prime Minister, William Ewart Gladstone, 'Jesus, pro me perforatus' ('Rock of ages, cleft for me') and 'Scis te lassum? Scis languentem?' ('Art thou weary, art thou languid'). The second of these was originally a Greek hymn, translated into English by Neale, whose *Hymns of the Eastern Church* (1862) introduced English-speaking readers to what Neale called 'this huge treasure of divinity ... a glorious mass of theology'.[7] As Leon Litvack has pointed out, Neale turned from Rome to Greece in his quest for 'Sobornost' or unity, that unity which he found so lacking in the fragmented and irritable British churches.[8] The result was hymns such as 'The day of resurrection', 'The day is past and over', and the hymn by St Andrew of Crete:

> Christian! Dost thou see them
>   On the holy ground,
> How the troops of Midian
>   Prowl and prowl around?

Who the troops of Midian might have been was not specified. This was one of the great advantages of these hymns: such imagery could be applied to whoever was the opposing party at the time, or used to support one's own side:

> Through many a day of darkness,
>   Through many a scene of strife,
> The faithful few fought bravely,
>   To guard the Nation's life.

This is from a celebrated Victorian hymn, 'Thy hand, O God, has guided', written by Edward Hayes Plumptre, Fellow of Brasenose College, Oxford, Professor at King's College London, and then Dean of Wells. Who 'the faithful few' were would have depended on where you stood in the turbulent and faction-ridden Victorian Church.

Nor was the insatiable appetite for controversy confined to the Protestant–Catholic divide or to High Church and Low Church. The Congregationalists in 1855 were torn apart by Thomas T. Lynch's *The Rivulet; or, Hymns for Heart and Voice*, an inoffensive collection of hymns which saw God in nature ('Flowers will not cease to speak, | And tell the praise of God'). The book was denounced by John Campbell, the editor of two Congregationalist magazines, the *British Banner* and the *Christian Witness,* as 'miserable garbage': the hymns were 'crude, disjointed, unmeaning, unchristian, ill-rhymed rubbish'.[9] The reason for such wild rage was evidently the insecurity of the Congregationalists (who lacked the stability of the official status of the Church of England and the *Book of Common Prayer)* in the face of doubt, science, and rational thought. Campbell identified the Tübingen school as the source of the problem:

While the Magazines were under his care they [the readers] need fear nothing from Germany. He discarded all such speculations. He had burned, he might say, reams of a speculative nature. He had dropped anchor in Westminster, where he found matter in abundance, in the Confession of Faith, in the Shorter and Larger Catechisms.[10]

'Westminster' refers to the Westminster Confession, the great statement of independent faith in the seventeenth century; and Campbell's furious response to Lynch's work was a return to the violent passions of those days. All that Lynch was doing was preaching a doctrine of God as found in the beauty of the natural world, a churched Wordsworthian creed. To Campbell, nothing less than the gospel of the atonement through the saving blood of Jesus Christ would suffice. And Campbell, like others after him, was a book-burner.

So far, this account has been dominated by the squabbles of men, and it is time to consider briefly the place of women. Although there were some women, as Richard Jenkyns has shown,[11] who were excellent at Greek (notably George Eliot), it was men who primarily appropriated Latin and Greek as languages of a cultivated man. Women, with some exceptions, were thought to be less capable of the required intellectual effort. It was generally thought, with Mr Stelling in *The Mill on the Floss,* that girls had 'a great deal of superficial cleverness; but they couldn't go far into anything. They're quick and shallow.'[12] The most poignant example from the world of the Victorian hymn was Dora Greenwell, who wrote hymns that are still sung, such as, 'And art thou come with us to dwell'. Her brother William was a noted antiquarian and a Canon of Durham Cathedral. She received from him what might be called the Maggie Tulliver treatment:

I remember I read one book (I forget which) and said, 'Dora, I cannot see your aim. What is it you want to tell people? You seem to be in earnest, but what is the conclusion? You roll your subject over and over, and then you stop. I don't believe you know yourself what you want to teach!'[13]

The bland assurance of 'I forget which' speaks volumes. It is hardly surprising that one of Dora's hymns should begin 'I am not skilled to understand | What God has willed, what God has planned'; nor that her life seems to have been one of frustration and unhappiness. Nor is it surprising that Christina Rossetti's 'In the bleak mid-winter' should end with

What can I give him,
   Poor as I am?
If I were a shepherd
   I would bring a lamb;
If I were a wise man
   I would do my part;
Yet what I can I give him—
   Give my heart.

A distinguished modern hymn writer, Elizabeth Cosnett, has pointed out that 'when a woman wrote these words women were largely excluded from the professions and from higher education'.[14] And yet the women hymn writers of the nineteenth century, such as the Unitarian Sarah Flower Adams ('Nearer, my God to Thee'), Frances Ridley Havergal ('Take my life, and let it be'), and Anna Laetitia Waring ('In heavenly love abiding'), produced texts that have continued to inspire generations of hymn-singers. The greatest of them all, however, was the translator Catherine Winkworth. She was one of many women writers who translated German hymns, which makes an interesting confluence of two streams: the growing confidence of women writers and the Reformed tradition of German hymnody.

In addition to translations of individual works such as Schiller's *Die Räuber* and Bürger's *Lenore,* there was a lively general interest in German philosophy, aesthetics, and theology throughout the nineteenth century. In hymnology the first great consequence was Carlyle's essay in *Fraser's Magazine* (1831) entitled 'Luther's Psalm'. The psalm in question was 46, beginning in Luther's version 'Ein feste Burg ist unser Gott' and in Carlyle's translation 'A safe stronghold our God is still'. Carlyle described Luther as

> A man ... not only permitted to enter the sphere of Poetry, but to dwell in the purest centre thereof: perhaps the most inspired of all Teachers since the first Apostles of his faith; and thus not a Poet only but a Prophet and God-ordained Priest, which is the highest form of that dignity, and of all dignity.[15]

Carlyle's comments were written immediately after Catholic emancipation, and they can hardly have pleased those, like Keble and Newman, who were hard at work at Oxford on the writings of the Church Fathers. But the reference to Luther as a 'God-ordained Priest' would hardly have delighted the episcopally ordained priests of the English church either. Carlyle's brief essay, with its magnificent psalm, was 'a plague on both your houses' rebuke to the effete clergy of all denominations and shades of belief. It was followed, however, by translations of hymns with a much more strident agenda. Richard Massie, who published *Martin Luther's Spiritual Songs* in 1854, introduced his translations with a lengthy preface, carrying the message that at the Reformation 'the light of the Gospel had by God's grace again risen upon benighted Christendom':

> For my own part, the longer I live, the more I learn to bless God for the Reformation and the Reformers, and the more I feel convinced that in a firm adherence to their doctrines and principles, so admirably embodied in our Articles, Liturgy, and Homilies, lies the best safety of our Church amid the perils which surround her.[16]

German hymns and theology were therefore part of a Protestant agenda (except for extremists such as Campbell). The man who did more than any other to introduce them into England was Christian Carl Josias Bunsen, the scholarly and cultured ambassador to the Court of St James. Before entering the diplomatic service, Bunsen had been a theologian and historian, and had published a vast treasury of German hymns and prayers, *Versuch eines allgemeinen evangelischen Gesang- und Gebetbuchs, zum Kirchen- und Hausegebrauch* (Hamburg, 1833). He made the acquaintance of Frances Elizabeth Cox, encouraging her to produce her *Sacred Hymns from the German* (1841); and Susanna Winkworth, whom he persuaded to translate an anthology of German mystical prose writers, *Deutsche Theologie,* resulting in *Theologica Germanica* (1854). He then encouraged the greatest of all German hymn translators, Susanna's sister Catherine, to produce *Lyra Germanica* (First Series, 1855, Second Series, 1858).

The Winkworth sisters were from an evangelical background, modified by the gentler teaching of their mother,[17] and even more modified by a year's study in Dresden. They had been taught German by William Gaskell, and met Bunsen through the Gaskells and their circle of Unitarian intellectuals in Manchester. Five of Catherine's translations were in the first edition of *A&M* in 1861: two years later she produced, with the assistance of two distinguished musicians, Otto Goldschmidt and William Sterndale Bennett, *The Chorale Book for England,* containing such hymns as 'Praise to the Lord, the Almighty, the King of Creation' and 'Jesu, priceless treasure'. Bunsen's response shows how closely the endeavour was bound up with Reformation ideology: 'her really wonderful translations seem to promise to effect what hitherto has proved impossible—namely, to *naturalize* in England the German *Hymns,* the most immortal literary fruit of the Reformation'.[18]

Cox and the Winkworth sisters were three of many women translators of German texts. Hymn translators included Eleanor, Lady Fortescue (*Hymns, Mostly Taken from the German,* 1843), Henrietta Joan Fry (*Hymns of the Reformation by Dr M. Luther and Others from the German,* 1845, 1853), and Jane Montgomery Campbell, who translated 'Wir pflügen und wir streuen' ('We plough the fields and scatter'). The pre-eminence of Luther was reaffirmed by a series of small books published in Edinburgh by two sisters, Jane Laurie Borthwick and Sarah Laurie Findlater, entitled *Hymns from the Land of Luther* (1854, 1855, 1858, 1862), including 'Be still my soul: the Lord is on thy side'. Rich in experience and individual interpretation of Scripture, the German hymns were a powerful contrasting element to the Latin hymns from the Breviaries.

A&M, in its comprehensive way, managed to satisfy many of these conflicting demands, and it sold very well indeed. The compilers said that they could not send forth their *Appendix* of 1868 'without the expression of their deep gratitude to Almighty God for the marvellous success with which He has been pleased to bless their former work' (p. iii). A second edition followed in 1875, with a Supplement added in 1889. Into these successive editions went the great hymns of the Victorian Church, 'Thy hand, O God, has guided', 'Alleluia, sing to Jesus', 'For all the saints who from their labours rest', 'The Church's one foundation'. The effect of singing these was sometimes quite extraordinary. When the last-named was sung at a service in St Paul's Cathedral during the third Lambeth Conference in 1888, the effect was described as 'almost appalling'.

Sung by a large congregation, some people say this hymn was really more than they could bear. 'It made them feel weak at the knees, their legs trembled, and they really felt as though they were going to collapse.'[19] Similarly, the singing of 'The day thou gavest, Lord, is ended' at the service for the Diamond Jubilee of Queen Victoria in 1897 had a great effect. When she chose it, the Queen can have been under no illusions about the British Empire: although the procession contained representatives from half the world, coloured red on the map, participants in services all over the country sang

> So be it, Lord; thy throne shall never,
> Like earth's proud empires, pass away.

Kipling's 'Recessional', written on the same occasion, was a reminder that the magnificence of the procession and the power of the naval review were transient:

> The tumult and the shouting dies;
>   The captains and the kings depart:
> Still stands thine ancient sacrifice
> An humble and a contrite heart.

The hymn (brilliantly linking 1897 to Psalm 51), which was included in the *English Hymnal* of 1906, was one of the hymns written at the end of the century which strove to remind the singers of national life and political responsibility, although the greatest of these, Chesterton's 'O God of earth and altar' and Scott Holland's 'Judge eternal, throned in splendour', date from the first years of the twentieth century. But they emerge from a late Victorian movement, the Christian Social Union, which sought to promote better conditions for the poor and a more equable distribution of wealth. The Salvation Army, the 'Missions', and the 'Settlements', together with some devoted clergy of all denominations, all tried to do something to minister to the material welfare of the underprivileged: while clergy such as Percy Dearmer, later an editor of the *English Hymnal* and *Songs of Praise,* was deeply affected by the dockers' strike of 1889. Ben Tillett, the leader of the dockers, was a chapel-goer; and there is some truth in the adage that the beginnings of the Labour Party owed more to Methodism than to Marx. But this is hardly revealed in hymns until Chesterton's plea for a society that would unite 'prince and priest and thrall'.

Notes

1 *The Autobiography of Isaac Williams, B.D.,* ed. by Sir George Prevost (London: Longmans, Green, 1892), p. 37.
2 G. B. Tennyson, *Victorian Devotional Poetry* (Cambridge, MA, and London: Harvard University Press, 1981), pp. 122–23.
3 J. H. Newman, 'Keble', in *Essays Critical and Historical,* 2 vols (London: Pickering, 1872), 11, 421–53. Keble, said Newman, 'did that for the Church of England which none but a poet could do: he made it poetical' (p. 442).
4 F.W. Faber, preface to *Hymns* (1849), repr. in *Hymns* (London: Burns & Oates, 1862), pp. xiii-xviii (p. xvi).
5 John Julian, *A Dictionary of Hymnology* (London: Murray, 1892), p. 787.
6 J. M. Neale, *A Short Commentary on the Hymnal Noted* (London: Masters, 1852), p. iv.
7 J. M. Neale, *Hymns of the Eastern Church* (London: Hayes, 1862), p. xli.
8 Leon Litvack, *J. M. Neale and the Quest for Sobornost* (Oxford: Clarendon Press, 1994).
9 William White, *Memoir of Thomas T. Lynch* (London: Isbister, 1874), pp. 109–10.
10 Albert Peel, *These Hundred Years: A History of the Congregational Union of England and Wales, 1831–1931* (London: Congregational Union of England and Wales, 1931), p. 220.
11 Richard Jenkyns, *The Victorians and Ancient Greece* (Oxford: Blackwell, 1980).
12 George Eliot, *The Mill on the Floss, Book 11,* chapter 1, Stereotype Edition (London and Edinburgh: Blackwood, 1894), p. 135.
13 Quoted in Constance L. Maynard, *Dora Greenwell: A Prophet for Our Own Time in the Battleground of Our Faith* (London: Allenson, 1926), p. 122.
14 'A (Female) Bookworm Reads Some Hymns', *Bulletin of the Hymn Society of Great Britain and Ireland,* 205 (October 1995), 172–84.
15 Repr. in Thomas Carlyle, *Critical and Miscellaneous Essays,* 5 vols (London: Chapman and Hall, 1899), 11, 160–64 (pp. 160–61).
16 Richard Massie, *Martin Luther's Spiritual Songs* (London: Hatchard, 1854), pp. vi, xiii.
17 Margaret J. Shaen, *Memorials of Two Sisters, Susanna and Catherine Winkworth* (London: Longmans, Green, 1908), pp. 8–9.
18 Shaen, p. 139.
19 Wesley Milgate, *Songs of the People of God,* 'A companion to *The Australian Hymn Book/With One Voice'* (London: Collins, 1982), p. 154. Unfortunately, Milgate does not give the source of this extraordinary account.

23 The Very Idea: Epic in the Head (2008)

Herbert F. Tucker

The Very Idea: Epic in the Head

In *The Critic as Artist* (1890), Oscar Wilde has his proxy Gilbert list among the topics canvassed by the self-conscious Greeks of Alexandria "the artistic value of the epic form in an age so modern as theirs."[1] Looking back two millennia to the good old days when modernity was really new, Wilde is kidding as usual; and as usual he means what he says. For his contemporaries the mind of classical Greece was more than a laughing matter; to them it mirrored the mind of nineteenth-century Britain as surely as Gilbert's dialogue with Ernest mirrors the mind of Oscar Wilde to us. Wilde's joke partook of an uncanny logic that, disclosing the familiar within the foreign, had pervaded reflection on the "value of the epic form" for a hundred years. Around 1890 epic in Britain happened to be entering the one fallow period within what this book will show was a continuously fertile Romantic and Victorian history; but it was not only towards the end of the long nineteenth century that the genre fell under suspicion of anachronism. Such suspicion has shadowed epic as long as it has been modern: if not since Wilde's Alexandria, then certainly since the decades flanking 1700 when John Dryden and Alexander Pope elaborated "Augustan" poetry within a London neoclassically renovated. For these authors, as for their Renaissance forerunners and their successors into our time, the exemplary career of that premier Augustan poet and direct Alexandrian heir Virgil established the composition of an epic as the last rite of passage to full poetic majority, the summative test of art. This was a test that, during the twelve decades covered by this book, more major British poets than not approached with fear and trembling.[2] The trepidation that accompanied a poet's approach to epic, and that even where it is not corroborated in a preface or surviving letter always leaves a trace somewhere in the resulting poem, came only half from self-doubt. The other half came from doubts that were entertained on every hand about the genre itself.

From 1858, close to the midpoint of our story, the Laureate-in-Chief speaks for all his tribe: "I wish that you would disabuse your own minds and those of others, as far as you can, that I am about an Epic of King Arthur. I should be crazed to attempt such a thing in the heart of the 19th Century."[3] Alfred Tennyson's gruff deprecation is not about King Arthur, or chivalry, or antiquity of subject as such. In fact the legendary matter of Arthur formed the substance of a book comprising four *Idylls of the King* that he would publish the next year; and he would do so fully confident that, whatever else he had made his new book into, it was not an epic. Instead, Tennyson's apprehensiveness was "about an Epic," whether hazarded on this theme or any other.

That way madness lay, he knew; yet he also knew it was a way his contemporaries suspected he was tempted to try. And they were right: within another decade the leading Victorian bard's *furor poeticus* would drive his Arthurian poem into epic territory after all, by the feat of generic conversion that frames our Chapter 10 below. If the gambler's malaria of hope and prudence, denial and recklessness, thus afflicted an author basking in every honor his era could bestow, we may safely regard Tennyson's generic hand-washing as the symptom of a contagion that none might escape.

Nor even now are we who apply the stethoscope of literary history to "the heart of the 19th Century" immune to the stress that made Tennyson's murmur. We bring to the very idea of epic a rash of doubts that are not only similar to those presented in the nineteenth century but continuous with them, for reasons rooted in the modernity that our moment shares with that not so very bygone time.[4] Like the Romantics and Victorians we want to belong to the sort of unified community that once embraced epic as its own; and yet that is not what we want at all. We endorse, and we discredit, the thought that our lives acquire meaning through participation in a large, whole, and absorbing history, whose collective dimension has an importance that as modern individuals we both covet and mistrust. Stirred even to applause by the epic poet's mission to symbolize "the accepted unconscious metaphysic of his age" (so one circumspect analyst called it at the close of the period this book covers), as regards our own age we harbor an acute reluctance to subscribe to anything of the kind.[5] For all of us, in the twenty-first century as in the nineteenth, the prospect of writing an epic poem devoted to such a mission—in truth, even the prospect of faithfully *reading* one—savors of a dare; embarked upon, it has about it the feeling of a stunt; and the result, whatever other qualities it may claim, cannot well avoid being regarded as a freak. So a book that goes on at such length as the one I have written, pursuing a redundantly confessed literary anachronism "in an age so modern," owes its reader an apology.

Mine, of course, has been underway for four paragraphs now. By diagnosing the ambivalence that epic prompted in Romantic and Victorian minds as a syndrome in which we still participate, I mean to purchase interest in the genre. Our suspicion about epic's modern irrelevance should itself prompt suspicion, or at least curiosity, about the mix of respect and aversion that keeps the genre in pious modern quarantine as a literary irrelevance. The long conspiracy to make the ongoing appeal of epic look like a sideshow attraction, safely off the common reader's beaten path, operates with maximum force where that reader has been schooled in our standard literary history. Such a scholar imbibes a lesson that comes in several versions, not always compatible with each other but invariably militating against the project of this book. The splendor of epic, so the lesson runs, is a glory that *was*.[6] For the severe purist it vanished millennia ago when literacy broke up the world of oral narrative; but on most accounts epic has enjoyed one or more visitations of second wind in literary and eventually print dispensations: Virgil's Rome, Dante's Italy and then Tasso's, the England of Spenser and, at the end of the line, Milton. Occasionally advocates have petitioned for a post-Miltonic stay of execution into the eighteenth or early nineteenth century.[7] In the end, though, literary history must have its victim. At whatever point the historian fixes, thereupon the date of epic prolixity was out, the curfew tolled the knell, and the genre gave up the ghost—either as a natural casualty of great old age or as a sacrifice exacted to consecrate the birth of that modern consciousness from whose vantage literary history is perennially put together.

This latter explanation of the death of epic takes most compact, memorable (and for now probably inexpugnable) shape in triumphalist accounts of the history of the novel. These accounts depict prose fiction as the genre in which modernity stands forth over epic's dead body.[8] Like the axioms of modern history from which the depiction borrows much of its formidable power (the rise of the middle class and of empirical science, the supplanting of feudalism by markets and monarchy by democracy), this account of generic supersession is equally amenable to explanatory models of lineal handoff and of revolutionary overthrow. Standard literary history's relative indifference as to causes suggests that *how* the change occurred matters less to the historian than the founding presumption *that* it occurred. As a practical matter the two models often coexist, for example in E. M. W. Tillyard's definitive generic histories of major narrative in English, where *The English Epic and Its Background* yields with the years—the 1700s, to be specific, when he tells us "the epic impulse left poetry for the novel"—to *The Epic Strain in the English Novel*.[9]

It is among the virtues of Tillyard's work to wield frankly the judgments about literary value that, often more covertly but in all cases necessarily, underpin work along this line of literary-historical argument. Evaluative judgments are required to police the scene as soon as it is conceded—as on overwhelming evidence it must be conceded— that works of conspicuously epic shape and aspiration have continued to appear, on a nearly annual basis, years after whatever generic expiration date the gazette of literary history has announced. Explaining this teeming evidence away obliges the historian to turn critic, round up the intruding senile delinquents and convict them of failing to observe the clearly posted criteria, or—by a less contestable, more candidly authoritarian indictment—of lacking the epic genre's authentic character or spirit, which *ex hypothesi* has passed away beyond human recovery. In any case the capital verdict against epic is a foregone conclusion dialectically entailed on generic traditionalism by the privilege it accords, wittingly or not, to the inviolable uniqueness of the modern.

From this dialectical entailment, and the act of critical judgment that it may flourish or harbor but cannot dispense with, has sprung a revivalist movement that also deserves our notice here. This movement subscribes to a heterodox exceptionalism maintaining that, under circumstances sufficiently extraordinary, epic can make a comeback after all. No matter when it died—which it certainly did do, the revivalist holds, way back somewhere in an inhospitable past—it was born again in the second quarter of the twentieth century. In its broadest and strongest form the argument privileges the century of modernism over the half-millennium of modernity: it pursues, that is, a corollary of twentieth-century modernism's self-definition as the unprecedented maker-new of all things, including the literary genres and media. The Great War having eviscerated and flattened European civilization, a generic reconfiguration took place, the hard-line exceptionalist affirms, such that James Joyce's *Ulysses* made richer sense as an epic than as a novel, or that Ezra Pound's ambition for the *Cantos* became not eccentric to its culture but chorically representative.[10] Alternatively, the rise of new media—cinema in particular—fostered a change in the relations among producers and consumers of major narrative that made epic possible once more in the twentieth century, on radically changed terms of page and screen.[11]

When it is formulated at full strength, this heterodox revision of epic traditionalism effects a drastic historical severance. It awards to the revived genre a contemporary inclusiveness across the culture, like Dante's or Homer's once upon a time; but such breadth of reference comes at the forfeit (a steep one for literary history) of longitudinal continuity down the centuries. Reluctance to pay this forfeit may explain the appeal of a weaker variant of exceptionalism, which rests content to champion not an entire avant-garde but a single resuscitated work. This or that major poem, it is argued, turns out miraculously to make the grade, winning out in spite of adverse odds—and indeed in the face of the criterion of cultural centrality on which stronger accounts, be they traditionalist or modernist, insist.

Traveling light, and requiring little more than the toolkit of evaluative critique, this gambit is historically adaptable in a way that the strong-modernist heterodoxy is not. With its help critics can airlift William Wordsworth's *The Prelude,* say, or Elizabeth Barrett Browning's *Aurora Leigh* over the frontier without confronting the intellectual structure that keeps the embargo in force. Like other modes of literary history by special indulgence, this one serves to confirm business as usual: it leaves intact the arrangement that entombs epic beneath the cornerstone of the modern.

[...]

From the Romantic edge of doom epic pulled back circa 1830, around the inaugurally Victorian hour of national reform, and rescued out of the mode of totalitarian judgment the genre's forensic and deliberative capacity, coupled with a marked new interest in dramatic modes friendly to exchange and debate (Ch. 7). This identification of the national interest with diversity-management thereupon fanned epic outwards, with the 1840s, into an apparently postnationalist outsourcing of Britishness; this development both reflected the geographic expansion of empire and subjoined to it a bid for the *translatio imperii* from Roman, Greek, and more racily Aryan origins into the keeping of a Britain now imagining its dynasty in collective terms larger than the national (Ch. 8). The expansionist impulse splashed into the 1850s as epic spasmody, a buffo recrudescent Romanticism whose star flamed out for good in the most entertaining of Victorian culture wars but whose influence remained to fertilize the most abidingly original anglophone poetry of the mid-century (Ch. 9). To this textural poetics of style succeeded in the next decade a structural poetics of myth. Fed by new discourses of culturalist comparatism that arose with empire's steady traffic, the mythological epic of the 1860s witnessed some of the Victorians' profoundest literary inquiry into the terms and costs of group allegiance (Ch. 10). This structural rigor abated across the last third of the century: as comparatism declined into collecting, the global portrait gallery or anthology of eras became a characteristic epic form, underwritten by a finally imperialist ideal of civilized progress. Broad yet slack, such provincially complacent metropolitanism met its generic rebuke in a dissenting minority tradition of epic narratives in tragic mode (Ch. 11). The genre's slumber at the very *fin-de-siècle* gave way at last to an Edwardian efflorescence: around 1905 several major works returned, as if preconcertedly, to themes deriving from British history and resumed, as if presciently, the unfinished business of national assessment within a now ominous context of world-historical struggle (Ch. 12).

So runs, in breathless and faceless summary, the long proof of nineteenth-century epic that fills the chapters ahead. It is a sketch whose internal variation I hope will suggest how adaptable the genre turned out to be, and how responsive it remained to contemporary concerns as they arose and changed with the decades. Only more searching acquaintance with individual works can bear out a further general proposition about all this generic variety: that the combination of the nineteenth-century epic poem's esteem value (confessedly superlative) with its market value (ordinarily minimal, though with spectacular exceptions) freed poets to take creative risks with narrative that their novelist and historian contemporaries in prose could seldom afford.[15] The poets were moreover impelled to such liberties, by the complex of ambition and doubt that, as we saw at starting, was indissolubly attached to epic's very idea. Both in themselves and in their chosen generic vehicle, the epoists of the nineteenth century had something to prove.

Modern thinking about the epic genre exhibits remarkable stability, not because it is in some final way correct but because it is modern: the problem it perennially addresses is not the essence of epic but the accidence of modernity. The working definition of epic that critics in our time take for granted—even the least theoretical of us can reluctantly produce it if we have to—reposes on fundamentals that would have won approval at once from their counterparts two centuries ago. At the point where our survey starts, the era of the French Revolution, there had lately occurred a deep shift in epic's theoretical premises, one that the last section of this chapter will rehearse as the replacement of a formal by a cultural criterion for epic unity. The orientation towards the genre that resulted from this shift consistently subtended the many poems the rest of the book takes up; nor has any rival orientation arisen to challenge it seriously in the hundred years since the eve of World War I, where our survey concludes.[16] It is tempting to ascribe a record so signally unanimous, when it occurs in a field like literary theory that thrives on contention, to forces other than consciously intellectual. Our unanimity as theorists of epic savors of codependency with the unanimity that, we all agree, is constitutive of epic itself.

For it is the very idea of epic to tell a sponsoring culture its own story, from a vantage whose privilege transpires through the successful articulation of a collective identity that links origins to destinies by way of heroic values in imagined action. *Consensus* furnishes the currency of an epic system where rendition of the generally acknowledged merges through explanation of the generally understood into prescription of the generally regulative—which then feeds back into the system to start the self-reinforcing cycle of facts, truths, and norms all over again. To narrate the tale of the tribe is at once to receive an order, to describe an order, and to issue an order, in a powerful gyrostabilized loop that, if we may judge from the recent history of epic theory, sheds a portion of steadying influence on all who move within its orbit.

The clearest sign of this exponential consensus inhabiting epic theory is that it furnishes the enduring reference point from which leading disputes in epic studies during the past two centuries are to be grasped. As debate over the unity of Homer raged across the nineteenth century between single-source unitarians and text-shredding, palimpsest-decoding analysts, both sides gravitated alike to theses rooted in a shared postulate of cultural coherence. The ideas of order in archaic and in classical Greece that were invoked, respectively, by the unitarian and the analyst differed from each other greatly; but it was to those ideas of order, to the explanatory power of Aegean or Athenian society's imputed wholeness, that either party in the Homeric dispute appealed when clinching its case.[17] A century later, in renewed pursuit of unsolved Homeric questions, and in the teeth of resistance from diehard *littérateurs,* an ethnographically bolstered generation of epic oralists introduced performative ideas about medium and venue that changed much in epic studies.[18] Yet these ideas left untouched, if they did not indeed strengthen, basic assumptions about the group mentality whose systematic intelligibility let the *Odyssey, Beowulf,* or *Chanson de Roland* speak. As the twentieth century grew older these assumptions would escort into the canon further oral-epic congeners from Africa, native America, and other cultural sites formerly invisible from the scholarly mainstream. Such canon-diversification has been facilitated in our time by the way controversy *about* epic interpretation has tended to migrate *inside* epic interpretation: the tensed density of mixed message we have learned to read in Virgil or Milton, H.D. or Derek Walcott, has substituted a complex for a simple unity as the expected point of epic reference.[19] Still, a unity it remains, the expression of a cultural system conflicted but not transcended; and on major poetry that treats imperial metropole or island outpost we continue to train, under conditions of globalization, species of the holistic thinking that has long attached to the epic idea.

That idea, as these reflections will suggest, is rather a neutral enabler of debate than a partaker; its taproot plunges well beneath the weather. We may confirm this neutrality in another register by considering the twentieth-century theorists of genre who remain most influential within studies of narrative. Not long after our *terminus ad quem* Gyorgy Lukács and Mikhail Bakhtin produced monumentally synthetic studies of the novel, whose leverage relied on the unwobbling fulcrum of the same generic idea that concerns us here.[20] Each of these theorists stakes his modernity, and that of the great novels he admires, on the *fait accompli* of a generic coup: the deposition of both epic and that inviolable societal unison which the idea of epic presupposes. The subtlety Lukács and Bakhtin evince as theorists and readers of fiction quite deserts them whenever they look back, now with regret and now with relief, on the tumbled monolith that was epic. Such blindness is a price forthrightly paid down for their insight into novels, and it need detain us no longer than to observe that a great deal of what Lukács and Bakhtin say about the prose fiction of the nineteenth century will also find exemplification among the period's verse epics.

The point to stress at present is that these leading modern epiphobes start from the same premise that during the next generation served such distinguished epiphile successors in narrative theory as Erich Auerbach and Northrop Frye.[21] Auerbach in *Mimesis* works details of story technique up into cultural history, on the strength of a conviction that the complex forms of major narrative coincide, in Flaubert as in Homer, with the complex forms of a rich social whole. Frye, primarily concerned in *Anatomy of Criticism* to place the epic system within a literary system larger still, nevertheless rests his running reference to extra-literary contexts on a conviction which is basically identical with Auerbach's—and Bakhtin's and Lukács's too. The epiphobe, seeing the continence of epic from outside, is struck by the exclusiveness on which its defining cultural fusion depends; the epiphile, reading instead from within, is struck by how inclusive the system is, and of how many different constituents. Like the rest of the contestants just enumerated, both parties agree to disagree, poising a difference comparatively superficial upon bedrock assumptions about epic's culturally consensual regimen that everybody has been making for a long time.

From this basis in cultural consensus flow most of the generic criteria that determine whether a given work gets discussed in this book.[22] First among these criteria is, to put it flatly, *length;* to put it roundly, *scope*. No mere count of lines or pages can decide when an epic scope has been attained or even—since in this matter it is sometimes right to take the wish for the deed—whole-mindedly aspired to. Length and scope do vouch for each other, though, once we cross a threshold where the reader is identifiably addressed as the member of a collectivity that knows itself as such in historical time. That is because the textual embodiment of such knowledge takes time; and the measure of time in print is in the first instance a matter of massed, bound volume. "A Poem, in Twelve Books" does not just log a bibliographic inventory but makes a clear promise of large and general reference. Such promise balloons out as the numbers go up—in the chapters ahead consideration of poems in 24, 28, 30, and 48 books awaits the persevering reader—and even when the numbers go down to 9 or 7 or 4, and nomenclature retrenches from book to canto, the practice of quantitative enumeration *per se* sustains a qualitative expectation, which to this day our colloquial honorific "great" and its synonyms may illustrate.[23]

The promise of epic scale is also made literally visible along linear and spatial dimensions; that the poetic line should be long and the page full was a serious matter, and not just to visually oriented epoists like Blake and Morris. Still more commonly poets aspired to analogous effects in soundspace: while the genre's license for magniloquence carried no security against its explosion in incompetent hands, a skilled epic verse maker could, even within relatively small compass, build up an orotundity that adequated scope to ambition on faith. The specimen or approval epics that dot our early chapters earn credit in proportion as they render for the duration, albeit at episodic rather than full scale, a world whose intended auditorium hums with the communal significance, on an at least implicitly world-historical stage, of the persons and action they sing. This intention accredits, if not the fragment poem as such, then the epicizing subset of that Romantic genre for which John Keats's *Hyperion* stands in vocal splendor as nonpareil exemplar.[24]

A further means of epic aggrandizement, perhaps the most telling of all, was genre-absorption. That it takes all kinds to make an epic is a commonplace.[25] But the commonplace has critical work to do when we come to assess the rival claims of the epic and the romance, or the epic and the novel, as Romantic and Victorian poets respectively had frequent occasion to do. These genres were the major predators at the top of the literary food chain, and in Scott, Eliot, and Hardy (to look no further) we find them grappling or repelling each other in a contest that our received literary history has often been too quick to call in favor of the modern challenger. Even where an upstart contender for generic supremacy did not engrossingly concern a given poet, the older genre still had to eat in order to live; and the meal that epic made of pastoral, georgic, ode, ballad, soliloquy, epigram, oratory, epistle, *et cetera* was a standing narratological demonstration of its definitive roominess—a generic amplitude from which poetry's shuffling preference today for the nondescript "long poem" seems a regrettable declension into one thin dimension.

Mention of a few limiting cases omitted from the following pages may frame this issue of size most efficiently. Neither Samuel Taylor Coleridge's "Rime of the Ancyent Marinere" 1798 at the opening phase of our story is included, nor Wilde's "Ballad of Reading Gaol" 1898 at the end. This is not because their balladry as such counts against them, but because each poet's quite different adaptation of the ballad tradition for a modern purpose dilutes that tradition's collectivity, for the sake of an individualized psychology that is traumatically agonized by a personal rhythm pitting obscure guilt against imperfect atonement. (An argument that lobbied harder than I can do on behalf of these works' collective spokesmanship would, of course, be making my generic point the other way round.) When we turn to Christina Rossetti's "Goblin Market" 1862 the juvenile clip of the verse is more nearly an *ipso facto* disqualifier, but again the real problem lies with how extensive an audience interpellation the poem performs. Rossetti's radiant parable expands within a horizon not civic and multiple but domestic and familial: a limiting circumstance that the overtly epicizing manner and content of several standout similes in the poem underscore, in effect, by contrast. "The Wreck of the *Deutschland*" by Gerard Manley Hopkins requires a closer call, since here the lineation is nothing if not rangy, and since the two narrative episodes of the poem, by what might be called sprung diegesis, amplify in respectively metaphysical and national directions the given topic of church/state enmity. If this ode were Blake's and dated 1795, it might have found room in the chapter following this one; but Hopkins wrote it in 1875, by which point the imperial culture that epic had to bespeak or denounce asked of an ocean-going tale the wider scope of a collectivity differently conceived. For an English epic of that late date Hopkins's greater lyric was just too short-sighted along the dimensions that counted.[26]

A criterion easier to apply but harder to defend in principle is that of verse. Even the most obvious defense, the overwhelming respect that nineteenth-century literary culture paid to the ennobling power of meter and rhyme, is not airtight: François de Fénelon's *Télémaque* and James Macpherson's Ossian productions were in prose, yet they were regularly invoked as epic poems well before our story begins. So, at our balance point between Romantic and Victorian dispensations, was Thomas Carlyle's *French Revolution,* and by a most prosy reader at that, John Stuart Mill.[27] Also, of course, that ingratiating but not illegitimate pretender to the epic throne, the nineteenth-century novel, which as late as 1853 Matthew Arnold affected to call "the domestic epic."[28] Although each of Scott's two earliest verse romances plays an important part in our story, and his prosody therein cast an influence both long and wide, merely to demur at his switch into prose with *Waverley* savors of pedantry. Bypassing the series of novels which that epochal book inaugurated is admittedly like getting off on a mere technicality. Just that is what we do below, nonetheless, even as place is found along the way for brief notice of a number of inferior novels that happened to be written in verse. The historical novel and the extended prose history are genuine and challenging highlands of epic territory whose nineteenth-century summits we sight at times but do not attempt.[29] The focus here remains the epic poem in verse, if for no better reason than sheer expediency in setting limits to a study that few readers will wish longer than it already is.

Notes

1   *Literary Criticism of Oscar Wilde,* ed. Stanley Weintraub (Lincoln: University of Nebraska Press, 1968) 210. Wilde is right about the Alexandrians, whose development of the idyll form as a modern compromise with old epic influenced Victorian poetry strongly. See H. M. McLuhan, "Tennyson and the Romantic Epic," in *Critical Essays on the Poetry of Tennyson,* ed. John Killham (London: Routledge and Kegan Paul, 1960) 86–95; Robert Pattison, *Tennyson and Tradition* (Cambridge, Mass.: Harvard University Press, 1979) 15–39; Richard Jenkyns, *The Victorians and Ancient Greece* (Cambridge, Mass.: Harvard University Press, 1980) 21–38. John Kevin Newman, *The Classical Epic Tradition* (Madison: University of Wisconsin Press, 1986), maintains that Alexandrian modes of coping with epic persist through Chaucer and Milton into 19th-cent. fiction and 20th-cent. film. On the Victorian tendency to regard the ancient Greeks as cultural contemporaries see Frank Turner, *The Greek Heritage in Victorian Britain* (New Haven and London: Yale University Press, 1981); Linda Dowling, *Hellenism and Homosexuality in Victorian Oxford* (Ithaca and London: Cornell University Press, 1994). About ancient Rome an *a fortiori* case might simply instance Matthew Arnold's 1857 lecture "On the Modern Element in Literature," which cites next to no post-classical authors and finds its paragon of modernity in Virgil.

2   In Robert Burns, George Crabbe, Gerard Manley Hopkins, and the two Rossettis, we may number on the fingers of one hand those who declined the challenge — bearing in mind that, while many failings converged to block Coleridge's long-meditated epic, lack of interest was not among them.

3   Letter of 11 Dec. 1858 to Ticknor and Fields, his publisher in America: *The Letters of Alfred Lord Tennyson,* ed. Cecil Y. Lang and Edgar F. Shannon, Jr. (Cambridge, Mass.: Harvard University Press, 1981–90) 2: 212.

4   The argument of this chapter converges with those of two recent books that came to my notice after I had composed it. For Robert Crawford, *The Modern Poet: Poetry, Academia, and Knowledge since the 1750s* (Oxford: Oxford University Press, 2001), the modernity of poetry after the Enlightenment inheres in its being both scholarly and wild, "at once ancient and *à la mode*". Similarly, Simon Dentith in *Epic and Empire in Nineteenth-Century Britain* (Cambridge: Cambridge University Press, 2006) investigates "various reworkings of a problematic" that hinges on "the interdependence, which is to say the incompatibility, of modernity with epic," whereby "consciousness of the archaism of epic entails a concomitant consciousness of the modernity of the present era" (3–4, 13).

5   Lascelles Abercrombie, *The Epic* (London: Secker, 1914) 39. In *Imagination and Power: A Study of Poetry on Public Themes* (London: Chatto and Windus, 1971), Thomas R. Edwards discusses the "complicated self-awareness" that epic induces. "It associates us gratifyingly with past greatness, with heroes who are *our* heroes; yet it also reminds us soberingly that it all *is* past, that we are less than our heritage. It allows us an imaginative association with greatness even as it makes us recognize that we are ordinary men—and it allows us some comfort in this rueful understanding" 11.

6   Thus Robert Scholes and Robert Kellogg in their classic *The Nature of Narrative* (New York: Oxford University Press, 1966) hand their readers the sobering news up front: "The epic poem is as dead as the dinosaur" 11. A generation later for J. B. Hainsworth in *The Idea of Epic* (Berkeley:

University of California Press, 1991), that "the genre died" (viii) is a fact to be explained and not a proposition to be tested. This commonplace forms a springboard for much livelier discussion in Frederick T. Griffiths and Stanley J. Rabinowitz, *Novel Epics: Gogol, Dostoevsky, and National Narrative* (Evanston: Northwestern University Press, 1990). Conceding that epic is "long dead, indeed recurrently dead," these authors propose that the genre "maintains its preeminence as the victim of choice for the dominant literary form," through the "millennial parasitism whereby it thrives through the nostalgia and condescension of its various replacements until they are themselves replaced" (12, 15).

7   See R. D. Havens, *The Influence of Milton on English Poetry* (Cambridge, Mass.: Harvard University Press, 1922): "The epic may ... be said to have been moribund throughout the second quarter of the nineteenth century and to have died soon after. It has never revived" 313. The coincidence of publication date between Havens's study, and *Ulysses* and *The Waste Land*, opens onto the modernist developments I proceed to discuss.

8   The *locus classicus* for such an account is Ian Watt, *The Rise of the Novel: Studies in Defoe, Richardson, and Fielding* (Berkeley: University of California Press, 1957). See also, *inter alia*, Thomas E. Maresca, *Epic to Novel* (Columbus: Ohio State University Press, 1974); Paul Hunter, *Before Novels: The Cultural Contexts of Eighteenth -Century English Fiction* (New York: Norton, 1990) 338–51. *Per contra*, Martin Mueller (*The Iliad*, London: Allen and Unwin, 1984, 192) crisply remarks that the two "critical facts for an understanding of the life of the *Iliad* in the nineteenth century" are the epic's "opposition to the bourgeois novel" and "the boys' school as the template for the cult of the heroic." The best contemporary study, David Quint's *Epic and Empire: Politics and Generic Form from Virgil to Milton* (Princeton: Princeton University Press, 1993), embraces the standard account axiomatically: when "the fortunes of a martial aristocracy ... waned in the seventeenth century, the classically modeled epic poem gave way to the 'modern' romance and the novel" 360. Already at the turn of the 19th cent, the supersession of epic by novel was an undisputed fact to John Millar in *An Historical View of the English Government* (London: Mawman, 1803) 4: 326–34.

9   Tillyard, *The English Epic and its Background* (London: Chatto and Windus, 1954) 14, again 109, 147, 528–31; and *The Epic Strain in the English Novel* (London: Chatto and Windus, 1958).

10 See Hugh Kenner, *The Pound Era* (Berkeley: University of California Press, 1971); Paul Fussell, *The Great War and Modern Memory* (New York: Oxford University Press, 1975); Mary Ellis Gibson, *Epic Reinvented: Ezra Pound and the Victorians* (Ithaca: Cornell University Press, 1995); Vincent Sherry, *The Great War and the Language of Modernism* (New York: Oxford University Press, 2003). A vigorous antirevivalist case waiving the verse/prose distinction is mounted for literature from across the Atlantic by John P. McWilliams, Jr., in *The American Epic: Transforming a Genre, 1770–1860* (Cambridge: Cambridge University Press, 1989).

11 See Derek Elley, *The Epic Film: Myth and History* (London: Routledge, 1984). Quint builds the coda to his book (*Epic and Empire,* 361–68) on a reading of Eisenstein's *Aleksandr Nevsky.*
    [...]

15 Franco Moretti, *Modern Epic: The World-System from Goethe to Garcia Marquez,* tr. Quintin Hoare (London and New York: Verso, 1996), reverses Bakhtin's valuation of the respective flexibilities of the major modern narrative genres: "the polyphonic form of the modern West is not the novel, but if anything precisely the epic, which specializes in the heterogeneous space of the world-system, and must learn to provide a stage for its many different voices" 56.

16 Donald M. Foerster, *The Fortunes of Epic Poetry: A Study in English and American Criticism 1750–1950* (n.p.: Catholic University of America Press, 1962), discerns little change across the 19th cent. in "the prevalent view as to the attributes of a truly great poem," which "was not pronouncedly different from what it had been in the time of Pope" 192. Since the span covered by Foerster's study, the stolid aplomb with which C. M. Bowra opens *From Virgil to Milton* (London: Macmillan, 1967) has yet to be seriously disturbed: "In the disputable and usually futile task of classifying the forms of poetry there is no great quarrel about the epic" 1.

17 Witness, on either side of the Homeric question—as of our period of study here—F. A. Wolf, *Prolegomena ad Homerum* 1795 and Andrew Lang, *Homer and His Age* 1906.

18 Albert B. Lord, *The Singer of Tales* (Cambridge, Mass.: Harvard University Press, 1960) both summarizes and further contributes to this phase of epic studies. Its chief figure, Milman Parry, is discussed in Dentith, *Epic and Empire,* 196–98.

19 A development ably discussed in Joseph Farrell's review of Quint's *Epic and Empire* and of
Susanne Wofford's *The Choice of Achilles: The Ideology of Figure in the Epic* (Stanford: Stanford
University Press, 1992): *Bryn Mawr Classical Review* 4 1993 481–89.

20 Lukács, *The Theory of the Novel: A Historical-Philosophical Essay on the Forms of Great Epic
Literature* 1920, tr. Anna Bostock (Cambridge, Mass.: MIT Press, 1971); Bakhtin, *The Dialogic
Imagination,* tr. Caryl Emerson and Michael Holquist (Austin: University of Texas Press, 1981),
esp. ch. 1 ("Epic and Novel," 1941). Admittedly Lukács breaches his own generic firewall when,
on the final page of *The Theory* he glimpses Tolstoy glimpsing "the form of the renewed epic"
152. By 1936, he would apply "epic" as a term of Marxist honor to describe the extremity of the
Russian novelist's "pre-revolutionary" critique of an emergent capitalization of human relations:
see "Tolstoy and the Development of Realism," in *Studies in European Realism,* tr. Edith Bone
(London: Hillway, 1950) 148–78. On this last point and its historical circumstances see Galin
Tihanov, *The Master and the Slave: Lukács, Bakhtin, and the Ideas of Their Time* (Oxford:
Clarendon Press, 2000) 114–22; with equivalent and salutary "astonishment" Tihanov notes both
Lukács's failure to show historically how it happened that the novel broke loose from the epic
120 and Bakhtin's programmatic insistence on the utter change which that break, whenever it took
place, produced *ipso facto* clear across the genres 146. As Masaki Mori curtly remarks in *Epic
Grandeur: Toward a Comparative Poetics of the Epic* (Albany: State University of New York
Press, 1997), the works that Bakhtin is prepared to call epics "essentially belong to the sphere of
anthropology. Bakhtin's argument would exclude all the major epic works in the West" 35. See
also Griffiths and Rabinowitz, *Novel Epics,* 18–28; Dentith, *Epic and Empire,* 114–18.

21 Auerbach, *Mimesis: The Representation of Reality in Western Literature* 1946, tr. Willard R. Trask
(Princeton: Princeton University Press, 1953); Frye, *Fearful Symmetry: A Study of William Blake*
(Princeton: Princeton University Press, 1947) and *Anatomy of Criticism: Four Essays* (Princeton:
Princeton University Press, 1957).

22 The ground I tread in this section, smooth already with many footprints, is recently, and very
systematically, measured out in Hermann Fischer, *Romantic Verse Narrative: The History of a
Genre,* 1964, tr. Sue Bollans (Cambridge: Cambridge University Press, 1991) 15–24.1 have no
quarrel with Fischer's flexibly cautious weighing of epic's generic properties; given what has been
said already here, it would be a surprise if I did. But I can give no quarter to Fischer's refusal to
make room in the epic genre for *The Prelude* ("subjective, biographical") and *Don Juan* (Byron is
not "representative of his age"), or to his categorical denial that "an epic set in an individualistic,
capitalist society" is so much as imaginable. Thus, in literary studies at least, *facile est communia
proprie dicere,* while the devil is in the details of particular analysis and judgment: *hic labor, hoc
opus est.*

23 For Roberts, *Long Poems,* length is an epic criterion especially applicable to poetry from the
19th cent., for reasons to do with the inflationary debasement attending the sublime and the
historical sense (3, 10–14); G. Headley, "The Early Nineteenth-Century Epic: The Harvey Thesis
Examined," *Journal of European Studies* 21 1991, doubts "that length as such can be a defining
characteristic" 201.

24 Among our poets here Landor and Tennyson tie for second place in doing what Emile Deschamps
said in 1828 that Alfred de Vigny had done in the *Kurzepos* genre: "Il a su être grand sans être
long": quoted in William Calin, *A Muse for Heroes: Nine Centuries of the Epic in France* (Toronto
and Buffalo: University of Toronto Press, 1983) 319. On the generic dialectic of fragmentation
with totality see Balachandra Rajan, *The Form of the Unfinished: English Poetics from Spenser
to Pound* (Princeton: Princeton University Press, 1985); also Thomas McFarland, *Romanticism
and the Forms of Ruin: Wordsworth, Coleridge, and Modalities of Fragmentation* (Princeton:
Princeton University Press, 1981); Marjorie Levinson, *The Romantic Fragment Poem: A Critique
of a Form* (Chapel Hill: University of North Carolina Press, 1986); Anne Janowitz, *England's
Ruins: Poetic Purpose and the National Landscape* (Oxford: Blackwell, 1990).

25 As Joseph Trapp put the matter in his Latin *Lectures on Poetry* (1711–1719, tr. 1742, the "Epic
Poem ... comprehends within its Sphere all the other Kinds of Poetry whatever": quoted in
William Keach, "Poetry, after 1740," in *The Cambridge History of Literary Criticism,* vol. 4, ed.
H. B. Nisbet and Claude Rawson (Cambridge: Cambridge University Press, 1997) 119. The topos
is still vivid towards the end of our period for Andrew Lang in *Homer and the Epic* (London:
Longmans, 1893): "The epic is thus the sum of all poetry—tragedy, comedy, lyric, dirge, idyll,

are all blended in its great furnace into one glorious metal, and one colossal group"—into which group he goes on to recruit the "romance" and "tale" into the bargain 7.

26 The poems I thus exclude have indeed been read, like Eliot's *The Waste Land* at the end of our period, as epics. See, e.g., Karl Kroeber, "'The Rime of the Ancient Mariner' as Stylized Epic," *Transactions of the Wisconsin Society of Sciences, Arts, and Letters* 46 1957 179–89; Dorothy Mermin, "Heroic Sisterhood in 'Goblin Market,'" *Victorian Poetry* 21 1983 107–18.

27 Mill's review of Carlyle, from the *London and Westminster Review* 27 (July 1837) 17–53, is reprinted in Mill's *Essays on French History and Historians,* ed. John M. Robson and John C. Cairns (Toronto and London: University of Toronto Press, 1985).

28 Arnold, Preface to *Poems* 1853: *The Complete Poems,* 2nd edn. Kenneth and Miriam Allott (London: Longman, 1979) 658.

29 I take greater liberties of this kind in ch. 14 of the Victorian volume (ed. Kate Flint) in the forthcoming *Cambridge History of English Literature.*

24 'Transcripts of the Private Heart': The Sonnet and Autobiography (2005)

Joseph Phelan

One of Elizabeth Barrett's earliest efforts in the sonnet form was prompted by Benjamin Robert Haydon's portrait 'Wordsworth on Helvellyn',[1] and her revaluation of a form she had previously disdained or ignored is bound up with her renewed admiration for Wordsworth at this stage of her career.[2] Her letters of this period are full of references to him as a kind of 'king' or ruler, as is 'The Book of the Poets', the survey of the history of English poetry she published in *The Athenaeum* in 1842: '[Of] all poets ... who have been kings in England, not one has swept the purple with more majesty than this poet, when it hath pleased him to be majestic. *Vivat rex*'.[3] She singles out his sonnets for particular praise, stating that he has surpassed all of his great precursors in his use of the form: '[The] greatest poets of our country, – the Shakespeares, Spensers, Miltons, – worked upon high sonnet-ground, [but] not one opened over it such broad and pouring sluices of various thought, imagery, and emphatic eloquence as he has done.'[4] Barrett was, moreover, at this time wrestling with problems similar to those which had produced Wordsworth's own turn towards the sonnet forty years earlier. There are signs in her work around this time of an increasing ambivalence towards the large-scale poetic projects into which she had previously poured most of her energies. Marjorie Stone emphasises the transgressive nature of the 'Romantic Prometheanism' of much of Barrett's early work, her determination to write herself into the male tradition of epic poetry.[5] But this ambition was clearly waning by the early 1840s. The title poem of her 1838 volume, *The Seraphim and other poems,* is an ambitious and overwrought attempt to describe Christ's passion and death from the point of view of two watching angels, but by 1842 Barrett was seeking to distance herself from it, describing it in a letter to Benjamin Robert Haydon as 'almost the worst poem' in the collection.[6] The decision to lead the 1844 volume with 'A Drama of Exile' indicates a similar ambivalence about her own epic ambitions. On the one hand the poem, which continues the story of the Fall after the expulsion from Paradise, seems to challenge comparison with Milton's epic; but on the other hand it highlights the extent to which Barrett is herself an 'exile' from this epic tradition. This conflict is articulated in the impassioned Preface to the collection:

> I had promised my own prudence to shut close the gates of Eden between Milton and myself, so that none might say I dared to walk in his footsteps. He should be within, I thought, with his Adam and Eve unfallen or falling, – and I, without, with my EXILES, – I also an exile! It would not do. The subject, and his glory covering it, swept through the gates, and I stood full in it, against my will, and contrary to my vow, – till I shrank back fearing, almost desponding; hesitating to venture even a passing association with our great poet before the face of the public.[7]

The Promethean attempt to steal Milton's fire is here transformed into a stereotypically feminine gesture of passivity and weakness; she is literally overpowered by the force of Milton's genius, and tackles the subject 'against her will' and 'contrary to [her] vow'. This note of apology continues throughout the remainder of the Preface; she is 'too low' and too weak – 'the weakest', in fact – to be suspected of a genuine challenge to Milton's poetic authority.

This adoption of a stereotypically, almost exaggeratedly feminine subject position in the defence of her work points to some of the reasons for Barrett's decision to scale down her poetic ambitions at this stage of her career. Like Wordsworth during the first decade of the nineteenth century, she was faced with a set of profoundly uncongenial external circumstances; but in her case these circumstances derived almost entirely from the fact of her gender. Biographical accounts of Barrett's life stress the extent to which her early life was characterised by a refusal to accept the limitations placed on the lives of girls and women; but following the death of her brother in 1840, and her father's increasingly tyrannical and irrational behaviour towards his children thereafter, she seems to have decided to become the very embodiment of the passive, suffering femininity fetishised by Victorian society. She had, as she puts it in some of her earliest letters to Robert Browning, decided to 'stand still in her stall', confining herself to her room 'like Mariana in the moated grange'.[8] This gesture was not a simple retreat into femininity, however; it was both retreat and defiance, and like Wordsworth's withdrawal from his society found its perfect poetic embodiment in the sonnet's paradoxical combination of freedom and self-imposed restriction. Her attention may have been drawn to this dimension of Wordsworth's sonnets by Sir Henry Taylor's remarkable review-essay on 'The Sonnets of William Wordsworth' in the *Quarterly Review* for 1842, discussed in the first chapter.[9] Barrett must have read this review; it includes the first publication of the notorious 'Sonnets upon the Punishment of Death', which she refers to in 'The Book of the Poets' (also published in 1842) as 'a misplaced "Benedicite" over the hangman and his victim'.[10] Picking up on Wordsworth's 'comparison mutually illustrative' between the sonnet form and voluntary self-restraint, Barrett presents herself in the 1844 sonnets as a kind of prisoner, accepting the limitations of her position and seeking in them the raw material for her imaginative life. Chastening her 'exuberant and discursive imagination' she takes up the mantle of the 'poetess' left vacant by her recently deceased contemporaries Felicia Hemans and L.E.L., inviting the reader to see her sonnets as a record of profound and imperfectly articulated personal suffering; in the Preface she states that her poems have her 'heart and life' in them, and represent 'the completest expression' of her personal being 'to which [she] could attain'.[11] But the narrative trajectory of the series also suggests a residual dissatisfaction with this role, and points to the desire to regain the possibility of fuller and freer utterance.

The first poem of the sequence, 'The Soul's Expression', takes up and intensifies the Wordsworthian apprehension of the paradoxical relation between freedom and limitation in the sonnet's form:

> With stammering lips and insufficient sound
> I strive and struggle to deliver right
> That music of my nature, day and night
> With dream and thought and feeling interwound,
> And inly answering all the senses round
> With octaves of a mystic depth and height
> Which step out grandly to the infinite

> From the dark edges of the sensual ground.
> This song of soul I struggle to outbear
> Through portals of the sense, sublime and whole,
> And utter all myself into the air:
> But if I did it, – as the thunder-roll
> Breaks its own cloud, my flesh would perish there,
> Before that dread apocalypse of soul.

Barrett here transforms the sonnet into something like a Romantic or even prophetic fragment, pointing beyond itself to the inarticulable sublime. The first eight lines exploit the latent musical pun in the term octave to produce a syntactically complex and disorientating conceit. The poet 'strives and struggles' – a telling redundancy – to deliver the 'music' of her nature. This music 'inly' answers 'all the senses round'; this could mean either that it answers all the senses which surround it; or it could be a continuation of the underlying musical metaphor, suggesting that the senses are singing a 'round' which is answered by the poet's inmost nature. Similarly, the 'octaves of a mystic depth and height' intoned by the poet's soul step out towards the infinite '[from] the dark edges of the sensual ground'. This last word combines the musical metaphor – the senses are a 'ground' or *basso continuo* against which the soul's music defines itself – with the traditional notion that the soul has the ability to escape from the earthbound senses. These ambiguities, and indeed the syntactic complexity of the octave, reinforce the notion articulated more simply and clearly in the sestet; that the attempt to 'outbear' the soul's music in its pristine completeness would produce a 'dread apocalypse of soul', destroying both poet and poem. Like the prophet Isaiah, she can only speak to 'this people' with 'stammering lips' and with 'another tongue'.[12] Human beings must accept the limitations of their condition; their work can point towards the 'infinite', but cannot hope to embody it adequately. The sonnet form is an emblem of the inescapability of this condition.

It is, as the remainder of the series makes clear, the poet's 'suffering' which gives her access to the boundless depths of the sublime. This use of suffering as a source of the sublime has a considerable Romantic heritage, and is explicitly alluded to in the Preface to 1844, where Barrett states that 'A Vision of Poets' is intended 'to indicate the necessary relations of genius to suffering and self-sacrifice', and that 'if knowledge is power, suffering should be acceptable as a part of knowledge'.[13] Burke asserts that he knows of 'nothing sublime which is not some modification of power', and the sublimity in this case comes from the poet's powerlessness to resist the grief and suffering which have been inflicted on her by a higher power.[14] A number of the sonnets illustrate the 'depth and height' of this suffering by emphasising their inability to articulate it fully within the confines of the sonnet form. In 'Grief', for instance, the poet highlights the peculiar fitness of 'artificial' and inorganic forms for the representation of the deepest kinds of suffering. A grief that can express itself in tears is one which holds out hope of recovery; a tearless grief, on the other hand, is silent and changeless:

> I tell you, hopeless grief is passionless;
> That only men incredulous of despair,
> Half-taught in anguish, through the midnight air
> Beat upward to God's throne in loud access
> Of shrieking and reproach. Full desertness,
> In souls as countries, lieth silent-bare
> Under the blanching, vertical eye-glare

Of the absolute Heavens. Deep-hearted man, express
Grief for thy Dead in silence like to death –
Most like a monumental statue set
In everlasting watch and moveless woe
Till itself crumble to the dust beneath.
Touch it; the marble eyelids are not wet:
If it could weep, it could arise and go.

A form which was able to mimic the progress of the poet's grief, and so hold out the possibility of change and recovery, would be false to the absolute and inconsolable suffering that the poet is trying to represent. The sonnet, in contrast, is a form which advertises its own artificial and inorganic status, like the 'monumental statue' which crumbles slowly into dust under the 'vertical eye-glare/ Of the absolute Heavens', and so paradoxically becomes the ideal medium for the representation of 'hopeless grief'.[15]

This emphasis on the inadequacy of the form that Rossetti later called a 'moment's monument' is, however, in tension with the tendency of the sonnets to form themselves into a biographical sequence. There is in the collection a kind of progress away from suffering and towards consolation; and this progress, in turn, calls into question the appropriateness of the sonnet form and the limitations and restrictions implied by it. The poem cited above, for instance, is followed immediately by one in which the poet invokes the possibility of a specifically religious consolation – 'Speak THOU, availing Christ! – and fill this pause' (l. 14) – and in the next poem, 'Comfort', this religious consolation offers the possibility of the redemptive 'tears' that had previously been deemed impossible:

Speak to me as to Mary at Thy feet!
And if no precious gums my hands bestow,
Let my tears drop like amber while I go
In reach of Thy divinest voice complete
In humanest affection – thus, in sooth,
To lose the sense of losing. (ll. 5–10)

This theme of religious redemption continues with the mini-sequence of poems on Peter's denial of Christ, which again focus on the healing power of tears and imply that the poet's earlier 'hopeless grief' was itself a kind of impious denial of Christ's mercy; and in 'Fururity' the unnamed cause of the poet's grief becomes an 'idol' that God has deliberately broken in order to prevent earthly love from usurping the place of its heavenly counterpart. This religious consolation is accompanied by a restatement and revaluation of some of the images used in the earlier poems. In 'Substitution' the song of the nightingale is one of the many things that cannot give comfort to the grieving poet, but in 'Exaggeration' it is the poet's excessive emphasis on 'the ills of life' that prevents her from hearing its song:

… near the alder brake
We sigh so loud, the nightingale within
Refuses to sing loud, as else she would.
O brothers, let us leave the shame and sin
Of taking vainly, in a plaintive mood,
The holy name of GRIEF! – holy herein,
That by the grief of ONE came all our good. (ll. 8–14)

The monumental and artificial aspects of the sonnet, so appropriate for highlighting the inexpressibility of 'hopeless grief', become an impediment when that grief has been superseded. The form now begins to signify a kind of imprisonment, the endless repetition of a gesture which has lost its basis in experience. This sense of frustration is indicated merely by the titles of some of the later sonnets: 'Discontent', 'Patience taught by Nature', 'Exaggeration', and, most strikingly, 'The Prisoner'. The last of these poems 'answers' in some respects the earlier sonnet 'Irreparableness', in which the poet explains the reasons behind her renunciation of the world. The 'nosegays' she had gathered in her wandering have decayed in her over-eager hands, and she cannot go '[back] straightway to the fields to gather more' (1. 10). This voluntary renunciation has now been transformed into an involuntary imprisonment which exiles the poet from life and nature:

> I count the dismal time by months and years
> Since last I felt the green sward under foot,
> And the great breath of all things summer-mute
> Met mine upon my lips. Now earth appears
> As strange to me as dreams of distant spheres
> Or thoughts of heaven we weep at. Nature's lute
> Sounds on, behind his door so closely shut,
> A strange wild music to the prisoner's ears,
> Dilated by the distance, till the brain
> Grows dim with fancies which it feels too fine:
> While ever, with a visionary pain,
> Past the precluded senses, sweep and shine
> Streams, forests, glades, and many a golden train
> Of sunlit hills transfigured to divine.

In its context, this can be seen as a rewriting of the Prefatory Sonnet's assertion that 'the prison unto which we doom/ Ourselves, no prison is'. There is no suggestion here of the benefits of voluntary confinement; the poet's incarceration gives rise only to a passionate longing for life outside the prison. This sense of unease finds a formal echo in the mid-line endings of the first two sentences, which make the poem as a whole sit uncomfortably across the Petrarchan schema.

The later poems of the series, including 'The Prisoner', manifest a profound dissatisfaction with the passive and exaggeratedly 'feminine' subject position into which the poet has written herself. There are repeated attempts to transform the poet's own experiences into the material for more general reflections; the curious and awkward 'Work and Contemplation', for example, begins with the Wordsworthian image of the 'maid at the wheel', but ends with a tentative and apologetic movement towards the Miltonic public sonnet; and the pair of poems on George Sand both illustrate and attempt to move beyond the identification of femininity with passivity and suffering. This dissatisfaction becomes a more overt and fully narrativised struggle in Barrett's next (and last) series of sonnets, *Sonnets from the Portuguese* (1850). The cultural affiliations of this series indicate Barrett's determination to recover or rather create a distinctively female tradition. In assuming the traditionally masculine role of the unworthy and hopeless lover and in writing poems of 'conjugal' rather than illicit love Barrett is following the lead of the Italian female sonnet writers of the sixteenth century, in particular Vittoria Colonna;[16] and in using the idea of translation from the Portuguese as a disguise she is again paying homage to Felicia Hemans, who translated a number of Camoens' sonnets.[17] The connection between the two writers is made clear in one of her letters to the man who was to become her husband during the six years between these two groups of sonnets, Robert Browning:

> [Talking] of poetesses, I had a note yesterday (again) which quite touched me ... from Mr. Hemans – Charles, the son of Felicia ... Do you not like to hear such things said? and is it not better than your tradition about Shelley's son? and is it not pleasant to know that that poor noble pure-hearted woman, the Vittoria Colonna of our country, should be so loved and comprehended by some ... by one at least ... of her own house? Not that, in naming Shelley, I meant for a moment to make a comparison – there is not equal ground for it. Vittoria Colonna does not walk near Dante – no. And if you promised never to tell Mrs Jameson ... nor Miss Martineau ... I would confide to you perhaps my secret profession of faith – which is ... which is ... that let us say and do what we please and can ... there *is* a natural inferiority of mind in women – of the intellect ... not by any means, of the moral nature – and that the history of Art and of genius testifies to this fact openly.[18]

Using Hemans-Colonna as the model for the *Sonnets from the Portuguese* is, however, still a profoundly ambivalent gesture, as this letter indicates. After making grand if implicit claims for Felicia Hemans as the equivalent of Shelley, Barrett quickly resumes her more usual posture of humility and ends up confessing to her future husband her conviction that there is a 'natural inferiority of mind in women' which the history of the arts makes abundantly clear. This combination of assertive appropriation of traditionally male subject positions and reinforcement of traditionally feminine roles is also enacted in the *Sonnets from the Portuguese* themselves. The abject self-abasement of the 1844 sonnets has gone, but it has not been replaced by a straightforward rejection of the passive, imprisoned, suffering model of femininity.

A number of recent critics have described the *Sonnets from the Portuguese* as a narrative of self-emancipation; the poet begins by portraying herself as 'the object of man's love', wavers for most of the series 'between objectifying herself and claiming her own creative and sexual subjectivity', and ends up substituting her own distinctively female voice for 'the conventions of the male tradition'.[19] By the end of the series this inversion of gender roles allows her to depict her husband in the traditionally female guise of the protecting angel: 'New angel mine, unhoped for in the world' (42, 1. 14). The thematic and metaphorical continuities between these poems and the 1844 sonnets have, however, been largely overlooked;[20] and these continuities complicate this narrative of emancipation, highlighting the extent to which Barrett's new female persona retains important features of her old one. The very first poem of the *Sonnets from the Portuguese* alludes to the 1844 sonnets on George Sand, the figure who was for Elizabeth Barrett a fascinating and horrifying illustration of the consequences of a complete rejection of conventional femininity. Her attempt to 'break away the gauds and armlets worn/ By weaker women in captivity' is, for Barrett, a 'vain denial':

> ... that revolted cry
> Is sobbed in by a woman's voice forlorn, –
> Thy woman's hair, my sister, all unshorn
> Floats back dishevelled strength in agony.

('To George Sand: A Recognition', ll. 5–8)

The same trope of women's hair as the visible embodiment of their femininity – both their 'dishevelled strength' and their weakness – recurs in the first of the *Sonnets from the Portuguese;* here it is the 'mystic Shape' of Love which draws the poet 'backward by the hair' away from her grief-obsessed fixation with death and towards renewed life. There is, then, no possibility of self-emancipation. The poet's liberation from her prison has to be achieved, in a by now familiar paradox, through total submission to the 'mastery' of another, and in particular that of her future husband. He is represented throughout as a prince and a king, but he also becomes, in a potentially blasphemous appropriation of the language of Protestant theology, a kind of God, redeeming her from her own profound unworthiness with his freely given and unmerited love. She continually describes herself, in a return to the language of Hemans, as 'low' – 'There's nothing low/ In love, when love the lowest' (10, ll. 9–10) – and this sense of her own unworthiness sometimes takes extreme forms. After having accepted the love of her Beloved, she asks what shape he would like her to assume:

A hope, to sing by gladly? or a fine
Sad memory, with thy songs to interfuse?
A shade, in which to sing – of palm or pine?
A grave, on which to rest from singing? Choose. (17, ll. 11–14)

Dorothy Mermin has suggested that these lines function as 'an incisive commentary on male love poems … since the alternatives require not only the woman's passivity and silence but her absence and finally her death'.[21] But there is little support for such an overtly satirical reading in the context of this sonnet. A number of the surrounding poems make the point that the poet has '[yielded] the grave' for the sake of her new love, and given up her 'near sweet view of Heaven, for earth with thee!' (23, ll. 13–14). The self-abnegation of sonnet 17 is earnest and straightforward; like the redeemed sinner, the poet is perfectly willing to sacrifice her life for her redeemer's sake.

In the most famous of these sonnets – 'How do I love thee?' – Barrett asserts the continuity between her old and new selves: 'I love thee with the passion put to use/ In my old griefs, and with my childhood's faith' (43, ll. 9–10). Such continuity means that the narrative of emancipation staged by the *Sonnets from the Portuguese* does not only represent 'the transformation of woman from muse/helpmeet/object into poet/creator/subject', but also something much closer to the myth of rescue developed and sustained by Elizabeth Barrett and Robert Browning during their courtship.[22] It is, moreover, only in the light of this continuity that the rhetorical gestures of the closing sonnets acquire their full resonance. In thanking those who have 'paused a little near the prison-wall/ To hear my music in its louder parts' (41, ll. 3–4) the poet is troping on the image of herself as a prisoner, and of the sonnet as a kind of imprisonment, developed in the earlier series. The last poem similarly recalls the language of 'Irreparableness', in which the poet had described how 'the nosegay' she plucked decayed in her hands because too 'warmly clasped':

My heart is very tired, my strength is low,
My hands are full of blossoms plucked before,
Held dead within them till myself shall die. (11. 12–14)

Now it is her 'Beloved' who brings flowers to her 'close room'; and her own sonnets, withdrawn from her 'heart's ground', become in turn her flowers:

    ... take them, as I used to do
    Thy flowers, and keep them where they shall not pine.
    Instruct thine eyes to keep their colours true,
    And tell thy soul their roots are left in mine. (44, ll. 11–14)

This metaphor embodies the sonnet's status for Barrett and her contemporaries; it has its 'roots' in the poet's real life, but like a cut flower it is 'withdrawn' from that living process to serve as a lifeless but poignant memento. The *Sonnets from the Portuguese* are retrospectively organised by this metaphor into the record of a superseded stage of the poet's life; the form associated with imprisonment, limitation and confinement is being left behind for ever; and the echoes of the earlier sequence reinforce the message that her future will not simply 'copy fair' her past. Barrett – by now Barrett Browning – in fact abandoned the sonnet form after *Sonnets from the Portuguese* in favour of freer and more expansive forms of utterance.[23]

In leaving the 'close room' of the sonnet behind, however, Elizabeth Barrett left a legacy which can be compared in importance to Wordsworth's. The *Sonnets from the Portuguese* are one of the nodal points of the form during the century, a moment at which a number of different features come together to produce a new orientation. They highlight the extent to which sonnet writers were beginning to become self-conscious about the biographical readings their work would attract, and indeed to conform to the 'confessional' model retrospectively imputed to Shakespeare, Milton and the other masters of the form. Natalie Houston has pointed out the way in which these sonnets construct an 'effect of authenticity' through their rhetoric of intimacy, detailed private allusion and direct personal address: 'Whether or not the poems were intended for publication, their rhetoric presents them as part of a private conversation'.[24] This self-consciousness also manifests itself in the establishment of defensive strategies against the prying eyes of the critic, though the flimsiness of Barrett's pretence that she was merely the translator of her sonnets was seen through more or less instantly.[25] Both these features – the rhetoric of authenticity and the establishment of ever more sophisticated defence mechanisms – will become important later in the century. In addition, the explicit narrativisation of the *Sonnets from the Portuguese* indicates the growing recognition of the potential affinities between serial lyric utterances and the hegemonic literary form of the period, the novel. In making her sonnets tell the archetypal romance story, with herself as Cinderella and Robert as Prince Charming,[26] Barrett was giving her readers a ready-made narrative into which her individual experience could be inserted, and paving the way for the various experiments with lyric sequences which she and her contemporaries and successors would carry out during the middle years of the century. Finally, and perhaps most importantly, the *Sonnets from the Portuguese* represent the first sustained attempt to revive the Petrarchan amatory sonnet sequence in the nineteenth century. Such sequences were commonplace during the Elizabethan period, and there is an element of self-conscious literary antiquarianism about the *Sonnets from the Portuguese* which manifests itself in the sequence's occasionally Spenserian vocabulary ('enow', 'certes') and parallels the kind of antiquarianism which gave rise to the sonnet revival in the eighteenth century. This super-imposition of nineteenth-century life and morals onto the early Renaissance template of the amatory sonnet sequence provided Barrett's successors in the final quarter of the nineteenth century with a powerful and resonant model for the exploration of contemporary beliefs and illusions about love and marriage.

Notes

1 See 'On a Portrait of Wordsworth by B.R. Haydon', published in the *Athenaeum* (29 October 1842) and reprinted as the third of the sonnets of 1844. There are a few sonnets in the 1838 volume, but none in the earlier collections.

2 This point is also made by Amy Billone; see '"In Silence Like to Death"; Elizabeth Barrett's Sonnet Turn', *Victorian Poetry* 39 (2001), pp. 533–50.

3 *The Complete Poetical Works of Elizabeth Barrett Browning* (London: Smith, Elder and Co., 1907), p. 648; the letter of 30 Apr 45 to Cornelius Matthews, in which EBB calls Wordsworth 'the prince of poets', and relates an anecdote concerning his meeting with Queen Victoria with the words 'And so do queens speak to Kings!'

4 Barrett, *Poetical Works,* p. 649.

5 Marjorie Stone, *Elizabeth Barrett Browning* (Basingstoke: Macmillan, 1995), ch. 2.

6 Letter of 20 October 1842; her hatred for it intensified with time; by 1853 she was describing the whole collection as 'that horrible ghost of the Seraphim which makes me sicker than other ghosts when I see it on a table'; Scott Lewis ed., *The Letters of Elizabeth Barrett Browning to Her Sister Arabella,* 2 vols (Waco, Texas: Wedgestone Press, 2002), ii, p. 21.

7 *Poetical Works,* pp. xi–xii

8 Letters of 15 Jan. and 7 June 1845; R. Barrett Browning ed., *The Letters of Robert and Elizabeth Barrett Browning* (London: John Murray, 1930), 1, pp. 7, 91.

9 See above, pp. 17–18.

10 Barrett, *Poetical Works,* p. 649.

11 *Poetical Works,* p. xiv.

12 Isaiah 28:11.

13 Barrett, *Poetical Works,* p. xiii.

14 Edmund Burke, *A Philosophical Enquiry into the Origin of Our Ideas of the Sublime and Beautiful* (London: R. and J. Dodsley, 1759), p. 110; on Barrett's development of the Romantic motifs of the Double and the Sublime as a way of articulating her sense of her relation to the male poetic tradition, see John Woolford, 'Elizabeth Barrett and the Wordsworthian Sublime', *Essays in Criticism* 45, 1 (1995), 36–56.

15 Amy Billone notes some verbal resemblances between this poem and Wordsworth's 'Composed upon Westminster Bridge'; 'Sonnet Turn', 541–3.

16 Vittoria Colonna's husband Ferrante D'Avalos died in 1525; she wrote a series of sonnets in his memory; see Vittoria Colonna, *Rime,* ed. Alan Bullock (Giuseppe Laterza e figli: Roma, 1982). Colonna is used as one example of the poetry of 'conjugal love' in Elizabeth Barrett's friend Anna Jameson's *The Romance of Biography; or, Memoirs of Women Loved and Celebrated by Poets,* 3rd ed. (London: Saunders and Otley, 1837), vol. 2.

17 The *Sonnets from the Portuguese* appeared immediately after Barrett's poem 'Catalina to Camoens' in the 1850 edition of her poems, as she pointed out in a letter to her sister Arabella; see Lewis, *EBB to Arabella,* 1, pp. 368–9. Felicia Hemans translated twenty of Camoens' sonnets into English. The question of Barrett's indebtedness to Camoens is discussed at length in Barbara Neri, 'A Lineage of Love: The Literary Bloodlines of Elizabeth Barrett Browning's *Sonnets from the Portuguese'*, *Studies in Browning and His Circle* 23 (2000), 50–69.

18 Letter of 2–3 July 1845; Daniel Karlin ed., *Robert Browning and Elizabeth Barrett; The Courtship Correspondence* (OUP, 1989), p, 78.

19 Helen Cooper, *Elizabeth Barrett Browning, Woman and Artist* (Chapel Hill and London: The University of North Carolina Press, 1988), p. 102; see also Angela Leighton, *Elizabeth Barrett Browning* (Brighton; Harvester, 1986).

20 There is an interesting account of some of the intertextual relations between the two sequences in Sharon Smulders, '"Medicated Music": Elizabeth Barrett Browning's *Sonnets from the Portuguese'*, *Victorian Literature and Culture* 23 (1996), 193–213; Smulders argues that Barrett Browning actualises the trope of feminine infirmity in order to chart her own emergence from a 'genre plagued by infirmity'.

21 'The Female Poet and the Embarrassed Reader; Elizabeth Barrett Browning's *Sonnets from the Portuguese'*, *English Literary History* 48 (1981), 354.

22 Cooper, *Woman and Artist,* p. 100; on the myth of rescue see Daniel Karlin, *The Courtship of Robert and Elizabeth Barrett Browning* (Oxford: OUP, 1985).

23 There are a number of other sonnets in the 1850 *Poems,* but almost none thereafter.

24 Natalie M. Houston, 'Affecting Authenticity: *Sonnets from the Portuguese* and *Modern Love'*, *Studies in the Literary Imagination* 35 (2002), 99–122.

25 Now I am going to speak to you about those sonnets. I have had a letter from dear Mr. Kenyon, and he and Mr. Forster detected them as well as you – and a letter from American speaks of 'the Portuguese sonnets *so called,*' – and a letter from Mrs. Payne disapproves of the 'blind' and tells me that the open truth would have been 'worthier of me' ... by which I am a little, just a little, vexed. The truth is that though they were written several years ago, I never showed them to Robert till last spring ... I felt shy about them altogether ... even to him. I had heard him express himself strongly against 'personal' poetry and I shrank back – As to publishing them, it did not enter my head. But when Robert saw them, he was much touched and pleased – and, thinking highly of the poetry, he did not like, ... could not consent, he said, that they should be lost to my volumes: so we agreed to slip them in under some sort of veil., and after much consideration chose the 'Portuguese'. Observe – the poem which precedes them, is 'Catarina to Camoens'. In a loving fancy, he had always associated me with Catarina, and the poem had affected him to tears, he said, again and again. So, Catarina being a Portuguese, we put 'Sonnets from the Portuguese' – which did not mean (as we understood the double-meaning) *'from the Portuguese language'* ... though the public (who are very little versed in Portuguese literature) might take it as they pleased. (Lewis, *EBB to Arabella,* 1, pp. 368–9).

26 Margaret Reynolds has suggested that 'the tone and the imagery which colours the *Sonnets [from the Portuguese]* is derived from a fairytale stock; there are palaces inhabited by her princely lover, gifts of ruby crowns and golden thrones, magic kisses which wake the enchanted Sleeping Beauty ... '; 'Love's Measurement in Elizabeth Barrett Browning's *Sonnets from the Portuguese,'Studies in Browning and His Circle* 21 (1997), 54–5.

25 The Divided Self and the Dramatic Monologue (2012)

Richard Cronin

D.G. Rossetti made the first draft of 'Jenny', his brother William Rossetti recalled, 'before the end of 1847', but that first draft was very different from the poem that Rossetti finally published in 1870: it was 'short, and was merely in the nature of general reflection – not (as now) of semi-dramatic monologue'.'Jenny' was one of the poems violently attacked by Robert Buchanan in his paper for the *Contemporary Review*, 'The Fleshly School of Poetry'.[2] It is, Buchanan allows, 'in some respects the finest poem in the volume', a poem 'suggested', he observes with a truly remarkable effrontery, by poems of Buchanan's own, especially 'Artist and Model' (1867). Nevertheless, Rossetti's poem is vitiated by the complexity of its speaker's responses to the young prostitute. Buchanan pities Jenny's plight when 'such a poet as this comes fawning over her, with tender compassion in one eye and aesthetic enjoyment in the other!' That response is acute enough, and in his reply Rossetti does not quarrel with it. Instead, he argues that Buchanan has mistaken the genre of the poem. It is not, as Buchanan supposes and as William Rossetti suggests that it had been in its first draft, a 'soliloquy'. Rossetti recognizes that even friendly readers (Ruskin for one) would have preferred it had he delivered his thoughts on prostitution while dispensing with 'the situation which', in the poem as published, 'serves it as framework'. The poem is spoken after the speaker has returned with Jenny to her room, as she falls asleep with her head on his knee. Rossetti defends his decision to write the poem as a monologue by insisting that the poem demanded 'an *inner* standing-point': 'the self-questionings and all-questionings' that the situation prompts 'can come with full force only from the mouth of one alive to its whole appeal, such as the speaker put forward in the poem, – that is, of a young and thoughtful man of the world. To such a speaker, many half-cynical revulsions of feeling and reverie, and a recurrent presence of the impressions of beauty (however artificial) which first brought him within such a circle of influence, would be inevitable features of the dramatic relation portrayed'.[3] Rossetti accepts, and repeats in more turgid prose, Buchanan's account of how the poem works. He insists only that Buchanan has failed to recognize its dramatic character.

In the earliest draft of the poem that survives, a text that probably dates from 1860, Rossetti has already introduced the 'situation' that serves as the 'framework' of the poem, and the '*inner* standing point', but both are developed far more fully in the text that Rossetti finally published in 1870. The room to which Jenny has brought the young man is realized with painful clarity when dawn breaks to reveal a 'pier-glass scrawled with diamond rings' (322):

> Glooms begin
> To shiver off as lights creep in
> Past the gauze curtains half drawn-to,
> And the lamp's doubled shade grows blue.

(311–14)

That double shadow is rendered with a fine painterly precision, and the same quality informs the '*inner* standing point' too, as when the young man looks at Jenny as if she were a High Renaissance Madonna:

> Fair shines the gilded aureole
> In which our highest painters place
> Some living woman's simple face,
> And the still features thus descried
> As Jenny's long throat droops aside, –
> The shadows where the cheeks are thin,
> And pure wide curve from ear to chin, –
> With Raffael's or Da Vinci's hand
> To show them to men's souls, might stand,
> Whole ages long, the whole world through,
> For preachings of what God can do.

(230–40)

His artist's eye is just as evident when he sees her as a woman of quite another kind, a Magdalen rather than a Madonna, 'Your silk ungirdled and unlac'd / And warm sweets open to the waist' (48–9). It is when he sees her as pitiable, as the victim of male lust, that his vision becomes blurred:

> Fresh flower, scarce touched with signs that tell
> Of Love's exuberant hotbed: – Nay,
> Poor flower left torn since yesterday
> Until tomorrow leave you bare;
> Poor handful of bright spring-water
> Flung in the whirlpool's shrieking face.

(12–7)

The lack of clarity (the wild flowers and hothouse flowers, the stream and the whirlpool reveal the speaker's confusion more clearly than they illuminate Jenny's situation) seems defensive. The imprecision helps him to avoid implicating himself in the behaviour that he condemns. The speaker never manages to resolve his conflicting responses, and looks at Jenny throughout the poem, to borrow Buchanan's devastating statement of the case, 'with tender compassion in one eye and aesthetic enjoyment in the other!'

It cannot be otherwise because Jenny is at once a person and a commodity. When she falls asleep with her head on his knee, she claims the protection to which her trust in him entitles her, and yet her body is what he has paid for. Jenny's room cannot be, like the room in Donne's 'The Sunne Rising', an erotic space perfectly sealed against the outside world. At dawn noises begin to intrude into the room, amongst them the sound of 'an early wagon drawn / To market' (304–5), but the sound fails to alert the young man to the fact that market values operate within the room just as ruthlessly as outside it.

The poem's 'framework' and its 'inner standing-point', it emerges, are thoroughly entangled. The speaker cherishes the flimsy, self-exculpatory fiction that Jenny might be equally fond of sex and money, that the economic and the erotic might be complementary. In the very first lines of the poem the thought becomes catchy:

> Lazy, laughing, languid Jenny,
> Fond of a kiss and fond of a guinea.
>
> (1–2)

Two extra unstressed syllables in the second line, two dactyls instead of two trochees, give it a jaunty swing. In Jenny's dreams, he guesses, men and money feature all but interchangeably:

> Whose person or whose purse may be
> The lodestar of your reverie?
>
> (20–1)

The thought remains with him in the poem's conclusion. He places coins in Jenny's hair as she sleeps and imagines how they will tumble about her when she rises, a 'Danaë for a moment there'. (376) Danaë was impregnated by Zeus when he defeated her father's security measures by transforming himself into a shower of gold, but the allusion serves only to accentuate the social distance between the speaker and his subject. Jenny, after all, is very unlikely to be familiar with classical mythology. The thought prompts another heartless pun – 'Jenny, my love rang true!' (377) –, from which even the perpetrator flinches, achieving as he does so at long last a fragile self-knowledge: 'And must I mock you to the last, / Ashamed of my own shame?' (380–1).

He leaves the money for Jenny even though he has not had sex with her (he rather prides himself on his self-restraint). He imagines her thankful that he has not been 'drunk or ruffianly' and has allowed her just to rest with her head upon his knee. (66–7) Denying himself the pleasure of penetrating her body, he has occupied himself during the night by attempts to penetrate her mind. He imagines her thoughts, her history, and, when she falls asleep, her dreams. She is, in a repeated metaphor, a book, a book that he spends the night reading. If he were to speak aloud his thoughts, 'the pages of her brain' might open, but only momentarily, as 'a volume seldom read / Being opened halfway shuts again' (158–61). As he gazes at her, he thinks,

> You know not what a book you seem,
> Half-read by lightning in a dream!
>
> (51–2)

Later, it is the book's contents rather than the light that it is read by that seem lurid. Women, the speaker admits, might be better qualified to read Jenny than he is himself, because their gaze would be uncomplicated by desire. But in the world as it is constituted she is a text that they are forbidden from looking into. Her heart is like a rose pressed within the pages of a pornographic book,

> Where through each dead rose-leaf that clings,
>   Pale as transparent psyche-wings,
> To the vile text, are traced such things
>   As might make lady's cheek indeed
> More than a living rose to read.
>
> (257–61)

A very different kind of book comes to mind when the cheeks of Aurora Leigh's strait-laced aunt are said to have a colour 'like a rose in a book / Kept more for ruth than pleasure' (2, 285–6), but in *Aurora Leigh* just as persistently as in 'Jenny' people are likened to books. Romney Leigh, Aurora tells him with some astringency, is a 'holy book', 'reserved for mild-eyed saints to pore upon' (2, 837–8), whereas she is herself '[t]oo light a book for a grave man's reading!' (5, 41). Lady Waldemar's over-familiarity prompts a more extended metaphor:

> Sweet heaven, she takes me up
> As if she had fingered me and dog-eared me
> And spelled me by the fireside half a life!
>
> (5, 1053–5)

People are like books in these poems because understanding them requires an act of interpretation, and it is often an act of some complexity. When Rossetti's speaker compares Jenny to a book, he inevitably offers himself too as a text that the reader is invited to construe, and the process does not stop there. Robert Buchanan read the poem as a text through which he could divine Rossetti's own character, and Rossetti was appalled by the interpretative methods that he deployed, but it would be hard to claim that Buchanan's project was in itself illegitimate.

In *Aurora Leigh* there, is a teasing relationship between Elizabeth Barrett Browning's poem and Aurora's poem that at last brings her the fame that she has sought. In Rossetti's poem relationships are still more vexed. The poem's instability is nicely caught by William Rossetti when he describes it as a 'semi-dramatic; monologue'. Some lines are spoken to Jenny on the assumption that she is awake:

> Well, handsome Jenny mine, sit up,
> I've filled our glasses, let us sup.
>
> (89–90)

Other lines seem spoken, but to a Jenny believed to be sleeping: 'Why, Jenny, you're asleep at last!' (171). Still other lines are presented as unspoken thoughts:

> Suppose I were to think aloud, –
> What if to her all this were said?
>
> (156–7)

But the status of a large majority of the poem's lines is unfixed, and offered to the reader to puzzle over. The same might be said of the poem's tetrameter couplets. In poems that distinguish between poet and speaker, the verse form employed has to be assigned to one or the other. The Duke in Browning's 'My Last Duchess' (1842), for example, is surely, despite the suggestions of some critics to the contrary, unaware that he is speaking in couplets. The verse form, so muffled by enjambment that it all but defeats the ear, stands as a formal guarantee of the distinction between the Duke's speech and the poem that Browning makes of it. The couplets frame the Duke for the reader's appalled and delighted inspection. When Browning's Fra Lippo Lippi (1855) breaks into couplets, on the other hand, they are his rather than Browning's:

> Flower o'the quince,
> I let Lisa go, and what good in life since?

(55–6)

It is Lippo Lippi who chooses to punctuate his speech with these 'whiffs of song' (52) that, just as powerfully as his style of painting, express his outlook on life. 'A Grammarian's Funeral' (1855) is a more complex example, which may be why the poem has puzzled its readers as to whether Browning shares or satirizes the admiration that the students who speak the poem claim to feel for their master. The poem is a marching song, sung by the grammarian's students as they carry the body of their master to its proper resting place on the summit of a mountain, elevated high above the humble dwellers on the plain. 'Step to a tune', (25) they urge each other, claiming the poem's metre as their own. In its interlocked quatrains, iambic pentameters alternate with dimeter lines made up of a dactyl followed by a trochee. The dimeters are almost wholly regular, but the pentameters are so various that it is little more than an act of faith to describe them as iambic. The swing of the poem is repeatedly threatened by lines, to quote the poem, of 'Accents uncertain' (54), which might express the difficulty of the climb ('Step two abreast, the way winds narrowly' (91), but seem more tellingly to betray a lurking suspicion that the grammarian's life of scholarship does not inspire in his students the single-minded admiration that they profess. The young scholars' song has an exuberance that makes them unlikely celebrants of a life lived 'Dead from the waist down' (132). But do the poem's iambic lines that seem to reach after 'New measures, other feet' (39), betray the suspicion that the students cannot quite bring themselves to make explicit that the life of the mind is not much of a life after all, or do they signal Browning's dry suspicion that the young men find it easier to praise such a life than to emulate it?

'Jenny' raises similar problems. Its tetrameter couplets are not clearly assigned either to the speaker or the poet. The opening couplet may have a jaunty, aphoristic quality that it seems easier to ascribe to the speaker, but elsewhere the couplets seem, as in 'My Last Duchess', to offer a formal guarantee that the poem is subject to a control of which the speaker is quite unaware. Rossetti has a tendency, for example, to muffle a rhyme by dividing a single couplet between verse paragraphs, and he sometimes uses rhymes so approximate that they can scarcely be heard (the most extreme example rhymes 'bare' with 'spring-water' (15–6)). By contrast, he also finds place for a number of obtrusively rhymed triplets:

> Poor little Jenny, good to kiss, –
> You'd not believe by what strange roads
> Thought travels when your beauty goads
> A man to-night to think of toads!

(299–302)

Such uncertainties may simply point to the history of the poem's composition, revealing the poem as a palimpsest, a reflective lyric incompletely rewritten as a dramatic poem, but they also work more positively. They keep the reader constantly alert to the status of the poem as text, and to the act of reading as an act of interpretation. The poem's speaker is a student, a reader, his room unlike Jenny's 'full of books' (23), and yet Jenny's room offers him no escape from print:

> All golden in the lamplight's gleam, –
> You know not what a book you seem.

(51–2)

And if Jenny is a book to the young man, so he is to the poem's reader, and a book just as elusive, a book that, just like Jenny herself, 'opened halfway shuts again'. (159)

When John Ruskin accused him of obscurity, Robert Browning mounted a vigorous self-defence. He encouraged Ruskin 'to keep pace with the thought tripping from ledge to ledge', and 'not stand poking your alpenstock into the holes, and demonstrating that no foot could have stood there – suppose it sprang over them?' Browning was describing a poetic style defined not by connections but by gaps, and, as he recognized, the most significant gap was between the poet and his speaker. The relationship, he admitted, might be uncertain, he might 'put Robert Browning' into his speakers: 'If so, *peccavi* [I have sinned]: but I don't see myself in them at all events.'[4] The challenge with which Victorian poets present their readers very often has its origin in the decision, common to so many Victorian poems, from Elizabeth Barrett Browning's *Aurora Leigh* to Tennyson's *Maud* to D.G. Rossetti's 'Jenny', to distinguish poet and speaker. The most distinctive generic innovation made by Victorian poets is, as everyone has recognized, the dramatic monologue, but it has proved impossible to define just what is distinctive about it. Either the qualifications for membership are so strict (in a famous article Ina Sessions argued that the perfect dramatic monologue must display seven distinct features[5]) that only a handful of poems, almost all of them by Browning, qualify, or Victorian poems with fictitious speakers become impossible to distinguish from poems with fictitious speakers written in any other period. But looked at in a different way the problem disappears. The dramatic monologue is the exemplary Victorian verse form because so many Victorian poems share some of its characteristics.

The poem most often identified as the first Victorian dramatic monologue, Tennyson's 'St Simeon Stylites', was written in 1833, some years before the Queen's accession. The use by poets of fictitious speakers was already common, as, for example, in Felicia Hemans's *Records of Woman* (1828), in which many of the poem's titles, such as 'Arabella Stuart' and 'Properzia Rossi', simply name their speakers. Tennyson's difference is signalled in Edward FitzGerald's recollection of how he would recite the poem 'with grotesque Grimness, especially at such passages as "Coughs, Aches, Stitches, etc." laughing aloud at times.'[6] The dramatic monologue, as FitzGerald intimates, is commonly a performance. The reader of 'St Simeon Stylites', for example, is invited to examine the self-delusion of a man who believes that he equips himself for heaven by choosing to spend his life on a pillar, on the assumption that sainthood is available for purchase by the man prepared to pay the price in self-mortification, but he is invited still more strongly to relish the gusto with which Tennyson assumes the character:

> Good people you do ill to kneel to me.
> What is it I can have done to merit this?
> I am a sinner viler than you all.
> It may be I have wrought some miracles,
> And cured some halt and maimed; but what of that?

(131–5)

Tennyson's friend, W. H. Thompson was concerned that the poem might be thought 'unwholesome', 'the description of [Simeon's] sufferings being too minute for any but those whom the knowledge of the Art holds above the subject.' But in this, as in most dramatic monologues, the reader is given little opportunity to forget the poet's 'Art'. St Simeon on his latest, and as he hopes his last pillar, is raised sixty feet above the ground, from where he looks down on those on whose behalf he suffers:

> But thou, O Lord,
> Aid all this foolish people; let them take
> Example, pattern: lead them to thy light.

> (218–20)

He is a grotesque compound of egotism and vanity, shut up in a hallucinatory world in which weird shapes 'with colt-like whinny and with hoggish whine' (174) drown out his prayers, and yet he never loses sight of how he is regarded by the admiring spectators, amongst whom he seems to include not only the 'good people' down below but God and all his angels. The poem is satirical, but, for all that, there is an odd complicity between the poet and his speaker. The fierceness of Tennyson's mockery of Simeon, performing with so much energy his own saintliness, cannot quite prevent the reader from noticing that Tennyson is playing the role of Simeon, and playing it just as vigorously. Odd complicities of this kind are characteristic of the dramatic monologue. Browning's first dramatic monologue, 'Johannes Agricola' (1836), was probably written two years after 'St Simeon Stylites', but Tennyson's poem was not published until 1842. It must be a coincidence, then, that Tennyson and Browning should both have chosen as the speakers of their first monologues a religious fanatic (Johannes Agricola, the first of the antinomians, held that the elect were exempt from the moral law). In the 1830s Wordsworth stood unchallenged at the head of the profession that Tennyson and Browning aspired to join, and it is possible to read these, the very first Victorian monologues, as a mordant response to the belief so closely associated with Wordsworth that the poet's true function was as the dispenser of religious truths.

The speaker of Browning's second monologue, 'Porphyria's Lover' (1836), is a murderer. So too is the speaker of the monologue of his that critics have agreed on identifying as the most perfect representative of the genre, 'My Last Duchess'. He is a murderer at any rate if that is how the Duke's nonchalant remark should be interpreted (Browning himself suggested, surely disingenuously, that he might simply have ordered that his wife be shut up in a convent):

> I gave commands;
> Then all smiles stopped together. There she stands
> As if alive.

> (45–7)

Dramatic monologues are very often spoken from the margins, from what Tennyson's Tithonus (1860) calls the 'limit of the world' (7), whether those margins be ethical or social or geographical or historical. Browning's Duke, for example, is not only a murderer, but an aristocrat, the bearer of a 'nine-hundred-years-old-name', and the ruler of a city state in late Renaissance Italy, in all which respects he would have been as marginal to most of Browning's readers as to Browning himself. Enjambment is so extreme that the ear scarcely registers that the poem is written in pentameter couplets. Rhyme and metre serve formally to secure the difference between the poet and the speaker, but they do not build between the two a fence high enough to keep them quite apart. The charge that the poem brings against the Duke is that he found it intolerable that his wife responded with a 'spot / Of joy' on the cheek to each and every instance of the vital beauty that she admired in everything around her, the selfsame beauty for which she herself, although she seems quite unconscious of it, was remarkable:

> The dropping of the daylight in the West.
> The bough of cherries some officious fool
> Broke in the orchard for her, the white mule
> She rode with round the terrace.

(26–9)

The free play of her responses is itself an outrage to the Duke's demand that she find her only satisfaction in being the object of his regard. In death, when 'the faint / Half-flush that dies along her throat' (18–9) persists only in its reproduction by Fra Pandolf, the portrait painter, her behaviour has at last been brought into conformity with her husband's demands. Now she is dead, her image is displayed as, when, and to whom the Duke chooses, 'since none puts by / The curtain I have drawn for you, but I' (9–10). By the Duke's command the Duchess has been reduced to her painted reproduction, but the Duke's deadening hand has fallen on himself too. The poem ends as the Duke and the envoy go downstairs together, the Duke pointing out another prized item from his collection:

> Notice Neptune, though,
> Taming a sea horse, thought a rarity,
> Which Claus of Innsbruck cast in bronze for me!

(54–6)

This is the Duke as he sees himself, superhuman tamer of women, and as the reader sees him, a man who, because he is so wholly trapped within his own egotism, and because he can understand no relation other than ownership, has cast his flesh and blood in bronze, becoming not so much a man as a statue of a man. Beauty for the Duke is fixed and dead: for Browning as for the Duchess it is quite otherwise. Browning says so directly in poem after poem, and he says as much in this poem too, in the movement of the verse at once so swift and so decisive. And yet does the poem quite eradicate the suspicion that the pleasure with which Browning uncurtains his Duke for the reader's perusal has an affinity with the pleasure that the Duke takes in displaying to chosen guests the portrait of his Duchess? The dramatic monologue distinguishes poet and speaker and one effect is to make it possible for them to develop unexpected and even uncomfortable relations one with another. The envoy, an emissary from the Count with whose daughter the Duke is negotiating a marriage, remains silent throughout the poem, his responses sometimes signalled ('not the first / Are you to turn and ask thus' (12–3)), but always opaque. The Duke gives the envoy a superb performance of the role that he has spent his life perfecting, the role of himself, but he is offered no clue as to how his performance is received, and in this too his predicament mirrors the poet's. It is, I think, significant that the dramatic monologue should first have been developed in the 1830s, when poets enjoyed such small sales, when publishers were so reluctant to issue their work (Edward Moxon was in that decade the only London publisher prepared to bring out volumes written by a single poet, and he did so usually on the basis that the poet bore the costs) that they can only have suspected that they were talking, like so many speakers of dramatic monologues, to themselves.

'My Last Duchess' is one of the simpler of Browning's dramatic monologues. It is hard, for example, to imagine a reader for whom the Duke's moral character is problematic. The poem's reader is unchallengingly confirmed in his prejudices against foreigners, aristocrats, autocrats, and wife-murderers. It is almost as hard to imagine a reader not charmed by the Duchess even in the Duke's representation of her. But even so the poem has prompted very different readings. The most obvious question that the poem raises is why the Duke should divulge to the emissary of the woman that he plans to marry that he has had his last wife killed. Ina Sessions believes that he is speaking by design, intending that the envoy should pass on to his future bride his view of the behaviour that will be expected of her, and of the consequences of any failure to satisfy those expectations. It may be, on the other hand, as Robert Langbaum supposes, that the Duke is displaying with characteristic flamboyance his utter disregard of how those he considers his inferiors might respond to him. But I suspect that most readers these days will prefer, like Alan Sinfield, to believe that the Duke is in the grip of a compulsion that impels him to rehearse the story of his last marriage no matter how inopportune the occasion.[7] That is my own preference, but my point is that the poem offers very little to support my preferred reading against those I find less persuasive, no more, perhaps, than the suggestion that the Duke may be rehearsing a speech that he has made many times before:

>   for never read
> Strangers like you that pictured countenance,
> The depth and passion of its earnest glance
> But to myself they turned ...
>
>   (6–9)

Dramatic monologues almost inevitably focus the reader's attention on the act of reading, and on the question of how and with what confidence the reader may arrive at a judgement of a speaker by examining that speaker's words. The speakers of dramatic monologues are always judged in their absence, their voices encountered not directly but in transcript. To read the poem is to listen to the voice of its speaker, but that voice can only ever be reconstructed by the reader from its printed trace. Every dramatic monologue offers a lesson in responsible reading.

Notes

1   *Works of Dante Gabriel Rossetti,* ed. W.M. Rossetti (London: Ellis, 1911), p. 649.
2   *Contemporary Review,* 18 (August, 1871), 334–50.
3   D.G. Rossetti, 'The *Contemporary Review* and the Stealthy School of Criticism: A Letter to Robert Buchanan, Esq. (Alias Thomas Maitland, Esq.)', London, 1871, reprinted in *Victorian Poetry* 41. 2 (2003), pp. 207–27.
4   Quoted in W.G. Collingwood, *Life of John Ruskin* (Boston: Houghton Mifflin, 1902), pp. 164–5.
5   Ina Beth Sessions, 'The Dramatic Monologue', *PMLA,* 62. 2 (1947): 503–16.
6   Hallam Tennyson, *Alfred Lord Tennyson: A Memoir,* 2 vols (London: Macmillan, 1897), 1, p. 193, footnote.
7   Ina Beth Sessions, 'The Dramatic Monologue', p. 510: Robert Langbaum, *The Poetry of Experience: The Dramatic Monologue in Modern Literary Tradition* (London: Chatto and Windus, 1957), pp. 82–5; Alan Sinfield, *Dramatic Monologue* (London: Methuen, 1977), p. 5.

Part VI
Emotion, Feeling, Affect

Emma Mason

Nineteenth-century poetry and poetics is in thrall to the question of what, how and why we feel. As twenty-first century readers, we are regularly confronted with a scientific 'measuring' of feeling by a media spellbound by magnetic resonance imaging and other neuroscientific technologies that ostensibly 'explain' the experience of feeling. Nineteenth-century readers, however, caught between the contradictions of a polite sensibility that produced a raw-nerved middle class, and an expanding industrialized economy dependent on the seeming exploitation of feeling, continually pressed the question of where and why feeling occurs. Is feeling individual or social, bodily or of the mind, moral or unhealthy? Does feeling refer to sense perception, the haptic or proprioceptive? An inner experience one fine-tunes by engaging with art, religion, science or politics? Or an outward expression marked by tears, laughter or blushes? Many poets writing in the period explored specific kinds of feeling, the meanings of which resonate with modern definitions (love, joy, sadness, jealousy); other poets focused on feelings the meanings of which have significantly changed (enthusiasm, affection, sentiment, benevolence). Some of these writers responded to philosophical, scientific and medical treatises on feeling; others were more interested in feelings about space and place, from eroded rural landscapes to factories and workhouses. Karl Marx, for example, described the nineteenth-century workplace as a site of affective alienation, one that, in valuing commodities and capital over well being and self-knowledge, cut workers off from the emotional experience of their labour, the products they produced and their fellow workers. Those who sought refuge from this industrialized workplace in rural economies were similarly subjected to long hours and the continual erosion of the landscape on which they worked and emotionally invested. Broadside balladeers bemoaned the horror of the workhouse with as much feeling as elegists mourned the dead, while the expression of feeling commanded further formal returns in the sonnet's revision of romance and the spasmodics' somatic rhythms. Strong feeling was a hallmark of both popular and less mainstream verse, and poetry was equally referred to as the cure, foundation, trigger and heart of all manner of emotions, feelings and affects.

While critics find the history of the emotions a compelling field in the early twenty-first century, their critical precursors struggled with it. As Isobel Armstrong noted in 1977 looking back on a twentieth-century aversion to the study of emotion, the 'search to render the "feel" of feelings in poetry verbally' is missing from modern criticism in a way it isn't from nineteenth-century poetry.[1] Armstrong's influential work on Victorian poetry contributed to what critics now refer to as the 'affective turn', restoring emotion to a literary critical field that had become dependent on the idea of itself as a feeling-free intellectual 'discipline' pioneered by university-educated men. Worried that literary studies was over-identified with reading practices associated with a feminized model of sentiment and leisure, early twentieth-century critics weathered an ontological crisis about the relevance and meaning of the field. For critics like F. R. Leavis, I. A. Richards, John Crowe Ransom, T. S. Eliot, W. K. Wimsatt and Monroe Beardsley, literary criticism should be cerebral and quantifiable: the New Criticism movement, with its emphasis on form over feeling, steered readers away from emotional and psychological interpretation. Yet, as Armstrong writes in a later work, *The Radical Aesthetic* (2000), emotion is at once form and feeling, sensual and rational, material and immaterial. By using the active word 'affect', which connotes the impact and effect of feelings on people, she gestures to all aspects of vital being – 'emotions, feelings, passions, moods, anxiety, discharge of psychic energy, motor innervation, pleasure, pain, joy and sorrow, rapture, depression' – belonging as they do 'to mind and soma, straddling conscious and unconscious just as they straddle mind and physiology'.[2]

Against the New Critics, Armstrong cites A. E. Housman's discussion of poetry's 'symptoms': tears, gooseflesh and tightness in the throat. Housman's poet 'experiences affect and transfuses it into the poem: the reader encounters the poem and through it traces back to the author's original state, sensing a "vibration corresponding to what was felt by the writer"'.[3] This model of vibrational correspondence recalls the eighteenth-century philosopher David Hartley's reading of sensation, one that influenced William Wordsworth and Samuel Taylor Coleridge's reading of poetic feeling, which in turn held appeal for Housman. No wonder Richards was rumoured to have exited from one of Housman's Cambridge lectures, mumbling: 'This has put us back ten years'.[4] While Plato's famous warning that the listener of poetry should guard against its allure enjoyed a revival by the beginning of the twentieth century, nineteenth-century readers and writers alike were invested in poetry's rhythmic and metrical properties as a stay against such seduction.[5] Writing in his *Biographia Literaria* (1817), Coleridge described poetry as 'the blossom and the fragrancy of all human knowledge, human thoughts, human passions, emotions, language'; while a year later, William Hazlitt called it the trace of life and movement itself, that which 'puts a spirit of life and motion into the universe. It describes the flowing, not the fixed'.[6] For the religious poet, John Keble, poetry helped to temper feeling, 'a kind of medicine divinely bestowed upon man: which gives healing relief to secret mental emotion'; while Laetitia Elizabeth Landon conceived of it as obligatory 'passion', claiming 'I should almost define poetry to be the necessity of feeling'.[7] John Stuart Mill stressed that even though 'poetry is feeling confessing itself to itself in moments of solitude', it is still '*overheard*' and so shared.[8] Other critics, like Robert Buchanan, worried that 'bad' poetry was little more than 'the mere fiddlededeeing of empty heads and hollow hearts … the true indication of falser tricks and affectations which lie far deeper. They are trifles, light as air, showing how the wind blows'.[9] Sydney Dobell admitted that words 'rhythmically combined affect the feelings of the poetic hearer or utterer', but considered the imagination a kind of muscle that 'by a reflex action', might at least negotiate its impact.[10] And even at the end of the century, W. B. Yeats still insisted that 'an emotion does not exist, or does not become perceptible and active among us, till it has found its expression, in colour or in sound or in form'.[11]

However varied these definitions might be, all have in common an emphasis on feeling, emotion and affect as that which is experienced rather than owned: nineteenth-century poetry and the context in which it was written are heightened in an awareness of this experience as a social and shared one. The period inherits two distinct readings of feeling: one Cartesian (mind and body are distinct, and mental phenomena thus non-physical); the other non-dualist (experience co-arises from the mutual dependence of mind and body). Adam Smith argued for the first, and located sympathy as the basis of social feeling and the driver behind whom we choose to feel for; Spinoza favoured the second, claiming that the mind has no power over affects, which humans 'imagine' through the experience of the body.[12] For Smith, feeling is affectionate and benevolent; for Spinoza it is raw and energetic.[13] Both theories, however, present emotion, feeling and affect as generated through relationships and disseminated through interaction with others: as Teresa Brennan argues, affect is not insulated within private moments, but rather transmitted back and forth between humans who change the way those feelings are then absorbed by others.[14] Despite the apparent emotional hesitation within lines like Emily Brontë's 'I could not speak the feeling' or Tennyson's 'I sometimes hold it half a sin' / To put in words the grief I feel', they nevertheless share the specifics of anxiety or grief with the poetry reader.[15] Nineteenth-century poetry and poetic theory alike repeatedly attempt to articulate how this expression and reception works in corporeal, textual and imaginative terms. The period's obsession with feelings and the implications of potential definitions for ethics, psychology, religion, philosophy and art are drawn out in the extracts this three-part chapter introduces. The first section explores 'feeling' and 'emotion' through Wordsworth's influential writing on poetry; the second compares how the relationship between 'feeling' and 'thought' signifies for the nineteenth-century and modern reader; and the third considers the emphasis nineteenth-century writers place, not on individuated, private feeling, but on emotion as inherently social and shared.

Feeling and emotion

The etymological histories of the words 'feeling' and 'emotion' are bound to each other. While 'feeling' can mean both tactual sensation and the bodily faculty by which one perceives and senses the world by touching and feeling it, it also signifies the 'condition of being emotionally affected'. 'Emotion', by contrast, derives from the Latin *emotio* and Middle French émotion, both of which connote a negative sense of displacement, agitation, unrest, commotion or disturbance. By the eighteenth century, the English word 'emotion' translated such disturbance into the movement and motion of the body, mind and blood, bringing together physical sensation with intuitive contemplation. Associated with mental as well as physical processes, emotion came to define a sensation that lasts longer than the more immediate 'feeling', although both feeling and emotion are often set against terms like reason, rationality and empirical knowledge. The history of the emotions is charged with competing stories about feeling and emotion, even though many eighteenth and nineteenth-century poets elided their work with these terms: poetry is feeling and feeling is poetry. The most often quoted of these accounts is Wordsworth's 1802 'Preface' to the *Lyrical Ballads*:

> I have said that poetry is the spontaneous overflow of powerful feelings: it takes its origin from emotion recollected in tranquillity: the emotion is contemplated till, by a species of reaction, the tranquillity gradually disappears, and an emotion, kindred to that which was before the subject of contemplation, is gradually produced, and does itself actually exist in the mind. In this mood successful composition generally begins.[16]

Wordsworth's formula distinguishes everyday emotions, which we remember in the quieter moments of our day, from related emotions, which arise once this period of contemplation is over. That is, when we are most at peace, emotions arise that we start to think about, and so 'react' to them both physically and mentally: these 'reactions' disturb the initial calm (tranquillity disappears) and we are left with a related but purer form of the initial emotion, which then sits in our 'mind' and produces a 'mood'. In this mood, Wordsworth argues, we are ready to write. While for Wordsworth, poems are not fountain-like wells of emotion (poems do not have their own feelings), they do provide sites that ideally capture the process by which humans feel emotion. The sound, rhythm, metre and music of poetry all grant access to joyful and painful feeling through a form likely to be read over and over, he argues, and in doing so, the reader undergoes the contemplation necessary to produce his or her own emotion. This is especially important in a newly industrial and capitalist world that denies many humans the time or environment in which the peaceful remembering of emotions might occur. If poetry arises from the remembered emotions of the poet, then the reader of poetry is granted a space in which to remember his or her own feelings.

In a separate note on his poem, 'The Thorn', Wordsworth introduces two further terms into the discussion, defining poetry as both 'passion' and 'the history or science of feelings'.[17] While 'passion' once referred to Christ's suffering, by the end of the eighteenth century it signified a particularly strong or overpowering feeling or emotion, one that is fitful, agitated or excited. This definition underlines Wordsworth's sense that feeling is volatile and unsettled, and that poems, far from sedating such feeling, actually help to generate and transfer it. Poems do not 'express' feeling, but rather musically arrange words as 'things, active and efficient, which are of themselves part of the passion' and that come to life in specific historical and 'scientific' (social) moments of reading. Feeling is not universal, then, but shared in particular instants through a poetic language that stresses the emotional content of the world over its other concerns. As he writes in his 1815 'Preface', the 'business of poetry' is 'to treat of things not as they *are*, but as they *appear*; not as they exist in themselves, but as they *seem* to exist to the *senses*, and to the *passions*'. Reading for personal feeling, Wordsworth acknowledges, might tempt the reader into a 'world of delusion', one he or she should guard against through the committed and repeated 'study' of poetry. Only when poetry is 'comprehended *as a study*' can it protect against petty worries and more serious suffering, also yielding the capacity to differentiate sensational, empty feeling from feeling that teaches readers about their lives and worlds.[18] In attending to and carefully studying poetry, the reader is almost bound to think and feel at once, recognizing the mutuality of these two faculties distinct from that which is free of thought (un-thoughtful in both senses of that word) and so without feeling.

The argument resounds in Wordsworth's poetry: the first book of *The Prelude* alone makes countless references to the relationship between feeling and thought, and presents the two in words readers today might associate with the other term. In the opening lines, for example, the narrator relates 'trances of thought and mountings of the mind / Come fast upon me': 'trances' and 'mountings', for example, both invoke emotional states of being hypnotized and lifted up, and which are not usually associated with rational thought.[19] Similarly, Wordsworth's description of the 'mind' blurs feeling and thinking to conjure a kind of dynamism or energy that makes the human tick, one that we experience like harmonious music and translate into 'calm existence':

> The mind of Man is fram'd even like a breath
> And harmony of music. There is a dark
> Invisible workmanship that reconciles
> Discordant elements, and makes them move
> In one society. Ah me! that all
> The terrors, all the early miseries
> Regrets, vexations, lassitudes, that all
> The thoughts and feelings which have been infus'd

Into my mind, should ever have made up
The calm existence that is mine when I
Am worthy of myself![20]

    The mind brings together thoughts and feelings by 'reconciling' them into a 'society', a word that connotes connection, participation and alliance. This sense of connection is underlined by the 'early miseries' Wordsworth lists – regret, irritation, exhaustion; these are experiences we register with both heart and head, and have the ability to reconfigure into tranquillity through the 'mind'. 'Mind', then, signifies the oneness of thought and feeling – we 'recognize' their impact on us in 'the beatings of the heart' – but remember this impact in 'the tenderness of thought'.[21] Feeling, thinking, emotion, reason exist in a continuum for Wordsworth, but how does he keep this continuity in play and why does it fracture for the modern reader?

Feeling and thought

For Wordsworth, feelings only 'revolt from the sway of reason' when they go undisciplined by contemplation or study. Modern readers tend to split feeling from thought, the subjective from the objective, assuming that feeling is a surface registering of a deeper reasoned response. Reasoned thought, the argument goes, serves as an authoritative check to the otherwise chaotic potential of feeling. The contention is exemplified in Wimsatt and Beardsley's 1949 attack on emotive criticism, 'The Affective Fallacy', wherein they suggest that reading for feeling is vague, 'raw, unarticulated, imprecise' because, on the one hand, emotion is relative and 'personal' and, on the other, too dependent on different knowledges, experiences and anthropologies. For them, the 'affective critic' is doomed either to engage indulgently with 'his own experiences', or to attempt such a generalized theory that his 'search for evidence will lead him into the dreary and antiseptic laboratory'. One can guess that their discomfort with psychoanalysis would hold double with current neuroscientific readings of literature. Wimsatt and Beardsley do not ignore emotion (they in fact call for a more nuanced reading of emotion as 'pattern'), nor do they exclude context (they admit that literature tells us much about 'social history' and 'anthropology'). They do, however, attempt to create a fully 'objective' reading practice that excises feeling from criticism. In attempting to banish emotive, impressionistic or intuitive thinking about literature, one that 'induces' 'vivid images, intense feelings, or heightened consciousness', Wimsatt and Beardsley ignored what nineteenth-century writers recognized: that thinking is an emotional act just as feeling involves cognition.[22] While these writers are intent on taxonomizing feeling into varieties and degrees, they do not split it from thought so much as seek to explore how a sensation differs from an emotion in relation to the mind that processes it.

    If the etymology of emotion ties it to meanings of unrest, movement and disturbance, by the nineteenth century it had come to mean mental phenomena and memory as well as a physical reaction to external stimuli. By the 1820s, its adjectival form – 'emotional' – signified an excess of feeling and was associated with femininity and inevitably with women; 'emotionless', by contrast, came to mean cold and even cruel.[23] While the association of emotion with either too much or too little feeling did not put nineteenth-century readers off engaging with it, they were sensitive to the nuances of 'emotionology'. Passion, for example, which has already been noted as a site of strong and often negative feeling (suffering, pain, desire, anger), was balanced by affection, a morally 'finer' form of feeling connected to benevolence and sympathy.[24] Affection was social and reciprocal, as well as devotional and loving: it served as a counter to the assumed-to-be more dangerous 'enthusiasm', associated with the mad ravings of religious extremists (of Methodist or Roman Catholic persuasion, depending on the bias of the critic). Sentiment, by contrast, indicated a more refined and even 'affected' or inauthentic excess of feeling; while sensibility denoted a capacity for sensitive, appropriate and compassionate emotional response. The obsession with classifying and distinguishing emotions appealed across the intellectual spectrum too: some readers studied Alexander Bain's scholarly scientific text, *The Emotions and the Will* (1859) to assess what he identifies as eleven 'families of emotion'; while others were drawn to Robert Tyas' *The Sentiments of Flowers* (1836), which lists two hundred different 'sentiments' depicted through a variety of flora. The period's 'emotion culture' also touched on the way other discourses – morality, religion, education, gender, health, taste – were 'felt'. John Abercrombie's *The Philosophy of the Moral Feelings* (1833) and poems like Elizabeth Bonhote's *Feeling, or, Sketches from Life; A Desultory Poem* (1810) and 'Mrs' Stringer's *The Chain of Affection; A Moral Poem* (1830) revealed the extent to which feelings were associated with moral stability and social order. James Martineau's proclamation that 'worship is an attitude which our nature assumes, not for a purpose, but from an emotion' typifies the connection between feeling and religion, as does Mary Ann Stodart's 'heart-religion, coming from the heart, and travelling to the heart'.[25] Stodart's work is representative too of a nineteenth-century tendency to feminize and domesticate feeling as the duty of 'woman ... it is her part to soothe, to solace, and to sympathize' by softening and gentling the space of the home.[26] On the other hand, Herbert Spencer considered 'moral sentiments' beyond the emotional capacity of women and children, making the same social and cultural assumptions about biological difference as Stodart but from the opposite perspective.[27] Reading feeling through biological difference is not confined to nineteenth-century thinking, however: modern beliefs about feeling and thinking, hearts and heads, are often used as a basis to make distinctions about the way women and men behave, decision-make and relate. Whether modern accounts make these distinctions via culture (ideology produces women and men differently) or science (hormonal or neural differences account for gendered ways of behaving or responding to the world), such conjecture derives largely from the Victorians.

Nineteenth-century readers were also confronted with such divisions, but reflected on them differently. Coleridge, for example, associated poetic genius with androgyny just as Mary Wollstonecraft claimed that souls had no sex: while critics point out that both writers assume this ideally hybrid human is male, Coleridge and Wollstonecraft nevertheless imply a refusal to equate women with feeling and men with reason.[28] Sarah Ellis argued in *The Education of the Heart: Women's Best Work* (1869), for example, that women needed to be 'trained' to feel as Stodart expected them to, undermining the notion that biology and feeling are directly connected.[29] The phenomenon of the 'poetess' also implicitly challenged women's emotionality by associating the woman poet with linguistic effusion, spontaneity and excess, even as her performance was defined by careful versification. Poems by Landon and Felicia Hemans in particular were frequently compared to 'waters from a fountain, gushing', recalling Germaine de Stael's ad-libbing female laureate in her novel, *Corinne* (1807). Yet their 'improvisations' were informed by poetic, aesthetic and historical tradition, as well as being strategically published and marketed to a vast readership – men as well as women – who were eager to develop the same emotional intelligence.[30] Only a few decades earlier, for example, Henry Mackenzie's *The Man of Feeling* (1771) had ennobled the sentimental and weepy hero Harley by relating his story through the emotions he experiences in different relationships and encounters. By the nineteenth century, Harley's ability to feel had become so popular with readers that an 'Index to Tears' was appended to the novel for quick reference:

from Mackenzie's depiction of heroic weeping to Tennyson's grieving self-portrait as 'an infant crying in the night / An infant crying for the light', men were free to emote.[31]

Many male poets suffered for assuming too 'feminine' an emotive stance, however: Tennyson was pulled up by Manley Hopkins for his 'womanly' and 'amatory tenderness' towards the deceased Hallam in *In Memoriam*; and Dante Gabriel Rossetti was accused of 'fleshly' feeling by Robert Buchanan.[32] Where John Keats had been declared guilty of Cockney effeminacy for the expression of a refined feeling beyond his class, Tennyson and Rossetti were denounced for writing about coarse feeling below their cultural status.[33] Part of the anxiety about who could feel what in the period can be attributed to concerns about whether ideas once thought to regulate emotional experience (religion, morality, ethics) could still do so. The appeal of David Hartley to Wordsworth and Coleridge, for example, was his ostensible bringing together of theology and science in *Observations on Man* (1749) to argue that mental phenomena are produced by associations and vibrations felt and interpreted by the body and mind. For Hartley, humans make sense of their worlds by receiving signals about them that vibrate along the nervous system; these sensations are computed as we associate what we see, hear, touch, taste and smell into a sequence of correspondences that then form thoughts, values and judgments. This implies an implicit connection between mental events (thoughts, feelings) and physical events (vibrations in the brain): the immaterial and material are connected just as the motions of planets impact upon our presence in the universe. As Coleridge worked out, the implication of such a theory is that subjective experiences – of the mind and the heart – could be granted as objective a reality as things seen and touched, like rocks or trees.

For Hartley as for Coleridge, this provided a shared 'evidence' of God through the material 'reality' of faith and intuition. Poets writing in the wake of Hartley considered mental phenomena from beliefs and hunches to feelings and moods to be concrete and collective, and not, as some modern critics assume, immaterial and atomized.[34] From Hemans' religious reading, in which she aimed to 'enlarge ... the sphere of Religious Poetry, by associating with its themes more of the emotions, the affections', to Shelley's musical exposition, in which the poet is 'an instrument over which a series of external and internal impressions are driven, like the alternations of an ever-changing wind over an Aeolian lyre', poetry gathers readers into a communal and harmonious experience.[35] Like Wordsworth's musical integration of thought and feeling, nineteenth-century poetry produces as well as records civil relationships founded on 'social sympathies' through which humans co-exist and interact. As Marx states, if 'language, like consciousness, only arises from the need, the necessity, of intercourse with other men', and consciousness registers the 'immediate sensuous environment' and 'connection with other persons and things', then our feelingful awareness of our world is relational and collective.[36]

Social emotion

However affective experience is defined in nineteenth-century poetry, it is always social. Wordsworth and Coleridge knew as much when they gave their volume a hybrid form – *Lyrical Ballads* – to encompass the more reclusive lyric and the communal ballad. Poetry of this period relentlessly negotiates the relationship between form and feeling, and so entirely rejects the binary logic that splits off conscious knowing from visceral feeling. Coleridge's claim that poetry is 'a rationalized dream dealing to manifold Forms our own Feelings' does more than attribute a psychological or dream-like origin to verse; it suggests that our thoughts distribute or 'deal out' feelings that are readily articulated through the various forms poetry offers.[37] Poetry might regulate feeling, as Keble thought it could, trusting as he did in rhythm and metre to obliquely communicate with and about God free of enthusiasm or excess; or it might transform feeling into a text, shaping linguistic sites of energetic concentration and release. Either way it negotiates both familiar and unfamiliar feelings by disclosing the relationship between emotional states and material conditions, while also softening the experience of disturbing or difficult self-knowledge. The spasmodics, for example, were both popular for rhythmically mapping the fidgety, restless and alienated body for a society intrigued by emergent physiological knowledges, but also harshly critiqued for apparent insensitivity to the affective biography of human being.[38] Poetry also reached readers concerned with the feelings of non-human beings, specifically the pain animals experienced during scientific experiment. As Jed Mayer argues, the period's vivisection debates were centred on the question of animal emotion, particularly as it was staged in Charles Darwin's *The Expression of the Emotions in Man and Animals* (1872), wherein human and animal feelings were linked. Public compassion for animals is a defining emotion of the nineteenth century, from dog-worship to the outcry at Jumbo's sale to the allegedly cruel circus owner, P. T. Barnum, in 1882.[39] Christina Rossetti's religious devotion to all aspects of creation, for example, is as much to do with a 'green' commitment to species and antivivisectionism as to her religious faith.[40] Rossetti's description of her poems as 'records' of 'sensation, fancy' echoes Hemans' focus on the word 'record', notably in *Records of Woman* (1828), which itself 'comes from the Latin *cor/cordis*, for heart, as conventional symbol of the humane and social feelings'.[41]

Even poems that beg to be read as mysterious or esoteric riddles addressed to veiled addressees end up inviting the reader to reflect on their expression, and in doing so forge a social pact with them. Joseph Freiherr von Eichendorff's lyric 'Mondnacht' (1835) is a notoriously enigmatic and moody example, its hermitic intensity incarnated in its language ('It was as though the heavens / Had silently kissed the earth, / Such that in the blossom's lustre, / She was caught in dreams of them ...') and redoubled in Robert Schumann's romantic setting of the poem.[42] While 'themes' are self-evident – romantic love, the relationship between heaven and earth, the dream-life of the mind, nature and the soul – their emotional content is not: it is almost impossible to relate the 'feelings' here without reducing them to cliché. As Theodor Adorno observes in his essay on Eichendorff, the reader of feeling threatens to collapse 'Mondnacht' into a predetermined message of 'romance' or 'love of nature' by either embracing such content as profound and authentic, or rejecting it as shallow and saccharine. Adorno recalls his schoolteacher's dismissal of Eichendorff's image of the sky kissing the earth as 'trivial'; by contrast, a participant in a recent study of music psychology stated that the lines evoke a 'mystical experience ... an enchantment'.[43] Adorno moves beyond this impasse by suggesting that the critic stave off the oblivion of individual taste by subordinating the narrative to the interpretive, and so turning the work of affects back on the reader. That poetry should enable readers to face and reflect upon emotion without defensiveness is a desperately urgent task for Adorno, writing as he was in the context of post-war Germany: if people

> allow themselves more of their affects and passions, if they do not once again repeat in themselves the pressure that society exerts upon them, then they will be far less evil, far less sadistic, and far less malicious than they sometimes are today.[44]

The question holds import too for our own neoliberal moment, one that champions individual choice as a freedom of market transactions, but in doing so demotes social relationships, welfare provisions and environmental sustainability in the name of capital value. This brutal commercialization of human experience and feeling is forewarned, not only by Marx, but by many of the poets commented on in this volume. Nineteenth-century poetry might appear to line up as a precursor to the commodification of feeling, its pathos and sentimentality satisfying the reader just enough to distract and benumb. Yet, as this discussion suggests, the focus of the period's poetry and poetics on emotion as the medium of reading and thinking invites the reader of the past and present to interrupt the assurances of subjective feeling to reflect instead on its consequences for relationship and community.

Notes

1   Isobel Armstrong, 'The Role and Treatment of Emotion in Victorian Criticism of Poetry', *Victorian Periodicals Newsletter*, 10 (1977), 3–16 (p. 14).
2   Isobel Armstrong, *The Radical Aesthetic* (Oxford: Blackwell, 2000), p. 108; and see Richa Dwor, *Jewish Feeling: Difference and Affect in Nineteenth-Century Jewish Women's Writing* (London: Bloomsbury, 2015); Tamara Ketabgian, 'Affect', in Juliet John (ed.), *Oxford Bibliographies in Victorian Studies* (New York: Oxford University Press, 2011); and Gregory J. Seigworth and Melissa Gregg, 'An Inventory of Shimmers', in Mellissa Gregg and Gregory J. Seigworth (eds), *The Affect Theory Reader* (Durham, NC and London: Duke University Press, 2010), pp. 1–25.
3   Armstrong, *Radical Aesthetic*, p. 109, quoting A. E. Housman, 'The Name and Nature of Poetry (1933).
4   Richard Aldington, *A. E. Housman and W. B. Yeats: Two Lectures* (Hurst, Berkshire: Peacocks Press, 1955), p. 11.
5   Plato, *The Republic* (London: Penguin, 2007).
6   S. T. Coleridge, *Biographia Literaria* (1815–17), chapter XV, in H. J. Jackson (ed.), *Samuel Taylor Coleridge: The Major Works* (Oxford: Oxford World Classics, 2008), p. 325; William Hazlitt, 'On Poetry in General,' *Lectures on English Poets and The Spirit of the Age* (London: J. M. Dent, 1910), pp. 3–18 (p. 3).
7   John Keble, *Lectures on Poetry 1832–1841*, trans. E. K. Francis, 2 vols (Oxford: Clarendon Press, 1912), p. 22; Letitia Elizabeth Landon, 'On the Character of Mrs Hemans' Writings,' *New Monthly Magazine*, 44 (1835), in Jerome McGann and Daniel Riess, *Letitia Elizabeth Landon: Selected Writings* (Ontario: Broadview, 1997), pp. 173–186 (p. 173).
8   John Stuart Mill, 'What is Poetry', in Edward Alexander (ed.), *Literary Essays* (Indianapolis, IN: Bobbs-Herrill, 1967), p. 56.
9   Robert Buchanan [Thomas Maitland], 'The Fleshly School of Poetry: Mr D. G. Rossetti', *The Contemporary Review*, October, 1871; http://www.rossettiarchive.org/docs/ap4.c7.18.rad.html
10 Sydney Dobell, *Thoughts on Art, Philosophy, and Religion, Selected from the Unpublished Papers of Sydney Dobell* (London: Smith, Elder, & Co, 1876), pp. 36–37.
11 William Butler Yeats, 'The Symbolism of Poetry,' from *Ideas of Good and Evil* (London: A. H. Bullen, 1903), p. 244.
12 Adam Smith, *Theory of the Moral Sentiments* (1759), 2 vols (Edinburgh: Bell and Bradfute Lackington, Allen and Co, 1808); Benedict de Spinoza, *Ethics* (1677), trans. George Eliot (Salzburg: University of Salzburg, 1981).
13 On Smith and Spinoza, see Isobel Armstrong, 'George Eliot, Spinoza, and the Emotions,' in Amanda Anderson and Harry E. Shaw (eds), *A Companion to George Eliot* (Oxford: Wiley-Blackwell, 2013), pp. 294–308.
14 Teresa Brennan, *The Transmission of Affect* (Ithaca, NJ: Cornell University Press, 2004).
15 Emily Brontë, 'Alone I sat; the summer day' (1837), in Derek Roper (ed.), *The Poems of Emily Brontë* (Oxford: Clarendon Press, 1996); Alfred Tennyson, *In Memoriam* (1850), in Erik Gray, (ed.), *In Memoriam,* Norton Critical Editions (New York: W. W. Norton, 2003), verse 5, ll. 1–12.
16 William Wordsworth, 'Preface to *Lyrical Ballads, with Pastoral and Other Poems* (1802)', in Stephen Gill (ed.), *William Wordsworth: The Major Works* (Oxford: Oxford World Classics, 2008), p. 611.
17 William Wordsworth, 'Note to "The Thorn" (1800)', in Gill (ed.), *Wordsworth*, p. 594.

18 William Wordsworth, 'Essay, Supplementary to the Preface (1815)', in Gill (ed.), *Wordsworth*, p. 641.

19 William Wordsworth, *The Prelude* (1805), in M. H. Abrams, Stephen Gill, Jonathan Wordsworth, (eds), *The Prelude 1799, 1805, 1850: Authoritative Texts, Context and Reception, Recent Critical Essays,* Norton Critical Editions (New York: W. W. Norton, 1979), Book 1, l. 20.

20 Wordsworth, *The Prelude*, Book 1, ll. 351–361.

21 Wordsworth, *The Prelude,* Book 1, l. 441; l. 600.

22 W. K. Wimsatt and M. C. Beardsley, 'The Affective Fallacy', *The Sewanee Review*, 57.1 (1949), 31–55 (pp. 34, 39, 44, 45).

23 See 'Emotion', University of Pittsburgh Keyword Project: http://keywords.pitt.edu/keywords_defined/emotion.html

24 See Francis Hutcheson, *An Essay on the Nature and Conduct of the Passions and Affections with Illustrations on the Moral Sense* (1728), 3rd edn (1742) (Gainesville, FL: Scholars' Facsimiles and Reprints, 1969).

25 James Martineau, *Hymns for the Christian Church and Home* (London: Longman, Brown, Green and Longmans, 1859), p. 8; Mary Ann Stodart, *Every Day Duties: In Letters to a Young Lady* (London: Seeley and Burnside, 1840), p. 206.

26 Stodart, *Every Day Duties*, p. 16.

27 Herbert Spencer, 'Morals and Moral Sentiments' (1852), in *Essays: Scientific, Political and Speculative* (London: Williams and Norgate, 1891).

28 Theresa Kelley, 'Women, Gender and Literary Criticism', in Marshall Brown (ed.), *The Cambridge History of Literary Criticism: Volume 5, Romanticism* (Cambridge: Cambridge University Press, 2000), pp. 321–337 (p. 330).

29 Sarah Ellis, *The Education of the Heart: Women's Best Work* (London: Hodder and Stoughton, 1869), p. 206; and see Gesa Stedman, *Stemming the Torrent: Expression and Control in the Victorian Discourses on Emotion 1830–1872* (Farnham: Ashgate, 2002).

30 Linda H. Peterson, 'Rewriting *A History of the Lyre*: Laetitia Landon, Elizabeth Barrett Browning and the (Re)Construction of the Nineteenth-Century Woman Poet,' in Isobel Armstrong and Virginia Blain, ed., *Women's Poetry Late Romantic to Late Victorian* (Basingstoke: Macmillan, 1999), pp. 115–132.

31 Tennyson, *In Memoriam*, verse 56, ll. 18–19.

32 Manley Hopkins, 'The Poetry of Sorrow', *The Times* (November 28, 1851), p. 8, issue 20971; Buchanan, 'Fleshly School'.

33 See Jeffrey N. Cox, *Poetry and Politics in the Cockney School: Keats, Shelley, Hunt and their Circle* (Cambridge: Cambridge University Press, 1998).

34 For example, see Helen Vendler's statement that 'Lyric is the genre of private life: it is what we say to ourselves when we are alone', in *Poems, Poets, Poetry: An Introduction and Anthology* (Boston, MA: St Martin's, 2002), p. xlii.

35 Felicia Hemans, 'Preface,' *Scenes and Hymns of Life, with Other Religious Poems* (Edinburgh: William Blackwood; London: T. Cadell, 1834), vii; and P. B. Shelley, *A Defence of Poetry* (1821), in Zachary Leader and Michael O'Neill (eds), *Percy Bysshe Shelley: The Major Works* (Oxford: Oxford World Classics, 2009), p. 675.

36 Karl Marx, 'Part I: Feuerbach. Opposition of the Materialist and Idealist Outlook', in *The German Ideology* (1845), https://www.marxists.org/archive/marx/works/1845/german-ideology/ch01a.htm

37 Seamus Perry (ed.), *Coleridge's Notebooks: A Selection* (Oxford: Oxford University Press, 2002), p. 66.

38 See Jason Rudy and Charles LaPorte, ed., 'Spasmodic Poetry and Poetics', *Victorian Poetry*, special issue, 42.4 (2004).

39 See Harriet Ritvo, *The Animal Estate: The English and Other Creatures in the Victorian Age* (Cambridge, MA: Harvard University Press, 1987).

40 Emma Mason, '"Whales and All that Move in the Waters": Christina Rossetti's Ecology of Grace', in Wendy Parkins (ed.), *Victorian Sustainability* (Farnham: Ashgate, 2016).

41 Gary Kelly (ed.), 'Introduction', *Felicia Hemans: Selected Poems, Prose and Letters* (Ontario: Broadview, 2002), pp. 15–85 (pp. 28–29).

42 Joseph Freiherr von Eichendorff, 'Mondnacht' (1837), trans. K. Winter as 'Moonlit Night' http://www.henleusa.com/en/schumann-anniversary-2010/schumann-forum/mondnacht.html;   see Robert Schumann, *Liederkreis*, op. 39 (1840).

43 Theodor W. Adorno, *Notes to Literature: Volume 1*, trans. Shierry Weber Nicholsen (New York: Columbia University Press, 1991), p. 56; Alf Gabrielsson, *Strong Experiences with Music: Music is Much More Than Just Music*, trans. Rod Bradbury (Oxford: Oxford University Press, 2011), pp. 223–234.

44 Theodor W. Adorno, 'Discussion of Professor Adorno's Lecture "The Meaning of Working Through the Past"', *Critical Models: Interventions and Catchwords* (New York: Columbia University Press, 1998), pp. 295–306 (pp. 299–300).

26 Preface to *Lyrical Ballads, with Pastoral and Other Poems* (1802)

William Wordsworth

The principal object, then, which I proposed to myself in these Poems was to chuse incidents and situations from common life, and to relate or describe them, throughout, as far as was possible, in a selection of language really used by men; and, at the same time, to throw over them a certain colouring of imagination, whereby ordinary things should be presented to the mind in an unusual way; and, further, and above all, to make these incidents and situations interesting by tracing in them, truly though not ostentatiously, the primary laws of our nature: chiefly, as far as regards the manner in which we associate ideas in a state of excitement. Low and rustic life was generally chosen, because in that condition, the essential passions of the heart find a better soil in which they can attain their maturity, are less under restraint, and speak a plainer and more emphatic language; because in that condition of life our elementary feelings co-exist in a state of greater simplicity, and, consequently, may be more accurately contemplated, and more forcibly communicated; because the manners of rural life germinate from those elementary feelings; and, from the necessary character of rural occupations, are more easily comprehended, and are more durable; and lastly, because in that condition the passions of men are incorporated with the beautiful and permanent forms of nature. The language, too, of these men is adopted (purified indeed from what appear to be its real defects, from all lasting and rational causes of dislike or disgust) because such men hourly communicate with the best objects from which the best part of language is originally derived; and because, from their rank in society and the sameness and narrow circle of their intercourse, being less under the influence of social vanity they convey their feelings and notions in simple and unelaborated expressions. Accordingly, such a language, arising out of repeated experience and regular feelings, is a more permanent, and a far more philosophical language, than that which is frequently substituted for it by Poets, who think that they are conferring honour upon themselves and their art, in proportion as they separate themselves from the sympathies of men, and indulge in arbitrary and capricious habits of expression, in order to furnish food for fickle tastes, and fickle appetites, of their own creation. [Wordsworth's note: "It is worth while here to observe that the affecting parts of Chaucer are almost always expressed in language pure and universally intelligible even to this day".]

I cannot, however, be insensible of the present outcry against the triviality and meanness both of thought and language, which some of my contemporaries have occasionally introduced into their metrical compositions; and I acknowledge, that this defect, where it exists, is more dishonorable to the Writer's own character than false refinement or arbitrary innovation, though I should contend at the same time that it is far less pernicious in the sum of its consequences. From such verses the Poems in these volumes will be found distinguished at least by one mark of difference, that each of them has a worthy *purpose*. Not that I mean to say, that I always began to write with a distinct purpose formally conceived; but I believe that my habits of meditation have so formed my feelings, as that my descriptions of such objects as strongly excite those feelings, will be found to carry along with them a *purpose*. If in this opinion I am mistaken, I can have little right to the name of a Poet. For all good poetry is the spontaneous overflow of powerful feelings: but though this be true, Poems to which any value can be attached, were never produced on any variety of subjects but by a man, who being possessed of more than usual organic sensibility, had also thought long and deeply. For our continued influxes of feeling are modified and directed by our thoughts, which are indeed the representatives of all our past feelings; and, as by contemplating the relation of these general representatives to each other we discover what is really important to men, so, by the repetition and continuance of this act, our feelings will be connected with important subjects, till at length, if we be originally possessed of much sensibility, such habits of mind will be produced, that, by obeying blindly and mechanically the impulses of those habits, we shall describe objects, and utter sentiments, of such a nature and in such connection with each other, that the understanding of the being to whom we address ourselves, if he be in a healthful state of association, must necessarily be in some degree enlightened, and his affections ameliorated.

[...]

The Reader will find that personifications of abstract ideas rarely occur in these volumes; and, I hope, are utterly rejected as an ordinary device to elevate the style, and raise it above prose. I have proposed to myself to imitate, and, as far as is possible, to adopt the very language of men; and assuredly such personifications do not make any natural or regular part of that language. They are, indeed, a figure of speech occasionally prompted by passion, and I have made use of them as such; but I have endeavoured utterly to reject them as a mechanical device of style, or as a family language which Writers in metre seem to lay claim to by prescription. I have wished to keep my Reader in the company of flesh and blood, persuaded that by so doing I shall interest him. I am, however, well aware that others who pursue a different track may interest him likewise; I do not interfere with their claim, I only wish to prefer a different claim of my own. There will also be found in these volumes little of what is usually called poetic diction; I have taken as much pains to avoid it as others ordinarily take to produce it; this I have done for the reason already alleged, to bring my language near to the language of men, and further, because the pleasure which I have proposed to myself to impart is of a kind very different from that which is supposed by many persons to be the proper object of poetry. I do not know how without being culpably particular I can give my Reader a more exact notion of the style in which I wished these poems to be written than by informing him that I have at all times endeavoured to look steadily at my subject, consequently, I hope that there is in these Poems little falsehood of description, and that my ideas are expressed in language fitted to their respective importance. Something I must have gained by this practice, as it is friendly to one property of all good poetry, namely, good sense; but it has necessarily cut me off from a large portion of phrases and figures of speech which from father to son have long been regarded as the common inheritance of Poets. I have also thought it expedient to restrict myself still further, having abstained from the use of many expressions, in themselves proper and beautiful, but which have been foolishly repeated by bad Poets, till such feelings of disgust are connected with them as it is scarcely possible by any art of association to overpower.

[...]

Taking up the subject, then, upon general grounds, I ask what is meant by the word Poet? What is a Poet? To whom does he address himself? And what language is to be expected from him? He is a man speaking to men: a man, it is true, endued with more lively sensibility, more enthusiasm and tenderness, who has a greater knowledge of human nature, and a more comprehensive soul, than are supposed to be common among mankind; a man pleased with his own passions and volitions, and who rejoices more than other men in the spirit of life that is in him; delighting to contemplate similar volitions and passions as manifested in the goings-on of the Universe, and habitually impelled to create them where he does not find them. To these qualities he has added a disposition to be affected more than other men by absent things as if they were present; an ability of conjuring up in himself passions, which are indeed far from being the same as those produced by real events, yet (especially in those parts of the general sympathy which are pleasing and delightful) do more nearly resemble the passions produced by real events, than any thing which, from the motions of their own minds merely, other men are accustomed to feel in themselves; whence, and from practice, he has acquired a greater readiness and power in expressing what he thinks and feels, and especially those thoughts and feelings which, by his own choice, or from the structure of his own mind, arise in him without immediate external excitement.

But, whatever portion of this faculty we may suppose even the greatest Poet to possess, there cannot be a doubt but that the language which it will suggest to him, must, in liveliness and truth, fall far short of that which is uttered by men in real life, under the actual pressure of those passions, certain shadows of which the Poet thus produces, or feels to be produced, in himself. However exalted a notion we would wish to cherish of the character of a Poet, it is obvious, that, while he describes and imitates passions, his situation is altogether slavish and mechanical, compared with the freedom and power of real and substantial action and suffering. So that it will be the wish of the Poet to bring his feelings near to those of the persons whose feelings he describes, nay, for short spaces of time perhaps, to let himself slip into an entire delusion, and even confound and identify his own feelings with theirs; modifying only the language which is thus suggested to him, by a consideration that he describes for a particular purpose, that of giving pleasure. Here, then, he will apply the principle on which I have so much insisted, namely, that of selection; on this he will depend for removing what would otherwise be painful or disgusting in the passion; he will feel that there is no necessity to trick out or to elevate nature: and, the more industriously he applies this principle, the deeper will be his faith that no words, which his fancy or imagination can suggest, will be to be compared with those which are the emanations of reality and truth.

But it may be said by those who do not object to the general spirit of these remarks, that, as it is impossible for the Poet to produce upon all occasions language as exquisitely fitted for the passion as that which the real passion itself suggests, it is proper that he should consider himself as in the situation of a translator, who deems himself justified when he substitutes excellences of another kind for those which are unattainable by him; and endeavours occasionally to surpass his original, in order to make some amends for the general inferiority to which he feels that he must submit. But this would be to encourage idleness and unmanly despair. Further, it is the language of men who speak of what they do not understand; who talk of Poetry as of a matter of amusement and idle pleasure; who will converse with us as gravely about a *taste* for Poetry, as they express it, as if it were a thing as indifferent as a taste for Rope-dancing, or Frontiniac or Sherry. Aristotle, I have been told, hath said, that Poetry is the most philosophic of all writing: it is so: its object is truth, not individual and local, but general, and operative; not standing upon external testimony, but carried alive into the heart by passion; truth which is its own testimony, which gives strength and divinity to the tribunal to which it appeals, and receives them from the same tribunal. Poetry is the image of man and nature. The obstacles which stand in the way of the fidelity of the Biographer and Historian, and of their consequent utility, are incalculably greater than those which are to be encountered by the Poet, who has an adequate notion of the dignity of his art. The Poet writes under one restriction only, namely, that of the necessity of giving immediate pleasure to a human Being possessed of that information which may be expected from him, not as a lawyer, a physician, a mariner, an astronomer or a natural philosopher, but as a Man. Except this one restriction, there is no object standing between the Poet and the image of things; between this, and the Biographer and Historian there are a thousand.

Nor let this necessity of producing immediate pleasure be considered as a degradation of the Poet's art. It is far otherwise. It is an acknowledgment of the beauty of the universe, an acknowledgment the more sincere because it is not formal, but indirect; it is a task light and easy to him who looks at the world in the spirit of love: further, it is a homage paid to the native and naked dignity of man, to the grand elementary principle of pleasure, by which he knows, and feels, and lives, and moves. We have no sympathy but what is propagated by pleasure: I would not be misunderstood; but wherever we sympathize with pain it will be found that the sympathy is produced and carried on by subtle combinations with pleasure. We have no knowledge, that is, no general principles drawn from the contemplation of particular facts, but what has been built up by pleasure, and exists in us by pleasure alone. The Man of Science, the Chemist and Mathematician, whatever difficulties and disgusts they may have had to struggle with, know and feel this. However painful may be the objects with which the Anatomist's knowledge is connected, he feels that his knowledge is pleasure; and where he has no pleasure he has no knowledge. What then does the Poet? He considers man and the objects that surround him as acting and re-acting upon each other, so as to produce an infinite complexity of pain and pleasure; he considers man in his own nature and in his ordinary life as contemplating this with a certain quantity of immediate knowledge, with certain convictions, intuitions, and deductions which by habit become of the nature of intuitions; he considers him as looking upon this complex scene of ideas and sensations, and finding every where objects that immediately excite in him sympathies which, from the necessities of his nature, are accompanied by an overbalance of enjoyment.

To this knowledge which all men carry about with them, and to these sympathies in which without any other discipline than that of our daily life we are fitted to take delight, the Poet principally directs his attention. He considers man and nature as essentially adapted to each other, and the mind of man as naturally the mirror of the fairest and most interesting qualities of nature. And thus the Poet, prompted by this feeling of pleasure which accompanies him through the whole course of his studies, converses with general nature with affections akin to those, which, through labour and length of time, the Man of Science has raised up in himself, by conversing with those particular parts of nature which are the objects of his studies. The knowledge both of the Poet and the Man of Science is pleasure; but the knowledge of the one cleaves to us as a necessary part of our existence, our natural and unalienable inheritance; the other is a personal and individual acquisition, slow to come to us, and by no habitual and direct sympathy connecting us with our fellow-beings. The Man of Science seeks truth as a remote and unknown benefactor; he cherishes and loves it in his solitude: the Poet, singing a song in which all human beings join with him, rejoices in the presence of truth as our visible friend and hourly companion. Poetry is the breath and finer spirit of all knowledge; it is the impassioned expression which is in the countenance of all Science. Emphatically may it be said of the Poet, as Shakespeare hath said of man, "that he looks before and after." He is the rock of defence of human nature; an upholder and preserver, carrying every where with him relationship and love. In spite of difference of soil and climate, of language and manners, of laws and customs, in spite of things silently gone out of mind and things violently destroyed, the Poet binds together by passion and knowledge the vast empire of human society, as it is spread over the whole earth, and over all time. The objects of the Poet's thoughts are every where; though the eyes and senses of man are, it is true, his favorite guides, yet he will follow wheresoever he can find an atmosphere of sensation in which to move his wings. Poetry is the first and last of all knowledge—it is as immortal as the heart of man. If the labours of men of Science should ever create any material revolution, direct or indirect, in our condition, and in the impressions which we habitually receive, the Poet will sleep then no more than at present, but he will be ready to follow the steps of the man of Science, not only in those general indirect effects, but he will be at his side, carrying sensation into the midst of the objects of the Science itself. The remotest discoveries of the Chemist, the Botanist, or Mineralogist, will be as proper objects of the Poet's art as any upon which it can be employed, if the time should ever come when these things shall be familiar to us, and the relations under which they are contemplated by the followers of these respective Sciences shall be manifestly and palpably material to us as enjoying and suffering beings. If the time should ever come when what is now called Science, thus familiarized to men, shall be ready to put on, as it were, a form of flesh and blood, the Poet will lend his divine spirit to aid the transfiguration, and will welcome the Being thus produced, as a dear and genuine inmate of the household of man. It is not, then, to be supposed that any one, who holds that sublime notion of Poetry which I have attempted to convey, will break in upon the sanctity and truth of his pictures by transitory and accidental ornaments, and endeavour to excite admiration of himself by arts, the necessity of which must manifestly depend upon the assumed meanness of his subject.

[…]

The sum of what I have there said is, that the Poet is chiefly distinguished from other men by a greater promptness to think and feel without immediate external excitement, and a greater power in expressing such thoughts and feelings as are produced in him in that manner. But these passions and thoughts and feelings are the general passions and thoughts and feelings of men. And with what are they connected? Undoubtedly with our moral sentiments and animal sensations, and with the causes which excite these; with the operations of the elements and the appearances of the visible universe; with storm and sun-shine, with the revolutions of the seasons, with cold and heat, with loss of friends and kindred, with injuries and resentments, gratitude and hope, with fear and sorrow. These, and the like, are the sensations and objects which the Poet describes, as they are the sensations of other men, and the objects which interest them. The Poet thinks and feels in the spirit of the passions of men. How, then, can his language differ in any material degree from that of all other men who feel vividly and see clearly? It might be *proved* that it is impossible. But supposing that this were not the case, the Poet might then be allowed to use a peculiar language, when expressing his feelings for his own gratification, or that of men like himself. But Poets do not write for Poets alone, but for men. Unless therefore we are advocates for that admiration which depends upon ignorance, and that pleasure which arises from hearing what we do not understand, the Poet must descend from this supposed height, and, in order to excite rational sympathy, he must express himself as other men express themselves. To this it may be added, that while he is only selecting from the real language of men, or, which amounts to the same thing, composing accurately in the spirit of such selection, he is treading upon safe ground, and we know what we are to expect from him. Our feelings are the same with respect to metre; for, as it may be proper to remind the Reader, the distinction of metre is regular and uniform, and not like that which is produced by what is usually called poetic diction, arbitrary, and subject to infinite caprices upon which no calculation whatever can be made. In the one case, the Reader is utterly at the mercy of the Poet respecting what imagery or diction he may choose to connect with the passion, whereas, in the other, the metre obeys certain laws, to which the Poet and Reader both willingly submit because they are certain, and because no interference is made by them with the passion but such as the concurring testimony of ages has shewn to heighten and improve the pleasure which coexists with it.

It will now be proper to answer an obvious question, namely, why, professing these opinions, have I written in verse? To this, in addition to such answer as is included in what I have already said, I reply in the first place, because, however I may have restricted myself, there is still left open to me what confessedly constitutes the most valuable object of all writing whether in prose or verse, the great and universal passions of men, the most general and interesting of their occupations, and the entire world of nature, from which I am at liberty to supply myself with endless combinations of forms and imagery. Now, supposing for a moment that whatever is interesting in these objects may be as vividly described in prose, why am I to be condemned, if to such description I have endeavoured to superadd the charm which, by the consent of all nations, is acknowledged to exist in metrical language? To this, by such as are unconvinced by what I have already said, it may be answered, that a very small part of the pleasure given by Poetry depends upon the metre, and that it is injudicious to write in metre, unless it be accompanied with the other artificial distinctions of style with which metre is usually accompanied, and that by such deviation more will be lost from the shock which will be thereby given to the Reader's associations, than will be counterbalanced by any pleasure which he can derive from the general power of numbers. In answer to those who still contend for the necessity of accompanying metre with certain appropriate colours of style in order to the accomplishment of its appropriate end, and who also, in my opinion, greatly under-rate the power of metre in itself, it might perhaps, as far as relates to these Poems, have been almost sufficient to observe, that poems are extant, written upon more humble subjects, and in a more naked and simple style than I have aimed at, which poems have continued to give pleasure from generation to generation. Now, if nakedness and simplicity be a defect, the fact here mentioned affords a strong presumption that poems somewhat less naked and simple are capable of affording pleasure at the present day; and, what I wished chiefly to attempt, at present, was to justify myself for having written under the impression of this belief.

But I might point out various causes why, when the style is manly, and the subject of some importance, words metrically arranged will long continue to impart such a pleasure to mankind as he who is sensible of the extent of that pleasure will be desirous to impart. The end of Poetry is to produce excitement in co-existence with an overbalance of pleasure. Now, by the supposition, excitement is an unusual and irregular state of the mind; ideas and feelings do not in that state succeed each other in accustomed order. But, if the words by which this excitement is produced are in themselves powerful, or the images and feelings have an undue proportion of pain connected with them, there is some danger that the excitement may be carried beyond its proper bounds. Now the co-presence of something regular, something to which the mind has been accustomed in various moods and in a less excited state, cannot but have great efficacy in tempering and restraining the passion by an intertexture of ordinary feeling, and of feeling not strictly and necessarily connected with the passion. This is unquestionably true, and hence, though the opinion will at first appear paradoxical, from the tendency of metre to divest language in a certain degree of its reality, and thus to throw a sort of half consciousness of unsubstantial existence over the whole composition, there can be little doubt but that more pathetic situations and sentiments, that is, those which have a greater proportion of pain connected with them, may be endured in metrical composition, especially in rhyme, than in prose. The metre of the old Ballads is very artless; yet they contain many passages which would illustrate this opinion, and, I hope, if the following Poems be attentively perused, similar instances will be found in them. This opinion may be further illustrated by appealing to the Reader's own experience of the reluctance with which he comes to the re-perusal of the distressful parts of *Clarissa Harlowe*, or *The Gamester*. While Shakespeare's writings, in the most pathetic scenes, never act upon us as pathetic beyond the bounds of pleasure an effect which, in a much greater degree than might at first be imagined, is to be ascribed to small, but continual and regular impulses of pleasurable surprise from the metrical arrangement. On the other hand (what it must be allowed will much more frequently happen) if the Poet's words should be incommensurate with the passion, and inadequate to raise the Reader to a height of desirable excitement, then, (unless the Poet's choice of his metre has been grossly injudicious) in the feelings of pleasure which the Reader has been accustomed to connect with metre in general, and in the feeling, whether cheerful or melancholy, which he has been accustomed to connect with that particular movement of metre, there will be found something which will greatly contribute to impart passion to the words, and to effect the complex end which the Poet proposes to himself.

If I had undertaken a systematic defence of the theory upon which these poems are written, it would have been my duty to develop the various causes upon which the pleasure received from metrical language depends. Among the chief of these causes is to be reckoned a principle which must be well known to those who have made any of the Arts the object of accurate reflection; I mean the pleasure which the mind derives from the perception of similitude in dissimilitude. This principle is the great spring of the activity of our minds, and their chief feeder. From this principle the direction of the sexual appetite, and all the passions connected with it take their origin: It is the life of our ordinary conversation; and upon the accuracy with which similitude in dissimilitude, and dissimilitude in similitude are perceived, depend our taste and our moral feelings. It would not have been a useless employment to have applied this principle to the consideration of metre, and to have shewn that metre is hence enabled to afford much pleasure, and to have pointed out in what manner that pleasure is produced. But my limits will not permit me to enter upon this subject, and I must content myself with a general summary.

I have said that Poetry is the spontaneous overflow of powerful feelings: it takes its origin from emotion recollected in tranquillity: the emotion is contemplated till by a species of reaction the tranquillity gradually disappears, and an emotion, kindred to that which was before the subject of contemplation, is gradually produced, and does itself actually exist in the mind. In this mood successful composition generally begins, and in a mood similar to this it is carried on; but the emotion, of whatever kind and in whatever degree, from various causes is qualified by various pleasures, so that in describing any passions whatsoever, which are voluntarily described, the mind will upon the whole be in a state of enjoyment. Now, if Nature be thus cautious in preserving in a state of enjoyment a being thus employed, the Poet ought to profit by the lesson thus held forth to him, and ought especially to take care, that whatever passions he communicates to his Reader, those passions, if his Reader's mind be sound and vigorous, should always be accompanied with an overbalance of pleasure. Now the music of harmonious metrical language, the sense of difficulty overcome, and the blind association of pleasure which has been previously received from works of rhyme or metre of the same or similar construction, an indistinct perception perpetually renewed of language closely resembling that of real life, and yet, in the circumstance of metre, differing from it so widely, all these imperceptibly make up a complex feeling of delight, which is of the most important use in tempering the painful feeling, which will always be found intermingled with powerful descriptions of the deeper passions. This effect is always produced in pathetic and impassioned poetry; while, in lighter compositions, the ease and gracefulness with which the Poet manages his numbers are themselves confessedly a principal source of the gratification of the Reader.

[...]

I have one request to make of my Reader, which is, that in judging these Poems he would decide by his own feelings genuinely, and not by reflection upon what will probably be the judgment of others. How common is it to hear a person say, "I myself do not object to this style of composition or this or that expression, but to such and such classes of people it will appear mean or ludicrous." This mode of criticism, so destructive of all sound unadulterated judgment, is almost universal: I have therefore to request, that the Reader would abide independently by his own feelings, and that if he finds himself affected he would not suffer such conjectures to interfere with his pleasure.

If an Author by any single composition has impressed us with respect for his talents, it is useful to consider this as affording a presumption, that, on other occasions where we have been displeased, he nevertheless may not have written ill or absurdly; and, further, to give him so much credit for this one composition as may induce us to review what has displeased us with more care than we should otherwise have bestowed upon it. This is not only an act of justice, but in our decisions upon poetry especially, may conduce in a high degree to the improvement of our own taste: for an accurate taste in poetry, and in all the other arts, as Sir Joshua Reynolds has observed, is an acquired talent, which can only be produced by thought and a long continued intercourse with the best models of composition. This is mentioned, not with so ridiculous a purpose as to prevent the most inexperienced Reader from judging for himself, (I have already said that I wish him to judge for himself;) but merely to temper the rashness of decision, and to suggest, that, if Poetry be a subject on which much time has not been bestowed, the judgment may be erroneous; and that in many cases it necessarily will be so.

[...]

27 Lecture 1 and Lecture 40 from *Lectures on Poetry* (1832–41)

John Keble

THERE are many pleas which I might naturally put forward in this Introduction in order to win a kindly criticism for this slight work of mine; but I see that I have urged nearly all of them in my Inaugural Lecture. Yet I confess there is one thing which I did not anticipate. I did not foresee that in these last few years it would be perils threatening the Church, more than perils threatening the State which would withdraw the minds of us all from the delights of quiet literary study. Yet so it has been, and had I not been encouraged by the opinion of those to whose judgement I chiefly defer on such a point that there is a real possibility that discussions on poetry may not be without profit even in the sphere of religion, I should neither at the outset have undertaken the task of delivering these lectures, nor have decided now to publish them.

I fear too, that I may be blamed for undue delay in their publication: but they needed long and careful revision: and if at length they are free—would that I could think so—of any serious blemishes, I should wish my readers to give the whole credit of that to a dear friend, well skilled himself in these literary studies, who has been generous enough to burden a life which has tasks enough of its own with the further task of correcting my mistakes.

[...]

Lecture 1

The mind indeed, oppressed and overcome by a crowd of great thoughts, pressing in upon it at one and the same time, knew not where to turn, and sought for some such relief and solace for itself as tears give to the worn-out body. And this is to feel the same craving as I ascribed to men torn by violent passion; but there was this difference, the latter shrunk, through shame, from any speech: the former feeling is higher and nobler, and therefore is neither able nor willing to be expressed in the speech of daily life.

I say therefore that that Almighty Power, which governs and harmonizes, not heaven and earth only, but also the hearts of men, has furnished amplest comfort for sufferers of either kind in the gift of Poetry. I will not now take pains to consider what Poetry fully means: even were I able to define it exactly, this is not the fitting opportunity: there are two points only, and points which no one will traverse, which I should wish to be allowed to assume as axiomatic; the first, that Poetry, of whatever kind, is, in one way or other, closely associated with measure and a definite rhythm of sound: the second, that its chief aim is to recall, to renew, and bring vividly before us pictures of absent objects: partly it has to draw out and bring to light things cognate or similar to each object it represents, however slight the connexion may be; partly it has to systematize and explain the connexion between them: in a word, it is the handmaid to Imagination and Fancy. In both of these processes it exhibits, assuredly, wonderful efficacy in soothing men's emotions and steadying the balance of their mind. For while we linger over language and rhythm, it occupies our minds and diverts them from cares and troubles: when, further, it gives play to Imagination, summons before us the past, forecasts the future, in brief, paints all things in the hues which the mind itself desires, we feel that it is sparing and merciful to the emotions that seethe within us, and that, for a while, we enjoy at least that solace which Dido once fruitlessly craved, to her woe:

> a transient grace
> To give this madness breathing-space.[1]

But how can the needs of modest reserve, and that becoming shrinking from publicity before noticed, be better served than if a troubled or enthusiastic spirit is able to express its wishes by those indirect methods best known to poets? At all events, it is remarkable how felicitous are the outlets which minds moved by strong excitement, and aspiring by a kind of blind impulse to high ideals, have sometimes found for themselves, by following the leadings of measure and rhythm, as they first offered, like a labyrinthine clue. They needed, in fact, some clue to guide them amid a thousand paths to take the right, and this clue, as every one can see, scansion and measure, simply in themselves, are well able to supply.

Let us therefore deem the glorious art of Poetry a kind of medicine divinely bestowed upon man: which gives healing relief to secret mental emotion, yet without detriment to modest reserve: and, while giving scope to enthusiasm, yet rules it with order and due control. But while all unanimously acclaim its eminent efficacy in this regard, it has occurred to no one, as far as I know, to make use of this special feature as the starting-point for explaining the origin of Poetry, and as the means of dividing it into its various branches. Yet I think both that this can be done and done with advantage. And therefore I have decided, with such care and accuracy as in me lie, to make the attempt. The road is clear then, gentlemen, for me to develop my views such as they are, and commend them to your kind indulgence: I have myself experienced that indulgence on many occasions in the past, and it will, I know, never be denied to any one who may err simply through the failings of natural ability, not for lack of taking pains: and I earnestly beg and pray you to hear the speaker and to judge of what is said, with fair and generous mind.

[...]

Lecture 40

Since it is clear, or at least a probable hypothesis, that in the highest of all interests, on which alone depends the final happiness of the race of man, poetry was providentially destined to prepare the way for Revealed Truth itself, and to guide and shape men's minds for reception of still nobler teaching, it is consistent to see the same principle at work in what I may call less important departments of its influence I cling to the belief that, in each several age of the world, in each several region of the earth, true and genuine Poetry has, by its silent influence, fostered sincere and grave piety. We shall not readily find an instance of any state, provided indeed it enjoy the advantage of stable law and morality, which has changed its existing religious belief for a more serious and holier creed, unless the tone of its favourite poets has first undergone a change. And assuredly, wherever religion has been weakened, there men fall back into the condition in which our ancestors were before embracing Christianity. There is no reason, then, why they should not be raised gradually to a better life by the same means and method, namely, by a new order of Poetry.

For instance (to keep to our own country), remember that renowned circle of writers who flourished among ourselves in the time of Elizabeth. Was not the tone and temper of poets and of poetry such as, even though the writers were unconscious of it, exactly accorded with the healthier religious spirit which was destined to prevail in the reign of Charles? To particularize—Shakespeare, the greatest of them all, the delight of all the world, especially of young England, did he effect nothing, who sometimes by jest, sometimes by bitter satire, lashed chiefly those very mischiefs which, in the age immediately following, were to work such, fatal harm in our State? Who always seems to be in his best and happiest mood when some hypocrite in religion or some disloyal subject is being put to shame. And did not the youth who grew up in studious love of Spenser enter with well-prepared minds into the contest with those turbulent foes who were wont to assail royal ladies and priests of religion with insult and abuse?

I say nothing of another fact, which nevertheless must have had great influence; on the one side we see men who estimate all things after a certain inborn sense of right and fitting; and, on the other, those who, like all the Epicurean school, look for some visible and material gain from every action. Now the noble poems of Shakespeare and Spenser had not merely taught men to shun the multitude, but, much more important, lifted their minds to piety and religion: for each of them always tests what can be seen by reference to a standard of heavenly truth, whether he is treating of the deeds and affairs of men or the splendid charm of earth and sky: and this has always been the chief aim of the Catholic Church, though after her own mystical and lofty fashion. And so, in this respect also I should hold that splendid harvest of great poems to have led the way to a sounder religious belief.

Thus much as to the fact itself: let us now briefly consider the causes of it. For it is hard to believe that these two—Poetry and Theology—would have proved such true allies unless there was a hidden tie of kinship between them; nor could we possibly place a nobler crown upon our whole work, than by briefly developing the essential principle and quality which they have in common.

And here, as so often before, we must go back to the very beginning and foundation of all Poetry. Our conclusion was, that this divine art essentially consisted in a power of healing and restoring overburdened and passionate minds. It follows that the more deeply any feeling penetrates human affections, and the more permanently it influences them, the closer are its relationships and associations with Poetry. Now, partly the very nature of religion in itself, partly the actual confession of all who can be supposed to have the faintest sense of true piety, impress on us the fact that nothing takes such entire possession of the human heart, and, in a way, concentrates its feeling, as the thought of God and an eternity to come: nowhere is our feeble mortal nature more conscious of its helplessness; nothing so powerfully impels it, sadly and anxiously, to look round on all sides for remedy and relief. As a result of this, Religion freely and gladly avails itself of every comfort and assistance which Poetry may afford: such as the regularity, the modulations, the changes of rhythm; the use of language sometimes restrained, sometimes eager and passionate; and all those other methods which all men feel after, but only a few can express. Moreover, a true and holy religion will turn such aids to the fullest account, because it, most of all, feels itself overwhelmed in the presence of the boundless vastness of the Universe: and this is so both when in early days, before Truth itself was fully revealed, simple untrained races were being taught by some dim outlines and types, and when more advanced believers are being trained to find utterance and language worthy to express their gratitude for God's great mercies to them.

Moreover, from this common weakness there springs a common use of this external world and of all objects which appeal to the senses. And in this regard it is marvellous how Piety and Poetry are able to help each other. For, while Religion seeks out, as I said, on all sides, not merely language but also anything which may perform the office of language and help to express the emotions of the soul; what aid can be imagined more grateful and more timely than the presence of Poetry, which leads men to the secret sources of Nature, and supplies a rich wealth of similes whereby a pious mind may supply and remedy, in some sort, its powerlessness of speech; and may express many things more touchingly, many things more seriously and weightily, all things more truly, than had been possible without this aid? Conversely, should we ask how, pre-eminently, 'came honour and renown to prophetic bards and their poems,'[2] it is Religion that has most to be thanked for this. For, once let that magic wand, as the phrase goes, touch any region of Nature, forthwith all that before seemed secular and profane is illumined with a new and celestial light: men come to realize that the various images and similes of things, and all other poetic charms, are not merely the play of a keen and clever mind, nor to be put down as empty fancies: but rather they guide us by gentle hints and no uncertain signs, to the very utterances of Nature, or we may more truly say, of the Author of Nature. And thus it has come to pass, that great and pre-eminent poets have almost been ranked as the representatives of religion, and their sphere has been treated with religious reverence. In short, Poetry lends Religion her wealth of symbols and similes; Religion restores these again to Poetry, clothed with so splendid a radiance that they appear to be no longer merely symbols, but to partake (I might almost say) of the nature of sacraments.

There is, too, another strong tie of kinship which binds these two together, in that each is controlled by a tone of modest and religious reserve. For, on the one hand, all who carefully try to imitate Nature are forced to observe a certain restraint and reserve: at least thus far, that, like her, they approach each stage of beauty by a quiet and well-ordered movement, not suddenly or, to use a mathematical phrase, *per saltum* (as do those who have no scruple in appearing boldly in public); and, on the other hand, the whole principle of piety, such at least as is wisely governed, is ordered by the rule divinely laid down in Holy Scripture, that things of highest worth should, for the most part, not be offered to listless and unprepared minds; but only be brought into the light when the eyes of those who gaze on them have been disciplined and purified. Thus the controlling Power which tempers and orders all things has compelled each, by a kind of decree, not to permit any one to have full fruition of the beauteous form and features of Truth, except his devotion be such as leads him to take zealous pains to search her out. Certainly no one who has been trained in this principle from his earliest years and into whose mind it has sunk deeply will ever allow himself to expose the sacred mysteries either of Nature or Religion to public view without regard to the temper and training of his hearers. He would rather be charged with obscureness than pour forth all truths, secret and open alike, without restraint; he would rather be criticized as wanting in ability than wanting in reserve.

Lastly, both in Poetry and in Religion, an indefinably tender and keen feeling for what is past or out of sight or yet to come, will ever assert and claim a high place of honour for itself. For those who, from their very heart, either burst into poetry, or seek the Deity in prayer, must needs ever cherish with their whole spirit the vision of something more beautiful, greater and more lovable, than all that mortal eye can see. Thus the very practice and cultivation of Poetry will be found to possess, in some sort the power of guiding and composing the mind to worship and prayer: provided indeed the poems contain nothing hurtful either to religion or morality.

I think we have now shown ample reason for believing that, since the relationships between Poetry and Religion are so close and so varied, it was by no mere accident, but by divine providence, that the former has often paved and prepared the way for the latter. And it follows that whatever is wont to corrupt and undermine Religion will to a great degree correspond with that which injures and degrades poets and poetry. For men may either praise in their poems things unworthy: and this may be compared with the error of those who make gods of earthly and perishable things: or they may praise worthy things not whole-heartedly, but rather out of imitation and fashion: and this is, as you know, the most discreditable of all faults in matters of piety or religion. Such men are called hypocrites, the term being borrowed from the stage: and hence we may infer that as these have only the empty show of virtue, so the others have only an empty form of Poetry, and that each is very far indeed from the reality.

Now as the faults in the two are so much alike, we may well consider whether the remedy will not be much the same in each case. In each the most important precept is this: be on your guard against the belief that anything is effected by mere admiration, without effort and action on your own part. No poet will ever be great who does not constantly spend time and toil in studying the beauty of earth and sky so as to make every detail of the whole bear upon the object, of his own love and enthusiasm: nor will any one make the slightest progress in holiness and piety who is content with the empty praises of good books or good men and makes no attempt to imitate them in his own life. In the second place, when a man has once chosen the field of work for which his true bent best fits him, let him keep bravely and persistently to it; let him not, by restlessly flitting from subject to subject, waste his powers and fail of all result: and, most important of all, let him not stain good with evil, pure with impure. These are the mottoes for those who aim either at being wise men in life or at winning renown in literature as poets. To both alike will apply the saying, 'put your whole heart into what you are doing': let it be something simple and clearly defined, something for which eye and mind will be on the watch at all times.

But on so well known a theme I am afraid that I may easily weary you by saying too much, and, indeed, I am under some apprehension that the same criticism may be made upon the greater part of these lectures. And so, at length to place some sort of crown upon the whole work, and at the same time not to end without a word of happy augury and a kindly hope—that would indeed be very unfitting in one whom, unworthy as he is, you have so highly honoured and with whose imperfect performance you have borne so indulgently—this one thing I desire to impress upon, and commend to all my younger hearers.

Only then will Poetry be fitly followed and studied, when those who love it remember that it is a gift to mankind, given that, like a "high-born handmaid, it may wait upon and minister to true Religion; and therefore it is to be honoured, not with lip-service, but really and truly, with all modesty, constancy, and purity. On this wholly depends the hope we venture to cherish to-day, that, in years to come, that deeper loftier note of Poetry which has for so many years been sounded in our ears may have good fruit and issue to the happy increase of those studies which are peculiarly termed Divine. May God grant, if this may perchance be His own will, that it be not hindered, even in the smallest degree by fault or failure on the part of any one of us!

Notes

1 *Aen.* iv. 433 (Conington).
2 Hor. *A. P.* 400.

28 The Role and the Treatment of Emotion in Victorian Criticism of Poetry (1977)

Isobel Armstrong

My subject is the Victorians' *feelings* about the feelings in poetry, the emotions they liked and the emotions they did not like. They believed in the expression of emotion in poetry—theoretically, at least—and needed to see emotion as the fundamental of poetic experience for poet and reader alike. And yet they had a very powerful distrust of emotion. In this paper I shall look at the significance of this divided feeling about emotion, and this will lead me to consider a connection, frequently made in Victorian criticism, between feeling correctly (or what the Victorians considered to be correctly) and seeing the external world accurately. My examination of the connection between feeling and seeing leads me on to consider the idea of imagery developed by critics, and so one arrives at a theory of symbol latent in Victorian criticism, a theory which in some ways resembles modern conceptions of symbol, but which was never fully developed. There were, I shall suggest, psychological and religious reasons which together provided a check on an aesthetic conception of symbol. Though the Victorians had all the theoretical equipment for it to do so, the idea of symbol such as we know did not emerge in the mid-nineteenth century.

[...]

The Victorians were not like us, but they worried about some of the same things. Hence our confusions and conflations. It is right to be aware of the large continuities of thought, but the emphases fall in very different places for the nineteenth and twentieth centuries. As my discussion of the treatment of emotion by critics of *In Memoriam* is in the context of an unexplored potential conception of symbol in the mid-nineteenth century it is as well to remind oneself of these differences from the start. The most manageable way of doing this is to group together a number of nineteenth and twentieth-century statements expressing some of the ideas which gather round the notion of symbol. These statements, about feeling and thought, particularity, image-making, can stand as touchstones for nineteenth and twentieth-century positions. My paper explores the reasons for the differences of emphasis.

First, Arthur Hallam and Lawrence. Hallam, in his famous review of Tennyson's *Poems, Chiefly Lyrical* (*Englishman's Magazine,* August, 1831), makes the post-Romantic distinction between head and heart, feeling and thought, a primal, pre-lapsarian organic response to life and art, and a fragmented response, the product of an "overcivilised condition of thought". Lawrence makes the same distinction but takes sides, assuming that the split is irreparable in our "idea-rotten", "spirit-rotten" society, and asks for the mass of people an education which *must* be "symbolical, mythical, dynamic".[1] Lawrence is against the mind, for the emotions. Hallam clearly feels that intellect and emotion *could* work harmoniously together, but only in ideal conditions now irreparably lost to us.

But repentance is unlike innocence; the laborious endeavour to restore has more complicated methods of action, than the freedom of untainted nature. Those different powers of poetic disposition, the energies of Sensitive, of Reflective, of Passionate Emotion, which in former times were intermingled, and derived from mutual support an extensive empire over the feelings of men, were now restrained within separate spheres of agency. The whole system no longer worked harmoniously, and by intrinsic harmony acquired external freedom; but there arose a violent and unusual action in the several component functions, each for itself, all striving to produce the regular power which the whole had once enjoyed.[2]

The primal consciousness in man is pre-mental, and has nothing to do with cognition. It is the same as in the animals. And this pre-mental consciousness remains as long as we have the powerful root and body of our consciousness. The mind is but the last flower, the *cul-de-sac*.[3]

Another pair: G. H. Lewes and T. E. Hulme: G. H. Lewes describes the "Principle of Vision" in the articles he began to contribute to the *Fortnightly* in 1865, "The Principles of Success in Literature". Lewes argues for vividness and particularity of image (using the word in a sense half way between description and metaphor). He is refuting Burke's suggestion that a drawing succeeds in raising emotion in proportion as it sacrifices clarity and distinctness. T. E. Hulme argues for the concreteness of images so that "in the realm of emotions you get imagination". Both writers reject a language which only produces "vanishing apparitions" (Lewes), "gliding through an abstract process" (Hulme), but Hulme's position is more extreme. Lewes thinks that words create pictures, but words are *signs* for things. There may be an intimate relationship between a sign and an object but there is nevertheless a distinct distance between words and the things to which they refer, a necessary severance created both by the psychological facts of perception and by the nature of language. Hulme, on the other hand, comes close to making language melt into experience. Words have an autonomous life because they *are* the experiences they describe and not signs for it. They do not make "an image [that is, picture in the mind] of the object", as Lewes says; they *are* the object, handing over "sensations bodily".

A work is imaginative in virtue of the power of its images over our emotions ... an artist produces an effect in virtue of the distinctness with which he sees the objects he represents, seeing them not vaguely as in vanishing apparitions, but steadily, and in their most characteristic relations ... . Note [of the description preceding the skating episode in *The Prelude*] how happily the one image, out of a thousand possible images by which November might be characterised, is chosen to call up in us the feeling of a lonely scene; and with what delicate selection the calm of summer nights, the "trembling lake" (an image in an epithet), and the gloomy hills, are brought before us ... . Instead of presenting us with an image of the object, they [poets, unlike Wordsworth] present us with something which they tell us is like the object—which it rarely is.[4]

Poetry ... is not a counter language, but a visual concrete one. It is a compromise for a language of intuition which would hand over sensations bodily. It always endeavours to arrest you, and to make you continuously see a physical thing, to prevent you gliding through an abstract process. It chooses fresh epithets and fresh metaphors ... [5]

Lastly, Keble and Yeats: Keble argues for the simultaneously compound experience that a non-literal or poetic reading of the Bible constitutes. Three Bibles, not one, emerge when we read on literal, moral and imaginative levels. (Though sometimes we have to abandon the literal meaning.) He points to the "complexity" of symbolic reading. Yeats describes the multiform "flickering" power of symbol, of emotions and associations which are continually re-combined and expressed in unique combinations of colour, sound and form. Both writers say that the fusion of a number of different symbols creates another, unique symbol and both say that the components of this new symbol have known and familiar associations which are absorbed into the fresh, unifying synthesis of experience which the symbol creates. However, Keble's analogy for this process, the combination of small items such as letters into larger units such as syllables and words is very much more static than Yeats' metaphor for symbol. Yeats chooses the flickering, mobile irradiation of light. For Yeats, symbol seems to transform, change and re-create significances in a way which is less fixed and invariable than for Keble. He says later that symbol is a continual "making and unmaking of mankind" which gives to symbol an autonomy and generative force which Keble does not seem to envisage.

> ... the manner in which, not seldom, the primary and simple ones [symbols] among them are varied and combined, as letters are combined into syllables, words, and sentences, retaining each somewhat of their original sound; or rather, as those compound derivatives which are made up of significant terms, each term modified, not changed, in its import.[6]

> ... take some line that is quite simple, that gets its beauty from its place in a story, and see how it flickers with the light of the many symbols that have given the story its beauty, as a sword-blade may flicker with the light of burning towers.
> All sounds, all colours, all forms, either because of their preordained energies or because of long association ... become, as it were, one sound, one colour, one form, and evoke an emotion that is made out of their distinct evocations and yet is one emotion.[7]

One could create innumerable such juxtapositions, though one does not really feel comfortable with them if they are made, in order to stress similarities rather than differences. But that would be to indulge in what one writer has called selective Victorianism. How, then, do discussions of feeling and seeing, of emotion and vision in *In Memoriam,* help to explain the Victorian refusal to pursue the symbolic implications of their theory?

In the first place, it is remarkable how frequently the word "calm", or words suggesting the same quality, turn up as an approving epithet. To extract this satisfaction, the reading of emotion in *In Memoriam* must have been highly selective, to say the least. (The complaints of monotony, weariness, repetition, are surely negative responses to the same selective reading.)

> ... the calmness of a settled and not overwhelming sorrow: settled equipoise ...
> (John Forster, *Examiner,* June 8, 1850, p. 356).[8]

> thoughts ... which flow in tranquil currents ...
> (*Britannia,* June 29, 1850, p. 410).

> ... that gentle mood of soul ...
> (*Christian Reformer,* N.S., VI [1850], 438).

... like a clearing sky ...

(Patmore, *Palladium,* 1 August 1850, p. 96).

... tenderness ... intellectual grace ... happy naiveté

(Gerald Massey, *Christian Socialist,* II [1851], 140).

The greatest heights are the fairest; the most universal minds the serenest, most healthful ... a calmly attuned voice ... the calm of a deep-toned landscape

(*Eclectic Review,* N.S., XXVIII [1850], 331, 335).

that sweet quiet pathos ... a holy pathos, which melts on the heart like dew

(*English Review,* XIV [1850], 80, 83).

One is reminded of the "calm veracity" Ruskin required of the poet who refused to indulge in the "pathetic fallacy", and of Arnold's 1853 Preface—"the calm, the cheerfulness, the disinterested objectivity ... ". One is reminded, indeed, of the high seriousness of the later touchstones (the *Eclectic* reviewer wrote of the "high earnestness" of *In Memoriam*). Arnold talked of Hawtrey's translation of the *Iliad* in *On Translating Homer* and described the reference to the death of Castor and Pollux (which became the first of the touchstones), as "suffused with a pensive grace", and the description might well have been used by an approving critic of *In Memoriam.*[9] Many critics questioned the morality of the revelation of feeling in *In Memoriam* and it is as if, to be acceptable, the emotion which was "overheard" (in Mill's definition of poetry), or which had what Lewes called the essential "nakedness" of true sincerity, could only be exposed if it possessed a kind of transparent serenity, limpidity, composure. It could not be raw, violent, messy, disturbing (in fact, most of the things one might reasonably expect of the expression of feeling).

One of the commonest words in critical vocabulary at this time is "deep", used so commonly and with such naturalness that it is almost imperceptible as a critical term. And naturally enough, critics tend to think of emotion in terms of the dead metaphor of flow, current, springs, wells, outlet, just as Wordsworth did when he talked of the spontaneous "overflow" of feeling. But now the "overflow" of feeling has to be controlled in proportion to its depth or even suppressed before it *can* overflow. Keble repeatedly talks of emotion in terms of flow and depth, as something necessarily "hidden" and "secret" (two of his favourite words, and used also by Mill in the phrases quoted at the beginning of this paper), and necessarily, inaccessible.

The theological notion of reserve comes to Keble's rescue as a solution to this psychological problem. Emotion can be expressed by "those indirect methods best known to poets": it can be displaced "without detriment to modest reserve" on to "particular places" so that these evoke emotion or constitute a sign or substitute for it.[10] Later on he says that poetry and religion are alike because they deal with deep feelings which are difficult to express, so that both use "this external world" and "all objects which appeal to the senses" as a symbolic language with which to express feeling.[11] A number of critics of *In Memoriam* concur in seeing the external world, the world of sense, as a means, if not of finding an objective equivalent for states of feeling, at least as a way of externalising emotion by allowing it to modify or mediate things seen with its peculiar qualities. Many of them praise the beauty of Tennyson's descriptions—"exquisite description" and "literal transcripts", as the *Inquirer* has it (June 22, 1850, p. 389)—and some go further and admire the "faculty of vision", distinctness of description, because it allows the external world to mirror states of feeling.

Interestingly, however, they admire such distinctness because it seems to stabilise, fix and anchor emotions in the palpable and concrete. It is a reassuring corroboration of being. It is a guarantee against an unfixed, self-enclosed and disorganised subjectivity. The external world is, as Arnold said of poetry much later, a consolation and a *stay*. To "apprehend" the "object", Stephen Daedalus says, when he talks about the idea of epiphany in *Stephen Hero,* "you must lift it away from everything else".[12] He speaks as if "the object" can only be contemplated if it is first unfixed, made contextless as far as the external world is concerned, and released into a dimension of pure aesthetic being. States of feeling "lifted away from everything else", objects "lifted away from everything else", will not do for most Victorian critics. Such autonomy would be too threatening. On the other hand, accurate description of the external world validates feeling because it is a bond between self and world. Notice how the word image, when it is used in the following passages of criticism of *In Memoriam,* hovers between meaning external picture and internal picture and comparison. It is as if critics did not wish to give up the anchor of the external world (though, interestingly, "image" in discussions of the psychology of perception seem to be used in the sense of an internal picture).[13]

> Creative sorrow [makes] ideal analogies to itself ... in familiar life ... . the capabilities of the *Actual* ... direct transcript of such [Nature] is developed by the poet's clear sight and artistic mastery, into the poetic and ideal ... *Definiteness* is with Tennyson an unfailing and remarkable part of his power. Every image, thought, picture, is rounded off into the objective. The most spiritual matters are brought within view. There is no verbal mystery ... clear is his sight
>
> (*Eclectic,* pp. 335–6).

> ... the subtlety of reflections and nobleness of thought which informs its fresh and graceful imagery ...
>
> (*Examiner,* p. 357).

> ... the heart should be opened ... the imagination should be suffered to dwell on the pictures indicated ... It is no new thing for the fancy of the poet to find in the outward world numerous echoes or representations that give back or image his inward feeling ...
>
> (*British Quarterly Review*, XII [1850], 292).

> The various aspects under which the poet contemplates his bereavement, suggest to him many charming pictures, and ideal resemblances drawn from the beaten path of human life, full of exquisite truth and beauty
>
> (*Sharpe's London Journal,* XII [1850], 120).

> [Emotion in *In Memoriam* is] noble [because it is free from] self-consciousness ... the outward world exists only as a magazine of symbols for revealing the inner world of man
>
> (Coventry Patmore, *North British Review*, XIII [1850], 551).

These passages are, of course, very much less interesting formulations of Hallam's wonderfully sensitive account of Tennyson's "picturesque" poetry. I would prefer to call these accounts "picturesque" rather than using Ruskin's term "pathetic fallacy" because I think that Ruskin's discussion in Volume III of *Modern Painters* is crude and oversimplified. He sees as mere personification the habit of investing the external world with human feeling it does not possess. Though his discussion is another important example of the distrust of emotion I have been exploring, he is too question-begging and dogmatic about "the difference between the ordinary, proper, and true appearances of things to us; and the extraordinary, or false appearances, when we are under the influence of emotion [like alcohol], or contemplative fancy; false appearances, I say, as being entirely unconnected with any real power or character in the object, and only imputed to it by us".[14] Hallam carefully protects his theory against unfixed subjectivity. States of feeling do indeed modify and transform the world, take it into themselves, turn it into metaphor—"the circumstances of the narration [i.e. its context] seem to have a natural correspondence with the predominant feeling, and, as it were, to be evolved from it by assimilative force". But then, unlike Ruskin, Hallam repeats his statement in reverse, moving not from internal state to external world but from external world to internal state. It is as if the "vivid, picturesque delineation of objects ... *fused* ... in a medium of strong emotion" provides a check on the subjectivity implied in the first statement. The intense particularity of external objects is not *evolved* from a state of mind but evokes emotion for itself. This is the very reverse of the symbolic "paysage intérieur" which McLuhan claims is prefigured in this review.[15] On the contrary, it is the "paysage extérieur" which carries feeling and protects it against its own return into the self. It does not stand for the complexities of inner feeling but is the object of out-going feeling, of the "energetic principle of love for the beautiful".

This is a psychological theory, then, but it pulls against a modern interpretation of symbol because it attempts to tether and stabilise both emotions and objects. Significantly, reviewers of spasmodic poetry do not attack the expression of feeling in itself but they claim that the feelings have taken on a violently diseased subjectivity approaching madness, a subjectivity which is always linked with the spasmodics' failure to create coherent images. The attack on the spasmodics, in fact, is almost invariably on their imagery, on a "monomaniac" disorganisation which leads to their "pouring forth floods of images and conceits" (W. E. Aytoun, *Blackwood's*, LXXV [1854], 349).[16] Aytoun made three hostile criticisms of the spasmodics before his parody, *Firmilian,* appeared, in which he makes a frontal attack as much on the unfixed cosmic metaphor in such poetry as on its morality. "You cannot tell what they would be at. You have a confused recollection of stars, and sunbeams, and moonbeams ... " (*Blackwood's, loc. cit.,* p. 534). They are images and states of feeling, in the words of Joyce, "lifted away from everything else". As one would expect, Patmore complained that "abstruse research" into the self and the "introverted vision" of such poets meant that "the out-flowing tides of feeling are checked and forced back" into the self (*North British Review,* XXVIII [1858], 238, 239, 237), so that the poet does not *see* clearly. It is not the poet's function to seek for beauty in his own mind which he then "confers on outer objects"; "The poet is, or should be, more of a seer of what God has already created, than a creator in the workshop of his own mind" (p. 231).

It is Kingsley who puts the matter most forcibly in *Fraser's Magazine,* XLVIII [1853], 452–466: the "tawdry spangles" (p. 454), the "vague and confused", "pancosmic metaphors" (p. 459) are caused by a self-regarding dislocation ("see what a highly organised and peculiar stomach-ache I have had") of the poet from the external world and *therefore* from God. The difference between diseased conceits and true images is

> that while both are analogies, the image is founded on an analogy between the essential properties of two things—the conceit on an analogy between its accidents. Images, therefore, whether metaphors or similes, deal with laws; conceits with private judgments

... Let it [poetry] set forth a real intercommunion between man and Nature, grounded on a communion between man and God, who made nature (pp. 462, 463).

Theological language is a bulwark against cosmic and psychological dislocation. Analogies, it seems, are *fixed*,—immovable: they have laws. This, for Kingsley, is a guarantee of sanity. So long as the natural world is given a "factitious life" (p. 461) from the poet and is regarded as mere phenomena for the sensations, poetry will move towards false passion and madness. "Real" passion, on the other hand (and we are back with the kinds of statement used of *In Memoriam*) is a paradoxical state in which "the very violence of the emotion produces perfect simplicity as the hurricane blows the sea smooth" (p. 461)—an extraordinarily idiosyncratic way of thinking of storm and upheaval, even if it is scientifically correct.

The impressive thing about the spasmodic controversy is the critics' willingness to debate *literary* qualities, qualities which stem from incoherence of feeling. The innumerable descriptions of the lawlessness, morbidity and madness of spasmodic poetry ("rant", "Bedlam, epilepsy, lunatic", are words used) were not, however, wholly metaphorical. Even in defending these poets the Coleridgean Gilfillan uses the vocabulary of lunacy. There is a persistent connection of the expression of emotion with insanity. "My brain is whirling like a potter's wheel", says Firmilian (*Blackwood's*, LXXV [1854], 550). It is interesting that Maudsley talks of a clinical category, *Neurosis Spasmodica*, in *The Physiology and Pathology of Mind* (1857), and describes the "tyranny of bad organisation" in language which coincides with the language of literary criticism current in the period.[17]

Dobell's lecture "On the Nature of Poetry" (1857) was obviously written with the attacks on spasmodic poetry in mind.[18] It is a systematic defence of metaphor (one of the most sophisticated Victorian accounts of metaphor I have read) as a symbolic equivalent of feeling and argues that metaphor *does* reconcile the mind and the external world, spirit with sense, the invisible with the visible; poetry *has* to be metaphorical. If the purpose of poetry is to express a mind, and if "To express is to carry out", then "To express a mind is to carry out that mind *into some equivalent*". Dobell is much more interested in what he calls the "indirect" or "compound" equivalents which create symbolic transformations of feeling than he is in the direct or simple expression of feeling ("As if, feeling love, I should say, 'I love'"). Language is the "vehicle" by which equivalents "can exist out of the mind" and language contains its own form of transformation within itself—metaphor. In fact, metaphor is the "law" or type of all poetic equivalents because in it one thing stands for another and the poem is therefore a "metaphor" of the mind which produced it[19] and ultimately a metaphor for God who is the perfect mind behind human minds.

With Dobell's essay one is back with Carlyle's preoccupation with the way in which Imagination plays into the "prose domain of sense". Dobell's terms are religious and psychological, but they are also aesthetic in a way which is unusual in Victorian criticism. I have talked so far about the pull away from an aesthetic view of symbol exerted by psychological accounts of feeling and seeing. There is a moral fear of mental disequilibrium. But one should not forget that the need to see the external world as a fixing and stabilising of feeling and the resistance to an autonomous, mobile "making and unmaking of mankind" in free-floating symbol was reinforced by religious conceptions of symbol which were very important to the Victorians. So there was a double check against the release of the object into untethered aesthetic being. I have already quoted Kingsley talking of the fixed laws of analogy: if one returns for a moment to discussions of *In Memoriam*, one finds that critics' accounts of the external world as analogue for psychological states often hover between a discussion of the psychological significance of "images" and "pictures" and the function of pictures and images as signs or emblems of spiritual ideas. Images or pictures have a religious significance because they express spiritual realities through the actual. It is worth remembering that *In Memoriam* was on the whole regarded as a religious poem, whether it was seen as a successful or unsuccessful religious work. There were exceptions to this interpretation—George Eliot's was one—but God is somewhere about, though He may have disappeared from the world: "it is a great proof of the depth, sincerity and simplicity of a man's faith when each sect of religion claims him as his own. The compliment becomes a little too extensive when sceptical philosophy puts in its claim as well" (Coventry Patmore, *Edinburgh Review,* CII [1855], 563).

There is a rather uncertain movement between psychological and spiritual or theological interpretations of Tennyson's "touching symbols, so many answering relationships ... " (*British Quarterly,* p. 292). The *Eclectic* reviewer (a confused discussion, this, but interesting because it is confused) uses the word "ideal" in a hazy way, and by his own testimony, talks loosely of a "vague" feeling for "the might of love, and the glory of Nature, and the majesty of life, and our human affinities with greatness" (p. 332): the union of "ideal and real", "objective beauty, such as spontaneously springs to the poet's footstep in traversing the realms of deep [emotional? spiritual?] and searching experience" (p. 333): "the real is steeped in the ideal of poetry" (p. 335): the poet's "clear sight" leads to "the poetic and ideal" (p. 336).

Nearer the point: "intensely English scenery"; "strivings to connect the seen and the unseen" (Forster, *Examiner,* p. 356); "analogies of moral beauty", though Tennyson fails to accept the "higher consolations" of religion (*Britannia,* p. 410); Tennyson respects the "dignity of Nature", seeing it with the clarity of the mystic (hence the accusations of transcendental mysticism), yet he has also discovered (back to Hallam's position) "new modes of viewing Nature" associated with his "new speculations on man" (Kingsley, *Fraser's Magazine,* XLII [1850], 246, 248); art has laws "as the same with those of religious life" because both poetry and religion are "sacred": subjectivity is turned on its head and called "the sacred expediency of self-sacrifice", so that the "symbols" which portray the "inner world of man" become spiritual symbols. What is required is a therapeutic release from the "loathsome independent life" of morbid feeling into spirituality (Patmore, *North British Review,* XIII [1850], 533, 551–2).

Such discussions enable us to move to a larger view of the relationship between art and religion in Victorian criticism. Keble felt that the affinity between poetry and religion makes for a wonderful interchange. Poetry provides religion with a language by going to the secret sources of Nature, religion gives poetry sanction by making Nature divine:

> In short, Poetry lends Religion her wealth of symbols and similes: Religion restores these again to Poetry, clothed with so splendid a radiance that they appear to be no longer merely symbols, but to partake (I might almost say) of the nature of sacraments.[20]

What he "almost" says in the Oxford lectures he really does say in Tract 89. Everyone has his own private poetry by making associations between his feelings and the works of nature. But our Lord has a "Poetry of His own" (p. 144) in which the visible necessarily embodies the invisible and there is a strict correspondence between "the words visible and invisible".[21] He invokes the "notion of a *Type*" (my italics) and transfers it to the world of sense.[22] Light visible is therefore the natural Type of God manifesting himself by his Son "as Isaac on the mountain was a historical Type of Our Lord yielding himself to death on the cross". And these Types have an invariably consistent significance. They are *fixed* and static and their "fixedness" guarantees their authority. Such symbols are kept firmly inside a theological context and significance and are unalterable.[23] Compare this with the Yeatsian "making and unmaking" of mankind through symbol.

It is, of course, from the model of sacramental thinking (a sacrament is traditionally the outward sign of an invisible grace) that our aesthetic account of symbol is derived. In Victorian criticism one is confronted with the fascinating development of a psychological account of symbol coexisting with a religious one. Neither quite congeals into an aesthetic account of experience. Even Carlyle's secularised "infinite" is some way away from the "soul" of the Ballast Office Clock in *Stephen Hero*. Even very different critics—Dobell, Lewes, Kingsley—defer to a religious sanction for art. Although T. E. Hulme was to characterise romanticism as "spilt religion", we are here, in the Victorian period, still dealing with religion which has not yet "spilt": it has not yet been aestheticised, as it has in Joyce. It is no surprise that some of the most subtle accounts of symbol occur in the work of theological writers, and particularly in the work of High Church or Tractarian writers. Nor is it surprising that the often brilliant insights of these writers did not spill over into poetics. Stabilised by the authority of a structure of belief, they could be reassuring: loosened from a theological account of the world, they could move towards a relativism and freedom which was disturbing. Here is Wilberforce on the identity of the Church and Christ's mystical body.

> Every organised body has some mode of giving expression to that pervading principle which renders it whole. A tree puts forth leaves, animal life discovers itself by sound and motion … And if the Church be not a mere aggregation of men, who meet by accident … but the living exponent of a spiritual power which renders it Christ's mystical body, then that quickening energy with which it is instinct, must have some means of utterance.[24]

Here is Newman, arguing with wonderful subtlety about the implications of the word "presence", the "real" and not literal and local presence of the blood and body of Christ in the sacrament of Communion. He argues for the absoluteness of the sense of spiritual presence as against the relativeness of physical presence. But in stressing the paradoxical subjectivity of this absoluteness he opens up—perhaps more widely than he knew—the whole question of symbolic meaning. Subjectivity for him is anchored by belief in God. Without this anchor, however, we are back with the threatening self-isolation the Victorians worked so strenuously to counteract. He argues that our physical perception of things depends on our relative relationship to them in space and time.

> The *presence*, then, of a thing is a relative word … it is a word of degree … very different from this is the conception that we form of the presence of spirit with spirit. The most intimate presence we can fancy is a spiritual presence in the soul; it is nearer to us than any material object can possibly be; for our body, which is the organ of conveying to us the presence of matter, sets bounds to its approach towards us. If, then, spiritual beings can be brought near to us … their presence is something *sui generis*, of a more perfect and simple character than any presence we commonly call local. And further, their presence has nothing to do with degrees of nearness; they are either present or not present, or, in other words, their coming is not measured by space, nor their absence ascertained by distance. In the case of things material, a transit through space is the necessary condition of approach and presence; but in things spiritual, (whatever be the condition) such a transit seems not to be the condition. The condition is unknown.[25]

"The condition is unknown": it may be that a sense of the mystery and difficulty of symbol inhibited Victorian criticism. I may seem rather small-minded, perhaps, in refusing to see the nineteenth century as thrusting forward to our own, but it does seem appropriate to look backwards and to ask how far Victorian criticism really was, in Lawrence's words, "symbolical, mythical, organic". I've attempted to look at the first of these terms. It may be that this look backwards could help us to see what was actually happening in Victorian poetry. Was *that* "symbolical, mythical, organic"? (I suspect the poetry both does and doesn't accord with its criticism in interesting ways.) Finally, though perhaps one discovers some of the naiveté as well as the subtlety of criticism from my perspective, one does discover something that is often missing from contemporary criticism—a search to render the "feel" of feelings in poetry verbally. It is as if we have lost this responsiveness in proportion to our critical self-consciousness. One might not entirely assent to these accounts of Tennyson, but one is made vividly aware of some of his qualities, of Tennyson's curious combination of "dream-driven" imagination and small-mindedness:

> We may liken him to the sea-shell which, sitting complacently and undistinguished amid the common-place ornaments of the mantle-piece, has only to be lifted to give forth from its smooth ear the far-rugged boom of the oceanbreakers
> (George Gilfillan, *Tait's Edinburgh Magazine*, XIV [1847], 229);

of *In Memoriam:*

> nature seems to be reflected in the depths of a clear lake, its surface gently rippled with the "breath of emotion, making the picture softer, and almost fairer than the truth
> (Patmore, *Edinburgh Review*, CII [1855], 506),

Notes

1 D. H. Lawrence, *Fantasia of the Unconscious* (Harmondsworth: Penguin Books, 1971), p. 77 (first published 1923).
2 Arthur Hallam, "On Some of the Characteristics of Modern Poetry" (first published August 1831) in *Victorian Scrutinies,* ed. Isobel Armstrong (London: The Athlone Press, 1972), p. 91, Cf. Schiller, *On the Aesthetic Education of Man,* transl. and ed. E. M. Wilkinson and C. A. Willoughby (Oxford, 1967), pp. 31, 33: "At that first awakening of the powers of the mind, sense and intellect did not as yet rule over strictly separate domains; for no dissension had as yet provoked them into hostile partition and mutual demarcation of their frontiers ... It was civilisation itself which inflicted this wound upon modern man ... ".
3 *Fantasia of the Unconscious,* p. 34.
4 G. H. Lewes, *Principles of Success in Literature,* ed. T. Sharper Knowlson (London: Gregg, 1892), pp. 59, 62, 64, 66.
5 T. E. Hulme, *Speculations* (London, 1924, 2d ed., 1958), p. 134.
6 John Keble, *Tracts for the Times, Tract* 89, 2d ed. (London, 1842), p. 179.
7 W. B. Yeats, "The Symbolism of Poetry", in *Essays and Introductions* (London: Macmillan, 1961), pp. 156–7 (essay dated 1900).
8 Attributions of authorship of discussions of *In Memoriam* are taken from *The Wellesley Index to Victorian Periodicals,* vols. I and II, or (in the case of weekly reviews) from E. F. Shannon, Jr., *Tennyson and the Reviewers* (Cambridge, Mass.: Harvard Univ. Press, 1952).
9 For a fuller discussion of the critical values behind Arnold's "touchstones" (which also indirectly illuminates discussion of *In Memoriam*) see John S. Eells, Jr., *The Touchstones of Matthew Arnold* (New Haven: Yale Univ. Press, 1955).
10 John Keble, *Oxford Lectures on Poetry, 1832–1841,* transl. and ed. Kershaw Francis (Oxford, 1912), I, 22.

11 *Oxford Lectures on Poetry,* II, 481.

12 James Joyce, *Stephen Hero,* ed. Theodore Spencer, rev. ed. (London: Cape, 1956), p. 217. Stephen's remark occurs in his discussion of the epiphany and his account of Aquinas and his three requirements for beauty—integrity, symmetry and radiance: "Consider the performance of your own mind when confronted with any object, hypothetically beautiful. You mind to apprehend that object divides the entire universe into two parts, the object, and the void which is not the object. To apprehend it you must lift it away from everything else: and then you perceive that it is one integral thing, that is *a* thing. You recognise its integrity".

13 See Johannes Müller's account of the ways in which we must deduce the externality of world to self: "Of the Senses", in *Visual Perception: The Nineteenth Century,* ed. William Dember (London: Wiley, 1964), pp. 62–65.

14 *English Critical Essays (Nineteenth Century),* ed. E. D. Jones (Oxford, O.U.P., 1916; reprinted 1950), p. 325. Ruskin's discussion of the pathetic fallacy is in volume III, pt. 4 of *Modern Painters* (1856).

15 Arthur Hallam, "On some of the Characteristics of Modern Poetry", *Victorian Scrutinies,* p. 93. See Marshall McLuhan's discussion of this essay in *Critical Essays of the Poetry of Tennyson,* ed. John Killham (London: Routledge, 1960), pp. 67–85.

16 For a fuller discussion of Aytoun's part in the spasmodic debate see Hark A. Weinstein, *William Edmonstoune Aytoun and the Spasmodic Controversy* (New Haven: Yale Univ. Press, 1968).

17 "There is, in fact, some inherent instability of nervous element, whereby the mutual reaction of the nerve-cells in the higher walks of nervous function does not take place properly, *and due consent and co-ordination* of function is replaced by *irregular and purposeless independent* reaction outwards: there is, as it were, *a loss of the pure self-control* of the individual nerve-cell, an inability of *calm self-contained* activity, subordinate or coordinate, and its energy is dissipated *in an explosive display,* which, like the *compulsive action of the passionate man,* surely denotes an irritable weakness" (2d ed., 1868, p. 257, my italics).

18 Sydney Dobell, "Lecture on the Nature of Poetry" (1857), in *Thoughts on Art, Philosophy, and Religion,* ed. John Nichol (London, 1876).

19 "On the Nature of Poetry", pp. 13, 21, 34, 40.

20 Keble, *Oxford Lectures on Poetry,* II, 481.

21 Keble, *Tract 89,* p. 165.

22 *Ibid.,* p. 167.

23 *Ibid.,* p. 179. The notion that religion could borrow the language of poetry and poetry the language of religion so that works of imagination could be validated and sanctified does not seem to have been confined to Tractarian thinkers. Jowett wrote to Frances Newman in the following terms in 1861: "Might not more use be made of Scripture as the vehicle of expressing truth? Our own words are weak and powerless when words which are thousands of years old seem almost divine. The higher spiritual element both in the Old and the New Testament works upon the mind in a very different way from statements or sentiments of morality" (unpublished letter, Balliol papers).

24 Robert Isaac Wilberforce, *The Doctrine of the Incarnation* (1848), Ch. XII, in *The Oxford Movement,* ed. E. R. Fairweather (New York and Oxford, 1964), p. 310.

25 John Henry Newman, *Tracts for the Times, Tract 90,* sect. 8, "Trans-substantiation": in *Tract 90,* ed. A. W. Evans (London, 1933), pp. 68–69.

29 Joy and Aesthetics: Coleridge to Wilde (2007)

Adam Potkay

Wordsworth concludes *The Prelude* with a tribute to Coleridge for helping him attain an intellectual joy in Nature or God, balancing his late adolescent intuition of the "deep enthusiastic joy, / The rapture of hallelujah sent / From all that breathes and is" (13.261–63). But well before 1805 Coleridge had abandoned any belief he might have had in philosophic joy. He dismissed any hope for joy in his own life except for what he could find through imagining the immediate joys of others, especially beings very unlike himself – pure maidens and young children, or more particularly Sara Hutchinson and his first-born son, Hartley.[1] Pure joy, for Coleridge, must come without self-consciousness or philosophical baggage, and without the erotic longing he felt for Sara Hutchinson. And it must come through grace. Whereas Wordsworth sings the glad independence of vagrants, idiots, sapient beasts, and unruly children, as well as of the philosophic mind, Coleridge, by contrast, grants joy to God's fowls, God's fools, and Gospel-like children – especially the ones in his own backyard. Incapable of pure or immediate joy, Coleridge meditates on the mediation of joy – and, by extension, any emotion – in aesthetic production and reception. Indeed, the implicit message of Coleridge's art seems to be that aesthetic joy rises above, even as it registers nostalgia for, ordinary life. His poems of joy – I will focus on "This Lime-Tree Bower My Prison," "The Nightingale," and *Dejection: An Ode* – are also poems on what it means, sympathetically or imaginatively, to participate in another being's emotional life and yet to transcend that life in the very act of aesthetic mediation. Coleridge relies on the belief that there must be unmediated, unselfconscious life out there, but this life – which he later calls, anticipating Nietzsche, the Bacchic – serves in his poetry only as stuff for his own Minervan talent to work upon: "Bacchus expressed the organic energies of the Universe which work by passion – a joy without consciousness; while Minerva, &c., imported the preordaining intellect."[2] Coleridge's reader, in turn, becomes his collaborator in imagining Bacchic energies through the preordaining mind.

What is the self's fundamental experience of joy? Coleridge maintained that to some degree joy always dissipates one's *idea* of a self. The "deeper" a joy the more it "dims" the self's cognitive grasp of itself. Coleridge arrived at this insight through an ingenious reading, or strong misreading, of a line and a half from "Tintern Abbey":

– and the deep power of Joy
We see into the *Life* of Things –

i.e., By deep feeling we make our *Ideas dim* – & this is what we mean by our Life – ourselves. I think of the Wall – it is before me, a distinct Image – here. I necessarily think of the *Idea* & the Thinking I as two distinct & opposite Things. Now let me think of *myself* – of the thinking Being – the Idea becomes dim whatever it be – so dim that I know not what it is – but the Feeling is deep & steady – and this I call *I* – identifying the Percipient & the Perceived.[3]

In this 1801 meditation on "Tintern Abbey," Coleridge deflects Wordsworth's lines from their natural climax in "things" to emphasize "life" – not the life of things, but that of the percipient individual. Joy is the deep feeling that, dimming the idea of self, becomes the self.

Take this one step further: if the power of joy relates inversely to the clarity of idea, then pure joy would make one perfectly unclear about one's own thinking self. The deepest joy would be the joy that obliterates self-comprehension. This is de-individuating joy of a very different sort from Spinoza's joy in thinking clearly the way that God does, understanding the causal determinations of things (*The Ethics,* Part V). Coleridge had by 1801 passed beyond the rationalist philosophy of joy to which he introduced Wordsworth in 1797–98, probably within their "Spy-Nozy" talks.

Yet self-forgetful joy, prize it as he will, is something Coleridge rarely claims to feel. He once claims to have felt something like joy at a point in life when he was forgetting his earlier "thought" of millennial "joy and love" harbored in relation to the French Revolution. In "France: An Ode," written in March–April 1798 and originally published as "THE RECANTATION," Coleridge repudiated ever having "cherish'd / One [millenialist] thought," and contrasted vain intellection with an epiphany of "feeling" in nature, "among the winds" and "upon the waves." Coleridge concludes his poem by apostrophizing liberty along the English seashore:

And there I felt thee! On yon sea-cliffs verge,
Whose pines just travell'd by the breeze above,
Had made one murmur with the distant surge –
Yes! as I stood and gaz'd, my forehead bare,
And shot my being thro' earth, sea, and air,
Possessing all things by intensest love –
O LIBERTY! my spirit felt thee there!

There's an odic enthusiasm in these lines, but also an elegiac note in their evocation of joy in being. The chiasmus of "there I felt thee" and "felt thee there" lend further closure to a feeling that already seems to lie in a distant past; contrast the completion of Coleridge's joy to Wordsworth's use of the imperfect tense in "Tintern Abbey": "And *I have felt* / A presence that disturbs me with the joy / Of elevated thoughts … " Wordsworth speaks of a recurrent feeling, one with the potential of continuing on into the future, that prompts philosophic joy, while Coleridge consigns his thoughtless feeling to a moment in the past, a seashore snapshot.

To recompense joys lost, Coleridge lights on an aesthetic practice of sympathetic joy. Sympathetic joy is not in itself a new idea – along with sympathetic sorrow it became a hallmark of eighteenth-century sentimentality, the mark of the man (and only later the woman) of feeling from Parson Adams onwards. Laurence Sterne apostrophized in *A Sentimental Journey through France and Italy:* "Dear sensibility! source inexhausted of all that's precious in our joys, or costly in our sorrows! … that I feel some generous joys and generous cares beyond myself – all comes from thee, great – great SENSORIUM of the world! which vibrates, if a hair of our heads but falls upon the ground, in the remotest desert of thy creation."[4] Sterne's "sensibility" connects all humans in sympathetic sharing; it is the "sensorium" or divine switchboard through which all individual perceptions come together.

Yet while Sterne captivates with imagery, he leaves unanswered a basic question – what does it mean to rejoice or suffer with another person? Is it actually to share the other person's perception, or at least a dimmer version of that perception? That is, are joys and sorrows transferable or communicable? Or, alternatively, is sympathy an intellectual attitude towards another person's feeling – a mode of assessing and responding not only to what someone else might be feeling but also to whether or not that person deserves to feel that way? (The sufferings of a criminal tend, after all, to elicit less sympathy than those of an innocent victim.) Within eighteenth-century moral philosophy, Adam Smith advanced this latter notion of sympathy as intellectual attitude while David Hume propounded the former model of sympathy as perceptual sharing. Yet for Smith and Hume sympathy remained an element of ethics – neither applied it, at least systematically, to aesthetics.

Moreover, for Smith – as for Rousseau, and indeed for most sentimental literature of the eighteenth-century – sympathy meant, in practice, pity or compassion for the suffering of others rather than rejoicing in their joy. This served to keep the sympathetic imagination, for all its purely aesthetic potential, firmly tied to ethics. Rousseau held that the rules of natural right and the foundation of civic virtue originate in pity or compassion, emotions through which we sympathetically identify with beings in pain.[5] Smith defined sympathy as "our fellow-feeling with any passion whatever," but in practice he treats it chiefly as an empathetic attitude towards pain, sorrow, and "the dread of death, the great poison to happiness, but the great restraint upon the injustice of mankind." Joy, by contrast, is something of an ethical embarrassment for Smith: it is a "selfish passion," and any expression of "extravagant joy" incites "a sentiment of envy [that] commonly prevents us from heartily sympathizing" with the joyous person.[6] "We are generally most disposed to sympathize with small joys and great sorrows," Smith concludes in a sentence that reflects the literary practice of sentimentalism as it developed into the 1790s. Wordsworth's first published poem, *Sonnet on seeing Miss Helen Maria Williams weep at a Tale of Distress* (1787), chimes in with the sympathetic suffering then in vogue: "That tear proclaims – in thee each virtue dwells, / And bright will shine in misery's midnight hour."[7] The seventeen-year-old Wordsworth evidently sought to establish his ethical alongside his poetic credentials, showing his tender heart to be the taproot of his own virtue as well as his literary malleability. He would later abandon such modishness in favor of a dry-eyed focus on human joy, a theme he probably derived in good measure from Coleridge.

Coleridge, insofar as he treated sympathy with joy rather than sympathy with suffering, served to free the imagination from ethical service. What does it mean to rejoice with others? Coleridge, in describing his own vicarious emotion, suggests a definition of joy that is purely aesthetic, dissevered from the pursuit of the good: "sometimes / 'Tis well to be bereft of promis'd good, / That we may lift the soul, and contemplate / With lively joy the joys we cannot share." The lines are from "This Lime-Tree Bower my Prison" (July 1797), in which Coleridge imaginatively participates in a country walk with his house guests Mary and Charles Lamb, visiting from London, and William and Dorothy Wordsworth. Coleridge particularly addresses his friend Charles Lamb, conjuring his perceptions and his joy:

> Live in the yellow light, ye distant groves!
> And kindle, thou blue Ocean! So my Friend
> Struck with deep joy may stand, as I have stood,
> Silent with swimming sense; yea, gazing round
> On the wide landscape, gaze till all doth seem
> Less gross than bodily: and of such hues

> As veil the Almighty Spirit, when he makes
> Spirits perceive his presence.

The speaker imaginatively (re-)creates his friend's joy and expresses an attitude, itself joyous, towards it. The joy-inspiring beauty Coleridge imagines is roughly comparable to a Turner painting of sea vista dissolving into yellow light, though here the light is analogous to divinity. Charles's "deep joy" (which Coleridge does not unambiguously claim ever to have felt himself in his moments of silent standing) is in the de-limited and as-it-were divine natural scene. He becomes (like) a "spirit," perhaps an angel, as it takes an angel's heart "for full adequate sympathy with Joy" – to recall the quip in which Coleridge contrasted joy with merely ethical compassion ("for compassion a human Heart suffices").[8] The whole scene may be read as an allegory for the aesthetic and, from Shaftesbury to Schiller, its metaphysical underpinnings: through the consensual apprehension of beauty we intuit that a rational law or Logos pervades all things, and somehow fits them to us.[9]

The difference between the imagined joy of Charles Lamb and the speaker's own joyous attitude towards it is that the former is immediate, and the latter a self-conscious reflection on deliquescent consciousness. Charles's idea of self dims, his senses swim, the material world blurs into the divine: such is the joy Coleridge ordains for his friend. "This Lime-tree Bower my Prison" sets the Dionysian joy wished upon Charles against the speaker's own Minervan joy of aesthetic contemplation (as spectator of Charles-in-nature) and of artistic act (as maker of the poem). The "lively joy" of aesthetic contemplation is different from the emotional experience of joy, the joy he "cannot share," because in ordinary situations the cognitive object of joy is an unmediated experience (here, union with nature, fulfillment in beauty), while the object of aesthetic joy is primarily the beauty or admirableness of mimesis itself, of prospect and description, before any superadded pleasure the poet/reader might find empathetically through a character such as Charles is imagined to be, overflowing with joy. Of course, Coleridge's aesthetic joy depends upon the silence of the Lambs. Coleridge's poem is a one-sided conversation, an eloquent outpouring to an absent auditor. Charles's subjectivity becomes an object of contemplation only after first being created. Works of art don't speak back; friends, however, often do. In this case Charles complained to Coleridge of being mischaracterized as "gentle-hearted" in a poem he called "your *Satire* upon *me*."[10] Charles, generally uninterested in rural beauty, would prove himself a great singer of metropolitan joy, writing to Wordsworth: "I often shed tears in the motley Strand from fullness of joy at so much Life."[11] So much for gentle Charles hungering after nature "in the great city pent."

After "This Lime-Tree Bower" Coleridge projected joy onto others who couldn't answer back and accuse him of impropriety: birds, ideal maidens, and young children. Human joy in nature becomes the privilege of "purity," the boon of the carefree child and rightly circumstanced virginal maid, to be shared reflectively by the learned poet and his reading audience. The figures of the maiden and child enter together in "The Nightingale," a conversation poem from April–May 1798. Hartley is the "dear babe" upon whom Coleridge wishes joy in nature and especially in the song of the nightingale. The maiden of the poem is just that: "a most gentle Maid" who lives by an uninhabited castle and a grove full of nightingales. According to the speaker of "The Nightingale," the babe and the grove-maiden are open to the joy of the nightingale's song through blissful ignorance of a literary prejudice, prominent in Milton's *Penseroso,* that associates the bird with grief and melancholy.[12]

The ironies of Coleridge's poem are many: first, does either the silent maiden or babbling baby really find joy in the nightingale? All we have is the speaker's suggestion that they do, and they serve in his poem more as exemplar than as characters. Second, finding joy in a birdsong is structurally the same thing as finding melancholy there. With a wink to his readers, Coleridge exposes melancholy in nature as fallacious so that he may project joy there. A third irony in a poem that ostensibly sets natural observation above imitation of earlier authors is that its "gentle maid who dwelleth … hard by the castle" steps right out of literary romance. The dweller in nature is ever a literary construction.

Coleridge concludes with a prayer for infant Hartley: "But if that Heaven / Should give me life, his childhood shall grow up / Familiar with these songs, that with the night / He may associate joy!" The poem's final irony is that "these songs" are, besides those of the nightingale, a body of lyric poems stretching back to the twelfth century and extending to "The Nightingale." Coleridge almost surely knows – even his poetic speaker alludes to knowing – the alternative literary tradition in which the nightingale sings not of pain but of vernal and often amorous "joy." This tradition, presumably the "different lore" his speaker claims to have "learnt," stretches from the Provençal troubadours through the Minnesingers, whom Coleridge read in German during his residence in Göttingen (March–June 1799), and Petrarch, whom we know Coleridge to have read in Italian by 1804.[13] Although much of Coleridge's knowledge of Continental nightingale lore would be acquired after he wrote "The Nightingale" in the spring of 1798, he would at this early date have had some inkling of this poetic tradition through English literary echoes: in Chaucer, in Sidney, in Drayton, and in Milton himself, we find the "merry," "amorous-descanting" and "joy"-inspiring nightingale.[14]

In this tradition the nightingale – typically, as in Coleridge's poem, a *male* nightingale – expresses the joy of vernal nature and its fecundity. The nightingale incites the poet to sing and rejoice with it as far as he is able to do so, erotic relations among humans being fraught with perils (fear, jealousy, false rumors) unknown to birds. The topos of the joyous nightingale arose full-blown in the earliest troubadours, especially Bernart de Ventadorn, who employs the bird prominently in his poetic corpus.[15] In *"Amics Bernartz de Ventadorn,"* Bernart imagines being exhorted by a fellow troubadour: "Bernart de Ventadorn, my friend, how can you refrain from singing, when you hear the nightingale have such pleasures night and day? Hear the joy [*joi*] it expresses! It sings all day and night beneath the flower; it understands love better than you." Bernart answers, in the guise of a tired-out lover, "I prefer sleep and rest to the nightingale's voice." Another poem begins: "When the fresh grass and the leaves appear … and the nightingale lifts its high, clear voice and moves its songs, I have joy from him, and joy from the flower, and joy from me and greater joy from my lady." After this promising opening, however, the speaker complains he is "dying of grief," "consumed by desire," and yet afraid of seeming at all forward in the presence of his lady.

The nightingale's simple and inviting *joi* contrasts with the poet's complex emotion of sorrow and joy – a complex emotion that is itself sometimes called, in troubadour argot and the Siculo-Tuscan poetry it influenced, *joi* or *gioia,* the deferred desire more desirable than any immediate gratification. Bernart's counterpoint between the *simple joi* of birds and the more complex *jei* of human lovers persists, in a more lugubrious key, in the *Canzoniere* of Petrarch;[16] it extends as well to Book 4 of *Paradise Lost* (lines 736–75), in which Milton contrasts the post-coital bliss of an unfallen Adam and Eve, "lull'd by Nightingales," with the ills that beset *eros* after the Fall: "the bought smile/ Of Harlots, loveless, joyless, unindear'd, / Casual fruition … Court Amours." Courtiers in particular, but sinful humans more generally, have much to learn from the Edenic nightingale and the original couple over whom it presided.

In Bernart, in Petrarch, in Milton, and finally in Coleridge we find nightingales singing not with melancholy but with unselfconscious joy, a joy the poet might share more fully were he not fully human. Humans, for their part – especially male poets – are subject to flashes of hearing the joy of things, but more apt to project winter onto spring because of the inner turmoil that comes from unfulfilled and often misdirected erotic longing. In erotic suffering there may lie a type of mixed or adulterated joy, as Coleridge recognized in a 1803 notebook jotting concerning Asra: "Why we two made to be a Joy to each other, should for so many years constitute each other's melancholy – O! but the melancholy is Joy –."[17] But Coleridge's fullest meditation on the chances for pure joy, and the odds stacked against the learned poet, is *Dejection: An Ode* (1802, rev. 1817).

In the *Dejection* ode Coleridge resolves the ironies of "The Nightingale": the ode acknowledges that the source of joy as well as dejection is from within, and that each passion has the power to transform nature in its own image. This, too, is a trope from troubadour verse: as Bernart wrote, "My heart is filled with such joy / That it transfigures everything for me."[18] Joy, in "wedding" mind to nature, clears away fallen creation and gives the percipient a new and perfected world. M. H. Abrams rightly calls the wedding central to the ode an internal apocalypse, Christian eschatology (the marriage of the Lamb and the New Jerusalem) transformed into perceptual event.[19] Yet the poem is not as naturalized as Abrams maintains. An inner joy is not necessarily a self-generated one; for Coleridge, we'll see, joy is noticeably "given." What Coleridge wishes upon his internal audience – Sara Hutchinson, referred to simply as "Lady" – is akin to the God-given (or God-withheld) joy imagined in Christian *tristitia* poems such as Thomas Scott's ode, "Dejection": "Ah! never, never shall I taste the joy / Which to thy children, Lord, belong!"; "To me, alas! the light of morning gay, / Like gloom of midnight is display'd: / To me thy noontide and thy western ray, / Is all but melancholy shade."[20] In Coleridge's poem transfiguring joy may be construed as a sublimation of the poet's own sexual drive and the anxieties inscribed in the very circumstances of the poem's publication. First published in the *Morning Post* on William Wordsworth's wedding day and the seventh-year anniversary of his own unhappy marriage to Sarah Fricker, and drawing upon his earlier, erotically-charged verse epistle to Sara Hutchinson (*A Letter to –*), *Dejection: An Ode* is Coleridge's intra- and extra-poetic effort to transmute marriage into metaphor, *joi* into Christian joy, material necessity into spiritual liberty – in short, for the poet as for his ideal reader, the constraints of lived experience into the freedom of art.[21]

The poem's "Lady" may be given joy, but it comes at the cost of agency. She has no consciousness except for the joy that drops from heaven on her humble, faceless state, a joy contemplated aesthetically by the poet who professes joylessness in the poem's first movement (stanzas 1–3). In the poem's second movement, stanzas 4–5, the speaker identifies inner joy as the key to external harmony, addressing the "Lady" as someone who has experienced this truth:

> IV
> O Lady! we receive but what we give,
> And in our life alone does nature live:
> Ours is her wedding-garment, ours her shroud!
> And would we aught behold, of higher worth,
> Than that inanimate cold world allow'd
> To the poor loveless ever-anxious crowd,
> Ah! from the soul itself must issue forth,
> A light, a glory, a fair luminous cloud
> Enveloping the Earth –

And from the soul itself must there be sent
A sweet and potent voice, of its own birth,
Of all sweet sounds the life and element!

V
O pure of heart! thou need'st not ask of me
What this strong music in the soul may be!
What, and wherein it doth exist,
This light, this glory, this fair luminous mist,
This beautiful, and beauty-making power.
Joy, virtuous Lady! Joy that ne'er was given,
Save to the pure, and in their purest hour,
Life, and Life's Effluence, Cloud at once and Shower,
Joy, Lady! is the spirit and the power,
Which wedding Nature to us gives in dow'r
A new Earth and new Heaven,
Undreamt of by the sensual and the proud –
Joy is the sweet voice, Joy the luminous cloud –
We in ourselves rejoice!
And thence flows all that charms or ear or sight,
All melodies the echoes of that voice,
All colours a suffusion from that light.

Joy, in "wedding" mind to nature, clears away fallen creation and gives the percipient a new and perfected world. Coleridge's reader becomes, as it were, his "wedding guest," led through fields of light far from the natural terrors to which the Ancient Mariner summoned his guest; and which briefly reappear in the "tragic sounds" of the *Dejection* ode's seventh stanza, reminders of what lies in unsanctified nature.

Coleridge retained something of joy's Christian context. His is not Emily Dickinson's natural joy that "Dowered – all the World –," nor Louise Bogan's joy as wholly inner resource:

Henceforth, from the mind,
For your whole joy, must spring
Such joy as you may find
In any earthly thing,
And every time and place
Will take your thought for grace.[22]

Coleridge, though crucial to this later tradition, worked within the theological framework of grace. He is closer in spirit to Luther than to Bogan. Yet he insisted, in a way most Christian writers of his day did not, on joy as an interior event. The climactic line of the *Dejection* ode's fifth stanza – "We in ourselves rejoice!" – does not mean "we self-reliantly rejoice," or still less "we rejoice in the idea of our selves." On the contrary, its meaning is akin to Coleridge's corresponding line in *A Letter to* –, "we ourselves rejoice!" (line 319), with an "in" added to distinguish this rejoicing from the physical jubilation of, say, the Book of Psalms or, closer to home, Dissenter enthusiasts from whom Coleridge felt an abiding need to distance himself. One Dissenter Coleridge knew well, Anna Letitia Barbauld, anticipated

Coleridge on the transformational power of religious joy: "Joy is too brilliant a thing to be confined within our own bosoms; it burnishes all nature, and with its vivid colouring gives a kind of factitious life to objects without sense or motion." Yet Barbauld's joy, unlike Coleridge's, demands bodily expression: "The devout heart ... bursts into loud and vocal expressions of praise and adoration."[23] *Dejection,* still more than the earlier *Letter,* represents an inward turn, an abstraction from corporeal expression of any kind. For Coleridge, even that immediate joy he projects but claims not to feel is regulated, if not by the intellect then by a kind of spiritual propriety.

Both the *Letter* and *Dejection* agree that joy does not spring from the mind, an autochthon, but rather must be *given:* "Joy, virtuous Lady!" (in the *Letter,* "Joy, innocent Sara!"), "Joy that ne'er was given/ Save to the pure, and in their purest hour." This joy is not self-generated or even self-aware. Rather, the self seems a "pure" vessel for a joy that's poured in – by whom? God seems the likeliest giver, and Coleridge, to eliminate any uncertainty about this, added to *Dejections* final address to Sara a line not found in the *Letter,* calling her (as he had earlier called Wordsworth in an intermediate version of the poem) "O simple spirit, guided from above." "From above" makes it clear not only that God's the giver, but that he's a transcendent God. (Wordsworth may have been thinking of Coleridge's poem when he invoked "God, the giver of all joy" in the 1805 *Prelude* [6.614]). Sara's duty is ideally to receive: "Dear Lady! friend devoutest of my choice, / Thus may'st thou ever, evermore rejoice." The counter-factual nature of Sara's joy appears more clearly in the *Letter* – "Thus, thus should'st thou rejoice!" – and still more clearly in Mary Hutchinson's transcript of the poem, in which "should'st" appears as "would'st."[24] Sara *would* rejoice *were* she freed from adult cares and human dread.

Notes

1 I am indebted to George Gilpin's survey of "The Surrogates: Child and Maiden" in *The Strategy of Joy: An Essay on the Poetry of S. T. Coleridge* (Salzburg: University of Salzburg, 1972), pp. 93–167.

2 S. T. Coleridge, *Shakespearean Criticism,* 2 vols, ed., T. M. Raysor (London: Dent, 1960), 2, p. 6.

3 S. T. Coleridge, *Notebooks,* 5 vols, ed., Kathleen Coburn et al. (Princeton: Princeton University Press, 1957–2003), 1, p. 921.

4 Laurence Sterne, *A Sentimental Journey through France and Italy and Continuation of the Bramine's Journal,* ed., Melvin New and W. G. Day. Vol 6 (2002) of *The Florida Edition of the Works of Laurence Sterne,* 6 vols (Gainesville: University Press of Florida, 1978–2002), p. 155.

5 Rousseau treats pity or compassion as a counterpoint to *amour propre* in *Discourse on the Origin of Inequality* (1755); he elaborates on its ideal civic function in Book IV of *Emile* (1762), See the entry on "compassion" in N. J. H. Dent, *A Rousseau Dictionary* (Oxford: Blackwell, 1992), pp. 51–55.

6 Adam Smith, *The Theory of Moral Sentiments,* ed., D. D. Raphael and A. L. Macfie (Oxford: Clarendon, 1972), Part 1 ("Of the Propriety of Action"); my quotations are from pp. 10, 13, 40–41.

7 Wordsworth's early sonnet is printed with useful contextual materials, including Helen Maria Williams' "To Sensibility," in *Lyrical Ballads and Related Writings* ed., William Richey and Daniel Robinson (Boston: Houghton Mifflin, 2002).

8 Coleridge, *Notebooks,* 3, p. 3304.

9 Terry Eagleton summarizes this aspect of the (German) aesthetic: "Because these are objects which we can agree to call beautiful, not by arguing or analyzing but just by looking and seeing, a spontaneous consensus is brought to birth within our creaturely life, bringing with it the promise that such a life, for all its apparent arbitrariness and obscurity, might indeed work in some sense very like a rational law" (*The Ideology of the Aesthetic,* Oxford, Blackwell, 1990, p. 17).

10 Quoted in an editorial note to "This Lime-Tree Bower my Prison," S. T. Coleridge. *Poetical Works,* vol I, *Poems (Reading Texts),* ed. J. C. C. Mays (Princeton: Princeton University Press, 2001), 1, p. 350.

11 Quoted in Gill, *William Wordsworth: A Life* (Oxford: Oxford University Press, 1989), p. 210. On Lamb's assertion of his urban tastes against Lake-school aesthetics, see also Denise Gigante, *Taste: A Literary History* (New Haven: Yale University Press, 2005), pp. 89–116.

12 Homer describes the mourning song of the nightingale in *The Odyssey* 19.518–23. The best-known version of Philomela's transformation is Ovid. *Metamorphoses* 6.412–674. For a succinct overview of the many variations of the Philomela and Procne tale in Greek myth, see Timothy Gantz, *Early Greek Myth: A Guide to Literary and Artistic Sources* (Baltimore: Johns Hopkins University Press, 1993), pp. 235–41.

13 *Minne* ("love") lyrics containing joyful nightingales include Walther von der Vogelweide's "*Under der Linden*" and Neidhart von Reuental, "*Blozen wir den anger*" ("Bare was the Meadow'). We know from Coleridge's letters that he was reading Petrarch at some time before his departure for Malta in April 1804: see *Poetical Works* 1, p. 706–07 for his adaptation of a Petrarch sonnet ("*I dolci colli*"). For a thorough survey of the troubadours and minnesingers on the nightingale as a bird of joy, see Wendy Pfeffer, *The Change of Philomel: The Nightingale in Medieval Literature* (New York: Peter Lang, 1985).

14 See, for example, Chaucer's tale of Sir Thopas in *The Canterbury Tales* (a "tale / merier than the nightingale") or the description of the Knight's Squire in the *General Prologue* ("So hote he lovede, that by nightertale [night-time] / He slept namore than dooth a nightingale"); Sidney's "You Gote-heard Gods," lines 25–42; Drayton's "Rowlands Madrigall"; and especially Milton's early sonnet (based on Italian models), "O Nightingale, that on yon bloomy Spray." The "amorous descant" of the nightingale is from *Paradise Lost,* Book 4, l. 603.

15 Pfeffer cites a quantitative survey demonstrating that the nightingale is the most frequently cited bird in all troubadour poetry (p. 73). My following translations from Bernart's poems are from Pfeffer, pp. 85–88.

16 See especially Petrarch's canzone numbered in modern editions 310, "*Zefiro torna,*" and 311, "*Quel rosigniuol che si soava piagne,*" Imitating this last sonnet, Charlotte Smith – a poet with whom Wordsworth and Coleridge were familiar – produced a poem. "To a Nightingale," that begins as Petrarch's does not. "Poor melancholy bird," and continues on in a post-*Penseroso* vein.

17 Coleridge, *Notebooks,* 1, p. 1394.

18 Bernart, *Tant ai mo cor ple de joya,* quoted, above, ch. 2, p. 60.

19 M. H. Abrams, *Natural Supernaturalism: Tradition and Revolution in Romantic Literature* (New York: Norton, 1971), esp. pp. 1–70, 264–77.

20 The English word "dejection" translates the Latin *tristitia,* one of the principal sins in a tradition extending back to early medieval penitential literature: see *Medieval Handbooks of Penance,* ed. John T. McNeill and Helena M. Gamer (New York: Columbia University Press, 1938), pp. 18–19. *The Penitential of Finnian (c.* 525–550) explains that *tristitia* must be combated by its opposite, *gaudium:* "by contraries ... let us make haste to cure contraries and to cleanse away the faults from our hearts and introduce virtues in their places. Patience must arise for wrathfulness ... for dejection, spiritual joy" (*Medieval Handbooks,* pp. 92–93).

21 The 139-line *Dejection* ode first published in the *Morning Post* on October 4, 1802, is the public version of a very personal verse epistle. *A Letter to –,* 339 lines frankly addressed to Sara Hutchinson and dated April 4, 1802. My *Dejection* quotations are from *Sibylline Leaves* 1817 text, a revised and polished version of the poem that appeared in the 1802 *Morning Post.*

22 Emily Dickinson, *The Complete Poems,* ed. Thomas H. Johnson (Boston: Little, Brown and Company, 1960), no. 430; Louise Bogan, "Henceforth, From the Mind," in *The Blue Estuaries: Poems 1923–1968* (New York: Farrar, Straus and Giroux, 1968), p. 64.

23 Quoted in Jon Mee, *Romanticism, Enthusiasm and Regulation: Poetics and the Policing of Culture in the Romantic Period* (Oxford: Oxford University Press, 2003), p. 203.

24 Mary Hutchinson's transcript of *A Letter to –,* also known as "the Cornell manuscript," appears with critical apparatus in Stephen M. Parrish, ed., *Coleridge's Dejection: The Earliest Manuscripts and the Earliest Printings* (Ithaca: Cornell University Press, 1988) pp. 21–34.

30 Soul: Inside Hopkins (2009)

William Cohen

Even before his conversion, at twenty-two, to Roman Catholicism and his decision to enter the Jesuit priesthood, Hopkins was already uneasy with the materialist turn in contemporary psychology. In his undergraduate essay "The Probable Future of Metaphysics," he explicitly deprecates these developments, writing: "Material explanation cannot be refined into explaining thought and it is all to no purpose to show an organ for each faculty and a nerve vibrating for each idea, because this only shows in the last detail what broadly no one doubted, to wit that the activities of the spirit are conveyed in those of the body as scent is conveyed in spirits of wine, remaining still inexplicably distinct" (118). This sentence epitomizes Hopkins's approach to the question of materialism: he opposes it philosophically, and yet the terms in which he does so are inescapably material. He gives voice to the immateriality of spirit by describing it with the simile of an olfactory sensation – which is to say, of a sensory experience that brings the perceived object into the body of the subject. After his conversion, this uneasy preservation of the material as both source and evidence of an idealist principle was sublated in a conception of the divine as at once immanent in and transcendent of fleshly human existence. As Daniel Brown has established, Hopkins's training in British idealist philosophy served as a basis for these arguments,[1] which were augmented by his later discovery of the work of the medieval theologian Duns Scotus and by his own highly inventive prosody. This combination of intellectual interests, religious beliefs, and poetic practices enabled Hopkins to partake of the broader cultural strains of Victorian materialism I have been tracing and, at the same time, to appear to repudiate it – often by sublimating it into ecstatic, sometimes agonized, spiritual revelation. Yet throughout his writing, even when he seems most resolutely to abjure the flesh in favor of the spirit, Hopkins does not evade the sensuous terms of embodiment.

Jesuit practice supplies Hopkins with a means of reconciling the conflicting impulses in his account of human interiority toward, on the one hand, an ethereal spiritualism and, on the other, the manifest physicality of bodily sensation. In the letter he writes to his father announcing his conversion, Hopkins declares that at the core of his decision lies the dogma of transubstantiation, which captures this doubleness: the "literal truth of our Lord's words by which I learn that the least fragment of the consecrated elements in the Blessed Sacrament of the Altar is the whole Body of Christ."[2] Through the doctrine of Incarnation, which receives even greater attention in his oeuvre than transubstantiation, Hopkins works out the paradox of a God at once divine and embodied, and a humanity both transcendent and substantial. He elaborates on the relation of bodily form to spiritual essence in a later letter to Robert Bridges: "For though even bodily beauty ... is from, the soul, in the sense, as we Aristotelian Catholics say, that the soul is the form of the body, yet the soul may have no other beauty, so to speak, than that which it expresses in the symmetry of the body – barring those blurs in the cast which wd. not be found in the die or the mould."[3] Hopkins articulates one of the tenets of the materialist position: that "the soul is the form of the body." He means this in a sense akin to Freud's later proposition that the ego is "first and foremost a bodily ego" – that is, the subject's conception of his interior self conforms precisely to the contours of his external morphology. But Hopkins also makes the stranger suggestion that the soul is the die from which the body is cast – in other words, that the subject as embodied takes its form as an impression from a type of Platonic ideal, one conventionally imagined as formless. The mystery of Incarnation and its replication in the sacrament of the Eucharist encompass for Hopkins the inextricability of spirit from matter, indicating that the soul lends form to the flesh as much as the reverse. Understood in relation to the tradition I have been tracing, Hopkins's devotion to the divine, perhaps surprisingly, does nothing to diminish the primacy of the material.

In his poetic theory, Hopkins places special pressure on the space of the inside with the concept of "inscape." W. H. Gardner describes inscape as "a name for that 'individually-distinctive' form (made up of various sense-data) which constitutes the rich and revealing 'oneness' of the natural object."[4] In the movement between the inscape of an object and the human apperception of it through "instress" – and through the materialization and recapitulation of this process within poetic language itself – Hopkins identifies a tangible contiguity between human subjects and the world, interiority and the exterior. These features of Hopkins's Weltanschauung, familiar to readers acquainted with his poetry and prosody, are also manifest in his theological pronouncements. Yet despite overwhelming evidence that Hopkins conceives of instress as a somatic experience, critics have had little to say about its location within the human body, except to note that instress often involves the senses.[5] To the extent that the human body in Hopkins's work has received attention recently, it has tended to be discussed in terms of repressed or sublimated sexuality.[6]

In this chapter, I focus on Hopkins's understanding of the interior, and its interaction with the external world, as irreducibly corporeal. For Hopkins the body's material form limits – sometimes even degrades – spiritual existence, yet it is also the agency that enables experience of the divinely charged world, for the perceptual encounter of instress would be unimaginable without it. After establishing this doubleness, which generates the poet's alternately despairing and joyous account of embodiment, I turn to his depiction of sensory experience, which provides the means of mediating the problem of the body. Hopkins, I argue, attends to the sensory routes to the interior because they do three things: they bring the world into the body; they suggest ways of imagining objects in the world themselves *as* percipient bodies; and they make the human body itself an object of sensory apprehension. In short, bodily sensation affirms the status of the human subject as an object in the world – albeit a privileged one – which is both contiguous with other objects and mutually pervious to them. The reversibility of subjects and objects is key to Hopkins's poetic practice, his theology, and his implicit theory of knowledge, for it dramatizes the primacy of the body in human experience – even experience of the divine – and simultaneously elevates inanimate objects into agents integral to the human. While incorporation through the senses is a key theme in works like "The Windhover," the "Kingfishers" sonnet, and the other poems for which Hopkins is best known, I extend the argument to the journals in which he records observations of nature and philosophical speculations. The journal entries expand on problems distilled in the poems while shifting our attention from the theological and prosodic concerns predominant in the poetry. I focus on excerpts from the journals, reading them in tandem with Hopkins's poetry and spiritual exercises, to demonstrate how, in a relatively secular context, Hopkins understands sensory experience to break down boundaries between inside and outside and between subject and object. Such writings extend the fusion of spirit and matter, grounded in Catholic doctrine, manifest in his poetry.

My discussion of Hopkins's formulations – of perception as a physical encounter with the world, of visual sensation in particular in tactile terms, and of perceiving human subjects themselves as objects – relies implicitly on twentieth-century phenomenology's account of such concepts and specifically on the ideas of Maurice Merleau-Ponty, which I have outlined in chapter 1. Hopkins's conception of embodiment shares with Merleau-Ponty's an argument against the tradition of Cartesian rationalism, which posits a dualistic distinction between mind and body; Hopkins also shares with Merleau-Ponty an assessment of knowledge, in even its most abstract forms, as rooted in the body. For both writers, the sense of sight is deprivileged, partly through an emphasis on other senses, which bring the world into or onto the body directly, and partly through a reimagination of sight itself as a form of incorporation and touching. While Hopkins's theory of sensation bears affinities to Merleau-Ponty's, in always taking perception to be a form of proximate contact, Hopkins takes the eye itself as an object of visual and visceral interest – an interest that suggests productive connections with Bataille as well. Hopkins presents an account of the human subject that resembles Bataille's insofar as that subject's material substance yields an exalted debasement, a savoring of degradation (physical, emotional, and spiritual), and an explosion outward of inner matter. Hopkins at times anticipates and illustrates Bataille's notion of a subject not just threatened but shattered by the fact of his own substantial being; both writers find resources for a paradoxically derealized psychological and spiritual subjectivity in the very degradation they feel embodiment to entail. Rather than the spiritual transcendence of a devotional Hopkins – or even the radically sensual one who, as Julia Saville has argued, turns ascetic renunciation into a form of sexual ecstasy – this is Hopkins understood as fully embodied, both elevated and unmade by the material conditions of his existence.[7]

Hopkins's frame of reference for the enclosure of spirit within corporeal forms varies widely, with allegories of embodiment ranging from the contracted (a prison) to the expansive (a landscape).[8] In the poem "The Caged Skylark," for example, the analogy between bodily and spatial enclosure is positively carceral. Just as the bird is trapped in its cage, so human "spirits" are imprisoned in their bodies:

> As a dare-gale skylark scanted in a dúll cáge,
>   Man's mounting spirit in his bone-house, mean house, dwells –
>   That bird beyond the remembering his free fells,
> This in drudgery, day-labouring-out life's age. (122)[9]

Enclosure is negative through most of this poem, imagined in terms of cage, cell, and prison; the body, through the kenning in line 2, is the "house" for both "spirit" and "bone." The cage is "dull"; its inmates "droop deadly sometimes in their cells / Or wring their barriers in bursts of fear or rage." Although the outdoors, too, can form an enclosure, Hopkins nearly always prefers it to "being indoors," for the immediate connections the outdoors allows to natural forms. Some of the most famous lines in the Hopkins corpus (from the "Kingfishers" sonnet) reiterate the language of spatial inhabitation as a figure for the inscape of spiritual qualities within material frames: "Each mortal thing does one thing and the same: / Deals out that being indoors each one dwells" (115). Similarly pressing on the conventional terms in which a soul is imagined as imprisoned in the body, an entry from Hopkins's journal of 1873 describes a nightmare in which he feels paralyzed: "The feeling is terrible: the body no longer swayed as a piece by the nervous and muscular in-stress seems to fall in and hang like a dead weight on the chest. I cried on the holy name and by degrees recovered myself as I thought to do. It made me think that this was how the souls in hell would be imprisoned in their bodies as in prisons" (238).[10] The passage is both evocative and involuted: somehow "the body" itself "weigh[s] on the chest," the whole obstructing the part. Likewise, if condemned souls are "imprisoned in their bodies as in prisons," then the body is at once actually a prison and the figure for a prison. Explicitly linking the image of spiritual imprisonment within the body to the theory of instress, these lines implicitly point to the body as the channel to (and agent for) its spiritual contents: when denied the flexibility and movement of the corporeal frame, the soul is condemned to its enclosure, like the wretched in hell.

The body is the route through which human beings encounter the godhead; the problem is that the body also incarcerates the soul, corrupting it through the occasions the body supplies for taint and temptation. Moreover, even if, for degraded mortals like the poet, the body impedes spiritual liberty, it is necessary to the doctrine of Incarnation: by assuming the material form of human flesh, Christ fulfilled his divine function as embodied.[11] This paradox explains the turn taken in the last lines of "The Caged Skylark," which shift from calling the body a cage to proposing that it houses the "best" of man:

> Man's spirit will be flesh-bound when found at best,
> But úncúmberèd: meadow-dówn is nót distréssed
>   For a ráinbow fóoting it nor hé for his bónes rísen.

Although human subjects may be ineluctably embodied, it is possible, Hopkins suggests, with Christ as a model, for the "flesh-bound" "spirit" to inhabit the body "uncumbered" – which is to say, to be in the body but not wholly *of* the body. While most of the poem dwells on the caged bird as a figure for the enclosure of human souls, this condensed final stanza extends the allegory in two directions, one lower, the other higher. Man's spirit is bound to his flesh but need not be hindered by it, these lines state, just as the meadow is not "distressed" by the rainbow that appears to set a foot down on it (a verbal image that personifies, and so lends bodily form to, the inanimate), and just as Christ does not regret the necessity of coming to earth in bodily human form, from which he arose (that is, was bodily resurrected). The poet holds out hope that rather than being the prison house of the soul, the body might be its portal.

If the body is the untranscenciable vessel bearing the human soul, then the body's own portals – its sensory openings – are the means of both material and spiritual ingress to the subject. Like "The Caged Skylark," "The Candle Indoors" draws an analogy between human embodiment and an inhabited dwelling, linking them through the image of interior illumination, both visible and sacred. The sonnet opens:

> Some candle clear burns somewhere I come by.
> I muse at how its being puts blissful back
> With yellowy moisture mild night's blear-all black
> Or to-fro tender trambeams truckle at the eye. (133)

The body is the absent, implied connection between the image, rendered in spatial terms (illumination shines within a physical container), and its spiritual meaning: the candle illuminates a house just as divine truth illuminates a soul. The soul, however, resides within a body, as is indicated by the realization of "I," the speaker, in the "eye," whose placement at the end of sentence, line, and quatrain emphasizes the word. If the human body is only suggested in the allegory between house and soul, it returns as the perceptual medium for receiving light: the embodied subject of this vision is engaged in a dialectical exchange of reflection and refraction with the shimmering candle flame.[12] The sonnet's apostrophic second half invites the addressee into an illuminated "indoors," whose light might mend the dimming internal flame of faith:

> Come you indoors, come home; your fading fire
> Mend first and vital candle in close heart's vault;
> You there are master, do your own desire;
> What hinders?

Hopkins's innovation on the traditional figure of divine inspiration as light is to emphasize its sensory apprehension through a visual apparatus ("trambeams," "beam-blind") that takes vivid tactile metaphors. The result is an account of seeing as a proximate sensation: with its "yellowy moisture," the candle pushes away the blinding blackness of the night. Hopkins prefigures Merleau-Ponty in employing a model of what has come to be called haptic visuality, of seeing modeled on the example of touch, the sense whose reciprocal and reversible qualities are most immediately evident. Describing vision as "palpation of the eye," Merleau-Ponty, like Hopkins, lends it the tactile qualities of propinquity and direct contact.[13] Rather than supplying the subject mastery over what he sees, such embodied sight renders him an object, to himself and to others, even as it permits him to experience the other – equally embodied – as a subject as well.

Hopkins is alternately jubilant and fearful about the possibilities the senses hold for enlightenment. The piety of Hopkins's works and their intensely devotional resolutions are rooted in the sensual apprehension of the world. At times, this sensitivity is ecstatic, insofar as "The world is charged wíth the grándeur of God" ("God's Grandeur," 139): the poet celebrates the earthly wonders that make tangible the promise of divine redemption. Hopkins's poems celebrating sensory experience of the natural world date from early in his extant work, beginning with "The Habit of Perfection" (77) – an extended apophasis that provides a sensuous account of forswearing each of the organs of perception in favor of the intangible sensations of divinity – and culminating in "The Windhover" (120), whose sensory and verbal achievements are inextricably bound together.[14] Such accounts of body and soul richly appreciate the human perceptual appurtenances as inlets for beauty, pleasure, and intellection. Although the poet sometimes reproves himself for savoring his apprehension of the natural world, his eyes fix on the divine even when his hands are in the mud.

One consequence of Hopkins's emphasis on perceiving simultaneously divine and sublunary objects is that the relation between the subject and the object of perception blurs, and the observer's process of observation itself becomes as central a focus of reflection as the objects that prompt it. The effect resonates with Merleau-Ponty's "double sensation" and "flesh," the idea of a reciprocity entailed by the embodied subject becoming an object of perception, which is exemplified by the way in which a hand that touches is itself always simultaneously touched. Hopkins addresses related concepts in a passage from the first of the Ignatian spiritual exercises he wrote on retreat in 1880. This passage makes distinctions between what lies within human beings – whether in bodily, mental, or spiritual terms – and what lies outside; that these distinctions are fluid and shifting rather than absolute leads him to consider the means of communication, as well as boundary transgression, between inside and outside:

Part of this world of objects, this object-world, is also part of the very self in question, as in man's case his own body, which each man not only feels in and acts with but also feels and acts on. If the centre of reference spoken of has concentric circles round it, one of these, the inmost, say, is its own, is óf it, the rest are tó it only. Within a certain bounding line all will be self, outside of it nothing: with it self begins from one side and ends from the other. I look through my eye and the window and the air; the eye is my eye and of me and me, the windowpane is my windowpane but not of me nor me. A self then will consist of a centre *and* a surrounding area or circumference, of a point of reference *and* a belonging field, the latter set out, as surveyors etc say, from the former; of two elements which we may call the inset and the outsetting or the display.[15]

The subject of perception has become its own object: "man's ... own body" is the "centre of reference" in which perception, both sensual and spiritual, originates – but this "self" is perceptible to itself as well.[16] Much in Hopkins's account depends on prepositions, as he seeks to make syntactical sense of the overlapping, relational articulation between subject and world. When he reaches for a figure by which to represent this process, he imagines himself indoors, looking through a window at an outside scene and taking it back in, through windowpane and eye, to the centered self. Window and eye are like each other – each is a transparent medium through which an exterior object can reach the inner self – but the eye, as part of the body ("the eye is my eye and of me and me"), lies within that "certain bounding line" where "all will be self," while the window, its representation, lies beyond it ("not of me nor me"). This passage portrays the distinction between self and world by invoking an inside/ outside body boundary superimposed on that of indoors/outdoors: Hopkins instinctively equates "external" with an outside landscape (as the reference to "surveyors" indicates), where the invisible (but for him, palpable) "air" is located. Instressing – or, to use the terms he here coins, taking to the "inset" the "outset" scene – is seeing his own eye seeing. If this is an exploration of "the very self" of man, it is an emphatically embodied self.[17]

This perceptual theory informs a passage from a very early journal, dated January 23, 1866. The journals' apparently casual notation of sense impressions, particularly of natural forms, is often exceedingly complex and evocative; as J. Hillis Miller has suggested, these entries deserve to be approached as a species of prose poetry.[18] This particular entry richly meditates on relations between subjective interiors and the form of objects. In explicating it, one encounters a welter of implied connections between an apperceptive human body and the sense impressions made on it by the natural world – of instress in process. The passage opens by naming a trivial phenomenon or object, "drops of rain hanging on rails," and then, in an apparent effort to evoke the visual experience, proceeds through an elaborate series of associations inspired by both the object and the process of perceiving it. In its entirety, the entry reads:

Drops of rain hanging on rails etc seen with only the lower rim lighted like nails (of fingers). Screws of brooks and twines. Soft chalky look with more shadowy middles of the globes of cloud on a night with a moon faint or concealed. Mealy clouds with a not brilliant moon. Blunt buds of the ash. Pencil buds of the beech. Lobes of the trees. Cups of the eyes. Gathering back the lightly hinged eyelids. Bows of the eyelids. Pencil of eyelashes. Juices of the eyeball. Eyelids like leaves, petals, caps, tufted hats, handkerchiefs, sleeves, gloves. Also of the bones sleeved in flesh. Juices of the sunrise. Joins and veins of the same. Vermilion look of the hand held against a candle with the darker parts as the middles of the fingers and especially the knuckles covered with ash. (72)

By following the logic of this passage, we can witness Hopkins's imagination at work as it moves progressively deeper into the body. The prose advances through a series of associations, filling in some steps that the poetry, with its customary layering of condensed images and metaphors, often elides; but it shares with the poetry a conception of objects known through their effects on the interior of the observing subject.

After notation of the thing he has observed ("drops of rain"), the particular illumination of these drops leads Hopkins to assimilate the visual phenomenon to another object, "nails," and then to specify that he means a part of the human body, ("of fingers"). It may be that "rails" elicits "nails" simply because of rhyme, for the sequence of sounds throughout the phrase makes it seem as if he were trying out sounds and images together: rain/hanging/ fingers, rain/rails/rim, only/lower/lighted/like, and all the long vowels (rain, seen, only, lower, lighted, like).[19] The link to the next image – "screws of brooks and twines" – is unclear: certainly there is a play of light on water in both; perhaps from nails (before they are human nails) to screws (things that fasten); or by an implied analogy between watery natural objects and human, or human-made, ones: raindrops are to fingernails as brooks are to twines. The association within the compound "brooks and twines" itself is the spiral ("screw") pattern common to whirlpools in running water and bound thread. From these two image sets to the following description of faintly illuminated clouds at night, the bridge is the impression of texture created by light, as with nails in raindrops or shapes of running water. All three imply an inscape, an embodied essence in material objects: the perfection of shape the raindrops assume, the curling into "screws" of winding flows, and the interior of the cloud pushing out to its surface ("soft chalky look with more shadowy middles"). As in the poetry, the language in this line mimics and instantiates the objects' inscape with its bounding rhythm and condensed internal rhymes (soft/chalky/look, shadowy/globes, chalky/ shadowy, more/ middle, etc.). "Mealy clouds with a not brilliant moon" stays with nighttime clouds and reflected illumination, documenting the perceived textural consequence of a change in light, from chalky to mealy. As with the opening line, the refraction of light in water gives rise to a series of associations; clouds are a perennial favorite object of observation in Hopkins's journals.

Even beyond the potential spiritual allegories of light and water, as the passage progresses the subject of sensation begins to move forward in the description of the perceptual encounter in ways that suggestively illuminate other parts of Hopkins's corpus. The next phrase makes a leap in object – "blunt buds of the ash" – but it remains focused on the haptic impression made through visual perception of a natural object. Describing how the buds look – "blunt" – supplies an indication of how they might feel, and the name of the tree ("ash") resonates with the "chalky, mealy" clouds above, and with what follows. Moving from one variety of tree bud to another, Hopkins goes to "pencil buds of the beech," whose long, pointed, tipped buds indeed resemble pencils. He then pulls back to a more distant view of the tree as a whole and, at the same time, to the generic form: "lobes of the trees." But with "cups of the eyes," a surprising shift occurs. While the genitive syntax remains the same (x of the y), there is an important change in substance. In concentrating on the process of visual perception, Hopkins here moves from the perceived object to the perceiving agent. More precisely, he shifts to seeing the subject as itself an object, by reflexively considering the eyes, which are likened to, and reflect, the object (the trees) they see: the trees have lobes, the eyes have cups. Perhaps the trees are like ears in having lobes, indicating a move from one sensory organ to another. The "cups" are eyelids, which both protect and blind the viewer, literally (perceptually) as well as figuratively: as in "The Habit of Perfection," apprehension in the everyday world impedes transcendental perception of the "uncreated light." Hopkins now stays with the eyes, fascinated with the eyelids, strange cups that fold: "Gathering back the lightly hinged eyelids. Bows of the eyelids." He focuses intensively on the appearance of the eyelids themselves, anatomizing their mechanics and appreciating their form.

How, then, do we get from eyes back to pencils? From an object that is a container ("cups") to one that is a perimeter ("bows"), Hopkins moves to the outer edge with "pencil of eyelashes." The "lashes" sound like "ashes," both the preceding tree and the ash that ends the entry. The *OED* lists one relevant definition for *pencil,* "a small tuft of hairs, bristles, feathers, or the like, springing from or close to a point on a surface," noting that, from the nineteenth century on, it is only used in natural history. It may be that Hopkins intends the word in this sense, but both the earlier use of it in this passage ("pencil buds") and its common meaning – difficult as they are to reconcile with this context – are relevant. Hopkins, who not only wrote with a pencil but was accomplished at drawing with one too, here seems to move around the eyes to sketch them (from lids to lashes) and then puts the pencil itself – the instrument for rendering the image – *into* the picture.[20] The identification and mutual dependency between, on the one hand, the interior energy realized in the outward form of phenomenal objects and, on the other, the incorporative abilities of human sensory apprehension break down the boundaries between subject and object. This peculiar "pencil" reaches back to the "pencil buds of the beech" and moves beyond the merely metaphoric relation to secure the connection between trees and eyes – not least because pencils are made from trees, are trees remade into an object accommodated to the human hand, which recursively serves to record the image of trees for the consumption of the eye.

The surprise is that the process moves still further in: having penetrated the image, the pencil now seems to puncture the eye itself. And inside the body, Hopkins discovers – more body: "juices of the eyeball." Grotesquely literal as it seems, this reading is authorized by his poetry. In "Binsey Poplars," eyes and trees are associated metaphorically (being likened to eyes makes the fallen poplars seem fragile), as well as through the dialectical relation between perceiving subject and object:

"Ó if we but knéw whát we do
    Whén we delve or hew –
Háck and rack the growing green!
    Since Country is so tender
To tóuch, her béing só slénder,
That, like this sleek and seeing ball
But a prick will make no eye at all,
    Whére we, even where we mean
        To mend her we end her,
    Whén we hew or delve. (130)

Through the analogy between cutting down trees and puncturing an eye, the natural scene comes to be like a body, damaged irretrievably by even the most apparently insignificant alteration. "This sleek and seeing ball" may be not just the eye but the globe of the earth, capable of being "pricked" as well by such changes.[21] As a heuristic, we might think of Hopkins's process of sensation as stages of transformation: from "eyes see trees" (subject perceives object) to "eyes are like trees" (subject resembles, and so becomes, an object), to "trees puncture eyes" (object enters subject); his body is the switch point between self and world, immaterial and material ways of being.

Notes

1 See Daniel Brown, *Hopkins's Idealism: Philosophy, Physics, Poetry* (Oxford: Clarendon, 1997). See also Tom Zaniello, *Hopkins in the Age of Darwin* (Iowa City: University of Iowa Press, 1988), on the embeddedness of Hopkins's thought in contemporary controversies over evolutionary biology and affiliated debates about materialism.

2 October 18, 1866, *Further Letters of General Manley Hopkins,* ed. Claude Colleer Abbott, 2nd ed. (London: Oxford University Press, 1956), 92. He continues: "This belief once got is the life of the soul and when I doubted it I shd. become an atheist the next day. But, as Monsignor Eyre says, it is a gross superstition unless guaranteed by infallibility. I cannot hold this doctrine confessedly except as a Tractarian or a Catholic."

3 October 22, 1879, *The Letters of Gerard Manley Hopkins to Robert Bridges,* ed. Claude Colleer Abbott (London: Oxford University Press, 1970), 95.

4 Gardner continues: "And for that energy of being by which all things are upheld, for that natural (but ultimately supernatural) stress which determines an *inscape* and keeps it in being – for that he coined the name *instress* … . But *instress* is not only the unifying force *in* the object; it connotes also that impulse *from* the 'inscape' which acts on the senses and, through them, actualizes the inscape in the mind of the beholder (or rather 'perceiver,' for inscape may be perceived through all the senses at once). Instress, then, is often the *sensation* of inscape – a quasi-mystical illumination, a sudden perception of that deeper pattern, order, and unity which gives meaning to external forms." W. H. Gardner, introduction to *Poems and Prose of Gerard Manley Hopkins* (1953; Baltimore: Penguin, 1966), xx–xxi. The phrase quoted is from W. A. M. Peters, S.J., *Gerard Manley Hopkins: A Critical Essay towards the Understanding of His Poetry* (Oxford: Basil Blackwell, 1948), the first chapter of which has the classic discussion of these terms.

5 Peters gives the clearest explanation of inscape; Alan Heuser, *The Shaping Vision of Gerard Manley Hopkins* (Oxford: Oxford University Press, 1958), has a helpful discussion of Hopkins's spiritualization of the senses. On sensory and bodily experience in relation to Hopkins's spiritual and poetic cosmology, see also J. Hillis Miller, *The Disappearance of God: Five Nineteenth-Century Writers* (Cambridge, Mass.: Harvard University Press, 1963); and Daniel A. Harris, *Inspirations Unbidden: The "Terrible Sonnets" of Gerard Manley Hopkins* (Berkeley: University of California Press, 1982).

6 Lesley Higgins, "'Bone-house' and 'lovescape': Writing the Body in Hopkins's Canon," in *Rereading Hopkins: Selected New Essays,* ed. Francis L. Fennell (Victoria: English Literary Studies, 1996), 11–35, applies a Foucault-inspired approach to bodily discipline in Hopkins. On sexual and gay themes, see Julia F. Saville, *A Queer Chivalry: The Homoerotic Asceticism of Gerard Manley Hopkins* (Charlottesville: University Press of Virginia, 2000); David Alderson, *Mansex Fine: Religion, Manliness, and Imperialism, in Nineteenth-Century British Culture* (Manchester: Manchester University Press, 1998), chaps. 5 and 6; Joseph Bristow, "'Churlsgrace'; Gerard Manley Hopkins and the Working-Class Male Body," *FLH* 59 (1992): 693–712; Wendell Stacy Johnson, "Sexuality and Inscape," *Hopkins Quarterly* 3, no. 2 (July 1976): 59–65; Renée V. Over-holser, "'Looking with Terrible Temptation': Gerard Manley Hopkins and Beautiful Bodies," *Victorian Literature and Culture* 19 (1991): 25–53; Robert-Bernard Martin, *Gerard Manley Hopkins: A Very Private Life* (New York: G. P. Putnam's, 1991). Also on the body in Hopkins (specifically focused on feet), see R. J. C. Watt, "Hopkins and the Gothic Body," in *Victorian Gothic: Literary and Cultural Manifestations in the Nineteenth Century,* ed. Ruth Robbins and Julian Wolfreys (New York: Palgrave, 2000), 60–89.

7 Saville makes the most persuasive and thoroughgoing argument for sexual (and, by association, bodily) signification in Hopkins's poetry; she judiciously removes the question from issues of sexual identity and places it in the context of the poet's devotional practice of asceticism, as well as showing it to be integral to his poetic (specifically metrical) technique.

8 See, for example, the sonnet "In the Valley of the Elwy," whose layered inhabitation images – of house, land, and body – suggest an alignment of physical, sensory, and spiritual interiors.

9 All references to poems are to *The Poetical Works of Gerard Manley Hopkins,* ed. Norman H. MacKenzie (Oxford: Clarendon, 1990); poems are indicated by number in this edition.

10 Quoted in Raymond J. Ventre, "The Body Racked with Pain: Hopkins's Dark Sonnets," *ANQ* 13, no. 4 (2000): 41.

11 See Nathan Cervo, "'Sweating Selves': Hopkins' Rebuff of Gnosticism," *Hopkins Quarterly* 20, nos. 1–2 (Winter–Spring 1993): 44–51. By contrast with the caged skylark, the windhover and the

kingfisher become Christlike symbols of spiritual apotheosis and fully realized inscape, largely unavailable to flesh-hindered human beings.

12 In his commentary on this poem, MacKenzie quotes F. R. Leavis's reading of the line as "lines of light (caused, I believe, by the eyelashes) that ... converge upon the eye like so many sets of tram-rails. But 'tram' unqualified would suggest something too solid, so he adds 'tender'; and 'truckle' conveys perfectly the obsequious way in which they follow every motion of the eyes and of the eyelids." This is consistent with Hopkins's attention to the physical embodiment of the visual apparatus (of which eyelashes are sometimes the sign). The notion of tram rails converging, further conveyed by "trambeams," reinforces Hopkins's contention that perceptual reality resides in the subject, not the object of vision.

13 "The Intertwining – the Chiasm," in *The Visible and the Invisible,* ed. Claude Lefort, trans. Alphonso Lingis (Evanston, Ill.: Northwestern University Press, 1968), 133.

14 Geoffrey H. Hartman makes this argument in a classic reading of the poem, "The Dialectic of Sense-Perception," in *Hopkins: A Collection of Critical Essays,* ed. Geoffrey H. Hartman (Englewood Cliffs, N.J.: Prentice-Hall, 1966), 117–30. Hopkins recapitulates the tour of the senses on other occasions in *Sermons and Devotional Writings of Gerard Manley Hopkins,* ed. Christopher Devlin, S.J. (London: Oxford University Press, 1959), in an abject mode, through accounts of hell (136, 241–44).

15 *Sermons and Devotional Writings,* 127; italics in original.

16 For Merleau-Ponty, even if relations between subject and object are reciprocal and reversible, they do not collapse into each other: the distinction between the two is important, for subjects can perceive themselves as objects, and can perceive the role of objects in their own constitution as subjects, only if they remain distinct.

17 Walter J. Ong, S.J., in *Hopkins, the Self, and God* (Toronto: University of Toronto Press, 1986), cites this passage, writing that it shows how "the human body is both part of the self and part of the material object world" (39).

18 In *Disappearance of God,* Miller discusses the description of nature in Hopkins's journals (279–87), including the sound and image patterns that make "miniature poems, or poems in the rough" (280). Miller's work is the most prominent among the earlier phenomenological approaches, and the one most relevant to my study. Here and in a related earlier essay, "The Creation of the Self in Gerard Manley Hopkins," *ELH* 22, no. 4 (December 1955): 293–319, Miller does not name the theoretical impetus for his study, but he writes generally about the critical effort to decipher a writer's "consciousness" and worldview, in places appearing to draw on Merleau-Ponty's phenomenology of perception. Miller focuses on the way in which self and world are coextensive to show how they emanate from (and display the generous humanity of) authorial consciousness, rather than, as I do, regarding the embodiment of subjectivity as a way of decentering a coherent consciousness, in either authorial or characterological terms.

19 Similarly, in discussing the penultimate line, "This Jack, jóke, poor pótsherd, | patch, matchwood, immortal diamond," from "That Nature is a Heraclitean Fire and of the comfort of the Resurrection" (174), Paul Mariani calls it an "extraordinary incremental chiming catalogue which suggests in its own protean lexical shifts the profound theological idea of death, sacrifice, and transformation." Mariani, "The Sound of Oneself Breathing," in *Critical Essays on Gerard Manley Hopkins,* ed. Alison G. Sulloway (Boston: G. K. Hall, 1990), 54. On fingernails before candles as a natural symbol, see also the poem "Moonrise June 19, 1876" (103): "The móon, dwíndled and thinned to the frínge | of a fingernail held to the candle."

20 Storey notes in his preface to *Journals* that in the second volume of early diaries (in which this passage appears), "The entries are almost entirely in pencil" (xvi). In *The Pencil: A History of Design and Circumstance* (New York: Knopf, 1990), Henry Petroski documents the common use of wood for manufacturing pencils in nineteenth-century England.

21 "The ashtree growing in the corner of the garden was felled. It was lopped first: I heard the sound and looking out and seeing it maimed there came at that moment a great pang and I wished to die and not to see the inscapes of the world destroyed anymore." April 8, 1873, in *Journals,* 230.

Part VII
Religion

Jonathan Herapath

It is somewhat commonplace to describe the reign of Victoria as an age of huge religious anxiety when the traditional beliefs of the Christian faith began to look far less solid than they once had. There are a number of pressures under which traditional Christianity falls in the nineteenth century which, while they have their origins prior to this, come into much sharper and more widespread cultural focus during the period.

The foremost of these is perhaps the challenge from developments in scientific understanding of the origins of the universe. In retrospect, the biggest of these was Darwin's theory of evolution. *On the Origin of Species* has become a symbolic reference for Victorian loss of religious assurance, but it really was only one in a whole series of pieces of scientific research and theory stretching back over previous centuries that challenged traditional Christian belief (Darwin himself was of course building on the work of others before him, perhaps most famously Charles Lyell's *The Principles of Geology*). The trajectory from Copernicus to Kepler, Galileo, Newton, Lyell, Darwin and beyond raised serious challenges, questioning the biblical understanding of creation and the plausibility of stories of the miraculous, and requiring a marked shift in the way the origin, place and value of human beings in the universe was perceived. The effect of the scientific revolution over time was an increasing divergence between scientific revelation and religious revelation, and it became ever harder for Christianity to command belief in the supernatural phenomena which had epistemologically underpinned its entire existence and teaching for so many centuries.

Science was not the only area in which progress of knowledge came to challenge Christian faith. A highly damaging critique of the notion of unique divine revelation through scripture emerged slowly but inexorably as the eighteenth century turned into the nineteenth, through the so-called higher biblical criticism of scholars such Johann Eichhorn, Friedrich Schleiermacher, Ferdinand Bauer and David Strauss, whose *The Life of Jesus* (translated by George Eliot, and published in England in 1846) seeks to historicise the figure of Jesus arguing that the gospels should not be read as historical accounts, but understood within a mythical framework as the poetic products of the early Christian community. So many strands of thought, discovery and theory, some of which had their roots centuries earlier, can be seen to coalesce in the cultural and intellectual mind of the period; and the implications of these for traditional Christian belief certainly contributed to an increasingly widespread anxiousness over the status of religious faith.

However, it is also the case that religious life in the nineteenth century was intense. It gave rise to the Evangelical Revival and the Oxford Movement, two of the most successful religious movements in the history of the Church of England, whose influence on the life of the church was huge at the time and is still felt today. The religious emancipation acts of the late 1820s enhanced religious freedom of expression and enabled full participation in mainstream political and institutional life of Roman Catholics and 'non-conformists', both being previously excluded on the basis of their not being members of the Church of England and adherents to the 39 Articles of Religion that such membership required.

The pervasiveness of widespread religiosity is amply illustrated in literature. The period saw the foundation of nine religious newspapers between 1828 (*The Record*) and 1860 (*The Universe*); the circulation of the 90 (in)famous 'Tracts for the Times' published between 1833 and 1841 by Newman, Keble, Pusey, Williams and others of the group that became known at the time as the Tractarians and retrospectively as the Oxford Movement. Tens of thousands of sermons were published, either as single sermon pamphlets or in collected volume form, making sermons one of the most popular literary genres of the century. The *Book of Common Prayer* was part of the national consciousness and public vocabulary with many of its phrases and prayers known by heart. *Essays and Reviews*, a collection of essays reflecting on the possible implications for Christianity in the light of developing scientific research and influence of German higher criticism on the interpretation of biblical texts, sold more copies in the two years following its publication in 1860 than *On the Origin of Species*, published the previous year, did in twenty years. The bestselling volume of poetry throughout the entire century was not by Wordsworth, Tennyson, Browning (Elizabeth Barrett or Robert) or Arnold but by John Keble, whose volume of Christian devotional poetry, *The Christian Year* (1827), had sold upwards of half a million copies by 1900. The most ubiquitous of literary genres to benefit from cheap print, the novel, addressed many of the various religious issues of the century, from Mrs Patten struggling to understand Amos's Evangelical doctrine of sin in George Eliot's *Amos Barton*, to Mrs Humphrey Ward's portrayal of acute religious doubt in *Robert Elsmere* or Anthony Trollope's unflattering portrayal of Church of England clergy and politics in *The Barchester Chronicles*. There is no doubting that much religious debate and practice had a distinctly textual manifestation. Indeed, it could be said that in the nineteenth century religion took a decidedly literary turn. As Kirstie Blair says in the introduction to her *Form and Faith in Victorian Poetry and Religion*, included in this volume, 'canonical poets such as Tennyson, the Brownings, Hardy, Hopkins and Rossetti produced their religious poetry as part of a context of popular religious poetics'; the problem is, as she also points out, that this shared context is one that has mostly been lost.[1] This has no doubt been one of the reasons for the near total critical neglect of religious poetry, particularly devotional poetry.

Another must surely be that most critics have followed scholars like Bernard Richards in seeing religious poetry, and especially devotional poetry, as for the most part unworthy of attention, with only that poetry motivated by doubt and loss of faith being worth reading.[2] However, this attitude is increasingly being challenged. F. E. Gray argues that it is this lack of attention that has 'skewed our understanding of the significance of religious devotion to the century's creative work'.[3] Charles LaPorte, in his introduction to the book whose chapter on Browning is included in this volume, suggests that it has been very easy to see a number of canonical poems of faith and doubt as synecdochic of a simple secularisation, 'death of God' narrative. Writing in 2011, he says that today, however, the 'moribund condition of nineteenth-century British Christianity now seems far less evident than it has seemed to us during most of the intervening period'.[4] If this is true, it is due to the work of scholars like LaPorte, Blair, Gray et al.[5]; as Blair succinctly puts it, 'I am part of a group of scholars who are engaged in revisiting the Victorian poetry of faith and questioning critical embarrassment in the face of apparently outdated beliefs'. For her, 'it is time to reconsider Victorian poetry as a site for secure faith',[6] and her own contribution to this rehabilitation is her astute recognition that recent theoretical interest in form is of direct relevance to any discussion of Victorian religious culture, especially the interplay between the place and role of form in religious faith, practice and poetry.

The text that prefigures the reinvigoration of this field is G. B. Tennyson's landmark 1981 *Victorian Devotional Poetry*,[7] and it is perhaps ample proof of the claims made by Blair, LaPorte et al. in respect of the lack of interest in poetry of faith that the book made little critical impact at the time; according to the author, rather sinking without trace.[8] Tennyson's aim is not to try and rehabilitate Keble, Newman and Williams as poets who should be read today alongside Coleridge, Arnold, Swinburne, Tennyson, Wordsworth, the Brownings etc; rather he argues that it is important to appreciate the extent of the influence that Tractarian poetics had upon the subsequent literary landscape. It has already been noted that Keble's 1827 *The Christian Year* was the best selling volume of poetry throughout the whole of the nineteenth century, and although we might agree with Bernard Richards that this is an example of pious poetry that we would no longer read for its own sake, the fact that it was so widely read meant it both reflected and helped form the religious, literary and emotional sensibility of the century, and as such it is a text that contributes to a fuller understanding of the cultural experience of the period.

The group to which the poets of Tennyson's focus – Newman, Keble and Williams – belonged became known as The Oxford Movement and its priests, poets and theologians as the Tractarians. They emerged in 1830s Oxford with the aim of 're-catholicising' the Church of England.[9] It was however as much an aesthetic movement. Steeped as it was in a Romantic sensibility of affect, it was an 'affair of the heart and spirit'[10] whose 'greatest literary achievement was the formulation of a full-scale poetics'.[11] For Newman, 'man is less of a reasoning animal and more of a "feeling, contemplating one"'.[12] Likewise for Isaac Williams: 'religious doctrines and articles of faith can only be received according to certain dispositions of the heart' (Tract 87 Part V). This understanding of faith as having chiefly to do with emotion is directly inherited from Romantic poetic theory which saw poetry, famously, as the spontaneous overflow of powerful feelings, pouring forth from a (divinely) inspired imagination,[13] as well as from Robert Lowth's mid-eighteenth century *Lectures on the Sacred Poetry of the Hebrews*, in which he argues that sacred poetry both derives from a heightened emotion inspired by faith, and then which in turn also regulates that emotion though its form and language. For the Oxford Movement it is just such a recognition that mental emotion and passionate belief need to be regulated, and that poetry is the best form to do this that becomes a hallmark of Tractarian aesthetics. The process by which religious knowledge and the outpouring of spiritual emotion generated by such knowledge is both enacted and controlled was what Tractarian poets came to refer to as the notion of 'reserve'. In his Tracts 80 and 87, Williams identifies in scripture a withholding of divine truth, seeing in the figurative devices of parable, typology and analogy to be found throughout scripture 'instances of a veil thrown remarkably over moral and spiritual truth' (Tract 80). It is only reserve that can protect sacred truth; additionally it is the case, according to Williams, that reserve 'always accompanies all strong and deep feeling' and it is the distinguishing 'characteristic of genuine poetry' (Tract 87). While for Williams the 'doctrine of reserve' (as it became known) remained principally an idea of theological exposition, for John Keble it became additionally an aesthetic theory. Reflecting a Romantic, especially Wordsworthian, sense of poetry as sacrament, Keble argues that all poetry (or at least all of that written by the poets he refers to as Primary) proceeds by reserve as it seeks to calm a mind 'over-wrought' with emotion. In his 1838 review of J. G. Lock's *Memoirs of the Life of Sir Walter Scott*, he claims poetry as 'the indirect expression in words, most appropriately in metrical words, of some overpowering emotion, or ruling taste, or feeling, the direct indulgence whereof is somehow repressed'.[14] Here again then is the same idea of withholding suggested by Williams's 'veil', 'indirect', 'repressed'; the idea that it is poetry which is the medium best suited to the expression of those thoughts and feelings that are of such spiritual and emotional import that they threaten to overwhelm writer and reader alike with their intensity. Ordinary language is not capable of communicating the deepest longings and emotions of the human heart, especially in matters of faith, whereas poetry can express these things 'more touchingly', 'more seriously and weightily' because its language hints and suggests rather than defines and describes:

> Poetry lends to Religion her wealth of symbols and similes: Religion restores these again to Poetry, clothed with so splendid a radiance that they appear to be no longer merely symbols but to partake (I might almost say) of the nature of sacraments'.[15]

The indirectness of figurative language, through its codification of meaning, is what enables the awesomeness and mysteriousness of religious knowledge to be approached obliquely, the revelation and appropriation of divine knowledge becomes a process of measured decoding.

Tennyson may not have succeeded in reinvigorating critical interest in Keble, Newman or Williams – today they are as absent from all but the most extensive anthologies of Victorian poetry – however, the same is not true of Christina Rossetti. At the end of his book, Tennyson includes an appendix on Rossetti, suggesting that poetically she is 'the true inheritor of the Tractarian devotional mode in poetry',[16] and identifying particularly Keble's poetics of the modulation of intense religious and emotional longing as the key to reading Rossetti. Noting the dearth of critical attention[17] hitherto paid to the importance of Tractarian poetics to both her poetry and prose, he argues that the tendency previously had been to account for the religiosity so central to most of her work more exclusively in psychological terms. Recent years, however, have seen the emergence of a more thorough approach to the relationship between Rossetti's poetry and her devout faith, and much of this has acknowledged the importance of both Tractarian poetics generally and the doctrine of reserve more specifically.[18]

If reserve is about the figurative processes by which divine knowledge is revealed and received, then arguably there is no part of biblical revelation where it is more at work than in the astonishing and terrifying *Revelation of St John the Divine,* a text whose very title announces its intention but which, with the obvious exception of the *The Book of Psalms*, is the most poetic book of the bible, being a complex, kaleidoscope and multivalent matrix of symbol, analogy, numerology and metaphor. In 1892, Rossetti published the complete *The Face of the Deep: A Devotional Commentary on the Apocalypse* (see Chapter 32, this volume), her major work of devotional prose in which she offers clues to her understanding and inheritance of the doctrine of reserve further to that found, more famously, in her poetry.

One of the ways in which Rossetti enacts reserve in *The Face of the Deep* is to be explicitly reticent about trying to inquire too much into the mysteries of God's will and decrees, remembering that whilst ultimate, complete knowledge is never possible, the right attitude may however result in wisdom:

> Such a consideration encourages us, I think, to pursue our study of the Apocalypse, ignorant as we may be. Bring we patience and prayer to our quest, and assuredly we shall not be sent empty away. The father of lights may still withhold from us knowledge, but, He will not deny us wisdom.

Patience operates methodologically throughout the work enacting Keble's emphasis on 'indirect expression' and Williams's 'veil'. Revelation of religious knowledge can only ever be partial, and its figurative mediation through poetic text ascribes to revelation a quality of deferral; it is a 'quest'. Closely allied to this is a powerful notion of 'suspense'. Glossing Chapter VIII – 'And when He had opened the seventh seal, there was silence in heaven about the space of half an hour' – Rossetti seeks to wonder on its implication. She concludes 'If from the songs of heaven we learn to sing and make melody to the Lord with both voice and understanding, equally from the silence of heaven we may learn somewhat'. And what is learned is that:

> one may view this 'silence' as a figure of suspense. Reversing which proposition, I perceive that a Christian's suspense ought to present a figure of that silence. And if so, suspense should sustain my heart in heavenly peace even whilst fluttering over some spot of earth: and should become my method of worship.

So whilst it retains a strong notion of deferral central to Tractarian definitions of reserve, here, through its incorporation as a means of worship, Rossetti ascribes to reserve a more dynamic concept of practice. It maintains a sense of indirectness, but it is not solely concerned with denial and repression, what is not seen or not expressed, but instead becomes additionally a doctrine of praxis, a way of reading we might say whereby a sign of absence and lack (silence) becomes interpreted as positive presence (suspense), hermeneutically and pedagogically important: 'Faithful, hopeful, loving suspense would be rich in evidence of things not seen and not heard' (Ch. XVIII).

Prior to his conversion, Gerard Manley Hopkins had described himself as a 'Tractarian'. Indeed, in a letter to his father in October 1866 explaining his decision to become a Roman Catholic, he credits the influence of E. B. Pusey and H. P. Liddon, the leaders of the Movement since Newman's conversion to Rome in 1845, with having delayed his final decision to leave the Church of England even though he had already persuaded himself of the theological and ecclesiastical reasons to convert.[19] To Hillis Miller in *The Disappearance of God* however, theological and ecclesiastical reasons are not the main motivation for Hopkins's conversion to Roman Catholicism. Rather, like those of the other writers he includes, he sees Hopkins's conversion as a personal attempt to overcome the cultural crisis of faith, 'an attempt to avoid falling into the abyss of the absence of God... to escape the poetic destiny which paralyses such men as Matthew Arnold, and leaves them hovering between two worlds'.[20]

The discernible lingering of Tractarian poetics generally and, more specifically, the deployment of the doctrine of reserve in Hopkins's poetry is a matter of some debate.[21] Certainly, however, although he was an admirer of Rossetti, and influenced by her, reserve does not characterise his poetry as it does hers. His poetic voice is for the most part not one of emotional reticence and restraint but one which seeks by the sheer exuberance of its figurative and formal will to make present the living Christ: 'Each created thing is a version of Christ, and derives its being from the way it expresses Christ's nature in a unique way'.[22] For Hopkins, nature does not point beyond itself to God but actually contains God; his is a theological poetics of immanence rather than analogy: 'I do not think I have ever seen anything more beautiful than the bluebell I have been looking at. I know the beauty of our Lord by it'.[23] This is not religious knowledge deferred but actually manifested in the present moment. It is this acutely incarnational attitude which motivates Hopkins's poetry. And whether this produces emotion of overwhelming joy or overwhelming darkness, the intensity of such feeling is a poetic visceralness in contrast to the indirectness of Tractarian reserve. Hopkins's emotions are not veiled but arguably retain just the kind of overwroughtness that Keble and Williams sort to soothe and regulate.

It is possible that to many, Hillis Miller overplays the extent to which Hopkins's intense religiosity and the affective vibrancy of much of his religious poetry derives from a resistance to a God-less abyss. There is no doubting though that Hopkins's faith was a matter of intense personal struggle, especially towards the end of his life, in which he often felt the absence of God more strongly than His presence. It is just such anguish over the apparent inaccessibility of God which characterises the poetry of the period usually referred to as the poetry of 'faith and doubt'.

Nineteenth-century poets were often reflective and melancholic; and 'elegiac' became a ubiquitous genre of poetry in the period, performing more generalised laments of loss and regret alongside the more traditional mourning of the death of a specific person. Such poetry voices the melancholy felt by, among other things, the passing of time, love, youth or the the pre-industrial rural landscape. Additionally though, the elegiac also became the poetic medium of religious doubt and the difficulties of belief; Matthew Arnold's *Dover Beach* perhaps being the bleakest as well as the most famous. Others, like Arthur Hugh Clough's *Easter Day Naples 1849*, reflect the acute bitterness many felt at their loss of belief; while poems like James Thomson's *The City of Dreadful Night* reflect as well the more general mood of dejection brought on by a broader awareness of change, decay and transitoriness in the context of the regretful but growing sense that God had disappeared. However, it is not only in the more emblematic poems of faith and doubt that religious struggle is to be found. A similar elegiac quality can also be detected even in what must surely be the most devotional mode of all poetry – hymnody.

The liturgical context for which most hymns are primarily intended might suggest that they express orthodox Christian faith and tend to offer unambiguous reassurances of heavenly consolation for life's ills and suffering. However, the aimed-for reassurance is often more successful in the intention than in the execution, and their confrontation with the sadder realities of life or the difficulties of faith is what draws the reader's attention.

Commonly recurring themes in nineteenth century hymnody are the transitoriness of life and life as dominated by cares and sorrow. Take, for example, John Mason Neale:

> Brief life is here our portion;
> Brief sorrow, short lived care;
> The life that know no ending,
> The tearless life, is there.[24]

Or Henry Baker:

> There is a blessed home
> beyond this land of woe
> where trials never come
> Nor tears of sorrow flow.[25]

Or Godfrey Thring;

> True and everlasting are the glories there
> Where no pain nor sorrow, toil nor care is known.[26]

All of these make a sharp distinction between earthly life and heavenly existence. There is no shying away from the sadder experiences: life is seen wholly in negative terms as being short and characterised by struggles, cares and, above all, sorrow – a word used by every one of these writers. This is contrasted with not only the permanence of heaven but its appealing character as the complete opposite of earthly experiences, an antidote to present suffering. The heaven that is being reached for is absent though – it is 'there' not here, and located in the future.

Each of these hymns goes on to attempt a soothing resolution of these sentiments through an appeal to God's mercy or the deployment of traditional Christian motifs. However, the description of so much of human experience in such stark terms is never quite overcome by the voice of faith and remains a perturbing presence in the hymns, thus dislocating religious consolation as the dominant reading. This can be seen in one of the most famous hymns of the nineteenth century – 'Abide with Me' by Henry Francis Lyte – written probably in the summer of 1847 a few months before the author's death.

It is an intense, personal imagining of approaching death and a powerful expression of the shortness, swiftness and littleness of human life. Against this is set the needy expression of a faithful hope in an immutable, present God who will be the kind and protective companion of the speaker. The speaker is very much alone:

> Abide with me; fast falls the eventide;
> The darkness deepens; Lord with me abide.
> When other helpers fail and comforts flee,
> Help of the helpless, O abide with me.
>
> Swift to its close ebbs out life's little day;
> Earth's joys grow dim; its glories pass away;
> Change and decay in all around I see;
> O Thou who changest not, abide with me.[27]

The opening verse establishes immediately the solitary position of the speaker as well as his precarious mental position in his confrontation with his own mortality, taking the reader to the defining fact of not only the speaker's but every human being's life: the knowledge of death. In this certainty, the speaker raises his heartfelt plea for the comfort of the almighty, manifested in the prayer-like opening words – 'abide with me'. These words become the refrain found in every verse, repeated ten times through the course of the poem. Such accumulation, however, ultimately serves only to emphasise the lack of satisfactory response and merely fixes the plea in agonised stasis; dependent on the wager of faith and the hope of prayer. Such contingency throws the the poem back onto its own bleak assessment of the human condition which remains the affectively resonant centre of the poem. Thus, 'Abide with Me' ultimately resonates less as a hymn of the reassuring presence and protection of God, and more as a sad meditation on the poet's view of the human condition; its comfort lies in its ability to elegise experience common to all.

Despite becoming one of the most famous hymns of the nineteenth century and remaining hugely popular today, 'Abide with Me' was not without its detractors. John Julian, in his magisterial *Dictionary of Hymnology*, acerbically notes that Lyte's hymns are characterised by their sadness and tenderness and rarely display joy or gladness. John Ellerton also thought the hymn too intense and personal for congregational use.

These criticisms are interesting for their illustration that among important writers and editors of hymns there was clearly a view that hymns serve a particular function within the community of faith – fortifying and enlivening that faith. These have also no doubt contributed to the opinion among the majority of literary critics that hymns are a genre that belongs to the church and are of no interest outside of that context.

However, perhaps it is the very fact that hymns can be very personal, gloomy meditations on the difficulties of life and faith that accounts for the huge popularity of hymns like 'Abide with Me'; that they are loved precisely because of their ambiguities of feeling and faith. Some people did no doubt feel reassured by the expression of such ambiguities within the context of a simultaneous trust in an unchanging God. For others, though, it was precisely that rawness, subjectivity and melancholy they were criticised for that resonated with their own experience or view of the world, and which provided a different sort of comfort – a comfort of empathy rather than reassurance. Either way, the presence in some nineteenth-century hymnody of some of the emotional and psychological anxieties of life and of the difficulties of faith experienced by the age suggest that hymnody has more to offer the student of nineteenth-century poetry than has hitherto been recognised, and is another genre of devotional poetry where there is still much critical work to be done.[28]

Notes

1   Kirstie Blair, *Form and Faith in Victorian Poetry and Religion* (Oxford: Oxford University Press, 2012), p. 5.
2   Bernard Richards, *English Poetry of the Victorian Period 1830–1890*, 2nd ed. (Harlow: Longman, 2001), p. 182.
3   F. E. Gray, *Christian and Lyric Tradition in Victorian Women's Poetry* (New York: Routledge, 2010), p. 3.
4   Charles LaPorte, *Victorian Poets and the Changing Bible* (Charlottesville, VA.: University of Virginia Press, 2007), p. 1.
5   Other scholars engaged in this endeavour also include, among others, Emma Mason and Mark Knight, *Nineteenth-Century Religion and Literature: An Introduction* (Oxford: Oxford University Press, 2006), Tracy Fassenden, *Culture and Redemption: Religion, the Secular and American Literature* (Princeton, NJ: Princeton University Press, 2007) and Dinah Roe, *Christina Rossetti's Faithful Imagination* (Basingstoke: Palgrave Macmillan, 2006).
6   For the student probably the best place to start for a contextual overview of the relationship between religion and literature in the nineteenth century is with Mason and Knight (2006) (see Note 5 above) and then proceed to Blair (2012) (see Note 1 above) for how form faith and poetry combine in a wide range of poets both canonical and the neglected – Tennyson, Browning (Robert and Elizabeth Barrett), Keble, Rossetti, Newman, Hopkins, Arnold and others.
7   G. B. Tennyson, *Victorian Devotional Poetry: The Tractarian Mode* (Cambridge, MA.: Harvard University Press, 1981).
8   A comment Tennyson made in his afterword to a special edition of dedicated to Tractarian Poetics (*Victorian Poetry* 44.1, 2006). This is another very useful resource for the student interested in this field, containing articles on, among others, Hopkins, Charlotte Yonge, Women's Poetry, Keble and Frederick Faber.
9   The name Tractarians arose from one of the principal means by which the 'founders' of the Oxford Movement (John Keble, John Henry Newman, J. A. Froude, Isaac Williams and E. B. Pusey) disseminated their ideas – through a series of ninety pamphlets, 1833–1841, published under the collective title *Tracts for the Times*. Emma Mason provides a succinct account of the aims of the Oxford Movement in her 'Introduction' to the special edition of *Victorian Poetry* dedicated to Tractarian Poetry (see Note 8 above).
10   Tennyson, *Victorian Devotional Poetry*, p. 9.
11   Ibid., p. 10.

12 John Henry Newman, 'Tamworth Reading Room', in *Discussions and Arguments on Various Subjects* (London: Longmans and Green, 1911), pp. 293–5.

13 For William Wordsworth the imagination is 'reason in her most exalted mood' (*The Prelude* xiv.192) while for Samuel Taylor Coleridge, the imagination is 'the living Power and prime Agent of all human Perception, and as a repetition in the finite mind of the eternal act of creation in the infinite I AM' (*Biographia Literaria*, Chapter 13). For Stephen Pricket the Romantic conception of the imagination, especially that of Wordsworth and Coleridge, exerts an important philosophic influence on religious poetics in the nineteenth century. See Stephen Prickett, *Romanticism and Religion: The Traditions of Coleridge and Wordsworth in the Victorian Church* (Cambridge: Cambridge University Press, 1976).

14 John Keble, 'Life of Sir Walter Scott' (1838), in John Keble, *Occasional Papers and Reviews* (Oxford and London: James Parker and Co., 1877), pp. 1–80.

15 E. K. Francis (trans.), *Keble's Lectures on Poetry* vol. II (Oxford: Clarendon Press, 1912), p. 481.

16 Tennyson, *Victorian Devotional Poetry*, p. 198.

17 The exception to this is Raymond Chapman, *Faith and Revolt: Studies in the Literary Influence of the Oxford Movement* (London: Weidenfeld & Nicholson,1970), pp. 170–97.

18 See for example: Emma Mason, 'Christina Rossetti and the Doctrine of Reserve', *Journal of Victorian Culture* 7.2 (2002), 196–219.

19 Gerard Manley Hopkins, Letter to his father 16 October 1866 in Catherine Phillips (ed.), *The Oxford Authors: Gerard Manley Hopkins*, (Oxford: Oxford University Press, 1986), pp. 323–326.

20 J. Hillis Miller, *The Disappearance of God* (Chicago, IL: University of Chicago Press, 1963), p. 312.

21 For an overview of some of the issues, see Peter Groves, 'Hopkins and Tractarianism', *Victorian Poetry* 44.1 (2006), 105–112

22 Hillis Miller, *Disappearance*, p. 313.

23 H. House and G. Storey (eds.), *The Journals and Papers of Gerard Manley Hopkins* (Oxford: Oxford University Press, 1959), p. 199.

24 John Mason Neale (trans.), *Bernard of Cluny*, 1861, 'Brief Life is Here our Portion' in *The New English Hymnal* (Norwich: The Canterbury Press, 1986).

25 Henry Baker, 'There is a Blessed Home' in *Hymns Ancient and Modern* (Norwich: The Canterbury Press,1861 edition).

26 'Savior Blessed Savior' retrieved 27 July 2015 from www.hymnary.org/text/savior_blessed_savior_listen_while_we_si

27 Henry Francis Lyte, 'Abide with me' in *The New English Hymnal* (Norwich: The Canterbury Press, 1986).

28 The standard critical work on hymnody remains J. R. Watson's *The English Hymn: A Critical and Historical* Study (Oxford: Oxford University Press, 1997) but see also Ian Bradley, *Abide with Me: The World of Victorian Hymns* (London: SCM Press, 1997) and J. R. Watson, *An Annotated Anthology of Hymns* (Oxford: Oxford University Press, 2002). J. R. Watson's excellent article on hymns in the nineteenth century is also included in the present volume in Part V: Forms.

31 Tracts 80 and 87: On Reserve in Communicating Religious Knowledge (1838–40)

Isaac Williams

Tract 80: On reserve in communicating religious knowledge

Part I: 'From the example of our Lord'

1. General allusions to this mode of concealment.

The object of the present inquiry is to ascertain, whether there is not in GOD'S dealings with mankind, a very remarkable holding back of sacred and important truths, as if the knowledge of them were injurious to persons unworthy of them. And if this be the case, it will lead to some important practical reflections. [...]

As the first view, we have the remarkable fact of the many generations of the heathen world, in a state of great ignorance of many things which we know to be of the very highest importance to our well-being. In the next place, we may notice the silence observed, respecting a future and eternal life in the books of Moses, as one of "the secret things which belonged unto GOD." The fact that the Patriarchs were supported by an indefinite, but full assurance of GOD'S unfailing goodness, which could not cease with this life, will be a confirmation of this point; for it shows that it was in some measure revealed unto them, as they could bear it. In the next place, the numerous rites and types are instances of a veil thrown remarkably over moral and spiritual truth; for it is very evident that to David and others, they conveyed all the "secrets of wisdom," and spoke of "the hands *washed* in innocency," and "the *sacrifice* of a broken heart," and "the circumcision of the heart"—but it was through a veil. The expression "I am a stranger upon earth, hide not thy commandments from me," seem to imply, that the commandments being hid from him was the thing which the Psalmist apprehended from unworthiness; and the verse preceding, "open thou mine eyes, that I may behold the wondrous things of the law," and indeed the whole of the 119th Psalm, indicates something great and wonderful, contained in the commandments beyond the letter. Origen says (contr. Cels. p. 197.) "if the law of Moses had not any thing of a more latent meaning, the prophet would not have said, 'open mine eyes, that I may behold the wonderful things of thy law.' The descriptions of the Messiah's kingdom in the prophets were exactly of this kind, such as a carnal mind would take literally; a good man would see that God had something better for those that waited for Him."

[...]

4. The teaching by Parables.

I cannot but conceive that there must have been this intention of veiling truth in the Parables. It has been said indeed that they render moral truths more plain and easy, as well as more engaging; and that this was their purpose. But is this the case? They are easy to us, as all such things seem to be when explained; but were they so at the time? Was not the Crucifixion foretold nine times to the Apostles, and yet it was said distinctly that they did not understand it, although it does not appear to us, who know the circumstances, so difficult? Does not the place where the word parable occurs, often imply that this was its meaning or effect? […]

In speaking of a Parable as a veil, I would be cautious against mentioning anything as the end proposed in the operations of GOD: which, of course, to confine to one end and purpose, we may perceive would be quite impossible, as in the works of Nature; I would only say that the Parable did serve this purpose among others. Might it not be that the most spiritual and heavenly precepts were thus left to the rude and rough world, so that the veil of the figure might still be over them, though disclosing its import to any attentive and thoughtful person; performing thus by themselves through the wonderful wisdom of GOD, that which He has commanded us to observe, in not "giving that which is holy to the dogs," and not "casting pearls before swine."

This view of a parable as a veil of the truth seems generally confirmed by the Fathers. A Parable is explained by Theophylact (see Schleusner) as "a dark saying." Cyril (in the Catechesis vi.) says, "Is it only the GOD of the Old Testament who hath blinded the eyes of them that believe not? Hath not JESUS Himself said, 'therefore I speak unto them in Parables, that seeing they might not perceive.' Was it from hating them that he wished them not to see? Or, was it not that they were unworthy to do so, since they had closed their eyes?" and again, the same writer says, "To those who could not hear He spoke in parables, and privately expounded them to His disciples. The brightness of glory was for these; and blindness for unbelievers."

Clement of Alexandria says (Stromata, B. vi. p. 676.) "Neither Prophecy nor our Saviour Himself promulgated the divine mysteries in such a manner that they might easily be apprehended by all persons, but discoursed in Parables. Certainly the Apostles say concerning the LORD, 'that He spake all things in Parables, and without a Parable spake He not unto them.'" "And even in the law and prophets," he adds, "it was He that spake to them in Parables."

And Chrysostom in like manner. "Had He not wished them to hear and to be saved, He would have been silent, and not have spoken in Parables. But by this means He moveth them, by speaking things overshadowed and darkened." (Homil. on St. Matt. xiii.)

5. The manner of our Lord's Miracles,—their concealment, &c.

The miracles of our blessed LORD were the other mode of His teaching mankind and disclosing His Divinity—and will not all that has been said forcibly apply to them also? Would it not appear (if I may so express myself with reverence) that He walked about, infinitely desirous to communicate good, without any limit or measure of His own goodness or power, but yet bound, as it were, in some very wonderful manner, by the unfitness of mankind to receive Him? For as He is revealed to us as more than willing to forgive, but as it were unable to do so unless we repent; in like manner is He also as desirous to manifest Himself to us, but as it were unable to do so, unless we are fitly disposed for it. Is it not very observable that the miracles recorded were to the very utmost of the faith of the person seeking relief, but as it were unable to go beyond? By a word, and at a distance, if so asked, as in the case of the Centurion: by laying on His hand, if the request went to this, as in Jairus's daughter: by a more speedy cure of another intervening by touching the hem of His garment, if such the belief; and He is spoken of as unable to work miracles (except a few) because they believed not: A very memorable expression, which incidentally occurs as marking the sole bounds of His power and will. [...]

The frequent instances of our LORD forbidding them to mention His miracles, is usually accounted for by His not wishing to call the attention of the Jews, and provoke persecution on the one hand, and that the people might not make Him a King on the other, for which on more than one occasion we have an Evangelist's authority. But may we not see more in it than this? Forbearing to work miracles before some persons seems to be like that of keeping from them what was already done. [...]

And if we take the instance of those miracles which appear to have been the most public, those, for instance, of the loaves and fishes, with 5000 persons on one occasion, and 4000 on the other partaking of them; even here it would appear as if there was somehow a sort of secret character about the miracle, for the multitudes were afterwards following our SAVIOUR, because they ate the bread, but not considering the miracle; and of the disciples themselves, of whom it is said, (by some doubtless very important coincidence of expression by the four Evangelists on both occasions,) that they distributed the bread as it grew in their hands, it is said immediately after on the sea, that they considered not the miracle. It was not, therefore, even on this public occasion like an overpowering sign from heaven, but the Divine agency even here retiring in some degree from view, as in His natural providence.

Part II: The example of our Lord confirmed by His Moral Government

7. That Christ, as seen in the conduct of good men, thus conceals Himself.

There is another mode in which we may find (I would speak with reverence) the presence of JESUS CHRIST, as still in the world, and His manner of dealing with mankind, and that is in the usual conduct of good men, especially if such conduct is at all marked by any peculiarity, and such peculiarity increasing as they advance in strictness of life. And this I think we may find to be the case: for notwithstanding that a spirit of true charity has a natural desire to communicate itself, and is, of all things, the most expansive and extending, yet in all such cases, we may still perceive the indwelling of CHRIST in them, still seeking, as it were, to hide Himself; for, I think, they are all marked by an inclination, as far as it is possible, of retiring, and shrinking from public view. [...]

As our blessed SAVIOUR in various ways retired from the view of men, and hid His glories, so it is remarkable how little we know of the saints of GOD; of one of the most eminent of the disciples we know nothing, and next to nothing, of St. John's private history and character. Indeed, what little we do know of them is but as it were accidental, and the exception to the general rule, as in the letters of St. Paul: and even there, casual intimations greatly tend to shew our ignorance respecting them, as of the Revelations of St. Paul, of the time he spent in Arabia, and at Tarsus. Add to these, how many things are there, which more immediately respect our LORD Himself, the account of which, as St. John says, would have been more than the world could contain, yet all lost in silence. So also the things pertaining to the kingdom which were spoken for the forty days. "Verily, thou art a GOD that hidest thyself, O GOD of Israel, the SAVIOUR. (Is. xlv.)

It must have occurred to every one, with some surprise at first, how much the sacred people, having the visible presence of GOD among them, and containing, as it were, the eternal destinies of mankind, were overlooked by, and unknown to, the more polished and powerful nations of the world. Gibbon has not failed to take hold of this circumstance. And, in like manner, how little Christianity was noticed or known to heathen writers at a time when it was secretly changing the whole face of the world, the salt of the earth, and on which the earth depended for its existence. There may be something analogous to this in cases of unknown individuals still. And all such are examples of what Aristotle says of virtuous principle, "[εἰ γὰρ καὶ τῷ ὄγκῳ μικόν ἐστι, δυνάμει καὶ τθμότητι πολὺ μᾶλλον ὑπερέχει πάντων]," "though in external appearance it be but small, yet, in power and worth, it is very far indeed superior to all things." (Ethics, b. x. c. vii. ad finem.) In the second place, there is another circumstance, which would tend to produce the same effect, viz. that reserve, or retiring delicacy, which exists naturally in a good man, unless injured by external motives, and which is of course the teaching of GOD through him. Something of this kind always accompanies all strong and deep feeling, so much so that indications of it have been considered the characteristic of genuine poetry, as distinguishing it from that which is only fictitious of poetic feeling." It is the very protection of all sacred and virtuous principle, and which, like the bloom which indicates life and freshness, when once lost cannot be restored. Which is thus expressed in a Latin hymn;

> "Se sub serenis vultibus
> Austera virtus occulit:
> Timet videri; ne suum,
> Dum prodit, amittat decus."
> Paris. Brev. Comm. Mul.

Such a reserve on other subjects of sublime or delicate feeling is only a type of the same in religion; where, of course, from the very nature of the subject, it must be much greater, inasmuch as it comprehends all feelings and all conduct which are directed to Him who is invisible, and who reads the language of the heart, and to whom silence may often best speak. Every thing which has GOD for its end gives rise to feelings which do not admit of expression. This seems to be implied in the difference which Aristotle speaks of, when he says there are objects which are worthy of higher feelings than praise can express, and such we look upon with honour and veneration. We do, indeed, often speak of such with words of praise, as we do of the Supreme Being, but in so doing we stand upon lower ground, and rather turn to each other than to Him, and introduce relation and comparison, which necessarily must be drawn from human and inferior objects: but we then descend from the higher, but silent, impressions of awe, veneration, and wonder.

Tract 87: On reserve in communicating religious knowledge

Part V: The Principle Opposed to Certain Modern Religious Opinions

7. On eloquent preaching and delivery.

There is another important point in which the modern system is opposed to Scripture in breaking the spirit of reserve, *viz.*, in attaching so great a value to preaching as to disparage Prayer and Sacraments in comparison. According to this the Church of GOD would be the House of Preaching; but Scripture calls it the House of Prayer. But with regard to the subject of preaching altogether, it is, in the present day, taken for granted, that eloquence in speech is the most powerful means of promoting religion in the world. But if this be the case, it occurs to one as remarkable, that there is no intimation of this in Scripture: perhaps no single expression can be found in any part of it that implies it: there is no recommendation of rhetoric in precept, or example, or prophecy. There is no instance of it; no part of Scripture itself appears in this shape, as the remains of what was delivered with powerful eloquence. Many parts of it consist of poetry, none of oratory; and it is remarkable that the former partakes more of this reserve, the latter less so. It speaks of instruction, "precept upon precept, line upon line, here a little and there a little," but never of powerful appeals of speech. The great teacher of the Gentiles, in whom we would most of all have expected to find it, was "weak in bodily presence, and in speech contemptible;" and rendered so, it is supposed, by "a thorn in the flesh." Whereas, it would be thought by many now, that the great requisites for a successful minister are a powerful bodily presence and eloquent speech. Indeed, St. Paul says, that the effect of the words of men's wisdom would be to render the Cross of CHRIST of none effect. It is, moreover, observable, that in Scripture all the words denoting a minister of the Gospel throw us back on the commission. Such, for instance, is the word "Apostle," or "the Sent," which title is repeated with a remarkable frequency and emphasis, and united, in one instance, with the awful and high expression, "As my FATHER hath sent me, even so I send you." And the word "preaching," as now used, has a meaning attached to it derived from modern notions, which we shall not find in Scripture. "A preacher," indeed, properly conveys the same idea as "Apostle," and really signifies the same thing – "a herald;" for, of course, all the office of a herald depends on him that sent him, not so much on himself, or his mode of delivering his message. All other words, in like manner adopted in the Church, speak the same; they all designate him as one *ministering* or *serving* at GOD'S altar, not as one whose first object is to be useful to men; such, for instance, are the appellations of *diaconus, sacerdos*. It is curious that our word "minister," implying also the same, comes to be commonly used in the other sense, being applied, like that of preacher, to self-created teachers. Thus do men's opinions invest sacred appellations with new meaning, according to the change in their own views.

  If people in general were now asked what was the most powerful means of advancing the cause of religion in the world, we should be told that it was eloquence of speech or preaching: and the excellency of speech we know consists in delivery; that is the first, the second, and the third requisite. Whereas, if we were to judge from Holy Scripture, of what were the best means of promoting Christianity in the world, we should say obedience; and if we were to be asked the second, we should say obedience; and if we were to be asked the third, we should say obedience. And it is evident, that if the spirit of obedience exists, simple and calm statement of truth will go far. Not that we would be thought entirely to depreciate preaching as a mode of doing good; it may be necessary in a weak and languishing state; but it is the characteristic of this system as opposed to that of the Church, and we fear the undue exaltation of an instrument which Scripture, to say the least, has never recommended. And, indeed, if from Revelation we turn to the great teachers of morals which have been in the world, we shall be surprised to find how little they esteemed it useful for their purpose. The exceeding jealous apprehension of rhetoric which Socrates evinces is remarkable, as shown throughout the Gorgias. Nor does it ever seem to have occurred to the sages of old, as a means of promoting morality; and yet some of them, as Pythagoras and Socrates, made this purpose, *viz.*, that of improving the principles of men, the object of their lives: and the former was remarkable for his mysterious discipline, and the silence he imposed; the latter for a mode of questioning, which may be considered as entirely an instance of this kind of reserve in teaching.

Part VI: The System of the Church, One of Reserve

8. Untenable objections on the ground of our present position.

But there are some objections to this treatise, of a very obvious and simple kind, which it is difficult to know how to answer, as they arise from a strange misapprehension *in limine* of the nature of the subject: objections which, as was stated before, are necessarily implied in the very word revelation. It is thought, for instance, that the command, "Go ye into all the world, and preach the Gospel unto every creature," is an insurmountable objection to the whole argument. Whereas, it should be considered, that the whole matter under consideration is, not whether the Gospel is to be preached or not, for of course there could be no doubt among Christians on that subject, but respecting the most effectual mode of preaching it: without taking this for granted as the first axiom among Christians, viz. that the Gospel is to be preached, the whole inquiry has no meaning.

With rather more appearance of reason it is alleged, that our LORD'S conduct is no example for us in this case; as He has said, "what I tell you in the ear, that preach ye on the housetops;" and "men do not light a candle, and put it under a bushel, but on a candlestick, and it giveth light unto all that are in the house." Now if there was any weight in these passages against this reserve, it would be merely that of one Scripture expression opposed to another; for there are several commands in the same discourse of an opposite character, and therefore of course they admit of explanation without contradicting each other. The obvious meaning of these passages of course is "Think not that My kingdom is to be confined, as now it is, to you few alone, it is to be preached to all the world;" and such a declaration evidently does not interfere with this principle of holy reserve, as the guide and mode of doing this most sincerely and effectually. And indeed to the latter text it is added, as if showing us the way by which we were to extend the truth, "Let your light shine before men, that they may see your good works," as Chrysostom says, not of course that they were to display their works in any way, but that if they keep the fire burning within them, it necessarily must shine. And besides which it appears, on many occasions, when expressions of this kind are used, that they have a reference also to the day of Judgment; as if it had been said, "Wonder not that My ways are so much in secret, and that I require your works also to be done so much in secret, and unlike those of the Pharisees; a time is coming when every thing whatever shall be publicly made known, to all men and angels." As if it were in some measure an explanation given, that that great manifestation will be a counterpart to this reserve.

But that these expressions respecting the general knowledge of the Gospel throughout the world, do in no way affect this rule of reserve, will be evident if we consider the various periods of the Divine economy as various manifestations of CHRIST. And it will be easily perceived that they are all characterized by this same law. First of all the term manifestation is applied to our LORD'S appearing in the flesh; it is applied to Him at His birth; it is applied to the coming and calling of the Gentiles; it is applied to the Presentation in the temple; it is applied to our LORD at His Baptism: and to the first miracle He performed in Cana of Galilee. It is applied to Him more especially in His miracles and teaching. All these we celebrate in the Epiphany, as will be seen in the successive Gospels for that season; but how secretly and mysteriously were they all conducted? All these are manifestations of GOD seen in the flesh, our Immanuel. And all these are with this reserve. In like manner the preaching of the Gospel, and the extension of the Kingdom, are more fully manifestations of GOD; but as in the former cases CHRIST was known and acknowledged but by a very few, notwithstanding those manifestations of Himself; so is it now. It is evident that in some sense even now the manifestation of Himself must be according to some law of exceeding reserve and secrecy, for our LORD has said that if any man will keep His commandments He will love him, and will manifest Himself unto him; that He would "manifest Himself to His disciples, and not unto the world." Now as it is too obvious that many do not keep His commandments, therefore to many He is not manifested. So that to us all, even now our LORD observes this rule of concealing Himself even in His manifestations; and therefore all His manifestations in His Church are ways of reserve.

32 The Face of the Deep: A Devotional Commentary on the Apocalypse (1892)

Christina Rossetti

To My Mother, For the First time
To Her Beloved, Revered, Cherished Memory.

Prefatory Note.

If thou canst dive, bring up pearls. If thou canst not dive, collect amber. Though I fail to identify Paradisiacal "bdellium," I still may hope to search out beauties of the "onyx stone."

A dear saint – I speak under correction of the Judgment of the Great Day, yet think not then to have my word corrected – this dear person once pointed out to me Patience as our lesson in the Book of Revelations.

Following the clue thus afforded me, I seek and hope to find Patience in this Book of awful import. Patience, at the least: and along with that grace whatever treasures beside God may vouchsafe me. Bearing meanwhile in mind how "to him that knoweth to do good, and doeth it not, to him it is sin."

Now if any deign to seek Patience in my company, I pray them to remember that One high above me in the Kingdom of Heaven heads our pilgrim caravan.

> O, ye who love to-day,
> Turn away
> From Patience with her silver ray:
> For Patience shows a twilight face,
> Like a half-lighted moon
> When daylight dies apace.
>
> But ye who love to-morrow,
> Beg or borrow
> To-day some bitterness of sorrow:
> For Patience shows a lustrous face
> In depth of night her noon;
> Then to her the sun gives place.

8. *I am Alpha and Omega, the beginning and the ending, saith the Lord, which is, and which was, and which is to come, the Almighty.*

"I am Alpha and Omega." – Thus well-nigh at the opening of these mysterious Revelations, we find in this title and instance of symbolical language accommodated to human apprehension; for any literal acceptation of the phrase seems obviously and utterly inadmissible. God condescends to teach us somewhat we can learn, and in a way by which we are capable of learning it. So, doubtless, either literally or figuratively, throughout the entire Book.

Such a consideration encourages us, I think, to pursue our study of the Apocalypse, ignorant as we may be. Bring we patience and prayer to our quest, and assuredly we shall not be sent empty away. The Father of lights may still withhold from us knowledge, but He will not deny us wisdom.

"Open Thou mine eyes, that I may behold wondrous things out of Thy law."

If a letter of the alphabet may be defined as a unit of language, then under this title "Alpha and Omega" we may adore God as the sole original Existence, the Unit of Existence, whence are derived all nations, and kindreds, and people, and tongues; yea, all other existences whatsoever.

The title derived from human language seems to call especially upon "men confabulant" for grateful homage. As said of old the wise son of Sirach: "The Lord hath given me a tongue for my reward, and I will praise Him therewith." Or as the sweet Psalmist of Israel declared: "I will sing and give praise with the best member that I have."

Alas! That men often pervert their choicest gifts to their soul's dire destruction. For St. James bears witness against the tongue: "The tongue is a little member, and boasteth great things. Behold, how great a matter a little fire kindleth! And the tongue is a fire, a world of iniquity: so is the tongue among our members, that it defileth the whole body, and setteth on fire the course of nature; and it is set on fire of hell … The tongue can no man tame; it is an unruly evil, full of deadly poison."

O Lord Jesus Christ, Wisdom and Word of God, dwell in our hearts, I beseech Thee, by Thy most Holy Spirit, that out of the abundance of our hearts our mouths may speak Thy praise. Amen.

"The beginning and the ending"—"The beginning" absolutely and in every sense, antecedent to all, cause of all, origin of all.

Not so "the ending"; for by God's merciful Will whilst all creatures have a commencement, many abide exempt from any end, being constituted to share His own eternity. Yet in a different sense God is "the Ending" of all creation, inasmuch as all permanent good creatures converge to His Beatific Presence, find their true unalterable level at His right hand, rejoice in His joy, and rest in His rest for ever and ever. In Him all, out of Him none, attain to fulness of life immortal. "He that dwelleth in the secret place of the Most High, shall abide under the shadow of the Almighty."

Contrariwise, obstinate sinners who finally and of set purpose approach not unto Him by attraction of love, dash themselves against Him in endless rebellion of hatred; as miry waves upheaved over and over and over again against the Rock of Ages.

"Fear ye not me? Saith the Lord: will ye not tremble at My presence, which have placed the sand for the bound of the sea by a perpetual decree, that it cannot pass it: and though the waves thereof toss themselves, yet can they not prevail; though they roar, yet can they not pass over it?"

"If I ascent up into heaven, Thou art there: if I make my bed in hell, behold, Thou art there."

"The Almighty."—

O Lord Almighty, Who hast formed us weak,
    With us whom Thou hast formed deal fatherly;
Be found of us whom Thou hast deigned to seek,
    Be found that we the more may seek for Thee;
Lord, speak and grant us ears to hear Thee speak;
    Lord, come to us and grant us eyes to see;
Lord, make us meek, for Thou Thyself art meek;
    Lord, Thou art Love, fill us with charity.
O Thou the Life of living and of dead,
    Who givest more the more Thyself hast given,
Suffice us as Thy saints Thou hast sufficed;
    That beautified, replenished, comforted;
Still gazing off from earth and up at heaven,
    We may pursue Thy steps, Lord Jesus Christ.

Christ said: "I will forewarn you whom ye shall fear. Fear Him, which after He hath killed hath power to cast into hell; yea, I say unto you, Fear Him"—words to awaken fear: may it be a godly fear.

Meanwhile in these words of dread lies a great encouragement. The power to destroy us is limited to the Almighty, and He is the All-merciful.

"O God, Who declarest Thy almighty power most chiefly in showing mercy and pity; mercifully grant unto us such a measure of Thy grace, that we, running the way of Thy commandments, may obtain Thy gracious promises, and be made partakers of Thy heavenly treasure; through Jesus Christ or Lord. Amen."

"The Lord appeared to Abram, and said unto him, I am the Almighty God; walk before Me, and be thou perfect."— "When the Almighty scattered kings for their sake: then were they as white as snow in Salmon."

Because or God is Almighty, therefore can He demand of us purity and perfection, for by aid of His preventing grace we can respond to His demand. Thanks be to Him, through Jesus Christ our Righteousness.

How light a heart befits one whose burden the Almighty deigns to carry with him. "Why art thou so heavy, O my soul: and why art thou so disquieted within me? Oh, put thy trust in God."

[…]

CHAPTER VI.

1. And I saw when the Lamb opened one of the seals, and I heard as it were the noise of thunder, one of the four beasts saying, Come and see.

He who had been redeemed by the Blood of the Lamb, he in whose stead Christ had died, he whom Jesus loved, "saw when the Lamb opened one of the seals." What that Wise Master and Gracious Lord did St. John could endure to behold, however awful, terrible overwhelming in the result He could endure because he was beloved and because he loved.

Lord, me also Thou hast redeemed by Thy Blood, in my stead also Thou hast died, me also Thou lovest (for which sinner hast Thou not loved?); yet I exceedingly fear and quake lest I should fall away. Thou hast not ceased to be my Wise Master and my Gracious Lord; Thou lovest as Thou hast ever loved; alas, it is I who love not as St. John loved.

Son of God, have mercy upon us. O Lord, let Thy mercy be showered upon us. O Lord, have mercy upon us; have mercy upon us.

> Love still is Love, and doeth all things well,
> Whether he show me heaven or hell,
>> Or earth in her decay
>> Passing away
>> On a day.

> Love still is Love, tho' He should say, "Depart,"
> And break my incorrigible heart,
>> And set me out of sight
>> Widowed of light
>> In the night.

> Love still is Love, is Love, if He should say,
> "Come" on that uttermost dread day,
>> "Come" unto very me,
>> "Come where I be,
>> Come and see."

> Love still is Love, whatever comes to pass:
> O Only Love, make me Thy glass,
>> Thy pleasure to fulfil
>> By loving still
>> Come what will.

"Opened one of the seals."—Not the whole seven at once; not forthwith to recompense all, or to make an end of all consuming as in a moment. Rather as it were remonstrating with mankind again and again: "The day of the Lord is great and very terrible; and who can abide it? Therefore also now, saith the Lord, turn ye even to Me with all your heart,"—and saying especially concerning the elect, as of old concerning Israel: "In measure when it shooteth forth, Thou wilt debate with it: He stayeth His rough wind in the day of the east wind."

So the waters of the Deluge mounted stage by stage, affording time not for the bitterness of death only but also (please God!) for the salutary bitterness of repentance in sight of death.

O Merciful Redeemer, grant us repentance early in the morning, repentance at the third hour, at the sixth hour, at the ninth hour. O Most Merciful Saviour, grant us repentance at the eleventh hour; grant us the eleventh hour for repentance. According to Thy Mercy saving us Thou Who hast died our death and paid our penalty.

"As it were the noise of thunder"—that is; as appears, the voice of one of the Living Creatures. If we may assume that these speak in the order in which they are first named, then this thunderous voice appertains to him of the leonine aspect, with whom such a sound seems congruous. I have read how the natural lion setting his face toward the ground utters a tremendous reverberant roar far reaching and appalling: this celestial "Lion" now sets his face earthwards and summons all within hearing to "Come and see." For surely his word is not to St. John exclusively, through him to us upon whom the ends of the world are come.

But if those four "Living Creatures" rest not day and night, saying, "Holy, Holy, Holy, Lord Almighty, Which Was, and Is, and Is to come": how is it that one after another they now say "Come and see"? Perhaps partly to show us that charitable work interrupts not the flow of adoration. [Yet in such a case I must not be rash to utter anything with my mouth: for these are problems of heaven, while I am upon earth; therefore should my words be few.]

O Lord, Who hast proclaimed by Thy servant, "Come and see," blessed is the man whom Thou choosest and receivest unto Thee. Show us, I beseech Thee, wonderful things in Thy righteousness, O God of our salvation: Thou that art the hope of all the ends of the earth. For Jesus Christ's sake. Amen.

St. Paul has written: "Let the woman learn in silence with all subjection. But I suffer not a woman to teach," Yet elsewhere he wrote: "I call to remembrance the unfeigned faith ... which dwelt first in thy grandmother Lois, and thy mother Eunice."

To expound prophecy lies of course beyond my power, and not within my wish. But the symbolic forms of prophecy being set before all eyes, must be so set for some purpose: to investigate them may not make us wise as serpents; yet ought by promoting faith, fear, hope, love, to aid in making us harmless as doves. "Write the vision, and make it plain upon tables, that he may run that readeth it":—God helping us, we all great and small can and will run.

A commentator I have turned to explains the remainder of this chapter as referring to the establishment on earth of Christ's Kingdom, and to successive events in the history of imperial Rome. But since in Holy Scripture personage after personage, crisis after crisis, judgment after judgment, becomes at various points typical of some greater personage, crisis, judgment, thereafter to be looked for: I venture to trust that throughout this Book of Revelations underlying or parallel with the primary meaning, is often discernible a further signification which may be unfolded to us even while the other continues occult.

Nor surely need an ignorant man be accounted any great loser (so long as ignorance be his misfortune, not his fault) if Bible history becomes less his chronicle of individuals and nations than his parable of Christ and mankind. Abel will speak better things than ever when he is lost sight of in Christ. Isaac will be glorified when by his submission to death Christ is manifested and remembered. Moses will be sufficed when the Prophet like unto him supersedes him. Melchizedek and Aaron will vanish gloriously when by him. Melchizedek and Aaron will vanish gloriously when by them Christ stands revealed: so David before his Son and Lord: so Solomon before the Sole Builder and Maker. The Paschal Lamb, the Scapegoat, will have fulfilled their end when they lead a worshipper to Christ: the Day of Atonement will avail him to whom it shadows forth Good Friday. The Deluge engulfing the old world, the eternal fire of the Cities of the plain, the fall of Jericho, of Assyria, of Babylon, the rejection of ancient Israel, will make wise unto salvation him to whom they bring home the final Day of account; and who with condemned Achan gives God the glory, and with ruined Manasseh betakes himself to penitence and prayer.

Glory be to Thee O God, with Whom are the treasures of wisdom and knowledge, and Who impartest to every man severally as Thou wilt. Glory be to Thee in the Church by Christ Jesus for ever and ever.

[...]

CHAPTER VIII.

1. And when He had opened the seventh seal, there was silence in heaven about the space of half an hour.

There seems to be a sense in which heaven waits on earth; in which (if I dare say so) God waits on man. Thus heaven now keeps silence as a prelude to earthly events, portents, vicissitudes.

Yet need not this celestial silence convey to us (I conjecture) any notion of interruption in the day and night harmony of worship before the Throne, any more than time interrupts eternity. For because we dare not think of God Who "inhabiteth eternity" as changing to a habitation of time, we thence perceive that time and eternity co-exist, are simultaneous: if, that is, they be not rather different aspects of one and the same continuity.

If from the songs of heaven we learn to sing and make melody to the Lord with both voice and understanding, equally from the silence of heaven we may learn somewhat.

Whilst heaven kept silence it appears it may have been looking or preparing to look earthwards. And of old David declared: "I will keep my mouth with a bridle, while the wicked is before me. I was dumb with silence, I held my peace, even from good." Thus from Angels above and from a saint below, I may study that meekness of righteous indignation, that discretion of holy zeal, which brings not railing accusations nor risks doing harm even by good words.

Silence seems unnatural, incongruous, in heaven. On this occasion and remotely we may surmise it to be a result of the Fall, for when earth first saw the light in panoply of beauty the morning stars sang together and all the sons of God shouted for joy: sinless earth, for sinless it then seems to have been whether or not inhabited, called forth instead of silencing an outburst of celestial music.

I think one may view this "silence" as a figure of suspense. Reversing which proposition, I perceive that a Christian's suspense ought to present a figure of that silence.

And if so, suspense should sustain my heart in heavenly peace even whilst fluttering over some spot of earth; and should become my method of worship, when other modes fail me; and should be adopted by my free will, whenever by God's Will it befalls me; and should not hinder heaven from appearing heaven to me, or divorce me from fellowship with angels, or make me speak unadvisedly with my lips. Faithful, hopeful, loving suspense would be rich in evidence of things not seen and not heard; and would neither lag nor hurry, but would contentedly maintain silence during its imposed "half-hour." A shorter time? no, on pain of rashness: a longer time? no, on pain of sullenness.

This silence followed and waited upon an act of our Lord: "when He had opened the seventh seal"—"Unto Thee lift I up mine eyes, O Thou that dwellest in the heavens. Behold, as the eyes of servants look unto the hand of their masters, so our eyes wait upon the Lord our God, until that He have mercy upon us."

"About the space of half an hour."—Not finally, not for long. "Our God shall come, and shall not keep silence … . He shall call to the heavens from above, and to the earth, that He may judge His people … . And the heavens shall declare His righteousness."

> The half moon shows a face of plaintive sweetness
> 　　Ready and poised to wax or wane;
> A fire of pale desire in incompleteness,
> 　　Tending to pleasure or to pain:—
> Lo, while we gaze she rolleth on in fleetness

To perfect loss or perfect gain.

Half bitterness we know, we know half sweetness;
    This world is all on wax, on wane:
  When shall completeness round time's incompleteness
    Fulfilling joy, fulfilling pain?—
  Lo, while we ask, life rolleth on in fleetness
    To finished loss or finished gain.

[...]

CHAPTER XII.

*1. And there appeared a great wonder in heaven; a woman clothed with the sun,
and the moon under her feet, and upon her head a crown of twelve stars:*

The Preacher, the son of David, King in Jerusalem, has left on record: "I know that, whatsoever God doeth, it shall be for ever: nothing can be put to it, nor anything taken from it; and God doeth it, that men should fear before Him. That which hath been is now; and that which is to be hath already been; and God requireth that which is past." Thus the past which we know, presages the future which we know not.

And Greater than that King and Wiser that Preacher, our Lord Himself said to His disciples: "Have ye understood all these things? They say unto Him, Yea, Lord. Then said He unto them, "Therefore every scribe which is instructed unto the kingdom of heaven is like unto a man that is an house-holder, which bringeth forth out of his treasure things new and old." Now as every Christian "is instructed unto the kingdom of heaven," he cannot be destitute of a treasure whence to bring forth somewhat; new it may be, old it cannot but be.

Of this Apocalypse the occult unfulfilled signification will be new; the letter is old. Old, not merely because these eighteen hundred years it has warned us to flee from the wrath to come; but also because each figure appeals to our experience, even when it stands for some object unprecedented or surpassing.

A rose might preach beauty and a lily purity to a receptive mind, although the ear had not yet heard tell of the Rose of Sharon and Lily of the Valleys.

"A woman clothed with the sun, and the moon under her feet, and upon her head a crown of twelve stars."—Whatever else may here be hidden, there stands revealed that "great wonder," weakness made strong and shame swallowed up in celestial glory. For thus the figure is set before our eyes. Through Eve's lapse, weakness and shame devolved on woman as her characteristics, in a manner special to herself and unlike the corresponding heritage of man.

And as instinctively we personify the sun and moon as *he* and *she*, I trust there is no harm in my considering that her sun-clothing indicates how in that heaven where St. John in vision behold her, she will be made equal with men and angels; arrayed in all human virtues, and decked with all communicable Divine graces: whilst the moon under her feet portends that her sometime infirmity of purpose and changeableness of mood have, by preventing, assisting, final grace, become immutable; she has done all and stands; from the lowest place she has gone up higher. As love of his Lord enabled St. Peter to tread the sea, so love of the same Lord sets weak woman immovable on the waves of this troublesome world, triumphantly erect, despite her own frailty, made not "like unto a wheel," amid all the changes and chances of this mortal life.

Eve's temptation and fall suggest the suitableness and safety of much (though by no means of all) ignorance, and the wholesomeness of studying what is open without prying into what is secret. We have no reason to doubt that the forbidden fruit was genuinely "pleasant to the eyes": as such she might innocently have gazed upon it with delight, and for that delight might profitably have returned thanks to the Author and Giver of all good. Not till she became wise in her own conceit, disregarding the plain obvious meaning of words, and theorizing on her own responsibility as to physical and intellectual results, did she bring sin and death into the world. The Tree of the Knowledge of Good and Evil was as it were a standing prophet ever reiterating the contingent sentence, Thou shalt surely die. This sentence, plain and unmistakable, she connived at explaining away, and being deceived, was undone.

Eve exhibits one extreme of feminine character, the Blessed Virgin the opposite extreme. Eve parleyed with a devil: holy Mary "was troubled" at the salutation of an Angel. Eve sought knowledge: Mary instruction. Eve aimed at self-indulgence: Mary at self-oblation. Eve, by disbelief and disobedience, brought sin to the birth: Mary, by faith and submission, Righteousness.

And yet, even as at the foot of the Cross, St. Mary Magdalene, out of whom went seven devils, stood beside the "lily among thorns," the Mother of sorrows: so (I humbly hope and trust) amongst all saints of all time will stand before the Throne, Eve the beloved first Mother of us all. Who that has loved and revered her own immediate dear mother, will not echo the hope?

Again and eminently, the heavenly figure under consideration presents and image of the Church: "the King hath brought me into His chambers."

"Who is she that looketh forth as the morning, fair as the moon, clear as the sun, and terrible as an army with banners?" All glorious she is within by the Indwelling of the Holy Spirit, and effluent glory envelopes her as with the sun for a garment. The moon, set below, may never again eclipse the sun; yet inasmuch as the perfect life had to be developed out of the imperfect, the unchangeable out of the changeable, therefore the moon abides underlying that consummated glory. Twelve stars compose her crown, a twelvefold splendour. I have seen the Twelve Apostles suggested as the interpretation of this symbol; and well may it direct our thoughts to their glorious company, the illumination of their doctrine, the shining light of their example. Perhaps there will be no harm in an additional gloss. The eternal state of the Church Triumphant is expressed by her sun-vesture; the moon beneath her feet memorializes her temporal probation while militant in this world; the twelve stars may— may they not? For earth's day is as night when compared with heaven's day—may remind us of those twelve hours in the day during which she was bound to walk and work in accordance with our Lord's own words and practice. Thus her probation issues in glory, a glory all the more glorious because of that probation. "Give her of the fruit of her hands; and let her own works praise her in the gates." Or if *stars* seem too incongruous an emblem of any *daylight* hours; I call to mind both that there shall be no night there, and that certain benefactors have for their allocated dignity to shine as the stars for ever and ever: whereby stars take rank in the everlasting day.

Or rather, what real connection is there between stars and night more than between stars and day? Earth's shadows approach them not in their high places; nor so far as we can trace, affect them in any way, or do aught in their regard beyond revealing them to mortal ken. Our perception varies, not their lustre.

CHAPTER XIV

21. And there fell upon men a great hail out of heaven, every stone about the weight of talent: and men blasphemed God because of the plague of the hail; for the plague thereof was exceeding great.

[…]

Lord grant us grace to make Thy Goodness our trust: shutting our hearts against pride, our mouths against evil words, our ears against foul knowledge; and using Thy gifts to the promotion of Thy Glory and of man's salvation. For His Blessed sake in Whom we have all and are full and abound, Jesus Christ. Amen.

"Behold, I come as a thief."—This or a kindred expression our Blessed Master and after Him His Apostles and Evangelists have employed repeatedly in reference to the Second Advent and ensuing Judgment Day. SS. Matthew and Luke record in great measure the same Divine words, although spoken (it seems) on two separate occasions: "Watch therefore: for ye know not what hour your Lord doth come. But know this; that if the Goodman of the house had known in what watch the thief would come, he would have watched, and would not have suffered his house to be broken up. Therefore be ye also ready: for in such an hour as ye think not the Son of Man cometh." St. Paul reminds the Thessalonians: "Yourselves know perfectly that the day of the Lord so cometh as a thief in the night … . But ye, brethren, are not in darkness, that that day should overtake you as a thief." St. Peter forewarns the Church Catholic: "But the day of the Lord will come as a thief in the night."

Still more striking is the likeness of our present text to part of our Lord's message to the Church in Sardis (ch. Iii. 3, 4): "If therefore thou shalt not watch, I will come on thee as a thief, and thou shalt not know what hour I will come upon thee. Thou hast a few names even in Sardis which have not defiled their garments; and they shall walk with Me in white."

Blessed indeed then is he that watcheth! He shall escape overwhelming shame: yea, much more, he shall abide in eternal fellowship with Christ.

> Solomon most glorious in array
>   Put not on his glories without care:—
> Clothe us as They lilies of a day,
>   As the lilies thou accountest fair,
>   Lilies of Thy making,
>   Of Thy love partaking,
>   Filling with free fragrance earth and air:
>   Thou Who gatherest lilies, gather us and wear.

"Armageddon"—is, I see, interpreted "The destruction of the troops," and (on the same authority) is supposed to allude to the overthrow of Sisera and his hosts before Barak and his ten thousand (*see* Judges iv. 14, 15; v 19-21).

"And the seventh angel poured out his vial into the air."—I trust that since modern accuracy has not yet forbidden our speaking of sunrise and sunset, we may also venture on occasion to revive the Four Elements of my youth.

Three elements have in turn been smitten; earth by the first vial, water by the second and third, fire (the sun) by the fourth. Then recommencing the series; earth (perhaps, the world) by the fifth; water (Euphrates) by the sixth: but fire (if the dragon and the spirits of devils may be assumed to represent it) musters on the contrary its rebellious force apparently for a final effort; not recking that the kingdom and the battle and the great day are all alike "of God Almighty."

The seventh vial is poured out "into the air," that element which may be termed the vital breath both of man and of fire: and we are reminded of St. Paul's phrase: "The prince of the power of the air, the spirit that now worketh in the children of disobedience."

"And there came a great Voice out of the Temple of heaven."—I do not know whether I perceive or merely fancy a distinction. In previous passages (ch. xi. 19; xiv. 17; xv. 5) the Temple is spoken of as *in* heaven, the context having reference to God the Son, man's Redeemer and Judge. In this passage, "the Temple of heaven" (harmonizing with the words, "The heaven is My Throne") might seem to speak of heaven at large as being itself that Temple; and to do so at this point of the Revelation because the imminent Judgment and consummation will affect much more than humankind only. The Revised Version, however, by omitting the words "of heaven" precludes any such notion.

"It is done."—"God requireth that which is past."

Holy fear incites faith to humility, hope to prudence, love to obedience. Faith without humility presumes, hope without prudence misleads, love without obedience—there is no genuine love without obedience. "He that hath My commandments, and keepeth them, he it is that loveth Me," saith the Sole Fountain of Truth and Love.

> Fear, Faith, and Hope have sent their hearts above:
>   Prudence, Obedience, and Humility
>   Climb at their call, all scaling heaven toward Love.
> Fear hath least grace but great expediency;
>   Faith and Humility show grave and strong;
>   Prudence and Hope mount balanced equally.
> Obedience marches marshalling their throng,
>   Goes first, goes last, to left hand or to right;
>   And all the six uplift a pilgrim's song.
> By day they rest not, nor they rest by night:
>   While Love within them, with them, over them,
>   Weans them and woos them from the dark to light.
> Each plies for staff not reed with broken stem,
>   But olive branch in pledge of patient peace;
>   Till Love being theirs in New Jerusalem,
> Transfigure them to Love, and so they cease.
>   Love is the sole beatitude above:
>   All other graces, to their vast increase
> Of glory, look on Love and mirror Love.

"A great earthquake, such as was not since men were upon the earth."—The latter clause is perhaps a saving clause, reserving pre-Adamite convulsions of which geology (if I am not mistaken) appears to detect tremendous indications.

O Lord God Only Wise, keep us or deliver us, I beseech Thee, from ignorant assertions and ignorant denials, from confusing probabilities with certainties and opinions with beliefs. So be it to Thy Glory and our salvation, for the honour of Jesus Christ. Amen.

[…]

CHAPTER XVII

*3. So he carried me away in the spirit into the wilderness: and I saw a woman
sit upon a scarlet-coloured beast, full of names of blasphemy, having seven
heads and ten horns.*

He who exhibits is an angel, and he who inspects is a saint: yet does this exalted pair betake
themselves into "the wilderness," there and not elsewhere to set themselves face to face with
an impersonation of abominable wickedness. So likewise did their and our Divine Master do
when He deigned to confront Satan. And if the Standard Bearer among ten thousand, and if
the flower of His armies did thus, it leaves us an example that we should tread in their steps.

Some innocent souls there are who from cradle to grave remain as it were veiled and
cloistered from knowledge of evil. As pearls in their native deep, as flower-buds under
Alpine snow, they abide unsullied: the lot has fallen unto them in a fair ground. But for most
persons contact with evil and consequent knowledge of evil being unavoidable, is clearly so
far ordained: they must achieve a more difficult sanctity, touching pitch yet continuing clean,
enduring evil communications yet without corruption of good manners.

To each such imperilled soul, Angel and Apostle here set a pattern. If we too would gaze
unscathed and undefiled on wickedness, let us not seek for enchantments, but set our face
toward the wilderness. Strip sin bare from voluptuousness of music, fascination of gesture,
entrancement of the stage, rapture of poetry, glamour of eloquence, seduction of imaginative
emotion; strip it of every adornment, let it stand out bald as in the Ten stern Commandments.
Study sin, when study it we must, not as a relishing pastime, but as an embittering deterrent.
Lavish sympathy on the sinner, never on the sin. Say, if we will and if we mean it, Would
God I had died for thee: nevertheless let us flee at the cry of such, lest the earth swallow us
up also.

Wherever the serpent is tolerated there is sure to be dust for his pasture: he finds or he
makes a desolate wilderness of what was as the Garden of Eden. Only an illusion, a mirage,
can cause a barren desert to appear in our eyes as a city of palaces, an orchard of fruits.

This woman Babylon sits upon a scarlet beast, it appears not whether as upon a throne or
as upon chariot: if a throne, steadfast in evil; if a chariot, swift unto perdition. Moreover, in
a former verse we read of her as sitting "upon many waters": a point to be noted further on.

The woman and the beast by a foul congruity seem to make up a sort of oneness, after the
fashion of a snail and its shell. If she removes he is the motor; she is lifted aloft to the extent
of his height; her stability depends on his. In semblance he is her slave, in reality her master.

33 Gerard Manley Hopkins (1963)

J. Hillis Miller

Verily Thou art a God that hidest Thyself.

(Isaiah, 45:15)[1]

[...]

The central principle of Catholicism, as Hopkins sees, is the doctrine of the Incarnation. For him a basic difference between Catholicism and Protestantism is their divergent interpretations of the Sacrament of Communion. Protestantism has moved from the doctrine of transubstantiation toward the idea that the communion service is a commemoration of the Last Supper. The bread and wine are signs or symbols pointing toward something which remains absent. The Zwinglian interpretation of the Eucharist prepares the way for the situation in poetry and in life which is characteristic of nineteenth-century man, and is experienced by Hopkins before his conversion. The thinning of the meaning of the communion service spreads out to diminish the divine meaning of the whole world. The heavens no longer declare the glory of God. The deity retires to an infinite distance, and the universe becomes drained of spiritual presence and meaning. The creation becomes "a lighted empty hall," and poetry becomes the manipulation of symbols which, no longer participate in the reality they name.

Hopkins' conversion is a rejection of three hundred and fifty years of the spiritual history of the West, three hundred and fifty years which seem to be taking man inexorably toward the nihilism of Nietzsche's "Gott ist tot." Like the Catholic revival in Victorian England of which it is part, Hopkins' conversion can be seen as an attempt to avoid falling into the abyss of the absence of God. Hopkins, like other Catholic converts, is willing to sacrifice everything—family, academic career, even his poetic genius—in order to escape the poetic and personal destiny which paralyzes such men as Matthew Arnold, and leaves them hovering between two worlds, waiting in vain for the spark from heaven to fall.

In letters written at the time of his conversion and afterwards Hopkins emphasizes the doctrine of the Real Presence as the core of Catholicism. "The great aid to belief and object of belief," he writes in a letter, "is the doctrine of the Real Presence in the Blessed Sacrament of the Altar. Religion without that is sombre, dangerous, illogical, with that it is ... *loveable*" (L, III, 17). The doctrine of the Real Presence is, as Hopkins says in the letter written to his father announcing his conversion, the only thing which keeps him from losing his faith in God: "This belief once got is the life of the soul and when I doubted it I shd. become an atheist the next day" (L, III, 92). Belief in the Incarnation and its repetition in the Eucharist offer the only escape from a world which has been rendered universally "sordid" by the disappearance of God (L, III, 226). Christ, in condescending to take upon himself not only the pains of manhood, but also its meannesses, transfigured these degrading characteristics of human life and made them radiant with spiritual significance. Belief in the Incarnation makes it possible to face the full triviality of human life, but at the same time it redeems this triviality and makes it part of the imitation of Christ: "I think that the trivialness of life is, and personally to each one, ought to be seen to be, done away with by the Incarnation ... " (L, III, 19).

The doctrines of the Incarnation and the Real Presence are more than proof that there was and is some connection between the divine and human worlds. Ultimately, with the help of Scotus and other theologians, Hopkins broadens his theory of the Incarnation until he comes to see all things as created in Christ. This doctrine of Christ is a Catholic version of the Parmenidean theory of being, and it is the means by which Hopkins can at last unify nature, words, and selfhood.

To say that all things are created in Christ means seeing the second person of the Trinity as the model on which all things are made, nonhuman things as well as men. "We are his design," said St. Paul; "God has created us in Christ Jesus" (Eph., 2:10). To see things as created in Christ means seeing Christ as the Word, the Being from whom all words derive: "God's utterance of himself in himself is God the Word, outside himself is this world. This world then is word, expression, news of God. Therefore its end, its purpose, its purport, its meaning, is God and its life or work to name and praise him" (S, 129). Christ is the perfection of human nature, but he is also the perfection of birds, trees, stones, flowers, clouds, and waterfalls. He is, to give the Scotist term for this concept, the *natura communis,* the common nature who contains in himself all natures. He is the creative Word, the means by which God created all things. As Christopher Devlin puts it: "GMH thinks of Christ's created nature as the original pattern of creation, to a place in which all subsequent created being must attain in order to be complete" (S, 341). Each created thing is a version of Christ, and derives its being from the way it expresses Christ's nature in a unique way. All things rhyme in Christ.

This vision of Christ as the common nature is the culmination of Hopkins' gradual integration of the world. Christ is the model for all inscapes, and can vibrate simultaneously at all frequencies. He is the ultimate guarantee for the validity of metaphor. It is proper to say that one thing is like another only because all thing are like Christ. The long exploration of nature in Hopkins' journals leads to certain key entries in which he comes to recognize that everything expresses the beauty of Christ:

> I do not think I have ever seen anything more beautiful than the bluebell I have been looking at. I know the beauty of our Lord by it.
>
> (J. 199)

> As we drove home the stars came out thick: I leant back to look at them and my heart opening more than usual praised our Lord to and in whom all that beauty comes home.
>
> (J. 254)

Such passages reveal what is distinctively Scotist about Hopkins' vision of nature, and demonstrate the significance of that journal entry where he says: "just then when I took in any inscape of the sky or sea I thought of Scotus" (J. 221). Scotus, like Parmenides, and unlike St. Thomas, affirms the doctrine of the univocity of being.[2] Scotus refers to Parmenides, and defends, against Aristotle's attempted refutation, Parmenides' proposition that all being is one. (See S, 284, and Duns Scotus, *Oxoniense,* I, iii, 2 and viii, 3.) If Parmenides is the Greek philosopher who comes closest to Hopkins' intuition of nature, Scotus is the theologian who seems to him "of realty the rarest-veinèd unraveller" (P, 84). Like Parmenides, Scotus believes that the term "being" means the same thing when we ascribe it to God and when we ascribe it to any creature.

The difference between Scotus and Aquinas on this point is a complex technical matter, and authorities tend to stress their ultimate agreement, or the verbal nature of their disagreement.[3] Even so, it would perhaps not be falsifying too much to say that Scotus and Aquinas represent opposing tendencies of thought, and that these tendencies, if carried to their extremes, would lead to two radically different concepts of nature and of poetry.

The concept of the analogy of being leads to an hierarchical view of nature. Each thing, in this view, possesses only a material and created equivalent of the immaterial and uncreated attributes of God. Things are *analogous* to the nature of God, and each thing in nature stands not for the whole nature of God, but for a particular attribute of the deity. The book of nature is a set of hieroglyphs or symbols, each one of which tells us something specific about God, the lion his strength, the honey his sweetness, the sun this brightness. In short, the concept of the analogy of being leads to something like the view of nature on which medieval and Renaissance poetry, with its horde of specific symbols, is based.

The idea of the univocity of being leads to a different view of nature, and therefore to a different kind of poetry. In this view natural things, instead of having a derived being, participate directly in the being of the creator. They are in the same way that he is. Each created thing, in its own special way, is the total image of its creator. It expresses not some aspect of God, but his beauty as a whole. Such a view of nature leads to a poetry in which things are not specific symbols, but all mean one thing and the same: the beauty of Christ, in whom they are created.

Hopkins sometimes speaks as if he believes in the analogy of being, as when he says of created things: "They glorify God ... The birds sing to him, the thunder speaks of his terror, the lion is like his strength, the sea is like his greatness, the honey like his sweetness; they are something like him, they make him known, they tell of him, they give him glory ... " (S, 238). In spite of such passages, and in spite of places in Hopkins' poetry where he uses the specific symbolism of the Middle Ages and Renaissance, the main tendency of his vision is toward seeing inscapes as versions of the whole nature of Christ. Natural things are all, and all equally, charged with the grandeur of God, and this overwhelming fact is more important than anything specific about the nature of God which may be learned from the special qualities of created things: "All things therefore are charged with love, are charged with God and if we know how to touch them give off sparks and take fire, yield drops and flow, ring and tell of him" (S, 195). God's beauty is like an ubiquitous fluid or electric energy molding everything in the image of the Son.

This idea is the basic presupposition of Hopkins' nature poems. In "The Starlight Night," the night sky, with its treasure of stars, is like bright people or cities hovering in the air, like "dim woods" with "diamond delves," like "grey lawns cold where gold, where quickgold lies," like "wind-beat whitebeam," like "airy abeles set on a flare," like a flock of doves flying in a barnyard, like May blossoms on orchard trees, and like "March-bloom ... on mealed-with-yellow sallows" (P, 70, 71). The poem, like so many of Hopkins' nature poems, is made up of a list of natural phenomena set in apposition to one another. The poem says: "Look at this, and this, and then this!" The things listed are all metaphors of the night sky and of one another. They are parallel because they all equally contain Christ. "The Starlight Night" ends with the affirmation that the night sky and the things with which it has been compared are like barns which house the precious grain, Christ. Christ is the treasure within all things.

The octave of "As kingfishers catch fire" is sustained by the same presupposition. The fact that all things cry, "What I do is me: for that I came" is more than evidence that things express their inscapes by "doing" themselves. The echo here of the words of Jesus[4] tells us that in doing what they came for, in speaking themselves, nonhuman creatures are revealing their likeness to Christ and speaking his name. Like just men, kingfishers and dragonflies are of the truth, hear Christ's voice, and speak it again.

In the same way the basis of "The May Magnificat" is a comparison of the Blessed Virgin and nature. As Mary carried Christ within her and magnified him, all nature in May is quick with Christ, the universal instress which reveals itself in a thousand different inscapes: "This ecstasy all through mothering earth/Tells Mary her mirth till Christ's birth" (P, 82).

"Hurrahing in Harvest" is the most ecstatic expression of Hopkins' vision of the ubiquity of Christ in nature. The poem "was the outcome of half an hour of extreme enthusiasm" (L, I, 56). It was enthusiasm in the etymological sense, for the seeing of Christ everywhere in the earth and sky of this autumn scene was a supernatural harvest for the spectator. "Gleaning" Christ from the multitudinous spectacle, threshing him out from the husks which hid him, Hopkins took him as it were in the communion of love, and was himself lifted up into an inscape of Christ: "I walk, I lift up, I lift up heart, eyes, / Down all that glory in the heavens to glean our Saviour" (P, 74).

The doctrine of the common nature takes Hopkins one all-important step beyond the recognition that all things rhyme. The latter led to a sense that all nature is integrated, but is foreign to man. Hopkins' doctrine of Christ allows him to integrate man into the great chorus of created things. Man too is a scape of Christ, and reflects Christ's image back to Christ at the same time as he affirms his own selfhood. A man, like other created things, says "Christ" at the same time as he speaks his own name. All men are rhymes of Christ:

> … the just man justices;
> Kéeps gráce: thát keeps all his goings graces;
> Acts in God's eye what in God's eye he is —
> Christ —

> (P, 95)

In imitating Christ man is also imitating natural things, and expressing his kinship with them. To know nature is also to know oneself, for the natural world is a mirror in which a man may see hints and reflections of his own selfhood. Hopkins' epistemology presupposes a new version of the Presocratic "theory of sensation by like and like" (J, 130). I am a "scape" of the common nature, Christ. Each natural thing is also a scape of Christ. Therefore I contain in myself and recapitulate in little all the variety of the creation, kingfishers, dragonflies, stones, trees, flowers—everything. To know them is to know myself, for they are rhymes for me, and for my model, Christ.

Hopkins has at last completed the edifice which seemed destined to remain in fragments. Everything has been brought under the aegis of rhyme. In doing this he has brought into harmony his three theories of poetry. Poetry can be at once self-expression, the inscape of words, and the imitation of nature. To imitate natural things is to express the self, for are not all natural things created in the image of man, since man too is in the image of Christ? To express the self is to imitate nature, for the best means of self-expression is those exterior things which so naturally and delightfully mirror the self. To express the inscape of the self in terms of the inscapes of nature is also to express the inscapes of words. Christ is himself the Word, the origin of all language. He is what "Heaven and earth are word of, worded by" (P, 65). The inscapes of nature flow from Christ the Word, and the inscapes of language flow from the same source. There is a natural harmony between the sounds of words and their meanings, and a poet seeking to express the harmonies of one will naturally express the harmonies of the other. Far from being the place where we are forced to confront the unbridgeable gulfs between world, words, and self, poetry is the medium through which man may best express the harmonious chiming of all three in Christ.

Any definition of poetry, if pushed far enough, will lead back to Christ, for the ultimate origin and inspiration of poetry is the poet's love of God the Son. "Feeling, love in particular," says Hopkins in a letter of 1879, "is the great moving power and spring of verse and the only person that I am in love with seldom, especially now, stirs my heart sensibly and when he does I cannot always 'make capital' of it, it would be a sacrilege to do so" (L, I, 66). Christ is the only person Hopkins is in love with. His power to write poetry is directly related to his religious life, and when there is a failure of grace there is a failure of poetry. Certain experiences of grace are too personal and too sacred to be made public in poetry. It would be a sacrilege to do so.

This connection between grace and poetic inspiration is behind Hopkins' accounts of the origin of his own poetic gift. He often uses imagery of flowing water to describe poetic inspiration: "Every impulse and spring of art seems to have died in me ... " (L, I, 124); "Thinking over this matter my vein began to flow" (L, I, 136); " ... my vein shews no signs of ever flowing again" (L, I, 178); "It is now years that I have had no inspiration of longer jet than makes a sonnet" (L, I, 270). Poetry is like a well or a spring which is usually dry, but suddenly and miraculously begins to flow.

Sometimes inspiration is described not as a spring or fountain, but as the descent of a tongue of flame, "sweet fire the sire of muse" (P, 114). This form of inspiration, like the other, is experienced subjectively as a rush of feelings which gives birth to creative thought. The flame of inspiration is like a fecundating jet of emotion which "leaves yet the mind a mother of immortal song" (P, 114).

Flowing water, flame, impregnation—these three images are precisely the ones which, for Hopkins, also define the descent of God's grace. In "The Wreck of the Deutschland," remembering the tongues of fire at Pentecost (Acts, 2:1ff.), Hopkins describes his own experience of grace as being struck and burned with God's lightning, so that he was "laced with fire of stress," and "flash[ed] from the flame to the flame then, tower[ed] from the grace to the grace" (P, 56). The tongues of fire at Pentecost brought the gift of tongues to the apostles, and were themselves the breathing in both of grace and of the power to speak. In the same way stanza four of "The Wreck" associates grace, the Word, and the image of water (P, 56). The "gospel proffer" which constantly regenerates the soul and keeps it sweet is the "good news," the Word, Christ's gift. In another stanza the nun's "conception" of Christ (P, 65) is described as the mental conception and uttering of the Word. Once more the descent of grace is associated with the miraculous bestowal of a verbal gift.

"The Wreck of the Deutschland" is about both poetic inspiration and grace. The poem is divided into two parts, the first recalling the time when Hopkins himself was touched by the finger of God, the second describing the wreck and the salvation of the nuns. Imagining the nuns' death has brought back vividly to Hopkins his own parallel experience. Remembering it, he has relived it again, and God's grace has descended once more into his heart. This experience of the renewal of grace is at the same time the renewal of poetic inspiration. Hopkins' poetic gift, artificially cut off at the time of his conversion, begins to flow irresistibly again, and, with the permission of his superiors, he writes the first of the great poems of his maturity.

Hopkins has put into the poem itself, in a stanza which is a hyperbaton or suspense in the midst of the storm, an account of its genesis. The poet pauses in his objective description of the wreck, returns to himself, and expresses, in a series of breathless ejaculations, his subjective response to the storm (P, 61, stanza 18). The tears which are the expression of his emotion at reading an account of the wreck are the signs of the flowing of poetic inspiration. This flowing melts his hardness of heart, makes words break from him, and generates the poem. The poem, consequently, is a "madrigal start"; it is like one voice, in a song of many parts, singing in canon a repetition of another voice. Another example of the principle of rhyme! The "new rhythm" whose "echo" had long been haunting Hopkins' ear, and which he first "realised on paper" in "The Wreck"[5] was not merely a new poetic device. Sprung rhythm is a reverberation, in the beat and tension of the lines, of the pulsation of grace which inspired the poem. The true theme of "The Wreck of the Deutschland" is not the heroic death of the nuns. It is Hopkins' response to hearing of the wreck—the father of grace and the father of poetry moving his heart simultaneously. For the two fathers are the same.

This is so in a more subtle way yet. Christ operates as the immaterial cause of the "fine delight" which moves the heart and "fathers thought" (P, 114). He is also the motivating force behind a certain way of seeing nature which is necessary to the writing of poetry.

Here Hopkins' Scotism comes to the surface again. Following the subtle doctor, Hopkins distinguishes in a special way between three faculties of the mind: memory, understanding, and will. Will in this context is affective volition, "the faculty of fruition, by which we enjoy or dislike" (S, 174). The affective will moves toward a thing or repulses it after it has first been comprehended by the understanding. The understanding "applies to words; it is the faculty for grasping not the fact but the meaning of a thing … . This faculty not identifies but verifies; takes the measure of things, brings word of them; is called λόγος and reason" (S, 174). Before we can understand a thing we must apprehend it with our senses, and this first act of the mind is called "Memory." Memory, for Hopkins as for Scotus, applies to present and future as well as to past. Toward past things it is "Memory proper." Toward "things future or things unknown or imaginary" it is "Imagination." Toward present things memory is "Simple Apprehension," the "faculty of Identification." It is the primary direction of the mind toward a thing, a grasping of the bare fact that something is there before us rather than nothing: "When continued or kept on the strain the act of this faculty is attention, advertence, heed, the being *ware,* and its habit, knowledge, the being *aware.* Towards God it gives rise to *reverence,* it is the sense of the *presence* of God" (S, 174).

Ordinarily the mind moves rapidly from memory to understanding to will. Apprehending that there is something before it, the mind comprehends that thing with the reason, and then moves toward it or away from it, driven by the liking or disliking of the affective will. It is possible for the mind to prolong the stage of simple apprehension, and to remain hovering in that state in which it has grasped the fact that something is there, and may even have barely identified it, but has not yet gone on to analyze the thing with the understanding, and place it in a pre-existing concept. It is as if the mind were to remain at the stage of sensation, the awareness of color, texture, and form, rather than moving on to perception, the awareness that this is an ash tree, or a bluebell, or the moon rising. On awaking from sleep, says Scotus, sensation is likely to be particularly vivid, and simple apprehension may then be prolonged so that it can be identified as a separate experience. On awaking the mind is cut off from past and future, and in a daze of immediacy can concentrate on the present, distorting it neither with memory nor with expectation. The man waking from sleep apprehends what is really there before him, not the preexisting structures of reason and will. Scotus calls this act of simple apprehension "confused knowing." It is *visio existentis ut existens*, a vision of the existing thing as existing. In such visionary sensation we see what Scotus called the *species specialissima,* nature in the very process of being created in the image of its model, Christ. In simple apprehension man is aware of the being of a thing, its beauty, its presence, what it shares with all other things, and with God.[6] Simple apprehension "keeps warm / Men's wits to the things that are" (P, 103).

This way of seeing things is the origin of poetry. Instead of seeing an object as an example of an abstract category the poet must see it as if it had just been created, and then the depths of his being opens up to receive, in a flood of emotion, the being of the thing he sees. Vivid sensation is a "prize" which pierces to the heart of the poet's being, and "wakes" him to another level of existence, a level closer to the heart of creation.

In "Moonrise," one of Hopkins' most exquisite poetic fragments, the poet tells how he "awoke in the Midsummer not to call night," and saw the waning moon just rising from the bulk of "dark Maenefa the mountain." His half-awake state made him vulnerable to the impact of sensation, and the scene plunged through the superficial layers of his consciousness to reach a level of perpetual vigilance. The rhythm of the lines and their syntax echo this process of an ever-so-delicate entry of reality deeper and deeper through the senses to the heart:

> This was the prized, the desirable sight, 'unsought, presented so easily, Parted me leaf and leaf, divided me,' eyelid and eyelid of slumber.
>
> (P, 149)

To see things in terms of their existence is to see them at such a depth that it can be recognized that their creation is something which goes on constantly. A vein of the Gospel proffer holds a man in being and keeps him from falling into nothingness, and natural things are kept in existence by a similar process of continuous creation. Since all things are perpetually renewed by God the poet knows that "There lives the dearest freshness deep down things" (P, 70). The first days of the creation are always being re-enacted, and there is throughout nature, even now, "A strain of the earth's sweet being in the beginning / In Eden garden" (P, 71).

To see nature being created is to see things in terms of the common nature, the perfection toward which they all move. The *visio existentis ut existens* is the true source of poetry because only this way of seeing things can go behind mere intellectual recognition to a vision of all things as being continuously created in Christ.

A passage in "The Wreck of the Deutschland" makes clearer the importance of simple apprehension in the perception of Christ within nature:

> … tho' he is under the world's splendour and wonder,
> His mystery must be instressed, stressed;
> For I greet him the days I meet him, and bless when I understand.
>
> (P, 57)

These lines recapitulate the whole mental process from memory through understanding to will. "Instress" matches "greet": when I catch a glimpse of Christ in nature, "meet" him, I "greet" him. I respond to him, "kiss my hand" to him, instress my simple apprehension in answer to the stress felt from him (the "stroke and a stress that stars and storms deliver" in the next stanza). After the meeting of simple apprehension has been responded to by my kiss of greeting, this affirmation of my awareness leads me to "understand," and this understanding is finally ratified by an act of will going out, in desire, toward Christ in nature. This is the "blessing" of the last line, which matches the "stressed" of the line before. In this process the instress with which I prolong my simple apprehension and dwell on it is necessary to my comprehension of the presence of Christ under the world's splendor and wonder. His mystery must be instressed if nature is to be seen poetically.

The same assumptions lie behind another poem, in which Hopkins describes how ash-boughs "new-nestle at heaven most high." Such a scene is the most poetic thing he knows. As in "Moonrise," the initiation of the poetic act is spoken of as a deep and subtle penetration of the mind by natural objects. The mind must assimilate the world into its deepest recesses before the poetic *élan* is released:

> Not of all my eyes see, wandering on the world,
> Is anything a milk to the mind so, so sighs deep
> Poetry tó it, as a tree whose boughs break in the sky.

(P, 164)

Ash-boughs, which "touch heaven, tabour on it" (P, 165), are a supremely poetic sight because, in the yearning and reaching of the tiny new twigs and leaves toward the sky, the poet can see going on before his eyes the process of continuous creation. Earth is the mother of all things, but God is their father, and in the growth of the ash-boughs is visibly enacted the intercourse between heaven and earth. The moving toward heaven of the ash-boughs is their imitation of Christ. The incarnate God, mediator between heaven and earth, possessor of both a divine and a human nature, is the model for the double nature of all created things:

> … May
> Mells blue with snowwhite through their fringe and fray
> Of greenery and old earth gropes for, grasps at steep
> Heaven with it whom she Childs things by.

(P, 165)

The ash-boughs' imitation of Christ is also their imitation of us, for we too are fathered by heaven on mother earth in the image of Christ. A variant reading of the last two lines of "Ash-boughs" says just this: "it is old earth's groping towards the steep / Heaven whom she childs *us* by" (P, 165, my italics). Again Hopkins' doctrine of Christ binds together nature, poetry, and the poet.

Beginning with a sense of his own isolation and idiosyncrasy, Hopkins turns outside himself to nature, to poetry, and to God. Gradually he integrates all things into one chorus of many voices all singing, in their different ways, the name of Christ. Poetry is the imitation and echo of this chorus. Even the poet, by virtue of his share in the common nature, is assimilated into the melody of creation. The inscapes of words, the inscapes of nature, the inscape of the self can be expressed at once as the presence of Christ. The three ways of poetry are the same way, and the inspiration of poetry is always, in one way or another, the poet's affective response to the omnipresence of Christ.

The isolation of the poet in his selftaste has turned out to be apparent, not real, and Hopkins' early experience of the absence of God has been transformed into what is, in Victorian poetry, an almost unique sense of the immanence of God in nature and in the human soul. Neither Arnold, nor Tennyson, nor Browning is able to transcend so completely the spiritual condition of his age. Hopkins alone recovers a world like that of Eden before the fall, a world in which God, in the person of his Son, once more walks with man in the garden in the cool of the evening.

Notes

1 The passage from Isaiah is quoted by Hopkins as an epigraph to "Nondum," *Poems,* ed. W. H. Gardner, third edition (New York: Oxford University Press, 1948), p. 43; hereafter cited as "P."

2 See Cyril L. Shircel, *The Univocity of the Concept of Being in the Philosophy of John Duns Scotus* (Washington, 1942). Allan Bernard Wolter, *The Transcendentals and Their Function in the Metaphysics of Duns Scotus* (Washington, 1946), pp. 31–57, and Etienne Gilson, *Jean Duns Scot* (Paris, 1952). For the doctrine of analogy in Aquinas, see George P. Klubertanz, *St. Thomas Aquinas on Analogy* (Chicago, 1960).

3 See, for example, Gilson, *Jean Duns Scot,* pp. 101–103.

4 See John, 18:37: "Pilate therefore said to him: Art thou a king then? Jesus answered: Thou sayest that I am a king. For this was I born, and for this came I into the world; that I should give testimony to the truth. Everyone that is of the truth, heareth my voice."

5 Claude Colleer Abbott, ed., *The Correspondence of Gerard Manley Hopkins and Richard Watson Dixon* (London: Oxford University Press, 1955), p. 14; hereafter cited as "L, II."

6 See Christopher Devlin, ed., *The Sermons and Devotional Writings of Gerard Manley Hopkins* (London: Oxford University Press, 1959) p. 298, and Christopher Devlin, "The Image and the Word," *Month,* N.S., III (1950), 114–27, 191–202, especially 196–199.

34 Robert Browning's Sacred and Legendary Art (2011)

Charles LaPorte

Browning's Borrowed Catholicism and the cult of Saint Pompilia

Like many Victorians, Browning associated hagiography with Catholicism, with its distinctive cult of saints and its modern-day Virgin apparitions.[1] But he also associated it with the problems of the higher criticism and religious hermeneutics. Indeed, many mid-century Protestants viewed Catholicism as the mirror reflection of the higher criticism, a religious failing of the opposite extreme. This is plain from *Christmas-Eve*, in which an ungainly and somewhat absurd British chapel meeting reveals its true grace only through comparison with jarring and antithetical alternatives: the high Roman mass at St. Peter's, on the one hand, and the demythologizing German lecture hall at Göttingen on the other. (Conveniently for its Victorian readership, the poem offers British Protestantism as a sort of sensible middle-ground.) In an analogous manner, Arthur Hugh Clough's "Notes on the Religious Tradition" disparages the modern demystification of the Gospels as a sort of religious indiscretion directly antithetical to—and grotesquely mirrored by—"Romish" mystification:

> I do not see that it is a great and noble thing, a very needful or very worthy service, to go about proclaiming that Mark is inconsistent with Luke, that the first Gospel is not really Matthew's, nor the last with any certainty John's, that Paul is not Jesus, &c. &c. &c. It is at the utmost a commendable piece of honesty; but it is no new gospel to tell us that the old one is of dubious authenticity.
>
> I do not see either, on the other hand, that it can be lawful for me, for the sake of the moral guidance and the spiritual comfort, to ignore all scientific or historic doubts, or if pressed with then to the utmost, to take refuge in Romish infallibility, and, to avoid sacrificing the four Gospels, consent to accept the legends of the saints and the tales of modern miracles.[2]

(416)

To a mind like Clough's, Catholicism too plainly represented the flip side of the higher criticism: whereas the higher critics abdicate any claim to the traditional value of the scriptures, Catholics retain this only by abdicating their right to question history sanctioned by the Church, including "the legends of the saints and the tales of modern miracles." "Romish infallibility" affords a sort of solution to problems raised by the higher criticism, but Clough finds this solution more offensive than the original problem.

For his part, Browning was possessed of no more native sympathy than Clough for "Romish" religion, but he found in this antithesis between the "modern miracles" of

Catholicism and the ancient ones of biblical narrative a means of testing the relationship between poetry and religion. Nineteenth-century Catholic legend, so problematic for Clough, brought to life Browning's poetic ambition, and the "tales of modern miracles" disparaged by Clough provide Browning with the machinery of a modern mythical poetry. The earliest higher critics had consistently implied that the myths of scripture originally emerged because they could circulate freely in premodern "Oriental" cultures. In theory, at least, the modern West had become less fertile ground for religions movements. But religious legend continued to emerge in modern cultures. The new Mormon scriptures were clearly important in this respect, as was the hubbub recently created in 1839 (and, before that, 1751) by an apocryphal English-language book of Jasher passed off as the lost text mentioned in the Hebrew Bible. As F. Max Müller recounted of the story that Froude's *Nemesis of Faith* was publicly burnt at Oxford, "The story is interesting as showing how quickly a myth can spring up even in our own life-time."[3] And even as Clough composed his "Notes," the Virgin Mary was appearing before the faithful at Paris, Périgord, La Salette, Valence, and most recently at Rimini in Italy.[4] During the next five years, she would appear more famously at Lourdes, and by the 1870s she would regularly perform miracles throughout Germany and Italy, in Ireland and America.[5] Browning's *Red Cotton Night-Cap Country,* to which I will return, will depict these Virgin apparitions as a hazardous illusion on the part of the Catholic world, but, by contrast, *The Ring and the Book* seems to embrace the possibility of modern miracles, and the truth of virgin hagiography in particular.

What Browning so stunningly dramatizes in *The Ring and the Book* is that, in practice, the legends of the nineteenth-century Catholic Revival afford striking religious parallels to the ancient religious traditions that Clough invokes when he concedes that a biblical literature could "grow up naturally" among an illiterate people to express "religious truths of the highest import" ("Notes" 417). If biblical miracles might articulate "truths," then contemporary miracles might do so as well. *The Ring and the Book* carefully re-creates the religious enthusiasm that Clough decries, and its central figure, Pompilia, carefully negotiates the religious conundrum of those contemporary legends scorned by Clough. Browning makes with Pompilia a hagiography for a post–higher critical Protestant world; rather than wondering at the persistence of "modern miracles," as Clough does, he endeavors to harness their power. "Pompilia," in sum, solicits the very religious response that Clough associates with Catholic excess.[6]

Given the Roman setting of the drama and Browning's historical rigor, it makes sense that Pompilia's supporters would use their familiarity with martyr hagiography to articulate her story: thus the sympathetic half of Rome reveres her martyrdom in book 3 (111–12), Caponsacchi insists upon her sainthood in book 6 (1880–81), and Pope Innocent pronounces upon her holiness in book 10 (111–12), even requesting her postmortem intercession: "stoop thou down, my child, / Give one good moment to the poor old Pope / Heart-sick at having all his world to blame" (1005–7).[7] But we should not take for granted the frequency with which nineteenth-century enthusiasts of Browning's poem echo these ideas of Pompilia as "a saint, / Martyr and miracle!" (1.207–8). This hagiographical lens raises genuine questions about the nature of the higher critical history lesson provided in the first book of the poem. Anticipating by a few years John Dalberg-Acton's dry observation that "Kritik grew up on the lives of Saints," Browning asks his readers to grow up on them again.[8]

The Ring and the Book insists repeatedly upon the "facts" of its history: "Here it is all i' the book at last, as first / There it was all i' the heads and hearts of Rome" (1.414–17). Neither did the poet waver from his poem's most forceful historical claims. To Julia Wedgwood, his proofreader, he wrote steadfastly, "I think this is the world as it is," and of Pompilia, in particular, he insisted, "I assure you I found her in the book just as she speaks and acts in the poem."⁹ Clear evidence from Charles Hodell's *Old Yellow Book* (1908) and Beatrice Corrigan's *Curious Annals* (1956) has long confirmed Browning's finding of Pompilia to be selective in its emphases, but such evidence falls beside the point of Browning's generic experiment.¹⁰ The strongest Victorian responses to the poem clearly advance the generically constructed ideals of sanctity that the poem itself provides. "For Pompilia," bids Caponsacchi, "build churches, go pray!" (6.1880–81). And reviewers who subscribed to the English cult of poetry did not need to be told twice. What Browning's biographer Alexandra Sutherland Orr calls "the saintly glory of Pompilia" animates many Victorian reviews, and literary scholars discuss "Pompilia" as a hagiographic text *tout court* well into the twentieth century.¹¹ Still, it is one thing for the *Christian Examiner* of 1868 to describe "Pompilia" as "the most touching passage in the literature of our time" because Pompilia is a "perfect … saint" (306). It is quite another for Harriet Gaylord in 1931 to write of Pompilia's ability to "hallow lives," or for Kay Austen in 1979 to argue for Pompilia's real significance as "a Christian saint" (290), The *Christian Examiner* betrays the religious enthusiasm that animated nineteenth-century Browning societies, but Gaylord and Austen demonstrate something more important: the extraordinary effectiveness of Browning's poetic devices and the peculiar longevity of his religious effects.

Browning both asks readers to believe in the truth of this story and rewards their commitment to his hagiography. If his explicit claims to historical truthfulness seem difficult to reconcile to the fact that Pompilia's representation in the poem is a generically mediated event, still the genre anticipates this difficulty. The conflation of the generic and historical terms of saintly biography is the response that all hagiography solicits, because hagiography generates most enthusiasm and authority from readers willing to elide the space between textual representation and historical manifestation. The sympathetic and deliberately naive reading of Pompilia that began with Browning and prevailed for over a century is less a historical accident or misreading of this text than it is the calculated effect of the poem's construction as a virgin martyr hagiography.¹² Sacred literature animates religious experience by dint of its aesthetic and generic properties: the poem both insists and demonstrates that "the world as it is" requires the lens of genre.

Admittedly, the central features of Pompilia's history must generally coincide with the tropes of virgin martyrdom for this all to work. Female martyr hagiography seldom departs from its stock history of a pious young Christian beauty coveted, captured, and finally executed by an evil pagan nobleman. But not only does Pompilia resemble a textbook virgin martyr, we may even feel confident which textbook Browning liked best: his friend Anna Jameson's *Sacred and Legendary Art: Containing the Patron Saints, the Martyrs, the Early Bishops, the Hermits, and the Warrior Saints of Christendom, as Represented in the Fine Arts* (1848).¹³ This popular study generated widespread interest in Continental hagiography from the 1840s through the 1860s, and indeed made Jameson into what Adèle Holcomb calls "the first professional art historian."¹⁴ Jameson made a career of *Sacred and Legendary Art,* with supplementary volumes entitled *Legends of the Monastic Orders* (1850), *Legends of the Madonna* (1852), and the unfinished *The History of Our Lord* (1864).¹⁵ Throughout, Jameson organizes her thoughts by genre, and virgin martyrs receive particular attention as instances of quintessentially Catholic aesthetics: noteworthy for their primitive, Gothic, poetical nature.¹⁶ And although Jameson's interests remain ostensibly historical and artistic, she also takes note of contemporary hagiography such as the recently canonized St. Filomela, whose martyrdom by the pagan emperor Diocletian was discovered through the visions of a nineteenth-century mystic in one of the Catholic "modern miracles" so troubling to

Protestants and skeptics such as Clough (672). Browning might well have participated in Jameson's composition process for this work: she accompanied the Brownings to Italy on their famous journey of 1846 so that she could finish research for the manuscript.

Attention to the hagiographical basis for Pompilia's character, as represented by Jameson, explains several crucial and otherwise unaccountable additions to the story as Browning had it from his sources in the "Old Yellow Book." In virgin martyr hagiography, the nobleman is invariably a pagan, and the maiden invariably consecrated to Jesus. Invariably, too, he avenges his abortive love by putting her to death, just as she performs miracles or receives visits by angelic beings. The poem's descriptions of Pompilia's home life in Arezzo, then, suggest not the usual forms of Victorian domestic violence, but rather a sort of costume-drama pagan sacrifice: "all was sure / Fire laid and cauldron set, the obscene ring traced, / The victim stripped and prostrate: what of God?" (1.580–83).[17] While Browning's source material attests to domestic brutality of a "My Last Duchess" variety, yet *The Ring and the Book* freely switches genres, borrowing from Jameson's hagiography its depiction of Guido's Arezzo as "the woman's trap and cage and torture-place" (1.502) and the locale of "foul rite[s]."[18] According to *Sacred and Legendary Art,* St. Justina of Antioch and St. Celia were immersed into just such a cauldron as Browning describes (*SLA* 576, 586) and (having been miraculously preserved from scalding) subsequently put to death by knife and sword like Pompilia. (Celia, like Pompilia, also lives for three days that she might perform good works before being taken up to God.) St. Agnes is stripped and burned before decapitation (*SLA* 603), St. Agatha scourged and mutilated before being incinerated, and St. Euphemia smashed with a wooden mallet. Grotesque torture being strictly de rigueur for virgin martyrs, two saints depicted on the frontispiece of Jameson's volume 2—Lucia and Agatha—are identifiable only because they hold aloft body parts that were torn off by their persecutors.

Similar elements from the virgin martyr legends animate book 3, Browning's explanation of "how, to the other half of Rome, / Pompilia seemed a saint and martyr both!" (1.908–9). Here the genre is indicated by Monna Baldi's announcement of Pompilia's healing powers ("Her palsied limb 'gan prick and promise life / At touch o' the bedclothes merely,—how much more / Had she but brushed the body as she tried!" [3.55–58]), coupled by Maratta the painter's claim that "a lovelier face is not in Rome" (3.63).[19] "The Other Half Rome," skeptical of such popular credulity, remarks that Pompilia was never before considered a beauty, but still acknowledges that Pompilia endured at the hands of Guido the sort of trials that have traditionally qualified women for a place in the canon: "Thus Saintship is effected probably; / No sparing saints the process!" (3.111–12), and by the middle of the monologue, even uses the genre to defend her innocence: "If it were this? / How do you say? It were improbable; / So is the legend of my patron-saint" (3.1049–51). A contemporary Italian audience would be aware of the means by which "saintship is effected" and would know to what extent Pompilia's story fulfills them. They could not have been surprised when, by its end, he confidently claims of Pompilia that "The couple were laid i' the church two days ago, / And the wife lives yet by miracle" (3.1640–41).

Sympathetic voices in *The Ring and the Book* insist upon Pompilia's peerless beauty and affirm their faith in her miraculous powers. But unsympathetic voices contribute equally to this hagiography. Take Guido's extraordinary death row confession that he has always secretly subscribed to the paganism of his distant Roman ancestors:

I think I never was at any time
A Christian, as you nickname all the world,
Me among others: truce to nonsense now!

> Name me, a primitive religionist—
> As should the aboriginary be
> I boast myself, Etruscan, Aretine.

(11.1914–19)

This rhetorical gesture presents a radical departure from Browning's source documents. And though Browning must be allowed a degree of poetic license in Guido's character, here such license operates in generically precise ways, according to the conventions of *Sacred and Legendary Art*. Only a genuine "primitive religionist" can be expected to lay fire and set cauldron, to trace "the obscene ring" in the approved fashion. Guido's startling decision to emerge from the closet of paganism thus presents an independent—and otherwise extraneous—confirmation of Pompilia's claims to virgin martyrdom. The same might be demonstrated of Caponsacchi's role as the sort of comforting angel sent to the virgin martyr saints Catherine (*SLA* 473), Theclea (560), Dorothea (569), and Cecilia (584).

Finally, and triumphantly, Pompilia's own monologue in the poem's seventh book embraces the virgin martyr hagiography as its own most fitting antecedent. Pompilia prefaces her history with the exact details of her execution, the foremost credential for her canonization: "The surgeon cared for me, / To count my wounds,—twenty-two dagger-wounds, / Five deadly, but I do not suffer much" (7.37–39). Most female martyrs receive their death before submitting to marriage with pagan noblemen, it is true, but Pompilia maintains that utter innocence kept her from comprehending what St. Augustine calls "intercourse of the flesh": "—Well, I no more saw sense in what [Violante] said / Than a lamb does in people clipping wool" (7.386–87). Here and throughout, Pompilia presents herself as a holy innocent. She emphasizes that her marriage had always admitted questions of authenticity—"People indeed would fain have somehow proved / He was no husband: but he did not hear, / Or would not wait, and so has killed us all" (7.156–58)—and repeatedly yokes the circumstances of her marriage and murder so as to underscore the truth of the martyrdom in contradistinction to the dubiousness of the marriage.

Pompilia insists that her narrative requires a Continental religious perspective that departs from the everyday and the natural: "Thus, all my life,— / As well what was, as what, like this, was not,— / Looks old, fantastic and impossible" (7.198–200). As Herbert F. Tucker puts it, only a rhetoric of religious virginity permits the socially suspect flight from Arezzo with a handsome young priest.[20] Thus Pompilia doggedly associates herself with the virgin heroines of her religious culture, insisting that she was innocent, virtuous, beautiful, committed to God and to her virginity, and put to death for being just those things. Even for the sake of her newborn son, Gaetano, she specifies,

> ... I hope he will regard
> The history of me as what someone dreamed,
> And get to disbelieve it at the last:
> Since to myself it dwindles fast to that,
> Sheer dreaming and impossibility.

(7.108–12)

This appeal to the "fantastic and impossible" nature of her history is, of course, central to the hagiographical strategy of her monologue, and while it serves Pompilia to redeem her name from accusations of adultery, it also serves Browning to redeem his heroine for the British public. In either context, the strategy depends upon her tale's fantastic nature, for it is only the fantastic nature of hagiography that allows Pompilia to acknowledge circumstances that might solicit a less forgiving interpretation, and that allows Browning to present her as dazzlingly pure to a British readership accustomed to conceiving of female sexual virtue in more straightforward ways.

As her story nears its most socially questionable moment, then, her flight with Caponsacchi and their stay together in an inn at Castelnuovo, Pompilia appeals directly to the cultural power of virgin martyr hagiography:

> An old rhyme came into my head and rang
> Of how a virgin, for the faith of God,
> Hid herself, from the Paynims that pursued,
> In a cave's heart; until a thunderstone
> Wrapped in a flame, revealed the coach and prey:
> And they laughed—"Thanks to lightning, ours at last!"
> And she cried, "Wrath of God, assert His love!
> Servant of God, thou fire, befriend His child!"
> And lo, the fire she grasped at, fixed its flash,
> Lay in her hand a calm cold dreadful sword
> She brandished till pursuers strewed the ground,
> So did the souls within them die away,
> As o'er the prostrate bodies, sworded, safe,
> She walked forth to the solitudes and Christ:
> So I should grasp the lightning and be saved!
>
> (7.1389–1403)

Now, the deathbed audience to whom Pompilia recounts this tale may be presumed to know that when Guido overtakes the fugitive pair at Castelnuovo, Pompilia will indeed "grasp the lightning" of his sword in a failed attempt to kill her husband. And, given *The Ring and the Book*'s peculiar narrative structure, so do Browning's readers. Pompilia prefaces her attempt on Guido's life with this holy virgin story not to inform her listeners of the circumstances of her forthcoming encounter, but rather to provide the genre in which she wishes her Castelnuovo encounter understood: hagiographical narrative.[21] She who "grasp[s] the lightning" to strike "Paynims" must be a "virgin" with true "faith of God." Pompilia's acknowledged role model emerges "sworded [and] safe" from the episode, as Pompilia cannot, but many virgin martyrs initially resist subjugation to no ultimate avail. Guido serves nicely as the demon that haunted St. Justina and the dragon that devoured St. Margaret: he is Pompilia's "master, by hell's right" (1586), "the serpent towering and triumphant" (1589), "the old adversary." and, perhaps redundantly "the fiend" (1623).

In a moment of self-fulfilling prophecy toward the end of her monologue, Pompilia remarks of Guido, "I am saved through him / So as by fire; to him—thanks and farewell!" (1738–39). By this point, even her early mention of her "own five [patron] saints" (107) may retrospectively be considered to include herself. There exists no "St. Pompilia" in the Catholic canon, as Browning surely knew when in a final draft he revised the poem's manuscript from "my own four saints" to "my own five"; either the revised line contains an anachronism (listing two Saint Angelas, although just one was canonized by 1698) or it includes Pompilia herself in the company of Saints Francesca, Camilla, Vittoria, and Angela.[22] In either case, the manuscript alteration points to the prolusion of the Catholic cult of saints and to its handiness as a paradigm for one situated in Pompilia's circumstances. It both organizes diverse elements of her story and brings that story to life. And the final words of Pompilia's monologue—"And I rise"—helps bind us to such "old rhyme[s]" as the best generic model for her story.[23]

Despite the wonderful effectiveness with which Pompilia's history lends itself to virgin martyr hagiography, however, the visible factitiousness of her hagiography puts on display the limits, as well as the reaches, of a generic self-defense. Browning refuses to conceal the hand of the artist in this hagiographical creation, and he throws into jeopardy the saint hailed in Victorian reviews (and honored even in much subsequent criticism) by crafting her hagiography out of materials that prohibit its generic logic from operating cleanly. Thus, Pompilia's most ambitious attempts to free herself from culpability sometimes violate the rules of the very genre that establishes her innocence. Here the example of Pompilia's pregnancy and childbearing of Gaetano looms rather large.[24] It is both a consequence of the Victorian cult of motherhood and a tribute to the immense power of *The Ring and the Book's* hagiographical themes that critics and reviewers have so much understated the audacity of Pompilia's apparent claims to virgin motherhood, her means of reconciling sexual innocence to the fact that she was carrying someone's child when Guido overtook her at Castelnuovo. Almost none of the poem's contemporary reviewers expresses confusion about how Browning leaves this point ambiguous as does J. R. Mozley in *Macmillan's Magazine:*

> We accept for the present, and are content to accept, that view of the subject of the plot—the story of Pompilia—which Mr. Browning evidently means us to believe … . And thus we assume, as we are clearly intended to assume, that Guido was a desperate rascal … Pompilia a model of pure trustful innocence. *But yet it cannot but be observed that the story lends itself to another interpretation, which Mr. Browning has hardly done his utmost to ward off.*[25]

> (emphasis mine)

On one level, Mozley is plainly right. But Browning does not "ward off" the possibility of this other interpretation—that Gaetano is the child of Caponsacchi, and Pompilia is not "innocent" in the Victorian sense of the term—because that would destroy the generic experiment that he wishes to effect. Browning was interested in the operation of hagiography as a form that disambiguates such circumstances on its own terms and through its own literary power.

By way of analogy, here, one might think of the story of Strauss's groomsman, who famously quipped of the higher critic's celebrity marriage to the opera singer Agnes Schebest, "It is certainly a strong proof in favour of Strauss' theory, that so many untruths are circulated about his wedding—nay, that it is turned into a myth only a few days after the event."[26] While Strauss's *Leben Jesu* does not itself question the profusion of myth in the modern world, it raises this question nonetheless. In turn, Browning's *Ring and the Book* performs its own latter-day "proof in favour of Strauss' theory" whenever it elides meaningful distinctions between historical fact and poetic fancy. Possibly it does so especially when it elides these distinctions against unequal odds, as in the case of Pompilia's baby, whose appearance drives Pompilia to reach for the most extraordinary claims about her own purity. Pompilia initially suggests the notion of virgin motherhood only tentatively, suggesting that her son will have "No father that he ever knew at all, / Nor ever had—no, never had, I say! / That is the truth,—nor any mother left" (91–93). This early claim she hedges by parallel reflections upon their similar orphanhood: "I never had a father,—no, nor yet / A mother: my own boy can say at least / 'I had a mother whom I kept two weeks!'" (131–33). Yet 1,500 lines later, when her audience is moved by her rhetoric of saintliness and its hagiographical weight, she returns to this theme without any qualifications at all: "My babe nor was, nor is, nor yet shall be / Count Guido Franceschini's child at all— / Only his mother's, born of love not hate!" (1762–65). It is an extraordinary moment in the poem. She cannot identify the baby as that of Guido (the fiend) or of Caponsacchi (the angel) and so her rhetoric lays claim to a sort of religious parthenogenesis. But this claim is not, as some modern critics have supposed, the consummate example of hagiographical pretensions in a culture where the fantastic is taken for truth. It continues a hagiographical theme of innocence, certainly, but it also indicates where such hagiography must break down. Anyone can become a Catholic saint (at least in theory), but no one else can become the Virgin. However many virgin martyrs proliferate in the Christian tradition, there remains only one Virgin Mother, as Browning knew and as Anna Jameson reminds us by publishing as a separate volume her third work in the *Sacred and Legendary Art series: Legends of the Madonna*. The virgin birth entails what Hilary Mantel calls a "one-off by the deity," and the cultic diversity of the religion, sprawling elsewhere, remains bounded here.[27]

This disjunction between Pompilia's vindication in the virgin martyr tradition and the audacity of her pretensions to virgin birth thus exposes a philosophically richer character than either her admirers or her more recent detractors have acknowledged. When today's scholars (such as Walker) first began to question the cult of Pompilia, they called her disingenuous, pragmatic, and evasive, but her rhetoric does not add up to this. It amounts to the cultural power of a particular combination of tropes regardless of Pompilia's sincerity (which might be perfect), and without necessitating any deliberation on her character's part to deploy a generic strategy (beyond taking "an old rhyme" as a model for her demeanor at Castelnuovo). Anna Jameson once recounted having encountered on the streets of Paris a gaily dressed child in beads, flowers, and veils. "Rather surprised at her appearance, I asked her name; she replied blushing, *'Madame, je suis la sainte Vierge'* [Madam, I am the Holy Virgin]."[28] Even if Browning's Pompilia makes the same innocent mistake as Jameson's Parisian girl, she also reveals the problematics of self-canonization. Jameson's story is comical because it shows off the difference between the sacred and the mundane. "Pompilia" is sublime because it shows how religious texts can simultaneously admit and efface that distinction.

In this manner, the generic construction of religious and historical truths becomes essential to Browning's poetic vocation and to his reception as a poet. Browning agreed with Strauss that the Bible's sacred truths were literary, and he understood that Anna Jameson's hagiographies were, like the Gospels, literary sites where fact and embellishment become indistinguishable and still demand to be read as truth. He took seriously the possibility of finding truth in the "legends of the saints" of which Clough complained, and for the same reason. So "Pompilia" presents a clear and important extension of the logic of "A Death in the Desert" (1864), an earlier dramatic monologue that purports to represent the death speech of St. John the Evangelist. In a twist upon the Gospel of John, which records the author's presence at Christ's crucifixion ("And he that saw *it* bare record, and his record is true" [19:35 AV]), Browning's St. John concedes that he was not present at the crucifixion, while insisting upon the fundamental truth of that biblical account in which he claimed to be there.[29] The analogy between Pompilia's hagiography and St. John's Gospel ought to be plain: both are fantastic religious tales by authors who insist upon their truthfulness even as they reveal their own historical dubiousness. Browning, like his own St. John, elides the difference between the generic and historical elements of his religious text when he insists that Pompilia "is just as I found her in the book." And Browning's St. John performs exactly the ideal of poetic creation offered by *The Ring and the Book:* that to "write a book shall mean, beyond the facts, / Suffice the eye and save the soul beside" (12.862–63). For Browning, no literature could be more eye-sufficing and soul-saving than the Gospel of John, so it is all the more compelling that he takes a Johannine approach in his construction of "Pompilia." Like St. John with his gospel, Browning composes "beyond the facts."

Notes

1 This is clear even in the opening lines of *The Ring and the Book:* the poet finds his story at the bookstall next to "The Life, Death, Miracles of Saint Somebody," and "Saint Somebody Else, his Miracles, Death, and Life,—" (1.80–81).
2 Clough, *Prose Remains,* 416.
3 Muller, *Auld Lang Syne,* 88.
4 Another example is that of the recently discovered Saint Filomela, who appears in Anna Jameson's *Sacred and Legendary Art,* 672.
5 Blackbourn, *Marpingen,* 17–57.
6 Buchanan's *Athenaeum* article insists that "from the first to the last, Pompilia haunts the poem with a look of ever-deepening light" ("The Ring and the Book," 399–400). H.B. Forman of the *London Quarterly Review* agrees, claiming, "Pompilia is so little dependent on anything but the nobility of her character and treatment for the interest she excites, the exquisite pleasures her speech yields, and the genuine help to be got therefrom in breasting the troubles of every day, that we feel confident in the efficiency of time to make this work a popular poem" (356), and "Pompilia's character is one which makes analysis a superfluity by reason of its mere simplicity and purity … . With Pompilia, every reader must know, before he has turned many pages of her death-bed speech, that he is reading good and beautiful poetry, which places him face to face with a good and beautiful soul" ("Epic of Psychology," 353). John Morley's *Fortnightly Review* confirms the prevalence of this view: "When the first volume of Mr. Browning's new poem came came before the critical tribunals … it was pronounced a murky subject, sordid, unlovely, morally sterile … [yet] Pompilia convinced them that the subject was not, after all, so incurably unlovely" ("On 'The Ring and the Book,'" 544). Later in the century, *Sir Henry Jones keeps this hermeneutic alive* with his claims that "Pompilia shone with a glory that mere knowledge could not give" (*Browning,* 333). And Harriet Gaylord confirms its longevity with *Pompilia and Her Poet,* an unqualified encomium on Pompilia's "white soul" that went through three editions in the 1930s. Even John Doherty's almost entirely unsympathetic report in the *Dublin Review* nonetheless concedes. "The character of Pompilia … is itself an exquisite conception … a type of simplicity, innocence, and purity … . There is something of the supernatural in it" ("The Ring and the Book," 60). See also Austen, "Pompilia."
7 The historical witnesses to Pompilia's death provide warrant for Browning's idea. Her confessor Fra Celestino Angelo records, "I have discovered and marveled at an innocent and saintly conscience in that ever-blessed child," who "died with strong love for God … and with the admiration of all bystanders, who blessed her as a saint." Nicolo Constantio, Placido Sardi, and the Marquis Nicolo Gregorio similarly add. "We have witnessed her dying the death of a saint" (Hodell, *Old Yellow Book.* 45–48).
8 Dalberg-Acton, "German Schools of History."
9 Curle, *Robert Browning and Julia Wedgwood,* 152; Hodell. *Old Yellow Book.* 282.
10 Hodell, *Old Yellow Book;* Corrigan, *Curious Annals.* Such selectiveness need not betoken Browning's bad faith, however; the poem's structure dramatizes the inevitable selectiveness of any history.
11 The *London Quarterly Review,* for example, maintains that Pompilia's utter simplicity and purity make analysis "a superfluity," calling her monologue "good and beautiful poetry, which places [the reader] face to face with good and beautiful soul" (Forman, "Epic of Psychology," 353). The *Edinburgh Review* writes of the poem's protagonists. "In English literature the creative faculty of the poet has not produced three characters more beautiful or better for men to contemplate than these three [Caponsacchi, Pompilia, and the Pope]" ("The Ring and the Book," 91).
12 My argument complements, and in some instances qualifies, the following studies: Auerbach, *Romantic Imprisonment,* 92–106; Brown, "Pompilia: The Woman (in) Question"; Tucker,

"Representation and Repristination"; Walker, "Pompilia and Pompilia"; and Candace Ward, "Damning Herself Praisworthily."

13 The original *Sacred and Legendary Art* (hereafter *SLA*) went through ten editions and was reprinted into the twentieth century. In the manner of Lootens, Judith Johnston, and Clara Thomas, I refer to this work under this title, although "Sacred and Legendary Art" as an umbrella title also applies to Jameson's subsequent works in the same series. See Johnston, *Anna Jameson,* and Thomas, *Love and Work Enough.*

14 Holcomb, "Anna Jameson."

15 That the Brownings did not know the two-volume SLA is only academically possible, given the friends' familiarity with one another's work. EBB translated verse for AJ's 1844 *Athenaeum* essay on the Xanthian Marbles, and Jameson, in turn, quotes "The Cry of the Children" in both *SLA*, vol. 1, and *Legends of the Madonna.* Jameson's famous 1846 "I have also here a poet and a poetess" letter from Paris mixes expressions of pleasure at the Brownings' elopement with complaints about the difficulty of rapidly finishing *SLA* (see MacPherson, *Memoirs,* 228–29). Further, Bate MacPherson, AJ's niece, records in her memoirs that the Brownings were Jameson's "closest associates" when at Pisa and Florence, "working out the result of [Jameson's] studies, arranging and classifying the additions to her stories" (233). Finally, when EBB thanked AJ for the reception of the second publication in the *SLA* series (*Legends of the Monastic Orders*), she observes that Jameson's "books" will be "a necessity for art students" (Barrett Browning, *Letters,* 2:440–41).

16 Jameson, *SLA,* 468, 517, 61, 68, 74, 601, 8–9. All subsequent page numbers will be from this edition.

17 Melissa V. Gregory shrewdly points out that the generic logic of the dramatic monologue helps account not only for Victorian readers' visceral response to Browning's depictions of domestic violence but also for Browning's inclination to treat it in the first place ("Violent Lyric Voice").

18 See Austen, "Pompilia," and Friedman, "To Tell the Sun."

19 In this, as throughout, RB takes elements of the *Old Yellow Book* and expands upon them. There are only two references to Pompilia's beauty in the *Old Yellow Book,* and neither are particularly emphatic or convincing. Yet Sir Frederick Treves, even after admitting Browning's dearth of evidence for her appearance, can attest as though it were factual that "Pompilia, so the book affirms, was young, good and beautiful, with large dark eyes and a bounty of black hair. Her face was pale and her expression grave and griefful [*sic*], like that of our Lady of All the Sorrows" (250).

20 Tucker asserts that *The Ring and the Book* "represents virginity not as a stable condition, but as a conviction dynamically effected and reaffirmed" ("Representation and Repristination," 78).

21 Walker has suggested that such elements deflate any claims that Pompilia has to Christian sanctity just the contrary is true, because of the poem's generic tradition. For a good discussion of the poetic rendering of this episode, see Campbell, *Rhythm and Will,* 99–124.

22 Both this numeric issue and the manuscript's revision are indicated in the Ohio *Complete Works,* 7:346.

23 So as not to belabor the generic element of this argument, I have refrained from addressing the poem's hagiographical elements that are not specifically related to female virgin martyrs. William De Vane's St. George narrative is one such element. One might also trace the less-developed depiction of Caponsacchi and Pompilia as Saints Francis and Clare. Browning was very likely acquainted with Giotto's early-Renaissance illustration of Francis's Arezzo exorcism; if not, it is a striking coincidence that Caponsacchi relates having repeated a prayer of exorcism to relieve Pompilia's nightmares of her own personal Arezzo demon—"'Oh, if the God, that only can, would help! / Am I his priest with power to cast out fiends? / Let God arise and all his enemies / Be scattered!' By morn, there was peace, no sigh / Out of the deep sleep" (6.1300–1304). Anna Jameson details the lives of Francis and Clare in her *Legends of the Monastic Orders,* 278–309. She relates the tale of St. Francis's Arezzo exorcism on 298.

24 Pompilia's monologue must strategically avoid questions of sex if it is to present its resemblance to hagiography. Still, at one point, she does imply herself to be a victim of what today would be called marital rape, and it is not by accident that the "New Woman" writer Mona Caird cites copiously from *The Ring and the Book* in her 1890 *Fortnightly Review* critique of the institution of marriage: "The Morality of Marriage."

25 John Mozley, "The Ring and the Book," 546.

26 Strauss, *The Old Faith and the New*, xl.
27 The phrase is from Mantel, "'What Did Her Neighbours Say?'"
28 Erskine, *Anna Jameson*, 28–29.
29 For further analyses of this poem, see Roberts, "Me/Not-Me"; Shaffer, "*Kubla Khan*."

Works Cited

Auerbach, Nina, *Romantic Imprisonment: Women and Other Glorified Outcasts* (New York: Columbia University Press, 1985).

Austen, Kay, 'Pompilia: "Saint and Martyr Both"', *Victorian Poetry* 17 (1979), 287–301.

Blackbourn, David, *Marpingen: Apparitions of the Virgin Mary in Bismarckian Germany* (Oxford: Clarendon Press, 1993).

Browning, Elizabeth Barrett, *The Letters of Elizabeth Barret-Browning*, ed. by Frederick G. Kenyon, 3rd ed., 2 vols. (London: Smith Elder, 1897).

Buchanan, Robert, 'The Ring and the Book', *Athenaeum* 2160 (1869), 399–400.

Caird, Mona, 'The Morality of Marriage', in Andrea Broomfield and Sally Mitchell, *Prose by Victorian Women: An Anthology* (New York: Garland, 1996), 629–53.

Campbell, Matthew, *Rhythm and Will in Victorian Poetry* (Cambridge: Cambridge University Press, 1999).

Clough, Arthur Hugh, *Prose Remains of Arthur Hugh Clough* ed. by Blanche Clough (London: Macmillan, 1898).

Curle, Richard, *Robert Browning and Julia Wedgwood: A Broken Friendship as Revealed by their Letters* (New York: Frederick A. Stokes Company, 1937).

Dalberg-Acton, John, 'German Schools of History', *English Historical Review* 1 (1886).

Erskine, Beatrice, *Anna Jameson: Letters and Friendships 1812–1860* (London: T. Fisher Unwin, 1915).

Gregory, Melissa Valiska, 'Robert Browning and the Lure of the Violent Lyric: Voice, Domestic Violence and the Dramatic Monologue', *Victorian Poetry* 38.4 (2000), 491–510.

Hodell, Charles Wesley, *Old Yellow Book: Source of Browning's 'The Ring and the Book' in Complete Photo-Reproduction* (Washington DC: Carnegie Institute of Washington, 1908).

Holcomb, Adele, M., 'Anna Jameson: The First Professional Art Historian', *Art History,* 6:2 (1983), 171 – 87.

Jameson, Anna, *Sacred and Legendary Art: Containing the Patron Saints, the Martyrs, the Early Bishops, the Hermits and the Warrior Saints of Christendom*, 5th ed. (London: Longmans, Green, 1866).

Jameson, Anna, *Legends of the Madonna*, 4th ed. (London: Longmans, Green, 1876).

Johnston, Judith, *Anna Jameson: Victorian, Feminist, Woman of Letters* (Aldershot: Scolar Press, 1997).

MacPherson, Gerardine Bate, *Memoirs of the Life of Anna Jameson* (Boston: Roberts Brothers, 1878).

Mantel, Hilary, 'What Did Her Neighbours Say When Gabriel Had Gone', *London Review of Books* 31.7, 9 April (2009), 3–6.

Mozley, John Richards, 'The Ring and the Book', *Macmillan's Magazine,* 19 (1868–69), 159–94.

Müller, F. Max, *Auld Lang Syne* (New York: Charles Scribner & Sons, 1898).

Roberts, Adam, 'Me/Not-Me: The Narrator of a Death in the Dessert', in *Robert Browning in Contexts*, ed. by John Woolford (Winfield, KS: Wedgestone Press,1998).

Strauss, David Friedrich, *The Old Faith and the New: A Confession*, trans. by Mathilde Blind, 3rd English Edition, (London: Asher, 1874).

Thomas, Clara, *Love and Work Enough: The Life of Anna Jameson* (London: Macdonald, 1967).

Tucker, Herbert, *Virginal Sexuality and Textuality in Victorian Literature*, ed. by Lloyd Davies (Albany: SUNY Press, 1993).

Walker, William, '*Pompilia* and Pompilia', *Victorian Poetry* 22.1 (1984), 47–63.

35 Introduction to *Form and Faith in Victorian Poetry and Religion* (2012)

Kirstie Blair

This study started from a very simple and obvious premiss: when Victorian poetry speaks of faith, it tends to do so in steady and regular rhythms; when it speaks of doubt, it is correspondingly more likely to deploy irregular, unsteady, unbalanced rhythms. This also holds true of other aspects of poetic form, such as the conventionality or otherwise of poetic language, verse form, and genre, all of which are often more 'regular' (and regulated) in the poetry of faith. This may seem self-evident. It certainly did so to Victorian poets and critics. Writing at mid-century, Charles Kingsley argues in his diatribe against modern poetry:

> Without faith there can be no real art, for art is the outward expression of firm, coherent belief. And a poetry of doubt, even a sceptical poetry, in its true sense, can never possess clear and sound form, even organic form at all. How can you put into form that thought which is by its very nature formless?[1]

'Organic' form was a topic of keen discussion from the Romantic poets onwards, and is also a live issue in twenty-first century criticism. It is important to note that for Kingsley organic or natural form is not messy or unpredictable; it does not indicate its vitality through deviation. Denise Gigante's fascinating *Life: Organic Form and Romanticism* associates the concept of organic form with developments in the life sciences and suggests that it offers a methodology for reading 'certain seemingly formless poems', which presented a 'world in which material structures were plastic and subject to ongoing change'.[2] Without questioning that this association of the organic with the 'seemingly formless' persisted into the Victorian period, many nineteenth-century critics (as will become evident in succeeding chapters of this monograph) also understood organic form in terms of law. Coleridge wrote that organic form 'shapes as it develops itself from within' [*sic*], as opposed to 'mechanic' form which is predetermined and impressed upon substance from without. Yet he also observed in the same lecture that 'a living Body is of necessity an organized one' and that all living powers (including poetry) must therefore be circumscribed by rules.[3] George Eliot's 'Notes on Form in Art', written in 1868, associates the organicism of poetic form with 'rhythmic persistence', which 'creates a form by the recurrence of its elements in adjustment with certain given conditions':

> just as the beautiful curves of a bivalve shell are not first made for the reception of the instable inhabitant, but grow and are limited by the simple rhythmic conditions of its growing life.[4]

Conditions are 'given', development is 'limited' and predetermined—and these limits and conditions are associated with rhythmic recurrence. Eliot's account of poetic form is not concerned with religion, but for writers like Kingsley and many others, the fact that such 'simple rhythmic conditions' of life were set by God and in accordance with his laws could be taken for granted. He is the giver, and all organic life adjusts itself to his conditions. Poetry that accepted 'nature's laws as the laws of God', Kingsley suggested, would therefore indicate this not in formlessness but in order: 'There is a beautiful and fit order in poetry, which is part of God's order.'[5] Where there is form, there is faith.

Until recently, however, the forms of faith in Victorian poetry have received relatively little critical attention. Critics have recognized that twentieth-century studies of Victorian religion tended 'to underestimate the persistence of traditional religious beliefs in the face of admittedly discouraging, even demoralizing circumstances', and scholars of literature and religion have taken this on board.[6] Charles LaPorte, for instance, in his recent *Victorian Poets and the Changing Bible,* comments that much Victorian poetry— thinking especially of the well-worn classics of 'faith and doubt', such as *In Memoriam,* 'Dover Beach', poems by Robert Browning, Arthur Hugh Clough, and Thomas Hardy— 'lends itself exceptionally well to the Victorian secularization narrative', but suggests that this narrative itself is collapsing under the weight of renewed scholarship on Victorian religion:

> Such well-trodden literary histories of secularization, nonetheless, tend to lean heavily upon an idea that religion was actually dying in mid-century Britain. It should therefore be of interest to scholars of Victorian poetry and of Victorian literature more broadly that the moribund condition of nineteenth-century British Christianity now seems far less evident than it has seemed to us during most of the intervening period.[7]

Tracy Fessenden's comments on American literature and culture suggest that the tendency to impose a narrative of secularization onto nineteenth-century literature has also been evident in a US context:

> Far from attending to the presence of religion in literary contexts... students of religion-and-literature learned instead to seek after its absence, its displacement by or reconstitution as the newly empowered secular, freed from the trappings of ritual, the limitations of historical communities, or the embarrassments of outmoded belief.[8]

It is precisely the 'trappings of ritual', 'limitations of historical communities', and forms of 'outmoded belief that are the subject of this monograph, which attempts to show their continuing importance for studies of nineteenth-century literature and culture. In this, I am part of a group of scholars who are engaged in revisiting the Victorian poetry of faith and questioning critical embarrassment in the face of its apparently outdated beliefs. F. E. Gray's 2010 study of women's devotional poetry is another excellent example of such work. She also agrees that it is time to reconsider Victorian poetry as a site for secure faith:

> Over the last fifty years, scholars of Victorian literature on religious topics have tended overwhelmingly to focus on and privilege the poetry of questioning and of doubt, which I suggest has skewed our understanding of the significance of religious devotion in the century's creative work.[9]

This longstanding critical emphasis on the poetry of 'questioning and of doubt', as LaPorte similarly observes, is scarcely surprising. From a purely literary-critical perspective—leaving aside historical and cultural shifts in the twentieth century that may have made 'doubt' seem a more attractive prospect for study—it is both more difficult and, for formally engaged criticism, inherently less interesting, indeed less fun, to discuss poetry that militantly sticks to conventions and that takes its faith for granted, as opposed to the formally varied and often anguished questioning of, say, Arnold or Clough. Gray, for example, comments ruefully on the 'disheartening aesthetic quality' of much female devotional verse even while successfully arguing for its significance.[10]

Women's religious poetry and hymns have been at the forefront of the renewed interest in popular Victorian religious verse. Important general studies by Cynthia Scheinberg and Emma Mason have complemented several significant individual studies of Christina Rossetti and EBB, all of which tend to view religion as an enabling, even radicalizing, force for female poets.[11] Scheinberg's recovery of the Jewish contexts of poetry by both Anglo-Jewish and non-Jewish poets added a vital dimension to Victorian religious poetics as well as to our understanding of women's poetry as a genre. Mason's short study of Victorian women poets assumes that their religious beliefs and affiliations constituted an essential part of their poetic identity, a stance that has not always been common. In comparison to these and many other scholars in the field of women's devotional poetics, popular religious poetry by men remains comparatively neglected. With the honourable exception of G. B. Tennyson's important *Victorian Devotional Poetry: The Tractarian Mode,* among the most-discussed group, the Tractarians, only John Henry Newman and John Keble retain critical currency, and the latter more often for his influence on later poets than as a poet himself.[12] Writers such as Frederick Faber and Isaac Williams, considered in various chapters here, were widely read in their day but now suffer from near-total critical neglect, though there is much remaining to be said about the complex negotiations with religious ideals in their poetry. *Form and Faith in Victorian Poetry and Religion* only scratches the surface in relation to other, wildly popular, Victorian religious poets, like Robert Montgomery, who is briefly discussed in Chapter 3, and does not engage with poetry written by men now better known as religious controversialists, such as John Mason Neale, or Arthur Stanley. Hundreds of Victorian clergymen and priests wrote poetry, and the way in which it was contiguous with their religious profession has not been fully studied. Outside Anglicanism, strong traditions of dissenting and working-class religious verse and of Roman Catholic verse made their own contribution. To begin reading the forgotten works of Victorian religious poetry is to realize how much remains to be read, how a large class of works read by a considerable number of people has effactually faded from view.

One of the central arguments of this book, then, is that canonical poets such as Tennyson, the Brownings, Hardy, Hopkins, and Rossetti produced their religious poetry as part of a context of popular religious poetics, and indeed a context including not only poetry but also tracts, sermons, pamphlets, journal articles, and religious works of all descriptions. Victorian poets and their readers shared a vocabulary relating to contemporary religious debates that we have largely lost. And one of the keywords in this vocabulary was 'form'. Form, as it features in recent theoretical debates over the emergence of what has been sometimes controversially been termed 'new formalism', remains relatively undefined.[13] Angela Leighton's outstanding contribution to these debates, *On Form: Poetry, History and the Legacy of a Word,* opens by noting the many and various meanings that 'form' can hold in English, observing that 'The fact that so many senses whisper within earshot of form make it, somehow, dense and crowded.'[14] Leighton traces the historical weight that 'form' carries, as a term that came to be associated, from the mid-eighteenth century, with 'the growth of philosophical aesthetics and the Kantian emphasis on subjective perception'.[15] In literature, she suggests, there is a direct line from Romantic writing on form to that of Walter Pater and Oscar Wilde as form becomes 'one of the most precious terms in the history of aestheticism'.[16] Leighton's nuanced study and its excellent close readings of Victorian poetry make clear the legacy of this understanding of form as aesthetic, form for form's sake.

There is, however, a historical context lurking behind the use of 'form' in Victorian aestheticism that is more parochial, more specific to early to mid-Victorian debates; a context that Pater and Wilde would have been well aware of. Indeed, it is arguable that this context was written out of form's history partly because late Victorian aestheticism, and subsequently modernism, was so successful in appropriating form as its own. In her chapter reassessing Tennyson's influence on aestheticism, Leighton comments: '"I dread the losing hold of forms", Tennyson himself once declared in relation to his poetry.'[17] But Tennyson was not talking about his poetry. The extract from the *Memoir*, which opens 'The Last Chapter' on Tennyson's death, states:

> In his view of the Gospel of Christ he found his Christianity undisturbed by jarring of sect and of creeds; but he said, 'I dread the losing hold of forms. I have expressed this in my "Akbar". There must be forms, yet I hate the need for so many sects and separate services.'[18]

Although every use of 'form' in Tennyson is arguably related to his self-consciousness about poetic forms and their value, this statement is fundamentally about religious practices rather than aesthetic. What Hallam Tennyson does here is position Tennyson in relation to an issue that was still current in the 1890s, the question of the value or otherwise of forms in religious worship. Statements such as this and poems such as 'Akbar's Dream' locate Tennyson both as a religious liberal whose spirituality was above the petty concerns of 'sect and creeds', and as an advocate for the retention of form, a position generally considered more conservative and often more Anglican.

When Victorian writers like Tennyson discussed form they were doing so with the full consciousness that there was a bitter debate over form within and without the Church of England. In this debate also, form is never clearly defined, or rather, its definition depends upon the allegiance of the speaker. To those who viewed themselves as antagonistic to form in religion, a form was any fixed aspect of worship, and a 'formalist' someone who relied upon externals.[19] The Lord's Prayer, for instance, is a form. But so is the act of genuflection, or an organ voluntary, or an elaborately carved font, or a church building. All of these are related to the performance of faith; they are designed to convey and communicate the faith of the congregation, priest, musician, builder, or architect to God. Opponents of form tended to be drawn from Evangelical or dissenting religious traditions, which emphasized a personal and individual relationship with God, accessible without the trappings of organized religion. They viewed forms as lifeless external structures, repressive and limiting. Supporters of form, who correspondingly were much more likely to be somewhere on the Anglo-Catholic spectrum, argued in contrast that formal limits were enabling, in the sense that they allowed the speaker to express something inexpressible, and that formal structures acted as supports for human weakness besides creating a sense of historic continuity and community within the Church. They also maintained that, in the words of the controversial ritualist minister William Bennett:

> Every thing clothed in words is a *form:* the only difference is, that a Liturgy is a form
> known to the congregation—an extempore prayer, a form unknown to the congregation.[20]

Dissenters might claim a distaste for form, Bennett argued, but to worship without forms
was impossible. The way in which form was imagined by advocates for its importance, the
metaphors it attracted, varied considerably within this group, from those who embraced an
understanding of forms as adaptable, growing and changing, to those who described them in
terms suggesting fixed limits, restraints, or containment, like a box, or a set of fences. In just
one paragraph, for instance, the High Church minister A. J. Pigott observes that 'forms and
ceremonies' are:

> the fences of the Lord's vineyard... they are the shell that keeps the kernel of religion from
> contempt; they are the casket, in which the precious jewels of Christ's temple are encased;
> they are the leaves that grow upon the tree of life, and shield its flowers and fruits from this
> world's killing frosts; they are the body in which the soul of Christianity is enshrined.[21]

Fences and caskets are man-made, constructed objects designed to enclose and keep safe
(and to keep others out). Nutshells, leaves, and bodies are also all arguably protective devices,
but grown rather than made; and both leaves and bodies are soft, fragile, subject to change,
decay, and death. Pigott demonstrates the capability of many writers on form to hold relatively
incompatible views of its working with ease.

Victorian debates over religious form have significant implications for the discourses of
architecture, music, art, and linguistics, among others. It is in relation to poetic form, however,
that these debates are most important. As William McKelvy has recently noted, 'it was only in
the nineteenth century that the putative religious function of literature became a self-defining
subject for public debate', and poetry, still held to be the highest form of literature, was
particularly liable to be considered as a work of religion.[22] Moreover, it is not simply the case
that Victorian poetry was held to have a religious function, but that Victorian religion was held
to have a poetic function, and, as discussed throughout this study, these functions depended
upon form. Clough, as an Oxford undergraduate tempted by Tractarianism, wrote:

> And it is no harm but rather good to give oneself up a little to hearing Oxford people, and
> admiring their good points, which lie, I suppose, principally in all they hold in opposition
> to the Evangelical portion of society—the benefit and beauty and necessity of forms—the
> ugliness of feelings put on unnaturally soon and consequently kept up by artificial means,
> ever strained and never sober.[23]

Writing in 1838, Clough was at the start of historical and cultural developments which
brought form to prominence, and which would have a direct effect on the experience of
Christian worship in Britain. His letter comments on the Oxford Movement, but it is also
part of an exchange about the appropriateness or otherwise of discussing personal feelings in
poetry. In thinking about the value of religious forms, Clough is also considering the value
of forms in poetry, as aesthetically pleasing, morally helpful, and essential in managing and
shaping the spontaneous overflow of emotion. He demonstrates here an acute understanding
of the Tractarian view of form as a container for feeling, a safeguard or barrier, whose aim
was to regulate emotion and to calm it, to induce a steady state of quiet belief rather than
ramping up enthusiasm. But his letter also shows that questions of form in religion and in
poetry were not separable, because the two discourses were discussed as one.

To a reader interested in the alleged return of formalism in critical studies, these comments on the interdisciplinarity of form in Victorian Britain might resonate with recent discussions of a 'formalist' critical method that combines detailed close reading with the analysis of broader historical relations. 'What would a criticism look like that took *both* literary forms and socio-political relations seriously?', Caroline Levine asks in a summary of recent work on form.[24] In her own seminal 2006 *Victorian Studies* article, she partly answered this question through a reading of EBB's 'The Cry of the Children', defining her methodology as 'strategic formalism':

> Form, in my definition, refers to shaping patterns, to identifiable interlacings of repetitions and differences, to dense networks of structuring principles and categories… It does involve a kind of close reading, a careful attention to the ways that historical texts, bodies and institutions are organized—what shapes they take, what models they follow and rework. But it is all about the social: it involves reading particular, historically specific collisions among generalizing political, cultural, and social forms.[25]

Herbert Tucker's response to Levine's article further observed, via a virtuoso reading of EBB's metrics, that 'the generalization that is form goes all the way down to the unit, and thus that a fractal relation obtains between our micro and our macro analytics'.[26] In paying close attention to the interactions between form and content in Victorian religious poetics, and in linking these to broader religious (and thus also 'socio-political') formations, this book clearly adheres to the kind of methodology that Levine describes. Her essay hovers a little over the relation between the 'literary' and the 'social'. Initially they are 'comparable and overlapping patterns' which we can link 'as if they inhabited the same plane, as if poetic techniques and social formations were comparably iterable patterns, each struggling to impose order', but by the essay's conclusion, she argues that 'social forms and literary forms are always potentially embedded within one another'.[27] The focus on poetic and religious forms here enables me to argue the case more strongly: in relation to these particular literary and social formations, there is nothing potential or 'as if' about their interlacing. Victorian writers (rather like Levine) sometimes start from a position of comparing poetry and religion, but often end by assuming that the two are equivalents, operating by the same methods and under the strictures of divine law. What this suggests is that they already had a clear understanding that 'the generalization that is form goes all the way down to the unit'. Basing this understanding on the premiss of the existence of God makes it abundantly clear that the micro (the choice of metre for a particular poem) is bound up with the macro (the deep pulsations of the world, in Tennyson's famous phrasing).

Victorian religious practitioners—a category that includes religious poets—knew what was at stake in formal choices and were highly self-conscious about them, creating their own discussion of the ethical and political ramifications of form that effectively pre-empts the formalist discourse of twenty-first-century literary criticism. They were aware that poetic form would be read as shorthand for the poet's beliefs and allegiance. As Susan J. Wolfson argues in her influential *Formal Charges: The Shaping of Poetry in British Romanticism:*

> Formal elements do not exist 'apart' from but play a part in the semantic order, especially when issues of form—poetic or otherwise—are at stake. On such occasions, choices of form and the way in which it is managed often signify as much as, and as part of, words themselves.[28]

'Choices of form' do not only apply to poetry. To choose Gregorian chant over a contemporary hymn, for instance, signified a great deal in mid-Victorian England, as did selecting archaic Gothic font as appropriate for your poems, or opting to wear a crucifix in public. Such choices matter enormously to our reading of Victorian poetry. In reading a poem such as Coventry Patmore's 'Legem Tuam Dilexi' [In your law have I delighted], for instance, part of the series *The Unknown Eros* (1877), to what extent might we need to know that Patmore began his poetic career as an Anglican married to the daughter of a Congregationalist preacher, but at the time of writing this volume was not only a Roman Catholic convert himself but had remarried a staunch Catholic and seen his beloved eldest daughter enter a convent? Unlike many if not most of the poems discussed below, 'Legem Tuam Dilexi' does not seem immediately concerned with particular forms of religious worship and practice. But it does signally reflect on questions of containment versus freedom:

> And the just Man does on himself affirm
> God's limits, and is conscious of delight,
> Freedom and right;
> And so His Semblance is, Who, every hour,
> By day and night,
> Buildeth new bulwarks 'gainst the Infinite.
> For, ah, who can express
> How full of bonds and simpleness
> Is God,
> How narrow is He,
> And how the wide, waste field of possibility
> Is only trod
> Straight to His homestead in the human heart,
> …
> Therefore the soul select assumes the stress
> Of bonds unbid, which God's own style express
> Better than well,[29]

In this poem, free access to the infinite is represented as both potentially 'seditious' and destructive: nature, in the 'soft growth twice constrain'd in leaf and flower', is subject to God's compulsion, and man should exercise his free will in voluntarily submitting to the same constraints.[30] Besides the need for such bonds in protecting fragile organic life from the unimaginable force and power of God's Infinity, they prove the only way to access grace and true freedom. These are ideas that, as we will see, were a constant refrain in High Anglican and Catholic poetics in this period, to the extent that by the 1870s they were almost clichéd.

What is different about Patmore's expression of this theme, however, is that, as a general rule, important predecessors such as John Keble (whom Patmore greatly admired) used the formal constraints of poetry to bolster their subject matter by visibly and audibly signalling conformity to metrical norms, regularity, and stability. Patmore's Odes do not look like this genre of verse. Indeed, they look much more like the kind of restless, shifting verse forms in Browning's 'Christmas-Eve' or in some of Arnold's poems, where he actively laments the fact that 'limits we did not set / Condition all we do'; that is, much more like dissenting or 'doubting' poetry.[31] Yet Patmore evidently did not intend his poetic form to indicate any disagreement or doubt about the value of form and faith. Its seemingly unorthodox patterns instead almost defiantly proclaim the possibilities of freedom within bonds. As Basil Champneys observed on Patmore's acceptance of Roman Catholic dogma:

> To one advanced in spiritual ideas and instinctively orthodox, such authority was a charter of perfect freedom, and manifested itself as encouragement or confirmation rather than as limitation or repression. As the true poet with rhyme and metre, so he with dogma.[32]

The analogy between dogma and poetic form here is a nod to one of the key arguments asserted throughout this book, the commonly held association of poetic and religious forms. In this poem, Patmore experiments with form to attempt to embody his argument about the importance of 'narrowness', in that stretched-out lines like 'And how the wide, waste, field of possibility' indicate precisely through their varying possibilities of scansion a lack of firm law, which for Patmore as a Roman Catholic is profoundly threatening. The 'narrow' lines, such as 'Freedom and right' or 'Is God', have a contrasting firmness and definition.

This ode and the others in the collection illustrated Patmore's theories of timing and pause, 'isochrony' and catalexis in metre, as expressed in his 'Essay on English Metrical Law', in which, as metre primarily exists in the reader's mind, he or she would implicitly fill in the missing beats in each line to reach a harmonious rhythm.[33] After the line 'Is God', for example, there would be a significant pause for the reader to take in this concept, even as long as four beats, to make the line into a ten-syllable pentameter. Jason Rudy notes in his valuable account of Patmore's metrical theory that in practice the supposed regularizing system of isochrony was problematic at best: 'if the point of metre is to subdue and regulate, then isochrony must largely fail the test: what sort of regulation might come from a poem that most readers cannot scan?'[34] Yet as Joshua King comments in an excellent recent discussion of the relation between Patmore's metrical theory and his faith, poems such as 'Legem Tuam Dilexi' nonetheless strove to develop the 'association of metrical law with divine moral law' by calling upon the reader 'to affirm the connection by pausing'. King comments that in *The Unknown Eros:*

> Submitting his voice to the bonds of meter, the just reader will transform Patmore's style into God's style… His metrical law is ultimately written in the conviction of things that eye has not seen nor ear heard. Ironically, it therefore depends on not being seen or heard, and runs the risk, so often met with disappointment in Patmore's experience, of trusting the 'hearts' of others to catch the meaning from the silence.[35]

A failure to appreciate the underlying laws that shape 'Legem Tuam Dilexi', then, is a failure of the reader's faith, not the poem's.

Both Rudy and King note the strong links between Patmore's interest in metrical laws and Hopkins's experiments: indeed, Hopkins offered detailed comments on and suggested revisions to the odes in *The Unknown Eros,* which Patmore took very seriously. In these particular lines, the involuntary exclamation 'ah' in 'For, ah, who can express', which introduces a graceful pause into the line and signals both wonder at God's majesty and the speaker's loss of words, is like a version of Hopkins's important use of such exclamations in the final line of 'God's Grandeur' ('with ah! bright wings') and elsewhere. The soul that assumes the 'stress | Of bonds unbid', with an obvious nod to the stresses felt in metrical verse, might also recall Hopkins's much-discussed lines from 'The Wreck of the Deutschland', which link this felt stress with the Passion, 'Not out of his bliss | Springs the stress felt'.[36]

Given the growing body of criticism on Hopkins's prosody, this book does not revisit questions of sprung rhythm and its significance, though it should certainly be read in tandem with recent discussions.[37] But it is vital to note that for both poets, metrical experimentation was not a signifier of unorthodoxy, but rather perhaps—as Chapter 6 partially suggests—a signal of the greater freedom offered by the stricter orthodoxies of Roman Catholicism, as opposed to Anglicanism. In this sense dissenting poets, coming from a tradition strongly opposed to forms in worship, and Roman Catholic poets, who assume the undeniable and unassailable significance of form, might in the end have more in common with each other than with the Anglican centre.

Without a sense of where Patmore can be located on this religious spectrum, the context in which *The Unknown Eros* operates, the way in which it responds to contemporary debates about form in poetry as well as religion, cannot be fully appreciated. Of course, as Rudy points out, this is not to say that poetic form cannot sometimes operate, for the reader, in ways contrary to the poet's professed beliefs. While Tennyson, Rossetti, or the other more 'canonical' poets discussed below use formal elements in immensely subtle ways, most Victorian religious poets did not have the mastery of technique that would allow them to manage form with dexterity. My argument about the Brownings' writing of dissent into the forms of their verse, for instance, does not mean that the mass of less well-educated Victorian dissenting poets were capable of equally bold formal experiments, though it might mean that they were more likely to try.

There is substantial agreement between my readings of nineteenth-century poetics and those described by advocates of a 'new' formally alert criticism, and I am happy to agree with Wolfson that, without dwelling on methods in the remainder of this book, 'reading in this way itself constitutes a theoretical commitment', if at times one that is loosely defined.[38] Where this project differs from some of the recent writing on form, however, is not just that it concentrates on a relatively neglected socio-political context but also that it presents a historicized reading of form, in this religious context, as intentionally if not always successfully conservative. J. Paul Hunter argues (in an essay on eighteenth-century couplets) that new engagements with form have been hindered by a persistent critical tradition, linked in his view to New Criticism, which sees form as repressive:

> Because, according to this view, we know already what formal signals imply— which is about discipline, regulation, restraint, authority and repression—we should distrust ideas and attitudes forced into or represented in this framework. Beyond the dogmatic assumptions about me powerful, even dictatorial, nature of formal determination, the difficulty here is that conclusions about the forms themselves tend to derive from old formalist analysis carried on without historicist intervention, so that the descriptions are essentialist and based on outdated and faulty attempts to define and defend forms as holding and reinforcing traditional values.[39]

He concludes that 'perhaps the most important work that formalist theory needs now to perform is to undo some stubborn but unproved (often homological) assumptions about such key terms as *discipline, regularity,* and *constraint*'.[40] Taking up this challenge, Levine's essays are interested in 'collisions', in how literary forms and social formations 'are less likely to reinforce each other than to clash, interrupt or derail one another'. 'Literary forms participate in a destabilizing relation to social formations,' is one of her opening gambits, and the forms that 'matter most', she concludes, are 'formal encounters that surprise power out of its intended tracks'.[41] This is true, in the sense that such forms might matter: most *to us,* particularly if we are engaged in an effort to try to demonstrate why forms are vital and exciting objects or areas for literary study. But deliberately to approach literary forms— especially Victorian literary forms—with the view that they are disruptive and disorderly forces is again to value doubt over faith, and to take the exception for the rule. Hunter lambastes 'essentialist' understandings of form, though of course essentialist understandings are also historically contingent. Nothing could be more essentialist (and more alien to our current critical practice) than assuming that forms 'imply' the authority of a transcendent God. No literary form was less likely to disrupt the social formations in which it participated than a bog-standard piece of Victorian religious verse. It is arguable that the cumulative effects of bitter Victorian debates over form in faith did prove destabilizing to the Anglican Church, but not to Christianity more generally, and most of the figures discussed in this book were deeply socially conservative. Moreover, even when gifted poets, like Hardy or Hopkins, did quite deliberately use forms in disruptive ways, they were often reacting against a widely held cultural perception of forms as agents of discipline, regularity, and constraint, holding and reinforcing traditional values, and without understanding the stubbornness of this perception, we cannot appreciate their enterprise.

Raymond Williams argues in his important discussion of form in *Marxism and Literature* that 'stable traditional forms' are helpful in understanding how form can activate a collective relationship 'in the very-processes of composition and performance'. For literary form to acquire social meaning requires acts of 'communicative composition' via shared perceptions held by writers, performers, audiences, and readers. Williams continues:

> It is impossible to overestimate the significance which is then felt and shared. The hearing of certain traditional arrangements of words; the recognition and activation of certain rhythms; the perception, often through already shared themes, of certain basic flows and relations… all these are part of some of our most profound cultural experiences.[42]

Implicit in this comment is a reference to the operations of religion, in the performance of acts of worship and in its wider cultural circulation, particularly in literary texts. Williams's understanding of form (which has itself exerted a significant influence on recent formalist criticism) was shared by many of the Victorian writers cited below. It is precisely in the recognition of such rhythms, shared themes, and language that religious forms in this period found their force. Victorian religious poets activated this force, this profound cultural experience of recognition, through their own deployment of form, which itself often depended on their chosen stance with relation to traditional religious forms. Yet because Victorian religion was subject to internal and external pressures that partly exalted and partly undermined a sense of shared cultural forms, poets and religious writers also offer a commentary on their formal choices, in the awareness that this recognition might be under threat.

Notes

1   Charles Kingsley, 'Alexander Smith and Alexanda Pope', *Fraser's Magazine*, 48 (October 1853), 452–66, 460.
2   Denis Gigante, *Life: Organic Form and Romanticism* (New Haven: Yale University Press, 2009), 46, 48.
3   Samuel Taylor Coleridge, Lecture 8, *Lectures on Belles Lettres (1812–13),* in *Lectures 1808– 1819: On Literature,* ed. R. A. Foakes, 2 vols. (Princeton: Princeton University Press, 1987), i, 495, 494, *The Collected Works of Samuel Taylor Coleridge,* ed. Kathleen Coburn, vol. v. For

an important account of Coleridge and Wordsworth's perception of organicism, particularly in relation to Victorian religion, see Stephen Pricken, *Romanticism and Religion: The Tradition of Coleridge and Wordsworth in the Victorian Church* (Cambridge: Cambridge University Press, 1976), 101 *and passim.*

4   George Eliot, 'Notes on Form in Art', in *Selected Essays, Poems and Other Writings,* ed. A. S. Byatt and Nicholas Warren (Harmondsworth: Penguin, 1990), 231–40, 235. For an interesting meditation on organic form and reception, see T. J. Clark, 'More Theses on Feuerbach', *Representations,* 104 (2008), 4–7.

5   Kingsley, 'Alexander Smith and Alexander Pope', 463, 457.

6   David Morse, *High Victorian Culture* (Houndsmills: Macmillan, 1993), 218.

7   Charles LaPorte, *Victorian Poets and the Changing Bible* (Charlottesville, Va.: University of Virginia Press, 2011), quotation from draft chapter 2.

8   Tracy Fessenden, *Culture and Redemption: Religion, the Secular and American Literature* (Princeton: Princeton University Press, 2007), 1.

9   F. E. Gray, *Christian and Lyric Tradition in Victorian Women's Poetry* (New York: Routledge, 2010), 3.

10 Ibid. 5.

11 Cynthia Scheinberg, *Women's Poetry and Religion in Victorian England: Jewish Identity and Christian Culture* (Cambridge: Cambridge University Press, 2002). Emma Mason, *Women Poets of the Nineteenth Century* (Tavistock: Northcote House, 2006). On Rossetti, for instance, Mary Arseneau argues that 'it was within the confines of the conservative, traditional and authoritarian Anglo-Catholic Church' that the Rossetti women 'expressed their most egalitarian and reform-minded ideals'. 'Pews, Periodicals and Politics. The Rossetti Woman as High Church Controversialists', in David Clifford and Laurence Roussillion (eds.), *Outsiders Looking in: The Rossettis Then and Now* (London: Anthem, 2004), 97–114, 98.

12 G. B. Tennyson, *Victorian Devotional Poetry: The Tractarian* Mode (Cambridge, Mass.: Harvard University Press, 1981).

13 For helpful (and sceptical) introductions to this 'new formalism' see Marjorie Levinson, 'What is New Formalism?', *PMLA* 122 (2007), 558–69, and Derek Attridge, 'A Return to Form', *Textual Practice,* 22 (2008), 563–75. Besides the works listed below, significant contributions to this discussion include a special issue of *Representations* on form (104 (2008)).

14 Angela Leighton, *On Form: Poetry, Aestheticism and the Legacy of a Word* (Oxford: Oxford University Press, 2007), 3.

15 Ibid. 4. On the return of Kantian aesthetics in recent debates over formalism, see also Robert Kaufman, 'Everybody Hates Kant: Blakean Formalism and the Symmetrics of Laura Moriarty', in Susan J. Wolfson and Marshall Brown (eds.), *Reading for Form* (Seattle: University of Washington Press, 2006), 203–30.

16 Leighton, *On Form,* 9.

17 Ibid. 63.

18 Hallam Tennyson, *Alfred Lord Tennyson: A Memoir,* 2 vols. (London: Macmillan, 1897), ii. 420. All further references given in the text.

19 'Formalist' almost always has a negative connotation in this context. It has been used in this sense since at least the seventeenth century, as Raymond Williams observes in *Keywords: A Vocabulary of Culture and Society* (London: Harper Collins, 1976; rev. edn. 1988), 137–8.

20 William J. E. Bennet, *The Principles of the Book of Common Prayer Considered* (London: W. J. Cleaver, 1845), 7.

21 A. J. Piggot, *The Prayer-Book or Liturgy of the Church of England* (London: Joseph Masters, 1863), 27.

22 William McKelvy, *The English Cult of Literature: Devoted Readers 1770–1880* (Charlottesville, Va.: University of Virginia Press, 2007), 1.

23 To J. P. Gell, 8 May [1838], *The Correspondence of Arthur Hugh Clough,* ed. F. L. Mulhauser, 2 vols. (Oxford: Clarendon Press, 1957), i. 71.

24 Caroline Levine, 'Formal Pasts and Formal Possibilities in Victorian Studies', *Literature Compass,* 4 (2007), 1241–56, 1244.

25 Levine, 'Strategic Formalism: Towards a New Method in Cultural Studies', *Victorian Studies,* 48 (2006), 626–57, 632.

26 Herbert Tucker, 'Tactical Formalism: A Response to Caroline Levine', *Victorian Studies,* 49 (2006), 85–95, 93.

27 Levine, 'Strategic Formalism', 626, 647, 651.

28 Susan J. Wolfson, *Formal Charges: The Shaping of Poetry in British Romanticism* (Stanford, Calif.: Stanford University Press, 1997), 3.

29 Coventry Patmore, 'Legem Tuam Dilexi', in *The Poems of Coventry Patmore,* ed. Frederick Page (London: Oxford University Press, 1949). 405–8, 406.

30 Ibid. 405.

31 Matthew Arnold, 'Empedocles on Etna', 184–5, in *Matthew Arnold: A Critical Edition of the Major Works*, ed. Miriam Allott and R. H. Super (Oxford: Oxford University Press, 1988). Further references given in the text.

32 Basil Champneys, *Memoirs and Correspondence of Coventry Patmore,* 2 vols. (London: George Bell, 1900), ii. 18.

33 See *Coventry Patmore's 'Essay on English Metrical Law': A Critical Edition with a Commentary*, ed. Mary Augustine Roth (Washington, D.C.: Catholic University of America Press, 1961), *passim.*

34 Jason Rudy, *Electric Meters: Victorian Physiological Poetics* (Athens, Oh.: Ohio University Press, 2009), 122, see also 125 on catalexis.

35 Joshua King, 'Patmore, Hopkins and the Problem of the English Metrical Law', *Hopkins Quarterly,* 38.1–2 (2011), 31–49, 38–9.

36 'God's Grandeur', 14, and 'The Wreck of the Deutschland', 41–2, in *Gerard Manley Hopkins: The Major Works*, ed. Catherine Phillips (Oxford: Oxford University Press, 2002), 132. All further references are to this edition and will be given in the text.

37 For the Summer 2011 issue of *Victorian Poetry* on prosody, 49/2, ed. Meredith Martin and Yisrael Levin, so many proposals were received for essays on Hopkins that this special issue is now paired with an issue of *Hopkins Quarterly* (38/1–2). Besides those works cited in Chapter 6, see also Meredith Martin's chapter on Hopkins in the forthcoming *The Rise and Fall of Meter: Poetry and English National Culture* (Princeton: Princeton University Press, 2012) and her 'Hopkins's Prosody', *Hopkins Quarterly,* 38/1–2 (2011), 1–30: Peter L. Groves. '"Opening" the Pentameter: Hopkins's Metrical Experimentation', *Hopkins Quarterly*, 38/1–2 (2011), 93–110, and Summer J. Star's 'For the Inscape's Sake: Sounding the Self in the Meters of Gerard Manley Hopkins, forthcoming in Jason D. Hall (ed), *Meter Matters: Verse Cultures of the Long Nineteenth Century* (Columbus, Oh.: Ohio University Press, 2011).

38 Wolfson, *Formal Charges,* 1. Levinson argues that new formalism cannot be accurately described as a theory or methodology because it does not retheorize form, but that it does 'generate commitment to and community around the idea of form' – which is certainly one of the purposes of this study, besides being part of its historical subject matter ('What is New Formalism?', 560, 561).

39 J. Paul Hunter, 'Formalism and History: Binarism and the Anglophone Couplet', in Wolfson and Brown (eds.), *Reading for Form,* 129–49, 129–30.

40 Ibid. 130n.

41 Levine, 'Strategic Formalism', 632, 626, 639. This argument relates strongly to Russian formalism and its views on the defamiliarization created by form. See, for instance, Viktor Shklovsky on *Tristram Shandy* and 'the realization of form achieved by the violation of form': 'The Parody Novel: Sterne's *Tristram Shandy*', trans. Richard Sheldon, *Review of Contemporary Fiction,* 1 (1981), 190–211,192. Wolfson, Formal *Charges,* contains a useful reading of Russian Formalism, 7 and *passim.*

42 Raymond Williams, *Marxism and Literature* (Oxford: Oxford University Press,1977), 187–8.

Part VIII
Sexuality

Stefano Evangelista

Sex has been a prime subject in lyric poetry ever since the early days of Sappho, in the sixth century BC. Victorian poetry is therefore hardly unprecedented in devoting so much attention to the themes of desire, passion and sexual jealousy. The Victorians inherited a Romantic lyric tradition in which male poets like Byron and Shelley spoke frankly about sexual desire, sometimes linking it to radical social and political ideals as well as to ideologies of artistic freedom and freedom of expression. The dominant poetic forms of the Victorian period, such as the lyric and the dramatic monologue, carried over this Romantic interest in sex. Yet, poets were also increasingly keen to explore how sex is mediated and determined by social dynamics; that is, to investigate the role played by gender in the construction of sexuality. Much Victorian poetry upheld a conventional gender ideology that identified sex exclusively with reproductive heterosexuality, and directly or indirectly promoted the marginalisation of women. This set of conservative values is enshrined in Coventry Patmore's now infamous *The Angel in the House* (1856), which came to stand for what the twentieth century found oppressive and antiquated about their Victorian predecessors (Virginia Woolf thought it was the woman writer's duty to kill the 'angel in the house' inside her). For every poetic statement of conservative gender politics, though, there were acts of revision, resistance and, occasionally, defiance. So, Elizabeth Barrett's proto-feminist epic *Aurora Leigh* came out the same year as Patmore's poem. By the same token, the last two decades of the century, which saw a toughening of anti-homosexual legislation, were also the period that witnessed the emergence of a self-consciously homosexual poetics. The extracts in this section show that Victorian poetry did indeed talk about sex beyond the confines of bourgeois domestic culture, leaving a productive and sometimes challenging legacy to their twentieth- and twenty-first-century readers.

The treatment of sex in Victorian poetry is interlinked with the cultural phenomena that characterise the history of sexuality in the nineteenth century: the appearance of scientific theories of evolution and sexual selection, developments in psychology that would eventually culminate in psychoanalysis, the rise of the first organised movements for female emancipation and, most importantly, the transformation of the old notion of sex as an act into the modern concepts of sexuality and sexual identity. In this fast-changing world, it is unsurprising to find poets using sexuality in order to pose fundamental questions about the very nature of humanity, exploring the border between the normal and abnormal or 'perverse'. The French poet Charles Baudelaire set the tone for subsequent experiments in this field. His 1857 collection *Les Fleurs du mal* (The Flowers of Evil) – a landmark in the history of modern poetry – pointed to productive new ways of connecting sex and literary modernity. Through the calculated amoral treatment of controversial topics such as lesbianism and by repeatedly linking love to death and violence, Baudelaire deliberately set out to shock his first readers and, at the same time, reflect on the impossibility of fulfilment and redemption in the modern world. *Les Fleurs du mal* was promptly withdrawn from circulation and reissued in expurgated form after the author was found guilty of offending public morality. But censorship did not limit the influence of Baudelaire who, if anything, gained in counter-cultural capital as a result of the puritanical crusade against his work, and who is today largely credited as a key precursor of literary movements such as Decadence, Symbolism and Modernism. In the mid-nineteenth century, Baudelaire showed the way in which sex could be used to challenge the limits of representation. He also set the parameters for the complex relationship of mutual hostility and dependence that locks together the artistic *avant gardes* and the bourgeois reading public: the radical poet needs the middle class to set the limits of respectability and standards of taste that s/he aims to transgress, as well as being dependent on the public's readiness to be outraged (Baudelaire famously addressed his imagined reader as a 'hypocrite').

The chief nineteenth-century English heir of Baudelaire was A. C. Swinburne, who wrote the earliest review of *Les Fleurs du mal* to appear in the British press and who drew inspiration from the French poet in his own scandalous first collection, *Poems and Ballads* (1866). From the 1860s onwards, Swinburne and his older contemporary, the poet and pre-Raphaelite artist D. G. Rossetti, were at the forefront of a poetic experiment with the lyric as forum for controversial topics relating to eroticism and sexual morality. In Rossetti's 'Jenny', for instance, the speaker delivers a long passionate address to a prostitute who has fallen asleep with her head on his knee, while Swinburne's *Poems and Ballads* contains explicit instances of lesbianism, necrophilia and, most notably, long-drawn passages in which the poet/speaker details sado-masochistic fantasies of subjection to cruel *dominatrices*. The impact of these works may be gauged from Robert Buchanan's condemnatory essay 'The Fleshly School of Poetry', published under a pseudonym in the prominent, conservative-leaning periodical, *The Contemporary Review*, in 1871.

Buchanan, who was also a published poet, is offended by the poets' representation of women as *femmes fatales*, which he finds insulting to the female sex and condemns as the half-disguised projection of a troubling male fantasy. It is interesting to notice that in the twentieth century some feminist critics would concur with this diagnosis, albeit from a very different political position, unmasking the intensity of the male gaze that dominates Rossetti's and Swinburne's scenes of supposed female sexual empowerment. What seems to trouble Buchanan most, though, is the way in which this poetry unsettles a series of time-honoured distinctions: first and foremost that between high and low cultures (he objects to elevated poetic form being employed for the depiction of debased subject matter), but also between the beautiful and the grotesque, poetic genius and perversion, male and female, public and private writings. He condemns the fact that sex is not treated in conjunction with moral sentiments but as an end in itself, for the sake of pleasure and artistic excess. Ultimately, Buchanan's 'Fleshly School' is a diatribe against the aesthetic principles of art for art's sake, which enabled poets like Rossetti and Swinburne to liberate sexuality from biology, representing the body as an instrument of erotic pleasure rather than the subject of physical and social laws aimed at reproduction and the conservation of the species.

The 1860s also witnessed the explosion of sensation fiction – a phenomenon that attracted widespread condemnation in the periodical press. Critics were anxious about the wide and unregulated circulation of licentious, lowbrow material that often featured large doses of sex and violence. Buchanan's accusation of poetic sensationalism, which is repeated several times in the article, is an explicit nod to the debate around sensation fiction that was raging at this time: like the sensation novelists (almost all of them women), the 'fleshly' poets are alleged to pose a danger to unsuspecting readers by aiming their works at the nerves, the senses and what Buchanan calls the 'animal faculties' rather than trying to engage with the spheres of rationality, intelligence and good taste. In other words, their fault is to use literature to stimulate the body rather than the mind. Buchanan also applies to the 'Fleshly School' the same imagery of overindulgence, disease and contagion that was prevalent in anti-sensation arguments. On the strength of that, he claims that reading this type of poetry is noxious not only for the individual, whose mind and body are debilitated by it, but also for public health. The 'fleshly' poets are therefore, according to him, 'public offenders' and, this being the case, it becomes a political imperative that their work should be censored.

When assessing the moral and political agenda behind these accusations, it is important to pay close attention to the exact terms in which Buchanan conducts his attacks. Thus, for instance, it is striking to notice how systematically gendered Buchanan's rhetoric is when he accuses his male poets of hysteria (a condition that was almost exclusively associated with female physiology at this time), and when he speaks of their lack of manliness and virility. Rossetti and Swinburne's effeminacy as diagnosed by Buchanan is a civic, as well as psycho-sexual, category: it promotes weakness and absolves adult men of their responsibility towards the public good of the nation. The militaristic mentality of the Empire and its ideal of masculinity inflect Buchanan's critique at an implicit level. Both Rossetti and Swinburne replied publicly to Buchanan in essays entitled respectively 'The Stealthy School of Criticism' (1871) and 'Under the Microscope' (1872), in which they defended artistic freedom. The controversy over the 'Fleshly School', played out in the pages of the periodical press, shows how public and politicised the question of sexuality in Victorian poetry could become.

One of the poems to which Buchanan took particular exception was Swinburne's 'Anactoria' (he was not the only Victorian reviewer to do so), a dramatic monologue in which Sappho addresses one of her female lovers, the eponymous Anactoria, unleashing her sexual jealousy and extravagant passion. In *Victorian Sappho*, Yopie Prins shows that Victorian poets repeatedly turned to Sappho in order 'to define their lyric vocation'. Thus, to the classically-trained, technically-masterful Swinburne, Sappho represents the origin of the lyric tradition: she was the 'tenth muse', as she was sometimes called in antiquity, and, quite simply, the greatest poet who ever lived. As such, she was a crucial model and precursor against whom to measure one's own poetic achievement. 'Anactoria' incorporates translations of some of Sappho's extant poetic fragments into the modern lyric, establishing a dialogue between the past and the present, across the gulf of time and across languages, and reflecting on issues of memory and poetic fame. Assuming the identity of Sappho by ventriloquising her voice, Swinburne crosses the boundaries of gender: the lyric as practised by Swinburne is a poetic space where male and female meet and merge, giving rise to new and forever-shifting configurations of bodies and types of desire. The modern poem is therefore an overlap of voices, identities and ways of desiring, textually and sexually. It is for this reason that Prins situates Swinburne within a history of sexual politics associated with the lyric in which the Victorian period occupies a central position. The sense of gender confusion is further complicated by the open, deliberately sensational lesbian content of 'Anactoria', where eroticism is linked with violence, sadism, and verbal and physical abuse. Critical opinion is divided as to whether Swinburne's representation of lesbian desire constitutes a male voyeuristic fantasy or a truly radical intervention into gender politics, which successfully overthrows the power logic of a male-dominated tradition.

In any case, as Prins reminds us, discussions of homosexuality in Victorian literature need to be carefully historicised. For most of the Victorian period the word 'homosexual' did not even exist. It came into English towards the end of the century and initially its usage was restricted to the medical profession. It is possible that none of the Victorian poets that are most familiar to us today was even acquainted with the concept of 'homosexuality' as a signifier of a distinctive sexual identity. This of course does not mean that Victorian poets did not explore homoeroticism in their works. Yet, given the lack of a well-defined set of terms and a public discourse around same-sex love, not to mention the repressive legislation that made male homosexuality a criminal offence, homoerotic themes entered Victorian poetry tentatively and indirectly, in the form of ambiguity and silence or in fluid configurations in which they are compounded with other types of desire.

Tennyson's *In Memoriam* (1850) provides a prime example of this poetics of ambiguity. The famous elegy was written to commemorate Tennyson's friend Arthur Henry Hallam, who had died prematurely in 1833. The poem had a very long period of gestation, which is reflected in its length and the irregular structure of its final form. In *In Memoriam*, the absence of Hallam and Tennyson's grief become paradigmatic of a type of universal cultural pessimism – the feelings of misery and alienation that would also interest Baudelaire. The elegy puts forward a meditation on the very nature of desire and loss (and the relationship between the two), but it is difficult to ignore that the focus and object of that desire is a male body, and that the poem describes a tortured process of discovering and coming to terms with this impossible desire. Moreover, Tennyson repeatedly expresses his feelings for Hallam through language and imagery that are commonly associated with heterosexual romance.

These aspects of *In Memoriam* did not escape the attention of early Victorian critics. In his anonymous review published in *The Times* in November 1851, Manley Hopkins, the father of the poet G. M. Hopkins, laments a lack of manliness in Tennyson – that is, a tendency to indulge in psychological weakness and emotional display – that would become a staple in critical responses to the poet. Buchanan would associate this same supposed failing with Rossetti and Swinburne when he classed the 'Fleshly School' as a 'sub-Tennysonian' movement. More pointedly, though, Hopkins detects with anxiety an inappropriate tone of 'amatory tenderness' in the poem, where he finds a 'strange manner of address to a man, even though he be dead'. This gender transgression clearly upsets Hopkins, who finds the language of affection of *In Memoriam* displaced and mismanaged. He criticises Tennyson's habit of 'transferring every epithet of womanly endearment to a masculine friend', for which he finds precedents in classical and 'Oriental' poetry and, closer to home, in Shakespeare's sonnets. But these historical and/or foreign models are out of place in Victoria's England. The implication is that in modern English verse, the language of sentiment should be regulated strictly according to heterosexual desire. The review of *In Memoriam* highlights a clash of expectations regarding the sexual politics of mid-Victorian poetry: Tennyson makes it a site for experimenting with gender and different modes of desire; Hopkins wants it to be a means of restating and reinforcing the difference between the sexes. It is telling in this sense that Hopkins's accusation of gender ambiguity should be compounded with that of obscurity. Clarity as demanded by Hopkins is charged with moral significance: it is the duty to conform to conservative structures in gender as much as language, inasmuch as language is conceived as a natural expression of gender difference.

It is startling to see the veiled passion of *In Memoriam*, full of abstract metaphors and moments of sublimation, compared to the open homoeroticism of Shakespeare's sonnets. But it is important to remember again that Hopkins's accusation of effeminacy, like Buchanan's twenty years later, does not straightforwardly imply homosexuality in this historical context. Today's readers of *In Memoriam* are also faced with the question of how and where to draw the line between homoeroticism and romantic friendship. Should the ambiguous eros of the elegy be understood as a product of authorial intention? Did Tennyson mean to write about his physical love for Hallam? Does the poem reveal a desire that he was trying to repress? Or does *In Memoriam* hold a homoerotic content that is there in spite of the author's intention or sexual orientation? Recognising a homoerotic subtext in the poem, or its challenges to traditional gender structures, does not entail investigating Tennyson's own sexual orientation. Besides, literary texts contain meanings that are activated later on in history, in the process of reception, becoming available to readers who are far removed in time from the moment of composition. The best way of conceptualising the homoeroticism of *In Memoriam* is therefore to see it as *potential* rather than fully realized; as setting an enabling precedent for how the elegy would be used by late-Victorian authors such as Michael Field and A.E. Housman who, as we shall see, deliberately manipulate this poetic genre to express homoerotic sentiment.

In the second half of the century, the public emergence of homosexuality as an identity meant that there would be less scope for the type of ambiguity we have seen in Tennyson. In the history of the emergence of a public discourse around homosexuality, the Victorian scientific movement of sexology played a particularly prominent role. From the 1860s onwards, sexologists in Britain and other European countries (notably Germany) embarked on an ambitious project to come up with comprehensive taxonomies of sexual desires and behaviours. True to their scientific mentality, sexologists generally believed that homosexuality should not be stigmatised as a moral aberration but rather understood as a psychological phenomenon. In this sense, sexology was broadly progressive and sympathetic to the cause of homosexual emancipation: it went against social prejudice, refuting the connection between homosexuality, disease and unwholesome lifestyles. Equally importantly, sexology brought homosexuality into the public consciousness by talking about it openly, presenting readers with case studies that were in effect miniature autobiographies of *real* people, many of whom were perfectly functional members of society and content with, or unashamed of, their sexual behaviour. This is the ground out of which psychoanalysis would grow in the early twentieth century. But the assumption, widespread among early sexologists that homosexuality was a congenital condition, held a strong residue of a mentality that viewed same-sex attachments as a deviation from the norm or, to use the term favoured by hostile critics, as unnatural. By contrast to the essentialism of the Victorian sexologists, queer theorists today tend to see sexuality as socially constructed, highlighting elements of cultural conditioning and performance, transformation, parody and deconstruction.

Havelock Ellis is undoubtedly the foremost British sexologist, as well as being a respected literary critic and intellectual. In *Sexual Inversion* (1897), part of his encyclopaedic *Studies in the Psychology of Sex*, Ellis popularised the notion of the homosexual as 'invert', i.e. a healthy body with reversed gender traits. In his introduction, Ellis provides a history of homosexuality among educated, cultivated and socially powerful men that stretches from the Greek and Roman times to the present. He wants to show that homosexual orientation can coexist with elevated moral and artistic feelings and, in particular, with literary talent. Within the canon of English literature, Ellis mentions the Renaissance poet Richard Barnfield, the dramatist Christopher Marlowe and the philosopher and author Francis Bacon. He even detects traces of homosexual 'instinct' in Shakespeare, although he is understandably cautious about including such a key figure in his list of eminent literary inverts. Moving to more recent times, Ellis examines the cases of Byron, Walt Whitman and of course Oscar

Wilde. He also treats the question of Tennyson's friendship with Hallam, as manifested in *In Memoriam*: although he sees 'an element of sexual emotion' in their friendship, he discounts the presence of a 'definite homosexual impulse', concluding that 'homosexuality is merely stimulated by the ardent and hyperaesthetic emotion of the poet'.[1] On the surface Ellis therefore distances Tennyson from homosexuality, but his nonchalant connection between poetic feeling and homosexuality is actually a daring revisionary gesture that is meant to normalise the connection between elevated literary form and allegedly low sentiment to which Hopkins had so strongly objected in his review of the poem. *Sexual Inversion* was first published in a German translation (1896); the following year the first English edition was bought up and destroyed by Horatio Brown, the literary executor of the recently deceased John Addington Symonds, who appeared as co-author on the book's cover; the second English edition (1898), from which Symonds's name had been removed, was banned as obscene. Like Baudelaire in *Les Fleurs du mal*, Ellis engaged in a battle against censorship. But *Sexual Inversion* had a transparent political aim: to use the authority of science in order to make an intervention in the social and legal treatment of homosexual men and women whom Ellis, in a climactic conclusion to the introduction, estimated as numbering about one million in Britain alone.

An understanding of the legal context is crucial in order to appreciate the enormous personal risks taken by homosexual writers and critics at this point. In Britain, homosexuality was proscribed by law for the whole of the nineteenth century, but the real watershed in anti-gay legislation came with the so-called Labouchere Amendment (Section 11 of the Criminal Law Amendment Act of 1885), to which Joseph Bristow refers in his chapter, 'Wilde's Fatal Effeminacy'. The Labouchere Amendment criminalised 'gross indecency' between males whether it occurred in public or private, and made it punishable with a maximum sentence of two years' imprisonment with hard labour. The crux was in the formulation 'in private', which included sexual relationships between two consenting adult males, and in the lack of precise definition of what constituted 'gross indecency'. It is easy to see how, by making the private lives of gay men matters of public regulation, the new legislation opened the door to occurrences of blackmailing. Oscar Wilde was the most prominent writer to be sentenced under the Labouchere Amendment. When he was sent to gaol in 1895, Wilde lost most of what made him respectable and successful in the eyes of his contemporary society: his family, his material possessions and, at least for some decades, his reputation as an intellectual and man of letters. The Wilde trials were both public and spectacular events in that they created a stage for the display of homosexuality: Wilde, who before the trials had not been readily recognisable as 'homosexual' in the eyes of his contemporaries, became the type of what the twentieth century would come to identify, and even stereotype, as 'a gay man'. Bristow shows that the trials also established a connection between male homosexual desire and effeminacy that would have a long and influential afterlife. Post-Wilde, it would no longer be possible to accuse a poet of effeminacy, as Hopkins did with Tennyson or Buchanan with Rossetti and Swinburne, without calling into question their heterosexual orientation. What is at stake in the Wilde trials is therefore, as Bristow claims, no less than the formation of a new form of masculinity, which sharply diverges from the athletic, military, commercial and imperial ideals that had regulated male gender behaviour in the nineteenth century so far. According to Bristow, the public emergence of the degenerate homosexual male, identified with Wilde, had important social and political implications because it embodied a set of 'oppositional' values that threatened the fabric of British society. The connection between homosexuality and radical politics was made even more explicit in the work of Wilde's contemporary Edward Carpenter, in which socialism and homosexual emancipation went hand in hand.

In the late Victorian period, the emergence of homosexuality as a well-defined social identity triggered the circulation of the first explicitly homosexual poems. Given the enormous pressure exercised by repressive legislation, same-sex love could still only inhabit literature indirectly, in the form of allusion or, even more tantalisingly, in the form of silences and omissions. In Alfred Douglas's memorable formulation in his widely-cited allegorical poem 'Two Loves' (1894), homosexuality was 'the love that dare not speak its name'. Yet speak it did, and increasingly so in the course of the century, even when its actual name could not be mentioned in print. In the lyrical tradition, to speak about the innermost desires confers authority to the poet. Writing in this tradition, homosexual Victorian poets found themselves caught in a dialectics between revelation and concealment, in which the impulse to speak openly about sexual desire was coupled with the practical need to find strategies to mask it, making it invisible in the eyes of unsympathetic readers, that is, of the majority.

Some poets, like Housman, represented homosexual desire in a decidedly pessimistic vein. Many of the lyrics in *A Shropshire Lad* (1896) internalise the imagery of criminality, guilt and punishment promoted by the law. Housman's Shropshire (a microcosm of late-Victorian England) is a debased pastoral landscape in which desire can find no gratification, and in which physical contact between men is displaced in the form of violence and death. The legacy of homophobic legislation is also evident in Wilde's *Ballad of Reading Gaol* (1898), which Bristow discusses as representing 'a society of criminals wrongly punished for their love of the body'[2] – a love, he adds, that problematically subsists on the invisibility of the murdered woman. By alerting us to the fact that in Wilde's poem the discourse of solidarity and liberation feeds on aspects of the selfsame repressive sexual ideology that it seeks to undo, Bristow reminds us of the need to disentangle uncomfortable elements of misogyny or social exclusion from the transgressive or progressive thrust of homosexual writing.

Other poets resisted this form of cultural pessimism and strove instead to find idioms and poetic forms that made homoeroticism appealing, celebrating its ennobling feelings and stressing its spiritual component. Wilde (in his early poetry), John Addington Symonds and the so-called 'Uranian' poets of the late-Victorian decades all turned their backs on the grim reality of the present and looked instead to Ancient Greece as a utopian ideal in which the toleration of same-sex desire coexisted with a flourishing of artistic culture, philosophy and democracy. The word 'Uranian' harks back to the work of the German sexologist Karl Heinrich Ulrichs, who had used the term 'Urning' to designate what Ellis would call the 'invert' (a feminine soul in a masculine body, or *vice versa*). But the English Uranian poets consciously departed from the new doctors of sex who argued that the road to homosexual emancipation went through medicine and science. In contrast to the rationalism of science and the cold logic of the case study, they made large use of myth and a heightened aestheticism that disengaged homosexual eros from social concerns. The draw of the Hellenic ideal was especially strong among educated men, who were likely to have had some exposure to classical culture at school or university; and something of the homosocial and exclusive public-school ethos clings to much Uranian poetry, with its emphasis on pederastic (cross-generational) models of desire and pedagogy. Oscar Wilde tried, unsuccessfully, to appeal to the rhetoric of the Uranians when he defended homosexuality in court by referring to Plato and glossing the love that dares not speak its name as 'the noblest form of affection'.

Meanwhile, female same-sex relationships continued to be out of the reach of the punitive arm of the law. This comparative invisibility led to a paradoxical situation: while open sexual provocations like those launched by Rossetti and Swinburne would not have been tolerated from the pen of women poets (it is worth remembering that all through the century ambitious women writers, from the Brontës to Vernon Lee, adopted male pseudonyms in order to ensure an unbiased reception of their works), the language of intimacy and affection between women was less strictly policed than its male counterpart. The work of Michael Field provides the most glaring example of how women poets were able to circumvent cultural prohibition in expressing homoerotic feelings. Michael Field was the pseudonym for a poetic and sexual partnership between an aunt and a niece, Katharine Bradley and Edith Cooper, who privately boasted that they were 'closer married' than the more famous poetic duo, Elizabeth Barrett and Robert Browning, because unlike their heterosexual precursors they wrote their poems together, blending their separate identities under one signature. In *Victorian Sappho*, Prins examines Bradley and Cooper's fascination with Sappho's poetic fragments. Their collection *Long Ago* (1889), in which they wrote a series of modern poetic responses to Sappho, celebrates their eros in poems that stage a distinctly neo-pagan sensuality rooted in the lost world of ancient Lesbos. Michael Field's lesbian poetics is free from the sensationalism of Swinburne's 'Anactoria'. Their poems combine the aims of writing a modern lesbian identity, founded on physical and emotional intimacy, and celebrating a powerful female poetic tradition that stretches to the dawn of European civilisation.

The leading historian of sexuality, Michel Foucault, has described how the nineteenth century is caught in a dialectics between denying the existence of sex, and making it an object of study and public enquiry with a systematic zeal that amounted almost to an obsession. Victorian poetry exemplifies this complex discursive mechanism of repression and expression. On the one hand, today's readers encounter flagrant transgressions and instances of censorship that make sex a matter of public controversy, visible for all to see; on the other, they are faced with the task of disentangling fluid formations of desires and judging subtle gradations of gender difference, reading silences and other modes of euphemism and ambiguity, and cracking the codes that protected writers from public exposure. When navigating this sometimes alien and highly varied landscape, the real challenge is not to uncover what the Victorians did in bed (and wherever else they pleased, for that matter), but to explore the networks that connected sexuality to questions of aesthetics – that is, literary form – and ethics, recognising how these in turn lead to the sphere of politics.

Notes

1 Havelock Ellis, *Studies in the Psychology of Sex*, Vol. II (3rd ed.) (Philadelphia, PA: F. A. Davis Company, 1915).
2 Joseph Bristow, 'Wilde's Fatal Effeminacy', in *Effeminate England: Homoerotic Writing After 1885* (Buckingham: Open University Press, 1995), p. 48.

36 The Poetry of Sorrow (1851)

Manley Hopkins

"Before I had published, I said to myself 'You and I, Mr Cowper, will not concern ourselves much with what the critics say of our book.'" This was a brave, but a hasty resolve, which Mr Cowper very soon abandoned, and stood before the judge of the chief review in a most uncomfortable state of shiver. He was improved by the suffering. An ingenious person of the last century, the Rhymer of the Leasowes, compared criticism to a turnpike on the road to fame, where authors, after being detained for a few minutes, and relieved of some trifles of baggage, are permitted to proceed on their journey. Of late this critical turnpike has been very carelessly attended. Authors, finding it left on the jar, or wide open, have daringly carried through it any amount of luggage, contraband or plundered, without question or interruption. The public are not the only losers by this neglect. Few people, intellectually or morally, are benefited by having their own way. A true critic is a physician of the mind, and his treatment strengthens the constitution of an author.

Perhaps of modern poets Mr. Tennyson has met with fewest obstacles on the high-road to reputation. The famous horseman of Edmonton did not find his gate thrown back with a more generous abandonment of the tax. It is well that the critical result has not been equally unfortunate with the equestrian. Mr. Tennyson, retaining all his packages, grotesque and beautiful, has grown into the most resolute mannerist in England, except Mr. Carlyle. His faults of taste and language are stereotyped, and he now writes his affectations in capitals.

Our present remarks upon his errors and his merits will be confined to the latest production of his pen. The book of verses bearing the title of *In Memoriam* is a tribute to the genius and virtues of a most accomplished son of Mr. Hallam, the historian. Let the acknowledgement be made at once that the writer dedicated his thoughts to a most difficult task. He has written 200 pages upon one person – in other words he has painted 120 miniatures of the same individual, with much happiness of expression, great bloom and freshness of landscape illustration, and many touching scenes of busy and indoor life. English literature possesses no work which, in compass and unity, can be justly compared with *In Memoriam*.

This interesting field of fancy had not, indeed, been left untilled. Two of the most eminent and dear of our poets – Spenser and Milton – have bound up their names with the poetry of sorrow. Spenser's elegies are carefully elaborated, but look more like exercises than the fruitfulness of his pen. Certainly his theme was not always suggestive. The life of Lord Howard's daughter furnished few opportunities of poetical decoration; but the glory and exploits of Sidney might be supposed to be ample enough to tax the utmost power of the author. Neither of his offerings is worthy of the minstrel of *Faëry Land.* With the exception of some delicious rhymes, such as

> "To hear him speak and sweetly smile,
> "You were in Paradise the while,"

which are bathed in the colours and dew of his sunniest hours, the lamentation for the hero as for the lady is only a sparkling network of conceits, woven after the pattern of Ovid or Marino. For example, he thus accounts for the death of Sidney: – Mars, being dazzled by the flash of his armour, instantly makes an iron tube and loads it with thunder. The volley is fatal; the knight falls, and a phoenix, which had built its nest in an English cedar, carries up the news to Jupiter, and makes his ascent in a brilliant explosion of fireworks. But in one charm of verse Spenser seldom disappoints his reader. He is the most musical of poets; and, even in these colder strains of his ingenious learning, the melody flows with a clear, limpid, running murmur, that refreshes and soothes the ear, like a waterbrook in a green wood. He was the most accomplished master of what Pope called the "style of sound." What a tune there is in these lines:—

> "A gentle shepherd born in Arcady,
> "Of gentlest race that ever shepherd bore,
> "About the grassy banks of Hæmony,
> "Did keep his sheep, his little stock, and store;
> "Full carefully he kept them day and night,
> "In fairest fields; and Astrophel he hight."

And these also,—

> "Did never love so sweetly breathe
> "In any mortal breast before?
> "Did never muse inspire beneath
> "A poet's brain with finer store?"

His tears at least were melodious; and it was ever a true harp that hung on the willow tree.

Milton, in every way, surpassed the Serious Teacher whom he loved. He wept his friends with a more winning sorrow. His Latin elegy on *Deodati* contains two or three exquisite touches of natural description and tenderness. But the full tide of his imaginative regret flowed into the memorial of another friend, Mr. King. *Lycidas* is one of the noblest efforts of an author who heard few strains of a higher mood. As a whole, the composition is beyond praise, whether we regard the beauty of the allegory, the solemn lights of the fancy, or the organ-like symphony of the verse, which, however, has in it nothing monotonous. Exquisitely does the writer say—

> "He touched the tender stops of various quills."

For at one moment the grandeur and torrent of his inspiration overbear us, and then a sweet, gleeful note calls us to the shade of the trees, or the field-side, when the plough moves or the husbandman reposes. The Doric lay variegates the chant, and we step out of a cathedral into a flower garden.

Only one discord in Milton's poetry of grief grates upon the ear and offends it. His anti-church invective reads like an interpolation by Mr. W. J. Fox, or a stray note for Mr. Binney's sermon. It is worth a remark that the chief spot in the elegy on *Deodati* has likewise a religious connexion. Having placed his friend among the blessed spirits, with a crown about his head and a palm in his hand, he desecrates the scene by a headlong Bacchanal and the tossing of the thyrsus. At a considerable distance from *Lycidas*, in the *Poetry of Sorrow*, we might mention Dryden's tribute to Oldham as being among the most manly and dignified utterances that ever flowed from his full mouth.

It will be seen that Spenser and Milton agree in giving a pastoral tone to their mourning. Their framework is bucolic. With what skill and pathos the similitude is managed in *Lycidas* every reader of it knows. But the interest of the style must always rise out of the handling. We admire the poem not so much because, as in despite of, its plan. The pencil of Claude turns a crook into a scepter, and makes it kingly. We cannot but think that Johnson's objection was essentially sound, if only he had confined it to the parabolical form of the poem, without shutting his eyes to the grace of the execution. We regard it as a most happy judgment of Mr. Tennyson, that he resolved to forget *Lycidas*, and to place the charm of his own longer elegy in its biographical passages and domestic interiors. We hear nothing of Damon, and are thankful for the silence. The age, whether for better or worse, has left the pastoral behind it. Corydon is for ever out of the question with people who have anything to do; the close of the 18th century witnessed his burial. That rather insipid shepherd-swain, whom Pope patronized, will never lead his flock along the banks of the Thames since the South Western crossed it at Twickenham. Not even Theocritus could have outlived a viaduct.

In turning to consider these verses we will mention on the threshold two leading defects likely, in our opinion, to largely lessen the satisfaction of a reflective and tasteful reader. One is the enormous exaggeration of the grief. We seem to hear of a person unlike ourselves in failings and virtues. The real fades into the legendary. Instead of a memorial we have a myth. Hence the subject suffers loss even from its magnitude. The hero is beyond our sympathy. We think of the difference between Ariosto's charmed knight and Sir John Moore at Corunna. It is not Mr. Arthur Hallam, but the Admirable Crichton of the romancer, who appeals to our hearts. A rather apt illustration occurs to us. A friend of ours was once spirited up to try for the medal which Cambridge offered in honour of deceased her Chancellor. Having completed his task he showed it to an accomplished critic, who said, – "The lines are good, but I should have imagined that instead of a duke dying, the whole world had gone off in convulsions, your lamentation is so tremendous." The wailings of *In Memoriam* might have drawn forth a similar exclamation. The disproportion of phrase is sometimes ludicrous, and occasionally it borders on blasphemy. Can the writer satisfy his own conscience with respect to these verse?

> "But brooding on the dear one dead,
>   "And all he said of things divine,
>   "(*And dear as sacramental wine*
> "*To dying lips, is all he said.*)"

For our part, we should consider no confession of regret too strong for the hardihood that indicted them.

Soften it as you will, the feeling of untruthfulness cannot be removed. Nature and identity are wanting. The lost friend stalks along a giant of 11 feet, or moves a spiritual being, with an Eden-halo, through life. The difficulty set before a poet is to reconcile the imaginary with the actual; the epic with the prose of common men. Affection is not to transfigure the face by illuminating it; nor is the difficulty insuperable. Johnson met and overcame it in his verses of Mr. Levett, a medical practitioner among the poor. "Levett, Sir," he said, "was not rough, he was brutal." In every attempt to panegyrize his friend this stumbling-block of temper stood sheer in the way. How does he deal with it? He just rolls it into twilight. He retains the defect, but refines it. The real vulgarity is shaded into an elegiac fitness. Mark the delicacy with which the moralist underlines the poet:—

> "Yet still he fills affection's eye,
>   "Obscurely wise, and *coarsely kind;*
> "Nor, lettered arrogance, deny
>   "Thy praise to merit *unrefined.*"

The true expression of the character is preserved; not a feature, not a line is lost. The sick beggar in Green Arbour-court would have recognized the doctor, – and yet the repulsive manner seems to have rubbed off its squalor. This is the mastery of art, ennobling the disagreeable. We might think, if chronology would allow us, how imperative Cromwell might have been to Titian about his roughness and his scars, and how even the seam and the pimple would have grown heroic under the hand of the Venetian.

A second defect, which has painfully come out as often as we take up the volume, is the tone of—may we say so?—amatory tenderness. Surely this is a strange manner of address to a man, even though he be dead:—

> "So dearest, now thy brows are cold,
>   "I see thee what thou art, and know
>   "Thy likeness to the wise below,
> "Thy kindred with the great of old.

> "But there is more than I can see,
>   "And what I see I leave unsaid,
>   "Nor speak it, knowing death has made
> "His darkness beautiful with thee."

Very sweet and plaintive these verses are; but who would not give them a feminine application? Shakespeare may be considered the founder of this style in English. In classical and Oriental poetry it is unpleasantly familiar. His mysterious sonnets present the startling peculiarity of transferring every epithet of womanly endearment to a masculine friend,—his master-mistress, as he calls him by a compound epithet, harsh as it is disagreeable. We should never expect to hear a young lawyer calling a member of the same inn "his rose," except in the Middle Temple of Ispahan, with Hafiz for a laureate. Equally objectionable are the following lines in the 42d sonnet:—

> "If I could write the beauty of your eyes,
>   "And in fresh numbers number all your graces,
> "The age to come would say this poet lies;
>   "Such heavenly touches ne'er touched earthly faces."

Is it Petrarch whispering to Laura? We really think that floating remembrances of Shakspeare's sonnets have beguiled Mr. Tennyson. Many of these poems seem to be contrived, like Goldsmith's chest of drawers, "a double debt to pay," and might be addressed with perfect propriety, and every assurance of a favourable reception, to one of those young ladies with melting blue eyes and a passion for novels whom we found Mr. Bennet so ungallantly denouncing in a recent letter to his children.

We object to a Cantab being styled a "rose" under any conditions; but do not suppose that we would shut up nature, as a storehouse of imagery and consolation, from him who laments a lost companion of his school, or college, or maturer days, with whom he took sweet counsel and walked as a friend. Let Cowley weep for Harvey. Most exquisitely does the poet of all joy and sorrow write—

> "So are you to my thoughts as food to life,
> "Or as sweet-seasoned showers are to the ground."

The harvest of memory will come up abundantly, as the seed falls up and down life; the shadow of the familiar form glides over the landscape; the old field-path recalls him; and the warm homestead, the meadow stile, the windy sheepwalk, the gray church tower, the wrangling daw in the quarry,—each is dear and each has a voice, as having been seen with him and by him. But this source of interest requires to be opened with a sparing hand. It easily and quickly is corrupted into sentiment. We can appreciate the meditative rapture of Burns, who saw his "Jean" in the flower under the hedge; but the taste is displeased when every expression of fondness is sighed out, and the only figure within our view is Amaryllis of the Chancery Bar.

Another fault is not peculiar to *In Memoriam;* it runs through all Mr. Tennyson's poetry,—we allude to his *obscurity.* We are prepared to admit that certain kinds of writing are especially exposed to this accusation, and from causes beyond the oversight of the author. The emotions of the heart and of the fancy have their own dialect. This is always hard to be understood,—is frequently altogether unintelligible by ruder minds. The muses' court cherishes particular idioms. Johnson's regard for Collins—and he seems to have been deeply attached to him—supplied no key to the gorgeous verse. The *Faëry Queen* was honestly despised by Burleigh; Milton appeared every inch an usher, with no wand but a birch, to the Caroline wits; Thomson's pictures were positive daubs to the Gothic gentleman in a primrose suit at Strawberry-hill. There was no pretence in the dullness; eye and ear for colour and music were closed. It was the infirmity of their constitution. "We have heard an excellent discourse this morning, Dr. Johnson," said a pompous stranger to our stout friend, coming out of Lichfield Cathedral. "That may be, Sir," was the chilling reply, "but it is impossible that you should know it." The sarcasm will often be true in poetical history. Walpole reading *Milton* is the Lichfield story over again. There is a grace, a delicacy, a fragrance, and a light of sentiment and image which are altogether dark to the crowd. We will offer two examples. Cowper, in one of his letters, exclaims in a burst of rural tenderness—"*My eyes drink the rivers as they flow!*" and Blanco White furnishes a more charming illustration in a remark upon a woman carrying primroses by his window,—"They were primroses—new primroses—so blooming, so fresh, and so tender, that it might be said *that their perfume was received by the eye!*" The thought of both writers is nearly the same—exquisite and full of the deepest love; but how would it appear to a reader in whom the poetical element was wanting? Like cuneiform writing or a roll from Pompeii.

Again, a magnificent thought is likely to be obscure to the first glance; a mist hangs round it and shows its elevation. As in passages of emotional tenderness and taste there is a reflective light to be thrown from the reader's experience of corresponding sensations, so in images of sublimity a large perspective requires filling up. Perhaps the poetry of the world contains no grander description than Milton's of the advancing God—

"Far off His coming shone."

But the picture loses its splendour unless we people the vast field of time that lies between with legions of heavenly warriors, and light the cloudy edge of distant centuries with the blaze of Cherubim and the chariots of the Eternal. In such cases the obscurity melts before the observer. We will call Mr. Tennyson himself in support of our argument:—

"That which we dare invoke to bless;
    "Our dearest faith; our ghastliest doubt;
    "He, They, One, All; within, without;
    "The Power in darkness whom we guess;

"I found Him not in world or sun,
    "Or eagle's wing, or insect's eye;
    "Nor thro' the questions men may try
    "The petty cobwebs we have spun:

"If e'er, when faith had fall'n asleep,
    "I heard a voice—'Believe no more,'
    "*And heard an ever breaking shore*
    "*That tumbled in the Godless deep;*

"A warmth within the breast would melt
    "The freezing reason's colder part,
    "And like a man in wrath, the heart
    "Stood up and answer'd, 'I have felt.'

"No, like a child in doubt and fear:
    "But that blind clamour made me wise;
    "Then was I as a child that cries,
    "But, crying, knows his father near;

"And what I seem beheld again
    "What is, and no man understands;
    "*And out of Darkness came the hands*
    "*That reach thro' nature moulding men.*"—cxxii.

To that most literal gentleman whom Elia pleasantly ridiculed these verses would be simply so many inscriptions in an unknown tongue; but to the poetical eye their obscurity is the result of the illimitable expanse of mystery over which the poet sweeps. The very dimness helps to impress his mind with immensity.

The following invocation to the deputed friend would claim the benefit of the exception:—

"Come; not in watches of the night,
    "But when the sunbeam broodeth warm,
    "Come, *beauteous in thine after form,*
    "*And like a finer light on light,*"

Perhaps we might even include in this class the contrast in the 24th elegy between the happiness and sorrow of former and present days, where the poet inquires whether it is that the haze of grief magnifies joy—

> "Or that the past will always win
> "A glory from its being far;
> "And orb into the perfect star,
> "We saw not when we moved therein?"

For there is something striking and suggestive in comparing the goneby time to some luminous body rising like a red harvest moon behind us, lighting our path homeward.

Now, for all such cases of obscurity a very liberal allowance is to be made. The highest beauty does not always lie upon the surface of words. In whatever degree the difficulty of Mr. Tennyson's verse is to be explained by its depth the writer should be acquitted. But in a large number of passages the plea cannot be received. He is difficult not from excess, but want of meaning. Take a specimen:—

> "Oh, if indeed that eye foresee,
> "Or see (in Him is no before)
> "In more of life true love no more,
> "And Love the indifference to be;
>
> "So might I find, ere yet the morn
> "Breaks hither over Indian seas,
> *"That Shadow waiting with the keys,*
> *"To cloak me from my proper scorn."*—xxvi.

We ask seriously if that celebrated collector and critic Mr. M. Scriblerus would not have bought up this stanza at any price? Unquestionably it is worth its weight in lead for a treatise on Bathos. Lately we have heard much of keys both from the Flaminian Gate and Piccadilly, but we back this verse against Hobbs. We dare him to pick it. Mr. Moxon may hang it up in his window, with a 200*l.* prize attached, more safely than a Bramah. That a Shadow should hold keys at all, is a noticeable circumstance; but that it should wait with a cloak ready to be thrown over a gentleman in difficulties, is absolutely amazing. There is an allusion, at p. 69, which soars to the same height above our comprehension:—

> "That each, who seems a separate whole,
> "Should *move his rounds, and fusing all*
> *"The skirts of self again, should fall,*
> *"Remerging in the general Soul."*

Of the two mysteries, the Shadow with the cloak is probably the easier. We request the reader, who may be of an analytical turn, to try the above stanza for himself. Let him resolve it into prose. We have applied every known test, without detecting the smallest trace of sense, and are confident that the "blind clerk" at the General Post-office would abandon the effort when he came to *fusing the skirts of self.*

There is a fainter kind of obscurity which ought, so far as possible, to be cleared away. In this sort, also, Mr. Tennyson makes considerable demands upon our patience. Even a refined and educated reader is often puzzled to identify his exact allusion. This uncertainty is always injurious to poetical scenery. When Mason was writing *Caractacus* he was cautioned by his most accomplished friend to make every allusion so plain that it might immediately be understood; because, he said, we are not allowed to *hint* at things in general or particular history as in the Greek fables, which everybody is supposed to know. This stanza of Mr. Tennyson will show our meaning:—

> "And seem to lift the form, and glow
> "In azure orbits heavenly wise;
> "And over those ethereal eyes
> *"The bar of Michael Angelo."*

We shall not say if we comprehend the closing line. We can keep a secret. But we put it to the last young lady for whom Hayday bound the *Princess* in pink morocco to answer whether the *Bar of Michael Angelo* raises a distinct image to her mind, so distinct that, in her next lesson from Gavazzi, she will be able to put the passage into good Tuscan for the Father?

We may here observe that Mr. Tennyson frequently allows his amplitude of coloured and stately phrases to seduce him into line after line of grand sounding dactyls and spondees, out of which it is extremely hard to draw any message of wisdom or utterance of common sense. We string together three passages that might be mistaken for lumps of Statius or Nat Lee in their most turgid or twilight mood. Just listen how they tumble along with a heavy, splashing, and bewildering roll:—

> "On thee the loyal-hearted hung,
> "The proud was half disarm'd of pride,
> *"Nor cared the serpent at thy side*
> *"To flicker with his treble tongue."*—cviii.

> "For every grain of sand that runs,
> "And every span of shade that steals,
> "And every hiss of toothed wheels,
> "And all the courses of the suns."—cxv.

> "Large elements in order brought,
> "And tracts of calm from tempest made,
> *"And world-wide fluctuation sway'd*
> *"In vassal tides that follow'd thought."*—cx.

What is the meaning of the serpent with the tongue that flickers? and how can a fluctuation be swayed into "a vassal tide?"

A frequent source of mist and doubtfulness in language is a habit, either wilful or indifferent, of grammatical inaccuracy. Mr. Tennyson is quite autocratic in his government of words. Substantives are flung upon the world without the slightest provision for their maintenance; active and passive verbs exchange duties with astonishing ease and boldness, and particles are disbanded by a summary process unknown to Lindley Murray or Dr. Latham. Look at these instances out of many:—

"I brim with sorrow drowning song."—xix.

"Each voice four changes on the wind."—xxviii.

"Thine own shall wither in the vast."—lxxiv.

"A happy lover, who has come
  "To look on her that loves him well;
  "Who *lights* and rings the gateway bell,
"And *learns her* gone, and far from home."—viii.

Here it is evident that "*lights*" and "*learns*" are used with extreme incorrectness. The construction requires us to suppose that the lover arrives in a dark evening with a lantern, and gropes about the brick wall until he finds the bell. Just look at the circumstance as Jones might relate it to a young lady in the suburbs—"I got into the Kennington omnibus yesterday, and in the hope of finding you at home I light and ring the bell, and learn you gone." Would such an epistle be understandable? If the object of his devotion be a girl of spirit, she will instantly cut off six heads, and send Jones a copy of Mr. Edwards' *Progressive English Exercises* by the next post. Will the Germanic and cloud-compelling school permit us to recommend to their patient meditation a short saying of Hobbes, which need not be confined to Mr. Tennyson's ear?—"The order of words, when placed as they ought to be, carries a light before it, whereby a man may foresee the length of his period; as a torch in the night showeth a man the stops and unevenness of the way."

We turn with very sincere pleasure to notice some of the finer and purer qualities of this book and its author. We wish Mr. Tennyson to number us with his friends. First among his gifts we should place his mastery of diction. Words many, and of the finest dyes, from Greece and Italy, are heaped in his treasury. Whatever be the wants of his muse, her wardrobe is rich in every article of dress, laid up in myrrh and ivory. A single expression often shoots a sunbeam into a line and kindles a page. This quality establishes his claim to the title of a true poet. It stamps every honoured name of song and distinguishes it from the usurper's. It is like the hasty touch of Rembrandt, that struck his mind's life into canvas. The "shadowy gust" with which Thomson swept his corn-field was as much beyond the ablest versifier as the building of Pandemonium. We judge a genius by a word, as we might try a new mintage by the shape and the ring of its smallest coin. With these happinesses of expression the present Elegies are plentifully sprinkled. We gather several, beginning with an evening cloud-scene:—

"That rises upward always higher,
  "And onward drags a labouring breast,
  "And topples round the *dreary west,*
"*A looming bastion fringed with fire.*"—xv.

"And on the low dark verge of life,
"*The twilight of eternal day.*"—xlix.

"I falter where I firmly trod,
  "And falling with my weight of cares
  "Upon the *great world's Altar stairs*
"*That slope through darkness up to God.*"—liv.

"The chesnut *pattering to the ground*,"—xi.

"With blasts *that blow the poplar white*."—lxx.

"The gust that round the garden flew,
"*And tumbled half the mellowing pears*."—lxxxvii.

"When summer's hourly-mellowing change
"May breathe with many roses sweet
"*Upon the thousand waves of wheat,*
"*That ripple round the lonely grange*."—lxxxix.

"And Autumn laying here and there
"*A fiery finger on the leaves*."—xcvii.

"Unwatched the garden bough shall sway,
"The tender blossom flutter down,
"Unloved that *beech will gather brown,*
"*This maple burn itself away*."—xcix.

Sometimes Mr. Tennyson is apt to exceed the poetical liberty of reviving ancient manners of speech. Old words are old gold. Dryden, in particular, understood this way of setting his jewels. Its recommendations are strong. A phrase or epithet of early times brings its age with it. A pure Chaucerism is like a fresh nosegay flung suddenly on the table; but the beauty of the word should be decided. It must have something of the past centuries more winning than their wrinkles. In Mr. Tennyson's revivals this preciousness is not seldom absent. Take two instances,—

"A thousand wants
"*Gnarr* at the heels of men."—p. 157.

"And *burgeons* every maze of quick."—p. 178.

We know that both of these words are used by Spenser—the former in the sense of snarling or barking, the latter of springing forth or budding—but they have no merit whatever of their own; Spenser's pen does not consecrate them.

It is not necessary to commend the almost unbroken music of Mr. Tennyson's rhythm—nobody denies his ear. You are sure of a sweet sound, though nothing be in it. We will add that he is extremely successful in the endings of the short poems into which the memorial is broken. This is a merit of much importance. When Mason sent his elegy written in a garden to Gray, he objected to the last line as being flat and prosaic, whereas that above every other, he told him, ought to sparkle, or, at least, to shine. Accordingly, Gray exhorted him to twirl the sentiment into an apophthegm, to stick a flower in it, to gild it with a costly expression, and to make it strike the fancy, the ear, or the heart. Mr. Tennyson has, however unconsciously, followed the advice. Nor among his word-excellencies should we forget the pleasing effect of his word-repetitions—an art which poets of all countries and times have been fond of practising. Ovid's description of Apollo's chariot is a musical example, with its golden axle, its golden beam, and the outward rim of the wheels in gold; where the sound of the *aureus* is like a mellow note continually returning in the strain.

In conclusion, we offer only one observation by way of moral. Small as this book is, it may be abridged with profit. The kindest gift to a poet is a division of "2." We would not exclude the greatest names from a share in the privilege. What fierce grinning distortions of Dante might be driven out of Purgatory? What succulent episodes of Spenser or Camoens be lopped off? What dry shreds of Milton be tossed into a Baptist magazine? How the noble features of Dryden's genius would shine out if all his trade verses had been treated like Tonson's trade guineas, and *clipped!* Wordsworth's *Excursion* would pleasantly shorten into a summer walk, and Southey's 10 volumes reappear with infinite vivacity in a moderate 18mo. Whatever be the expansion of ancient song, compression is indispensable to a modern versifier. The circulation of his blood is too languid for a large body and scarcely reaches the extremities. His chances of fame in the future may be calculated by the thickness of his volume. Posterity will only preserve the choicer metal. Epic urns, with their glitter and baseness, will be broken up, while the ode and sonnet give forth their little gleams; and he will be the happy rhymer in the coming century, whose grain of gold, disengaged of its impurities, and not swollen out with alloy, has melted quite pure into a locket.

37 The Fleshly School of Poetry: Mr. D. G. Rossetti (1871)

Thomas Maitland [Robert Buchanan]

Mr. Rossetti has been known for many years as a painter of exceptional powers, who, for reasons best known to himself, has shrunk from publicly exhibiting his pictures, and from allowing anything like a popular estimate to be formed of their qualities. He belongs, or is said to belong, to the so-called Pre-Raphaelite school, a school which is generally considered to exhibit much genius for colour, and great indifference to perspective. It would be unfair to judge the painter by the glimpses we have had of his works, or by the photographs which are sold of the principal paintings. Judged by the photographs, he is an artist who conceives unpleasantly, and draws ill. Like Mr. Simeon Solomon, however, with whom he seems to have many points in common, he is distinctively a colourist, and of his capabilities in colour we cannot speak, though we should guess that they are great; for if there is any good quality by which his poems are specially marked, it is a great sensitiveness to hues and tints as conveyed in poetic epithet. These qualities, which impress the casual spectator of the photographs from his pictures, are to be found abundantly among his verses. There is the same thinness and transparence of design, the same combination of the simple and the grotesque, the same morbid deviation from healthy forms of life, the same sense of weary, wasting, yet exquisite sensuality; nothing virile, nothing tender, nothing completely sane; a superfluity of extreme sensibility, of delight in beautiful forms, hues, and tints, and a deep-sealed indifference to all agitating forces and agencies, all tumultuous griefs and sorrows, all the thunderous stress of life, and all the straining storm of speculation. Mr. Morris is often pure, fresh, and wholesome as his own great model; Mr. Swinburne startles us more than once by some fine flash of insight; but the mind of Mr. Rossetti is like a glassy mere, broken only by the dive of some water-bird or the hum of winged insects, and brooded over by an atmosphere of insufferable closeness, with a light blue sky above it, sultry depths mirrored within it, and a surface so thickly sown with water-lilies that it retains its glassy smoothness even in the strongest wind. Judged relatively to his poetic associates, Mr. Rossetti must be pronounced inferior to either. He cannot tell a pleasant story like Mr. Morris, nor forge alliterative thunderbolts like Mr. Swinburne. It must be conceded, nevertheless, that he is neither so glibly imitative as the one, nor so transcendently superficial as the other.

Although he has been known for many years as a poet as well as a painter—as a painter and poet idolized by his own family and personal associates—and although he has once or twice appeared in print as a contributor to magazines, Mr. Rossetti did not formally appeal to the public until rather more than a year ago, when he published a copious volume of poems, with the announcement that the book, although it contained pieces composed at intervals during a period of many years, "included nothing which the author believes to be immature." This work was inscribed to his brother, Mr. William Rossetti, who, having written much both in poetry and criticism, will perhaps be known to bibliographers as the editor of the worst edition of Shelley which has yet seen the light. No sooner had the work appeared than the chorus of eulogy began. "The book is satisfactory from end to end," wrote Mr. Morris in the Academy; "I think these lyrics, with all their other merits, the most complete of their time; nor do I know what lyrics of any time are to be called great, if we are to deny the title to these." On the same subject Mr. Swinburne went into a hysteria of admiration: "golden affluence," "jewel-coloured words," "chastity of form," "harmonious nakedness," "consummate fleshly sculpture," and so on in Mr. Swinburne's well-known manner when reviewing his friends. Other critics, with a singular similarity of phrase, followed suit. Strange to say, moreover, no one accused Mr. Rossetti of naughtiness. What had been heinous in Mr. Swinburne was Majestic exquisiteness in Mr. Rossetti. Yet we question if there is anything in the unfortunate "Poems and Ballads" quite so questionable on the score of thorough nastiness as many pieces in Mr. Rossetti's collection. Swinburne was wilder, more outrageous, more blasphemous, and his subjects were more atrocious in themselves; yet the hysterical tone slew the animalism, the furiousness of epithet lowered the sensation; and the first feeling of disgust at such themes as "Laus Veneris" and "Anactoria," faded away into comic amazement. It was only a little mad boy letting off squibs; not a great strong man, who might be really dangerous to society, "I will be naughty!" screamed the little boy; but, after all, what did it matter? It is quite different, however, when a grown man, with the self-control and easy audacity of actual experience, comes forward to chronicle his amorous sensations, and, first proclaiming in a loud voice his literary maturity, and consequent responsibility, shamelessly prints and publishes such a piece of writing as this sonnet on "Nuptial Sleep":—

> *At length their long kiss severed, with sweet smart:*
> *And as the last slow sudden drops are shed*
> *From sparkling caves when all the storm has fled,*
> *So singly flagged the pulses of each heart.*
> *Their bosoms sundered, with the opening start*
> *Of married flowers to either side outspread*
> *From the knit stem; yet still their mouths, burnt red,*
> *Fawned on each other where they lay apart.*

> Sleep sank them lower than the tide of dreams,
>   And their dreams watched them sink, and slid away.
> Slowly their souls swam up again, through gleams
>   Of watered light and dull drowned waifs of day;
> Till from some wonder of now woods and streams
>   He woke, and wondered more; for there she lay.

This, then, is "the golden affluence of words, the firm outline, the justice and chastity of form." Here is a full-grown man, presumably intelligent and cultivated, putting on record for other full-grown men to read, the most secret mysteries of sexual connection, and that with so sickening a desire to reproduce the sensual mood, so careful a choice of epithet to convey mere animal sensations, that we merely shudder at the shameless nakedness. We are no purists in such matters. We hold the sensual part of our nature to be as holy as the spiritual or intellectual part, and we believe that such things must find their equivalent in all; but it is neither poetic, nor manly, nor even human, to obtrude such things as the themes of whole poems. It is simply nasty. Nasty as it is, we are very mistaken if many readers do not think it nice. English society of one kind purchases the *Day's Doings*. English society of another kind goes into ecstasy over Mr. Solomon's pictures—pretty pieces of morality, such as "Love dying by the breath of Lust." There is not much to choose between the two objects of admiration, except that painters like Mr. Solomon lend actual genius to worthless subjects, and thereby produce veritable monsters—like the lovely devils that danced round Saint Anthony. Mr. Rossetti owes his so called success to the same causes. In poems like "Nuptial Sleep," the man who is too sensitive to exhibit his pictures, and so modest that it takes him years to make up his mind to publish his poems, parades his private sensations before a coarse public, and is gratified by their applause.

It must not be supposed that all Mr. Rossetti's poems are made up of trash like this. Some of them are as noteworthy for delicacy of touch as others are for shamelessness of exposition. They contain some exquisite pictures of nature, occasional passages of real meaning, much beautiful phraseology, lines of peculiar sweetness, and epithets chosen with true literary cunning. But the fleshly feeling is everywhere. Sometimes, as in "The Stream's Secret," it is deliciously modulated, and adds greatly to our emotion of pleasure at perusing a finely-wrought poem; at other times, as in the "Last Confession," it is fiercely held in check by the exigencies of a powerful situation and the strength of a dramatic speaker; but it is generally in the foreground, flushing the whole poem with unhealthy rose-colour, stifling the senses with overpowering sickliness, as of too much civet. Mr. Rossetti is never dramatic, never impersonal—always attitudinizing, posturing, and describing his own exquisite emotions. He is the "Blessed Damozel," leaning over the "gold bar of heaven," and seeing

> "Time like a pulse shake fierce
>   Thro' all the worlds;"

he is "heaven-born Helen, Sparta's queen," whose "each twin breast is an apple sweet;" he is Lilith the first wife of Adam; he is the rosy Virgin of the poem called "Ave," and the Queen in the "Staff and Scrip;" he is " Sister Helen" melting her waxen man; he is all these; just as surely as he is Mr. Rossetti soliloquizing over Jenny in her London lodging, or the very nuptial person writing erotic sonnets to his wife. In petticoats or pantaloons, in modern times or in the middle ages, he is just Mr. Rossetti, a fleshly person, with nothing particular to tell us or teach us, with extreme self-control, a strong sense of colour, and a careful choice of diction. Amid all his "affluence of jewel-coloured words," he has not given us one rounded and noteworthy piece of art, though his verses are all art; not one poem which is memorable for its own sake, and quite separable from the displeasing identity of the composer. The nearest approach to a perfect whole is the "Blessed Damozel," a peculiar poem, placed first in the book, perhaps by accident, perhaps because it is a key to the poems which follow. This poem appeared in a rough shape many years ago in the *Germ*, an unwholesome periodical started by the Pre-Raphaelites, and suffered, after gasping through a few feeble numbers, to die the death of all such publications. In spite of its affected title, and of numberless affectations throughout the text, the "Blessed Damozel" has great merits of its own, and a few lines of real genius. We have heard it described as the record of actual grief and love, or, in simple words, the apotheosis of one actually lost by the writer; but, without having any private knowledge of the circumstance of its composition, we feel that such an account of the poem is inadmissible. It does not contain one single note of sorrow. It is a "composition," and a clever one. Read the opening stanzas:—

"The blessed damozel leaned out
　　From the gold bar of Heaven;
Her eyes were deeper than the depth
　　Of water stilled at even;
She had three lilies in her hand,
　　And the stars in her hair were seven.

"Her robe, ungirt from clasp to hem,
　　No wrought flowers did adorn,
But a white rose of Mary's gift,
　　For service meetly worn;
Her hair that lay along her back
　　Was yellow like ripe corn."

This is a careful sketch for a picture, which, worked into actual colour by a master, might have been worth seeing. The steadiness of hand lessens as the poem proceeds, and although there are several passages of considerable power,—such as that where, far down the void,

　　　　"this earth
Spins like a fretful midge,"

or that other, describing how

　　　　"the curled moon
"Was like a little feather
Fluttering far down the gulf,"—

the general effect is that of a queer old painting in a missal, very affected and very odd. What moved the British critic to ecstasy in this poem seems to us very sad nonsense indeed, or, if not sad nonsense, very meretricious affectation. Thus, we have seen the following verses quoted with enthusiasm, as italicised—

"And still she bowed herself and stooped
　　Out of the circling charm;
Until her bosom must have made
　　The bar she leaned on warm,
And the lilies lay as if asleep
　　Along her bended arm.

"From the fixed place of Heaven she saw
　　Time like a pulse shake fierce
Thro' all the worlds. Her gaze still strove
　　Within the gulf to pierce
Its path; and now she spoke as when
　　The stars sang in their spheres."

It seems to us that all these lines are very bad, with the exception of the two admirable lines ending the first verse, and that the italicised portions are quite without merit, and almost without meaning. On the whole, one feels disheartened and amazed at the poet who, in the nineteenth century, talks about "damozels," "citherns," and "citoles," and addresses the mother of Christ as the "Lady Mary,"—

> "With her five handmaidens, whose names
>   Are five sweet symphonies,
> Cecily, Gertrude, Magdalen,
>   Margaret and Rosalys."

A suspicion is awakened that the writer is laughing at us. We hover uncertainly between picturesqueness and namby-pamby, and the effect, as Artemus Ward would express it, is "weakening to the intellect." The thing would have been almost too much in the shape of a picture, though the workmanship might have made amends. The truth is that literature, and more particularly poetry, is in a very bad way when one art gets hold of another, and imposes upon it its conditions and limitations. In the first few verses of the "Damozel" we have the subject, or part of the subject, of a picture, and the inventor should either have painted it or left it alone altogether; and, had he done the latter, the world would have lost nothing. Poetry is something more than painting; and an idea will not become a poem because it is too smudgy for a picture.

In a short notice from a well-known pen, giving the best estimate we have seen of Mr. Rossetti's powers as a poet, the *North American Review* offers a certain explanation for affectation such as that of Mr. Rossetti. The writer suggests that "it may probably be the expression of genuine moods of mind in natures too little comprehensive." We would rather believe that Mr. Rossetti lacks comprehension than that he is deficient in sincerity; yet really, to paraphrase the words which Johnson applied to Thomas Sheridan, Mr. Rossetti is affected, naturally affected, but it must have taken him a great deal of trouble to become what we now see him—such an excess of affectation is not in nature.[1] There is very little writing in the volume spontaneous in the sense that some of Swinburne's verses are spontaneous; the poems all look as if they had taken a great deal of trouble. The grotesque mediævalism of "Stratton Water" and "Sister Helen," the mediæval classicism of "Troy Town," the false and shallow mysticism of "Eden Bower," are one and all essentially imitative, and must have cost the writer much pains. It is time, indeed, to point out that Mr. Rossetti is a poet possessing great powers of assimilation and some faculty for concealing the nutriment on which he feeds. Setting aside the "Vita Nuova" and the early Italian poems, which are familiar to many readers by his own excellent translations, Mr. Rossetti may be described as a writer who has yielded to an unusual extent to the complex influences of the literature surrounding him at the present moment. He has the painter's imitative power developed in proportion to his lack of the poet's conceiving imagination. He reproduces to a nicety the manner of an old ballad, a trick in which Mr. Swinburne is also an adept. Cultivated readers, moreover, will recognise in every one of these poems the tone of Mr. Tennyson broken up by the style of Mr. and Mrs. Browning, and disguised here and there by the eccentricities of the Pre-Raphaelites. The "Burden of Nineveh" is a philosophical edition of "Recollections of the Arabian Nights;" "A Last Confession" and "Dante at Verona" are, in the minutest trick and form of thought, suggestive of Mr. Browning; and that the sonnets have been largely moulded and inspired by Mrs. Browning can be ascertained by any critic who will compare them with the "Sonnets from the Portuguese." Much remains, nevertheless, that is Mr. Rossetti's own. We at once recognise as his own property such passages as this:·—

"I looked up
And saw where a brown-shouldered harlot leaned
Half through a tavern window thick with vine.
Some man had come behind her in the room
And caught her by her arms, and she had turned
With that coarse empty laugh on him, as now
He *munched her neck with kisses, while the vine
Crawled in her back.*

Or this:—

"As I stooped, her own lips rising there
    Bubbled with brimming kisses at my mouth."

Or this:—

"Have seen your lifted silken skirt
Advertise dainties through the dirt!"

Or this:—

"What more prize than love to impel thee,
Grip and *lip* my limbs as I tell thee!"

Passages like these are the common stock of the walking gentlemen of the fleshly school. We cannot forbear expressing our wonder, by the way, at the kind of women whom it seems the unhappy lot of these gentlemen to encounter. We have lived as long in the world as they have, but never yet came across persons of the other sex who conduct themselves in the manner described. Females who bite, scratch, scream, bubble, munch, sweat, writhe, twist, wriggle, foam, and in a general way slaver over their lovers, must surely possess some extraordinary qualities to counteract their otherwise most offensive mode of conducting themselves. It appears, however, on examination, that their poet-lovers conduct themselves in a similar manner. They, too, bite, scratch, scream, bubble, munch, sweat, writhe, twist, wriggle, foam, and slaver, in a style frightful to hear of. Let us hope that it is only their fun, and that they don't mean half they say. At times, in reading such books as this, one cannot help wishing that things had remained for ever in the asexual state described in Mr. Darwin's great chapter on Palingenesis. We get very weary of this protracted hankering after a person of the other sex; it seems meat, drink, thought, sinew, religion for the fleshly school. There is no limit to the fleshliness, and Mr. Rossetti finds in it its own religious justification much in the same way as Holy Willie:—

"Maybe thou, let'st this fleshly thorn
Perplex thy servant night and morn,
        'Cause he's so gifted.
If so, thy hand must e'en be borne,
        Until thou lift it,"

Whether he is writing of the holy Damozel, or of the Virgin herself, or of Lilith, or Helen, or of Dante, or of Jenny the streetwalker, he is fleshly all over, from the roots of his hair to the tip of his toes; never a true lover merging his identity into that of the beloved one; never spiritual, never tender; always self-conscious and æsthetic. "Nothing," says a modern writer, "in human life is so utterly remorseless—not love, not hate, not ambition, not vanity—as the artistic or æsthetic instinct morbidly developed to the suppression of conscience and feeling; "and at no time do we feel more fully impressed with this truth than after the perusal of "Jenny," in some respects the finest poem in the volume, and in all respects the poem best indicative of the true quality of the writer's humanity. It is a production which bears signs of having been suggested by Mr. Buchanan's quasi-lyrical poems, which it copies in the style of title, and particularly by "Artist and Model;" but certainly Mr. Rossetti cannot be accused, as the Scottish writer has been accused, of maudlin sentiment and affected tenderness. The two first lines are perfect:—

> "Lazy Laughing languid Jenny,
> Fond of a kiss and fond of a guinea;"

And the poem is a soliloquy of the poet—who has been spending the evening in dancing at a casino—over his partner, whom he has accompanied home to the usual style of lodgings by such ladies, and who has fallen asleep with her head upon his knee, while he wonders, in a wretched pun—

> "Whose person or whose purse may be
> The lodestar of your reverie?"

The soliloquy is long, and in some parts beautiful, despite a very constant suspicion that we are listening to an emasculated Mr. Browning, whose whole tone and gesture, so to speak, is occasionally introduced with startling fidelity; and there are here and there glimpses of actual thought and insight, over and above the picturesque touches which belong to the writer's true profession, such as that where, at daybreak—

> "lights creep in
> Past the gauze curtains half drawn-to,
> And *the lamp's doubled shade grows blue.*"

What we object to in this poem is not the subject, which any writer may be fairly left to choose for himself; nor anything particularly vicious in the poetic treatment of it; nor any bad blood bursting through in special passages. But the whole tone, without being more than usually coarse, seems heartless. There is not a drop of piteousness in Mr. Rossetti. He is just to the outcast, even generous; severe to the seducer; sad even at the spectacle of lust in dimity and fine ribbons. Notwithstanding all this, and a certain delicacy and refinement of treatment unusual with this poet, the poem repels and revolts us, and we like Mr. Rossetti least after its perusal. We are angry with the fleshly person at last. The "Blessed Damozel" puzzled us, the "Song of the Bower" amused us, the love-sonnet depressed and sickened us, but "Jenny," though distinguished by less special viciousness of thought and style than any of these, fairly makes us lose patience. We detect its fleshliness at a glance; we perceive that the scene was fascinating less through its human tenderness than because it, like all the others, possessed an inherent quality of animalism. "The whole work" ("Jenny,") writes Mr. Swinburne, "is worthy to fill its place for ever as one of the most perfect poems of an age or generation. There is just the same life-blood and breadth of poetic interest in this episode of a London street and lodging as in the song of 'Troy Town' and the song of 'Eden Bower;' just as much, and no jot more,"—to which last statement we cordially assent; for there is bad blood in all, and breadth of poetic interest in none. "Vengeance of Jenny's case," indeed!—when such a poet as this comes fawning over here, with tender compassion in one eye and æsthetic enjoyment in the other!

It is time that we permitted Mr. Rossetti to speak for himself, which we will do by quoting a fairly representative poem entire:—

Love-Lily.

"Between the hand, between the brows,
    Between the lips of Love-Lily,
A spirit is born whose birth endows
    My blood with fire to burn through me;
Who breathes upon my gazing eyes,
    Who laughs and murmurs in mine ear,
At whose least touch my colour flies,
    And whom my life grows faint to hear.

"Within the voice, within the heart,
    Within the mind of Love-Lily,
A spirit is born who lifts apart
    His tremulous wings and looks at me;
Who on my mouth his finger lays,
    And shows, while whispering lutes confer,
That Eden of Love's watered ways
    Whose winds and spirits worship her.

"Brows, hands, and lips, heart, mind, and voice,
    Kisses and words of Love-Lily,—
Oh! bid me with your joy rejoice
    Till *riotous longing rest in me!*
Ah! let not hope be still distraught,
    But find in her its gracious goal,
Whose speech Truth knows not from her thought,
    Nor Love her body from her soul."

With the exception of the usual "riotous longing," which seems to make Mr. Rossetti a burthen to himself, there is nothing to find fault with in the extreme fleshliness of these verses, and to many people who live in the country they may even appear beautiful. Without pausing to criticise a thing so trifling—as well might we dissect a cobweb or anatomize a medusa—let us ask the reader's attention to a peculiarity to which all the students of the fleshly school must sooner or later give their attention—we mean the habit of accenting the last syllable in words which in ordinary speech are accented on the penultimate:—

"Between the hands, between the brows,
    Between the lips of Love-Lil*ee!*"

which may be said to give to the speaker's voice a sort of cooing tenderness just bordering on a loving whistle. Still better as an illustration are the lines:—

> "Saturday night is market night
> Everywhere, be it dry or wet,
> And market night in the Haymar-*ket*!"

which the reader may advantageously compare with Mr. Morris's

> "Then said the king
> Thanked be thou; *neither for nothing*
> Shall thou this good deed do to me;"

or Mr. Swinburne's

> "In either of the twain
> Red roses full of rain;
> She hath for bondwo*men*
> All kinds of flowers."

It is unnecessary to multiply examples of an affectation which disfigures all these writers—Guildenstern, Rosencranz, and Osric; who, in the same spirit which prompts the ambitious nobodies that rent London theatres in the "empty" season to make up for their dullness by fearfully original "new readings," distinguish their attempt at leading business by affecting the construction of their grandfathers and great-grandfathers, and the accentuation of the poets of the court of James I. It is in all respects a sign of remarkable genius, from this point of view, to rhyme "was" with "grass," "death " with "lièth," "love" with "of," "once" with "suns," and so on *ad nauseam*. We are far from disputing the value of bad rhymes used occasionally to break up the monotony of verse, but the case is hard when such blunders become the rule and not the exception, when writers deliberately lay themselves out to be as archaic and affected as possible. Poetry is perfect human speech, and these archaisms are the mere fiddlededeeing of empty heads and hollow hearts. Bad as they are, they are the true indication of falser tricks and affectations which lie far deeper. They are trifles, light as air, showing how the wind blows. The soul's speech and the heart's speech are clear, simple, natural, and beautiful, and reject the meretricious tricks to which we have drawn attention.

It is on the score that these tricks and affectations have procured the professors a number of imitators, that the fleshly school deliver their formula that great poets are always to be known because their manner is immediately reproduced by small poets, and that a poet who finds few imitators is probably of inferior rank—by which they mean to infer that they themselves are very great poets indeed.

Note

1 "Why, sir, Sherry is dull, naturally dull; but it must have taken him a great deal of trouble to become what we now see him—such an excess of stupidity is not in nature."—*Boswell's Life*.

38 Introduction to *Sexual Inversion* (1896/7)

Havelock Ellis

In modern Europe we find the strongest evidence of the presence of what may fairly be called true sexual inversion when we investigate the men of the Renaissance. The intellectual independence of those days and the influence of antiquity seem to have liberated and fully developed the impulses of those abnormal individuals who would otherwise have found no clear expression, and passed unnoticed.[1] Muret, for instance, a distinguished French humanist, was throughout his whole life the victim of his own homosexual impulses. He taught philosophy and civil law at Paris to crowds of students, but was charged with unnatural crime and thrown into the Châtelet. He resolved to starve himself to death, but, on being liberated by the help of influential friends, he went to Toulouse and taught Roman law until once more he was accused of an unnatural offense with a young man, and the two were condemned to be burned. Muret escaped, however, and fled to Italy, where he became the friend of many distinguished men, although similar charges pursued him to the last. Michelangelo, one of the very chief artists of the Renaissance period, we cannot now doubt, was sexually inverted. The evidence furnished by his own letters and poems, as well as the researches of numerous recent workers,—Parlagreco, Scheffler, J. A. Symonds, etc.,—may be said to have placed this beyond question.[2] He belonged to a family of five brothers, four of whom never married, and so far as is known left no offspring; the fifth only left one male heir. His biographer describes Michelangelo as "a man of peculiar, not altogether healthy, nervous temperament." He was indifferent to women; only in one case, indeed, during his long life is there evidence even of friendship with a woman, while he was very sensitive to the beauty of men, and his friendships were very tender and enthusiastic. At the same time there is no reason to suppose that he formed any physically passionate relationships with men, and even his enemies seldom or never made this accusation against him. We may probably accept the estimate of his character given by one of his latest biographers:—

> Michelangelo Buonarotti was one of those exceptional, but not uncommon, men who are born with sensibilities abnormally deflected from the ordinary channel. He showed no partiality for women, and a notable enthusiasm for the beauty of young men ... . He was a man of physically frigid temperament, extremely sensitive to beauty of the male type, who habitually philosophized his emotions, and contemplated the living objects of his admiration as amiable, not only for their personal qualities, but also for their esthetical attractiveness.[3]

A temperament of this kind seems to have had no significance for the men of those days; they were blind to all homosexual emotion which had no result in sodomy. Plato found such attraction a subject for sentimental metaphysics, but it was not until nearly our own time that it again became a subject of interest and study. Yet it undoubtedly had profound influence on Michelangelo's art, impelling him to find every kind of human beauty in the male form, and only a grave dignity or tenderness, divorced from every quality that is sexually desirable, in the female form. This deeply rooted abnormality is at once the key to the melancholy of Michelangelo and to the mystery of his art. His contemporary, the painter Bazzi, seems also to have been radically inverted, and to this fact he owed his nickname Sodoma. As, however, he was married and had children, it may be that he was what we should now call a psychosexual hermaphrodite. He was a great artist who has been dealt with unjustly, partly, perhaps, because of the prejudice of Vasari,—whose admiration for Michelangelo amounted to worship, but who is contemptuous toward Sodoma and grudging of praise,—partly because his work is little known out of Italy and not very easy of access there. Reckless, unbalanced, and eccentric in his life, Sodoma, if we may judge him by the interesting portrait in the Pitti Palace, was a man of neurotic type, full of nervous energy, and of deeply melancholic temperament. In his painting there is a peculiar feminine softness and warmth, and a very marked and tender feeling for masculine, but scarcely virile, beauty.

In the seventeenth century a notable Flemish sculptor, Jérôme Duquesnoy (whose still more distinguished brother François executed the Manneken Pis in Brussels), was an invert; having finally been accused of sexual relations with a youth in a chapel of the Ghent Cathedral, where he was executing a monument for the bishop, he was strangled and burned, notwithstanding that much influence, including that of the bishop, was brought to bear in his behalf.[4]

In more recent times Winkelmann, who was the initiator of a new Greek Renaissance and of the modern appreciation of ancient art, lies under what seems to be a well-grounded suspicion of sexual inversion. His letters to male friends are full of the most passionate expressions of love. His violent death also appears to have been due to a love-adventure with a man. The murderer was a cook, a wholly uncultivated man, a criminal who had already been condemned to death, and shortly before murdering Winkelmann for the sake of plunder he was found to be on very intimate terms with him.[5] It is noteworthy that sexual inversion should so often be found associated with the study of antiquity. It must not, however, be too hastily concluded that this is due to suggestion and that to abolish the study of Greek literature and art would be largely to abolish sexual inversion. What has really occurred in those recent cases that may be studied, and therefore without doubt in the older cases, is that the subject of congenital sexual inversion is attracted to the study of Greek antiquity because he finds there the explanation and the apotheosis of his own obscure impulses. Undoubtedly that study tends to develop these impulses.

In English history we find many traces of homosexual practices. In Norman times it seems to have flourished, as it always has wherever the Normans have gone. William Rufus was undoubtedly inverted. Edward II and James I were certainly abnormally attracted to their own sex.[6] Marlowe, whose most powerful drama, *Edward II*, is devoted to a picture of the relations between that king and his minions, is himself suspected of homosexuality. An ignorant informer brought certain charges of freethought and criminality against him, and further accused him of asserting that they are fools who love not boys. These charges have doubtless been colored by the vulgar channel through which they passed, but it seems absolutely impossible to regard them as the inventions of a mere gallows-bird such as this informer was.[7] Moreover, Marlowe's poetic work, while it shows him by no means insensitive to the beauty of women, also reveals a special and peculiar sensitiveness to masculine beauty. Marlowe clearly had a reckless delight in all things unlawful, and it seems probable that he possessed the psychosexual hermaphrodite's temperament. Shakespeare has also been discussed from this point of view. All that can be said, however, is that he addressed a long series of sonnets to a youthful male friend. These sonnets are written in lover's language of a very tender and noble order. They do not appear to imply any relationship that the writer regarded as shameful or that would be so regarded by the world. Moreover, they seem to represent but a single episode in the life of a very sensitive, many-sided nature.[8] There is no other evidence in Shakespeare's work of homosexual instinct such as we may trace throughout Marlowe's, while there is abundant evidence of a constant preoccupation with women. It is remarkable that, while Shakespeare thus narrowly escapes inclusion in the list of inverts, his great contemporary, Lord Bacon, according to Aubrey's statement in *Short Lives*, was a pederast.

A minor Elizabethan lyrical poet, whose work has had the honor of being confused with Shakespeare's, Richard Barnfield, appears to have possessed the temperament, at least, of the invert. His poems to male friends are of so impassioned a character that they aroused the protests of a very tolerant age. Very little is known of Barnfield's life; he was a country gentleman of means, who retired to his estate in Shropshire and apparently died unmarried. At a somewhat earlier period an eminent humanist and notable pioneer in dramatic literature, Nicholas Udall, to whom is attributed *Ralph Roister Doister*, the first English comedy, stands out as unquestionably addicted to homosexual tastes, although he has left no literary evidence of this tendency. He was an early adherent of the Protestant movement, and when head-master of Eton he was noted for his love of inflicting corporal punishment on the boys. Tusser says he once received from Udall fifty-three stripes for "fault but small or none at all." Here there was evidently a sexual sadistic impulse, for in 1541 (the year of *Ralph Roister Doister*) Udall was charged with unnatural crime, and confessed his guilt before the Privy Council. He was dismissed from the head-mastership and imprisoned, but only for a short time, "and his reputation," his modern biographer states, "was not permanently injured." He retained the vicarage of Braintree, and was much favored by Edward VI, who nominated him to a prebend of Windsor. Queen Mary was also favorable and he became head-master of Westminster School.[9] In more recent times Byron has frequently been referred to as experiencing homosexual affections, and I have been informed that some of his poems nominally addressed to women were really inspired by men. It is certain that he experienced very strong emotions toward his male friends. "My school-friendships," he wrote, "were with me passions." When he afterward met one of these friends, Lord Clare, in Italy, he was painfully agitated, and could never hear the name without a beating of the heart. At the age of 22 he formed one of his strong attachments for a youth to whom he left £7000 in his will. It is probable, however, that here, as well as in the case of Shakespeare, and in that of Tennyson's love for his youthful friend Arthur Hallam, although such strong friendships may involve an element of sexual emotion, we have no true and definite homosexual impulse; homosexuality is merely simulated by the ardent and hyperesthetic emotions of the poet. The same quality of the poet's emotional temperament may doubtless, also, be invoked in the case of Goethe, who is said to have written elegies which, on account of their homosexual character, still remain unpublished.

A great personality of our own time, who has been widely regarded with reverence as the prophet-poet of Democracy[10]—Walt Whitman—has aroused discussion by his sympathetic attitude toward passionate friendship, or "manly love" as he calls it, in *Leaves of Grass*. In this book—in "Calamus," "Drumtaps," and elsewhere—Whitman celebrates a friendship in which physical contact and a kind of silent voluptuous emotion are essential elements. In order to settle the question as to the precise significance of "Calamus," J. A. Symonds wrote to Whitman, frankly posing the question. The answer (written from Camden, N. J., on August 19, 1890) is the only statement of Whitman's attitude toward homosexuality, and it is therefore desirable that it should be set on record:—

> "About the questions on 'Calamus,' etc., they quite daze me. *Leaves of Grass* is only to be rightly construed by and within its own atmosphere and essential character—all its pages and pieces so coming strictly under. That the 'Calamus' part has ever allowed the possibility of such construction as mentioned is terrible. I am fain to hope that the pages themselves are not to be even mentioned for such gratuitous and quite at the time undreamed and unwished possibility of morbid inferences—which are disavowed by me and seem damnable."

It seems from this that Whitman had never realized that there is any relationship whatever between the passionate emotion of physical contact from man to man, as he had experienced it and sung it, and the act which with other people he would regard as a crime against nature. This may be singular, for there are many inverted persons who have found satisfaction in friendships less physical and passionate than those described in *Leaves of Grass*, but Whitman was a man of concrete, emotional, instinctive temperament, lacking in analytical power, receptive to all influences, and careless of harmonizing them.[11] He would most certainly have refused to admit that he was the subject of inverted sexuality. It remains true, however, that "manly love" occupies in his work a predominance which it would scarcely hold in the feelings of the "average man," whom Whitman wishes to honor. A normally constituted person, having assumed the very frank attitude taken up by Whitman, would be impelled to devote far more space and far more ardor to the subject of sexual relationships with women and all that is involved in maternity than is accorded to them in *Leaves of Grass*. Some of Whitman's extant letters to young men, though they do not throw definite light on this question, are of a very affectionate character,[12] and, although a man of remarkable physical vigor, he never felt inclined to marry.[13] It remains somewhat difficult to classify him from the sexual point of view, but we can scarcely fail to recognize the presence of a homosexual tendency, or tendency to psychosexual hermaphroditism, however latent and unconscious.

Concerning another great writer whose name may be mentioned without impropriety— Paul Verlaine, the first of modern French poets—it is possible to speak with less hesitation. A man who possessed in fullest measure the irresponsible impressionability of genius, Verlaine—as his work shows and as he himself admitted—all his life oscillated between normal and homosexual love, at one period attracted to women, at another to men. He was without doubt a psychosexual hermaphrodite. An early connection with another young poet, Arthur Rimbaud, terminated in a violent quarrel with his friend, and led to Verlaine's imprisonment at Mons. In after-years he gave expression to the exalted passion of this relationship—*mon grand péché radieux*—in *Lœti et Errabundi*, published in the volume entitled *Parallèlement*; and in later poems he has told of less passionate and less sensual relationships which were yet more than friendship, for instance, in the poem *"Mon ami, ma plus belle amitié, ma meilleure,"* in *Bonheur.* I may quote, as of some psychological interest, a few stanzas from Ces Passions, in Parallèlement:—

> Ces passions qu'eux seuls nomment encore amours
> Sont des amours aussi, tendres et furieuses,
> Avec des particularités curieuses
> Que n'ont pas les amours certes de tous les jours.

Même plus qu'elles et mieux qu'elles héroïques,
  Elles se parent de splendeurs d'âme et de sang
  Telles qu'au prix d'elles les amours dans le rang
  Ne sont que Ris et Jeux ou bésoins érotiques,

Que vains proverbs, que riens d'enfants trop gâtés.
  "Ah! les pauvres amours banales, animales,
  Normales! Gros goûts lourds ou frugales fringales
  Sans compter la sottise et des fécondités!"

In this brief glance at some of the ethnographical, historical, and literary aspects of homosexual passion there is one other phenomenon which must be mentioned. This is the curious fact that, while this phenomenon exists to some extent everywhere, we seem to find a special proclivity to homosexuality (whether or not involving a greater frequency of congenital inversion is not usually clear) among certain races and in certain regions.[14] In Europe it is probably best illustrated by the case of southern Italy, which in this respect is totally distinct from northern Italy, although Italians generally are franker than men of northern race in admitting their sexual practices. How far the homosexuality of southern Italy may be due to Greek influence and Greek blood it is not at present easy to say.

It must be remembered that, in dealing with a northern country, like England, homosexual phenomena do not present themselves in the same way as they do in southern Italy to-day, or in ancient Greece. In Greece the homosexual impulse was recognized and idealized; a man could be an open homosexual lover, and yet, like Epaminondas, be a great and honored citizen of his country. There was no reason whatever why a man who in mental and physical constitution was perfectly normal should not adopt a custom that was regarded as respectable, and sometimes as even specially honorable. But it is quite otherwise today in a country like England or the United States.[15] In these countries all our traditions and all our moral ideals, as well as the law, are energetically opposed to every manifestation of homosexual passion. It requires a very strong impetus to go against this compact social force which, on every side, constrains the individual into the paths of heterosexual love. That impetus, in a well-bred individual who leads the normal life of his fellow-men and who feels the ordinary degree of respect for the social feeling surrounding him, can only be supplied by a fundamental—usually, it is probable, inborn—perversion of the sexual instinct, rendering the individual organically abnormal. It is with this fundamental abnormality, usually called sexual inversion, that we shall here be concerned. There is no evidence to show that homosexuality in Greece was a congenital perversion, although it appears that Cœlius Aurelianus affirms that in the opinion of Parmenides it was hereditary. Aristotle also, in his fragment on physical love, though treating the whole matter with indulgence, seems to have distinguished abnormal congenital homosexuality from acquired homosexual vice. Doubtless in a certain proportion of cases the impulse was organic, and it may well be that there was an organic and racial predisposition to homosexuality among the Greeks, or, at all events, the Dorians. But the state of social feeling, however it originated, induced a large proportion of the ordinary population to adopt homosexuality as a fashion. So that any given number of homosexual persons among the Greeks would have presented a far smaller proportion of constitutionally abnormal individuals than a like number in England. In a similar manner—though I do not regard the analogy as complete—infanticide or the exposition of children was practiced in some of the early Greek States by parents who were completely healthy and normal; in England a married woman who destroys her child is in nearly every case demonstrably diseased or abnormal. For this reason I am unable to see that homosexuality in ancient Greece—while of great interest as a social and psychological problem—throws light on sexual inversion as we know it in England or the United States.

Notes

1 "Italian literature," remarks Symonds, "can show the *Rime Burlesche,* Beccadelli's *Hermaphroditus,* the *Canti Carnascialeschi,* the Macaronic poems of Fidentius, and the remarkably outspoken romance entitled *Alcibiade Fanciulle a Scola.*"

2 See Parlagreco, *Michelangelo Buonarotti,* Naples, 1888; Ludwig von Scheffler, *Michelangelo, Ein Renaissance Studie.* 1882; *Archivo di Psichiatria,* vol. xv, fasc. i, ii, p. 129; J. A. Symonds, *Life of Michelangelo,* 1893; Dr. Jur. Numa Praetorius, "Michel Angelo's Urningtum," *Jahrbuch fur sexuelle Zwischenstufen,* B. 2, 1899, pp. 254–267.

3 J. A. Symonds, *Life of Michelangelo,* vol. ii, p. 384.

4 See the interesting account of Duquesnoy by Eckhoud (*Jahrbuch für sexuelle Zwischenstufen,* B. 2, 1899), an eminent Belgian novelist who has himself lately been subjected to prosecution on account of the pictures of homosexuality in his novels and stories, *Escal-Vigor* and *Le Cycle Patibulaire.*

5 See Justi's *Life of Winkelmann,* and also Moll's *Die Konträre Sexualempfindung,* third edition, 1899, pp. 122–126. In this work, as well as in Raffalovich's *Uranisms et Unisexualité,* there will be found some account of many eminent men who are, on more or less reliable grounds, suspected of homosexuality. Other German writers brought forward as inverted by Moll and Raffalovich are Platen, K. P. Moritz, and Iffland. Platen was clearly a congenital invert, who sought, however, the satisfaction of his impulses in Platonic friendship; his homosexual poems and the recently-published unabridged edition of his diary render him an interesting object of study; see for a sympathetic account of him, Ludwig Frey, "Aus dem Seelenleben des Grafen Platen," *Jahrbuch für sexuelle Zwischenstufen,* B. 1, 1898, pp. 159–214. Raffalovich also traces homosexual episodes in the lives of Goethe, Molière, Montaigne, Alfieri, Casanova, etc. These writers also refer in the same connection to various kings and potentates, including the Sultan Baber; Henri III of France; Edward II, William II, James I, and William III of England, and perhaps Queen Anne and George III, Frederick the Great and his brother Heinrich, Popes Paul II, Sixtus IV, and Julius II, Ludwig II of Bavaria, and others. Kings seem peculiarly inclined to homosexuality. In this connection we may remember that, as Jacoby and many others have shown, monarchical families are much subject to degeneration.

6 Raffalovich very properly calls attention to the extraordinary manner in which the biographer of James I, in the *Dictionary of National Biography,* has been allowed to suppress the evidence for that monarch's homosexual practices, and to treat him as a model of personal purity in the most conventional sense.

7 See appendix to my edition of Marlowe in the Mermaid Series, first edition. For a study of Marlowe's "Gaveston," regarded as "the hermaphrodite in soul," see J. A. Nicklin, *Free Review,* December, 1895.

8 As Raffalovich acutely points out, the twentieth sonnet, with its reference to the "one thing to my purpose nothing," is alone enough to show that Shakespeare was not a genuine invert, as then he would have found the virility of the loved object beautiful.

9 These particulars are taken from the article on Udall in the *Dictionary of National Biography.*

10 It is as such that Whitman should be approached, and I would desire to protest against the tendency, now marked in many quarters, to treat him merely as an invert, and to vilify him or glorify him accordingly. However important inversion may be as a psychological key to Whitman's personality, it plays but a small part in Whitman's work, and for many who care for that work a negligible part.

11 I should add that some friends and admirers of Whitman are not prepared to accept the evidence of this letter. I am indebted to "Q." for the following statement of the objections:—
"I think myself that it is a mistake to give much weight to this letter—perhaps a mistake to introduce it at all, since if introduced it will, of course, carry weight. And this for three or four reasons:—
    "1. That it is difficult to reconcile the letter itself (with its strong tone of disapprobation) with the general 'atmosphere' of *Leaves of Grass,* the tenor of which is to leave everything open and free.

"2. That the letter is in hopeless conflict with the 'Calamus' section of poems. For, whatever moral lines Whitman may have drawn at the time of writing these poems, it seems to me quite incredible that the possibility of certain inferences, morbid or other, was undreamed of.

"3. That the letter was written only a few months before his last illness and death, and is the only expression of the kind that he appears to have given utterance to.

"4. That Symonds's letter, to which this was a reply, is not forthcoming; and we consequently do not know what rash expressions it may have contained—leading Whitman (with his extreme caution) to hedge his name from possible use to justify dubious practices."

I may add that I endeavored to obtain Symonds's letter, but he was unable to produce it, nor has any copy of it been found among his papers.

It should be said that Whitman's attitude toward Symonds was marked by high regard and admiration. "A wonderful man is Addington Symonds," he remarked shortly before his own death; "some ways the most indicative and penetrating and significant man of our time. Symonds is a curious fellow; I love him dearly. He is of college breed and education, horribly literary and suspicious, and enjoys things. A great fellow for delving into persons and into the concrete, and even into the physiological and the gastric, and wonderfully cute." But on this occasion he delved in vain.

12 Whitman's letters to Peter Doyle, an uncultured young workman, deeply loved by the poet, have been edited by Dr. Bucke, and published at Boston.

13 It appears, however, that he acknowledged having had several children.

14 Sir Richard Burton, who devoted special attention to this point, regarded the phenomenon as "geographical and climatic, not racial." His conclusions may thus be stated in his own words:—

"1. There exists what I shall call a 'Sotadic Zone,' bounded westward by the northern shores of the Mediterranean (N. lat., 43°) and by the southern (N. lat., 30°). Thus, the depth would be 780 to 800 miles, including meridional France, the Iberian peninsula, Italy and Greece, with the coast-regions of Africa from Morocco to Egypt.

"2. Running eastward the Sotadic Zone narrows, embracing Asia Minor, Mesopotamia, Chaldea, Afghanistan, Sind, the Punjaub, and Kashmir.

"3. In Indo-China the belt begins to broaden, infolding China, Japan, and Turkestan.

"4. It then embraces the South-Sea Islands and the New World, where at the time of its discovery, Sotadic love was, with some exceptions, an established racial institution.

5. Within the Sotadic Zone the vice is popular and endemic, held at the worst to be a mere peccadillo, while the races to the north and south of the limits here defined practice it only sporadically, amid the opprobrium of their fellows, who, as a rule, are physically incapable of performing the operation, and look upon it with the liveliest disgust." He adds: "The only physical cause for the practice which suggests itself to me, and that must be owned to be purely conjectural, is that within the Sotadic Zone there is a blending of the masculine and feminine temperaments, a crasis which elsewhere only occurs sporadically" (*Arabian Nights*, 1885, vol. x, pp. 205–254). The theory of the Sotadic Zone is interesting; but, as a critic has pointed out, it does not account for the custom among the Normans, Celts, Scythians, Bulgars, and Tartars, and, moreover, in various of these regions different views have prevailed at different periods. Burton was wholly unacquainted with the recent psychological investigations into sexual inversion.

15 It is true that in the solitude of great modern cities it is possible for small homosexual coteries to form, in a certain sense, an environment of their own, favorable to their abnormality; yet this fact hardly modifies the general statement made in the text.

39 Wilde's Fatal Effeminacy (1995)

Joseph Bristow

On 20 February 1892, after the curtain had dropped on the final act of *Lady Windermere's Fan,* Wilde presented himself before his audience to make some characteristically witty remarks on what had been a highly successful opening night:

> Ladies and gentlemen: I have injoyed [*sic*] this evening *immensely*. The actors have given a charming rendering of a *delightful* play, and your appreciation has been *most* intelligent. I congratulate you on the *great* success of your performance, which persuades me that you think *almost* as highly of the play as I do myself.[1]

According to the painter, Louise Jopling, the comedy was indeed 'gorgeously put on stage, and splendidly acted'.[2] More memorable still was the pose that Wilde struck when addressing his enthusiastic playgoers. He delivered his short and amusingly condescending speech while smoking a cigarette. Jopling observes that, at the time, Wilde's 'smoking of the cigarette was put down to a deliberate insult', although she herself attributes Wilde's behaviour to 'sheer nervousness''. Smoking in such a public manner, to be sure, caused several influential members of the audience considerable offence. The arch–conservative critic, Clement Scott, in a review published in the *Illustrated London News,* regarded Wilde's gesture as a complete affront to good manners. Imagining Wilde turning over in his mind how he might test the limits of propriety, Scott puts these arrogant words into the playwright's mouth: 'The society that allows boys to puff cigarette–smoke into the faces of ladies in theatre–corridors will condone the originality of a smoking author on the stage.'[3]

An increasingly fashionable item, the cigarette by the 1890s was superseding the hand–rolled cigar and the working–class clay pipe. In *Dorian Gray,* it features as a sure sign of aesthetic indulgence. Informing the painter, Basil Hallward, that he must not light a cigar, Lord Henry Wotton insists that he should smoke a cigarette. 'A cigarette', remarks Lord Henry, 'is a perfect pleasure. It is exquisite and leaves one unsatisfied' (p.70). No sooner has Lord Henry spoken these words than he assures Dorian Gray of the hedonism represented by the cigarette–smoking man. 'I represent to you', he says, 'all the sins you have never had the courage to commit' (p.70). Set alongside Scott's indignation at Wilde's public behaviour, Lord Henry's remarks suggest that these recently machine–rolled items were the focus of an unsettling shared interest in unrespectability among those who belonged to different classes. On his opening night, Wilde appears to be adopting the vulgar discourtesies of young men who engaged in rituals of resistance against those who wanted them kept at a safe distance. And it is doubtless the case that the hostility Wilde aroused on this occasion related to wider anxieties about the social and moral standards set by the theatre as a whole. As John Stokes has shown, the music–halls had gained greatest notoriety in the mid–1890s for allowing an undesirable traffic between respectable and unrespectable types, and it was in places such as the Empire in Leicester Square that people of a great diversity of social classes could mix.[4] In *Earnest,* Jack and Algernon promise to indulge their life of unnamed pleasures by considering a ten o'clock visit to the Empire (p.337). So intolerable was the situation at these kinds of theatre that purity campaigners such as Mrs Ormiston Chant petitioned for their closure. In Scott's eyes, Wilde's flagrant lack of decorum no doubt suggested that the middle–class St James's Theatre might be heading in the same direction. Blowing smoke in the public's face simply served to compound Scott's distaste for what had been a despicable drama, one that displayed a wholly contemptuous attitude towards 'that holiest and purest instinct with women': motherhood. Not only had Wilde presented himself before the public as no man of his class should have done, he had also produced a comedy in which it was acceptable for a young wife to desert her newly–born child and rush into the arms of a *'roué* admirer' because 'she has learned from the tittle–tattle of her friends that her husband has been false to her'. No doubt Lady Windermere struck him as repugnant as Nora in *A Doll's House* by Henrik Ibsen. In his review of the English production in 1889, Scott condemned Nora for 'doing a thing that one of the lower animals would not do'.[5]

A month after *Lady Windermere's Fan* had opened, *Punch* took the opportunity to lampoon Wilde's outrageous act of smoking in the public's face. Representing him in a manner similar to that of Jellaby Postlethwaite – the so–called 'Professor of Aesthetics' created by George du Maurier in the 1880s – the playwright in this 'Fancy Portrait' by Bernard Partridge is depicted in a languid pose, leaning against a pillar. At his feet lies a toppled statue of the Bard, set next to an open box of cigarettes. Rising above the author's head are three 'puffs' of smoke, each one making a neat pun that satirizes Wilde's reputation for arousing the unwarranted enthusiasm of his audience – here pictured as nothing more than the puppets, as Wilde had called them in the letter he published in the *Daily Telegraph.* This remark would prompt Charles Brookfield and J.M. Glover to stage a satire of Wilde entitled *The Poet and the Puppets* (1892). In Partridge's picture, underneath a caption imitating Wilde's camp style with the words 'Quite Too–Too Puffickly Precious', there is a short extract from a review in the *Daily Telegraph* drawing attention to the way in which 'his daintily–gloved fingers' held 'a still burning and half–smoked cigarette'. Like those illustrations by du Maurier that chide the arrogance of aesthetes such as Wilde, this 'Fancy Portrait' attacks the arrogance of a self-styled demi–god who exhibits a dandiacal narcissism that shows complete contempt for anyone but himself. Here he is indisputably the ego–maniac later to be despised by Nordau.

But if Wilde was incensing some sections of the theatrical establishment with his elegantly mocking pose of superiority, he won in equal proportions a great many admirers. A.B. Walkley, one of the most enlightened late Victorian drama critics, was only too aware that *Lady Windermere's Fan* drew many of its incidents from 'half a dozen familiar French plays'. He observed that 'its plot is always thin, often stale; indeed, it is full of faults'. Yet, in spite of his reservations, Walkley claimed that what distinguished Wilde's play from its contemporaries was its 'sparkling dialogue'.[6] This quality alone drew the crowds, breaking with the rather predictable exchanges that take the equally popular plays of Arthur Wing Pinero and Henry Arthur Jones to melodramatic fever pitch. Even if this comedy is not particularly 'good', argues Walkley, it is at least 'diverting'.

Three years later, Ada Leverson attended the premiere of *Earnest* on 14 February 1895. In her memoirs, Leverson recalls the air of anticipation among a 'rippling, glittering, chattering crowd'. Even if the play were to have unexpectedly failed to amuse them, she says, the audience could rest assured that the author was bound to make his mark during the evening's entertainment. 'Would he', Leverson remembers them asking, 'perhaps walk on after the play smoking a cigarette, with a green carnation blooming in his coat' or 'would he bow from a box and state in clear tones, heard all over the theatre, that Mr Wilde was not in the house?'[7] By this time Wilde was not just an author but also an integral part of the performance. Indeed, his whole reputation dating from the late 1870s, when he entered fashionable society as the chief protagonist of the 'Aesthetic Movement', was based on the idea of the male critic as an artist in his own right. This doctrine would come into its own in 'The Critic as Artist' where Gilbert insists that 'the highest Criticism, being the purest form of personal impression, is in its way more creative than creation' (p. 1027). When Wilde's comedies were staged in the early 1890s, he accomplished yet another categorical shift, making the dramatist into a performer. Endlessly promoting his spectacular personality, Wilde brought about a signal change in the relations between the artist and his audience. No longer was the artist the producer of culture, he was now an embodiment of it. In other words, he became the artwork while art itself, like the writings of the Bard, toppled over at his feet.

Wilde's calculated self–exhibition, however, had a much wider aim than simply drawing attention to his superiority to those he entertained. He was, as Scott observes, involved in gaining the admiration of a society whose values he never ceased to mock, often at the expense of his observers. Nothing was more to the point in this respect than the buttonhole Wilde wore while smoking in front of his audience in 1892. Although Scott was infuriated by the cigarette, he makes no mention of the green carnation, which a number of Wilde's associates sported on their lapels on the opening night. This is not so unexpected given that this unnaturally coloured bloom was, so the legend goes, the secret symbol of Parisian homosexuals.[8] Most spectators probably viewed this flower as yet another 'aesthetic' eccentricity, since Wilde had worn lilies and sunflowers ostentatiously when dressing up for the fashionable circles he moved in during the 1880s. Lillie Langtry, the famous actress, remembers Wilde's appearance at the opening night of one of his plays (she does not specify which one); he was 'wearing a black velvet jacket, a white straw hat in one hand and a lighted cigarette in me other'.[9] There are several similar accounts of Wilde's couture. Although it is common for critics to claim that Wilde's dress sense transformed from the unconventional exhibitionism of his early career to gentlemanly sobriety when his work reached the height of its popularity, descriptions such as Langtry's show that, right up until the time of the trials in 1895, Wilde did not present himself on important occasions in clothes that would allow him to pass as an ordinary man. Even when he had been embraced by the establishment, he remained a poser – true to the Delsartean tradition on which, according to Moe Meyer, he modeled his public persona.[10]

Ada Leverson, recalling Wilde's appearance at the close of *Lady Windermere's Fan*, states that 'he was dressed with elaborate dandyism and a sort of florid sobriety'. Like Langtry, she itemizes his garments, but draws attention to different details:

> His coat had a black velvet collar. He held white gloves in his small pointed hands. On one finger he wore a large scarab ring. A green carnation – echo in colour of the ring – bloomed savagely in his buttonhole, and a large bunch of seals on a black moiré ribbon watch chain hung from his white waistcoat. This costume, which on another man might have appeared perilously like fancy dress, seemed perfectly to suit him; he seemed at ease and to have a great look of the first gentleman in Europe.[11]

If Leverson's judgement that Wilde appeared like 'the first gentleman of Europe' is anything to go by (this was, in fact, the sobriquet given to the Prince Regent in the 1810s), then it would appear that Wilde's distinctive style involved taking a given form (such as comedy) and a given style (that of the gentleman) and renovating them. His ability to make exceptionally familiar things seem new depends on an aesthetics that is unavoidably vicarious. Sedgwick identifies this 'vicariating' impulse as a part of a sentimentalizing of the male body that underpins Wilde's homoerotic project.[12] This is a useful formulation for comprehending Wilde's late Victorian adaptation of a dandiacal style both in person and in writing. His work, argues Sedgwick, engages with a campness and an archness that ridicule the moral codes of respectable Victorian masculinity. These obviously theatricalizing aspects of Wilde's life and *oeuvre* served to question the founding categories in which the late bourgeois sphere understood the organization of gender. Appearing before his public, with all the appurtenances of the modern dandy, Wilde drove at the heart of the multiple denials and disavowals upon which respectable society was built. If too excessively dressed to be a gentleman, he none the less had the ingenuity to look like the only one in the house, reminding everybody else of their ordinariness.

Yet, as the outrage that always attended Wilde's career makes perfectly clear – most vividly, of course, in the trials of 1895 – his position as a mocking dandy was a hazardous one to maintain. In making himself so original, Wilde worked in perilous proximity to those conformists who so brutally accomplished his downfall. For not only did Wilde deride respectable society, he also needed its support to underwrite his success. In many respects, his performances in person and in print bear all the hallmarks of the endangered parodist, since parody was, by and large, Wilde's intellectual mode. Through a suave and incisive manipulation of proverbial sayings, he turned innumerable platitudes on their heads to lay bare the spurious assumptions upon which accepted moral wisdom was based. The most striking lines from his fiction, essays, and plays all adopt this parodic attitude. 'Only the shallow know themselves' and 'Industry is the root of all ugliness' are two of the more obvious 'Phrases and Philosophies for the Use of the Young' that exemplify a technique in rhetorical legerdemain that repeats throughout his *oeuvre*.

Nothing could bear out his distinctive dandiacal style more than his closing remarks to his audience in 1892 where he turns back their flattery upon themselves: 'I congratulate you on the *great* success of your performance.' Reversing roles, Wilde takes himself the customary voice of his appreciative theatregoers, making them realize that they too are also performers, ones who rarely see how they are acting out already scripted parts. 'Being natural', as we are told in *Dorian Gray,* 'is simply a pose' (p.20). Yet the denaturalizing poses that Wilde struck as an unrivalled parodist proved to be far less durable than one might be led to believe, particularly by those critics who view Wilde as a precursor of postmodern thought. When his pithy maxims, which brilliantly derided middle–class pieties, were set before him in the Old Bailey as evidence of his immorality, his ability to sustain his parodic style suffered immeasurable strain. A substantial difficulty for Wilde was that the pose he developed in the early 1880s was altogether too closely defined against the middle–class respectability he wished to flout. As Eagleton has said, he left a deep impression on his privileged public because it was making fun of what was only too familiar to them. His critique, in other words, was bound into – if not presupposed by – the very terms it wished to attack.

Let me explain this point more fully by taking issue with one of the most powerful analyses of Wilde's key rhetorical manoeuvre. In his wide–ranging study of sexual dissidence, Dollimore argues that Wilde's aesthetics and politics engage in a radical revision of received orthodoxies, and he implies that this process of inversion may be related to the sexual inversion classified by sexologists, such as Havelock Ellis and Richard von Krafft Ebing. Inversion provides an account of how femininity defines the psyche, if not physiology, of an anatomically male body, and how, by comparison, masculinity shapes the psychological contours of a body identified as female. In his account of Wilde's 'transgressive aesthetic', Dollimore warns that 'inversion is only a stage in a process of resistance whose effects can never be guaranteed and perhaps not even predicted'.[13] But, in seeking to align rhetorical strategy with sexual taxonomy, this series of suggestions about '(in)subordinate inversion' compounds some of the main protocols of post–structuralist thought, ones which have been immensely enabling in undoing binary oppositions, with an idea about homosexual desire that does not necessarily apply to Wilde. Rather, it is an elegant form of parody that operates within the very institutions that he so punishingly critiques. And the force of Wilde's parody is not as Dollimore might be indicating, one in which the world, in terms of the carnivalesque, is readily turned upside down.

But that is not to say that postmodern paradigms are irrelevant to Wilde's aesthetic practice. Recent theorizations of the parodic have a useful bearing on those aspects of his work that mock those cherished middle–class values which – as Dollimore himself shows – privilege depth over surface, and make specious claims on authenticity. In her powerful study of theories of sex, gender, and sexuality, Judith Butler stakes a large claim on the political advantages that may be won through strategic forms of parody. Although Butler recognizes that parody may on many occasions be the result of despair and hopelessness, she generally takes an optimistic view of its trans–formational possibilities. Butler points out how highly self–conscious gender performances such as gay male drag may disclose how the apparent 'original' is just as much a construction as the parodic 'copy' upon which it is modeled. 'The performance of drag', writes Butler, 'plays upon the distinction between the anatomy of the performer and the gender that is [help] being performed. It follows that the 'notion of parody' that Butler defends 'does not assume that there is an original which such parodic identities imitate'.[14] Parody may, in Butler's terms, serve to undermine the naturalizing assumptions that so often support our ideas of what constitutes a correct sex, gender, or sexual preference. But, as a number of commentators have remarked. Butler's argument that gender is a performance – something which comprises a set of props including dress, tone of voice, and styles of bodily comportment – lacks a social theory that would adequately explain the power differentials that necessarily obtain when men and women act out their genders.[15] Without an account of power in its structural, discursive, and institutional forms, this idea of 'gender performance' suggests that one could, as if by an act of will, change one's gender.

This objection has hardly escaped Butler's attention. She recognizes how gay male drag has often served to reinforce the very forms of misogyny that are often displaced on to male homosexuality. Experimentation with gender performance, then, necessarily operates within a field of constraints and opportunities. Wilde's career surely testifies to the intractable problems in finding a political space in which one might successfully mount a cultural critique through parody not least when it comes to devising visual and verbal forms where male same–sex desire could, at some intelligible level, be expressed. So let us be clear about one point. In Wilde's career homosexuality remains, not in the field of sexological inversion and theories of the 'third sex', but within the realm of the simulacrum, the feigned, and the forgery. Once we recognize how much of Wilde's work depends on ideas and acts of theft, it is possible to see how the criminality of same–sex desire is all the more outrageous because it could prove to be attractive to the very society that created 'monstrous laws' to ban it in public and in private. It should not surprise us, then, that the imperative to police male homosexuality intensified so alarmingly at this time because this type of desire threatened to expose the naturalized – that is, not natural – structure of respectable relations between the sexes. In asserting, much in the manner of Charles Baudelaire, that 'Dandyism is the assertion of the absolute modernity of Beauty' (p.1204), Wilde was partly trying to fashion homosexual desire in a guise that could be passed off as something else – the bachelor, the artist, the poser, the forger.

But, as *Earnest* shows, his dandies and their associates are rarely in contract of their destinies, and only in one work do they emerge as men with discernibly homoerotic interests. Early on in *Dorian Gray,* the painter Basil Hallward states regretfully that 'there is a fatality about all physical and intellectual distinction' (p.19). This is 'the sort of fatality', he adds, 'that seems to dog through history the faltering steps of kings' (p.19). The premonitory force of these words leads not only to his own death but also to the high gothic tragedy of the beautiful Dorian Gray whose portrait Hallward had so faithfully painted. Between these two men stands the arch figure of the dandy, Lord Henry Wotton, whose hedonistic philosophy casts a baleful influence upon them both. Lord Henry is the knowledgeable wit who draws on a rhetorically persuasive hoard of well–turned phrases. Yet the more we see of Wotton, the clearer it becomes that his desires are closely attached to crime. But his praise of the 'Hellenic ideal' exists only in theory. Lord Henry, after all, does not practice what he preaches. He finds in Dorian Gray the material he needs to conduct a practical experiment, to see if the beautiful boy will become either 'a Titan or a toy' (p.41).

The dandy, then, hardly exists on the front line of transgression. His crimes remain the substance of theory rather than practice. Indeed, the force of his political insurgency is blunted because of his class position. Although the dandy's identity had passed through several transformations in Victorian England, he still occupied a special place in the upper echelons of Society. As Victorian writers on the first and most influential dandy have made clear, Beau Brummell's career during the Regency depended on entering the aristocratic order from below. In this period, then, the dandy was a figure of ascendancy. When fashioning Lord Henry as his chief spokesman for the pursuit of pleasure, Wilde was bearing Baudelaire's definition of the dandy in mind. In claiming that 'Dandyism appears above all in periods of transition, when democracy is not yet all–powerful' Baudelaire regards this figure as one who is making a bid for those aristocratic values that dispense with work and money. In some respects, the dandy could be seen as the last bastion of the *ancien régime* before the 'rising tide of democracy … invades and levels everything'. That is why an apocalyptic tone issues from this style of man. 'Dandyism', writes Baudelaire, 'is a sunset' – brilliant but inevitably fading.[16] He is all the more fading when we remember that Wilde's dandies are generally men who are not on the ascendant, gaining entry into the most exalted circles. They are, instead, men who were born into the landed classes, and yet who have the prerogative to mock the idleness of the rich.

No one has made this point more forcefully than Regenia Gagnier whose pathbreaking study of Wilde examines the complex dynamic of his interaction with the Victorian world of cultural consumption. Tracing the genealogy of Wilde's dandiacal affiliations, Gagnier claims that Baudelaire 'see the dandy as an auricular artwork' – an artwork that, in Walter Benjamin's terms, strives to defend itself in the face of mass society.[17] Undoubtedly, this ideal fed directly into Wilde's aesthetics. But so too did Baudelaire's fatalism. Everywhere Wilde's dandies are at once aristocratic in their bearing, and yet in jeopardy of losing their reputations. This is certainly the case with the Regency poisoner, Thomas Griffith Wainewright, the subject of 'pen, Pencil, and Poison'. Wainewright was, we are told, a 'young dandy', one who 'sought to be somebody, rather than do something' (p.995). Yet in making his mark, Wainewright was compelled to thrive upon crime. Not without coincidence, so too does Wilde violate the protocols of authorship by thieving substantial portions of his essay from unacknowledged sources. Bent on self–invention, Wainewright powerfully suggested to Wilde that there was a mode of life that could exist outside 'the vulgar test of production' (p.995). Flatly opposed to the utilitarian values that had come to regulate the Victorian middle classes, Wilde extended Matthew Arnold's view that culture should be promoted as the alternative means through which social relations may be improved. That is why Lord Illingworth, who flaunts his mocking phrases in *A Woman of No Importance* (1893), resolutely declares that 'the future belongs to the dandy'. 'It is the exquisites', he argues, 'who are going to rule' (p.459). But this confident speech is delivered to a young man who will soon discover that he is Lord Illingworth's illegitimate son. Worse still, the son will come to reject his newly–found father once the dandy's treachery in siring a bastard comes to light, for Lord Illingworth is finally humiliated by the woman whom he once cruelly betrayed. The triumph of this drama assuredly goes to the mother, Mrs Arbuthnot, who strikes Lord Illingworth across the face with his own glove before returning victorious to her son and his fiancée. And it is in the woman who shall become Mrs Arbuthnot's daughter–in–law that the dandy comes up against his greatest rival in terms of both moral and dramatic power.

Notes

1   E.H. Mikhail (ed.) *Oscar Wilde: Interviews and Recollections,* 2 vols (Basingstoke, Macmillan, 1979), II, p.398. The quotation is also recorded in Hesketh Pearson, *The Life of Oscar Wilde* (London, Methuen, 1946), p.224.

2   Louise Jopling, *Twenty Years of My Life* (London, John Lane, 1925), reprinted in Mikhail (ed.) I, p.205.

3   Clement Scott, review of *Lady Windermere's Fan, Illustrated London News,* 27 February 1892, p.278, reprinted in Beckson, p.125.

4   John Stokes, *In the Nineties* (Hemel Hempstead, Harvester–Wheatsheaf, 1989), pp.54–93.

5   Scott, 'A Doll's House', *Theatre,* 14 (1889), pp. 1.9–22, reprinted in Michael Egan (ed.) *Ibsen: The Critical Heritage* (London, Routledge and Kegan Paul, 1972), p.114.

6   A.B. Walkley, review of *Lady Windermere's Fan,* 27 February 1892, pp.257–8, reprinted in Beckson, pp. 119–20.

7   Ada Leverson, 'The Last First Night', *The New Criterion,* January 1926, pp. 148–53, reprinted in Mikhail, II, p, 268,

8   Like many pieces of received wisdom about the homosexual codings associated with Wilde's life and art, the specific status of the green carnation has not as yet been verified. Research on this topic is currently being conducted by Joel H. Kaplan and Sheila Stowell for their forthcoming performance history of Wilde's dramas.

9   Lillie Langtry, *The Days I Knew* (London, Hutchinson, 1925), reprinted in Mikhail, II, p.257.

10 Moe Meyer, 'Under the Sign of Wilde: An Archaeology of Posing', in Moe Meyer (ed.) *The Politics and Poetics of Camp* (London, Routledge, 1994), pp.75–109. Meyer notes that the influence of Francois Delsarte's stylized rhetoric of bodily gestures can be first felt in Wilde's writings in the review of Whistler's work, 'The Relation of Dress to Art', that appeared in 1886.

11 Ada Leverson, in Mikhail, II, p.270.

12 Eve Sedgwick, *Epistemology of the Closet* (Berkeley: University of California Press, 2008), p. 152.

13 Jonathan Dollimore, *Sexual Dissidence: Augustine to Wilde, Freud to Foucault* (Oxford: Clarendon Press, 1991), p.66.

14 Judith Butler, *Gender Trouble: Feminism and the Subversion of Identity* (New York, Routledge, 1990), pp.137, 138.

15 Ed Cohen, for one, observes how Butler's exploration of 'gender performance' suggests that 'subversive bodily acts', such as drag, could be viewed as 'voluntaristic': 'Who Are "We": Gay "Identity" as Political (E)motion (A Theoretical Rumination)', in Diana Fuss (ed.) *Inside/Out: Lesbian Theories, Gay Theories* (New York, Routledge, 1991), p.83. Butler herself defends many of the controversial claims about 'gender performance' made in *Gender Trouble* in a subsequent collection of essays: *Bodies That Matter: On the Discursive Limits of 'Sex'* (New York, Routledge, 1993).

16 Charles Baudelaire, 'The Painter of Modern Life', in *The Painter of Modern Life and Other Essays,* ed. and trans. Jonathan Mayne (New York, Da Capo, 1989), p.28, 29.

17 Regenia Gagnier, *Idylls of the Marketplace: Oscar Wilde and the Victorian Public* (Aldershot, Scolar Press, 1987), p.82.

Works cited

Gilbert, Sandra M. and Gubar, Susan (1987–1989) *No Man's Land: The Place of the Woman Writer in the Twentieth Century*, 2 vols. New Haven, CT: Yale University Press.

Wilde, Oscar (1966) *Complete Works*, J. B. Foreman, ed. London: Collins.

40 'Declining a Name', Introduction to *Victorian Sappho* (1999)

Yopie Prins

The Victorian legacy of Sappho

Victorian Sappho combines a literary historical thesis, a theoretical argument about lyric, and a series of questions in the field of feminist criticism and gender studies. I trace the emergence of Sappho as an exemplary lyric figure in Victorian England, when the Sapphic fragments circulated in an increasing number of scholarly editions, poetic translations, and other literary imitations. Sappho of Lesbos became a name with multiple significations in the course of the nineteenth century, as the reconstruction of ancient Greek fragments attributed to Sappho contributed to the construction of Sappho herself as the first woman poet, singing at the origin of a Western lyric tradition. This idealized feminine figure emerged at a critical turning point in the long and various history of Sappho's reception; what we now call "Sappho" is, in many ways, an artifact of Victorian poetics. Reading the fragments in Greek alongside various English versions, I show how the Victorian reception of Sappho influenced the gendering of lyric as a feminine genre, and I consider why Victorian poets—male and female, canonical and noncanonical, famous and forgotten—often turned to Sappho to define their lyric vocation. In this book I reconfigure the study of Victorian poetry through the figure of Sappho, and I ask more generally how a history and theory of lyric might be declined in Sappho's name.

The Victorian period is an important moment in Sappho's reception because of its particular fascination with the fragmentation of the Sapphic corpus. While Greek fragments attributed to Sappho were collected and translated from the Renaissance onward, the recovery of "new fragments" of Sappho in the course of the nineteenth century coincided with a Romantic aesthetic of fragmentation and the rise of Classical philology, culminating in the idealization of Sappho herself as the perfect fragment. Out of scattered texts, an idea of the original woman poet and the body of her song could be hypothesized in retrospect: an imaginary totalization, imagined in the present and projected into the past. Of course Sappho has always been a figment of the literary imagination. Invoked as a lyric muse in antiquity and mythologized for posterity by Ovid, Sappho entered into the tradition of English verse through the Ovidian myth of her suicide, and until the early nineteenth century she was primarily known by English imitations of her two most famous poems, the "Ode to Aphrodite" and "Ode to Anactoria" (now identified by modern scholars as fragments 1 and 31).[1] The interest in Sappho as an increasingly fragmentary text of many parts is a distinctly Victorian phenomenon, however, as we see in an influential popular edition compiled by Henry Thornton Wharton in 1885, entitled *Sappho: Memoir, Text, Selected Renderings, and a Literal Translation*. Implicit in these "renderings" is the rending of Sappho as well. Wharton's book simultaneously composes a portrait of the woman poet and presents her as a decomposing text; Sappho is exhumed and deciphered from the crypt of ancient Greek. The close relationship between nineteenth-century philology and Victorian poetics produces this reading of Sappho, whose texts are made to exemplify the formal mechanism through which a body, person, subjectivity, and voice can be imagined as prior to, yet also produced by, a history of fragmentation.

The projected fantasy of a female body and a feminine voice through linguistic scattering, grammatical dismemberment, rhetorical contradiction—as well as other forms of disjunction, hiatus, and ellipsis—suggests why Sappho became exemplary of lyric in its irreducibly textual embodiment, and exemplary of lyric reading as well, in its desire to hypothesize a living whole from dead letters.[2] It is a Victorian legacy that continues well into the twentieth century, as is evident in the aestheticized fragmentation of Sappho in early Modernism. In *The Pound Era,* for example, Hugh Kenner notes that the young Ezra Pound read Wharton's *Sappho* carefully, and discovered in those pages a "muse in tatters."[3] Pound's 1916 poem "Papyrus," inspired by a newly discovered Sapphic fragment, is a meditation on lyric desire that makes Sappho synonymous with the desire for lyric:

> Spring … … …
> Too long … …
> Gongula … …

While the fragment points to a moment beyond itself—some idea to make the poem complete—surely the point(s) of the ellipses would also be to make the fragment itself into an aesthetic ideal. It is a literary representation of a literally fragmented text, in which time is suspended and meaning deferred, prolonging ("too long") the desire for something lost. Thus Pound also introduced Hilda Doolittle to the literary world in 1913 as a Sapphic fragment, with her name abbreviated into the elliptical letters H.D., the embodiment of an "Imagist" aesthetic inspired by Sappho's Greek. "It all began with the Greek fragments," H.D. later wrote, reflecting on a career that began with her poetic imitations of a Sappho whose initial appeal was perhaps more Victorian than Modernist (1979: 41).

Not only does the nineteenth-century legacy of Sappho manifest itself in early-twentieth-century poetry, it also influences later generations of scholars, translators, and critics. Taking Wharton's earlier edition as a model, *The Songs of Sappho: Including the Recent Egyptian Discoveries* was published in 1925, annotated by David Moore Robinson and translated into English verse by Marion Mills Miller, as part of an ongoing reconstruction of the Sapphic fragments in England. This desire to reconstruct Sappho led to the definitive edition of *Poetarum Lesbiorum Fragmenta* in 1955 by Edgar Lobel and Denys Page, displacing German philology with the authority of British scholarship. Page also published a Sappho commentary including "The Contents and Character of Sappho's Poetry," a long essay written very much in the English tradition of Wharton: here too, the contents of Sappho's poetry depend on how the character of Sappho is construed (Page 1955).[4] The creation of Sappho in the character of the woman poet continued in Mary Barnard's popular translation, published a few years later and widely read for decades. In *Sappho: A New Translation* (1958) Barnard emphasizes the fragmentary image of Sappho, but by arranging her translations in sequence she also reimagines the life and times of Sappho in an implicitly chronological narrative, from youth to old age. Thus revived from fragments, Sappho seems to speak directly to modern readers; even today, Mary Barnard's Sappho is read as if it *is* the voice of Sappho, taught in the classroom either as representative of "women's voices" in antiquity or as representation of a timeless "feminine voice" in poetry.[5]

If the tendency to invoke Sappho as a female persona with an original lyric voice seems overdetermined to us now, it is because this reading of Sappho is inherited from the end of the previous century and repeated at the end of our own.[6] Indeed, with the publication of several recent books on Sappho, the proliferation of new translations, and the reclamation of a Sapphic tradition by contemporary women poets and feminist critics, it would seem that another Sappho revival is well underway.[7] In *Sappho's Immortal Daughters* (1995), for example, Margaret Williamson constructs a Sapphic voice from the poems she reads as Sappho's daughters, the creative offspring of a woman poet who lived and sang in a community of women on the island of Lesbos. Although Sappho is lost, her songs survive to create the idea "of a specifically female poetic inheritance" (16) according to Williamson. She identifies herself as "a feminist academic writing in the twentieth century" (x) but also aligns her work with the late-nineteenth-century "Sappho enthusiast, Henry Wharton," who pored over the same texts: both scholars contribute to the long history of Sappho scholarship, knowing that "the chain will continue; other generations will recreate Sappho in their own image" (ix-x). Yet in articulating the differences between herself and Wharton, Williamson demonstrates how closely linked they are in the chain. She seems to be making the very same Victorian link, in fact, as she writes, "I have had my own stake in straining to recover that earlier woman's voice" (x). Here again, the Sapphic fragments create a desire to identify with Sappho, to personify the woman poet and give voice to her.

The postmodern reading proposed by Page duBois in *Sappho Is Burning* (1995) can be understood as another version of this Victorian yearning. In her "Fragmentary Introduction," duBois insists on Sappho as fragment: "When I use the proper name 'Sappho' I mean only the voice in the fragments attributed to her, only the assembly of poems assigned to her name. She is not a person, not even a character in a drama or a fiction, but a set of texts gathered in her name" (3). Nevertheless the figure of voice continues to haunt this invocation of Sappho, as if the texts "gathered in her name" might be recollected as a disembodied voice if not a living body. Throughout her book, duBois celebrates the Sapphic corpus as a body-in-pieces, resisting the temptation to construct a whole, but still insisting on an idea of Sappho that persists as obscure object of desire, forever out of reach. "Sappho herself persists elusively always as an absent source ... an origin we can never know. Her texts, as we receive them, insist on the impossibility of recapturing the lost body" (28–29). In turning to Sappho "herself" as the name for that absent origin, and metaphorizing "her texts" as part of the lost body, duBois returns us to the rhetoric of dismembering and remembering Sappho: as in Wharton's *Sappho,* textual mediation is sublimated into an organic figure.

The seemingly inevitable personification of Sappho does not mean, however, that Williamson and duBois imagine the same Sapphic persona. What is most Victorian about the current Sappho revival is, in fact, the contradictory features of this feminine figure. The simultaneous publication of both books in 1995, each imagining Sappho differently, points to the contradictions that constitute the very idea of a Sapphic voice; whose desire does it articulate, and what kind of desire? In a book review comparing these contrary visions of Sappho as communal lyric poet and Sappho as postmodern lyric subject, Mary Loeffelholz poses the question most forcefully: "To judge from the Sapphos conjured up by Williamson's and duBois's readings, the value of Sappho for present-day feminism is her power to sponsor dramatically different accounts of female or feminist desire, its pasts and possible futures" (1996: 15). A vision of Sappho as lesbian also emerges in *Sappho and the Virgin Mary* by Ruth Vanita (1996) and *Lesbian Desire in the Lyrics of Sappho* (1997) by Jane Snyder. But in their conversion of Sappho of Lesbos into a lesbian Sappho, there are differences as well: while Vanita imagines Sappho as ancestor for a lesbian literary tradition in England, with the

Victorian period as an important turning point for defining lesbian identity, Snyder imagines the more diffuse expression of homoerotic desire in the woman-centered world of Sappho.

Thus Sappho is variously invoked to authorize a female poetic tradition, or to embody postmodern fragmentation, or to affirm lesbian identity, but what these readings have in common is a (re)turn to Sappho as an exemplary, engendering figure for the reading of lyric. In *Victorian Sappho* I make a contribution to current Sappho studies as well as a critical intervention, as I seek to historicize and theorize in further detail the logic of lyric reading that has produced this idea of Sappho. My version of literary history relates Classical antiquity to the present time, while developing a focus on the late Victorian period as a crux or turning point; it is a literary history crucially inflected by gender as well, although in the course of my argument I will be calling into question some of the assumptions of feminist literary history. Questions about feminism, gender, and sexuality are central to my argument not only because Sappho has become synonymous with the woman poet—and throughout this book I emphasize the causes and effects of making that synonym seem self-evident—but also because such questions enable us to reread the canon of Victorian poetry from a new perspective. Rereading Victorian poetry, as Isobel Armstrong argues, means revising literary history as well: "The task of a history of Victorian poetry is to restore the questions of politics, not least sexual politics, and the epistemology and language which belong to it" (1993: 7). By demonstrating how sexual politics determine the production of Victorian poetry as well as its reception, *Victorian Sappho* offers a revisionary history of Victorian poetry and places contemporary lyric theory within that history. It is therefore not my interest to refute any particular reading of Sappho, but rather to spell out the implications of writing in the name of Sappho, in the last century and at the end of our own.

Who wrongs Sappho?

What is Sappho except a name? "No day will ever dawn that does not speak the name of Sappho, the lyric poetess," proclaims one of the poets in the Palatine Anthology (Sappho Test. 28, Campbell 28–29).[8] Even if Sappho no longer speaks, her name will be spoken in the future, and indeed, in another epigram from the Anthology, Sappho herself is made to speak again by reclaiming her name from the past: "My name is Sappho, and I surpassed women in poetry as greatly as Homer surpassed men" (Sappho Test. 57, Campbell 46–47). Projected from the past into the future and from the future into the past, "Sappho" is presented to us now, in the present tense, as a name that lives on. Yet that name also raises questions, not unlike "The Homeric Question" that haunted nineteenth-century Classical philologists, obsessively disassembling and reassembling Greek texts in the name of a poet who never quite existed in the authorial form they imagined. Just as "Homer" names an epic tradition composed by many voices over time and recomposed in the long history of being written and read, "Sappho" is associated with a lyric tradition originating in oral performance and increasingly mediated by writing.[9] What we call Sappho was, perhaps, never a woman at all; not the poet we imagine on the island of Lesbos in the seventh century B.C., singing songs to her Sapphic circle, but a fictional persona circulating in archaic Greek lyric and reinvoked throughout antiquity as "the tenth muse." If Homer was the Poet, the Poetess was Sappho, a name repeated over the centuries as the proper name for lyric poetry itself, despite the scattering of the Sapphic fragments.

Sappho survives as exemplary lyric figure precisely because of that legacy of fragmentation; the more the fragments are dispersed, the more we recollect Sappho as their point of origin. "The passage of time has destroyed Sappho and her works, her lyre and songs," writes Tzetzes, a Byzantine scholar who laments the loss of Sapphic song (Sappho Test. 61, Campbell 50–51). By the twelfth century most of the Sapphic corpus had already disappeared, yet Sappho reappears twice in his sentence, in the reiteration of the name: "both Sappho and the works of Sappho," καὶ ἡ Σαπφὼ καὶ τὰ Σαπφοῦς. The declension from nominative to genitive, from *Sapphō* to *Sapphous,* measures the decline from Sappho to Tzetzes, who can only invoke her name in his own time by declining it. Nevertheless "nouns and verbs may be known by their declining," as the *Oxford English Dictionary* reminds us; the verb "to decline" comes (via Latin) from the Greek "to bend" (*klinein*) and the preposition "down" (*de*), meaning "to turn away," "bend aside," "fall down," "deviate," "digress," "descend," "decay." In the case of Sappho, we are declining a name in every sense. Nominative, genitive, dative, accusative, vocative: the name that is Sappho, the name of Sappho, the name given to Sappho, the Sappho that we name, or what we address as "O, Sappho." This lesson in grammar teaches us that even a proper name is only known by its variants, not a fixed identity but a series of inflections. Each grammatical inflection gives another meaning to the name, turning it into a wayward genealogy: always a repetition with a difference, a variation on the name and a deviation from it, a perpetual re-naming.

The name appears in four of the Greek fragments currently attributed to Sappho, as we see in the modern Loeb edition of the Sapphic fragments, recompiled and retranslated by D. A. Campbell in 1982.[10] In fragment 65, for example, six letters slip through the ellipses to spell out "Sappho," as follows:

> . . . . .] . . . α[
> . . . . .] ρομε
> . . . . .] . ελασ[
> . ροτήννεμε[
> **Ψάπφοι,** σε φίλ[
> Κύπρωι β[α]σίλ[
> καίτοι μέλα δ . [
> ὄ]σσοις φαέθων[
> πάνται κλέος[
> καί σ' ένν Ἀχέρ[οντ

The reconstruction of the ancient Greek in Campbell's edition is followed by his tentative translation in English:

> ... (Andromeda?) ... Sappho (I love?) you ... Cyprus ... queen ... yet great ... all whom (the sun) shining ... everywhere glory ... and in the (house of) Acheron ... you ...

Campbell also offers an explanatory note after Sappho's name, to hypothesize a narrative context for this fragmentary text: "S[appho] is promised world-wide glory, probably by Aphrodite, the Cyprian." To make the Greek fragment readable, Campbell therefore reads it as Sappho's claim to fame, the great lyric poet radiating glory everywhere. The simple proclamation of the name, it would seem, is enough to reclaim Sappho as an unequivocal lyric subject. The name appears in the vocative, however, not in the voice of Sappho but as an address to Sappho: "Sappho, (I love?) you" (*Sapphoi, se phil ...*). The fragment speaks the name of Sappho as that which is bespoken (perhaps, beloved) by another; "Sappho" is the citation of a name, divided from itself.

In another fragment the vocative is used again to name Sappho, this time in the form of a question. Fragment 133 is a line (Ψάπφοι, τί τὰν πολύολβον, Ἀφροδίταν ... ;) partially reconstructed in Campbell's translation: "Why, Sappho (do you summon? neglect?) Aphrodite rich in blessings?" If in fragment 65 Aphrodite appears to confirm the name and fame of Sappho, in fragment 133 the relation between namer and named is more questionable. We do not know who speaks the name of Sappho, nor how Sappho speaks the name of Aphrodite; the verb is missing. Nevertheless the fragment is attributed to Sappho by Campbell, as if the name can be understood as an act of self-naming, as if Sappho can be identified with "Sappho." But even if we understand Sappho to be speaking (implicitly) in the first person in order to address herself (explicitly) in the second person in order to be named in the third person, how can the name confer identity without also deferring it? How do we refer the utterance back to Sappho? Only in the complex mediations between first, second, and third person can Sappho be named as a hypothetical lyric subject.

Likewise in fragment 94, "Sappho" is implicitly placed in quotation marks, disrupting the lyric utterance attributed to her. The name appears in a dialogue between parting lovers: "Sappho, truly, against my will do I leave you," says one, in a vocative that shows again how the name of Sappho is conferred from a position external to the first person lyric "I" (Ψάπφ', ἦ μάν σ' ἀέκοισ' ἀπυλίμπάνω). As the fragment continues, the "I" that responds exists only in relation to the one who has already addressed it: "And I answered: 'Go, be happy, and remember me'" (τάν δ' ἔγω ταδ' ἀμειβόμαν χαίροισ' ἔρχεο κἄμεθεν μέμναισ'). The very possibility of response is here predicated on the second-person address to "Sappho," producing a first-person "I" (ἔγω) who speaks in reply and then asks to be remembered by those who will repeat her name. Written into this scene of separation is the separation of naming from meaning, and the dispersal of the proper name. The memory of Sappho depends on the repetition of the name, no longer addressed to the second person but referring to it in the third person. The memory is more like a memorization, since to memorize a name—to make it repeatable—means that one must forget what it means: the "you" to whom it no longer refers, the one who has been left behind. Thus fragment 94 anticipates its own interruption: it predicts that Sappho must be forgotten, and already has been, in order to be called "Sappho."

While the question of the name may appear in these examples to be a function of their fragmentation, even the Ode to Aphrodite—the only complete poem in the Sapphic corpus—calls the name of Sappho into question. This famous ode begins with an invocation to Aphrodite and then stages a reversal of the invocation, when in turn the goddess invokes Sappho. In stanzas 3 and 4, the vocative "O Blessed One" (Sappho to Aphrodite) is reciprocated by the vocative "O Sappho" (Aphrodite to Sappho). Descending in her chariot drawn by sparrows, Aphrodite is recalled from the past to call Sappho by her proper name, in the present:

αἶψα δ' ἐξίκοντο' σὺ δ', ὦ μάκαιρα,
μειδιαίσαισ' ἀθανάτω προσώπω
ἦρε' ὄττι δηὖτε πέπονθα κὤττι
δηὖτε κάλημμι,

κὤττι μοι μάλιστα θέλω γένεσθαι
μαινόλᾳ θύμῳ τίνα δηὖτε πείθω
ἄψ σ' ἄγην ἐς Fὰν φιλότατα; τίς σ', ὦ
Ψάπφ', ἀδικήει;

> Quickly they came. And you O blessed one
>   smiling with your immortal face
>   asked what again did I suffer and what
>   again did I call for
>
> and what did I most want to happen
>   in my maddened heart. Whom again shall I persuade
>   to lead to your love? Who, O
>   Sapph', wrongs you?

With the shift from third-person description to second-person address, past tense to present tense, narrative to dialogue, the ode also seems to shift voices from Sappho to Aphrodite, who now speaks on behalf of Sappho. "Who, O Sapph', wrongs you?" she asks, ready to set aright the injustice that has left Sappho abandoned by the girl she loves.

This would also seem to be the moment when the name of Sappho is justified, set aright by writing the wrong that she suffers: through the fiction of Aphrodite's voice, we read a Sapphic signature that apparently authorizes Sappho as the writer of the poem, and authenticates her narrative of suffering. The Greek adverb δηὖτε (a contraction of two words, "now" and "again") appears three times in the Ode to Aphrodite, to emphasize that again Sappho has suffered, and again Sappho has asked for divine intervention, and again Aphrodite has to lead some girl back into her arms. Sappho is identified in Aphrodite's address by the repeatability of that scenario: what is happening now has happened before, and what happened then had already happened before, and so on. As John Winkler points out, the poem multiplies different versions of Sappho by setting up multiple relations between past and present. "The doubling of Aphrodite (present and past) and the tripling of Sappho (present, past, and ... pluperfect) leads like the mirrors in a fun house to receding vistas of endlessly repeated intercessions" (1990: 171). Where, in this infinite regress, is the original Sappho? Winkler tries to stop the mirror effect by suggesting that the poem can reflect Sappho back to us; he concludes that "the appearance of an infinite regress, however, is framed and bounded by another Sappho," by which he means "Sappho-the-poet," the one who appears to be in control of the poem (171).

But if the poem lets itself be signed in the name of "Sappho-the-poet," that signature is not of the author; another signs it, by repeating the name. Rather than authorizing Sappho, the Ode to Aphrodite reflects upon the rightful ownership of its signature. Is Sappho naming herself or being named, the origin of the name or its reiteration, the original or the copy? The narrative complexity of the Ode is not resolved ("framed and bounded," according to Winkler) by invoking Sappho-the-poet; to the contrary, it is produced by the invocation that leaves Sappho's name unresolved, in the form of a rhetorical question: "Who, O Sapph', wrongs you?" Here the question is not only "who" wrongs Sappho, but "who" is Sappho, other than the effect of a wrong that can never be written right in this poem? Even the name of Sappho is written wrong: a contraction makes the "o" at the end of "Sappho" disappear, while the vocative "O" makes it reappear at the beginning of the name. Thus Sappho becomes O Sapph' (ὦ Ψάπφ', in Greek), transposing the letters to spell the name out of order, and reversing the alphabet by placing the last letter first: the omega before the alpha, the end before the beginning, an alphabetical *hysteron proteron*. The disordering of the name destabilizes the authorial identity we might wish to ascribe to Sappho, for it shows that "Sappho" is subject to continual deformation and not a stable form: the Sapphic signature is made to appear by writing the name, in reverse, and in retrospect.

The Sapphic signature lends itself to infinite variations, not only in our interpretation of the Ode to Aphrodite but within the tradition of translating the Ode as well. In every version "Sappho" is transliterated, translated, transformed to produce yet another signature, in many languages over many centuries. Thus Wharton compiles various English translations in his late Victorian edition of the Sapphic fragments, an important book because it points to the proliferation of signatures in the name of Sappho. Each translator has placed the invocation to Sappho in a different context and then signed his own name to the text. What constitutes the Sapphic signature, in these examples, is the repetition of Sappho's wrong: "Tell me, my Sappho, tell me who?" (Ambrose Philips, 1711). "Alas, poor Sappho, who is this ingrate?" (Herbert, 1713). "Who, Sappho, who hath done thee wrong?" (John Herman Merivale, 1833). "Who hath wrought my Sappho wrong?" (F. T. Palgrave, 1854). "My Sappho, who is it wrongs thee?" (Edwin Arnold, 1869). "Who has harmed thee? O my poor Sappho" (T. W. Higginson, 1871). "Who thy love now is it that ill requiteth, Sappho?" (Moreton John Walhouse, 1877). "Who now, Sappho, hath wronged thee?" (J. Addington Symonds, 1893). "Who Sappho, wounds thy tender breast?" (Akenside, 1745). "Who doth thee wrong, Sappho?" (Swinburne 1866). Alongside these poetic versions a prose translation is also provided by Wharton himself, who signs his name below Sappho on the title page of his book: *Sappho: Memoir, Text, Selected Renderings, and a Literal Translation by Henry Thornton Wharton.* These various appropriations of the Sapphic signature demonstrate that the proper name of Sappho is no one's property, least of all the property of "Sappho." The name of Sappho is signed each time by someone other than Sappho, and each time it is written again by being written wrong.

Who writes Sappho?

In the course of this book, I develop a theoretical argument about the Sapphic signature as well as a historical account of its significations in Victorian poetry. By the end of the century, Sappho had become a highly overdetermined and contradictory trope within nineteenth-century discourses of gender, sexuality, poetics, and politics. Each chapter of *Victorian Sappho* proposes a variation on the name, demonstrating how it is variously declined: the declension of a noun and its deviation from origins, the improper bending of a proper name, a line of descent that is also a falling into decadence, the perpetual return of a name that is also a turning away from nomination. By placing the texts of Sappho within a Victorian context—declining the name yet again—*Victorian Sappho* contributes to the study of Sappho's reception: the *Nachleben* or afterlife. Rather than reconstructing the life of Sappho within the historical context of archaic Greece, *Nachleben* studies trace the afterlife by considering constructions of Sappho within other historical contexts, demonstrating how Sappho is continually transformed in the process of transmission. Indeed, in the proliferation of many Sapphic versions, new visions and revisions, Sappho emerges as an imitation for which there is no original. Sapphic imitations are a product of their own historical moment and no longer measured against—except perhaps to measure their distance from—the time of Sappho.

The most comprehensive recent study of Sappho's reception is Joan DeJean's *Fictions of Sappho: 1546–1937,* surveying a Sapphic tradition in France over four centuries. Her book has given new impetus to such reception studies, by moving beyond thematic reading to a critical account of "Saphon, Sappho, Sapho, Sappho, Sapphô, Psappha" as "a figment of the modern imagination" (1); the name is variously spelled and, as DeJean points out, "behind each spelling there is a story."[11] DeJean does not spell out the implications of Sappho's name for a critical understanding of *lyric,* however; as a "literary history à la Flaubert," her survey is broadly chronological in approach, narrative in emphasis, and focused primarily on French literature. Indeed, she tends to assume that English versions of Sappho merely recapitulate the French tradition, fifty years later: "The English discovery of Sappho reproduces so closely the structure of her entry into the French tradition a half-century earlier that an analysis of its unfolding would have been repetitive, without being essential to an understanding of the future of Sapphic fictions" (5).[12] Of course repetition always produces difference, and we can understand lyric as a historical form precisely because it depends on such repetition; I therefore argue that the fate of Sappho within English poetry is necessarily different from the French tradition, another way to predict "the future of Sapphic fictions" rather than a predictable repetition of the same.

In Victorian England, as we shall see, Sappho of Lesbos emerges as a proper name for the Poetess—and less properly, the Lesbian—according to a logic of lyric reading that distinguishes Victorian versions of Sappho from other Sapphic fictions. Sappho becomes an ideal lyric persona, a figure that provokes the desire to reclaim an original, perhaps even originary, feminine voice. Not only is Sappho personified by a reading that assumes a speaker and is predicated on the assumption of voice; as a personified abstraction, she comes to personify lyric at a time when it is increasingly read in terms of its personifying function. What I call "Victorian Sappho" is of course a double personification, identifying the lyric persona of Sappho with a historical period that is more commonly identified with the person of Queen Victoria, another proper name. I invoke Victoria alongside Sappho, in order to name the second half of the nineteenth century as a time when feminine figures and figurations of femininity contribute in complex ways to the formation of aesthetic categories, and more generally to the feminization of Victorian culture. The question of Sappho thus converges with nineteenth-century debates around "The Woman Question." Throughout the reign of Queen Victoria, Sappho represents different ideas of Victorian womanhood, and like the Queen she becomes a "representative" woman who embodies the very possibility of such representations, allowing them to multiply in often contradictory forms.[13] Indeed it is the repeatability of the Sapphic figure that marks it feminine, as the variations on the name—its successive differences from the nominative—point to a principle of differentiation that also produces gender difference. The cultural formations that cluster around this poetic form—and in particular, the construction of nineteenth-century female authorship on a Sapphic model—will reveal what is uniquely Victorian about Victorian Sappho.

I do not present the Victorian reception of Sappho according to a chronology that often shapes reception studies, since one important objective of my book is to define an approach to literary history that does not assume an "original" prior to the moment of its "reception." Rather than organizing the chapters to imply a developing tradition or a linear progression, I emphasize the continual recirculation of Sappho within Victorian poetry. My argument proceeds in a series of differential repetitions; after demonstrating how Sappho is to be read as a non-originary figure in the first chapter, the other chapters show in further detail how its repetition takes different historical forms: the doubling of the Sapphic signature by Michael Field, the Sapphic rhythms performed by Algernon Swinburne, the reiteration of Sappho's leap by various Victorian poetesses. By returning to the question of the name in each context, *Victorian Sappho* offers a more fully contextualized analysis of the structures of repetition outlined by Jacques Derrida in "Signature, Event, Context" (1977). An insistence on the structural necessity of repetition—manifested in the iterability of the singular mark, the nonsingularity of the event, the overdetermination of context—is evident in the organization of my argument, even as I seek to mobilize a familiar deconstructive reading of lyric in a less familiar, more historical direction.

I begin Chapter 1 with a Sapphic riddle, a paradox serving as my paradigm for the conversion of a female body into written letters that become vocal at the moment of their reception: when they are delivered to a reader, they seem to speak. But their arrival is unpredictable, as I show in a detailed analysis of fragment 31 of Sappho, first in Greek and then in a series of English translations. Every attempt to recuperate Sapphic voice repeats a break that is inscribed—indeed, prescribed—in this fragment: Sappho's tongue is broken, disarticulating a speaking subject even as it is also said to emerge. The repetition of the break nevertheless makes fragment 31 an exemplary lyric, I argue, and the most frequently translated text of Sappho; it is incorporated into an English lyric tradition from the seventeenth century onward, a tradition that is itself reincorporated into the Sapphic corpus by Wharton, who writes in the Preface to his third edition of *Sappho:* "As a name, as a figure pre-eminent in literary history, she has indeed never been overlooked" (xv). In Wharton's book the continual renaming of this figure allows Sappho to appear as a figure *for* translation: Sappho is simultaneous cause and effect of translation, and increasingly feminized in this process of transmission. Although Wharton introduces Sappho as the pure and unmediated voice of a woman poet who is the perfection of lyric song, his book demonstrates how Sapphic voice is mediated by text and marked feminine precisely because it does not speak. In this respect Wharton's *Sappho* is distinctively Victorian, as it reflects and influences a nineteenth-century ideology of lyric reading predicated on the figure of voice.

Wharton's first edition of *Sappho* in 1885 was the inspiration for a collection of Sapphic imitations entitled *Long Ago,* published in 1889 by "Michael Field," the pseudonym of Katherine Bradley and Edith Cooper. In Chapter 2, I argue that these two Victorian women—aunt and niece, who collaborated in writing poetry and considered themselves married—perform a self-doubling signature that unsettles conventional definitions of lyric as the solitary utterance of a single speaker. In Wharton's edition they discover not only the possibility for multiple signatures in the name of Sappho, but a space between Greek and English that allows for eroticized textual exchange. Fragment 2 of Sappho, an invitation to come to the island of Lesbos, becomes a lesbian topos in the Sapphic lyrics of Michael Field, allowing Bradley and Cooper to enter a metaphorical "field" of writing where the crossing out, over, and through of sexual identities can be performed. Bradley and Cooper writing as Michael Field, writing as Sappho, therefore appropriate a name that is simultaneously proper and improper, their own and not their own, and introduce the possibility of lesbian imitation not predicated on the assumption of voice. The reader is left to ponder the erotic appeal of Greek letters that spell out Sappho's name, without spelling it out completely. My chapter complicates the reclamation of Michael Field in the name of lesbian writing; such a reading depends on the rhetorical figure of antonomasia, taking a common noun for a proper name, and vice versa. Rather than identifying Lesbian Sappho with lesbian Sappho, the Sapphic lyrics in *Long Ago* enact the rhetorical conversion itself and remain suspended in that moment, both then and now.

The identification of, and with, Sappho as a "lesbian" figure is performed in yet another way by Algernon Charles Swinburne. The *succès de scandale* of his early Sapphic imitations encouraged readers to identify Swinburne with Sappho, and he is still read as the most important Victorian incarnation of Sappho. Swinburne invokes her as the greatest lyric poet who ever lived, his personal precursor and the proper name for all lyric song: "Name above all names. " While this act of nomination creates a line of descent from Sappho to Swinburne, his repetition of the name also turns Sappho into a figure for decadence and decline: a descending cadence that is heard only as an echoing rhythm, memorized by Swinburne and recorded in the writing of his own Sapphic imitations. Swinburne's Sappho,

I argue, is a rhythmicized body that disappears and reappears in the rhythms of its own scattering, according to a logic of disintegration and figurative reconstitution familiar from the Longinian treatise on the sublime. The subtext for this sublime reading of Sappho is not only fragment 31 (admired by Longinus), but also fragment 130: in both poems, the rhythmic force of eros, "the loosener of limbs," threatens to disarticulate the body of Sappho, while also articulating the Sapphic corpus into a perfect metrical body. Swinburne learns the fine art of suffering meter from Sappho, in a sublime scenario that I call "the Sapphic scene of instruction," played out in his Sapphic poems and in his flagellant verse as well. The beating of the body is internalized as the rhythm of poetry and transposed into the formal abstraction of meter: a written notation. The hyperbolic performance of this violent inscription can be understood as a perverse response to Victorian metrical theory, enabling Swinburne to constitute his own poetic corpus as a body of writing that materializes through and as meter. Initially abused by the critics for his Sapphic imitations, Swinburne presents himself as a body *for* abuse, rhythmically scattered and recollected like the fragments of Sappho. The reception of Swinburne at the turn of the century repeats the logic of Swinburne's Sapphic sublime and continues in current criticism on Swinburne.

Alongside the homoerotic Sapphism of Michael Field and the eroticized rhythms of Swinburne's Sapphic imitations, there also exists a tradition of Victorian women poets who turn to Sappho in order to perform the suffering of "woman" as an overdetermined heterosexual identification: doomed to die for love, Sappho becomes a proper name for the "Poetess." Prior to Wharton's edition of the Sapphic fragments in 1885, the popular reception of Sappho is primarily mediated by Ovid's "Sappho to Phaon," where Sappho laments her abandonment by the young ferryman Phaon, before leaping to her death from the Leucadian Cliff. The Sapphic signature in Ovid's elegiac epistle is a postscript to a suicide that has already occurred, and sets a precedent for the "posthumous" writing of nineteenth-century poetesses. Their Sapphic imitations circulate as postscripts to the postscript, in a seemingly endless series of Sapphic signatures: P.S. Sappho, P.P.S. Sappho, P.P.P.S. Sappho, and so on. In Chapter 4 I offer another perspective on literary history, by tracing the repetition of Sappho's leap in women's verse from the early to the late nineteenth century. I refer back to Mary Robinson, L. E. L. and Felicia Hemans as important Romantic precursors for Victorian poetesses such as Christina Rossetti and Caroline Norton, all of whom turn to Sappho as the personification of an empty figure. Nevertheless, this Sapphic (non) persona is increasingly invoked in the cause of woman toward the century, as it circulates on both side of the Atlantic in the poetry of American and British feminists, such as Elizabeth Oakes Smith, Mary Catherine Hume and Catharine Amy Dawson Scott. While these names have been mostly forgotten in the twentieth century, they give us an insight into the rhetorical complexity of sentimental lyric; indeed, the forgetting of nineteenth-century poetesses is predicted in their verse as the very means of its literary transmission.

There are in fact more Victorian Sapphos than I can name, and I do not offer a comprehensive survey; each would deserve a detailed analysis, well beyond the scope of one book. The historical scope of my argument does expand from chapter to chapter, however. In the first chapter, I place a single text within the context of a single book: after reading fragment 31 in theoretical terms, I show how this logic of lyric reading is writ large in Wharton's 1885 edition of Sappho. The second chapter places this influential Victorian text within the context of its reception toward the end of the nineteenth century, by showing how its textual logic is reworked in the Sapphic lyrics of Michael Field. The third chapter ranges more freely over four decades to show how Swinburne is read as one famously scandalous Victorian incarnation of Sappho. The fourth chapter spans the entire reign of Queen Victoria, in order to present a long succession of women who write within the conventions of nineteenth-century sentimental lyric. The poets I consider in this book have been selected for their relevance to larger critical debates within the field of Victorian poetry: the relationship between gender and genre, the intersection between philology and poetry, the possibility of collaborative and cross-gendered writing, the question of lesbian poetics, the sexual politics of Victorian Hellenism, the implications of Victorian prosody, the historical reclamation of women poets, the rhetorical and cultural function of sentimental lyric, and the theoretical claims of formalist reading. This final question about form can only be addressed in the performance of reading itself, and it informs the attention to detail in my readings in each chapter. While I do not assume knowledge of ancient Greek from my readers, the juxtaposition of English and Greek might nevertheless serve as a reminder of the difficulty of reading all poetry, even in English.

As I define a Sapphic strain in Victorian poetry, I therefore want to insist more strenuously on the theoretical questions raised by reading lyric, or lyric reading. If "reading lyric" implies that lyric is already defined as an object to be read, "lyric reading" implies an act of lyrical reading, or reading lyrically, that poses the possibility of lyric without presuming its objective existence or assuming it to be a form of subjective expression. Traditional definitions of lyric depend on a generic model that assumes the continuity of a speaker, as Jonathan Culler points out: "To assume that interpreting a lyric means identifying the speaker is to forget that the speaker is inferred from a voice, which is itself a figure here; but once one begins to consider the figure of voice, the question arises of how far the intelligibility of lyric depends on this figure and whether the generic model or reading strategy of the lyric is not designed to maintain the notion of language as the product of and therefore sign of the subject" (1988: 298). Lyric reading predicated on the figure of voice creates the possibility of identification of and with a speaker, in order to defend against readings that could make lyric less intelligible, more resistant to the recuperation of a lyric subject. Culler therefore questions "the generic model or reading strategy" that allows lyric to be associated with subjectivity, as does Paul de Man in his essay on "Anthropomorphism and Trope in the Lyric." "What we call the lyric, the instance of represented voice, conveniently spells out the rhetorical and thematic characteristics that make it the paradigm of a complementary relationship between grammar, trope, and theme," de Man observes, leading him to conclude that "the lyric is not a genre but one name among several to designate the defensive motion of understanding, the possibility of a future hermeneutics" (1984: 261). Here lyric serves as proper name—"one name among several"—for anthropomorphic (mis)reading, in which anthropomorphism is "not just a trope but an identification" that freezes an endless series of propositions into a single assertion: "no longer a proposition but a proper name" (241). The essay performs a lyrical unreading that would refuse such identification, revoking what is invoked in its title, namely "the Lyric," and de Man concludes with a series of self-qualifying negations that place lyric in opposition to "non-anthropomorphic, non-elegiac, non-celebratory, non-lyrical, non-poetic, that is to say, prosaic, or, better: *historical* modes of language power" (262).[14]

Victorian Sappho works simultaneously within and against this critique of lyric anthropomorphism. According to de Man's logic, when Sappho is identified with lyric as a genre we project "the possibility of a future hermeneutics" into the past: we read the Sapphic fragments not only as "the instance of represented voice" but as the very origin of lyric voice itself. Such a reading does indeed designate a defensive motion of understanding, the conversion of trope into anthropomorphism. Within the context of my argument, however, the proper name of Sappho can also be read propositionally. If Sappho is an anthropomorphism—

no longer a proposition but a proper name—nevertheless that name cannot be identified with a speaker, nor does it stop the chain of tropological transformations that de Man defines as reading. To the contrary, Sappho is an overdetermined trope within a history of continual transformation that never ends, enabling us to read lyric as structure for shifting identifications, rather than the fixing of an identification. To define another approach to lyric reading, it is not enough to question the complementary relationship between grammar, trope, and theme; we must question the historical relationship between gender and genre as well. While de Man opposes lyric to *"historical* modes of language power,"* what is at stake in *Victorian Sappho* is the undoing of this antithesis and an interest in reconstructing a history of lyric reading that de Man simultaneously assumes and erases. The effacement of gender in his theoretical account of lyric as a genre is, I argue, historically determined and itself a trace of the history that de Man claims does not fall properly within the domain of lyric.

To re-evaluate the genealogy of the genre assumed by contemporary lyric theory, and to demonstrate how *historical* modes of language power are always *gendered* as well, I propose a literary history that includes women poets, but also reflects further on the historical category of the "woman poet." As Denise Riley has argued in *"Am I That Name?" Feminism and the Category of "Women" in History,* the conversion of a proper name ("Woman") into a common name ("women") troubles the history of feminism, which instituted women as its founding category yet also found itself mediating "between the many temporalities of a designation." But if there is no originary woman, nevertheless "some characterisation or other is eternally in play," so that "the question then for a feminist history is to discover whose, and to what effects" (1988: 98). This is also the question for feminist literary history, and especially in feminist readings of women's poetry, where the characterisation of woman "in play" is already a personified rhetorical effect. Throughout my book a deconstructive critique of lyric is therefore coupled with feminist criticism: two approaches to critical reading that are not as incompatible as they might seem, insofar as both revolve around the problem of personification.

In an incisive analysis of the uncanny coupling of deconstruction and feminism, Barbara Johnson questions "whether there is a *simple* incompatibility between the depersonalization of deconstruction and the repersonalization of feminism, or whether each is not in reality haunted by the ghost of the other" (1987: 44). The return of the personal in de Man's work takes the form of personification, according to Johnson, who describes how the transference of personal agency to rhetorical entities in his prose allows him to achieve "an elimination of sexual difference." "By making personhood the property of an 'it,' de Man is able to claim a form of universality which can be said to inhere in language itself, and which is not directly subject to ordinary feminist critique, however gender-inflected language can in fact be shown to be" (45). I argue that the transfer of personhood to rhetorical entities— especially as performed in lyric—is not the elimination of sexual difference but another way to articulate the historical effects of gender. If we extend Johnson's argument into nineteenth-century women's verse, we will find a precedent for this version of personification, making personhood the property of an "it" named Sappho that is explicitly marked feminine. A reading that insists on repersonalizing this "it" as a person might fall under the category of "ordinary feminist critique," but as Johnson points out, "what is interesting about this attempt at personalization is how quickly it slides into an assumption of generalizability" (46). Thus, "while de Man's writing is haunted by the return of personification, feminist writing is haunted by the return of abstraction," with each making the other "both possible and problematic" (46). To recognize and analyze the complex relation between the two would be the beginning of an extraordinary feminist critique.

My purpose in *Victorian Sappho* is to develop an approach to reading lyric that is both rhetorically and historically inflected by gender. Sappho spells out an alternative to "what we call the lyric," not only within de Man's rhetorical formulation but also within the historical account offered by Joel Fineman for the invention of poetic subjectivity. In *Shakespeare's Perjured Eye,* Fineman describes a lyric subject "willed" to literary history by William Shakespeare, in the sonnets that pun repeatedly on the name of "Will." The speaking of the proper name allows the poet to be spoken about, and thus to be read as author: "Naming himself, therefore, the poet to himself becomes a 'he,' someone to be spoken about, a third person elsewhere from and different from his first and second person" (1986: 291). Although this act of self-naming is also an act of self-division, nevertheless it authorizes a lyric subject who is gendered male: the poet "finds his 'Will' at odds with his 'I,'" (291) yet what he finds—a "Will" and an "I"—are still "his." Indeed, Fineman cannot imagine a lyric subject other than one defined by the will he owns, even if that will also disowns him by producing internal difference. "Whatever might be different from Shakespeare's poetry of verbal difference would therefore have to find, outside language, another name," Fineman concludes; such a "hypothetical successor" would have to be "outside history" (ibid.: 296).

But suppose this hypothetical successor is a predecessor that has already found, in Sappho, another name? If Shakespeare represents one possible origin for a highly speculative history of the lyric subject, I nominate Sappho to represent another possible point of departure for a lyric tradition—equally specular—that does not locate the signature within the subject. Declining the name of Sappho does not place it "outside language" or "outside history," however, but in a different relation to both. Rather than defining a poet who to himself becomes a "he" by self-naming, the relationship between the personal pronoun and the proper name might be articulated, differently, to pose the question of feminine difference. The effects of that difference would not be circumscribed by a proper name that signifies the "will" of an authorial intention. A gendered perspective on lyric would not have to depend on the invention of a "she" who speaks her own name—say, Sappho—but could be discovered unpredictably elsewhere, in the Sapphic signature that circulates at the specific moment of its reception. The Sapphic signature I trace in the following pages is also mine, of course. Who writes Sappho, now? Who wrongs Sappho? Who, O Sapph'? I am inclined to answer, there is no choice but to go on declining the name.

Notes

1 Here and throughout the book, I refer to the Lobel-Page numbering of the Sapphic fragments.
2 I owe this formulation to Carolyn Williams.
3 Kenner describes in further detail how Pound used Wharton's edition of Sappho to develop a "poiesis of loss" and an "aesthetic of glimpses" (1971: 56, 71). On H. D.'s aesthetic of fragmentation, also inspired by Sappho, see Gregory 1998. On the Romantic fragment poem and the aesthetic of fragmentation in nineteenth-century England, see Levinson 1986.
4 DeJean (1989: 304–5) points out that Page promotes British Classical scholarship by referring to Victorian precursors such as John Addington Symonds. This Victorian scholarly tradition includes Wharton, who also draws extensively on Symonds in the introductory essay to his edition of Sappho.
5 For further discussion of Barnard's Sappho translations, see Prins 1997: 63–66.
6 Of course Sappho is not the only figure from archaic Greek lyric who is called upon to authorize a Western lyric tradition, as we see from a long tradition associated with Anacreon and the Anacreonta, or a Pindaric tradition associated with the epinician odes of Pindar. However, it is the privileging of Sappho as a point of "feminine" origin that makes twentieth-century readings of the Sapphic fragments a perpetuation of Victorian readings.

7   In addition to the books by duBois and Williamson, there has been a resurgence of interest in Sappho among Classical scholars; other recent books include Wilson 1996, Greene 1997a, 1997b. New translations of Sappho include Barnstone 1988, Balmer 1988, Roche 1991, Rayor 1991, Powell 1993. On the figure of Sappho in contemporary poetry, see Gubar 1984, Grahn 1985, Greer 1995, and Prins and Shreiber 1997: 187–259.

8   I refer to the Sappho Testimonia by number and by page, as they appear in Campbell 1982.

9   For a survey of "Homeric Questions," see Nagy 1992; for further discussion of Sapphic songs in performance, see Calame 1977 (tr. 1997), Nagy 1996: 87–103, and Stehle 1997.

10 Here and throughout, I follow the reconstruction of the Greek fragments as they appear in the Loeb edition of Sappho (Campbell 1982). English translations are my own, unless noted otherwise.

11 In addition to earlier surveys of Sappho's reception in Robinson 1923 and Rudiger 1933, other recent reception studies include Saake 1972, Lipking 1988, Fornaro 1991, Greer 1995: 102–46, Jay and Lewis 1996, and Greene 1997b.

12 Of course the wide scope of DeJean's book inevitably entails omissions, and she acknowledges that "concentration on the French Sapphic construct does not signify the exclusion of her presence in other national traditions" (4). Nevertheless she finds it "obvious that the French tradition has played throughout its development a privileged role as the nexus of [Sappho's] fictionalization" (5) and tends to assimilate other traditions into a French model.

13 On multiple representations of Queen Victoria in nineteenth-century England, see Munich 1996, Homans and Munich 1997, and Homans 1998; on the twentieth century as a "post-Victorian" age mourning various memories of the queen, see Dickson 1996; on the feminization of Victorian culture, see Psomiades 1997.

14 For further elaboration of de Man's theoretical account of lyric see Culler 1985; in Hosek and Parker 1985, see also de Man, "Lyrical Voice in Contemporary Theory" and Culler, "Changes in the Study of the Lyric." I owe my understanding of de Man's essay as a performance of "lyrical un-reading" to Virginia Jackson's brilliant reading of de Man, in chapter 2 of *Dickinson's Misery.*

Works Cited

Armstrong, Isobel, *Victorian Poetry: Poetry, Poetics and Politics* (London and New York: Routledge, 1993)

Balmer, Josephine, Tr., *Sappho: Poems and Fragments* (Secaucus: Meadowland Books, 1988)

Barnstone, Willis, Tr., *Sappho and the Greek Lyric Poets* (New York: Schocken Books, 1988)

Calame, Claude, *Choruses of Young Women in Ancient Greece: Their Morphology, Religious Role, and Social Functions*, trans. by Derek Collins and Jane Orion (Lanham: Rowman and Littlefield, 1997)

Campbell, D. A. *Greek Lyric, Volume 1: Sappho and Alcaeus* (Cambridge: Harvard University Press, 1982)

Culler, Jonathan, 'Changes in the Study of Lyric' in *Lyric Poetry: Beyond New Criticism*, ed. by Chaviva Hosek and Patricia Parker (Ithaca: Cornell University Press, 1985)

DeJean, Joan, *Fictions of Sappho: 1546–1937* (Chicago: Chicago University Press, 1989)

de Man, Paul, 'Lyrical Voice in Contemporary Theory' in *Lyric Poetry: Beyond New Criticism*, ed. by Chaviva Hosek and Patricia Parker (Ithaca: Cornell University Press, 1985)

Derrida, Jacques, 'Signature, Event, Context', *Glyph* 1 (1977), 172–97

Dickson, Jay, 'Surviving Victoria' in *High and Low Moderns: Literature and Culture 1889–1939*, ed. by Maria Dibattista and Lucy McDiarmid (Oxford: Oxford University Press, 1996)

duBois, Page, *Sappho is Burning* (Chicago: Chicago University Press, 1995)

Kenner, Hugh, *The Pound Era* (Berkeley: University of California Press, 1971)

Fornaro, Sotera, 'Immagini di Sappho', *Rose di Piera*, ed. by Francesca de Martino (Bari: Levante, 1991)

Grahn, Judy, *The Highest Apple: Sappho and the Lesbian Poetic Tradition* (San Francisco: Spinsters, Ink, 1985)

Greene, Ellen, ed., *Reading Sappho: Contemporary Approaches* (Berkeley: University of California Press, 1997)

Greer, Germaine, *Slip-Shod Sibyls: Recognition, Rejection and the Woman Poet* (London: Viking, 1995)

Gregory, Eileen, *H. D. and Hellensism: Classic Lines* (New York: Cambridge University Press, 1997)

Gubar, Susan, 'Sapphistries' *Signs*, 10.1 (1984), 43–62

Homans, Margaret, *Royal Representations: Queen Victoria and British Culture 1837–1876* (Chicago: University of Chicago Press, 1998)

Homans, Margaret and Munich, Adrianne, eds., *Remaking Queen Victoria* (Cambridge: Cambridge University Press, 1997)

Hosek, Chaviva and Parker, Patricia, *Lyric Poetry: Beyond New Criticism* (Ithaca: Cornell University Press, 1985)

Jay, Peter and Lewis, Caroline, *Sappho Through English Poetry* (London: Anvil Press Poetry, 1996)

Johnson, Barbara, *A World of Difference* (Baltimore: The Johns Hopkins University Press, 1987)

Levinson, Marjorie, *The Romantic Fragment Poem* (Chapel Hill: University of North Carolina Press, 1986)

Lipking, Lawrence, *Abandoned Women and Poetic Tradition* (Chicago: Chicago University Press, 1988)

Loeffelholz, Mary, 'One of the Boys?' *The Women's Review of Books*, 13.7 (1996), 15–16

Munich, Adrianne, *Queen Victoria's Secrets* (New York: Columbia University Press, 1996)

Nagy, Gregory, *Poetry as Performance: Homer and Beyond* (Cambridge: Cambridge University Press, 1996)

Nagy, Gregory, 'Homeric Questions', *Transactions of the American Philological Association*, 122 (1992) 17–60

Powell, Jim, *Sappho: A Garland* (New York: Farrar, Straus, Giroux, 1993)

Prins, Yopie, 'Sappho's Afterlife in Translation' in *Re-Reading Sappho: Reception and Transmission*, ed. by Ellen Greene (Berkeley: University of California Press, 1997)

Prins, Yopie and Shreiber, Maeera, eds., *Dwelling in Possibility: Women Poets and Critics on Poetry* (Ithaca: Cornell University Press, 1997)

Psomiades, Kathy Alexis, *Beauty's Body* (Stanford: Stanford University Press, 1997)

Rayor, Diane, Tr., *Sappho's Lyre: Archaic Lyric and Women Poets of Ancient Greece* (Berkeley: University of California Press, 1991)

Robinson, David M., *Sappho and Her Influence* (New York: Cooper Square Publishers, 1963)

Roche, Paul, Tr., *The Love Songs of Sappho* (New York: Signet Classic, 1991)

Rudiger, H., *Sappho, Ihr Ruf und Ruhm bei der Nachwelt* (Leipzig: Dieterich, 1933)

Saake, Helmut, *Sapphostudies: Forschungsgeschichte, Biografische und Literärische Untersuchungen* (Munich: Schoningh, 1972)

Snyder, Jane, *Lesbian Desire in the Lyrics of Sappho* (New York: Columbia University Press, 1997)

Stehle, Eva, *Performance and Gender in Ancient Greece: Nondramatic Poetry in its Setting* (Princeton: Princeton University Press, 1997)

Vanita, Ruth, *Sappho and the Virgin Mary: Same-Sex Love and the English Literary Imagination* (New York: Columbia University Press, 1996)

Williamson, Margaret, *Sappho's Immortal Daughters* (Cambridge: Harvard University Press, 1995)

Wilson, Lyn Hatherly, *Sappho's Sweetbitter Songs: Configurations of Female and Male in Ancient Greek Lyric* (New York: Routledge, 1996)

Part IX
Science

Greg Tate

Throughout the nineteenth century, poetry and science were often defined in opposition to each other. In 1834, for instance, John Stuart Mill wrote an essay 'On the Application of the Terms Poetry, Science, and Philosophy' in which philosophy is relegated to a brief discussion at the end of the piece; the main concern of the essay is to set out a comparison between science and poetry. Mill starts by describing poetry's 'adherence, in the elements of its most diversified combinations, to individual reality, to what has at some former period acted through the sense upon the feelings'; and he then asserts that 'this avoidance of the abstract and the general, is an essential attribute of all true Poetry: for the sole object of Poetry, as such—is to produce emotion'.[1] Mill presents an affective poetic theory here: poetry is defined by its dependence on personal feeling, both the poet's and the reader's. By representing the 'individual reality' of the poet's experiences and emotions, Mill suggests, poems can 'produce' similar feelings in their readers. Science, on the other hand,

> considers all objects under a totally different point of view from Poetry: it is the classification of individuals, the comprehension of general facts. Its object is not, by the exhibition of objects, in their individual proprieties, as they act upon the senses and feelings, to excite emotion; but, through the medium of general propositions, to furnish knowledge.[2]

According to Mill, the opposition between science and poetry is rooted in their different psychological and epistemological perspectives: poetry appeals to the subjective emotions of individuals, while science deals in factual and objective knowledge, which carries the same meaning for everyone. Mill's approach in this essay is, in his own sense of the term, scientific: he presents a systematic classification of two general and abstract terms, 'Poetry' and 'Science'. The work of individual poets and scientists in the nineteenth century complicates his classification, because they frequently borrow and reimagine each other's language and concepts, undermining the notion of an essential divide between the concerns and methods of science and of poetry. Still, the conceptual separation of the two was a persistent feature of nineteenth-century poetic theory, and any discussion of Romantic and Victorian poetry needs to acknowledge the importance of this separation.

The idea of an inherent disjunction between factual knowledge and poetic representation is ancient. The differences between the two were sharpened, however, in the nineteenth century, as the industrialisation of the British economy and the professionalisation of scientific research contributed to a widespread view that scientific method, and its technological applications, offered the best means of understanding and organising the world. The realist novel, which emerged as the most popular literary form of the century, also claimed a sort of empirical and scientific authority for its observations of the social realities of modern life. Poetry, to some extent, was assigned a similar authority: Mill suggests that poetic feeling, like scientific knowledge, begins with the action of external objects on the senses. At the same time, though, the rise of scientific thinking (and of the novel) was seen as a threat to poetry's cultural prestige, and poetry's advocates sought to defend it by arguing that poems ministered to the individual emotions and the creative imagination that science appeared to neglect. Probably the most famous assertion of this view is William Wordsworth's Preface to *Lyrical Ballads*, in which he identifies a 'contradistinction' between 'Matter of Fact, or Science' and a poetry founded on subjective memory and emotion.[3] Wordsworth was an important influence on Mill, and the appearance of Mill's 1834 essay in the *Monthly Repository*, a journal that campaigned for political reform, suggests that the poetry/science contradistinction which he inherited from Wordsworth was not simply a matter of intellectual interest. It had political implications too: these writers saw poetry as the most secure refuge for personal feeling in a utilitarian culture that was too exclusively preoccupied with individuals' physical and economic circumstances.

It is an axiom of Romantic aesthetic theory that, while the arts originate in, and represent, the psychological processes of the mind or spirit, the sciences are primarily concerned with the physical world. In his 'Treatise on Method', Samuel Taylor Coleridge writes that, in scientific work, 'the mental initiative may have been received from without; but it has escaped some critics, that in the fine arts the mental initiative must necessarily proceed from within'.[4] Although he recognises the value of scientific knowledge, Coleridge tends to privilege artistic expression, because it springs directly from the mind's active power of imagination, without intervention from external objects. Romantic thinkers typically identify poetry as the epitome of imaginative art; Immanuel Kant argues in his *Critique of Judgment* that '*Poetry* (which owes its origin almost entirely to genius and is least willing to be led by precepts or example) holds the first rank among all the arts. It expands the mind by giving freedom to the imagination' (author's italics).[5] Kant's definition of poetry as the free exercise of the imagination, independent of external 'precepts or example', places it in opposition to the factual objectivity and empirical methods of science. This view of poetry set the terms for discussions of the relation between literature and science both in the Romantic and in the Victorian periods. When Matthew Arnold responded to the scientist Thomas Henry Huxley's comments about education in the 1880s, for instance, their debate centred on the question of whether children were more in need of factual and practical instruction in science or of the aesthetic and imaginative education offered by literature.[6]

The argument that the goals of poetry and science were incommensurable, or even antagonistic, demonstrated its enduring popularity throughout the century. It is too neat and straightforward an argument, however, to encompass the various ways in which poets and scientists responded to each other's work, and a brief consideration of some important contextual issues reveals just how insufficient it is. The poetry/science opposition is too simple, first and foremost, because 'poetry' and 'science' are not, in themselves, simple terms. A diversity of poetic theories and poetic forms were in use within nineteenth-century culture, and 'science', as well as involving its older and more general meaning of systematic knowledge, also incorporated subjects ranging from chemistry and the developing social sciences of psychology and anthropology to disciplines, such as philology, which arguably may not be considered sciences today. In the nineteenth century, too, the conventions of training and qualification which separate the scientific disciplines from other intellectual practices were not firmly established. Science was commencing its process of professionalisation, but that process was ongoing, and so scientific knowledge was, on the whole, more accessible to non-scientists than it would be in the twentieth and twenty-first centuries. Concepts and terms might move with relative ease between literary and scientific texts, although not without being in some sense altered.

Another important issue, which remains relevant today, is that science, like poetry, is to some extent shaped by the social and political context in which it is practised, by the language in which it is expressed, and by the forms (scientific papers, textbooks, newspaper articles) in which it is disseminated. Although scientific knowledge is often presented as an objective record of external reality, Gowan Dawson and Sally Shuttleworth comment that 'science, as several scholars have pointed out, is intrinsically and inextricably textual, and relies on the same rhetorical structures and tropes found in all other forms of writing, including poetry, as well as being subject to a corresponding instability of meaning', and that scientists and poets in the nineteenth century 'frequently employed the same metaphors, themes, images, and ideological orientations'.[7] Instead of viewing poetry and science as inherently opposite, it is possible to identify them as two types of linguistic and cultural meaning, which share several of the same contexts and methods. Yet it would be an oversimplification to suggest that there are no differences between poetry and science, in the nineteenth century or now. George Levine argues that 'one of the primary functions of students of the relations between science and literature' is 'to attempt to reconstruct the difference' which distinguishes the two: 'having understood the ways they are like each other, we need to avoid the reductiveness of identity and try to figure out the ways in which they are not'.[8] In the study of nineteenth-century poetry and science, this process of figuring out demands a detailed consideration of how scientific concepts are altered by their representation in particular poems. It also involves thinking critically, and in a non-reductive way, about Romantic and Victorian definitions of the relation between poetry and science: these definitions are often more complex, and more revealing of the difficulties surrounding the issue, than they at first appear.

This is evident in 'Science Versus Poetry', published in *Chambers's Journal of Popular Literature, Science and Arts* in 1857. The title of the journal indicates how scientific and literary subjects were discussed side-by-side, and for a general readership, in the nineteenth-century periodical press. The title of the article, conversely, sets up not just an opposition but an antagonism between poetry and science: it implies that the methods and concerns of the two are somehow at odds with each other. Within the article itself, however, this seemingly straightforward stance begins to unravel and to merge with other perspectives on science and poetry. The second sentence of the article brings the two together by suggesting that both depend on 'exact accuracy of description', and that, together with its 'great variety of embellishment,' the writing of poetry also 'demands a correlative amount of knowledge in the poet'.[9] This proposes a close link between poetry and science by suggesting that poetic description, despite the figurative and metaphorical embellishments of its language, is founded, like science, on accurate information and on the interpretation of sensory data. The article's anonymous writer is drawing here on another important element of Romantic and Victorian poetics, which posits that poetry, instead of (or as well as) representing the unfettered workings of pure imagination, also depends on careful observation of the external world, and particularly of nature; Noel Jackson has recently examined the similarities and connections between this model of poetry and scientific method in the early nineteenth century.[10]

The 1857 article then proceeds to suggest that science and poetry are joined together by more than methodology, arguing that both are directed by the search for 'a knowledge of all things'. In 'earlier ages', it asserts, 'poetry and science were one and the same;

now they are at least twin-sisters'. This claim encapsulates another view of the relation between science and poetry which was prominent throughout the nineteenth century: in this historical argument, the two are presented as essentially identical, having a shared origin in an ancient unity of knowledge (typically assigned to classical Greece). Over the course of time, and particularly in the specialised and fragmented cultures of modernity, this unity is dissolved, and poetry and science are divided. Some writers claim that the gap between the two will widen further in the future, while others argue that it is possible to reintegrate them; the writer of the *Chambers's* article suggests instead that they will continue to exist in a close but not identical relation: 'the two must ever keep pace, and walk hand in hand together'. After this pronouncement of kinship and co-operation, however, and still in the first paragraph, the article takes up yet another perspective on science and poetry, claiming that

> whenever the poet, overstepping the modesty of nature, illustrates his verses with images founded on unnatural, or, which is the same thing, unscientific conclusions, the pleasure derived from the poetry is marred by the incongruous associations and distorted fancies presented to our minds.[11]

This is an example of the hierarchical arguments which were also a recurring feature of nineteenth-century debates about poetry and science: the two are presented as sharing similar goals and practices, but one is given epistemological priority and authority over the other, which is identified as ancillary or subordinate. In this case, the findings of science are not referable to the standards of poetry, but poetry is made to conform to the methods and strictures of science. Poems, according to this article, are most successful, and most pleasurable for readers, when their images are scientifically accurate, based on undistorted observations of nature. The writer of the article then tries to substantiate this claim by listing scientific mistakes made by various poets.

This piece demonstrates the diversity of arguments that contributed to nineteenth-century understandings of the relation between science and poetry. On the whole, though, despite its interest in poetry's factual and observational errors, and despite its oppositional title, the article focuses more on the similarities than on the differences between the two. In contrast to Mill's 1834 essay, it claims that poetry and science are directed towards the same goal: the investigation and description of the phenomena of nature. As Ashton Nichols notes, in his essay in this volume, one of the key developments of nineteenth-century science was to reposition humanity within nature, as new knowledge of comparative anatomy and natural history demonstrated the biological similarities and ecological connections between humans and other species. Connections such as these reinforce the notion that science and poetry are concerned with the same subject—a natural world which is also the most basic context for the actions and emotions of people—and Nichols argues that, in the early nineteenth century, poets and scientific writers 'consistently claim that human beings are contiguous with the natural world rather than distinct from it. They collapse the distinction between nature and culture at the same time that they point out similarities between and among all living things'.[12] Romantic poets, and their Victorian heirs, often use their writing to reflect on whether and how developments in natural and scientific knowledge may offer insight into cultural practices (such as poetry itself). It is possible to argue, then, that poetry and science in the nineteenth century, despite their evident and important differences, were each participating in the same larger enterprise: the examination of the links between nature and human psychology, society, and culture.

Support for this view can be found in a number of Romantic and Victorian poems, in which scientific theories are incorporated into the poet's account of the links between the natural world and personal experience. In Percy Bysshe Shelley's 'Mont Blanc' (1817), for example, the sublime grandeur of the mountain is presented as emblematic of the universal forces that animate, and link together, physical nature and the human mind:

> Is this the scene
> Where the old Earthquake-daemon taught her young
> Ruin? Were these their toys? or did a sea
> Of fire envelop once this silent snow?
> None can reply—all seems eternal now.[13]

Shelley draws here on contemporary 'catastrophist' theories of geology, which argued that the surface of the earth had been shaped by sudden and violent transformations (and which were later challenged by more gradual 'uniformitarian' models of geological change), to support his account of the power and mutability of nature. Although Shelley represents geological concepts using the figurative language typical of lyrical poetry, identifying the earthquake as a 'daemon', his interest in the scientific implications of the theories remains evident. Yet these lines also point to a gap or conflict between poetry and science. The rhetorical questions, and the irregular rhyme scheme which runs throughout the poem, identify 'Mont Blanc' as an expression of doubt, rather than certitude, about the workings of nature. Geological science argues that the mountain has been subject to change over vast stretches of time, but the speaker of the poem, when faced with its imposing size and sublimity, struggles to imagine that Mont Blanc is anything other than permanent and enduring: 'all seems eternal now'. There is a tension in these lines between the scientific interpretation of nature and the subjective response which the poem sets out to articulate. In some ways, then, and in contrast to Nichols's account, it may be argued that the scientific developments of the nineteenth century separated personal experience and cultural practices from the natural world rather than bringing them closer together.

As Gillian Beer suggests in her essay on Gerard Manley Hopkins, the 'recognition of a disjunction between natural processes and human patterns of expectation and design' was a characteristic feature of nineteenth-century debates about science.[14] Scientists often interpreted this disjunction as a mark of intellectual progress, a correction of inaccurate and unfounded assumptions by the objective precision of scientific observation and analysis. Poets, conversely, were often troubled by scientific knowledge, because it seemed to construct a model of the natural world which did not conform to, or which even threatened, religious or anthropocentric beliefs. The ambiguities of Shelley's 'Mont Blanc' indicate that this was a concern for Romantic poets, but the disjunction between natural science and personal experience was registered more acutely in Victorian poetry, as the Romantic celebration of nature was complicated by the unsettling implications of new scientific ideas. Perhaps the most important of these, simultaneously linking culture to nature and estranging them from each other, was the theory of evolution by natural selection, propounded in Charles Darwin's *On the Origin of Species*. While other theorists had put forward evolutionary models of the development of species before Darwin, his account of an essentially random evolutionary process, unfolding without purpose or progress over immense expanses of time, is an example of what the historian of science Thomas S. Kuhn famously termed 'paradigm changes', revolutionary shifts in scientific theory after which 'scientists are responding to a different world'.[15] Darwinian evolution changed the Victorians' scientific understanding of the world by positing the close proximity of humans to other animal species. This was not solely a scientific paradigm change, however, because Darwinism also had a profound effect on religious and social debates: evolutionary science upset received notions of humans' exceptional status in relation to the natural world, demanding a reconsideration of established understandings of religion, morality, and human nature.

Poets recorded and reflected on the intellectual turbulence surrounding Darwinism, and other scientific theories, in the language and the subject matter of their verse. Their considerations of developments in science also shaped the forms of their writing, as they examined whether new scientific knowledge might suggest or invite new approaches to or definitions of poetry. Jason Rudy considers one instance of this in his study of poetry's responses to theories of physiology and electricity, arguing that 'the electrical sciences came to offer the Victorians a valuable framework for reading and understanding poetry'.[16] Victorian poets, Rudy suggests, did not just write about physiology and electricity. Rather, new theories from the developing physiological and electrical sciences played a part in altering the ways in which poets understood and composed the rhythms of their verse, and the ways in which readers experienced them. The relation between poetry and science in the nineteenth century, however it was defined, was inescapably reciprocal: poets borrowed from, reflected on, and reimagined the concepts of science; but science also, to some extent, changed how poetry was understood within nineteenth-century culture, and how it was written.

To give one example, May Kendall's 'Lay of the Trilobite', a popular and still frequently anthologised Victorian poem, demonstrates the ways in which science in general, and Darwinian evolutionary theory in particular, contributed to the practice of poetry in the nineteenth century. First published in the satirical magazine *Punch* in 1885, Kendall's poem is voiced by a speaker who finds the fossilised remains of an extinct prehistoric animal. The poem's title, which juxtaposes the archaic and self-consciously literary word 'lay' with the scientific classification 'trilobite', implies a tension between poetry and science, and this implication is developed over the course of its first stanza:

> A mountain's giddy height I sought,
> Because I could not find
> Sufficient vague and mighty thought
> To fill my mighty mind;
> And as I wandered ill at ease,
> There chanced upon my sight
> A native of Silurian seas,
> An ancient Trilobite.[17]

This stanza makes use of more than one poetic convention. It is written in a version of traditional ballad metre, with alternating lines of iambic tetrameter and iambic trimeter. Set on a mountain similar to the peak apostrophised in Shelley's 'Mont Blanc', it also recalls the Romantic preoccupation with representing and celebrating the intercommunication between sublime nature and the human mind. Kendall's handling of form and language, however, satirises this Romantic trope, and her poem's own generic conventions. The strict regularity of the stanza's metre imbues it with an arch and humorous tone, and the repetition of 'mighty' pokes fun at the speaker's high opinion of his own mind as he seeks to commune with nature. The stanza's ironic and critical stance towards its speaker's Romantic pretensions, and arguably towards Romantic poetics more generally, is reinforced, in its closing lines, by the introduction of the scientific terms 'Silurian' (referring to a geological epoch) and

'Trilobite'. The humour in the stanza's conclusion is double-edged: on the one hand, the use of specialist terms is another example of the speaker's intellectual ostentation; on the other hand, the scientific language sounds out of place after the Romantic clichés of the first six lines, pointing to an alternative way of thinking about the natural world, which promises to undermine the speaker's self-involved confidence.

On seeing the fossilised trilobite, the speaker interprets it at first as evidence of the divine ordering of the universe that ensures his own superiority to the extinct animal. He celebrates 'the providential plan, / That he should be a Trilobite, / And I should be a man!'. At this point, however, the trilobite is given a voice in the poem, addressing the speaker directly and troubling his complacency by informing him

> How all your faiths are ghosts and dreams,
> How in the silent sea
> Your ancestors were Monotremes—
> Whatever these may be;
> How you evolved your shining lights
> Of wisdom and perfection
> From Jelly-fish and Trilobites
> By Natural Selection.

The trilobite's words collapse the distance which the poem's speaker tried to preserve between them: the very sound and presence of the trilobite's voice within the poem inescapably place the human speaker in dialogue with it. The content of the trilobite's argument, moreover, articulates a Darwinian worldview in which there is no essential difference or hierarchy between the two species: both have evolved their defining characteristics through the same process of natural selection. The trilobite's claims integrate the human and the natural worlds, but they are at the same time unsettling, because they suggest that any beliefs about God's 'providential plan' are 'ghosts and dreams', and that the most exceptional capacities of the human mind have evolved from less exalted organisms. Again, in this stanza, scientific ideas influence the way in which the poetry is written: the tension between belief in human perfection and the Darwinian perspective embodied in the trilobite is expressed in the rhymes between incongruous words: 'dreams' and 'Monotremes', 'perfection' and 'Natural Selection'. In these examples, the similarity of sound on which rhyme is founded highlights, by contrast, the dissimilarity between the speaker's dreams of faith and wisdom, and the scientific theory which threatens to undermine them.

As its speech progresses, the trilobite enumerates the problems and confusions inflicted on humans by politics, imperialism and war, before concluding its argument by comparing these sufferings to the straightforwardness of its own prehistoric life:

> But gentle, stupid, free from woe
> I lived among my nation,
> I didn't care—I didn't know
> That I was a Crustacean.
> I didn't grumble, didn't steal,
> I *never* took to rhyme:
> Salt water was my frugal meal,
> And carbonate of lime.
>
> (author's italics)

The trilobite pushes his claims further here, reversing the terms of the human speaker's argument and suggesting not that the two species are equal or equivalent, but that the trilobite's 'gentle, stupid' life is superior. The prehistoric trilobite was untroubled by politics, misery, or dishonesty, and it was also unconcerned with poetry: 'I *never* took to rhyme'. Through the dismissive emphasis which it places on 'never', the trilobite identifies poetry as one of the 'shining lights' that it presents not as the attainments but as the burdens of humanity. As John Holmes argues, Kendall's poetry demonstrates that 'science can be disillusioning, even disenchanting'.[18] In this poem, Darwinian evolutionary theory disillusions the speaker of his belief in human superiority by undermining the idea of a providential plan, and by showing that evolution by natural selection does not render a 'more' evolved species superior to others: the trilobite was arguably better suited to its specific habitat and environment than humanity is. Kendall's science in 'Lay of the Trilobite' is not particularly accurate: 'Monotremes' (egg-laying mammals) are not ancestors of humanity, and, when the poem was republished in Kendall's 1887 volume *Dreams to Sell*, she added a note acknowledging that the trilobite was not, in fact, a crustacean. Despite these factual errors, though, the poem addresses some of the most important theoretical concepts of Darwinian science, and incorporates them into a poem which appears to question the value of poetry itself. At the same time, it is of course significant that the trilobite's argument is written in verse (the word 'rhyme', with which it dismisses poetry, is itself a rhyme). Kendall uses poetry to explore the disillusioning implications of Darwinian evolution with a humour and intellectual self-consciousness which might not have been possible in a strictly scientific textual form.

This poem shows how poets in the nineteenth century made use of scientific concepts to inform their writing about nature, the human mind and poetry itself. Even as it incorporates elements of Darwinian evolutionary theory into its verse, the poem preserves the notion of an opposition or distinction between poetic and scientific ways of thinking; it reveals, therefore, how each specific exchange between science and poetry is capable of presenting more than one perspective on the relation between the two. It is important to recognise, as well, that these exchanges were not only instigated by poets. Many nineteenth-century scientists wrote and published poetry, employing it not just as a private recreation or as emotional self-expression, but as another means of working through and disseminating their scientific ideas.[19] Scientists also incorporated poetry into the fabric of their scientific arguments and writings, a practice which is evident in the geologist Gideon Mantell's *Thoughts on a Pebble*: the first chapter of the book employs quotations from Shakespeare, Sir Walter Scott, James Beattie, Mary Howitt, and, most prominently, Lord Byron. Although Mantell's book was written as an introduction to geology aimed at children, it was not uncommon for scientific texts of all types, from popularisations to textbooks to original treatises, to feature some poetry. Many of Mantell's quotations are inserted into his argument without comment, but at times, such as in this introduction to a quotation from Byron's *Childe Harold's Pilgrimage*, he gives a particular reason for making use of verse:

> Our noble poet, Lord Byron, in his sublime apostrophe to the Sea, has most eloquently enunciated the startling fact revealed by modern geological researches,—namely, that if the character of immutability be attributable to anything on the surface of our planet, it is to the ocean and not to the land!—[20]

There are several ways of interpreting Mantell's discussion of the 'noble poet', and the collaboration between poetry and geology which it announces. The geologist, arguably, credits Byron's poetry with significant scientific insight, as it expresses the same 'fact' that has been verified by 'modern geological researches'. In this interpretation, poetry and science are set on a footing of epistemological equality and mutual corroboration: they have equal and supporting stakes in the geological knowledge which the book presents. It may also be argued, conversely, that Mantell presents poetry here as mere eloquence, an expressive and fluent enunciation of a fact that has been 'revealed' and proven solely through the methods of scientific research. Poetry and science, in this reading, are placed in a hierarchical relation, in which poetry becomes little more than an adornment or embellishment of the objective truths of scientific knowledge.

Mantell's reference to the eloquence of poetry may, however, be a mark of respect rather than an expression of his belief in science's superiority. Despite the growing influence of scientific thinking, and of the technological applications of science, in nineteenth-century Britain, a widespread sense of scepticism or worry continued to surround scientific accounts of the world such as Darwinian evolution. Poetry, on the other hand, although it often reached no more than a small audience, retained its position in nineteenth-century culture as the epitome of artistic creativity, and as the articulation of enduring emotional and spiritual truths. Dawson and Shuttleworth note that nineteenth-century scientists recognised the prestige of poetic expression, and that their writings 'often made use of the enormous cultural authority of Victorian poetry to reinforce, as well as add respectability to, their often controversial scientific arguments'.[21] Poetry took on an active role in the dissemination of concepts from a range of scientific disciplines in the nineteenth century, converting the specialised and possibly troubling formulations of science into language that conveyed a cultural and emotional resonance which might not be realised in scientific writing. While poetry influenced the development of science, the communication between the two fields also worked in the opposite direction, as scientific concepts and practices contributed to changes in the theory, the formal practice and the language of nineteenth-century verse.

Notes

1 John Stuart Mill, 'On the Application of the Terms of Poetry, Science and Philosophy', *Monthly Repository* (new series) 8 (1834), 324.
2 Ibid., p. 327.
3 William Wordsworth, 'Preface to the Lyrical Ballads', in Stephen Gill (ed.), *William Wordsworth*, 21st-Century Oxford Authors (Oxford: Oxford University Press, 2010), p. 64.
4 Samuel Taylor Coleridge, 'Treatise on Method', in H. A. Jackson and J. R. de J. Jackson (eds), *Shorter Works and Fragments*, 2 vols (Princeton, NJ: Princeton University Press, 1995), I, 680.
5 Immanuel Kant, *Critique of Judgement*, trans. James Creed Meredith, ed. Nicholas Walker (Oxford: Oxford University Press), p. 155.
6 See: Matthew Arnold, 'Literature and Science' in R. H. Super (ed.), *Philistinism in England and America* (Ann Arbor, MI: University of Michigan Press, 1974), pp. 53–73 and Thomas Henry Huxley, 'Science and Culture', *Science and Culture and Other Essays* (London: Macmillan, 1881), pp. 1–23.
7 Gowan Dawson and Sally Shuttleworth, 'Introduction: Science and Victorian Poetry', *Victorian Poetry*, 41 (2003), 1–10.
8 George Levine, *Realism, Ethics and Secularism: Essays on Victorian Literature and Science* (Cambridge: Cambridge University Press, 2008), p.175.
9 William Chambers and Robert Chambers (eds.), 'Science versus Poetry', *Chambers's Journal*, 169 (March 1857), 198.
10 See: Noel Jackson, *Science and Sensation in Romantic Poetry* (Cambridge: Cambridge University Press, 2008).
11 Chambers and Chambers, 'Science *versus* Poetry', p. 198.
12 Ashton Nichols, *Beyond Romantic Ecocriticism: Towards Urbanatural Roosting* (London: Palgrave Macmillan, 2011), p. 22.

13 Percy Bysshe Shelley, 'Mont Blanc: Lines Written in the Vale of Chamouni', in Kelvin Everest and Geoffrey Matthews eds., *The Poems of Shelley 1804–1817* (London: Longman, 1989), pp. 542–549.

14 Gillian Beer, *Open Fields: Science in Cultural Encounter* (Oxford: Oxford University Press, 1996), p. 259.

15 Thomas S. Kuhn, *The Structure of Scientific Revolutions* 4th ed., (Chicago: Chicago University Press, 1962), p. 111.

16 Jason Rudy, *Electric Meters: Victorian Physiological Poetics* (Athens: Ohio University Press, 2009), p. 4.

17 For this and following quotations from Kendall's 'Lay of the Trilobite', see: May Kendall, 'Lay of the Trilobite', *Dreams to Sell* (London: Longmans Green & Co., 1887), pp. 7–10.

18 John Holmes, 'The Lay of the Trilobite: Rereading May Kendall' *19: Interdisciplinary Studies in then Long Nineteenth Century*, 11 (2010), p. 7.

19 See: Daniel Brown, *The Poetry of Victorian Scientists: Style, Science and Nonsense* (Cambridge: Cambridge University Press, 2013).

20 G. A. Mantell, *Thoughts on a Pebble, or a First Lesson in Geology* (London: Reeve, Benham and Reeve, 1849), p. 29.

21 Dawson and Shuttleworth, p. 9.

41 Science *versus* Poetry (1857)

William Chambers and Robert Chambers

Poetry has been well defined as

Truth severe in fairy fiction dressed;

for the office of the poet is to hold the mirror up to nature, and, like the painter, give a faithful reflection of whatever he may deem worthy of delineation; whether he reflects the truth of nature direct on the imagination of his reader, or the truth merely as it affects his own feelings and sentiments. Poetry, thus requiring exact accuracy of description, with great variety of embellishment, imperatively demands a correlative amount of knowledge in the poet. Indeed the word muse, as applied to poetical composition, is derived from a Greek phrase signifying to inquire; and as inquiry is the source or parent of all knowledge, the ancients considered the peculiar attribute of the presiding genius of poetry to be a knowledge of all things animate and inanimate, intellectual and corporeal. In every clime, and among every people, the poets were the first historians; and even laws, oracles, moral precepts, and religious rites, were in the earlier ages clothed in verse divine. Then poetry and science were one and the same; now they are at least twin-sisters; and though the onward strides of science are long and rapid, poetry may not, cannot lag behind—the two must ever keep pace, and walk hand in hand together. For, however difficult it may be to assign the definite limits of poetic licence, yet, whenever the poet, overstepping the modesty of nature, illustrates his verses with images founded on unnatural, or, which is the same thing, unscientific conclusions, the pleasure derivable from the poetry is marred by the incongruous associations and distorted fancies presented to our minds. The long muster-roll of qualifications requisite to constitute a poet, as detailed by Imlac to Rasselas, were probably never possessed by any human being; yet such is the inspiration of the art, that few aggressions against natural science are found among many volumes of immortal verse. Of these few, our object is to notice some, if not altogether for the instruction, may we hope for the amusement of the reader.

Hamlet argumentatively says: 'If the sun breed maggots in a dead dog,' and proceeds to draw an inference from his postulate, without in the slightest degree questioning its accuracy. That the sun had such a creative power, and the corruption of animal matter spontaneously produced insects, was the general opinion in the time of Shakspeare; and, in fact, a belief in what naturalists now term equivocal generation, is as ancient as the Augustan era of old Rome, when Virgil, for the benefit of husbandmen, minutely described the whole process of spontaneously producing a swarm of bees. A steer of two years old having first been killed, the poet, as translated by Dryden, thus proceeds:

They leave the beast, but first sweet flowers are strewed
Beneath his body, broken boughs, and thyme,
And pleasing cassia just renewed in prime.
This must be done ere spring makes equal day,
When western winds on curling waters play:
Ere painted meads produce their flowery crops,
Or swallows twitter on the chimney-tops.
The tainted blood, in this close prison pent,
Begins to boil, and through the bones ferment;
Then, wondrous to behold, new creatures rise,
A moving mass at first, and short of thighs;
Till shooting out with legs, and imped with wings,
The grubs proceed to bees with pointed stings,
And more and more affecting air, they try
Their tender pinions, and begin to fly.

In all probability, Virgil was deceived by the very great natural resemblance existing between the bee and the *syrphus,* a species of blow-fly; and though his contemporaries had full faith in the infallibility of his directions, it would be difficult to find any one, at the present day, so ignorant as to believe that insects could be produced in a foreign body, except from eggs previously deposited.

Among all the manifold marvels of nature, nothing is more wonderful than the varied changes insects undergo during their short existence. In the moth tribe, to which we more particularly wish to refer, the egg, deposited in a suitable locality, is in course of time hatched into a crawling, many-legged caterpillar. In this state, it eats voraciously, and casts its skin several times. Having arrived at its full growth as a caterpillar, it casts its skin for the last time, becoming a nymph or chrysalis, an oviform mass without external mouth, eyes, or limbs; and in deathlike torpor awaits its final transformation, when, bursting its cell, it flies forth a beautiful and perfect insect, to propagate its kind, and die in a few days, perhaps hours. This mysterious series of progressive perfectibility has frequently afforded both poet and philosopher a fine emblem of the immortality of the soul; but in the following lines the poet, reversing the real order of nature, erroneously describes the perfect moth as assuming the imperfect state of the nymph:

Thus the gay moth, by sun and vernal gales,
Called forth to wander o'er the dewy vales,
From flower to flower, from sweet to sweet, will stray,
Till tired and satiate with her food and play,
Deep in the shades she builds her peaceful nest,
In loved seclusion pleased at length to rest:
There folds the wings that erst so widely bore,
Becomes a household nymph, and seeks to range no more.

Darwin commits a somewhat similar error, when alluding to the 'old grub, time out of mind the fairies' coachmaker:'

So sleeps in silence the curculio, shut
In the dark chamber of the caverned nut;

Erodes with ivory beak the vaulted shell,
And quits on filmy wings its narrow cell.

Now, the curculio or weevil passes its larva state of existence only in the nut, and having eaten its way out, falls to the ground, where it becomes a chrysalis; and then undergoing its last change, acquires its 'filmy wings' in the earth, and not, as Darwin has it, in 'the vaulted shell.'

Few but have witnessed, in autumnal mornings, the filmy threads termed gossamer, which in some localities are so plentiful as to carpet the earth and clothe the hedges in their shining dew-besprinkled folds. It is now well known that this substance is the work of two species of spider, though naturalists are not as yet agreed with respect to the exact mode of its production. Our ancestors, however, held that gossamer was dew scorched by the sun. Spenser speaks of

The fine nets which oft we woven see
Of scorched dew;

and another poet thus alludes to the same phenomenon

As light and thin as cobwebs that do fly
In the blue air, caused by the autumnal sun,
That boils the dew that on the earth doth lie.

In an old romance, at one time the book of its season, but now completely forgotten, named *Mandeville,* the author describes a ruined castle inhabited by owls and bitterns. Now, though the bittern has been mentioned even in Scripture as the emblem of desolation, it is not the desolation of a ruined castle, but of some wild upland marsh, far from the dwellings of man, irreclaimable by his energies, and incapable of affording sustenance to the animals he domesticates. There the bittern abides in dreary solitude; and in the still nights of spring, ascending by a spiral flight to a great altitude, he serenades his mate, engaged in the maternal duties of the nest below: and it is a most extraordinary serenade. Let the reader fancy a burst of uncouth fiendish laughter, gratingly, piercingly loud, as if the bellow of a bull were mingled with the neigh of a horse, and he will have a faint idea of the wild boom of the bittern—as wild as the desert morass over which it resounds. As the bird booms, the listener really fancies that the unstable quagmire beneath his feet is shaken by the noise; and this circumstance may be accounted for by the general affection of the sentient system caused by the rude jar upon the ear, a feeling experienced with other harsh grating sounds. From a very early period, however, the popular notion has been that the bittern boomed by plunging his bill in the muddy marsh; and Thomson has not only adopted this absurd idea, but also ascribed the season of booming to an earlier part of the year than when it actually takes place:

As yet the trembling year is unconfirmed,
And winter oft at eve resumes the breeze,
Chills the pale morn, and bids his driving sleets
Deform the day delightless—so that scarce
The bittern knows his time, with bill engulfed,
To shake the sounding marsh; or from the shore

The plovers, when to scatter o'er the heath,
And sing their wild notes to the listening waste.

In the *Lady of the Lake,* a fine description of the solitary desolation of an ancient battle-field is sadly deteriorated by a simple error regarding the natural habit of a well-known bird:

The knot-grass fettered there the hand
Which once could burst an iron band;
Beneath the broad and ample bone,
That bucklered heart to fear unknown,
A feeble and a timorous guest,
The fieldfare, framed her lowly nest.

The fieldfare is truly a timorous guest, but it is a winter one. It never frames a nest in this country; and if it did remain with us during the summer, it would, like all the rest of its tribe, build in a tree, and not on the ground. Milton, in his *Lycidas,* in verses of singular elegance, almost offends our sensibilities by enumerating as 'vernal flowers' many which are the production of summer and early autumn:

Ye valleys low, where the mild whispers use
Of shades, and wanton winds, and gushing brooks,
On whose fresh lap the swart star sparely looks,
Throw hither all your quaint enamelled eyes,
That on the green turf suck the honied showers,
And purple all the ground with vernal flowers.
Bring the rathe primrose that forsaken dies,
The tufted crow-toe, and pale jessamine,
The white-pink, and the pansy freaked with jet,
The glowing violet,
The musk-rose, and the well-attired woodbine,
The cowslip wan that hangs the pensive head,
And every flower that sad embroidery wears:
Bid amaranthus all his beauty shed,
And daffodillies fill their cups with tears,
To strew the laureat hearse where Lycid lies.

The sense of hearing in the mole is well known to be most exquisite, and Shakspeare ably alludes to the fact; but he is in error with respect to the animal being blind:

Pray you, tread softly, that the blind mole may not
Hear a footfall.

The mole has eyes, and though a limited power of vision might seem sufficient for such a 'dweller in the dark,' it can see better than is generally imagined. After all, we can scarcely blame the great poet for merely repeating a very common error of his period; while, on the other hand, he declares that crickets can hear—a fact which was denied by entomologists down almost to the present day:

I will tell it softly, young crickets shall not hear me.

It was Brunelli, an Italian naturalist, who first proved that insects had a sense of hearing, by experimenting with crickets. He shut up several of these noisy, but not altogether unharmonious insects in an apartment where they would chirp all day, if he did not alarm them by knocking on the door; and at last he learned to imitate their chirp so well, that they regularly replied to him. Moreover, he confined a male cricket on one side of his garden, placing a female on the other, but at liberty; and as soon as the lady-cricket heard the merry chirp of her imprisoned beau, she made the best of her way to comfort and solace him.

It would be hypercritical to find fault with Shakspeare in *Midsummer Night's Dream,* where he makes Titania tell her fairy attendants to be kind and courteous to Bottom, and to

> Feed him with apricoks and dewberries,
> With purple grapes, green figs, and mulberries;
> The honey bags steal from the humble bees,
> And for night tapers, crop their waxen thighs,
> And fight them at the fiery glowworm's eyes,
> To have my love to bed and to arise.

In reality, the light of the glowworm is not in the head, but at the opposite extremity of its body. But Moore is certainly open to censure where one of his angels talks of

> the light
> The glowworm hangs out to allure
> Her mate to her green bower at night.

For both the winged male, as well as wingless females, and even their larvæ, also possess the light; and the best entomologists admit that they cannot satisfactorily explain the cause or object of the singular phosphorescent phenomenon exhibited by this insect.

The paper nautilus, *Argonauta Argo,* has long been a favourite simile, and a sad stumbling-block among the poetic race:

> Learn of the little nautilus to sail,
> Spread the thin oar, and catch the driving gale.

It is to Madame Jeannette Power, a French lady-naturalist, whose experiments and observations have received the highest praise from Professor Owen and other distinguished European *savans,* that we are indebted for the true history and nature of the argonaut. Keeping a quantity of these beautiful *cephalopods* in a large marine vivarium in Sicily, Madame Power was enabled to observe their habits with the greatest minuteness. The two velated dorsal arms, that the poets imagined to be sails, are in fact the covering of the shell, which they enclose like the mantle of the cowrie, and by their calcifying power, not only in the first instance form the shell, but afterwards keep it in repair. The so-called oars are not used when the animal is moving through the water, but protruded forwards from the head to be out of the way—the motion being in a backward direction, and produced, as in all the cuttle tribe, by the alternate expansion and contraction of the sac, and ejection of water through the siphon. A steam fishing-vessel, recently constructed at one of the Scotch ports, was propelled in a not very dissimilar manner.

A still more extraordinary wonder of the deep has been commemorated in poetry; Milton mentions that 'sea-beast'

> Which God of all his works
> Created hugest that swim the ocean flood.
> Him haply slumbering on the Norway foam,
> The pilot of some small night-foundered skiff,
> Deeming some island oft, as seamen tell,
> With fixed anchor in his scaly rind
> Moors by his side.

Yet we can scarcely blame Milton for alluding to this animal, the mythical kraken—

> On the deep
> Stretcht like a promontorie—

that had previously been described by Olaus Magnus and Bishop Pontoppidan. Gesner, too, the leading naturalist of the age, presents us with an engraving of it, in which the 'scaly rind' forms a prominent feature. Milton also qualifies his description with the words 'as seamen tell.' Undoubtedly, one of these seamen was Sinbad, the Arabian Ulysses, who, taking the animal for an island, landed to cook his dinner upon it, and in consequence nearly lost his life. The companions of St Brandanus, the Irish Sinbad, were taken in and done for in the very same manner by 'a great fish named Jasconye, which laboureth night and day to put his tail in his mouth, but for greatness he may not.'

Moore sings of an island, which, if more poetical than the one formed by the huge 'sea-beast slumbering on the Norway foam,' is quite as irreconcilable with common sense and the fixed laws of nature:

> Oh, had we some bright little isle of our own,
> In a blue summer ocean far off and alone,
> Where a leaf never dies in the still blooming bowers,
> And the bee banquets on through a whole year of flowers.

An island where a leaf never dies, and the flowers bloom all the year round, must be situated in the tropics, where there is almost no twilight, where the moment the sun sets, darkness covers the earth, and when it rises, day as suddenly succeeds to night. But Moore continues:

> Where the sun loves to pause
> With so fond a delay,
> That the night only draws
> A thin veil o'er the day.

These last lines accurately describe a summer night in the extreme northern islands of Scotland, or in Norway, where the slight depression of the sun beneath the horizon causes a short night, not of darkness, but of twilight. In fact, Moore, in the above lines, has combined two incompatible conditions—a perpetual summer and short night of twilight, the first found near the equator only, the last towards the pole.

Poets and moralists have in all times celebrated the industry and alleged foresight of the ant, upholding the tiny insect as a lesson and example to mankind. But although the diligence of the ant tribe is unquestionable, still it is well known now that the European ants at least do not lay up a store of food for the winter; nor do they require it, as they pass the cold weather in a state of torpidity. Still there can be no doubt that, in eastern climes, ants provide a store of provisions to last them over the rainy season, when they are unable to go abroad—just as several species of wasps in South America store honey, though their European representatives do not. In the *Transactions of the Entomological Society,* there is an interesting account of a tribe of ants, observed by Colonel Sykes, at Poonah, in India, which carefully dry and store up the seeds of a kind of grass (*panicum*), for no other imaginable purpose but for food. So the wise king was, morally and zoologically speaking, correct when he said: 'Go to the ant, thou sluggard; consider her ways and be wise: which having no guide, overseer, or ruler, provideth her meat in the summer, and gathereth her food in the harvest.'

42   Thoughts on a Pebble, or a First Lesson in Geology (1849)

Gideon Algernon Mantell

"Honoured, therefore, be thou, thou small pebble, lying in the lane; and whenever any one looks at thee, may he think of the beautiful and noble world he lives in, and all of which it is capable"

— LEIGH HUNT'S *London Journal*, p. 10

Well might our immortal Shakspeare talk of "*Sermons in stones;*" and Lavater exclaim, that "*Every grain of sand is an immensity;*" and the author of 'Contemplations of Nature' remark, that "*there is no picking up a pebble by the brook-side without finding all nature in connexion with it.*"

I shall confine my remarks to a *flint* pebble, as being the kind of stone familiar to every one. The pebble I hold in my hand was picked up in the bed of the torrent which is dashing down the side of yonder hill, and winding its way through that beautiful valley, and over those

> Huge rocks and mounds confus'dly hurl'd,
> The fragments of an earlier world,

Which partially filling up the chasm, and obstructing the course of the rushing waters, give rise to those gentle murmurings that are so inexpressibly soothing and delightful to the soul.

Upon examining this stone I discover that it is but the fragment of a much larger mass, and has evidently been transported from a distance, for its surface is smooth and rounded, the angles having been worn away by friction against other pebbles, produced by the agency of running water. I trace the stream to its source, half way up the hill, and find that it gushes out from a bed of gravel lying on a stratum of clay, which forms the eminence where I am standing, and is nearly 300 feet above the level of the British Channel. From this accumulation of water-worn materials the pebble must have been removed by the torrent, and carried down to the spot where it first attracted our notice; but we are still very far from having ascertained its origin. The bed of stones on the summit of this hill is clearly but a heap of transported gravel – an ancient sea-beach or shingle – formed of chalk-flints, that at some remote period were detached from their parent rock, and broken, rolled, and thrown together, by the action of the waves.

[…]

The composition of the Chalk, and the prevalence throughout that rock of the relics of animals that can only live in salt-water, prove incontestably that the chalk and flint were deposited in the sea; and that our beautiful South Downs, now so smooth and verdant, and supporting thousands of flocks and herds, and the rich plains and fertile valleys spread around their flanks, were once the bed of an ocean. It is also evident not only that such must have been the case, but also that the Chalk was deposited in the basin of a very *deep* sea – in the profound abyss of an ocean as vast as the Atlantic.

From the absence of gravel, shingle, and seabeach, it is certain that the white chalk-strata were formed at a great distance from sea-shores and cliffs; and this inference is confirmed by the swarms of shells termed *Ammonites* and *Nautili*, which we know from their peculiar structure were, like the recent pearly Nautilus, inhabitants of deep waters only. For these are chambered shells; that is, are divided internally by thin transverse shelly septa or plates, into numerous cells; the body of the animal occupied only the outer compartment, but was connected with the entire series of chambers by a tube or siphuncle, which passed through each partition. This mechanism constituted an apparatus which contributed to the buoyancy of these animals when afloat on the waves; for the Ammonites and Nautili were able to swim on the surface, or sink to the depths of the ocean at pleasure.

> The tender Nautilus who steers his prow,
> The sea-born sailor of his shell canoe,
> The Ocean Mab, the fairy of the sea,
> O'er the blue waves at will to roam is free.
> He, when the lightning-winged tornadoes sweep
> The surf, is safe, his home is in the deep;
> And triumphs o'er the Armadas of mankind,
> Which shake the world, yet crumble in the wind.
>
> BYRON, *The Island.*

The Ammonites, so called from the supposed resemblance of their shells to the fabled horn of Jupiter Ammon, are only known in a fossil state; but they must have swarmed in the ancient seas, for several hundred species have been discovered in the Chalk and antecedent strata, though none have been found in any deposits of more recent formation; at the termination of the chalk epoch the whole race, therefore, appears to have perished. The Ammonites are commonly termed *snake-stones*, from the origin ascribed to them by local legends; those of Whitby are well known.

> Thus Whitby's nuns exulting told –
> How that of thousand snakes, each one
> Was changed into a coil of stone,
> When holy Hilda prayed:
> Themselves, within their sacred bound,
> Their stony folds had often found.
>
> SCOTT'S *Marmion.*

The Nautili were the contemporaries of the Ammonites, and many kinds are found associated with those shells, in strata far more ancient than the Chalk; and several species of both genera, as we have previously shown, were inhabitants of the cretaceous ocean. When the Ammonites became extinct, the Nautili continued to flourish, and numerous examples occur in the strata that were deposited during the vast period which intervened between the close of the Chalk formation, and the dawn of the existing condition of the earth's surface. At the present time two or three kinds only are known in a living state, and these are restricted to the seas of tropical climes, and so seldom approach the shores, that but few specimens of the animals that inhabit the shells have been obtained.

The Nautilus, therefore, is one of those types of animal organization that have survived all the physical revolutions to which the surface of the earth was subjected during the innumerable ages that preceded the creation of the human race. This remarkable fact is portrayed with much force and beauty by Mrs. Howitt, in the following stanzas:

TO THE NAUTILUS.

> Thou didst laugh at sun and breeze
> In the new created seas;
> Thou wast with the reptile broods
> In the old sea solitudes,
> Sailing in the new-made light,
> With the curled-up Ammonite.
> Thou surviv'dst the awful shock,
> Which turn'd the ocean-bed to rock;
> And chang'd its myriad living swarms
> To the marble's veined forms.
> Thou wert there, thy little boat,
> Airy voyager! kept afloat,
> O'er the waters wild and dismal,
> O'er the yawning gulfs abysmal;
> Amid wreck and overturning,
> Rock-imbedding, heaving, burning,
> Mid the tumult and the stir,
> Thou, most ancient mariner!
> In that pearly boat of thine,
> Sail'dst upon the troubled brine.

We have thus acquired satisfactory proof that the flint of which our pebble is composed, was once fluid in an ocean teeming with beings, of genera and species unknown in a living state, and that it consolidated and became imbedded in the chalk, which was then being deposited at the bottom of the sea; hence the shells, corals, and other organic remains, which we now find attached to its surface, and enclosed in its substance. Thus much for the origin of the pebble; let us next inquire by what means it was dislodged from its rocky sepulchre, cast up from the depths of the ocean, and transported to the summit of the hill whence it was dislodged by yonder torrent. If we stroll along the sea-shore, and observe the changes which are there going on, we shall obtain an answer to these questions; for

> There is a *language* by the lonely shore-
> There is society where none intrudes,
> By the deep Sea, and music in its roar!

> BYRON

The incessant dashing of the waves against the base of the chalk-cliffs, undermines the strata, and huge masses of rock are constantly giving way and falling into the waters. The chalk then becomes softened and disintegrated, and is quickly reduced to the state of mud, and transported to the tranquil depths of the ocean, where it subsides and forms new deposits; but the flints thus detached, are broken and rolled by attrition in the state of the boulders, pebbles, and gravel, and ultimately of sand.

Now we must bear in mind, that had the chalk remained at the bottom of the deep sea in which it was originally deposited, it would not have been exposed to these destructive operations. It is therefore manifest, that at some very distant period of the earth's physical history, the bed of the Chalk-ocean was broken up, extensive areas were protruded above the waters, lines of sea-cliffs were formed, and boulders, sand, and shingle accumulated at their base. Subsequent elevations of the land took place, and finally, the sea-beach was raised to its present situation, which is several hundred feet above the level of the sea!

Every part of the earth's surface present unequivocal proofs that the elevation of the bed of the ocean in some places, and the subsidence of the dry land in others, have been, and are still going on; and that, in truth, the continual changes in the relative position of the land and water, are the effects of laws which the Divine Author of the Universe has impressed on matter, and thus rendered it capable of perpetual renovation:-

> Art, Empire, Earth itself, to change are doomed;
> Earthquakes have raised to heaven the humble vale,
> And gulfs the mountain's mighty mass entombed,
> And where the Atlantic rolls wide continents have bloomed.

BEATTIE

Our noble poet, Lord Byron, in his sublime apostrophe to the Sea, has most eloquently enunciated the startling fact revealed by modern geological researches, – namely, that if the character of immutability be attributable to anything on the surface of our planet, it is to the ocean and not to the land!-

> Roll on, thou deep and dark blue ocean — roll!
>   Ten thousand fleets sweep over thee in vain;
>   Man marks the earth with ruin — his control
>   Stops with the shore: — upon the watery plain
>   The wrecks are all thy deed, nor doth remain
>   A shadow of man's ravage, save his own,
>   When for a moment, like a drop of rain,
>   He sinks into thy depths with bubbling groan,
> Without a grave, unknell'd, uncoffin'd, and unknown!

> Thy shores are empires, changed in all save thee, —
>   Assyria, Greece, Rome, Carthage, what are they?
>   Thy waters wasted them while they were free,
>   And many a tyrant since; their shores obey
>   The stranger, slave, or savage, – their decay
>   Has dried up realms to deserts: – not so thou,
>   Unchangeable, save to thy wild waves' play —
> *Time writes no wrinkle on thine azure brow:*
> *Such as Creation's dawn beheld, thou rollest now!*

> Thou glorious mirror, where the Almighty's form
>   Glasses itself in tempests; in all time,

Calm or convulsed — in breeze, or gale, or storm,
Icing the pole, or in the torrid clime
Dark-heaving, boundless, endless, and sublime —
The image of Eternity — the throne
Of the Invisible; even from out thy slime
The monsters of the deep are made; each zone
Obeys thee: thou goest forth, dread, fathomless, alone!

I will conclude this "first lesson" with the following beautiful remark of an eminent living philosopher: – "To discover order and intelligence, in scenes of apparent wildness and confusion, is the pleasing task of the geological inquirer; who recognizes, in the changes which are continually taking place on the surface of the globe, a series of necessary operations, by which the harmony, beauty, and integrity of the Universe are maintained and perpetuated; and which must be regarded, not as symptoms of frailty or decay, but as wise provisions of the Supreme Cause, to ensure that circle of changes, so essential to animal and vegetable existence."

43 Helmholtz, Tyndall, Gerard Manley Hopkins: Leaps of the Prepared Imagination (1996)

Gillian Beer

John Tyndall was probably the most important single figure among the scientific community for those concerned with the relations between ordinary human perceptions and science. Thomas Henry Huxley had more combative presence, but whereas Huxley concentrated on evolutionary and anthropological processes. Tyndall was principally concerned with heat, light, sound, ether, matter. Through his writing the cosmological was articulated near at hand, and through his demonstrations the invisible and inaudible reaches of vibration that make up life were manifested, with the production of artificial blue skies and singing rods. It is not altogether surprising that spiritualists, whom he detested, sought to claim Tyndall as a medium. For the physical sciences, he asserted, it is necessary not only empirically to demonstrate but also to find a way beyond experience: 'The Germans express the act of picturing by the world *vorstellen*, and the picture they call a *Vorstellung*. We have no word in English which comes nearer to our requirements than *Imagination*.'[1] So although he emphasizes always materialism he is able to give a transcendental edge to that ordinarily unmystical concept: despite denying vitalism—and indeed all religious authority—he contrived to keep some dark space for an ordering, though not a pre-emptive, Intelligence.

This ambiguous position was not enough to ward off charges of atheism but it softened his cultural role and made his voice audible in circles that might otherwise have shut their ears. The distinguished mathematician J. J. Sylvester spoke of him as one 'whom Science and Poetry woo with an equal spell, and whose ideas have a faculty for arranging themselves in forms of order and beauty as spontaneously and unfailingly as those crystalline solutions from which ... he drew so vivid and instructive an illustration'.[2] Tyndall's imaginative eloquence and his power of seemly yet unexpected exposition gave him a major interpretative role in Victorian culture. He wrote in a style that gave pleasure to an extraordinary variety of readers and he published in a great array of journals, both technical and general.[3] Science, he held, 'not unfrequently derives motive power from an ultra-scientific source'.[4] He was both a highly respected and an innovative worker, constantly referred to in *Nature* during the 1870s particularly. His scientific education in Germany and his friendship with Helmholtz gave him, moreover, a much broader awareness of current possibilities in European science than a cultural chauvinist like P. G. Tait, whose later book on *Light* so irritated Hopkins.[5]

The particular urgency for Hopkins of John Tyndall's writing, in the light of Helmholtz, on sound, colour, the conserving and dissipation of energy, has been effaced. That effacing has obscured sources of conflict within Victorian experience, which find a peculiarly intense form in Hopkins's poetry and in his journals. Tyndall was not only an exceptionally alluring and widely published writer on scientific questions, he was also well known as a materialist, as one who refused the idea of miracles, and one who was not afraid to accept the epithet 'atheist'.[6] The present essay therefore brings to the surface a network of allusion and controversy, shared with other Victorian intellectuals, that in Hopkins's work becomes vehemently condensed.

'He was intimately versed in the whole range of scientific expression, and showed a preference for such terms as were most recondite and but seldom used.' So wrote Father John MacLeod, a younger contemporary, in the internal journal of the Jesuits in 1906.[7] This strain in Hopkins was no mere quaint attachment to the out of-the-way; it was rather an expression of his earnest familiarity with a field of experience more openly available to the Victorians than it is to us: the current work of scientists and the difficult, world-embracing meanings of their work. It is also a sign of his abiding fascination with the specificity of things, a specificity that is only at great cost brought into temper with authority.

In Roman Catholic circles at the time new developments in scientific theory were by no means always seen as being in conflict with established doctrine. In the late 1870s *The Month*, the main organ of educated Catholic opinion, was sanguine about the possibility of reconciling evolutionism with the teachings of the Church. In a review essay on St. George Mivart's *Lessons from Nature, as Manifested in Mind and Matter*, which refers back also to Mivart's earlier *Genesis of Species*, John Rickaby claims that Mivart 'had previously shown the complete harmony between the strictest orthodoxy and the theory of evolution'.[8] Hopkins himself had taken the same view of Mivart's work in a letter to his mother two years earlier in 1874: 'You should read St. George Mivart's *Genesis of Species*: he is an Evolutionist though he combats downright Darwinism and is very orthodox' (*Letters*, III, 128). Rickaby continues in *The Month*: 'It would he well too if Catholics would learn more accurately the real bearings of the relations between science and religion, and would never forget that it is impossible that dogma can conflict with physical science.'

This sanguine view is tempered in the next paragraph which looks back towards earlier conditions of Church authority: 'We are fortunate that in these troubled days of her journey through time, the Church has had no need to shield the faith of her children by laying restraint, as she has sometimes been obliged to do, on the free discussion of the discoveries of science.' Be that as it may, St. George Mivart was eventually excommunicated as a result of articles he wrote from the mid-1880s on, repudiating ecclesiastical authority.

That sequence of events illustrates both the openness of Catholicism to the latest scientific discoveries and the dangerous borderland trodden by all those within the Church who were interested in scientific explanation. All was well so long as the discoveries could be appropriated to an earlier body of approved knowledge or shown to issue from the words of earlier teachers—as the article under discussion concludes: 'It has been shown that the possibility of this latest discovery of the gradual evolution of species was prepared for in the teaching of the most honoured among the great minds which in all ages have devoted themselves to her service.' Indeed, in an article a few months later, 'St. Augustine and Scientific Unbelief', the writer invokes the difficulty of belief in recent physics as an analogy to difficulties of belief in transubstantiation. In each case it is necessary, he argues, to rely upon the authority of teachings that one cannot, unless especially trained and long practiced, encompass. The writer invokes Helmholtzian theory:

What pupil would be allowed to interrupt the very first lectures of his professor of physics by such premature questions as these: If heat is a mode of motion, how do we cool hot tea by stirring it? If light is propagated by modulations, how do we actually see the rays in straight lines? If musical harmony depends upon a certain regularity, proportion, and interlacement of atmospheric waves, how is it that these conditions are not utterly destroyed by the ever-varied modifying obstacles encountered in different concert rooms, and by the ever-varied relative position of the several instruments?[9]

The difficult novelty of current physics—whose formulation here draws directly on Tyndall's writing in *Sound*—demonstrates that the universe is full of unexpected and hidden phenomena for which authoritative interpretation is required.

An often-repeated claim among Victorian scientists, on the other hand, was that science was the love of truth 'for its own sake'. For example, in *Nature,* 1 May 1884, adjacent to a long article on 'The Krakatoa Eruption' whose after-sunsets so fascinated observers, including Hopkins, S. Newcomb distinguishes different attitudes to authority:

> If called upon to define the scientific spirit, I should say that it was the love of truth for its own sake. This definition carries with it the idea of a love of exactitude—the more exact we are the nearer we are to the truth. It carries with it a certain dependence of authority; because, although an adherence to authoritative propositions taught us by our ancestors, and which we regard as true, may, in a certain sense, be regarded as love of truth, yet it ought rather to be called a love of these propositions, irrespective of their truth. The lover of truth is ready to reject every previous opinion the moment he sees reason to doubt its exactness. (10)

The emphasis here on exact observation chimes in with Hopkins's work. Certainly, Hopkins was insistent that new circumstances heighten observation: in one of his contributions to *Nature* he points out that many attribute to the Krakatoa eruption effects already observable but not then paid much attention to: 'It is, however, right and important to distinguish phenomena really new from old ones first observed under new circumstances which make people unusually observant' (30 Oct. 1884, 636). Other of his contributions to *Nature* make essentially the same points: 'I may remark that things common at home have sometimes first been remarked abroad. The stars in snow were first observed in the polar regions; it was thought that they only arose there, but now everyone sees them with the naked eye on his coatsleeve' (*Nature* (16 Nov. 1882), 53). 'There seems to be no reason why the phenomenon should not be common, and perhaps if looked out for it would be found to be. But who looks east at sunset?'

You must first expect to find, or you must look from a point of view contrary to the ordinary, to make such discoveries, Hopkins indicates. New circumstances—the encounter with phenomena strained within the language and metrics of a poem, for example—can make things fresh. But though de-familiarization can make things *seem* new, Hopkins emphasizes that many of them were already there, all about us. The good sense of this argument also serves to keep most phenomena within the bounds of established knowledge. Newcomb's emphasis on the need to respond to new observations and discard old authorities tells against all that Hopkins had committed himself to.

The problem becomes clear in Hopkins's tart remarks on Tyndall's references to authoritative sources in the Belfast Address: 'I notice that he has no sense of the relative weights of authority: he quotes Draper, Whewell and other respectable writers for or against Aristotle, Bacon etc as if it were just the same thing and you were keeping at the same level—the Lord Chief Justice rules this way, his parlourmaid however says it should be the other, and so on.'[10]

Hopkins takes for granted that major writers of the past carry most weight and that there is a permanent class hierarchy in knowledge. Tyndall assumes that the more recent writers are more likely to be correct. This is not a matter of Hopkins being authoritarian and Tyndall flexible—though it may be that too. It is, rather, a confrontation between two *forms* of authority, one of them the more familiar to us now. Hopkins assumes that truth has a stable, though hermeneutic, form, whereas Tyndall adopts a progressive heuristic. In this pattern science steadily accrues true knowledge and discards error: the most recent is taken to be the most correct.

Hopkins was both fascinated by and resistant to evolutionism wherever he found it. He calls it 'a philosophy of continuity or flux' and insists on the need to uncover stable mathematical patterns. Indeed, Hopkins's formulation of such distinctions in acoustical terms in 1867 (before the start of *Nature* in 1869 when the discussion of such topics became widespread) suggests that he already knew something of the arguments in Helmholtz's *Tonempfindungen*, published in Germany four years earlier, most probably through Tyndall's *Sound* (1866), though also, less wide-rangingly, through Müller's work on the science of language.[11]

To the prevalent philosophy and science nature is a string all the differences in which are really chromatic but certain places in it have become accidentally fixed and the series of fixed points becomes an arbitrary scale. The new Realism will maintain that in musical strings the roots of chords, to use technical wording, are mathematically fixed and give a standard by which to fix all the notes of the appropriate scale.[12]

Yet that insistence, that need for fixing, springs from Hopkins's fascination with changeful forms, dappled things: whatever is fickle, freckled. Within Hopkins's responsiveness intellectual fields, expressed as physical and linguistic desires, knot and waver. He is drawn to natural history by its prinked exactness of observation, to physics by its charged meteorological interpretations and its insistence on waves, vibrations, patterns, beyond the ordinary range of our senses: above all, perhaps, by its recognition that light, heat, and sound are all modes of motion. In the later poetry particularly that motion reveals itself threateningly as entropy, the rapid and increasing disorganization that makes less and less of energy available, squandering difference.

> Down roughcast, down dazzling whitewash, wherever an elm arches,
> Shivelights and shadowtackle in long lashes lace, lance, and pair.
> Delightfully the bright wind boisterous ropes, wrestles, beats earth bare
> Of yestertempest's creases; in pool and rutpeel parches
> Squandering ooze to squeezed dough, crúst, dust; stánches, stárches
> Squadroned masks and manmarks treadmire toil there
> Fóotfretted in it. Million-fuelèd, nature's bonfire burns on.
> But quench her bonniest, dearest to her, her clearest-selvèd spark
> Mán, how fást his fíredint, his mark on mind, is gone!

In Hopkins's poetry all parts of speech incline to verbs. Not only does he form verbs such as 'swarthed', 'sheaved', but adjectives and nouns often take on simultaneously the functions of verbs and present participles so that everything is de-stabilized, rushing onwards or oscillating. Everything is charged with motion. To take a typical, and lesser-known, example (*c*.1878), where even the first word 'furl' is a record of process, feasibly either verb or noun as the eye alights upon it, and the line-ending poises 'down' momentarily as substantive the soft covering of the leaf, before the enjambement loosens it as adverbial, downward motion:[13]

The furl of fresh-leaved dogrose down
His cheeks the forth-and-flaunting sun
Had swarthed about with lion-brown
    Before the Spring was done

Or like a juicy and jostling shock
    Of blue bells sheaved in May
Or wind-long fleeces on the flock
    A day off shearing day.

The fascination with the manifest and with its hidden energy of form, the suggestion that light and pitch are related, that out of the white solar rays kingfishers catch fire and shining comes from shook foil, the discussion of the blue of the sky and its meaning (Mary's colour) are not Hopkins's alone. All these concerns are spread through the pages of *Nature* in the 1870s and 1880s, and are explored from the mid-century in the writing of people like Tyndall and greater theorists such as Faraday, Rayleigh, Clerk Maxwell, and Helmholtz. They vibrate in Hopkins's language and in his metrical experiments too. Those metrical experiments have been profusely studied; more remains to be thought through in relation to energy physics. From considerations of space, however, I have chosen to reserve that topic for a future essay.

    Nor were the pages of *Nature* entirely devoid of poetry themselves. Hopkins's first letter to the journal (16 Nov. 1882, 53) was triggered by a discussion of 'rayons de crépuscule' in the previous issue, 9 November 1832 (30). Immediately adjacent in that issue is an article on James Clerk Maxwell's life and major scientific contribution which ends by quoting the opening of Maxwell's 'Paradoxical Ode to Hermann Stoffkraft'. Maxwell's sardonic survey of his contemporaries' (unsuccessful) attempts to dislodge the soul from matter and energy, though metrically more conservative, has a semantic vigour and precision not unlike Hopkins's own:

My soul's an amphicheiral knot,
  Upon a liquid vortex wrought
By Intellect, in the Unseen residing.
  And thine doth like a convict sit,
  With marlinspike untwisting it,
Only to find its knottiness abiding;
  Since all the tools for its untying
  In four-dimensioned space are lying,
  Wherein thy fancy intersperses
  Long avenues of universes,
  While Klein and Clifford fill the void
  With one finite, unbounded homaloid,
  And think the Infinite is now at last destroyed.

The temper of *Nature* in its early days was open, various, conversational, enquiring, making room for interested amateurs and conducting controversies without great pulling of rank. *Nature's* early ideals were set out in the first issue (4 Nov.1869):

Men of science work not for themselves, or for their scientific fellows, but for mankind; and that only mischief can come of it if they whose business it is to ask Nature her secrets are hindered from telling the world all that they think they hear. It is impossible to separate science from other knowledge and from daily life: all new discoveries especially must have ties with every part of our nature. (13)

During the first volumes of *Nature* a spirited correspondence recurred concerning the correlations of music and colour, alongside meteorological observations, discussion of comets and sunspots, the flight of birds and 'wingmanship' (*Nature*, 1870, 431), the flowering of winter plants, lumeniferous ether, electrical shining. The laws of thermodynamics, in particular, set a puzzle that moved in contrary directions and engaged those outside the scientific community, suggesting at once an energetic rush towards inertia and a teased-out system of interpenetrating waves that produced systems of extraordinary complexity without losing the individual impulse. These, at least, were the terms in which writers like Tyndall made such knowledge available to their contemporaries, as I shall illustrate. So my argument here is not a matter of finding single sources, or of simply assigning priorities (though I do seek to establish the reading of particular and hitherto undiscussed works, and their significance in Hopkins's creativity). As important is feeling the energy available to Hopkins in the scientific, secular world around him, and in which he participated.

Hopkins's fascination with philology, and the importance of language history to his poetry, is well known. Scientists, like Maxwell and Clifford and Sylvester, were as much fascinated in this period with philology as were poets. The mathematician W. K. Clifford, following William Barnes, translated *Erkenntnistheorie* as 'Ken-lore'; J. J. Sylvester in his Presidential Address to the Mathematical and Physical Section of the British Association in 1869 argued that there is a close connection between mathematics and philology:

The relation between these two sciences is not perhaps so remote as may at first appear; and indeed it has often struck me that metamorphosis runs like a golden thread through the most diverse branches of modern intellectual culture, and forms a nature link of connection between subjects in their aims so remote as grammar, philology, ethnology, rational mythology, chemistry, botany, comparative anatomy, physiology, physics, algebra, versification, music, all of which under the modern point of view, may be regarded as having morphology for their common centre.[14]

Hopkins writes sympathetically of William Barnes's re-made Anglo-Saxon English in which 'degrees of comparison' become 'pitches or suchness'.[15] The quaint phrase, in which 'degrees of comparison' take on an acoustical intensity, has a particular aptness for my discussion. Hopkins's ear is tuned to 'sensations of tone' in his contemporaries' scientific work.

Hopkins several times alludes directly to Tyndall in his letters (whose name he spells Tyndal), and always with mixed responses. Tyndall generated in Hopkins an uneasy crossing of emotions-admiration of his eloquence, fellow feeling with a fine observer, enjoyment of his imaginative passion, dismay at his materialist system of explanation, and an unfettered enjoyment of Tyndall's power of imaging fresh knowledge.

Writing to his mother on 20 September 1874, Hopkins added a long postscript concerning John Tyndall's Belfast address to the British Association for the Advancement of Science. This Address roused widespread controversy because of Tyndall's insistence that materialism offered a sufficient creative explanation of the history of the universe and of mankind. Tyndall warned of the tendency of religion, both in the past and potentially, to 'exercise despotic sway over ... intellect' (216). In the Address he outlined a history of the search for knowledge, seeing it as a primal impulse, a desire for causality. Within that history, religion and the role of adversary—first anthropomorphizing, and then inhibiting, the free exploration of observed phenomena. In particular, Tyndall dwells on the case of Giordano Bruno: 'Struck with the problem of the generation and maintenance of organisms, and duly pondering it, he came to the conclusion that Nature in her productions does not imitate the technic of man' (212).

This recognition of a disjunction between natural processes and human patterns of expectation and design Tyndall sees as one of the characterizing gains of science. Bruno was, Tyndall recounts, a martyr to these values. Originally a Dominican monk, he was accused of heresy, fell into the hands of the Inquisition, and was eventually burnt at the stake. It is not surprising that Hopkins found the piece disquieting, not to say infuriating.

It is Tyndall's willingness *not* to know that troubles Hopkins: it is not only that the looks back to an obscure origin, he looks forward with the same content to an obscure future— to be lost "in the infinite azure of the past" (fine phrase by the by)."[16] Yet Tyndall casts epistemophilia as profoundly natural and emphasizes its evolutionary capacity: 'An impulse inherent in primeval man turned his thoughts and questionings betimes towards the sources of natural phenomena. The same impulse, inherited and intensified, is the spur of scientific action today' (209).

Tyndall proves, nevertheless, to be unwilling quite to shed the passional life that finds expression equally in religion, in sexual love, in 'Awe, Reverence, Wonder'. 'You who have escaped from these religions into the high-and-dry light of the understanding may derive them' (216). But high-and-dry light is not Tyndall's medium; be prefers the liberal oscillation within sentences, the vigour of metaphor, and the ardent re-composition of ideas. To that degree his views temptingly ran alongside the religious even while they repudiated religious authority. That makes it possible for Hopkins to sustain a fellow feeling with him which gives sustained access to a range of ideas apparently at odds with Hopkins's own profession: 'I fear he must be called an atheist, but he is not a shameless one: I wish he might come round' (*Letters,* III, 128). Moreover, for Hopkins, confident of the incarnation and to whom the mass was an act of transubstantiation, materialism was always less threatening than was mentalism. Materialism simply did not go far enough: it understood inscape but not instress.

Notes

1 *The Academy: A Weekly Review of Literature, Science, and Art* (22 Aug. 1874), 212.
2 J. J. Sylvester, *The Laws of Verse together with the Inaugural Presidential Address to the Mathematical and Physical Section of the British Association of Exeter* (London, 1870), 103.
3 Generalist journals to which Tyndall contributed include: *The Westminister Review, The Academy, The Contemporary Review, Macmillan's Magazine, The Fortnightly Review, Fraser's Magazine, Longman's Magazine, The Nineteenth Century, New Review.*
4 *The Academy* (22 Aug 1874), 216.
5 P. G. Tait, *Light* (Edinburgh, 1884). Hopkins disliked what he perceived as Tait's tone of condescension and—strikingly—his mentalism rather than materialism, his failure to apprehend the richness of the material world: 'they end in conceiving only of a world of formulas, with its being properly speaking in thought, towards which the outer world acts as a sort of feeder, supplying examples for literary purposes' (*Letters,* III, 139–40, 7 Aug. 1886). Tait was an important correspondent and friend for Clerk Maxwell, but Tyndall's obdurate enemy. Despite Hopkins's impatience with the book he might have found (and perhaps did) the discussion of different kinds of light valuable: 'Reflection from the surface of metals, and of very highly refractive substances such as diamond, generally gives at all incidences elliptically polarized light' (230).
6 In response to a Catholic critic of his Belfast Address Tyndall wrote: 'I do not fear the charge of Atheism; nor should I even disavow it, in reference to any definition of the Supreme which he,

or his order, would be likely to frame.' *Fragments of Science,* vol. II, 10th impression (London, 1889), 205.

7 Fr. John MacLeod, 'The Diary of a Devoted Student of Nature', *Letters and Notices* (Apr. 1906), 390, collected in Gerald Roberts (ed.), *Gerard Manley Hopkins: The Critical Heritage,* (London, 1987), 64–5.

8 *The Month and Catholic Review,* 8 (May–Aug 1876), 107.

9 *The Month 9* (Sept.–Dec. 1876), 202–3. This discussion appears to draw directly on Tyndall's *Second,* esp. at 282–3 where Tyndall discusses Helmholtz and uses the same example. The same writer, John Rickaby, whose brother Joseph had earlier written a critique of Tyndall's Belfast Address in *The Month,* gives a hostile account of Tyndall in his next essay, 'The Reign of Mist' 281–96, but a much more appreciative account in the following volume, 10, (Jan.–Apr. 1877), in an essay on 'Evolution and Involution' (269–85). There he writes that the physicist has been able to reduce the 'primary phenomena' of 'material force' to undulations or modes of motion; and by discovering the principle of 'the conservation of energy'—the counterpart to the principle of the indestructibility of matter—he has come to see the close bond of union—that exists between the workings of the several forces of nature, and the constant transformations that take place between them, at least as regards their outward manifestations. The pure physicist, as such, goes no further than the external effects; according to Professor Tyndall 'the convertibility of natural force consists solely in the transformations of dynamic into potential and of potential into dynamic energy. In no other sense has the convertibility of force, at present, any scientific meaning' (276). Zaniello, *Hopkins in the Age of Darwin,* has an informative discussion of the Rickaby brothers in his chapter on 'The Stonyhurst Philosophers'.

10 *Letters,* III, 128. Hopkins read Tyndall's essay in *The Academy* (19 Aug 1874), 109-19. This journal devoted a quarter of its space to science, which 'includes Natural Philosophy, Theology, and the Science of Language'.

11 For discussion of the relations between evolutionary and language theory in this period see my 'Darwin and the Growth of Language Theory', in John Christie and Sally Shuttleworth (eds.), *Nature Transfigured: Essays in Literature and Science* (Manchester, 1989), 152-70, repr. as Ch. 5 above.

12 The Probable Future of Metaphysics', *Journals and Papers,* 120, See e.g. the discussion, in Part 3, of *On the Sensations of Tone,* 2nd edn. (London, 1885), 369: 'Then, again, we have seen that the reason why a chord in music appears to be the chord of a determinate root, depends as before upon the analysis of a compound tone into its partial tones, that is, as before upon those elements of a sensation which cannot readily become subjects of conscious perception.'

13 The *Poetical Works of Gerard Manley Hopkins,* ed. by Norman H. Mackenzie (Oxford: Oxford University Press, 1990), 154.

14 *The Laws of Verse of Principles of Versification Exemplified in Metrical Translations: together with The Inaugural Presidential Address ... of the British Association* (London, 1870), 130.

15 *The Letters of Gerard Manley Hopkins to Robert Bridges,* ed Claude Colleer Abbon, rev. edn. (Oxford, 1955), 163. Hereafter *Letters,* I.

16 *Letters,* III, 128.

44 'Physiological Poetics', Introduction to *Electric Meters: Victorian Physiological Poetics* (2009)

Jason Rudy

O for a Life of Sensations rather than of Thoughts!
—John Keats, letter to Benjamin Bailey (1817)

Man acts by electricity.
—Alfred Smee, *Instinct and Reason: Deduced from Electro-biology* (1850)

Nearly five hundred years separate the florentine poet Angelo Poliziano from the American Charles Olsen, but the two agree in their understanding of poetry as a dynamic, charged mode of communication. Echoing Plato, Poliziano describes poetry as working like a magnetic stone, exerting its "hidden force" on readers; for Olsen, poetry "is energy transferred from where the poet got it ... by way of the poem itself to, all the way over to, the reader" (Poliziano, 125; Olsen, 240).[1] The discerning reader confronts in both Poliziano and Olsen two possible—and somewhat contradictory—directives for poetic experience. The first treats literature figuratively and understands poetry to be *like* a magnet, *like* the transfer of energy. The experience of reading poetry in this model remains primarily an intellectual endeavor; the individual who picks up Tennyson's *In Memoriam,* for example, feels the tug of strong emotion because she has thought strongly about Tennyson's words and the ideas and feelings they represent. The energy transferred from poem to reader occurs here through the medium of the thinking brain. Not so for the second model of poetic experience, which erases the distance between the poem and the reader and understands poetry quite literally *as* magnetic, a direct transfer of energy. In this instance, the reader of *In Memoriam* feels Tennyson's charge of thought/feeling as it moves—magnetically, electrically—from page to body. The reader remains mostly unconscious of the transference of energy; she experiences the poem viscerally, intimately, bodily. This second model of poetic experience, which locates the body as central to the individual's encounter with a poem, rests at the heart of *Electric Meters.* This book tells the history of physiological poetics in the British nineteenth century, focusing on the period between 1832 and 1872 as the height of Britain's poetic engagement with bodily modes of experience.

Indeed, the history of Victorian poetry is in no small part a history of the human body. Whether we look to Alfred Tennyson's "poetics of sensation," the midcentury "Spasmodic" phenomenon, or the so-called fleshly school of the 1870s, Victorian poetry demands to be read as physiologically inspired: rhythms that pulse in the body, a rhetoric of sensation that readers might feel compelled to experience. Like Poliziano and Olsen, Victorian poets turned to various manifestations of electricity—lightning strikes, electric shocks, nerve impulses, telegraph signals—to articulate the work of physiological poetics. The electrical sciences and bodily poetics, I argue, cannot be separated, and they came together with especial force in the years between the 1830s, which witnessed the invention of the electric telegraph, and the 1870s, when James Clerk Maxwell's electric field theory transformed the study of electrodynamics. Because much of nineteenth-century electrical theory had to do with human bodies, and specifically with the ways that individual human bodies might be connected to one another, electricity offered Victorian poets a figure for thinking through the effects of poetry on communities of readers. Electricity, in other words, serves in the nineteenth century as a tool for exploring poetry's political consequences. Scholars have long identified the political work of Victorian poetry, just as they have recognized the astonishing physicality of Victorian poetics.[2] *Electric Meters* insists that these phenomena be understood as two sides of the same coin, and it uses electricity as a model for reading that aesthetic and physiological conjunction.

More specifically, I argue that Victorian readers understood the connections between bodily and poetic experience in ways that took more seriously the unself-conscious effects of poetic form. "Physiological poetics" thus refers to the metrical, rhythmic, and sonic effects that, along with other formal poetic features, were increasingly imagined as carrying physiological truths. Whereas the predominant eighteenth-century model of poetic transmission privileged the mind's interpretive role (the brain acting as mediator between the poem and the individual), nineteenth-century readers gave credit to the body as an arbiter of poetic truths. Whether one ought to read Poliziano and Olsen figuratively or literally, then, depends on the period in which one encounters their texts. Readers prior to the physiological trends of the Victorian period were more likely to opt for figuration, to understand a poem's semantic presence but not its mimetic facility. In contrast, the Victorian poets and critics at the center of this study err on the side of the literal: the poem is itself a magnetic force, "a high energy-construct" (Olsen, 240).

Poetry and electricity

Through the 1860s and '70s, while devising equations to describe the physical relations among electricity, magnetism, and light—the consequences of which formed an important cornerstone for Einstein's theory of relativity—James Clerk Maxwell also found an occasional spare moment to compose poetry.[3] His verses are neither entirely serious nor of the sort that rewards extended reflection, but they remain suggestive of the curious, persistent interplay through the nineteenth century between poetry and electricity. Maxwell composed the following riff on Tennyson's "The Splendour Falls," one of the great lyrics from *The Princess,* in 1874:

> The lamp-light falls on blackened walls,
>   And streams through narrow perforations,
> The long beam trails o'er pasteboard scales,
>   With slow-decaying oscillations.
> Flow, current, flow, set the quick light-spot flying,
> Flow, current, answer light-spot, flashing, quivering, dying.
>
> (quoted in Campbell and Garnett, 409)

Maxwell refers here to the mirror galvanometer developed in the 1850s by William Thomson (later Lord Kelvin), a device used to measure the flow of electric current through submarine telegraph cables. The galvanometer was crucial for transatlantic telegraphy, as it enabled the reading of very weak electric currents.[4] The sonic resonances of Tennyson's bugle song, "Blow, bugle, blow, set the wild echoes flying," thus become in Maxwell's hands the flow of electricity through a cable, which is then made visible by the "oscillations" of a "lamp-light ... on blackened walls." Maxwell does not mean for us to take his verse too seriously; entitled "Lectures to Women on Physical Science" (part I), the poem is at least as concerned with the erotics of instruction as it is with physics ("O love!" the speaker apostrophizes in the third stanza, "you fail to read the scale / Correct to tenths of a division" [410]).[5] But if Maxwell turns to poetry to interject some play into the laboratory—"A little literature helps to chase away mathematics from the mind," he writes in November 1863 (quoted in Campbell and Garnett, 253)—many of his less scientific contemporaries did the reverse, turning to electricity and the physical sciences to inspire new ways of thinking about poetry. This book will show, among other things, why in the nineteenth century Tennyson's echoing bugle song might so seamlessly have been aligned with the pulses of an electric telegraph. More broadly, I demonstrate how the electrical sciences came to offer the Victorians a valuable framework for reading and understanding poetry.

Electricity has long been a privileged figure for those describing the ineffable qualities that make poetry *poetic*. Percy Shelley tells us that poetry "startle[s]" with "the electric life which burns within ... words," and this electric life is precisely what enables poetry, in Shelley's view, to rejuvenate language and thought (Shelley, 7:140). This figurative yoking of electricity and poetry articulates some of the most pressing concerns of nineteenth-century poetic theory. Newly harnessed as a tool of industry, science, and communication (the electric telegraph being the most important of electricity's new uses), electricity serves as a touchstone for nineteenth-century poets reflecting on the complex interactions of thought, emotion, and physiological experience. From the earliest electrical experiments, electricity has been depicted as having physiological and noncognitive effects on those who encounter it (the shock of an electric current, say), and poets throughout history have turned to the same language of bodily shock in describing "lyrical" experience. "Like a lightning flash," writes Longinus, "[the sublime] reveals, at a stroke and in its entirety, the power of the orator"; Longinus's primary example of such sublime power is the poetry of Sappho, which "gather[s] soul and body into one, hearing and tongue, eyes and complexion; all dispersed and strangers before" (Longinus, 23–24). Through the "shock" of a felicitously placed word, a compelling linguistic friction, or a moving rhythmic pressure, poetry transmits, lightning-like, new truths to its readers.

The following chapters will demonstrate that in different ways, Mary Robinson, Felicia Hemans, Alfred Tennyson, Elizabeth Barrett Browning, Gerard Manley Hopkins, Algernon Swinburne, and Mathilde Blind look to electricity to make sense of poetry's effects on the human body, distinguishing themselves from their predecessors in their overriding concern with physicality, with the material human body through which we experience poetry. Yet this physicality must be read within a larger political framework for nineteenth-century poetry and poetic theory. Whitman's "body electric" is only the most familiar of nineteenth-century poetic elisions between physiology and electricity, elisions that ask us to think about affinities between bodily affect and poetic communication, between physiological shock and intellectual absorption, and between individual experience and communal consciousness. In Maxwell's rewriting of Tennyson, for example, the telegraph's pulsing electric current represents a mode of communication already implicit in the original poem. Tennyson's "The Splendour Falls" transforms into poetic language, rhythm, and sound the echoing of a bugle song Tennyson heard over a lake in Killarney, Ireland, during an 1848 visit (H. Tennyson, 1:291–93): "Blow, bugle, blow, set the wild echoes flying, / Blow, bugle; answer, echoes, dying, dying, dying" (ALT, 2:231). This work of transformation—a transcription of sonic waves into written form—becomes in Maxwell's poem the translation of an oscillating light into a telegraphic message (the telegrapher "reads" letters from the to-and-fro swaying of the lamplight). Both poems explore the intersection of poetry with sensory experience and different modes of communication. The following chapters foreground such intersections of poetry, physiology, and the electrical sciences, suggesting how "physiological poetics" both depend on and enhance the phenomenon I call "electric meters," the complex interplay of poetic form and electrical epistemologies (ideas or structures of thought inspired by the work of electricity).

In focusing on the interplay of physiology and electricity, I remain true to scientific history. The human body is very much at the heart of the earliest electrical experiments, and it was often by means of their own bodies that scientists, from roughly the 1740s on, came to understand the nature of electric charges (Delbourgo, 25–30). I want to emphasize from the outset the distance in these experimental moments between bodily feeling (experiencing the electric shock) and thoughtful engagement with scientific ideas (thinking through electrical theories, hypotheses, and physical laws). Electricity becomes a compelling literary figure in part due to the gap between physiological experience and mental cognition. Consider, for example, the language Benjamin Franklin uses to describe an electrical shock, an accident that occurred during an experiment in 1750: "It seem'd an universal Blow from head to foot throughout the Body, and followed by a violent quick Trembling in the Trunk, which went gradually off in a few seconds. It was some Minutes before I could collect my Thoughts so as to know what was the Matter ... . My Arms and Back of my Neck felt somewhat numb the remainder of the Evening, and my Breast-bone was sore for a Week after, as if it had been bruised" (letter to William Watson, 4 February 1750; quoted in Cohen, 94). Franklin does not lose consciousness from the shock, but at the moment of electrification his physical body takes center stage, fully pushing his active mind to the wings. Only after "some Minutes" can Franklin "collect [his] Thoughts" as he gradually awakens from his stupor, the point at which he becomes conscious of what happened. Franklin's physiological experience makes apparent the truth of electricity's vast power, yet only subsequently is Franklin's brain able to perceive the truth of his experience; the electric shock imposes a temporal gap between experience and cognition.

Franklin's mishap was accidental, but attempts to make sense of electrical shocks and their noncognitive effects on the human body were surprisingly common in the mid-1700s. Perhaps the most infamous of these experiments transpired in 1746, when Jean-Antoine Nollet, a French scientist who was soon to become the foremost European expert on electricity, amassed a circle of nearly two hundred Carthusian monks, each linked to his neighbors by a twenty-five-foot line of iron wire. When Nollet connected the ends of the wires to a rudimentary electric battery, a great communal spasm among the monks offered spectators one of the most important scenes in eighteenth-century science. "It is singular," wrote Nollet after the experiment, "to see the multitude of different gestures, and to hear the instantaneous exclamation of those surprised by the shock" (quoted in Heilbron, 312).[6] Like the temporal lapse between Franklin's physiological experience of the electric shock and his conscious realization of what had happened, Nollet here achieves knowledge only subsequent to and at a distance from the violent, noncognitive physiological experiences of the Carthusian monks. Nollet's experiment both demonstrates the communicative potential in electricity (the circuit of electrified monks might be thought of as leading ultimately to the development of the electric telegraph in the 1830s) and suggests the necessarily physiological nature of such communication.

Nollet's and Franklin's experiments also resonate with a mounting interest in the physiology of poetic experience. Writing in 1757, Edmund Burke frames his discussion of *Paradise Lost* with language that echoes, and seems to make use of, contemporary electrical science: "The mind" of Milton's reader "is hurried out of itself, by a crowd of great and confused images" (Burke 1968, 62). Poetry communicates not by conscious thought but "by the contagion of our passions" (175). Those genuinely affected by poetry experience emotional shocks that, in their disjunction from conscious thought, seem not unlike the electric pulses enjoyed by Nollet's monks. "If the affection be well conveyed," Burke concludes, "it will work its effect without any clear idea; often without any idea at all of the thing which has originally given rise to it" (176). Burke's language looks forward to the poetics of sensibility that soon would dominate eighteenth-century aesthetics, imagining poetry as affective experience transmitted, via spoken language, from composing poet to reading individual. My point here is not to suggest that eighteenth-century science makes the physiology of poetic experience suddenly visible. Poetry has always, in various ways, been associated with bodily experience, from Longinus's exhortations on Sappho's sublimity, to Poliziano's magnetic attachments, to the "heavenly harmony" celebrated in Dryden's 1687 "Song for St. Cecilia's Day." But there can be little doubt that the poetics of sensibility push physiology to the foreground of poetic theory in new and increasingly demonstrative ways, setting the scene for the Victorians' all-out engagement with a poetics of the body. We witness this attention to physiology in reading John Stuart Mill's 1833 assertion that poetry represents "thoughts and words in which emotion spontaneously embodies itself"; poets, he concludes, are "those who are so constituted, that emotions are links of association by which their ideas, both sensuous and spiritual, are connected together" (Mill, 1:356). Across the nineteenth century, poets and literary critics grappled with this notion of embodied lyricism, from Arthur Hallam's poetics of sensation in 1831 to Robert Buchanan's 1871 critique of the "fleshly" school of poetry. In the many permutations of these thoughts, poetry remains a bodily experience, felt like an electric shock through and through.

It is as physiological experience that poetry facilitates the "association"—in Mill's words, which intentionally reference the associationist tradition of Locke, Hume, Hartley, and others—of "ideas ... sensuous and spiritual." The very qualities of associationist philosophy that made Coleridge wince—that is, its privileging of the "primary sensations" and its skepticism of "an infinite spirit ... an intelligent and holy will" (Coleridge, 75)—were for Mill and many of his Victorian peers fundamental to poetic practice in its ideal form.[7] This ideal remains in circulation today: for example, with Barbara Hardy's suggestion that lyric poetry "does not provide an explanation, judgment or narrative; what it does provide is feeling, alone and without histories or characters" (Hardy 1977, 1), and Susan Stewart's description of lyric creation as "the transformation of sense experience into words" (Stewart, 26). The continuity among these writers rests in their understanding of poetry as physiological and essentially noncognitive. Within this mode of poetic interpretation, a mode that came to dominate poetic practice in the nineteenth century, electricity most powerfully stands as a figure for poetic experience. But electricity is not simply a trope used to describe or to elaborate a poetic function. In the nineteenth century, electricity was the most prominent figure for a more widespread and pervasive interest in communication, from William Cooke and Charles Wheatstone's invention of the electric telegraph to Alexander Bain's analysis of nerve impulses in the human body. The nineteenth century, as John Durham Peters has argued, "saw unprecedented transformations in the conditions of human contact," which played out through new technologies for transmitting and recording information (Peters, 138). Recent work by Paul Gilmore, Richard Menke, Laura Otis, and

Katherine Stubbs has suggested how profoundly and variously these electrical technologies, and the electric telegraph in particular, altered the Victorian literary landscape.[8] But this literary history has almost exclusively focused on prose fiction as the object of analysis.[9] It was inevitable that poets, too, would take an interest in these advances, and that they would come to think differently about their work as a result. Jay Clayton's recent insight into the intensely physical nature of telegraphic communication—a physicality that Friedrich Kittler, among others, overlooks—suggests in part why poets would have had an especial investment in this new technology; much as "the telegraph links hand, ear, and letter with remarkable power" (Clayton, 68), this book shows how Victorian poets ultimately came to see their work as physiologically based, as connecting intimately and instantaneously word, mind, and body.[10]

The Victorians' physiological approach to poetry manifests both thematically and, more important, as a part of poetry's formal structure. Rhythm in particular becomes a key element for poetic communication, suggesting through its stress and release a physiological give and take that, like a telegraphic transmission, connects individuals via bodily sensation. In this approach to Victorian poetics, I build on the work of critics who in the past decade have reinvigorated the study of poetic form, and drawn attention to the necessary interactions between form and the human body. Matthew Campbell's *Rhythm and Will in Victorian Poetry* (1999), for example, encourages readers to experience rhythm as "more than just a sound," to understand poetic impulses as permitting "the speaker to express an experience of the activity of the body" (Campbell, 18). Kirstie Blair's *Victorian Poetry and the Culture of the Heart* (2006) situates such bodily rhythmic experiences within the Victorian physiological sciences. Blair shows how rhythm pervades Victorian scientific discourse and comes to be understood "as an organic force, related to bodily movements and hence able to influence the breath or heartbeat of both poet and reader" (Blair, 2006, 17). Yopie Prins's work on meter has pushed our understanding of form in new and important directions, most especially by way of her notion of a "linguistic materialism" that allows voice to "materialize" in Victorian poetry "through the counting of metrical marks" (Prins, 2000, 92).[11] These studies suggest that nineteenth-century advances in the physiological sciences had a particular influence on poets, who understood their work to be connected necessarily to the human body and its functions. Yet with few exceptions, poetry has remained peripheral to the recent surge of interest in literature and physiology. In Anne Stiles's fine collection of essays, *Neurology and Literature, 1860–1920*, for example, "literature" means almost exclusively prose, and the novel in particular. Nicholas Dames's provocative inquiry into what he calls "physiological novel theory," though important as a focused reading of Dames's genre of choice, has implications beyond the study of the novel. In fact, the three Victorian theorists whom Dames identifies as central to physiological novel theory—Alexander Bain, George Henry Lewes, and E. S. Dallas (Dames, 9)—all made important contributions to the theorization of poetics.[12] Even when writing about essays explicitly on the nature of poetry—Paul Valéry's lecture "Propos sur la poésie" and George Eliot's "Notes on Form in Art"—Dames resists acknowledging that it was often to poetry that nineteenth-century thinkers turned when considering the connections between literature and physiological affect (Dames, 26–27, 49). In a way unprecedented in the Western tradition, nineteenth-century poets understood what Derek Attridge calls "the psychological and physiological reality" that poetic rhythm conveys to "reader[s] and listener[s] alike" (Attridge, 1990, 1016). Recent studies in the field of cognitive poetics by Reuven Tsur and Andrew Elfenbein articulate in modern terms ideas that surfaced first among Victorian thinkers such as Bain, Lewes, and Dallas, among many others.[13]

The physiological thrust of Victorian poetics develops in tandem with, and in necessary relation to, a series of formal poetic innovations. Bridging the genteel refinements of neoclassicism and the radical austerity of modernism, the nineteenth century was a period of audacious poetic experiment, much of which has been glossed over and dismissed as either aesthetically deficient or atypical of the period. While critics have long recognized the importance of the dramatic monologue as a Victorian invention, comparatively little attention has been given to the period's metrical and rhythmic innovations. Those formal innovations that *do* get attention—Whitman's early nod toward free verse, for example, and Hopkins's invention of "sprung rhythm"—are most often identified as not belonging to the arc of nineteenth-century poetics (Hopkins especially has long been read as a "modern" poet, an anomaly of the Victorian period).[14] This blindness to the diversity of Victorian prosody has resulted in a proliferation of critical misreadings: a longstanding refusal, for example, to take seriously the contributions of the Spasmodic poets; an insistence that poets such as Hopkins and Swinburne somehow stood outside the general trends of British poetics; a resistance to perceiving the crucial role of Romantic women poets in Victorian reading practices.[15] From the metrical novelty of Coleridge's "Christabel" (1816) to Coventry Patmore's midcentury attempts to bring classical quantitative verse into English, nineteenth-century prosody surprises with its creativity and its willingness to break with the often rigid formality of earlier periods.[16] The Victorians' formal dexterity must be read within the context of the period's engagement with both physiology and the electrical sciences. Within this broader historical and cultural context, the century's more outlandish experiments (Sydney Dobell's "Spasmodic" poetics and Patmore's quantitative verse) seem somewhat less outlandish, whereas a number of more familiar works (Tennyson's *Princess* and Barrett Browning's *Aurora Leigh*) emerge as more extraordinary than might once have been thought.

Electric Meters thus enters the ongoing conversation around physiology and literature to help make sense of the enormous shifts in British poetics that occur across the nineteenth century, and to explicate more specifically the cultural and political nature of these changes. It has often been suggested that Victorian poetry can be distinguished from that of earlier periods by poets' attempts to communicate differently, for example, via the dramatic monologue or the prose poem. More broadly, according to Isobel Armstrong, "The effort to renegotiate a content to every relationship between self and *the* world is the Victorian poet's project" (Armstrong, 7). In the nineteenth century, there can be no greater figure for interpersonal communication—the negotiation of self and world—than electricity, and no greater manifestation of this phenomenon in literary form than poetic rhythm. Accordingly, the chapters that follow track the shifts in poetic theory, from the Romantic poetess tradition through to late-Victorian figures such as Hopkins and Swinburne, that engage both philosophically and formally with the electrical sciences and technologies. In positioning their work within scientific discourses, Victorian poets and poetic theorists negotiate the cultural and political dynamics inherent in artistic, and specifically poetic, transmission.

Notes

1. My thanks to Gerard Passannante for directing me to Poliziano's work. In Plato's *Ion*, Socrates explains the work of poetic experience—"an inspiration ... divinity moving you"—to be "like ... a magnet"; just as a magnetic force can pull through a chain of iron rings, so too the strength of "the Muse" works through the poet, by way of the poem, to the reader (Plato, 1:107).

2. On the politics of Victorian poetry, the most important recent studies include Armstrong 1993; Kuduk Weiner 2005; and Reynolds 2001. On the physiology of Victorian poetry, see Blair 2006b; M. Campbell 1999; and Prins 2000.
3. Basil Mahon describes the significance of Maxwell's equations: "The theory predicted that every time a magnet jiggled, or an electric current changed, a wave of energy would spread out into space like a ripple on a pond. Maxwell calculated the speed of the waves and it turned out to be the very speed at which light had been measured. At a stroke, he had united electricity, magnetism and light" (Mahon, 1–2). I am indebted to Michelle Boswell for introducing me to Maxwell's poetry.
4. James Munro's 1891 *Heroes of the Telegraph* describes the mirror galvanometer: "[It] consists of a very long fine coil of silk-covered copper wire, and in the heart of the coil, within a little air-chamber, a small round mirror, having four tiny magnets cemented to its back, is hung, by a single fibre of floss silk no thicker than a spider's line. The mirror is of film glass silvered, the magnets of hair-spring, and both together sometimes weigh only one-tenth of a grain. A beam of light is thrown from a lamp upon the mirror, and reflected by it upon a white screen or scale a few feet distant, where it forms a bright spot of light. When there is no current on the instrument, the spot of light remains stationary at the zero position on the screen; but the instant a current traverses the long wire of the coil, the suspended magnets twist themselves horizontally out of their former position, the mirror is of course inclined with them, and the beam of light is deflected along the screen to one side or the other, according to the nature of the current. If a *positive* electric current ... gives a deflection to the *right* of zero, a *negative* current ... will give a deflection to the left of zero, and *vice versa*" (Munro, 99–100).
5. Tennyson's version of the line—"O love, they die in yon rich sky"—highlights by contrast Maxwell's playfulness.
6. Tom Standage reviews Nollet's experiment and its aftermath in *The Victorian Internet* (1–2). On Nollet's relation to eighteenth-century science, especially his rivalry with Franklin, see Riskin 2002, 69–103; and Delbourgo 2006, 39–40.
7. Chapter 2 examines Mill in detail, with especial attention to the empiricist/associationist debate within his poetic theory. For more on Coleridge's ambivalent relation to materialism, associationist philosophy, and the sciences, see A. Richardson 2001, 39–65; and Roe 2001.
8. See Gilmore 2002a, 2002b, 2004; Menke 2005 and 2008; Otis 2001; and Stubbs 2003. Gilmore's thoughts on the connections between aesthetics and electricity have been especially helpful to my thinking.
9. Menke's *Telegraphic Realism*, for example, argues that "new media and information systems offered inspiration for reimagining how the world might register *in prose*" (Menke 2008, 7; emphasis mine); those studies that bring poetry into the conversation, such as Menke's "Media in America" and Gilmore's "Telegraph in Black and White," discuss the thematic appearance of electric technologies in nineteenth-century poetry but not their formal implications.
10. Kittler elaborates his views on nineteenth-century technologies of communication in *Gramophone, Film, Typewriter* and *Discourse Networks*. Clayton roundly critiques Kittler's dismissive account of the telegraph (2003, 65–70).
11. See also Prins's reading of Swinburne's use of rhythm and meter (Prins 1999, 121–56) and Alice Meynell's late-Victorian experiments with a "poetics of pauses" (Prins 2005, 264). Other important recent work on Victorian rhythm includes Catherine Maxwell's work on Swinburne (2003 and 2006) and Catherine Robson's reading of Felicia Hemans's "Casabianca" (2005).
12. Alexander Bain's *English Composition and Rhetoric* (1866) includes a lengthy chapter on poetry (257–94) and E. S. Dallas authored one of the key midcentury studies of poetry and poetic form, *Poetics* (1852).
13. Tsur 1998; Elfenbein 2006. See also Attridge 1982 and Stewart 2002. Elfenbein's essay embraces both novel theory and poetics.
14. F. R. Leavis claimed (erroneously) that "Hopkins has no relation to ... any nineteenth-century poet" (Leavis, 26).
15. There are, of course, exceptions. Recent work on the Spasmodic poets has done much to overturn the longstanding prejudices against them (see LaPorte and Rudy 2004). Romantic women poets have benefited from some recent and long-overdue critical attention (see especially Armstrong 1993; Leighton 1992; Lootens 1996; Mason 2006; Ross 1989; and Wolfson 2006).
16. See Prins 2000 for an overview of the period's experimentation.

Works cited

Armstrong, Isobel, *Victorian Poetry: Poetry, Poetics and Politics* (New York: Routledge, 1993)

Attridge, Derek, *The Rhythms of English Poetry* (London: Longman, 1982)

Attridge, Derek, 'Rhythm in English Poetry', *New Literary History*, 21 (1990), 1015–37

Bain, Alexander, *English Composition and Rhetoric: A Manual* [1866] (New York: D. Appleton, 1855)

Barker-Benfield, G. J., *The Culture of Sensibility: Sex and Society in Eighteenth-Century Britain* (Chicago: University of Chicago Press, 1992)

Blair, Kirstie, *Victorian Poetry and the Culture of the Heart* (Oxford: Clarendon, 2006)

Burke, Edmund, *A Philosophical Enquiry into the Origin of Our Ideas of the Sublime and Beautiful* [1757], ed. James T. Boulton (Notre Dame: University of Notre Dame Press, 1968)

Campbell, Lewis and William Garnett, *The Life of James Clerk Maxwell* (London: Macmillan, 1884)

Campbell, Matthew, *Rhythm and Will in Victorian Poetry* (Cambridge: Cambridge University Press, 1999)

Clayton, J., *Charles Dickens in Cyberspace: The Afterlife of the Nineteenth Century in Postmodern Culture* (Oxford: Oxford University Press, 2003)

Cohen, Bernard, *Benjamin Franklin's Experiments* (Cambridge, MA: Harvard University Press, 1941)

Coleridge, Samuel Taylor, *Biographia Literaria* (London: J. M. Dent, 1817)

Dallas, E. S., *Poetics: An Essay on Poetry* (London: Smith, Elder and Co., 1852)

Dames, Nicholas, *The Physiology of the Novel: Reading, Neural Science and the Form of Victorian Fiction* (Oxford: Oxford University Press, 2007)

Delbourgo, James, *A Most Amazing Scene of Wonders: Electricity and Enlightenment in Early America* (Cambridge, MA: Harvard University Press, 2006)

Elfenbein, Andrew, 'Cognitive Science and the History of Reading', *PMLA*, 121 (2006), 484–502

Gilmore, Paul, 'Aesthetic Power: Electric Words and the Example of Frederick Douglas', *American Transcendental Quarterly*, 16 (2002a), 291–311

Gilmore, Paul, 'The Telegraph in Black and White', *English Literary History*, 69 (2002b), 805–33

Gilmore, Paul, 'Romantic Electricity, or the Materiality of Aesthetics', *American Literature*, 76 (2004), 467–94

Hardy, Barbara, *The Advantage of Lyric: Essays on Feeling in Poetry* (Bloomington: Indiana University Press, 1977)

Heilbron, J. L., *Electricity in the 17th and 18th Centuries: A Study of Early Modern Physics* (Berkeley: University of California Press, 1979)

Kittler, Friedrich, *Gramophone, Film, Typewriter* [1986], trans. Geoffrey Winthrop-Young and Michael Wutz (Stanford: Stanford University Press, 1999)

Kuduk Weiner, Stephanie, *Republican Politics and English Poetry 1789–1874* (New York: Palgrave, 2005).

Laporte, Charles and Jason Rudy, eds, 'Spasmodic Poetry and Poetics', special issue of *Victorian Poetry*, 42 (2004)

Leavis, F. R., 'Gerard Manley Hopkins' [1932], in *Hopkins: A Collection of Critical Essays*, ed., Geoffrey H. Hartman (Englewood Cliffs, NJ: Prentice Hall, 1966)

Leighton, Angela, *Victorian Women Poets: Writing against the Heart* (Charlottesville: University Press of Virginia, 1992)

Longinus, *On the Sublime*, trans. A. O. Prickard (Oxford: Clarendon, 1906)

Lootens, Tricia, *Lost Saints: Silence, Gender and Victorian Literary Canonization* (Charlottesville: University Press of Virginia, 1996)

Mahon, Basil, *The Man Who Changed Everything: The Life of James Clerk Maxwell* (Chichester: Wiley, 2003)

Mason, Emma, *Women Poets of the Nineteenth Century* (Tavistock: Northcote, 2006)

Maxwell, Catherine, 'Swinburne: Style, Sympathy, and Sadomasochism', *Journal of Pre-Raphaelite Studies*, 12 (2003), 86–96

Maxwell, Catherine, *Swinburne* (Tavistock: Northcote, 2006)

Menke, Richard, 'Media in America, 1881: Garfield, Guiteau, Bell, Whitman', *Critical Inquiry*, 31 (2005), 638–64

Menke, Richard, *Telegraphic Realism: Victorian Fiction and Other Information Systems* (Stanford: Stanford University Press, 2008)

Mill, John Stuart, *Collected Works*, ed. John M. Robson and Jack Stillinger, 19 vols (Toronto: Toronto University Press, 1981)

Munro, John, *Heroes of the Telegraph* (London: Religious Tract Society, 1891)

Olsen, Charles, *Collected Prose* (Berkeley: University of California Press, 1997)

Otis, Laura, 'The Other End of the Wire: Uncertainties of Organic and Telegraphic Communication', *Configurations*, 9 (2001), 181–206

Peters, John Durham, *Speaking into the Air: A History of the Idea of Communication* (Chicago: University of Chicago Press, 1999)

Plato, *The Dialogues of Plato*, trans. Benjamin Jowett, 4 vols (Clarendon: Oxford, 1953)

Prins, Yopie, *Victorian Sappho* (Princeton: Princeton University Press, 1999)

Prins, Yopie, 'Victorian Meters', in *Cambridge Companion to Victorian Poetry*, ed. Joseph Bristow (Cambridge: Cambridge University Press, 2000), 89–113

Prins, Yopie, 'Patmore's Law, Meynell's Rhythm', in *The Fin-de-Siècle Poem: English Literary Culture and the 1890s*, ed., Joseph Bristow (Athens: Ohio University Press, 2005), 261–84

Poliziano, Angelo, *Silvae*, trans. Charles Fantazzi (Cambridge, MA: Cambridge University Press, 2004)

Reynolds, Matthew, *The Realms of Verse 1830–1870: English Poetry in a Time of Nation-Building* (Oxford: Oxford University Press, 2001)

Richardson, Alan, *British Romanticism and the Science of the Mind* (Cambridge: Cambridge University Press, 2001)

Riskin, Jessica, *Science in the Age of Sensibility: The Sentimental Empiricists of the French Enlightenment* (Chicago: University of Chicago Press, 2002)

Robson, Catherine, 'Standing on the Burning Deck: Poetry, Performance, History', *PMLA*, 120 (2005), 148–62

Roe, Nicholas, 'Introduction: Samuel Taylor Coleridge and the Sciences of Life', in *Samuel Taylor Coleridge and the Sciences of Life*, ed. Nicholas Roe (Oxford: Oxford University Press, 2001), 1–21

Ross, Marlon B., *The Contours of Masculine Desire: Romanticism and the Rise of Women's Poetry* (Oxford: Oxford University Press, 1989)

Shelley, Percy Bysshe, *The Complete Works*, ed. Roger Ingpen and Walter E. Peck, 10 vols (New York: Gordion Press, 1965)

Standage, Tom, *The Victorian Internet: The Remarkable Story of the Telegraph and the Nineteenth Century's On-line Pioneers* (New York: Walker and Co., 1998)

Stewart, Susan, *Poetry and the Fate of the Senses* (Chicago: University of Chicago Press, 2002)

Stubbs, Katherine, 'Telegraphy's Corporeal Fictions', in *New Media 1740–1915*, ed. Lisa Gitelman and Geoffrey B. Pingree (Cambridge: MIT Press, 2003), 91–111

Tennyson, Alfred, *The Poems of Tennyson*, ed. Christopher Ricks, 3 vols (Harlow: Longman, 1987)

Tennyson, Hallam, *Alfred Lord Tennyson: A Memoir*, 2 vols (New York: Macmillan, 1897)

Tsur, Reuven, *Poetic Rhythm: Structure and Performance; An Empirical Study in Cognitive Poetics* (Berne: Peter Lang, 1998)

Wolfson, Susan, *Borderlines: The Shiftings of Gender in British Romanticism* (Stanford: Stanford University Press, 2006)

45 April: Poetry and Science & Nature as Culture, Culture as Society (2011)

Ashton Nichols

Realize thy Simple Self; Embrace thy Original Nature.

—Tao Te Ching, 19

So I convince myself—might it actually be true?—that I can hear the sap rising when I stand close to the towering oak tree by the front door of the cabin. I press my ear to the rough bark to be sure. Do I hear it, or is that just the blood pumping in my ears? The green treetops all around me are literally exploding along the hillsides now, across the river bottom and up the edges of the valley, reaching all the way to the mountain ridge-tops beyond. The trees on the crest of the Roost's low mountain—from 1,000 to 1,200 feet in altitude—are still caught in the cold of winter, but one five-pointed flower (a blue periwinkle, my field guide says) has unfolded its petals on the forest floor. A large mat of thick moss shoots spiky pistil-stalks above soft and spongy moss-tops. The light carpet of gentle greens—this moss-bed, a few lichens, and the earliest of the spring grasses—spreads out across the ground into the distance, like a rolling carpet of motley.

Butter-yellow forsythias burst their bud-tops all around me. Another periwinkle pushes its pointy leaves upward. The leaves unwrap and unfold, each plant revealing a startling purple-blue flower within. Drab—almost gray—ivy grows greener along the walls of the cabin and around the rocks that form the Roost's pathways and rustic yard. Near the ridge line behind the cabin, a huge pileated woodpecker works hard against the bark of a spreading oak tree. The huge bird *ham-hammers* until he can latch his massive beak under a slab of lichen-covered bark. Then he pops the rough slab off the tree, sending it crashing to the forest floor. When this hardworking woodpecker finds a wriggling, fat white grub in the oak tree, he buries his thick beak deep into the softer inner wood and pops the moist blob of squirming insect life into his mouth. Then he shakes his wide woodpecker-head rapidly up and down—up and down again—as he swallows.

Unfolding red maple blossoms unfurl to become more blossoms and shimmering leaves. Each quaking-aspen bud opens as a cluster of heart-shaped green leaves, quivering and quavering in the sun. White dogwood blossoms unfold to spread out as glorious leaf-flowers (dogwood flowers are actually modified leaves). Countless shades of green—the green of untold flowers and twigs and shoots and leaves—will soon fill the whole forest: first slowly (day-by-day) and then faster (days turning into weeks), but always silently and steadily, always without the aid of any human being. The plant world performs its magic so slowly and soundlessly that human beings barely notice, unless they take the time to watch carefully. Watch these buds and shoots every day, and the scene changes: imperceptibly at first, then noticeably, and finally with the evidence of a total transformation. Sit very still, observe one flower or vine-tip long enough, and it is possible to literally watch it unfold. I can almost sense these individual cells swelling and dividing.

For the first time in the early months of my "natural" year, the bug world is also waking up in earnest. A few gnats skitter across my face and hit my hands in the sunlit clearing. A thin, silvery moth crawls up the rock wall of the cabin. A larger moth flutters near the porch lamp, where he had alighted and rested last night. More wasps are waking up as well, still stumbling along the window ledges and eaves. Some of them crawl slowly and then halt, as though they are still too cold to move or have forgotten how to fly. One white-faced hornet buzzes by the side of the house, rising and falling, testing his thin, still-warming wings. A small white butterfly dances among dead brown leaves and pale green shoots on the hillside behind me, darting from forsythia blossom to forsythia blossom, taking advantage of the first bright gush of nectar before the full flowering of spring. Soon, bigger butterflies will emerge to challenge this small white-sulfur for supremacy on the hillside.

As I cock my head to one side, I can suddenly hear the spring migration of countless April birds. Flapping and gliding masses come through trees and shrubs, along rocky ledges all around me, sometimes like a distant breeze, sometimes like a full-blown flutter of feathery leaves on the wing. First come small clouds of multicolored, skittery warblers, then a tight bundle of rusty, thudding robins. All at once, there are literally dozens of songs and calls echoing in the curve of the hillside, filling the air around me with the only sounds amid an otherwise silent world around me. There is nothing remarkable here beyond these diurnal and seasonal matters of fact, just the ordinary miracle of morning.

A white-throated sparrow calls from far off in the distance. The dozen notes of his special song are as sweet as the clang of the most delicate wind chime: plaintive and clear, high pitched with an unmistakable meter, like a well-known and often-remembered poem: *I-I Pea-bod-y, Pea-bod-y, Pea-bod-y, I.* To the north, in this hemisphere, the ornithologists say *O-O Can-a-da, Can-a-da, Can-a-da-a.* Always and everywhere the conspicuous towhee can also be heard: a slurry, slurping *che-wink, che-wink,* followed by an unmistakable, clattery *drink-your-tea, drink-your-tea-he-he.* Suddenly, a melodious wood thrush breaks through— the nightingale of the eastern American forests—louder than all the rest, sweet and liquid: singing *here-I-am, here-I-am.* This song is as sweet and melodious as any sound offered in any forest in the world. Meanwhile, the cardinals have stayed around all winter. They have no need to migrate. They manage to find resilient winter seeds, or small shrubs and tree buds, right through all of the short, cold days of winter. The swirling birds around me are now so thick in the low bushes and trees that their wing-beats sound like wind. In fact, their wings are among the loudest sound I hear in the greening woods of morning. All afternoon I find fallen feathers scattered in the forest around me.

Poetry and science

When Mary Shelley sought to explain Victor Frankenstein's reason for creating his monster, she wrote that a "new species" would bless its human creator for existence. What did Mary think the word "species" meant in 1816? By this time, throughout Europe and North America, poets and natural historians were hinting at the biological connectedness of all living things, even without the precise scientific details that would allow them to explain such links. When Coleridge refers to "the one Life, within us and abroad, / Which meets all Motion, and becomes its soul, / A Light in Sound, a sound-like power in Light" ("The Eolian Harp" 26–28), he is imagining a naturalized version of a divine force, but he is clearly not describing any version of the Judeo-Christian God. Erasmus Darwin might have called Coleridge's "one Life" a "vegetative" energy, an *élan vital,* which pervades all living things ("all objects of all thought, / And rolls through all things" as Wordsworth would add in "Tintern Abbey" [1798, 102–3]). In "The Eolian Harp," Coleridge describes "all of animated nature" as "organic Harps diversely fram'd" and refers to the animating principle as "Plastic and vast" (36, 37, 39). The phrase "animated nature" was widely used by natural historians to distinguish those aspects of creation that were responsible for their own motion (*anima* deriving from the word that means "breath" or "wind") from inanimate objects, those without *anima* (*spirit*-less equals *breath*-less). To lack a spirit meant to lack a breath. There was nothing magical here, nothing immaterial. The phrase "animated nature" also hinted at a vital principle that distinguished living from nonliving things.

These authors, poets, and early scientists, consistently claim that human beings are contiguous with the natural world rather than distinct from it. They collapse the distinction between nature and culture at the same time that they point out similarities between and among all living things. Even a brief survey of well-known Romantic writings reveals how frequently the claims of early-modern science were connected to ideas and images drawn from these poets. When, for example, Percy Shelley says, in 1816, that "Nought may endure but Mutability" ("Mutability" 16), he is arguing, much as a scientist might, that change is the only constant in the physical universe. Shelley's statement concludes another poem about the Eolian harp or lyre—a wind-vibrated musical instrument—that gives "various response to each varying blast" of the breeze (6). Such a claim is a poetic restatement of a scientific principle that stretches from the flux of Heraclitus to Heisenberg's Uncertainty Principle. In the material world, change is the only thing that remains ever the same: change of seasons, change of form, change of characteristics, and change of state: $E=mC^2$ was Einstein's version of this same truth.

Shelley, for example, believes in a unifying principle that can link the force (energy) of the wind to the materiality (matter) of the objects that the wind affects. In his poem "The Cloud," he describes how each sky-born cloud is an example of natural renewal, an image that affirms the permanence of transience. In the process, the poet— for the first time in any work of literature—offers the precise details of what scientists call the hydrologic cycle, in verse. "The Cloud" accurately describes how each sky-borne collection of H_2O molecule takes shape out of vapor drawn from the ocean waters (by the heat of the sun) and then replenishes those same waters when it falls back to the earth and sea: "I pass through the pores, of the ocean and shores; / I change, but I cannot die" (75–76). With each of these cycles of watery renewal, the cloud notes its ability to laugh at its own "cenotaph" (81), its own tomb. Shelley takes his readers beyond any personal or egocentric longing for eternal life; instead, he grants "immortality" of cyclical, natural process. This is nature's only promise of eternal life, but for Shelley it is a sufficient one:

> All things that we love and cherish,
> Like ourselves must fade and perish;
> Such is our rude mortal lot—
> Love itself would, did they not.

("Death" 1–4)

Likewise, in each hydrological cycle, the cloud repeats a process of making and unmaking that represents, not only a version of immortality, but also the world's only form of permanence: "Like a child from the womb, like a ghost from the tomb, / I arise and unbuild it again" (83–84).

Shelley's cloud image, and its cycle of building and rebuilding, can be linked directly to current science's idea of the hereditary germplasm, that aspect of genetic material that survives the death of each individual and continues from life to life. Like the water in any cloud, each creature's genetic imprint—its DNA—is a direct copy of the hereditary cells of its parents and of countless individuals stretching back through time. Most of my own direct ancestors are centuries and millennia dead, but their DNA, their hereditary imprint, survives in me: in my eye color, my baldness, my height, even in the details of my personality. In this sense, I contain material strains (or replicated versions) of the actual germplasm that was contained in the bodies of my predecessors. Everything in me—except for mutations that I may have added—I owe to them. This germplasm stretches far back beyond humans and hominids to every creature, of every kind, that gave rise to the species I became, and even to me. The biological permanence I possess *is* the coiled DNA (arising from my parents into me and from me into my offspring) that I have already passed on to my children at the moment of their conception and—potentially—to their children and their children's children as well. Shelley, confronted with the precise details of twenty-first century genetics would probably ask, "What more immortality might I need than this?" His answer, in "The Cloud" and elsewhere in his work, is resounding and persuasive: "none."

Shelley's "Sensitive Plant" presents another example of the science of natural history invoked for poetic purposes. The sensitive plant (*Mimosa pudica*), as Erasmus Darwin had noted in his *Botanic Garden* (1791), posed a continuing scientific mystery because its visible movements seemed so much like those of an animal. Sensitive plants possessed rudimentary forms of sensation; they responded to touch and folded up their leaves (some observers said they "slept") at night. The earlier Darwin had said, "Naturalists have not explained the immediate cause of the collapsing of the sensitive plant; the leaves meet and close in the night during the sleep of the plant … in the same manner as when they are affected by external violence" (*Botanic* 2: 40). A plant that can be said to "sleep," even metaphorically, easily provides Shelley with a botanical example of more widely organic, and even human, characteristics. Earl Wasserman points out that "the sensitive plant was one of the most frequent examples of those ambiguous border-forms sharing both vegetable and animal characteristics" (157). Such forms broke down the integrity of the "Great Chain of Being" by suggesting that "fitness" was a matter of practical success, not of objective or ideological standards. Venus flytraps—brought to Europe first from the swamps of the southeastern United States—could capture, kill, and digest whole insects. Erasmus Darwin's "Loves of the Plants" linked the sex lives of flowers directly to the sex lives of humans. Some plants are polygamous, while others are adulterous. Some flowers are seductive, and others are chaste. Such links between organic forms reach all the way to humans.

Shelley's "Power"—like Coleridge's "a sound-like power in Light" and Wordsworth's "motion and a spirit, that impels / All thinking things, all objects of all thought, / And rolls through all things" ("Tintern Abbey" 101–3)—is in front of me all the time: in rocks, in trees, in everything I see. This is why Romantic writers were so often described as pantheistic; they located their versions of divinity in the world of nonhuman nature, or they imagined capital-"N"-Nature possessing all of the "spirituality" that any human might need. Shelley is, however, not like the twenty-first-century nature lover who says that she gets in touch with her spiritual side during long walks in the springtime woods. Shelley clearly distinguishes "Power" from the effects of power in such a way that the two can never be confused with one another. For him, it is only the effects of "power" that are ever fully evident in the human realm: "Power *in likeness* of the Arve comes down" ("Mont Blanc" 16; italics added). Such Romantic natural power is sometimes seen as synonymous with the life force, the *élan vital*, what Dylan Thomas later calls "The Force that Through the Green Fuse Drives the Flower" (a Romantically ecocritical poem if there ever was one). Authors and readers claim to—or get to—experience this Romantic "spiritual" power through the five senses, but Romantic authors and Romantic readers both claim to be receptive to the presence of this power—some more than others—even if that possibility requires a "sixth" sense. This is the same force, of course, that can be sensed by each Romantic's *sensorium* (the sum of all five physical senses) through the vehicle of clouds, mimosa plants, skylarks, and nightingales.

Other borders—between the living and the nonliving, the organic and the inorganic, plants and animals—are comparable to the barrier that separates Shelley's unseen "Power" from its visible effects in nature. The *Cyclopedia* compiled by Ephraim Chambers in 1728 described the sensitive plant as "an herb sufficiently known to the world for its remarkable property of receding from the touch, and giving signs, as it were, of animal life"; similarly, the natural historian Soames Jenyns compared the sensitive plant to a "shell-fish," noting that the "lowest" animal and the "highest" plant are both distinguished by sensitivity—this bivalve opens "to receive the water which surrounds it," just as the sensitive mimosa is observed "shrinking from the finger" that touches it (Wasserman 157n). All sensitive plants embody a general anxiety about hybrids (half-and-half organisms) that plagued early naturalists. If everything had been separately created and then uniquely placed in its proper spot along the Great Chain of Being—by divine fiat—how might an organism look like a plant but behave like an animal? In the process of exploring such curious cases, early naturalists found apparent species boundaries to be much less absolute than had been previously imagined. A plant (the mimosa) might move like an animal. An animal (the sea anemone) could behave much like a plant. Which was which, who was what? It would take Charles Darwin, and then Gregor Mendel, to resolve this particular border dispute.

Shelley's "Ode to the West Wind" includes another of the most powerful Romantic depictions of sympathetic interactions across an apparent natural boundary. In one of his typical border-crossing images, Shelley claims that the wind that influences plants on the land can have a comparable effect on plants in the sea. Shelley imagines undersea plants responding to the terrestrial change of seasons brought about by the West Wind:

> The sea-blooms and the oozy woods which wear
> The sapless foliage of the ocean, know
> Thy [the wind's] voice, and suddenly grow grey with fear,
> And tremble and despoil themselves: O hear!
>
> (*Shelley* 3.39–42)

Shelley's science is not accurate here, but his impulse is proto-ecological, as he indicates in his own footnote: "The phenomenon alluded to ... is well known to naturalists. The vegetation at the bottom of the sea, of rivers, and of lakes, sympathises with that of the land in the change of seasons, and is consequently influenced by the winds which announce it" (Nichols 311). Plants in the sea enter into a natural cycle that includes plants on land. In addition, terrestrial plants have literal sympathy for aquatic ones. What happens on land influences what happens beneath the waves. Scientists have now proven how right Shelley was, even though he may have been wrong in his specifics; what happens on land has a direct impact on what happens under the sea: natural climate and human pollution both produce versions of Shelley's sympathetic interactions between various parts of the ecosystem. Even the modern term "ecosystem" suggests just the sorts of connectedness that Shelley and other Romantic writers intuited, and sought to describe, in the nonhuman world.

Ideas about the relationship between the natural world and human culture have been part of English literary criticism since its beginnings in the eighteenth century. Coleridge, another of those Romantic poets and critics who consistently and carefully scrutinizes literary representations of the natural world, praises Prince Hamlet's focus on the smallest physical detail in his naturalistic surroundings, noting that "attention to minute sounds,—naturally associated with the recollection of minute objects ... gives a philosophic pertinency ... and ... really is, the language of nature" (*Shakespeare* 347–48). In a related way, Shelley's prose essay "On Love" notes that

> Hence in solitude, or in that deserted state when we are surrounded by human beings, and yet they sympathise not with us, we love the flowers, the grass and the waters and the sky. In the motion of the very leaves of spring in the blue air there is then found a secret correspondence with our heart. There is eloquence in the tongueless wind and a melody in the flowing of brooks and the rustling of the reeds beside them which by their inconceivable relation to something within the soul awaken the spirits to a dance of breathless rapture, and bring tears of mysterious tenderness to the eyes like the enthusiasm of patriotic success or the voice of one beloved singing to you alone. Sterne says that if he were in a desart [*sic*] he would love some cypress. (*Poetry and Prose* 504)

Ever since this Romantic idea of a direct (if "secret") organic correspondence between human emotions and the objects of the natural world, imaginative writers in English have sought to explore and explain the connection between humans and nature for literary effect. Some of the greatest passages in English poetry and imaginative prose—since 1820—have emerged out of this belief in Shelley's "secret correspondence" between the brooks, the weeds, the wind, and the human "heart."

My point is not that Shelley anticipates the precise details of subsequent thinking—much of his science is simply wrong—but only that his awareness of natural history allows him to imagine nature as an interdependent realm (depending on the relationship between and among it parts) while also seeing wild nature and human culture as interdependent systems, eventually leading to the idea of urbanature. Of course, this notion of an interdependence between human mental activity and organic nature also drives the imaginative impulse in poems like Shelley's "Ode to the West Wind," Keats's "Ode to a Nightingale," and Coleridge's "Frost at Midnight." In each of these poems, the human speaker longs to possess, or link to, a nonhuman energy that he identifies with the wind, the bird, or the frost. The force that causes the wind to blow, in Shelley's poem, is credited with planting "winged seeds" in the ground, bringing them to life in the spring, driving "loose clouds" across the sky, dropping "rain and lightning," even causing waves to roll the entire length of the ocean along the "Atlantic's level powers." One unified power causes all of these natural effects, but this power is nothing more than a series of physical processes contained in nature, what John Locke and others had called "natural law." Shelley, as the speaker of his poem, addresses the wind self-consciously and says, in effect, "I feel a sense of connection to the power within these natural processes linked to the West Wind. Now let me be even more fully identified with that power" ("Oh! lift me as a wave, a leaf, a cloud!" 53). Let me feel its force directly and grow more forceful in the process, "Be thou, spirit fierce, / My spirit! Be thou me, impetuous one!" (61–62). In all such Romantic poems, the speaker longs to identify with, or to be identified with, a nonhuman object or force that possesses a power the poet lacks: be it wind, bird, or frost. Numerous other Romantic poems rely on similar versions of natural forces: waterfalls, sunsets, and skylarks, even glow-worms.

Biology, the science that would eventually explain the physical facts behind such Romantic "nature" poems, came into being early in the nineteenth century—the term originated around 1800 (*OED*)—and helped to show how the 1859 world of Darwin's *On the Origin of Species* differed so greatly from the 1735 world of Linnaeus's *Systema Natura*. Biology did not determine destiny in the nineteenth century—as it seems to do so often in our own cultural moment—but Romantic natural history helps us see how the "Nature" of Isaac Newton and Linnaeus becomes, via Wordsworth and Shelley, the "nature" of Stephen Hawking and Stephen Jay Gould. If species are mutable, as Darwin and Mendel prove them to be, then all species are connected in ways that no static view of creation could allow. As we now know, through DNA testing, every species is genetically linked to every other species, alive or dead, extant or extinct. In addition, the barrier that once appeared to separate species from one another has now been replaced by a dynamic system that produces new species out of older ones, evolution via natural selection. The mimosa is related to all of the motile animals it mimics. The biochemical processes that cause its leaves to open and close are directly related to the nervous impulses of the animals it seems to imitate. The nightingale (we now know) does sing for a biological reason, and that reason is related to the very issues that are lurking in Keats's human mind: the search for a mate, the need to declare the range over which he has control, and the necessity to reproduce before "a few, sad, last gray hairs" (25) disappear. Hairs for the human, like feathers for the bird, announce the end of those shared expectations of lifespan and species reproduction.

One implication of genetic inheritance is that there is, in one sense, no such thing as a species at all; or rather, many species are regularly transforming themselves into new forms, new species and subspecies, new aspects of biological creation. If every species emerged out of earlier species, then it is precisely the liminal border states— subspecies, varieties, subpopulations, transitional forms—that reveal points of contact between one species and another: domestic dog and wild wolf, coyote and coy-dog cross, competitive chimpanzee and cooperative bonobo, primitive Neanderthal and sophisticated Cro-Magnon. Mary Shelley did not know precisely what a "species" was when she published the term in the first edition of *Frankenstein* in 1818, but neither did the Comte de Buffon, Erasmus Darwin, or Charles Darwin. The word "species" is a generalized word we use to describe populations that share genetic material and are unable to breed with other species. But the crossing of the complex borders between species and among species is precisely the point at which new species emerge. Romantic anxiety about species was not merely the result of uncertainty about the origins of organic nature. Such anxiety was part of a much wider cultural movement away from an atomized view of discrete natural types toward the current model of nature as an organic whole, what scientists now call an ecological system.

Romantic writers were not always good scientists, nor did all of their literary images derive from accurate scientific information. But sensitive plants, western winds, and the idea of new species chart a pervasive paradigm shift, away from a "Nature" that was static and unchanging toward a "nature" characterized by dynamic links among all living things. Such a view is much closer to the contemporary claim that nature is not here for human beings, but that human beings are—in one sense at least—here for nature, as part of its continuing processes. It now does make sense for me to say that I am here *for* nature; I am part of the vast web of genetic links and animate inter-relatedness that Shelley, Keats, and Coleridge (among others) clearly intuited in their writings. Twenty-first century cultural emphasis on ecology links directly to many of these earlier Romantic thinkers. In the century before Charles Darwin, scientists and writers saw human beings as organisms with important connections to their surroundings. These same connections, as science has come to understand, have profound implications for life on the planet that human beings share with the rest of the living world.

Works cited

Buffon, George Louis Leclerc, Comte de. *Barr's Buffon: Buffon's* Natural History; *containing a theory of the Earth.* 10 vols. London: J. S. Barr, 1792.

Buffon, George Louis Leclerc, Comte de. *The Natural History of Insects, compiled from Swammerdam, Brookes, & Goldsmith.* 1792. [bound with Buffon, *System*].

Buffon, George Louis Leclerc, Comte de. *The System of Natural History Written by the Celebrated Buffon.* Perth: R. Morison, 1791.

Coleridge, Samuel Taylor. *Anima Poetae: From the Unpublished Note-books of Samuel Taylor Coleridge.* Ed. E. H. Coleridge. Boston: Houghton Mifflin, 1895.

Coleridge, Samuel Taylor. *Coleridge's Poetry and Prose.* Ed. Nicholas Halmi, Paul Magnuson, and Raimonda Modiano. New York: Norton, 2004.

Coleridge, Samuel Taylor. *Notes and Lectures upon Shakespeare and Some of the Old Poets and Dramatists with Other Literary Remains.* Vol. 1. Ed. Mrs. H. N. Coleridge. London: William Pickering, 1849.

Darwin, Charles. *Charles Darwin's Letters: A Selection.* Ed. Frederick Burkhardt. Cambridge: Cambridge UP, 1996.

Darwin, Charles. *Darwin,* Ed. Philip Appleman. 3rd ed. New York: Norton, 2001.

Darwin, Charles. *On the Origin of Species by Means of Natural Selection.* London: John Murray, 1859.

Darwin, Erasmus. *The Botanic Garden: A Poem, in Two Parts.* Part I "The Economy of Vegetation." Part II: "The Loves of the Plants." London: Joseph Johnson, 1791.

Darwin, Erasmus. *Phytologia; or the Philosophy of Agriculture and Gardening,* London: Joseph Johnson, 1800.

Darwin, Erasmus. *The Temple of Nature; or, The Origin of Society. A poem, with Philosophical Notes.* London: Joseph Johnson, 1803.

Darwin, Erasmus. *Zoonomia; or, The Laws of Organic Life.* 2 vols. London: Joseph Johnson, 1794. Vol. 2, 1794.

Keats, John. *The Complete Poems.* Ed. Miriam Allott. London: Longman, 1975.

Keats, John. *Lamia, Isabella, The Eve of St. Agnes, and Other Poems.* London: Taylor and Hessey, 1820.

Keats, John. *Selected Poem and Letters.* Ed. Douglas Bush. Boston: Houghton Mifflin, 1959.

Linnaeus, Carolus. *Systema Natura.* Stockholm: Laurentii Salvii Holmiae, 1735.

Locke, John. *Two Treatises on Civil Government.* London: Routledge, 1887.

Nichols, Ashton. *Romantic Natural Histories.* Boston: Houghton Mifflin, 2003. Print

Shelley, Mary. *The Frankenstein Notebooks.* Ed. Charles E. Robinson. 2 vols. New York: Garland, 1966.

Shelley, Mary. (with Percy Bysshe Shelley). *The Original Frankenstein: Two New Versions.* Ed. Charles E. Robinson. New York: Vintage Random House, 2008 (1816–17).

Shelley, Percy Bysshe. "Essay on a Future State." *Essays, Letters from Abroad, Translations and Fragments.* Ed. Mary Shelley. 2 vols. London: Moxon, 1852.

Shelley, Percy Bysshe. *Poetical Works.* Ed. Mary Shelley. London: Moxon, 1839.

Shelley, Percy Bysshe. *Shelley's Poetry and Prose.* Ed. Donald H. Reiman and Neil Fraistat. New York: Norton, 2002.

Wasserman, Earl, *Shelley: A Critical Reading.* Baltimore: John Hopkins University Press, 1977.

Index

When the text is within a note, this is indicated by page number, 'n', note number
e.g. Stedman, E.C. 47–53nn2&5, 54n9

Where a character is discussed in the text, the character is indexed, followed by the name of the work
in parentheses
e.g. Lord Walter *(Aurora Leigh)* 115–16

men of science 260–1, 447
Menander 18
Mendel, G. 465, 467
Merleau-Ponty, M. 292, 294, 299nn16&18
Mermin, D. 93, 232
Merwin, W.S. 189
metaphors: emotion 271–2, 273, 275–6,
286, 294, 296–7; forms 228, 231, 233,
238–9; periodization 26, 45, 52; politics
125, 136, 143; prosody 175, 179; religion
304, 330–1, 353; science 423, 449, 464;
sexuality 364, 406, 413; what constitutes
poetry 55, 66, 104
metaphysical criticism 19
meter *see* metre
metre: metrical accent 166; metrical
composition 73, 86, 148, 155–62, 257,
262–3; metrical feet 179–82; metrical form
86–7, 154n20, 158 *see also* English metre
Michelangelo 389–90
Middlemarch (Eliot, G.) 135
Miles, A.H. 90–1, 92, 95nn9&22
Miles, R. 55–63
Mill, James 33, 58
Mill, J.S.: emotion 246, 273; epic genre 221;
physiological poetics 421–2, 424, 455;
what is poetry? 58, 73–80
Miller, J.H. 295, 299n18, 305–6, 329–37
Milton, J.: aesthetic joy 284–5; Elizabeth
Barrett Browning 111, 119; epic genre 196,
216, 219; periodization 11, 27; poetics
205; prosody 155, 160, 165, 177; science
434, 435–6, 455; sexuality 369–71, 373,
379; sonnets 198, 226–7, 230, 233; what
constitutes poetry 68–9, 70, 85–6
mimetic representation 66
minnesingers 285, 289n13
miracles: dramatic monologues 241;
periodization 11; religion 312–13, 316,
338–9, 340–1; science 443, 462
missionary work 207–8
Mivart, St G. 444
modern traditionalism 22–3
Modernism: epic genre 196, 217–18, 223n7,
224n13; periodization 10; religion 352;
science 457; sexuality 362, 405; E.C.
Stedman 47
Moers, E. 117
Mont Blanc (Shelley) 425, 426, 464
Moonrise (Hopkins) 335–6
Moore, T. 435–6
moral government 313–14
Mormonism 339
Morris, Sir L. 14–15
Morris, W. 59, 220, 380–1, 388
Mozart, W.A. 77, 85
Mozley, J.R. 344

Mukherjee, A. 107–14
muscular Christianity 39
My Last Duchess (Browning) 36, 239–40,
242–4, 341

Nachleben (afterlife) 411
Nadira (sultana in *The Zenana*) 102–4
narrative painting 79
narrative theory 220
nationalism 112, 122, 131, 139–41, 143
natural selection 425, 427–8, 467
Nature 443, 445–8
nature 461–7
Nature and Elements of Poetry, The
(Stedman) 49–50
nautili 435, 439–40
Nautilus, To the (Howitt) 440
Neale, J.M. 209–10, 306, 351
neo-classicism 55, 457
New Woman poetry 92
Newcomb, S. 445
Newman, J.H.: emotion 278; hymns 206,
208–9, 212; religion 302–4, 305, 308n9
Newton, I. 24, 162, 301, 467
Nichols, A. 424–5, 461–7
Niebuhr, B.G. 20
Nietzsche, F. 52, 128n10, 194, 281, 329
Nightingale, The (Coleridge) 281, 284–6
nightingales 57, 229, 284–6, 289nn12–15,
462, 465–7
No Newspapers (Coleridge, M.E.) 187–8
Nollet, J.-A. 454–5
Nora (*A Doll's House*) 397
Northern Star 129–31

objectivity 25–7, 28–9, 109, 135, 273, 422 *see
also* subjectivity
Observations on Man (Hartley) 251
Ode to Anactoria (Sappho) 404
Ode to Aphrodite (Sappho) 404, 409–11
Oenone (Tennyson) 39–41, 44–6
O'Gorman, F. 9–16
Old Man Travelling (Wordsworth) 189–90
Olney Hymns (Newton & Cowper) 207, 209
On Joseph Rayner Stephens (E.H.) 129–30
On the Origin of Species (Darwin) 301–2,
425, 467
One Day in Every Year (Coleridge, M.E.) 189
ontology 1, 127, 247
Orestes 18
Oriental poetry 364, 372
origin of metre 156
Orthometry (Brewer) 187
Ovid 370, 378, 404, 414

Pallas Athene (*Oenone*) 40, 41–2, 44–5
parables 35, 221, 303, 312, 322

travel writing 96–7
tri-syllable rhymes 157, 159
Trilobite, Lay of the (Kendall) 426–8
triviality 18, 111, 164, 252, 257, 330
troubadours 205, 285–6, 289nn13&15
true poetry 74–6, 204, 258–9, 421
Tucker, H.F.: criticism 123; dramatic
  monologues 199; epic genre 196, 215–25;
  religion 342, 347n20, 354
Turner, J.M.W. 78, 284
Tyndall, J. 174, 443, 445–9, 449nn5&6, 450n9

Udall, N. 391
Ulysses 13, 45, 436
Ulysses (Joyce) 23, 217, 223nn7&12
utilitarianism 56, 57–8, 205, 402, 422

Veley, M. 185
Verlaine, P. 392
vernaculars 113, 143, 145
Victorian American culture 47, 50–1
Victorian criticism 51, 107, 270–9
Victorian hymns 195, 206–13
Victorian Poetry: Poetry, Poetics, Politics
  (Armstrong) 6, 32, 41, 57, 93, 107, 407,
  458
Victorian poets: forms 199, 221, 241;
  periodization 14, 33; religion 349, 351;
  science 426, 451–2, 456–7; sexuality
  363–4, 367, 404; what constitutes poetry
  57, 59
Victorian Poets (Stedman) 48, 53n2
Victorian Sappho 404–7
Virgil 56, 205, 215–16, 219, 431–2

Wainewright, T.G. 401–2
Walker, J. 136–7
Walkley, A.B. 397
Ward, A. (pseudonym) 384
Warren, A.H. 56
Waste Land, The (Eliot) 22–3, 196, 223n7,
  225n26
Watson, J.R. 55, 194–5, 206–14, 309n28
Weber, G. 167
Wharton, H.T. 404–6, 411, 413–14, 417nn3&4
Whitman, W.: periodization 29, 50, 52, 53n5;
  science 453, 457; sexuality 365, 391–2,
  394nn10&11

Wilde, O. 3; critical categories 92; epic
  genre 215, 221; periodization 14; religion
  352; sexuality 366–7, 396–403
Williams, I. 207–8, 304–6, 308n9, 311–17,
  351
Williams, P. 112, 143
Williams, R. 136, 358
Williamson, M. 406, 418n7
Wilson, J. 83
Winckelmann, J.J. 390
Windhover, The (Hopkins) 291, 294
Winkworth sisters 212–13
Winter's Tale, The (Shakespeare) 156
Wolfson, S.J. 354, 357
Woman of No Importance, A (Wilde) 402
Women Poets of the Victorian Era (Sharp)
  60, 90
women writers: hymns 197, 211–12;
  sexuality 361, 368; women's poetry 60,
  90, 93–4, 98, 103
women's poetry: critical categories 59–60,
  89–94, 95nn9&22; politics 111, 118;
  religion 351; sexuality 416
Wopsle, Mr (*Great Expectations*) 132–3
Wordsworth, W. 2–4; aesthetic joy 281–4,
  286, 288n7, 289n16; emotion 246–7,
  247–9, 251, 271, 273; forms 196, 197–8,
  204, 211, 218, 242; *Lyrical Ballads*
  preface 257–64; periodization 10–12,
  24–5, 27; politics 109; prosody 148,
  155, 157–61, 165, 169n32, 189–90;
  religion 302–3, 309n13, 359n3; science
  422, 463–4, 467; sexuality 379; sonnets
  226–7, 230, 233, 234nn1&3; what
  constitutes poetry 55–6, 58–9, 61, 73,
  82–7
Wotton, Lord Henry (*Dorian Gray*) 396, 401
Wreck of the Deutschland, The (Hopkins)
  221, 333–4, 335, 356

Yeats, W.B.: emotion 246, 272, 278;
  periodization 9, 12, 45; printed voice
  81–2, 88n11; romanticism 23, 26, 28–9,
  30nn9&12

Zenana, The (Landon) 101–4
Zilara (character in *The Zenana*) 102–4
Zwingli, H. 329

Taylor & Francis eBooks

Helping you to choose the right eBooks for your Library

Add Routledge titles to your library's digital collection today. Taylor and Francis ebooks contains over 50,000 titles in the Humanities, Social Sciences, Behavioural Sciences, Built Environment and Law.

Choose from a range of subject packages or create your own!

Benefits for you

» Free MARC records
» COUNTER-compliant usage statistics
» Flexible purchase and pricing options
» All titles DRM-free.

Benefits for your user

» Off-site, anytime access via Athens or referring URL
» Print or copy pages or chapters
» Full content search
» Bookmark, highlight and annotate text
» Access to thousands of pages of quality research at the click of a button.

REQUEST YOUR **FREE** INSTITUTIONAL TRIAL TODAY

Free Trials Available
We offer free trials to qualifying academic, corporate and government customers.

eCollections – Choose from over 30 subject eCollections, including:

Archaeology	Language Learning
Architecture	Law
Asian Studies	Literature
Business & Management	Media & Communication
Classical Studies	Middle East Studies
Construction	Music
Creative & Media Arts	Philosophy
Criminology & Criminal Justice	Planning
Economics	Politics
Education	Psychology & Mental Health
Energy	Religion
Engineering	Security
English Language & Linguistics	Social Work
Environment & Sustainability	Sociology
Geography	Sport
Health Studies	Theatre & Performance
History	Tourism, Hospitality & Events

For more information, pricing enquiries or to order a free trial, please contact your local sales team:
www.tandfebooks.com/page/sales

 Routledge
Taylor & Francis Group

The home of
Routledge books

www.tandfebooks.com